PRAISE FOR *The Best of* Outside

"Engaging, sharp-eyed reports on the people, places, politics, art, literature, and natural history of the great and not-so-great outdoors."
—*Miami Herald*

"There's a reason *Outside* magazine has received the National Magazine Award for general excellence . . . it's the writing. . . . Whether you're in need of a good laugh, a sobering thought, or just plain entertainment, you're likely to find it in *The Best of* Outside."
—*North Coast Sports*

"*Outside* has long been known for its writing; it has been nominated for National Magazine Awards 16 years in a row and won six."
—*The New York Times*

"Original and engaging reports on travel, adventure, sports, and the environment. . . . *The Best of* Outside represents the finest the award-winning magazine has to offer: thirty-one stories that range from high action to high comedy."
—*Women's Magazine*

"This book glitters . . . highly recommended."
—*Library Journal*

"*Outside* writers offer unique insights and powerful prose. I shake my head in wonder at the strength and clarity of such writing; I know I'll visit this book again and again. So should you."
—*Bookpage*

"*The Best of* Outside is filled with the serious and the thoughtful, the humorous and the outrageous. . . . A must for anyone who enjoys provocative outdoor adventure writing."
—*Wisconsin Bookwatch*

The Best of Outside

Outside magazine has been in publication since 1977. It
has received six National Magazine Awards, including the
award for reporting in 1997 and the award for general
excellence in both 1996 and 1997.

THE BEST OF

THE FIRST 20 YEARS

The Editors

of *Outside* Magazine

VINTAGE DEPARTURES

Vintage Books

A Division of Random House, Inc.

New York

FIRST VINTAGE DEPARTURES EDITION, SEPTEMBER 1998

Most of the material in this book has been previously
published in *Outside* magazine.

The Library of Congress has cataloged the Villard Books
edition as follows:
The best of Outside: the first twenty years /
the editors of Outside magazine.
P. cm.
ISBN 0-375-50064-2 (acid-free paper)
1. Outdoor recreation.
2.Outdoor recreation—United States.
3.Outside (Santa Fe, N.M.)
I. Outside (Santa Fe, N.M.)
GV191.6.O94   1997
796.5—dc21   97-22666

Vintage ISBN 0-375-70313-6

Random House Web address: www.randomhouse.com

Printed in the United States of America
10 9 8

Contents

THE WORLD OUT THERE

Introduction

The difference between journalism and literature is that journalism is un-
readable and literature is not read.

— OSCAR WILDE

"Nobody who loves to hunt feels absolutely hunky-dory when the quarry goes
down," wrote Thomas McGuane in his now classic "The Heart of the Game,"
published in *Outside*'s inaugural issue twenty years ago and reprinted here.
"The remorse spins out almost before anything and the balancing act ends on
one declination or another. I decided that unless I become a vegetarian, I'll get
my meat by hunting for it. . . . I've seen slaughterhouses, and anyway, as Sitting Bull said, when the buffalo are gone, we will hunt mice, for we are hunters
and we want our freedom."

Freedom was what *Outside*'s editors sought as well, as that first issue made
abundantly clear. In this particular landscape, freedom meant an editorial ability to range near and far: Alongside McGuane's elegant, richly personal con-
sideration of hunting were an article on the shock-troop ethos of Greenpeace;
an examination of the egg; a melancholy report from paradise lost on the island of Kauai; reviews of the Minox 35EL camera, the Hi-Roller cowboy hat
from Texas Hatters, and *The Hallucinogenic and Poisonous Mushroom Guide*; and
a decidedly short story (188 words) by Richard Brautigan about a bicyclist and
two dogs on a roof. Obviously no one was looking to get typecast at *Outside*; not
only would the magazine entertain a full array of subjects, but it would also air
a wide spectrum of opinion as well—the better to keep the reader guessing and
preserve, as editor-at-large David Quammen would put it years later, "the ca-
cophonous disunity of souls." The one fixed requirement was that the writer,
every writer, be skillful enough to pull it all off.

That the magazine was trying to stake out some wide-open territory in
which to conduct its business, that it had journalistic and literary ambitions,
was largely a response to the banality of much that was available to people
who loved the outdoors and loved to read, circa 1977. Among magazines there
were the traditional hunting and fishing and camping monthlies, some respectable if earnest back-to-the-land journals, and lest we forget, the long-
standing "men's adventure" periodicals, which were still happily serving their

readers a never-ending bounty of flesh-eating headhunters, exploding volcanoes, and blood-crazed wild beasts. There seemed to be no magazines about the outdoors that would have published the more lyric offerings of a contemporary Twain or Melville or Dinesen or Conrad, wilderness folks all. In fact, there was no publication that saw itself as a general-interest magazine about the outdoors and placed a premium on reporting and thinking and storytelling. To *Outside*'s editors and writers, there was no more perfect arena in which to probe the complexities of the human condition than the natural world, the world as it really is out there. And there was no better method of exploration than the long and demanding process of reporting and then writing—truly writing—about it. "I write because I hold the conviction, smarmy as it might seem, that we must give back to that from which we take," Bob Shacochis, the National Book Award winner and *Outside* contributing editor, has said. "Take a penny, leave a penny. What I've most taken from in my life is the banquet table of literature. What most fulfills my sense of worth are my own attempts to contribute to the timeless feast, to keep the food replenished and fresh . . . 'There are no old myths,' the writer Jim Harrison once said, 'only new people.' "

The great Oakland Raider George Blanda once observed, "You stay in this game twenty-two years and things are gonna happen." Happily for us, they seem to have been happening right from the beginning. Through the years, the magazine has continued to interpret its mission broadly, seeking to evolve with the times, its readers' changing interests, and its writers' and editors' intuitions. Thus far, it seems to be working: What early critics deemed a charming if naive little enterprise that would never attract great writers, let alone a large and committed audience, has been nominated for National Magazine Awards in each of the last fifteen years, winning six times, three of them in the last couple of years. But whatever we've achieved in our better moments comes compliments of the magazine's ambitious roots—and the skilled writers that those ambitions led us to discover and publish. We've been profoundly fortunate to provide an environment for some of the finest writers of a few generations: Norman Maclean, James Salter, Annie Proulx, Robert Stone, David Quammen, Jane Smiley, Edward Abbey, Barry Lopez, Tim Cahill, William Kittredge, William Burroughs, Bob Shacochis, Susan Orlean, Barry Hannah, Jim Harrison, Ian Frazier, Jonathan Raban, Thomas McGuane, Bill Bryson, Peter Matthiessen, Chip Brown, Randy Wayne White, Bill McKibben, Donald Katz, Kate Wheeler, Mark Kramer, Garrison Keillor, Craig Vetter, James Hamilton-Paterson, Willian Finnegan, Edward Hoagland, Jon Krakauer, and many others.

Spouting such a list probably seems a little like boasting, and perhaps it is.

But what I'm trying to get across here is how privileged we are. *Outside* may be (as I'm prone to prattle on about) a great license to be curious, but it would be another magazine altogether without this particular corps of writers. What *Outside*'s authors share is not so much a style of writing as an attitude—about themselves and the planet at large. An attitude that is fiercely independent and often irreverent, touched by irony yet also generous and inclusive. These writers marvel at much of what they discover—whether at the far ends of the earth or lurking in the backyard—yet they are also, properly, saddened and angered by some of what they find. They resist compartmentalizing their experiences, understanding that what we see and do outside is an integral part of life, a life crammed with contradictions and maddening, intriguing shadings. Thus they aim high, creating pieces not merely to entertain on the subject at hand—knocking around the forests of Belize, summiting Mount Everest, homesteading in Montana, evading the snapping jaws of the Komodo dragon—but to explore our behavior, our values, our judgments, our place in the natural order of things. These people know how to watch and listen and tell a story.

They also know how to revel in the simple awkward act of being human, and they aren't shy about advertising their screwups; misadventure in the right hands can make for a memorable tale. And so it is that we see McGuane on an uncharacteristically lackadaisical hunting trip, tucked under a cottonwood to wait for whitetail deer, fast asleep. "I woke up a couple of hours later, the coffee and early morning drill having done not one thing for my alertness. I had drooled on my rifle and it was time for my chores back at the ranch."

One of the painful truths about magazine journalism is that these flashes of humor and grace—some of the best writing of our times—often get heaved with the trash at the end of each month. Collecting it again between two covers is immensely satisfying for obvious reasons, yet what a trying experience: selecting only one piece per writer when some of these authors, like our former "Natural Acts" columnist David Quammen, have been contributing on an almost monthly basis for a decade and a half, even two. Many worthy writers, sad to say, could not be represented here—blame it on space and story mix. And so we grit our teeth against those hard cuts, at least until anthology time comes round again.

In the meantime, special thanks are owed to my colleagues in the editorial ranks—past and present—who have lent their ideas, their wisdom, their passion, their endurance, and their skills with a nubby No. 2 Mirado Black Warrior. In particular to Larry Burke, *Outside*'s owner and publisher, for his remarkable support all these years, and to Greg Cliburn, John Tayman, Hal Espen, Susan Casey, Hampton Sides, Adam Horowitz, Brad Wetzler, Susan Smith, Gretchen Reynolds, Mike Grudowski, Michael Paterniti, John Rasmus, Alex

Heard, Dan Ferrara, Kathy Martin O'Neil, Andrew Tilin, Eric Hagerman, Will Dana, Lisa Chase, Donovan Webster, Terry McDonell, Marshall Sella, Dan Coyle, Marilyn Johnson, Michael McRae, Michelle Stacey, David Schonauer, Alison Carpenter Davis, Todd Balf, and Amy Goldwasser. Many of the writers in this collection are indebted to these people, and so am I. My thanks as well, and most importantly, to Laura Hohnhold, with whom I've had the pleasure of working for twelve years now. Much of the effort and taste and sensibility in this anthology are hers.

Last, enormous gratitude to our readers, who continue to help us prove that Oscar Wilde had it wrong.

—Mark Bryant, editor

THE SPORTING LIFE

THE HEART OF THE GAME

by THOMAS McGUANE

Hunting in your own backyard becomes with time, if you love hunting, less and less expeditionary. When Montana's eager September frosts knocked my garden on its butt, the hoe seemed more like the rifle than it ever had before, the vegetables more like game.

My nine-year-old son and I went scouting before the season and saw some antelope in the high plains foothills of the Absaroka Range, wary, hanging on the skyline; a few bands and no great heads. We crept around, looking into basins, and at dusk met a tired cowboy on a tired horse followed by a tired blue-heeler dog. The plains seemed bigger than anything, bigger than the mountains that seemed to sit in the middle of them, bigger than the ocean. The clouds made huge shadows that traveled on the grass slowly through the day.

Hunting season trickles on forever; if you don't go in on a cow with anybody, there is the dark argument of the deep freeze against headhunting ("You can't eat horns!"). But nevertheless, in my mind, I've laid out the months like playing cards, knowing some decent whitetails could be down in the river bottom and, fairly reliably, the long windy shots at antelope. The big buck mule deer—the ridge-runners—stay up in the scree and rock walls until the snow drives them out; but they stay high long after the elk have quit and broken down the hay corrals on the ranches and farmsteads, which, when you're hunting the rocks from a saddle horse, look pathetic and housebroken with their yellow lights against the coming of winter.

Where I live, the Yellowstone River runs straight north, then takes an eastward turn at Livingston, Montana. This flowing north is supposed to be remarkable; and the river doesn't do it long. It runs mostly over sand and stones once it comes out of the rock slots near the Wyoming line. But all along, there are deviations of one sort or another: canals, backwaters, sloughs; the red willows grow in the sometime-flooded bottom, and at the first elevation, the cottonwoods. I hunt here in the early fall for the whitetail deer, which, in recent years, have moved up these rivers in numbers never seen before.

When I first start hunting in the fall, I'm not used to getting up so early. I won't get up that early to fish, not three or four in the morning just to be out in the middle of nowhere at first light.

The first morning, the sun came up hitting around me in arbitrary panels as the light came through the jagged openings in the Absaroka Range. I was moving very slowly in the edge of the trees, the river invisible a few hundred yards to my right but sending a huge sigh through the willows. It was cold and the sloughs had crowns of ice, thick enough to support me. As I crossed one great clear panel, trout raced around under my feet and a ten-foot bubble advanced slowly before my cautious steps. Then passing back into the trees, I found an active game trail, cut across lots to pick a better stand, sat in a good vantage place under a cottonwood with the ought-six across my knees. I thought, running my hands up into my sleeves, this is lovely but I'd rather be up in the hills; and I fell asleep.

I woke up a couple of hours later, the coffee and early morning drill having done not one thing for my alertness. I had drooled on my rifle and it was time for my chores back at the ranch. My chores of late had consisted primarily of working on screenplays so that the bank didn't take the ranch. These days the primary ranch skill is making the payment; it comes before irrigation, feeding out, and calving. Some rancher friends find this so discouraging they get up and roll a number or have a slash of tanglefoot before they even think of the glories of the West. This is the New Rugged.

The next day, I reflected upon my lackadaisical hunting and left really too early in the morning. I drove around to Mission Creek in the dark and ended up sitting in the truck up some wash listening to a New Mexico radio station until my patience gave out and I started out cross-country in the dark, just able to make out the nose of the Absaroka Range as it faced across the river to the Crazy Mountains. It seemed maddeningly up and down slick banks and a couple of times I had game clatter out in front of me in the dark. Then I turned up a long coulee that climbed endlessly south and started in that direction, knowing the plateau on top should hold some antelope. After half an hour or so, I heard the mad laughing of coyotes, throwing their voices all around the inside of the coulee, trying to panic rabbits and making my hair stand on end despite my affection for them. The stars tracked overhead into the first pale light and it was nearly dawn before I came up on the bench. I could hear cattle below me and I moved along an edge of thorn trees to break my outline, then sat down at the point to wait for shooting light.

I could see antelope on the skyline before I had that light; and by the time I did, there was a good big buck angling across from me, looking at everything. I thought I could see well enough, and I got up into a sitting position and into the sling. I had made my moves quietly, but when I looked through the scope the antelope was 200 yards out, using up the country in bounds. I tracked with him, let him bounce up into the reticle and touched off a shot. He was down and still, but I sat watching until I was sure.

Nobody who loves to hunt feels absolutely hunky-dory when the quarry goes down. The remorse spins out almost before anything and the balancing act ends on one declination or another. I decided that unless I become a vegetarian, I'll get my meat by hunting for it. I feel absolutely unabashed by the arguments of other carnivores who get their meat in plastic with blue numbers on it. I've seen slaughterhouses, and anyway, as Sitting Bull said, when the buffalo are gone, we will hunt mice, for we are hunters and we want our freedom.

The antelope had piled up in the sage, dead before he hit the ground. He was an old enough buck that the tips of his pronged horns were angled in toward each other. I turned him downhill to bleed him out. The bullet had mushroomed in the front of the lungs; so the job was already halfway done. With antelope, proper field dressing is critical because they can end up sour if they've been run or haphazardly hog-dressed. And they sour from their own body heat more than external heat.

The sun was up and the big buteo hawks were lifting on the thermals. There was enough breeze that the grass began to have directional grain like the prairie and the rim of the coulee wound up away from me toward the Absaroka. I felt peculiarly solitary, sitting on my heels next to the carcass in the sagebrush and greasewood, my rifle racked open on the ground. I made an incision around the metatarsal glands inside the back legs and carefully removed them and set them well aside; then I cleaned the blade of my hunting knife with handfuls of grass to keep from tainting the meat with those powerful glands. Next I detached the anus and testes from the outer walls and made a shallow puncture below the sternum, spread it with the thumb and forefinger of my left hand and ran the knife upside down clear to the bone bridge between the hind legs. Inside, the diaphragm was like the taut lid of a drum and cut away cleanly so that I could reach clear up to the back of the mouth and detach the windpipe. Once that was done I could draw the whole visceral package out onto the grass and separate out the heart, liver, and tongue before propping the carcass open with two whittled-up sage scantlings.

You could tell how cold the morning was, despite the exertion, just by watching the steam roar from the abdominal cavity. I stuck the knife in the ground and sat back against the slope, looking clear across to Convict Grade and the Crazy Mountains. I was blood from the elbows down and the antelope's eyes had skinned over. I thought, this is goddamned serious and you had better always remember that.

There was a big red enamel pot on the stove; and I ladled antelope chili into two bowls for my little boy and me. He said, "It better not be too hot."

"It isn't."

"What's your news?" he asked.

"Grandpa's dead."

"Which grandpa?" he asked. I told him it was Big Grandpa, my father. He kept on eating. "He died last night."

He said, "I know what I want for Christmas."

"What's that?"

"I want Big Grandpa back."

It was 1950-something and I was small, under twelve say, and there were four of us: my father, two of his friends, and me. There was a good belton setter belonging to the one friend, a hearty bird hunter who taught dancing and fist-fought at any provocation. The other man was old and sick and had a green fatal look in his face. My father took me aside and said, "Jack and I are going to the head of this field"—and he pointed up a mile and a half of stalks to where it ended in the flat woods—"and we're going to take the dog and get what he can point. These are running birds. So you and Bill just block the field and you'll have some shooting."

"I'd like to hunt with the dog." I had a 20-gauge Winchester my grandfather had given me, which got hocked and lost years later when another of my family got into the bottle; and I could hit with it and wanted to hunt over the setter. With respect to blocking the field, I could smell a rat.

"You stay with Bill," said my father, "and try to cheer him up."

"What's the matter with Bill?"

"He's had one heart attack after another and he's going to die."

"When?"

"Pretty damn soon."

I blocked the field with Bill. My first thought was, I hope he doesn't die before they drive those birds onto us; but if he does, I'll have all the shooting.

There was a crazy cold autumn light on everything, magnified by the yellow silage all over the field. The dog found birds right away and they were shooting. Bill said he was sorry but he didn't feel so good. He had his hunting license safety-pinned to the back of his coat and fiddled with a handful of 12-gauge shells. "I've shot a shitpile of game," said Bill, "but I don't feel so good anymore." He took a knife out of his coat pocket. "I got this in the Marines," he said, "and I carried it for four years in the Pacific. The handle's drilled out and weighted so you can throw it. I want you to have it." I took it and thanked him, looking into his green face, and wondered why he had given it to me. "That's for blocking this field with me," he said. "Your dad and that dance teacher are going to shoot them all. When you're not feeling so good, they put you at the end of the field to block when there isn't shit-all going to fly by you. They'll get them all. They and the dog will."

We had an indestructible tree in the yard we had chopped on, nailed steps to and initialed; and when I pitched that throwing knife at it, the knife broke in two. I picked it up and thought, *this thing is jinxed.* So I took it out into the crab-apple woods and put it in the can I had buried along with a Roosevelt dime and an atomic-bomb ring I had sent away for. This was a small collection of things I buried over a period of years. I was sending them to God. All He had to do was open the can, but they were never collected. In any case, I have long known that if I could understand why I wanted to send a broken knife I believed to be jinxed to God, that I would be a long way toward what they call a personal philosophy as opposed to these hand-to-mouth metaphysics of who said what to who in some cornfield twenty-five years ago.

We were in the bar at Chico Hot Springs near my home in Montana: me—a lout poet who had spent the day floating under the diving board while adolescent girls leapt overhead; my brother John had glued himself to the pipe, which poured warm water into the pool and announced over and over in a loud voice that every drop of water had been filtered through his bathing suit.

Now, covered with wrinkles, we were in the bar, talking to Alvin Close, an old government hunter. After half a century of predator control he called it "useless and half-assed."

Alvin Close killed the last major stock-killing wolf in Montana. He hunted the wolf so long he raised a litter of dogs to do it with. He hunted the wolf futilely with a pack that had fought the wolf a dozen times until one day he gave up and let the dogs run the wolf out the back of a shallow canyon. He heard them yip their way into silence while he leaned up against a tree; and presently the wolf came tiptoeing down the front of the canyon into Alvin's lap. The wolf simply stopped because the game was up. Alvin raised the Winchester and shot it.

"How did you feel about that?" I asked.

"How do you think I felt?"

"I don't know."

"I felt like hell."

Alvin's evening was ruined and he went home. He was seventy-six years old and carried himself like an old-time Army officer, setting his glass on the bar behind him without looking.

You stare through the plastic at the red smear of meat in the supermarket. What's this it says here? *Mighty Good? Tastee? Quality, Premium, and Government Inspected?* Soon enough, the blood is on your hands. It's inescapable.

It is New York City and the beef freaks are foregathering at Bruno's Pen and

Pencil. In the kitchen the slabs quiver. In the dining room deals sear the air. Princess Lee Radziwill could be anywhere, fangs aloft to hit the meat that Bruno's Pen and Pencil's butcher's slaughterhouse killed for the Princess. The cow's head and lightless eyes twirl in the rendering vat as linen soars to the Princess's dripping lips.

Aldo Leopold was a hunter who I am sure abjured freeze-dried vegetables and extrusion burgers. His conscience was clean because his hunting was part of a larger husbandry in which the life of the country was enhanced by his own work. He knew that game populations are not bothered by hunting until they are already too precarious and that precarious game populations should not be hunted. Grizzlies should not be hunted, for instance. The enemy of game is clean farming and sinful chemicals, as well as the useless alteration of watersheds by promoter cretins and the insidious dizzards of land development whose lobbyists teach us the venality of all governments.

A world in which a sacramental portion of food can be taken in an old way—hunting, fishing, farming, and gathering—has as much to do with societal sanity as a day's work for a day's pay.

For a long time, there was no tracking snow. I hunted on horseback for a couple of days in a complicated earthquake fault in the Gallatins. The fault made a maze of narrow canyons with flat floors. The sagebrush grew on woody trunks higher than my head and left sandy paths and game trails where the horse and I could travel.

There were Hungarian partridge that roared out in front of my horse, putting his head suddenly in my lap. And hawks tobogganed on the low air currents, astonished to find me there. One finger canyon ended in a vertical rock wall from which issued a spring of the kind elsewhere associated with the Virgin Mary, hung with *ex-votos* and the orthopedic supplications of satisfied miracle customers. Here, instead, were nine identical piles of bear shit, neatly adorned with undigested berries.

One canyon planed up and topped out on an endless grassy rise. There were deer there, does and a young buck. A thousand yards away and staring at me with semaphore ears.

They assembled at a stiff trot from the haphazard array of feeding and strung out in a precise line against the far hill in a dog trot. When I removed my hat, they went into their pogo-stick gait and that was that.

"What did a deer ever do to you?"

"Nothing."

"I'm serious. What do you have to go and kill them for?"

"I can't explain it talking like this."

"Why should they die for you? Would you die for deer?"

"If it came to that."

My boy and I went up the North Fork to look for grouse. We had my old pointer Molly, and Thomas's .22 pump. We flushed a number of birds climbing through the wild roses; but they roared away at knee level, leaving me little opportunity for my over-and-under, much less an opening for Thomas to ground-sluice one with his .22. We started out at the meteor hole above the last ranch and went all the way to the national forest. Thomas had his cap on the bridge of his nose and wobbled through the trees until we hit cross fences. We went out into the last open pasture before he got winded. So, we sat down and looked across the valley at the Gallatin Range, furiously white and serrated, making a bleak edge of the world. We sat in the sun and watched the chickadees make their way through the russet brush.

"Are you having a good time?"

"Sure," he said and curled a small hand around the octagonal barrel of the Winchester.

"A guy in a New York paper said I was destroying you with my lifestyle."

"What's a lifestyle?"

"It's a word they have. It means, how you go around acting."

He said, "Oh."

"The same guy said the movies gave us four hundred thousand dollars."

My son looked at me sharply. "What did you do with it?"

"I never got it."

"Who is this guy?"

"Name of the *Village Voice.*"

"Is he a liar, liar with his pants on fire?"

"He's a yellow journalist."

"What's that?"

"Filth."

"What happened to all that money?"

"I don't know. Somebody forgot to pass it on. Then the journalist blamed it on me."

"That Marlon Brando got it," Thomas said.

"I don't think so. All he wanted was to be an Indian. We needed more for him to be a cowboy, but he wanted to be an Indian."

"He had the suit."

"I think that was our problem. I think he already had the suit."

"Can he hunt?" asked my son.

"I don't think so, Tom."

The rear quarters of the antelope came from the smoker so dense and finely grained it should have been sliced as prosciutto. My Canadian in-laws brought edgy, crumbling Cheddar from British Columbia and everybody kept an eye on the food and tried to pace themselves. The snow whirled in the windowlight and puffed the smoke down the chimney around the cedar flames. I had a stretch of enumerating things: my family, hayfields, saddle horses, friends, thirty-ought-six, French and Russian novels. I had a baby girl, colts coming, and a new roof on the barn. I finished a big corral made of railroad ties and 2 × 6s. I was within eighteen months of my father's death, my sister's death, the collapse of my marriage, the recutting of a film I'd made by ham-fisted producers, and the turning of a compact Western I'd written into utter rat shit by the puffy androids of *avanti* cinema. Finally, the fabrications of these birdbrains were being ascribed to me by such luminaries as John Simon, masochistic *New York*'s house Nazi, and Rex Reed, the Prince of Mince. Still, the washouts were repairing; and when a few things had been set aside, not excluding drugs and paranoia, a few features were left standing, not excluding lovers, children, friends, and saddle horses. In time, it would be clear as a bell. I did want venison again in the winter and couldn't help but feel some old ridge-runner had my number on him.

I didn't want to read and I didn't want to write or acknowledge the phone with its tendrils into the zombie enclaves. I didn't want the New Rugged; I wanted the Old Rugged and a pot to piss in. Otherwise, it's deteriorata with mice undermining the wiring in my frame house, sparks jumping in the insulation, the dog turning queer, and a horned owl staring at the baby through the nursery window.

It was pitch black in the bedroom and the windows radiated cold across the blankets. The top of my head felt this side of frost and the stars hung like ice crystals over the chimney. I scrambled out of bed and slipped into my long johns, put on a heavy shirt and my wool logger pants with the police suspenders. I carried the boots down to the kitchen so as not to wake the house and zapped the percolator on. I put some cheese and chocolate in my coat, and when the coffee was done I filled a chili bowl and quaffed it against the winter.

When I hit the front steps I heard the hard squeaking of new snow under my boots and the wind moved against my face like a machine for refinishing hardwood floors. I backed the truck up to the horse trailer, the lights wheeling against the ghostly trunks of the bare cottonwoods. I connected the trailer and pulled it forward to a flat spot for loading the horse.

I had figured that when I got to the corral, I could tell one horse from another by starlight; but the horses were in the shadow of the barn and I went in feeling my way among their shapes trying to find my hunting horse, Rocky, and trying to get the front end of the big sorrel who kicks when surprised. Suddenly Rocky was looking in my face and I reached around his neck with the halter. A 1,300-pound bay quarter horse, his withers angled up like a fighting bull, he wondered where we were going but ambled after me on a slack lead rope as we headed out of the darkened corral.

I have an old trailer made by a Texas horse vet years ago. It has none of the amenities of newer trailers. I wish it had a dome light for loading in the dark;

but it doesn't. You ought to check and see if the cat's sleeping in it before you load; and I didn't do that either. Instead, I climbed inside of the trailer and the horse followed me. I tied the horse down to a D-ring and started back out, when he blew up. The two of us were confined in the small space and he was ripping and bucking between the walls with such noise and violence that I had a brief disassociated moment of suspension from fear. I jumped up on the manger with my arms around my head while the horse shattered the inside of the trailer and rocked it furiously on its axles. Then he blew the steel rings out of the halter and fell over backward in the snow. The cat darted out and was gone. I slipped down off the manger and looked for the horse; he had gotten up and was sidling down past the granary in the star shadows.

I put two blankets on him, saddled him, played with his feet, and calmed him. I loaded him without incident and headed out.

I went through the aspen line at daybreak, still climbing. The horse ascended steadily toward a high basin creaking the saddle metronomically. It was getting colder as the sun came up and the rifle scabbard held my left leg far enough from the horse that I was chilling on that side.

We touched the bottom of the basin and I could see the rock wall defined by a black stripe of evergreens on one side and the remains of an avalanche on the other. I thought how utterly desolate this country can look in winter and how one could hardly think of human travel in it at all, not white horsemen nor Indians dragging travois, just aerial raptors with their rending talons and heads like cameras slicing across the geometry of winter.

Then we stepped into a deep hole and the horse went to his chest in the powder, splashing the snow out before him as he floundered toward the other side. I got my feet out of the stirrups in case we went over. Then we were on wind-scoured rock and I hunted some lee for the two of us. I thought of my son's words after our last cold ride: "Dad, you know in 4-H? Well, I want to switch from Horsemanship to Aviation."

The spot was like this: a crest of snow crowned in a sculpted edge high enough to protect us. There was a tough little juniper to picket the horse to, and a good place to sit out of the cold and noise. Over my head, a long, curling plume of snow poured out, unchanging in shape against the pale blue sky. I ate some of the cheese and rewrapped it. I got the rifle down from the scabbard, loosened the cinch and undid the flank cinch. I put the stirrup over the horn to remind me my saddle was loose, loaded two cartridges into the blind magazine and slipped one in the chamber. Then I started toward the rock wall, staring at the patterned discolorations: old seeps, lichen, cracks, and the madhouse calligraphy of immemorial weather.

There were a lot of tracks where the snow had crusted out of the wind; all deer except for one well-used bobcat trail winding along the edges of a long rocky slot. I moved as carefully as I could, stretching my eyes as far out in front of my detectable movement as I could. I tried to work into the wind but it turned erratically in the basin as the temperature of the new day changed.

The buck was studying me as soon as I came out on the open slope; he was a long way away and I stopped motionless to wait for him to feed again. He stared straight at me from 500 yards. I waited until I could no longer feel my feet or finally my legs. It was nearly an hour before he suddenly ducked his head and began to feed. Every time he fed I moved a few feet, but he was working away from me and I wasn't getting anywhere. Over the next half-hour he made his way to a little rim and, in the half-hour after that, moved the twenty feet that dropped him over the rim.

I went as fast as I could move quietly. I now had the rim to cover me and the buck should be less than a hundred yards from me when I looked over. It was all browse for a half-mile, wild roses, buck brush, and young quakies where there was any runoff.

When I reached the rim, I took off my hat and set it in the snow with my gloves inside. I wanted to be looking in the right direction when I cleared the rim, rise a half step and be looking straight at the buck, not scanning for the buck with him running sixty, a degree or two out of my periphery. And I didn't want to gum it up with thinking or trajectory guessing. People are always trajectory guessing their way into gut shots and clean misses. So, before I took the last step, all there was to do was lower the rim with my feet, lower the buck into my vision and isolate the path of the bullet.

As I took that step, I knew he was running. He wasn't in the browse at all, but angling into invisibility at the rock wall, racing straight into the elevation, bounding toward zero gravity, taking his longest arc into the bullet and the finality and terror of all you have made of the world, the finality you know that you share even with the Princess and your babies with their inherited and ambiguous dentition, the finality that, any minute now, you will meet as well.

He slid a hundred yards in a plume of snow. I dressed him and skidded him by one antler to the horse. I made a slit behind the last ribs, pulled him over the saddle and put the horn through the slit, lashed the feet to the cinch Ds, and led the horse downhill. The horse had bells of clear ice around his hooves and, when he slipped, I chipped them out from under his feet with the point of a bullet.

I hung the buck in the open woodshed with a lariat over a rafter. He turned slowly against the cooling air. I could see the intermittent blue light of the television against the bedroom ceiling from where I stood. I stopped the twirling of the buck, my hands deep in the sage-scented fur, and thought: This is either the beginning or the end of everything.

SEPTEMBER 1977

THE LAST PORK CHOP

by EDWARD ABBEY

IN MEDIAS RES, ALASKA; JUNE 24

We watch the little Cessna roar down the gravel bar toward the river, going away. At full throttle, into the wind, pilot and airplane are fully committed—they must take off or die. Once again the miracle takes place, the fragile craft lifts itself from the ground and rises into the air, noisy as a bumblebee, delicate as a butterfly. Function of the airfoil, pulled forward by a whirling screw. And I am delighted, one more time, by the daring of my species and the audacity of our flying machines. There is poetry and music in our technology, a beauty as touching as that of eagle, moss campion, raven, or yonder limestone boulder shining under the Arctic sun.

The airplane diminishes downriver, banks, and turns through a pass in the hills and is gone, out of sight, suddenly silent, ephemeral and lovely as a dream.

I notice now that we have been left behind. Two of us, myself and Dana Van Burgh the Third, a handsome, hearty river guide who looks a bit like Paul Mc-Cartney or maybe one of Elvis Presley's possible sons. The Cessna is bound for an Eskimo village called Kaktovik ("fish-seining place") about a hundred miles away on the most dismal, desperate, degraded rat hole in the world—Barter Island. If all goes well the plane will return in two hours with more of our equipment and two or three more members of our party. Our expedition. Mark Jensen's Alaska River Expeditions, Haines, Alaska.

The river at our side, more crystalline than golden, is called the Kongakut, and the plan, if all goes right, is to float down this river in two rubber rafts to another straight gravel bar eighty miles away. There, ten days from now, the airplane will pick us up and ferry us back—to Kaktovik, and Barter Island. Something to look forward to. But the river is alive with Arctic char and grayling, first-rate primeval fishing waters, and in the valley and among the treeless mountains around us roam the caribou, the wolf, the Dall sheep (close cousin to the bighorn), the moose, and of course the hypothetical grizzly bear. Himself, *Ursus arctos horribilis*. So they say.

If I seem skeptical about the bear it is because after several efforts I have yet to see with my own eyes a grizzly in the wild. I spent a summer as a fire lookout in Glacier National Park in Montana, and I saw a few black bears but not one grizzly. Even hiking alone, after dark, through alder thickets on a mountain trail, I failed to attract the GRIZ (the plural form of which is GRIZZ). I sweated up another mountain trail behind Douglas Peacock, himself half-grizzly, to a secret place he calls the Grizzly Hilton, where he has filmed, encountered, and *talked with* many grizzlies, but we saw nothing except flies, mosquitoes, and the devil's club, a mean, ugly plant with hairy leaves, thorny stems, a fist of inedible yellow berries on its top. Ten days on the Tatshenshini River in the wilderness of the Yukon and southeast Alaska again failed to produce an authentic grizzly bear. I even tried the Tucson Zoo one time, but the alleged grizzly (if such there be) refused to emerge from its den in the rear of the cage. I could see a single dark paw with ragged claws, a host of loitering flies, nothing more.

The grizzly bear is an inferential beast.

Of course I've seen the inferential evidence—the photographs and movies, the broad tracks in the sand, the deep claw marks on a spruce tree higher than I could reach, the fresh bear shit steaming like hot caviar on the trail. And I've heard and read the testimony of many others. What does it come to? Inference. If "p" then "q." It could all be a practical joke, a hoax, even a conspiracy. Which is more likely? asked Mark Twain (I paraphrase): that the unicorn exists or that men tell lies?

The grizzly bear is a myth.

The high peaks of the Brooks Range stand behind us, to the south, barren of trees, dappled with snowfields and a few small glaciers. To the east is Canada, perhaps a hundred miles away. The nearest city in that direction would be Murmansk. Murmansk, Russia. The nearest city to the west is also Murmansk.

The nearest city in any direction is Fairbanks, about 600 miles to the south-west. (If you are willing to allow Fairbanks a place in the category of city. And why not? We are a generous people.) The nearest permanently inhabited or reinhabited town, after Kaktovik up there in the Beaufort Sea, is an Athabas-can Indian settlement called Arctic Village, a couple of hundred miles away on the other side, the southern, wetter side, of the Brooks Range.

After the Australian outback, this is the most remote spot on which I've managed to install myself, on this particular planet, so far. But it seems benign here, especially, the river flowing nearby, its water clean enough to drink, di-rectly, without boiling or purifying. Imagine the rare, almost-forgotten plea-sure of dipping a cup into a river—not a stream but a river—and drinking the water at once, without hesitation, without fear. There are no beaver in the Brooks, no domestic cattle, no permanent humans, and extremely few tran-sient humans, and therefore no coliform bacteria. So far.

And the sun keeps shining, circling, shining, not so intensely as in the desert or at high elevations (we're only 2,500 feet above sea level here), but more per-sistently. With a doughty, dogged persistence—that midsummer sun will never go down.

We gather firewood. Timberline begins at sea level on the north side of the Brooks Range divide, but there is a scrubby growth of willow, shoulder high, along the crystal river, and little groves of small, slender cottonwoods—like baby aspens—tucked in sheltered corners here and there. We garner drift-wood, enough for a couple of days, from the gravel bar.

Dana stops, hearing a noise in the willow thicket downstream. A noise like the thump and thud of heavy feet. He faces that way, watching intently. The noise stops. I look the other way, upstream and to both sides, afraid of some-thing *fierce* creeping up on us from behind.

"It ain't wilderness," says my friend Doug Peacock, "unless there's a critter out there that can kill you and eat you."

Two pump-action short-barreled shotguns lie on our duffel a hundred feet away, loaded with 12-gauge slugs. Back at the Barter Island airstrip Dana had explained the shotguns in the following way to one of our passengers:

"You fire the first shot in front of the GRIZ, into the ground, to scare him away. If he don't scare but keeps advancing you wait until you can't stand it anymore, then shoot to kill. First a shot to knock him down, next a shot to fin-ish him off."

I like Dana's phrase, *Until you can't stand it anymore . . .* Thoroughly subjec-tive but admirably rational.

The noise we heard is not repeated; Dana and I surmise that the sound came from a lone caribou browsing on willow leaves. We finish our work. Erecting my own tent out on the gravel bar close to the river, where the breeze is breezier and the mosquitoes scattered, I happen to glance up and see a file of caribou—twelve or fifteen of them, moving rapidly down the open mountain-side on the other side of the Kongakut Valley. They appear to be heading for an acre field of overflow ice, the white *Aufeis*, as the Germans call it, which covers much of the bottom land a half-mile to our north. I watch them for a while through my binoculars. Pale brown or yellowish in color, as big as elk, each animal carries an impressive rack of antlers (not horns) on its head, the cow and yearling as well as the bull. They look to me like storybook reindeer, exactly the kind that Santa Claus once harnessed to his sleigh. The caribou gather on the ice and linger there, perhaps to escape for a time the flying swarms of devils that infest the grass, flowers, shrubs, heather, and bracken of the tundra-upholstered hillsides.

The Cessna returns, circles once, floats down upon the rough shingle of the gravel bar, bounces to another hair-raising stop in an aura of dust. A door is opened from within, disgorging our trip leader, Mark Jensen; another half-ton of baggage; the pilot; and a lawyer. A lawyer on the Kongakut River? Everybody has to be somewhere, said the philosopher Parmenides, explaining his theory of the plenum. Her name is Ginger Fletcher, and she comes from Salt Lake City, where she works as a public defender. She's that kind of lawyer, public-spirited, and a smart, lively, good-looking young woman to boot. (I list her more conspicuous attributes in random order of importance.) Later, when she opens a bottle of schnapps from her bag, we name her Ginger Schnapps.

Mark Jensen, like so many professional outdoors people, is one of those depressingly youngish types (thirty-four years old) with the body of a trained athlete, hands like Vise-Grips, and a keen mind bright with ideas and full of enthusiasm for any project that promises the rewards of difficulty. He has the usual array of primary skills, being a first-class boatman, fisherman, hunter, camp cook, mountain climber, and so on and so forth. He has hair like Robert Redford and a sort of Robert Mitchum high-bridged nose that gives him, in profile, the classical heroic Homeric look. Life is not fair. In compensation he addresses everyone as "mate" or "partner," which fools no one. Enough of these *Übermenschen*. I wish that Fran Lebowitz or Nora Ephron were here. My sort of people.

Jensen smiles, opens a big thermos jug, and pours each of us a cupful of hot, smoking coffee. Our pilot, young Gil Zemansky, Ph.D. (biology), gulps his quickly; we pivot his aircraft around by hand, nose into the wind, and off he roars in all-out effort, racketing over the stones and gravel at fifty miles an hour, heading toward the willow thicket, the boulders, the river, departing Earth as before at the last plausible moment. He has one more trip to make, three more passengers to bring us, before his work is done and the day ends.

But of course, I remind myself, it's late June in the Arctic; this day will not end, not for us. For us that sun will never go down.

We carry the baggage off the landing strip, build up the fire, start a two-gallon pot of coffee, eat a snack before supper. Or is it lunch? Ginger puts up her tent back in the caribou-cropped willows. We watch more caribou trickle over the mountain to join their friends on the ice field. A golden eagle sails overhead and the gulls come and go, hoping for someone to catch and gut a fish.

I realize that I have described all of these people, including the pilot, as young. Compared to me they are. Everywhere I go these days I seem to find myself surrounded by younger and younger humans. If one keeps hanging about, as I do, then the temporal horizon expands, the pursuing generations extend toward infinity. But why should I care? Sagging into my late middle age, I have discovered one clear consolation for my stiffening back (I never could touch my toes anyway, and why should I want to?), my mildewed pancreas, my missing gallbladder, my *panza de cerveza*, my cranky and arthritic Anglo-Saxon attitudes. And the consolation is this, that I am content with my limitations.

Unsuspecting, the caribou come to meet us, a herd of twenty-five or so. Anxious and bug-harassed creatures, they usually keep on the move. They pass us, their big ungulate feet clicking, then stop, turn, go the other way, as finely attuned to one another's movements and emotions as a school of minnows. Watching them at close range, I can see the velvet on their antlers, the large glowing eyeballs, the supple muscles, the spring and tension in their step. Each animal moves within its personalized cloud of gnats, flies, mosquitoes, every insect probing for entrance into an eye, nostril, ear, mouth, vagina, pizzle, rectum, or wound. I do not envy the caribou. North of here on the calving grounds, the bear and wolves are attacking their newborn at this very hour. The natives hound them on snowmobiles (or snow machines, as Alaskans say), shooting them down by the thousands with high-powered, scope-sighted rifles ("subsistence hunting"). Even the golden eagle, according to some Alaska Fish and Game officials, will attack and kill a caribou calf. Nobody envies the caribou. But like fruit flies, rabbits, alley cats, street rats, and the human race, caribou possess one great talent for survival: not intelligence or the power of reasoning, but fertility—a high rate of reproduction.

Once more our aerial taxicab returns, unloading the balance of the 1983 Kongakut expedition: John Feeley, a schoolteacher from a little town called Whittier in southern Alaska; Maurine Bachman, a legal secretary from Anchorage; and Mike Bladyka, an anesthesiologist from Los Angeles. Good people, happy to be here. All of us but John have been on a river trip with Mark Jensen before. Obeying the territorial, nesting instinct, each man sets up his tent first thing. Maurine moves in with Ginger. John uncases his rod and goes fishing. Mike joins the crowd in the cook tent, out of the wind, to manufacture the salad for our first wilderness dinner. I too do my part: I sit on my ammo can and activate my word processor. It's a good one. User-friendly, cheap, silent, no vibrations or radiation, no moving parts, no maintenance, no power source needed, easily replaceable, fully portable, it consists of a notebook and a ball-point pen from DESERT TREES, 9559 N. CAMINO DEL PLATA, TUCSON, ARIZ. The necessary software must be supplied by the operator, but as friendly critics have pointed out, an author's head is full of that.

For dinner we get by on soup, salad, spaghetti and sauce with meatballs. We drink no beer on this trip. When air freight costs one dollar a pound beer is not cost-effective; we subsist on wine, whiskey, schnapps, and, best of all, the 40-degree, immaculately conceived waters of the Kongakut River.

The sun angles sidewise behind some western peaks. But there is no sunset, no evening. Not even a twilight. The bald, unmediated light continues to shine on the mountainsides east of the river. There are a couple of wristwatches in our group, but no one refers to them. There seems no point to it. At last, and reluctantly, one by one, we let the wind or the mosquitoes or fatigue—it's been a long day—worry us into our tents.

The light inside my translucent nylon dome is bright enough to read a book by. The mosquitoes gather outside the netting of my doorway, poking their Pinocchio noses through the interstices, sniffing at me like bloodhounds. A few have followed me inside. I hunt them down, one at a time, and pinch their little heads off. For such resolute, persistent, vicious, bloodthirsty animalcules, they are surprisingly fragile. As individuals. One slap on the snout and they crumple. Collectively, they can drive a bull moose insane. I feel no remorse in extinguishing their miserable lives. I'm a cold-hearted bleeding heart. Yet I know that even the mosquito has a function, you might say a purpose, in the great web of life. Their larvae help feed fingerlings, for example. Certain of their women help spread the viruses and parasitic protozoa that give us dengue, yellow fever, and malaria, for example, keeping in control the human population of places like Borneo, Angola, and Italy. No organism can be condemned as totally useless.

Nevertheless, one does not wish them well. I would not kill them all, but I will certainly kill every one I can catch. Send them back where they came from.

We sleep. I dream that I hear robins, 300 miles north of the Arctic Circle. Dreaming of Home, Pennsylvania.

JUNE 25

Today we climb a mountain. We follow a brook up a deep ravine, over the rocks and a deep-pile carpet of tundra, lupine, buttercups, forget-me-nots, campion, mountain avens, bayrose, eight-petal dryas, kinnikinick, saxifrage ("stone-breakers"), woolly lousewort (a favorite of mine), Labrador tea, drunken bumblebees, piles of caribou droppings like chocolate-covered almonds, pictographic lichen on the limestone, and many little yellow composites. What are these? asks Ginger. Don't know, says Mark. Water gurgles under the rocks. Call it a virus, says Dana; that's what doctors do when they don't know. Ain't that right, Doc? Doctor Mike smiles, chuffing along with me in the rear guard of the party. Aside from myself, he is the only person here over the age of thirty-five.

We scramble up a pile of scree and eat lunch on the summit, 2,500 feet above the river, 5,000 feet above sea level. Snowy peaks lift hoary heads (as John Muir would say) in most—not all—directions. We are in that part of the Brooks Range called the Romanzof Mountains, which recalls the former colonizers of the Alaskan territory. To the Russians Alaska must have seemed like merely a two-bit extension of Siberia. Extreme East Slobbovia. No wonder they parted with it so cheaply.

Americans think Alaska is big. The Northwest Territories of Canada are bigger. Siberia is one and a half times bigger than both combined. So much for surface extension. If the state of Utah—which consists mostly of mountains, plateaus, mesas, buttes, pinnacles, synclines, anticlines, folds, reefs, canyons, and vertical canyon walls—were ironed out flat it would take up more room on a map than Texas. What does that prove? It's what is there, or here, now, that matters.

So much for chauvinism. Most of the mountains around us, so far as we know, have never been climbed by anybody but the Dall bighorns. The majority have not even been named, except for the most prominent, like Michelson (9,239 feet) and Chamberlin (9,020).

We return to camp by a different route, finding fresh bear sign on the way: torn-up sod, where the bear was rooting for marmots and ground squirrels; a well-trod bear trail; a messy pile of bear dung. Dana carries his shotgun slung on shoulder, but we stay alert as we march along. There is an animal out here that is bigger than we are.

We tramp through a mile of muskeg at the foot of the hills. Muskeg consists of tussocks of balled-up grass, each tussock the size of a human head, all rooted in a bog. It is difficult to walk among them in the soft muck, even more difficult to walk upon or over them. We lurch and stumble through the mire, and as we advance great shimmering hosts of mosquitoes rise eagerly from the weeds to greet us. Alaska is not only the biggest of the fifty states, it is also the boggiest and buggiest. Dripping in sweat and the greasy oil of insect repellent, we stagger on. Takes guts to live in Alaska, no doubt about it. I am favorably impressed, once again, by the pluck and hardihood of these people, both native and white. I wonder though, sometimes, about their native intelligence.

We reach camp, the fresh breeze, the welcome hard ground of the gravel beach, and wade into the icy river for a drink, then a shampoo, a bath—ladies upstream, men downstream.

Shivering in the wind, I dry myself with my cleanest dirty shirt. Forgot to bring a towel. The wind is coming up the river, as usual, from the north and the frozen Arctic Sea; I can feel that chill malignancy penetrate the marrow of my bones. Hurriedly I dress, layering on a shirt, a hooded sweatshirt, and a parka. When I feel warm the wind stops.

And *they* come out again. I wait. One slap on the arm kills nine. Forgot to bring cigars. I reach for the repellent.

We have Mexican food for supper, preceded by a pitcher of margaritas iced with snow carried down from the mountain in a daypack by Mike, a thoughtful and foresighted man. We drink to his health. Life is rough on the Last Frontier. Don't feel quite right myself, but it's only a matter of acclimatizing: When I left Tucson three days ago the temperature was 106 in the shade; at Salt Lake City, where we paused for a day and a night, it was 65 degrees and stormy; at Fairbanks (elevation 448 feet), where I stayed for two nights, the air was humid, muggy, and close to 90 degrees—and hotter than that in my little cell at the El Sleazo Hotel on the banks of the Chena River. From Fairbanks by DC-3 to Barter Island, on the edge of the Arctic ice pack, we found ourselves in the heart of the wind-chill factory—even the Eskimos were wearing their parkas; and now on the river, where the wind comes and goes, the temperature seems to fluctuate from subfreezing to 80 and back again. No one complains about the weather except me, and I do it inwardly only; can't let the others know that the most sissified rugged outdoorsman in the West is now squatting among them on his ammo can, huddled in thermal long johns, wool pants, wool shirt, flannel sweatshirt, wool ski cap, and a flannel-lined hooded parka.

Before turning in for the sun-bright night I requisition a handful of aspirin from the expedition infirmary; Mark also doses me with 10,000 milligrams of vitamin C and other huge jellied capsules, spansules, and suppositories, each about horse-size. "Can't get sick on us, mate," he says. "You know there are no germs north of the Arctic Circle."

"Of course not," I agree. "But one could always show up." Crawling into my geodesic tent, sliding into my antique, greasy, duct-tape-mended mummy bag, I say to myself, No germs, eh? Well, if I were a germ I wouldn't want to live here either.

The sun shines all night long.

JUNE 26

I awaken by degrees to the sound of robins chirping in the cherry trees of Home, Pennsylvania. Impossible. But when I emerge from my cocoon the first thing I see is a fat robin redbreast bouncing along on the gravel bar. How could such a small, harmless, innocent bird travel so far? Or as Jensen says, how many fpm (wing flaps per minute) to cover 3,000 miles?

Mark has caught an 18-inch char for breakfast. Six or seven pounds. He packs it with lemon, paprika, and butter; wraps it in aluminum foil; and bakes it on a grill over the low driftwood fire. The flesh is firm, sweet, pink, something like fresh salmon but better, not so oily, much like the Dolly Varden we used to eat, years ago, from that little lake—Akakola—below the Numa Ridge fire lookout in Glacier Park. The Dolly Varden, in fact, is a type of char.

Today we set out on the Kongakut. We inflate, rig, and load the two neo-prene rafts; strike tents; police the site. Like all good professional outfitters, Mark Jensen practices no-trace camping. Everything noncombustible is ham-mered flat with a stone and packed out. The ashes from the fire, collected on the metal fire pan, are dumped into the river, where they will end their chemic lives blended with the Arctic Ocean. Even our footprints—since we've made camp on the flood plain—will be obliterated by the next rise in the river.

We launch forth. Check the time by Maurine's quartz crystal wristwatch: 2:00 P.M. in Fairbanks. We have again failed to crack the noon barrier. But here, where high noon lasts for hours, it does not matter.

We float downstream through the treeless hills, among the golden tundra mountains. It's something like boating through Colorado at 13,000 feet. We see golden plovers out on the flats, another golden eagle overhead. And the gulls. And the robins. And a raven.

"My favorite bird," says Mark. "Smart, talented, handsome—"

"Like you," says Ginger.

"Like me. When I—" He points to the high mountainside on our left. "Sheep."

A herd of Dall bighorns is grazing up there, a dozen of them, ewes, lambs, rams with curling horns. Placid, motionless, they watch us—phantom beings out of nowhere—drifting through their world.

"When I come back," continues Mark, "I want to come back as a raven."

"Crawling with lice," Ginger points out. "Smelling like a dead fish."

"With a beak even bigger than the beak you've got now," says Maurine. "Proportionately speaking."

Smiling, Mark stands up between the oars to survey the channel ahead. Like most Alaskan rivers the Kongakut is shallow, broad, and braided, hard to read, forcing the boatman to search constantly for the one navigable channel among many false options. Following us in the second boat, Dana watches carefully. Only Mark has seen this river before.

All goes well today. In the evening we make camp on another bar, a pleasant site with limestone cliffs overlooking the river, a grove of little ten-foot cotton-woods on the other shore, a vista upriver of the valley we have come through and the splendid craggy snowy mountains beyond. The classic alpine-Arctic scene—photogenic, fundamental, perfect.

Why are there almost no trees on the North Slope of the Brooks? The reason is the permafrost two feet below the surface, a substratum of rocklike ice that prevents trees from sinking roots. Only close to the river, where the ground is warmer, can the dwarf willows and midget cottonwoods take hold.

Years ago I was employed briefly as a technical writer for the Western Electric Company in New York City. The company had a contract with the War Department to prepare training manuals for the workers building the Arctic radar stations and air bases of the Distant Early Warning System. One hundred of us sat at desks in one huge office ten floors above Barclay Street in lower Manhattan. Fluorescent lights glared down upon our bent, white-shirted backs. (All technical writers were required to wear white shirts. With tie.) Since my security clearance had not yet come through, I was assigned the menial task of editing the manual called *How to Dispose of Human Sewage in Permafrost*. I told the boss I wanted to be sent to the Arctic in order to conduct firsthand field studies. He told me that my job was spelling, grammar, and punctuation, not shit research. I returned to my desk among the other stuffed, bent white shirts—we all faced in the same direction—and stared moodily out the window for two weeks, watching the sun go down over Hoboken, New Jersey.

The boss came to me. "Abbey," he said, "do you really want to work for Western Electric?" "No sir," I said, "not really." "I thought not," he said. "We're letting you go as of 1700 hours today." I could have kissed him—and knowing New York, I probably should have. "That's all right, sir," I said. "I'm leaving right now, as of 1330 hours." And I did. Spent the afternoon at the White Horse Tavern on Hudson Street, then with cronies at Minsky's Burlesque in Newark. Reported to my wife, drunk and happy, at 2200 hours with what was left of my first and final Western Electric paycheck. Pointed the old Chevy pickup south and west at 2300 hours and headed for Arizona. Never did learn how to dispose of human sewage (is there any other kind?) in permafrost.

But I know now. What they do on Barter Island, at least, is dump it into a sewage lagoon two feet deep, chlorinate the water, and drink it. And how do they dispose of general garbage on the North Slope? They don't; they leave it on the surface, where it becomes the highest and most scenic feature of the landscape.

Beef Stroganoff for supper. The Russian influence lingers on in nostalgia-loving Alaska.

Loaded with aspirin and more of Jensen's horse medicine, I retire early to my tent, still feeling lousy. Forgot the towel, forgot the cigars, forgot to bring a book. So I borrow a paperback from Maurine, something called *Still Life With Woodpecker*. Yes, that appears to be the title. I glance at the blurbs, the summary on the back cover. "You didn't bring anything for grown-ups?" She has not. "Did anybody?" I ask the group.

Dana offers me a book called *The Dancing Wu Li Masters,* by a Mr. Gary Zukav. "How about a Gideon's Bible? Or a dictionary?" Mark offers his ammo-can edition of Merriam-Webster. "Already read that one," I say. I borrow the first two, ungrateful bastard, and sulk off. The wind has died; a number of dancing Wu Li masters follow me into my tent. I slaughter them and bed down with Tom Robbins and Mr. Gary Zukav. *Ménage à trois . . . de poupée . . . entente . . .*

JUNE 27

Breakfast goes by in a blur. We load the boats, shove off, glide down the current between walls of turquoise-colored *Aufeis.* Horned white sheep crawl upon the distant hillsides like woolly maggots. Clouds cover the sun; the Arctic wind comes sweeping up the river. Dana strains at the oars, sweating hard to keep up with Mark while I sit huddled in the bow swaddled in layers of Pendleton and polyester and self-pity. "Let me know if you see a GRIZZ," I growl, nodding off. He nods.

Hours pass, along with some gravel bars, a few willow thickets, more walls of ice. This is the kind of thing, I say to myself, that no one actually wants to do. And afterward you're not even glad you did it. Unlike the infantry, or suicide, or exploratory surgery. I become aware of danger ahead. Trouble: I look up hopefully.

Mark has beached his rubber raft on a most unlikely, rough, difficult spot. Emphatically, he signals Dana to bring his boat alongside. "Ready for a fast landing," Dana says, pulling hard toward shore. I pick the coiled bowline from under my rubber boots. We grate onto the ice and gravel. I stagger out with the rope and hold the boat against the violent tug of the current. Dana jumps out, and we heave the boat higher onto the gravel. There is nothing here to tie up to: All hands are summoned to drag both boats out of the river.

Mark talks quietly to Dana. Followed by John, they go off to investigate something ahead. All that I can see, from where we have landed, is the river funneling into a narrow channel between vertical walls of blue ice six to ten feet high. Fifty yards ahead the river swerves around a bend, going out of view within the icy walls. We have stopped at the last possible takeout point short of a full commitment to the ice canyon.

"What seems to be the trouble here?" I ask, holding out my GI canteen cup. Ginger is pouring hot coffee from the thermos jug. My hands shake with cold; I need both hands to hold my cup steady.

"Don't know," she says. "Mark said he doesn't like the looks of the river here."

"Looks like the same old Styx to me," Mike says from deep within his parka hood. I'm glad to see that he, too, is feeling the cold. Los Angeles. He and I, the only southwesterners in the party, are equally thin-blooded.

Mark, Dana, John come back. Mark looks somber, an unusual expression for his habitually cheerful face. "We'll camp here, mates."

"Here? On the ice?"

He points to the left bank, beyond the ice. "Over there." We unload the boats and carry our gear and baggage to dry land, then come back for the boats. By then we've seen what the problem is. Not far beyond the bend the river goes *under* the ice, emerging a hundred feet beyond. If we had gone on in the boats we would have been trapped and drowned beneath the ice, or, if flushed through, we would probably have died of hypothermia before we found dry matches and sufficient wood to get a big fire going.

"I had this feeling," Mark says.

JUNE 28

I totter down the hill from my tent and join the jolly bunch around the breakfast fire. Mutely, sadly, I hold out my tin cup; someone pours coffee into it. "How's it going, partner?" our leader says.

"Great," I mumble, "great."

I swallow my coffee and watch Ginger and Mike squabbling politely over Mark's last blueberry pancake. You take it, she says. Naw, you take it, Mike says. They remind me, in my fluish delirium, of my friend Kevin Briggs, another river rat, and his

Parable of the Last Pork Chop

My friend Kevin is a stout, husky fellow, and, being a graduate student of philosophy and literature, he is always hungry. One day he and five classmates were invited to lunch by their teacher, Ms. Doctor Professor H. A kind, well-meaning, but frugal woman, Professor H. seated her six guests at the dining table in her home and set a platter holding exactly seven pork chops at the head of the table. Kevin, seated on her right, too hungry to waste time counting the pork chops, helped himself to two from the top and passed the platter on. Professor H. meanwhile had gone back to her kitchen. She returned with the mashed potatoes and gravy just as the platter had nearly completed its round of the table. One pork chop remained. She sat down. The young man on her left, who had not yet served himself, looked at the last pork chop, then at his hostess. She looked at him. Both laughed awkwardly. You take it, he said. Oh no, she said, you take it. I'm really not hungry, he said. I'm not either, really, she said. Kevin, by this time, had gobbled down everything on his plate; he reached across the table with his fork and stabbed the last pork chop. I'll eat it, he said. And he did.

Moral? He who hesitates is second? No, Kevin explained to me, not at all. Remember the words of our Lord and Savior: "To him that hath much, much shall be given. But verily, from him that hath little, that little shall be taken away" (Matt. 13:12).

Mark Jensen, looking at me, says, "We'll stay here a couple of days. Who wants to climb another mountain?"

I creep back to my tent. I read the borrowed books.

Hours later I am roused from a deep stupor by Mark, bringing me with his own hands a bowl of hot celery soup and a plate containing chunks of fish with noodles and mashed potatoes. It looks good, and I am hungry.

"How's it going, partner?"

"Fine, Mark, fine. Say, this is damn good fish. You catch another char?"

"That's turkey. Out of a can."

"Damn good. See any GRIZZ?"

"Had a glimpse of one going over the next ridge. Only for a minute. A true silvertip—we could see the fur shining on the shoulder hump. You should've been there, mate."

"I know. What else?"

"Lots of sheep. A wolf. A lone bull caribou."

"Sure sorry I missed that bear."

"We thought of you, mate. If I'd had a good rope with me I'd have lassoed the son of a bitch and drug him back here. Better take some more of these pharmaceuticals."

JUNE 30

Another gay, sunny, brisk, breezy Arctic morning. We carry the boats to the river, since the river will not come to us, and proceed as before, downstream. My flu has entered its terminal phase and I am ready to meet my Maker, eyeball to eyeball, way up here on top of the world, as we say in these parts.

The top of the world. But of course the giddy, dizzying truth is that the words *top* and *bottom*, from a planetary point of view, have no meaning. From out here in deep space, where I am orbiting, there is no top, there is no bottom, no floor, no ceiling, to anything. We spin through an infinite void, following our curving path around the sun, which is as bewildered as we are. True, the infinite is incomprehensible—but the finite is absurd. Einstein claimed otherwise, I know, but Einstein was only a mortal like us. No ceiling, no floor, no walls. . . . We are 350 miles north of the Arctic Circle, and we flow as we go, like spindrift, like bits of Styrofoam, through the outliers of what Mark says is the northernmost mountain range in the world, i.e., on Earth. Will we ever get back to downtown Kaktovik?

I think of the Eskimos there, holed up all day inside their $250,000 air-freighted prefab modular houses (paid for with oil royalties), watching *Mr. Rogers' Neighborhood* on their brand-new color-TV sets. A few grinning kids race up and down the dirt street, among the melting snowbanks, on their Honda ATCs. What we call "road lice" back in the Southwest. (Girls love horses. Little boys love machines. Grown-up men and women like to walk.) The kids seem to have nothing else to do. A dead bowhead whale—rare species—lies rotting on the waterfront, partially dismembered. Slabs of whale blubber—*muktuk*—are stacked in the yard of each house, along with the empty plywood crates, the diesel spills, the oil drums, the Skiddoo parts, the caribou antlers, the musk-ox bones, the wolf pelts, the moose heads, the worn-out rubber boots, the tin cans and liquor bottles and loose papers and plastic potsherds. In each yard lies one howling arthritic Husky dog, token souvenir of former days, short-chained to a stake out of reach of the muktuk. The dogs are never released from the chain.

And the wind blows day and night, forever, out of the north, from beyond the dead whale on the beach, from beyond the mangled ice floes, out of the infinite wastes of the most awesome sight in the North: that pale, cold, no-man's-land, that endless frozen *whiteness* leading as far as eye can perceive out over the Beaufort Sea and into the Arctic Ocean. Toward the Pole.

What will happen to these people when the North Slope oil gives out? The Eskimos and other Alaskan natives still enjoy the hunt, as much or more than ever, and when they do go hunting, on their screaming packs of snow machines, they kill everything that moves, or so I was told. But this kind of hunting, whether of land or sea animals, depends upon technology and access to the cash nexus—money. (The musk ox, for example, had to be reintroduced from Canada into the Arctic National Wildlife Refuge because the natives, equipped with white man's machines and armed with white man's weapons, had exterminated the local herds.) Impossible to imagine, I was told, that the new generations would or could return to the traditional nomadic way, using primitive weapons, following the game in its seasonal migrations from Alaska to Canada and back, surviving in hide tents and sod huts under the snow as their ancestors—their still-living grandparents—had done. Unimaginable. When the oil money is gone, they'll all move to the slums of Fairbanks, Anchorage, and Seattle, join the public welfare culture, before consenting to such romantic humiliation. Can't blame them; until the coming of the white man the natives spent half their lives on the edge of starvation. Famine was common. Now, despite alcoholism, violence, suicide, their population is growing—and fast.

What happens to these people when they migrate to the city? I think of "Two Street" (Second Avenue), Fairbanks, which resembles the center of Flagstaff or Gallup on a Saturday night. There is even a "Navajo Taco Stand" on one corner, selling genuine Athabascan tacos (fry bread, shredded lettuce, and hamburger), and the street is lined with grim little bars jam-packed with brawling Indians and Eskimos. Just like down home: the Club 66 in Flag, the Eagle in Gallup, or the Silver Dollar in Bluff, on the edge of the Navajo reservation.

We camp today at a broad open place that Mark has named Velvet Valley. Under a spiny, purple, crenellated mountain that looks like Mordor, like the Hall of the Mountain King, like Darth Vader's childhood playpen, like the home of the Wicked Witch of the North, extends a lovely valley clothed in golden tundra, a million bloody blooming flowers, the lambent light of the midnight sun. (I dislike that word *lambent*, but it must be employed.) A soft, benevolent radiance, you might say, playing upon the emerald green, the virgin swales of grass and moss and heather and Swede-heads.

The Arctic wind blows merrily; it takes four of us to get the cook tent up, our only communal shelter. I scrounge for firewood with the others, and soon we've got a good fire burning near the entrance to the tent, a big meal under way inside.

More time slippage. We'd eaten lunch at five in the afternoon, we're having dinner at eleven. Time, says Einstein, is a function of space. Or, said another philosopher, time is but the mind of space. How true. And is everything finally only relative? It is not. The light is fixed and absolute. Especially the Arctic light. We'll eat dinner at eleven and have a midnight snack in Seward's Icebox at four in the morning if we bloody well feel like it. Who's to stop us?

The sun shines all night long.

JULY 3

John and Mark catch a big char and a small grayling for breakfast. A fine kettle of fish.

We go for a walk up the Velvet Valley, through the willows, through the muskeg, up onto the tundra, deep into the valley. Flowers everywhere, each flower concealing a knot of mosquitoes, but we're accustomed to the little shit-heads by now; they don't bother us; we rub on the bug juice and let the insects dance and hover—patterns of organic energy made visible—in futile molecular orbits one inch from the skin. Like the flies in Australia the mosquitoes here become simply part of the atmosphere, the decor, the ambience. We ignore them.

A ram watches us from a high point of rock; his flock grazes above. Mark kneels by a mountain stream trying to photograph the cross-hatched ripples of converging currents. Dana glasses the high ridges for bear, shotgun at his side. John is fishing back at the river. Mike, Maurine, and Ginger are eating cheese and crackers and identifying the many flowers, with the help of a guidebook, that I have not mentioned. I sit on the grass scribbling these notes, with a clump of Siberian asters fluttering at my elbow.

This is what I am writing:

Alaska is not, as the state license plate asserts, the Last Frontier. Alaska is the final big bite on the American table, where there is never quite enough to go around. "We're here for the megabucks," said a construction worker in the Bunkhouse at Kaktovik, "and nothing else." At the Bunkhouse the room and board cost $150 a day, on the monthly rate, but a cook can earn $10,000 a month. Others much more. Alaska is where a man feels free to destroy an entire valley by placer mining, as I could see from the air over Fairbanks, in order to extract one peanut butter jar full of gold dust. Flying from Barter Island to the Kongakut, Gil Zemansky showed me the vast spread of unspoiled coastal plain where Arco, Chevron, and others plan oil and gas exploration in the near future, using D-7 bulldozers pulling sledges, thus invading the caribou calving grounds and tearing up the tundra and foothills of the Arctic National Wildlife Refuge, last great genuine wilderness area left in the fifty United States. In southeast Alaska the U.S. Forest Service is allowing the logging companies to clear-cut and decimate vast areas of the Tongass National Forest, home of our national bird and officially, ostensibly, the legal property of the American public—all of us.

Last Frontier? Not exactly: Anchorage, Fairbanks, and outposts like Barter Island, with their glass-and-aluminum office buildings, their airlift prefab fiberboard hovels for the natives and the workers, their compounds of elaborate and destructive machinery, exhibit merely the latest development in the planetary expansion of space-age sleaze—not a frontier but only one more high-tech slum. For Americans, another colony. Alaska is the last pork chop.

Down the river, through the portal of the mountains into the foothills, approaching the coastal plain, we float northward in our little air-filled boats. Seeing that I have come back to life, the literary natives on shipboard badger me with bookish questions. I am happy to oblige.

ˉ What's the best book about Alaska? The best book about the North, I say, is *The Call of the Wild*. In the language of critics, Jack London captures there the essence of the mythos of the wilderness. No, my companions say, the best book about Alaska. *Winter News*, I say, by John Haines—pure poetry; and by pure I mean poetry about ordinary things, about the great weather, about daily living experience, as opposed to technical poetry, which is concerned mainly with prosody—with technique. (One of my favorite lectures.) Don't lecture, they say;

what about prose—books in prose. (I sense a trap about to snap.) I pause for a moment, pretending to reflect, and say *Going to Extremes*, by Joe McGinnis. A brilliant book. Mandatory for anyone who wants a sense of what contemporary life in Alaska is like. My opinion does not sit well with the locals. No! they say, McGinnis writes only about the sensational. Alaska is a sensational place, I reply. He's a scandalmonger, they say. Alaska is a scandalous place, I say; McGinnis tells the truth. How much time have you spent in Alaska? they want to know. About four weeks, all told, I answer. They smile in scorn. Four weeks of observation, I explain, is better than a lifetime of daydreaming. What about *Coming Into the Country*? someone asks. I had to admit that I had started on that book but never finished it. McPhee, I explain, is a first-rate reporter, but too mild, too nice, too cautious—no point of view. More questions. You like Robert Service? I love him. But, says one inquisitor, I don't think you really love Alaska, do you? The most attractive feature of Alaska, I say, is its tiny, insignificant human population—thanks to its miserable climate. I like the mountains, the glaciers, the wildlife, and the roominess, I hasten to add—or I would if the bugs would stop crowding me. I think you are a geographical chauvinist, she says, a spatial bigot. Special? Spatial. Well, I confess, I'll admit I've lived too long in the Southwest; I should have saved that for last. Then what are you doing in Alaska? she says.

Me?

You.

Slumming, I explain.

Quiet, whispers Mark, resting on the oars. Look over there.

We look where he points. Three wolves are watching us from another bar beside the river, less than a hundred feet away. Three great gray shaggy wolves, backlighted by the low sun, staring at us. Silently we drift closer. Gently, Mark pulls the boat onto the gravel, where it stops. Don't get out, Mark whispers. The wolves watch, the cameras come out, the wolves start to move away into the willow thicket and toward the open tundra. A whistle stops the last one as it climbs the bank. I stare at the wolf through my binoculars, the wolf stares at me; for one still, frozen, sacred moment I see the wild green fire in its eyes. Then it shrugs, moves, vanishes.

We drift on, silently, down the clear gray waters. After a while my friend says to me: When's the last time you saw something like that in Arizona? In your whole crowded, polluted, stinking Southwest?

Me?

You.

Moi?

Vous.

Another pause. Never did, I say.

You ought to be ashamed of yourself.

I am.

You ought to take back everything you've said.

I take it all back. (*But*, I think, all the same . . .)

Now the river tangles itself into a dozen different channels, all shallow. The main channel runs straight into a jungle of willow. We unload the boats, portage them and our gear around the obstruction. As I'm lugging two ten-gallon ammo cans across the damp silt I see a pair of tracks coming toward me. Big feet with claw marks longer than my fingers. The feet are not so long as mine, but they are twice as wide. Double wides, size 10-EEEE. I stop and look around through the silence and the emptiness.

Old Ephraim, where are you?

He does not appear.

We go on. We camp for the day and the daytime night at what Mark calls Buena Vista—a grand view upriver of the Portal, Wicked Witch Mountain, the hanging glaciers of the high peaks beyond. Char-broiled char for supper.

John and I go for a long walk into the hills, over the spongy tundra, taking one of the shotguns with us. Peacock can face his bear with only a camera; I want firepower. As we walk uphill toward the sun we see the mosquitoes waiting for us, about two and a half billion of them hovering in place above the field, the little wings and bodies glowing in the sunlight. "It looks like a zone defense," John says. But they part before us, lackadaisical atoms unable to make up their pinpoint minds, yielding before our scent and our more concentrated nodules of organic energy, as Alan Watts would say. John is a quiet fellow, likable, attractive despite his Yasser Arafat–type beard. He tells me a little about life in Whittier, Alaska. To get to his classroom in winter he walks from his bachelor apartment in a dormitory through an underground tunnel to the adjacent but separate school building. The wind outside, he says, would knock you down; when there is no wind the snow comes up to your armpits. Yet Whittier is in the far south of central Alaska—the balmy part. (You have to be balmy to live there.) When the one road out of town is closed he buckles on touring skis and glides five miles over the pass to the railway station for a ride to the heart of Anchorage. He likes his life in Whittier. (He says.) Likes his students, the bright and lively Indian kids. Doesn't mind the isolation—he's a reader of books. Is fond of snow, ice, wind, mountains, the soft summer—bugs and icicles both. How long do you plan to stay there? I ask him. Oh, another year, maybe two. Then where? Oh . . . back to the other world.

JULY 4

Mark celebrates with four blasts of the shotgun, shattering the morning air. Thinking a GRIZ is raiding the camp, I go running back only to see our leader and the others drinking coffee around the fire. Mark is always drinking coffee, and he makes strong coffee, stout, vigorous, and powerful. "Listen, mate," he says, explaining his secret formula, "you don't need *near* as much water to make coffee as some people think."

John stands by the river with his camera, photographing another dead fish. He lost most of his rod to the Kongakut days ago but didn't let that stop him; he attached his reel and a new line to his rod case and went on fishing. We've had char and grayling coming out our ears for a week. We're up to our asses in fish. But good—beats bacon and beans by a country mile. And I *like* bacon and beans.

Last stop on the river. We're encamped at the place known as Caribou Pass, near another straight gravel bar on which Gil Zemansky will land to pick us up for the last flight to Barter Island, where we then will catch the Air North DC-3 for the journey over the Brooks Range to Fairbanks and points south.

Caribou Pass—but where are the caribou? They're supposed to be massing out on the coast 100,000 strong. So far the biggest bunch we've seen was 25 head. But here is where they should pass, through these low hills, on their annual trip into the Yukon and south from there to the edge of the forest, where they spend—where they endure, somehow—the dark, six-month Yukon winter.

On the hill above us, a mile away, stands a white wall-tent and a little below it four small bivouac tents: Bear Camp. A squad of wildlife students from the University of Alaska is living up there, trapping (alive) and identifying the rodents in the tundra, watching for the caribou herds, the wolves, the GRIZZ. Mark has told them about my grizzly problem, and when a young, blond-haired, brown-skinned man named Mike Phillips comes rushing down the hillside I climb up the hill to meet him. A male grizzly, he reports, one mile east of Bear Camp. He rushes up the hill; I trudge after him. When I get there, on the high point, the bear has disappeared. Down in that willow thicket along the creek, says Mike, pointing. We glass the area for an hour, but the bear is gone. Probably took off behind the ridge, Mike explains, and crossed over the divide. Of course it would, I think, knowing that I was coming. The grizzly bear, I explain to Mike, is apocryphal, like the griffin, the centaur, and the yeti. You wouldn't think so, he replies, if you'd been with me two days ago. And he tells me about the scene at the caribou birthing grounds, the leisurely, arrogant GRIZZ he'd observed circling the great herd, chasing the cows and devouring some of the newborn young.

We watch for another hour, but the grizzly does not show. I return to the river. There I find my own party staring at a spectacle two miles away on the hillside west of the river. A big herd of caribou, 2,000, 3,000 of them, a compact animal mass, is advancing steadily to the south. If they go up the side valley over there they'll be blocked by the mountains; if they come our way they'll have to pass within a quarter-mile of where we stand, waiting and hoping.

But something, we can't see what, spooks the herd, and after milling in confusion for a few minutes the caribou reach consensus and reverse direction, returning north the way they had come, jogging along at a smart pace. Within ten minutes the entire herd is out of sight. The caribou, like the grizzly, is an unpredictable animal. It refuses to be guided by precedent, or reason, or common sense, or the wishes of a delegation of tourists.

An albino mosquito lands on my forearm. She walks nervously back and forth on my naked skin, searching for the ideal pore to probe for blood. I wait. She selects a spot she likes; the needle nose, like the drooping snout of a supersonic jet, comes down and enters. Slight prickling sensation. I hear an audible snorkeling sound—but no, I must be imagining that. I am about to slap the little thing into eternity, into its next cycle on the meat-wheel of life, when something stays my hand. Let this little one live, a voice says in my inner ear. Just once, be merciful. I hesitate. Another voice says, Don't let that Buddhist karma run over your Darwinian dogma: Mash the brute. But still I hesitate, and as I do the tiny albino withdraws her dildo, waggles her wings, and floats off into the mob. God only knows what ghastly plague I may have loosed upon humanity and the caribou by letting that one go. But I feel good about it.

We deflate and unrig the rafts, roll them up into snug bundles, stack boats, oars, rowing frames, ammo boxes, rubber bags, icebox, tents, and other dunnage at the downwind end of the imaginary airstrip.

The Cessna comes, and the ferry operation to Barter Island begins. Mark assigns me the third and final flight, giving me four extra hours on the shore of the Kongakut. Last chance. Last chance for what? I know what but dare not bait the gods by even thinking of it. Last chance for an understanding with the Spirit of the Arctic, that's what.

We wait. The plane comes and goes again with most of the cargo and all passengers but Maurine, John, and me. Two more hours.

John sleeps. Maurine is reading a book and watching the hills and meditating. I go for a walk beside the river, over the gravel bars and through the willow, heading north. The cold green waters rush past at my side, breaking over the rocks with a surflike turbulence, bound for the northern sea. A mile beyond the airstrip I am cut off by a headland. I stop and look back. The shining river races toward me. The velvet-covered hills rise on either side; the great jagged wall of the Brooks extends across the southern horizon—700 miles of largely unknown mountains, reaching across Alaska from the Yukon to the Bering Sea. The end of the Rockies. The final American wilderness.

Where is he?

The willow leaves flash their silvery undersides in the wind; McCone poppies and the purple lupine and red bayrose and yellow composites dance on the hillsides. Wordsworth would enjoy the spectacle. I think. But he might not care much for what I'm waiting for. Expecting. Both shotguns lean on the last pile of duffel where John lies sleeping, out of sight, out of hearing. I am unarmed, ready, open. Let it come.

Two shrikes watch me from the willows. Three screaming gulls pursue a golden eagle high above the river, diving and pecking at its head, trying to turn it into a bald eagle. I long to see that eagle flip on its back in midair, snatch one of those gulls in its deadly talons, and—*rip its head off!* But the eagle sails on in a straight, steady airline toward the hills, and the gulls drop away, bored.

My bear does not come.

As the plane takes off Gil Zemansky says, "I'm going to show you something." He banks and turns off course and enters a pass through the foothills west of the river. We fly a thousand feet above the lion-colored tundra. Little ponds and bog holes wink, sparkle, glitter in the light.

We cross another ridge. And there below, suddenly, the hills appear to be in motion, alive, as if the skin of the earth had begun to crawl over its rockbound bones. A broad river of caribou streams in waves west-southwesterly up the ridges and through the valleys, all its elements in rapid, parallel advance. It takes me a moment to realize that I am looking down on the greatest mass movement of untamed four-hoofed animals I may ever see. It's like the stampede of the wildebeest on the Serengeti Plain.

"My God," I say, "how many?"

Gil banks and circles, looking down. "Hard to tell. It's only a part of the Porcupine River herd. Maybe 40,000, maybe 50,000."

John and Maurine are busy taking pictures. I'm too excited to get out my binoculars. "Any GRIZZ down there?"

Gil looks again. "Bound to be a few," he says. "But they blend in so well we'd never see them."

He circles one more time, then takes a bearing northwest for Barter Island and Kaktovik, over the last foothills and 2,000 feet above the coastal plain. Well, I'm thinking, now I'm satisfied. Now I've seen it, the secret of the essence of the riddle of the Spirit of the Arctic—the flowering of life, of life wild, free, and abundant, in the midst of the hardest, cruelest land on the northern half of Earth.

And then as we approach the coast and the flat, small island at its edge, the frozen sea appears again, that curving rim of bland, silent *whiteness* stretching on and on and on, unbroken, toward the stillness of the polar climax—and beyond. And I know at last that I have seen but little of the real North, and of that little, understood less.

We don't know what it means.

LA MATADORA REVISA SU MAQUILLAJE

(The Bullfighter Checks Her Makeup)

by SUSAN ORLEAN

I went to Spain not long ago to watch Cristina Sánchez fight bulls, but she had gotten tossed by one during a performance in the village of Ejea de los Caballeros and was convalescing when I arrived. Getting tossed sounds sort of merry, but I saw a matador tossed once, and he looked like a saggy bale of hay flung by a pitchfork, and when he landed on his back he looked busted and terrified. Cristina got tossed by accidentally hooking a horn with her elbow during a pass with the cape, and the joint was wrenched so hard that her doctor said it would need at least three or four days to heal. It probably hurt like hell, and the timing was terrible. She had fights scheduled each of the nights she was supposed to rest and every night until October—every night, with no breaks in between. It had been like this for her since May, when she was elevated from the status of a novice to a full *matador de toros*. The title is conferred in a formal ceremony called "taking the *alternativa*," and it implies that you are experienced and talented and that other matadors have recognized you as a top-drawer bullfighter. You will now fight the biggest, toughest bulls and will probably be hired to fight often and in the most prestigious arenas. Bullfighting becomes your whole life, your everyday life—so routine that "sometimes after you've fought and killed the bull you feel as if you hadn't done a thing all day," as Cristina once told me. When Cristina Sánchez took her alternativa, it caused a sensation. Other women before her have fought bulls in Spain. Many have only fought little bulls, but some did advance to big animals and become accomplished and famous, and a few of the best have been declared full matadors de toros. Juanita Cruz became a matador in 1940, and Morenita de Quindio did in 1968, and Raquel Martinez and Maribel Atienzar did in the eighties, but they all took their alternativas in Mexico, where the standards are a little less exacting. Cristina is the first woman to have taken her alternativa in Europe and made her debut as a matador in Spain.

There was a fight program of three matadors—a corrida—scheduled for the Madrid bullring the day after I got to Spain, and I decided to go so I could see some other toreros while Cristina was laid up with her bad arm. One of the three scheduled to perform was the bastard son of El Cordobes. El Cordobes had been a matador superstar in the sixties and a breeder of several illegitimate children and a prideful man who was so possessive of his nickname that he had once sued this kid—the one I was going to see—because the kid wanted to fight bulls under the name El Cordobes, too. In the end, the judge let each and every El Cordobes continue to be known professionally as El Cordobes.

The kid El Cordobes is a scrubbed, cute blonde with a crinkly smile. Outside the rings where he is fighting, vendors sell fan photos of him alongside postcards and little bags of sunflower seeds and stuffed-bull souvenirs. In the photos, El Cordobes is dressed in a plaid camp shirt and acid-washed blue jeans and is hugging a good-looking white horse. In the ring, he does some flashy moves on his knees in front of the bull, including a frog-hop that he times to make it look like he's going to get skewered. These tricks, plus the renown of his name, have gotten him a lot of attention, but El Cordobes is just one of many cute young male matadors working these days. If his knees give out, he might have nothing.

On the other hand, there is just one Cristina, and everyone in Spain knows her and is following her rise. She has gotten attention far outside of Spain and on television and in newspapers and even in fashion magazines; other matadors, even very good ones, fuse in the collective mind as man-against-bull, but every time Cristina kills a bull she forms part of a singular and unforgettable tableau—that of an attractive, self-possessed young woman elegantly slaying a large animal in a somber and ancient masculine ritual—and regardless of gender she is a really good matador, and she is being painstakingly managed and promoted, so there is no saying where her celebrity will stop. This is only her first season as a full matador, but it has been a big event. Lately El Cordobes or his publicist or his accountant has been igniting and fanning the rumor that he and Cristina Sánchez are madly in love, with the hope that her fame will rub off on him. She will probably be more and more acclaimed in the four or so

years she plans to fight, and she will probably be credited with many more pu-
tative love affairs before her career is through.

Before the fight in Madrid, I walked around to the back of the bullring and
through the *patio de caballos*, the dirt-floored courtyard and stable where the
picadors' horses and the donkeys that drag away the dead bull after the fight
relax in their stalls and get their hair combed and get fed and get saddled. I was
on my way to the bullfighting museum—the Museo Taurino—which is in a
gallery next to the stalls. It was a brilliant day with just a whiff of wind. In the
courtyard, muscle men were tossing equipment back and forth and unloading
a horse trailer. Another twenty or so men were idling in the courtyard in the
few pockets of shade or near the locked door of the matadors' chapel, which is
opened before the fight so the matadors can stop in and pray. The idlers were
older men with bellies that began at their chins and trousers hiked up to their
nipples, and they were hanging around just so they could take a look at the
bulls for tonight's fight and see how they were going to be divvied up among
the three matadors. Really, there isn't a crumb of any piece of bullfighting that
goes unexamined by aficionados like these men. I lingered for a minute and
then went into the museum. I wandered past the oil portraits of Manolete
and Joselito and of dozens of other revered bullfighters, and past six stuffed
and mounted heads of bulls whose names were Paisano, Landejo, Mediaonza,
Jocinero, Hermano, and Perdigón—they were chosen for the museum because
they had been particularly mean or unusual-looking or because they had
killed someone famous. Then I stopped at a glass display case that had in it a
picture of the matador Juanita Cruz. The picture was an eight-by-ten and
looked like it had been shot in a studio. Juanita Cruz's pearly face and her
wedge of a chin and her pitch-black hair with its tiny standing waves were
blurred along the edges, movie-star style. She looked solemn, and her eyes
were focused on middle space. In the case next to the picture were her pink
matador knee socks and her mouse-eared matador hat and one of her bullfighter suits. These are called *traje de luces*, "suit of lights," and all toreros wear
them and like to change them often; Cristina has half a dozen, and Juanita
Cruz probably owned twenty or so in the course of her bullfighting career. This
one was blush pink with beautiful gold piping and sparkly black sequins. It had
the classic short, stiff, big-shouldered, box-shaped matador jacket but not the
caprilike trousers that all matadors wear, because Juanita Cruz fought in a
skirt. There is no such thing as a matador skirt anymore—Cristina, of course,
wears trousers. I looked at the skirt for a while and decided that even though it
looked unwieldy it might actually have been an advantage—in a skirt, you can
bend and stretch and lunge with a sword unconstrained. On the other hand, a
skirt would have exposed so much fabric to the bull that in a fight it would have
gotten awfully splashed and smeared with blood. Every matador has an assis-

tant who is assigned to clean his suit with soap and a toothbrush after every fight. Juanita Cruz was popular and well accepted even though she was an anomaly, but late at night, as her assistant was scrubbing her big bloody skirt, I bet he cursed the fact that she had been wearing so much fabric while sticking swords into bulls.

I went to visit Cristina at home the morning before she was going to be fighting in a corrida in a town called Móstoles. It was now a week since her injury, and her elbow apparently had healed. Two days earlier, she had tested it in a fight in Cordobes and another the following day in Jáen, and a friend of mine who reads Madrid's bullfight newspaper told me Cristina had gotten very good reviews. It turns out that I was lucky to catch her at home, because she is hardly there during the bullfighting season—usually she keeps a rock star schedule, leaving whatever town she's in with her crew right after she fights, driving all night to the next place on her schedule, checking into a hotel, sleeping until noon, eating lunch, watching some television, suiting up, fighting, and then leaving again. She was going to be at home this particular morning because Móstoles is only a few miles from Parla, the town where she and her parents and sisters live. She had come home the night before, after the fight in Jáen, and was planning to spend the day in Parla doing errands. The corrida in Móstoles would start at six. The assistant who helps her dress—he is called the sword boy, because he also takes care of all her cutlery—was going to come to the apartment at five so she could get prepared and then just drive over to the bullring already dressed and ready to go in her suit of lights. Parla is an unglamorous place about forty minutes south of Madrid; it is a kernel of an old village that had been alone on the wide open plains but is now picketed by incredibly ugly high-rise apartment buildings put up in the midsixties for workers overflowing the available housing in Madrid. The Sánchez apartment is in a slightly less ugly and somewhat shorter brick building on a busy street, on a block with a driving school, a bra shop, and a bank. There is no name on the doorbell, but Cristina's father's initials are barely scratched into a metal plate beside it. These days it is next to impossible to find Cristina. The nearly unmarked doorbell is the least of it. Cristina has a magician press agent who can make himself disappear and a very powerful and self-confident manager—a former French bullfighter named Simon Casas—who is credited with having gotten her into the biggest bullrings and the best corridas in the country but is also impossible to find and even if he were findable he would tell you that his answer to your request to speak to Cristina is no. He is especially watchful of her international exposure. Simon Casas didn't know I was coming to see Cristina in Parla and he might have disapproved simply to be disapproving, and after I saw him later that afternoon in Móstoles, prowling the perimeter of the bullring like an irritable wild animal, I was that much gladder I'd stayed out of his way.

Anyway, Cristina wasn't even home when I got there. I had driven to Parla with my translator, Muriel, and her bullfighter husband, Pedro, who both know Cristina and Cristina's father, Antonio, who himself used to be a bullfighter—if it sounds like just about everyone I encountered in Spain was or is a bullfighter, it's true. No one answered the doorbell at the apartment. Cristina's car wasn't around, so it looked like she really was gone. A car seems to be the first thing matadors buy themselves when they start making big money—that is, when they start getting sometimes as much as tens of thousands of dollars for a major fight. The bullfighter car of choice is a Mercedes, but Cristina bought herself a bright red Ford Probe, which is much sportier. She also bought her mother a small business, a gift store. We decided to wait a bit longer. Pedro killed time by making some bullfight business calls on his cellular phone. Just as we were debating whether to go looking for Cristina at her mother's store, Mrs. Sánchez came around the corner, carrying a load of groceries; she said Cristina was at the bank and that in the meantime we could come upstairs. We climbed a few flights. The apartment was tidy and fresh-looking and furnished with modern things in pastel tones, and in the living room there were a life-size oil painting of Cristina looking beautiful in her suit of lights, two huge photographs of Cristina in bullfights, one of her as a civilian, a large photograph of the older Sánchez daughter getting married, and a big-screen TV. On almost every horizontal surface there was a bronze or brass or pewter statuette of a bull, usually bucking, its withers bristling with three or four barbed harpoons called *banderillas,* which are stuck in to aggravate him before he is killed. These were all trophies from different corridas and from Cristina's stint as a star pupil at the Madrid bullfighting school. Lots of Cristina's stuff was lying around the room. On the dining table were stacks of fresh laundry, mostly white dress shirts and white T-shirts and pink socks. On the floor were a four-foot-long leather sword case, three hatboxes, and a piece of luggage that looked like a giant bowling-ball bag, which is a specially designed case for a matador's $20,000 suit jacket. Also, there was a small black Kipling backpack of Cristina's, which cracked me up because it was the exact same backpack that I was carrying.

Mrs. Sánchez was clattering around in the kitchen, making Cristina's lunch. A few minutes later, I heard the front door scrape open, and then Cristina stepped into the room, out of breath and flustered about being late. She is twenty-five years old and has chemically assisted blond hair, long eyelashes, high cheekbones, and a tiny nose. She looks really pretty when she smiles and almost regal when she doesn't, but she's not so beautiful that she's scary. This day, she was wearing blue jeans, a denim shirt with some flower embroidery, and white slip-on shoes with chunky heels, and her hair was held in a ponytail by a sunflower barrette. She is not unusually big or small. Her shoulders are square and her legs are sturdy, and she's solid and athletic-looking, like a forward on a field hockey team. Her strength is a matter of public debate in Spain. The weakest part of her performance is the very end of the fight, when she's supposed to kill the bull with one perfect jam of her sword, but she often doesn't go deep enough or in the right place. It is said in certain quarters that she simply isn't strong enough, but the fact is that many matadors mess up with the sword. When I brought it up, she shook her head and said, "People who don't understand the bullfighting world think you have to be extremely strong, but that's not the case. What is important is technique and experience. You have to be in good shape, but you don't have to match a man's strength. Besides, your real opponent is the bull, and you can never match it in strength."

Her mother came in and out of the room a few times. When she was out, Cristina said in a low voice, "I'm very happy with my family, but the time comes when you have to be independent." The tabloids have reported that she has just bought a castle on millions of enchanted acres. "I bought a small piece of property right near here," she said, rolling her eyes. "I'm having a house built. I think when I come back from my winter tour in South America I'll be able to move in."

What I really wanted to know was why in the world she decided to become a bullfighter. I knew she'd grown up watching her father fight, so it had always been a profession that seemed normal to her, even though at the ring she didn't see many girls. Plus she doesn't like to sit still. Before she started training to be a matador, she had worked in a beauty parlor and then as a typist at a fire-extinguisher factory, and both jobs drove her crazy. She is a very girly girl—she wears makeup, she wants children, she has boyfriends—but she says she was only interested in jobs that would keep her on her feet, and coincidentally those were jobs that were mostly filled by men. If she hadn't become a matador, she thinks she would have become a trainer at a gym, or a police officer, or perhaps a firefighter, which used to be her father's backup job when he was a bullfighter, in the years before he started advising her and became a full-time part of her six-person crew. She didn't become a woman matador to be shocking or make a feminist point, although along the way she has been shunned by some of her male colleagues and there are still a few who refuse to appear in a corrida with her. Once, in protest, she went to Toledo and instead of having a corrida in which three matadors each killed two bulls, she took on all six bulls herself, one by one. She said she wants to be known as a great matador and not an oddity or anecdote in the history of bullfighting. She simply loves the art and craft of fighting bulls. Later that day, when I saw her in the ring, I also realized that besides loving the bullfight itself, she is that sort of person who is illuminated by the attention of a crowd. I asked her what she'll do after she retires from the ring in three or four years. "I want to have earned a lot of money and invested it wisely," she said. "And then I want to do something in the movies or on TV."

She mentioned that she was eating early today because she had a stomachache. With a fight almost every night for months, I suppose there would be nights when she felt crummy or wasn't in the mood. Cristina laughed and said, "Yeah, sometimes you do feel like, oh God, I don't have the slightest desire to face a bull this afternoon!" Personally, I'm not a huge coward, but the phrase "desire to face a bull" will never be part of my life, any afternoon, ever. I figured that nothing must scare her. She shook her head and said, "Failure. My greatest fear is failure. I'm a woman who is a fighter and I always think about trying to surpass myself, so what I most fear is to fail."

Just then, Mrs. Sánchez came into the room and said the sandwiches were ready, so Cristina started to get up. She paused for a moment and said, "You know, people think that because I kill bulls I have to be really brave, but I'm not. I'm a sensitive person, and I can get super-terrified. I'm afraid of staying home by myself, and I get hysterical if I see a spider." I asked if bulls ever haunted her dreams, and she said, "I don't dream much at all, but a few times I've dreamed that a bull was pursuing me in the ring, up into the stands. And the night before my debut in Madrid, I did dream of bulls with huge, twisted horns."

I had seen the first bullfight of my life a few days earlier, on that night in Madrid, and it was a profound education. I learned that I should not eat for several hours beforehand and to start looking away the minute the picadors ride in on their stoic-looking blindfolded horses, because their arrival signaled that the blood and torment would begin. At first, in Madrid, I had been excited because the Plaza de Toros is so dramatic and beautiful, and also the pageantry that began the corrida was very nice, and when the first bull galloped in, I liked watching it bolt around the ring and chase the matador and his assistants until they retreated behind the small fences around the ring that are there for their protection. The small fences had targets—bull's-eyes, actually—painted on them. The bull would ram into them with its horns and the fence would rock. The more furious bulls would ram again and again, until the matador teased them away with a flourish of his cape. The bulls were homely, with little heads and huge briskets and tapered hips, and they cornered like schoolbuses and sometimes skidded to their knees, but they had fantastic energy and single-mindedness and thick muscles that flickered under their skin and faces that didn't look vicious at all and were interesting to watch. Some of the fight was wonderful: The matador's flourishes with the shocking pink and bright yellow big cape and his elegance with the small triangular red one; the sound of thousands of people gasping when the bull got very close to the cape; the plain thrilling danger of it and the fascination of watching a bull be slowly hypnotized; the bravery of the picadors' horses, which stood stock-still as the bull pounded them broadside, the flags along the rim of the ring flashing in the late-afternoon light; the resplendence of the matador's suit in that angling light, especially when the matador inched one foot forward and squared his hips and arched his back so that he was a bright new moon against a sky of sand with the black cloud of a bull racing by. I loved the ancientness and majesty and excitement of it, the way bullfighting could be at once precious and refined yet absolutely primal and raw. But beyond that I was lost and nauseated and knew I didn't understand how so many people, a whole nation of people, weren't shaken by the gore and the idea of watching a ballet that always, absolutely, unfailingly ends with a gradual and deliberate death. I didn't understand it then, and I doubt I ever will.

In the little brick bullring in Móstoles, Cristina killed two bulls well but not exceptionally—for the first kill the judge awarded her one of the bull's ears, but for the second she got no award at all. A once-in-a-lifetime sort of performance would have earned two ears, a tail, and a hoof. After that second fight Cristina looked a little disgusted with herself, and she hung back and talked for several minutes with her father, who was standing in the crew area, before she came out and took the traditional victory walk around the ring. She was clearly the crowd favorite. People wave white handkerchiefs at bullfights to indicate their support; in Móstoles it looked like it was snowing. As she circled the ring, men and women and little kids yelled, *"Matadora! Matadora!"* and *"Olé, Cristina!"* and tossed congratulatory sweaters and flowers and shoes and blazers and sandwiches and a Levi's jacket and a crutch and a cane, and then a representative of a social club in Móstoles stepped into the ring and presented her with an enormous watermelon.

After the fight, Cristina left immediately for Zaragoza, where she would have her next fight. I went back to Madrid to have dinner with Muriel and Pedro. Pedro had just finished his own fight, and he looked very relaxed and his face was pink and bright. The restaurant, Vina P, was practically wallpapered with old and new fight posters and photographs of bullfighters and some mounted bulls' heads. Its specialty was slabs of beef—since the animals killed in bullfights are butchered and are highly sought after for dining, the specialty of the house might occasionally be straight from the bullring. Pedro said Vina P was a bullfighters' restaurant, which means it is the rough equivalent of a sports bar frequented by real athletes in the United States. Before I got to Spain I imagined that bullfighting was an old and colorful tradition that was preserved but isolated, a fragile antique. Cristina Sánchez would be honored, but she would be in the margins—it would be as if she were the very best square dancer in America. Instead, she looms, and bullfighting looms. There are tons of restaurants in every city that are bullfighter and bullfight-aficionado hangouts, and there are pictures and posters of bullfights even in the restaurants that aren't, and there are bullfight newspapers and regular television coverage, and every time I turned around I was in front of the headquarters of some bullfight association. At a gas station in a nowhere place called Otero de Herreros the only bit of decoration I saw was a poster for an upcoming fight; it happened to have a picture of Cristina on it. The biggest billboards in Madrid were ads for Pepe Jeans, modeled by Francisco Rivera Ordóñez, Matador de Toros. Mostly because of Cristina, bullfight attendance is up and applications to the Madrid bullfighting school are up, especially with girls. The Spanish tabloids are fat with bullfighter gossip, and they are really keen on Cristina. That night while we were eating dinner, Pedro noticed a gorgeous young man at another table and whispered that he was a Mexican pop singer and also Cristina's old boyfriend, whom she'd recently broken up with because he'd sold the story of their relationship to the press.

I had planned to leave Spain after the fight in Móstoles, but when I heard that Cristina was going to fight soon in a town that was easy to get to, I decided to stay a few more days. The town was called Nava de la Asunción, and to get there you head north from Madrid over the raggedy gray Sierra de Guadarrama and then onto the high golden plain where many fighting bulls are raised. The occasion for the fight was the Nava town fair. According to the local paper, "peculiar and small amateur bullfights used to be done in the fenced yards of local houses until for reasons of security it was recommended to do away with these customs." The bulls were always chased through the fields in the morning so the townspeople could see what they were like. The paper said, "Traditionally there are accidents because there is always a bull that escapes. There is maximum effort put out to be sure that this does not occur, even though it is part of the tradition." It also said, "To have Cristina Sánchez in Nava is special." "The Party of the Bulls—Cristina Sánchez will be the star of the program!" "Cristina Sánchez will show her bullfighting together with the gifted Antonio Borrero 'Chamaco' and Antonio Cutiño—a great bill in which the star is, without a doubt, Cristina Sánchez."

Nava is the prettiest little town, and on the afternoon of the fight there was a marching band zigzagging around and strings of candy-colored banners hanging along the streets, popping and flapping in the wind. Just outside the bullring a few vendors had set up booths. One was selling soft drinks, one had candy and nuts, one had every manner of bullfighter souvenir: T-shirts with matador photos, pins with matador photos, photo cigarette lighters and key chains, autographed photos themselves, and white hankies for waving at the end of the fights. Of the nine photo T-shirts, seven were of Cristina. Six were different pictures of her either posing in her suit of lights or actually fighting. The other one was a casual portrait. She was dressed in a blue blouse trimmed with white daisy embroidery, and her blond hair was loose and she appeared to be sitting in a park. A nun came over to the souvenir booth and bought a Cristina photo-hankie. Big-bodied women with spindly little daughters were starting to gather around the booth and hold up first one Cristina T-shirt and then another and finally, sighing, indicate that they would take both. Skittery little boys, sometimes with a bigger boy or their fathers, darted up and poked through the stuff on the table and lingered. After a while, a couple of men pushed past the throng, lugging a trunk marked C. SÁNCHEZ toward the area under the bleachers where the matadors and picadors were getting ready. Now and then, if you looked in that direction, you could catch a glimpse of someone in a short sequined jacket, and until the band came thundering by, you could hear the hollow clunking of hooves and the heavy rustling of horses and donkeys.

The tickets were expensive whether you bought one for the sunny side or the shade, but every row was packed and every standing-room spot was taken. The men around me were smoking cigars and women were snacking on honey-roasted peanuts, and every few minutes a guy would come through hawking shots of Cutty Sark and cans of beer. Young kids were in shorts and American basketball-team T-shirts, but everyone else was dressed up, as if they were going to a dinner party at a friend's. At 5:30, in slanting sunlight, the parade of the matadors and their assistants began. Each of them was dressed in a different color, and they were dazzling and glinting in the sun. In a box seat across the ring from the entrance gate were the sober-looking judge and three girls who were queens of the fair, wearing lacy white crowns in their hair. Antonio Borrero "Chamaco" fought first, and then came Cristina. She was wearing a fuchsia suit and had her hair in a braid and had a look of dark focus on her face. When she and her assistants entered the ring, a man stood up in the stands and hollered about how much he admired her and then an old woman called out that she wanted Cristina to bless a little brooch she had pinned on her shawl.

The bull came out. He was brownish black, small-chested, wide-horned, and branded with the number 36. Cristina, the other two matadors of the day, and Cristina's picadors and banderilleros spread out around the ring holding hot-pink capes, and each one in turn would catch the bull's attention, tease him into charging, and then the next person would step forward and do the same. It was like a shoot-around before a basketball game. Meanwhile, the matadors had a chance to assess the bull and figure out how fast he moved and if he faked right and passed left or if he seemed crazy. This bull was a sprinter, and all around the ring the capes were blooming. Then two picadors rode out and positioned their horses at either end of the ring, and as soon as the bull noticed one, he roared toward it, head down, and slammed into the padding that protected the horse's flank. The picadors stabbed the bull with long spears as he tangled with the horse. After he was speared several times by each picador, he was lured away by the big capes again. A few moments later, the ring cleared, and a banderillero sprinted into the ring carrying a pair of short, nicely decorated harpoons. He held them high and wide. Eventually the bull lunged toward the banderillero, who ducked out of the way of the horns and planted the banderillas into the bull's withers. Then a second banderillero did the same thing. The bull was panting. The band burst into a fanfare, and then Cristina came out alone, carrying a small red heart-shaped cape. She stood at attention and tipped her hat to the judge—asking permission to kill the bull—and then turned and glanced just slightly toward her father, who was standing between the seats and the ring. The bull stood motionless and stared at her. For ten minutes or so she seduced him toward her, and just as he thought he was about to kill her, she diverted him with dizzying, rippling, precise swings of her cape—first a windmill, then a circle, then a chest pass, where the bull rushes straight toward and then under the cape. As the bull passed her, Cristina's back was as arched as a scythe. When the bull was swooning, she stood right in front of him, rubbed his forehead lightly with the flat of her sword, and then spread her arms, yelled something, and dropped down on one knee. The bull looked like he might faint.

Then she started getting ready to kill him. She walked over to her sword boy and traded him for her longest, sharpest blade. The band was toodling away on some brassy song, and after a moment she glowered and thrust her hand up to stop it. She drew the bull toward and past her a few more times. On one pass, she lost her grip on her cape and her father shot up from his seat and the crew raced in to help her, but without even looking up she waved them away. Then the bull squared up and she squared up. His fat beige tongue was now hanging out, and a saddle-blanket of blood was spreading from the cuts that the picadors and the banderilleros had made. Cristina's eyes were fixed with a look of concentration and command, and her arm was outstretched, and she lined up the bull, her arm, and her sword. She and the bull had not seen each other before the fight—matadors and bulls never do, the way grooms avoid brides on their wedding day—but she now stared so hard at him and he at her that it looked as if each was examining the other through and through.

• • •

When it was over, she got flowers, wineskins, berets, bags of olives, loafers, crutches, more wineskins, hundreds of things shoved at her to autograph, and both of the bull's black ears. The bull got two recumbent laps of the ring, hauled around by a team of donkeys, and there was a butcher with a five-o'clock shadow and black rubber hip boots waiting for him as soon as the team dragged him through the door. When the whole corrida was finally over, a left-over bull was let loose in the ring, and anyone with nerve could hop in with him and fool around. Most people passed on that and instead filed out of the stands, beaming and chatting and slapping backs and shaking hands. Just outside the front gate was a clean white Peugot van with CRISTINA SÁNCHEZ stenciled in script on the front and the back, and in it were a driver and Cristina and Cristina's father and her crew, still dressed in their sumptuous fight clothes, still damp and pink-faced from the fight. Cristina looked tremendously happy. The van couldn't move, because the crowd had closed in around it, and everyone was waving and throwing kisses and pushing papers to autograph through the van's windows, and for ten minutes or so Cristina signed stuff and waved at people and smiled genuinely and touched scores of outstretched hands. It was such a familiar picture of success and adoration and fame, but it had a scramble of contradictory details: Here was an ancient village with a brand-new bullring, and here was a modern new car filled with young and able people wearing the uniforms of a sport so unchanging and so ritualized that except for the fresh concrete and the new car and the flushed blond face of Cristina it all could have been taking place a hundred years in the future or a hundred years ago.

At last Cristina whispered *"No más"* to the driver, and he began inching the van down the driveway and then out toward the highway, and soon you could only see a speck in the shape of the van. The town of Nava then returned to normal. Cristina was going on to fight and fight and fight until the end of the European season, and then she planned to fly to South America and fight and then to Mexico and fight and then to return to Spain and start the season again. Once someone suggested that she try to get a Nike contract, and once she told me that she would love to bring bullfighting to America. But it seems that bullfighting is such a strange pursuit and the life bullfighters lead is so peculiar and the sight and the sound and the smell of the whole thing is so powerful and so deadly that it could only exist where strangeness is expected and treasured and long-standing and even a familiar part of every day.

It was now deep evening in Nava, and the road out had not a single street-light. Outside town the road cut through huge unlit pastures, so everything in all directions was pure black. No one was on the road, so it felt even more spooky. Then a car pulled up behind me, and after a moment it sped up and passed. It was a medium-size station wagon driven by a harried-looking man, and there was a shaggy dappled-gray pony standing in the back. The man had the interior lamp turned on, maybe for the pony, and it made a trail of light I could follow the whole way back to Madrid.

DECEMBER 1996

INTO THIN AIR

by JON KRAKAUER

Straddling the top of the world, one foot in Tibet and the other in Nepal, I cleared the ice from my oxygen mask, hunched a shoulder against the wind, and stared absently at the vast sweep of earth below. I understood on some dim, detached level that it was a spectacular sight. I'd been fantasizing about this moment, and the release of emotion that would accompany it, for many months. But now that I was finally here, standing on the summit of Mount Everest, I just couldn't summon the energy to care. It was the afternoon of May 10. I hadn't slept in fifty-seven hours. The only food I'd been able to force down over the preceding three days was a bowl of Ramen soup and a handful of peanut M&M's. Weeks of violent coughing had left me with two separated ribs, making it excruciatingly painful to breathe. Twenty-nine thousand twenty-eight feet up in the troposphere, there was so little oxygen reaching my brain that my mental capacity was that of a slow child. Under the circumstances, I was incapable of feeling much of anything except cold and tired.

I'd arrived on the summit a few minutes after Anatoli Boukreev, a Russian guide with an American expedition, and just ahead of Andy Harris, a guide with the New Zealand–based commercial team that I was a part of and someone with whom I'd grown to be friends during the past six weeks. I snapped four quick photos of Harris and Boukreev striking summit poses, and then turned and started down. My watch read 1:17 P.M. All told, I'd spent less than five minutes on the roof of the world.

After a few steps, I paused to take another photo, this one looking down the Southeast Ridge, the route we had ascended. Training my lens on a pair of climbers approaching the summit, I saw something that until that moment had escaped my attention. To the south, where the sky had been perfectly clear just an hour earlier, a blanket of clouds now hid Pumori, Ama Dablam, and the other lesser peaks surrounding Everest.

Days later—after six bodies had been found, after a search for two others had been abandoned, after surgeons had amputated the gangrenous right hand of my teammate Beck Weathers—people would ask why, if the weather had begun to deteriorate, had climbers on the upper mountain not heeded the signs? Why did veteran Himalayan guides keep moving upward, leading a gaggle of amateurs, each of whom had paid as much as $65,000 to be ushered safely up Everest, into an apparent death trap?

Nobody can speak for the leaders of the two guided groups involved, for both men are now dead. But I can attest that nothing I saw early on the afternoon of May 10 suggested that a murderous storm was about to bear down on us. To my oxygen-depleted mind, the clouds drifting up the grand valley of ice known as the Western Cwm looked innocuous, wispy, insubstantial. Gleaming in the brilliant midday sun, they appeared no different than the harmless puffs of convection condensation that rose from the valley almost daily. As I began my descent, I was indeed anxious, but my concern had little to do with the weather. A check of the gauge on my oxygen tank had revealed that it was almost empty. I needed to get down, fast.

The uppermost shank of the Southeast Ridge is a slender, heavily corniced fin of rock and wind-scoured snow that snakes for a quarter-mile toward a secondary pinnacle known as the South Summit. Negotiating the serrated ridge presents few great technical hurdles, but the route is dreadfully exposed. After fifteen minutes of cautious shuffling over a 7,000-foot abyss, I arrived at the notorious Hillary Step, a pronounced notch in the ridge named after Sir Edmund Hillary, the first Westerner to climb the mountain, and a spot that does require a fair amount of technical maneuvering. As I clipped into a fixed rope and prepared to rappel over the lip, I was greeted by an alarming sight.

Thirty feet below, some twenty people were queued up at the base of the Step, and three climbers were hauling themselves up the rope that I was attempting to descend. I had no choice but to unclip from the line and step aside.

The traffic jam comprised climbers from three separate expeditions: the team I belonged to, a group of paying clients under the leadership of the celebrated New Zealand guide Rob Hall; another guided party headed by American Scott Fischer; and a nonguided team from Taiwan. Moving at the snail's pace that is the norm above 8,000 meters, the throng labored up the Hillary Step one by one, while I nervously bided my time.

Harris, who left the summit shortly after I did, soon pulled up behind me. Wanting to conserve whatever oxygen remained in my tank, I asked him to reach inside my backpack and turn off the valve on my regulator, which he did. For the next ten minutes I felt surprisingly good. My head cleared. I actually seemed less tired than with the gas turned on. Then, abruptly, I felt like I was suffocating. My vision dimmed and my head began to spin. I was on the brink of losing consciousness.

Instead of turning my oxygen off, Harris, in his hypoxically impaired state, had mistakenly cranked the valve open to full flow, draining the tank. I'd just squandered the last of my gas going nowhere. There was another tank waiting for me at the South Summit, 250 feet below, but to get there I would have to descend the most exposed terrain on the entire route without benefit of supplemental oxygen.

But first I had to wait for the crowd to thin. I removed my now useless mask, planted my ice ax into the mountain's frozen hide, and hunkered on the ridge crest. As I exchanged banal congratulations with the climbers filing past, inwardly I was frantic: "Hurry it up, hurry it up!" I silently pleaded. "While you guys are screwing around here, I'm losing brain cells by the millions!"

Most of the passing crowd belonged to Fischer's group, but near the back of the parade two of my teammates eventually appeared: Hall and Yasuko Namba. Girlish and reserved, the forty-seven-year-old Namba was forty minutes away from becoming the oldest woman to climb Everest and the second Japanese woman to reach the highest point on each continent, the so-called Seven Summits.

Later still, Doug Hansen—another member of our expedition, a postal worker from Seattle who had become my closest friend on the mountain—arrived atop the Step. "It's in the bag!" I yelled over the wind, trying to sound more upbeat than I felt. Plainly exhausted, Doug mumbled something from behind his oxygen mask that I didn't catch, shook my hand weakly, and continued plodding upward.

The last climber up the rope was Fischer, whom I knew casually from Seattle, where we both lived. His strength and drive were legendary—in 1994 he'd climbed Everest without using bottled oxygen—so I was surprised at how slowly he was moving and how hammered he looked when he pulled his mask aside to say hello. "Bruuuuuuuce!" he wheezed with forced cheer, employing his trademark, fratboyish greeting. When I asked how he was doing, Fischer insisted he was feeling fine: "Just dragging ass a little today for some reason. No big deal." With the Hillary Step finally clear, I clipped into the strand of orange rope, swung quickly around Fischer as he slumped over his ice ax, and rap-pelled over the edge.

It was after 2:30 when I made it down to the South Summit. By now tendrils of mist were wrapping across the top of 27,890-foot Lhotse and lapping at Everest's summit pyramid. No longer did the weather look so benign. I grabbed a fresh oxygen cylinder, jammed it onto my regulator, and hurried down into the gathering cloud. Moments after I dropped below the South Summit, it be-gan to snow lightly and the visibility went to hell.

Four hundred vertical feet above, where the summit was still washed in bright sunlight under an immaculate cobalt sky, my compadres were dallying, memorializing their arrival at the apex of the planet with photos and high-fives—and using up precious ticks of the clock. None of them imagined that a horrible ordeal was drawing nigh. None of them suspected that by the end of that long day, every minute would matter.

In May of 1963, when I was nine years old, Tom Hornbein and Willi Unsoeld made the first ascent of Everest's daunting West Ridge, one of the great feats in the annals of mountaineering. Late in the day on their summit push, they climbed a stratum of steep, crumbly limestone—the infamous Yellow Band—that they didn't think they'd be able to descend. Their best shot for getting off the mountain alive, they reckoned, was to go over the top and down the South-east Ridge, an extremely audacious plan, given the late hour and the unknown terrain. Reaching the summit at sunset, they were forced to spend the night in the open above 28,000 feet—at the time, the highest bivouac in history—and to descend the Southeast Ridge the next morning. That night cost Unsoeld his toes, but the two survived to tell their tale.

Unsoeld, who hailed from my hometown in Oregon, was a close friend of my father's. I climbed my first mountain in the company of my dad, Unsoeld, and his oldest son, Regon, a few months before Unsoeld departed for Nepal. Not surprisingly, accounts of the 1963 Everest epic resonated loud and long in my preadolescent imagination. While my friends idolized John Glenn, Sandy Kou-fax, and Johnny Unitas, my heroes were Hornbein and Unsoeld.

Secretly, I dreamed of climbing Everest myself one day; for more than a decade it remained a burning ambition. It wasn't until my midtwenties that I abandoned the dream as a preposterous boyhood fantasy. Soon thereafter I be-gan to look down my nose at the world's tallest mountain. It had become fash-ionable among alpine cognoscenti to denigrate Everest as a "slag heap," a peak lacking sufficient technical challenge or aesthetic appeal to be a worthy objec-tive for a "serious" climber, which I desperately aspired to be.

Such snobbery was rooted in the fact that by the early 1980s, Everest's eas-iest line—the South Col/Southeast Ridge, or the so-called Yak Route—had been climbed more than a hundred times. Then, in 1985, the floodgates were flung wide open when Dick Bass, a wealthy fifty-five-year-old Texan with limited climbing experience, was ushered to the top of Everest by an extraordinary young climber named David Breashears. In bagging Everest, Bass became the first person to ascend all of the so-called Seven Summits, a feat that earned him worldwide renown and spurred a swarm of other amateur climbers to follow in his guided bootprints.

"To aging Walter Mitty types like myself, Dick Bass was an inspiration," Seaborn Beck Weathers explained during the trek to Everest Base Camp last April. A forty-nine-year-old Dallas pathologist, Weathers was one of eight paying clients on my expedition. "Bass showed that Everest was within the realm of possibility for regular guys. Assuming you're reasonably fit and have some disposable income, I think the biggest obstacle is probably taking time off from your job and leaving your family for two months."

For a great many climbers, the record shows, stealing time away from the daily grind has not been an insurmountable obstacle, nor has the hefty outlay of cash. Over the past half-decade, the traffic on all of the Seven Summits, and especially Everest, has grown at an astonishing rate. And to meet demand, the number of commercial enterprises peddling guided ascents of these mountains has multiplied correspondingly. In the spring of 1996, thirty separate expeditions were on the flanks of Everest, at least eight of them organized as money-making ventures.

Even before last season's calamitous outcome, the proliferation of commercial expeditions was a touchy issue. Traditionalists were offended that the world's highest summit was being sold to rich parvenus who, if denied the services of guides, would have difficulty making it to the top of a peak as modest as Mount Rainier. Everest, the purists sniffed, had been debased and profaned.

Such critics also point out that, thanks to the commercialization of Everest, the once hallowed peak has now even been dragged into the swamp of American jurisprudence. Having paid princely sums to be escorted up Everest, some climbers have then sued their guides after the summit eluded them. "Occasionally you'll get a client who thinks he's bought a guaranteed ticket to the summit," laments Peter Athans, a highly respected guide who's made eleven trips to Everest and reached the top four times. "Some people don't understand that an Everest expedition can't be run like a Swiss train."

Sadly, not every Everest lawsuit is unwarranted. Inept or disreputable companies have on more than one occasion failed to deliver crucial logistical support—oxygen, for instance—as promised. On some expeditions guides have gone to the summit without any of their clients, prompting the bitter clients to conclude that they were brought along simply to pick up the tab. In 1995, the leader of one commercial expedition absconded with tens of thousands of dollars of his clients' money before the trip even got off the ground.

To a certain degree, climbers shopping for an Everest expedition get what they pay for. Expeditions on the northern, Tibetan side of the mountain are considerably cheaper—the going rate there is $20,000 to $40,000 per person—than those on the south, in part because China charges much less for climbing permits than does Nepal. But there's a trade-off: Until 1995, no guided client had ever reached the summit from Tibet.

This year, Hall charged $65,000 a head, not including airfare or personal equipment, to take people up the South Col/Southeast Ridge route. Although no commercial guide service charged more, Hall, a lanky thirty-five-year-old with a biting Kiwi wit, had no difficulty booking clients, thanks to his phenomenal success rate: He'd put thirty-nine climbers on the summit between 1990 and 1995, which meant that he was responsible for three more ascents than had been made in the first twenty years after Hillary's inaugural climb. Despite the disdain I'd expressed for Everest over the years, when the call came to join Hall's expedition, I said yes without even hesitating to catch my breath. Boyhood dreams die hard, I discovered, and good sense be damned.

On April 10, after ten days of hiking through the steep, walled canyons and rhododendron forests of northern Nepal, I walked into Everest Base Camp. My altimeter read 17,600 feet.

Situated at the entrance to a magnificent natural amphitheater formed by Everest and its two sisters, Lhotse and Nuptse, was a small city of tents sheltering 240 climbers and Sherpas from fourteen expeditions, all of it sprawled across a bend in the Khumbu Glacier. The escarpments above camp were draped with hanging glaciers, from which calved immense serac avalanches that thundered down at all hours of the day and night. Hard to the east, pinched between the Nuptse wall and the West Shoulder of Everest, the Khumbu Icefall spilled to within a quarter-mile of the tents in a chaos of pale blue shards.

In stark contrast to the harsh qualities of the environment stood our campsite and all its creature comforts, including a nineteen-person staff. Our mess tent, a cavernous canvas structure, was wired with a stereo system and solar-powered electric lights; an adjacent communications tent housed a satellite phone and fax. There was a hot shower. A cook boy came to each client's tent in the mornings to serve us steaming mugs of tea in our sleeping bags. Fresh bread and vegetables arrived every few days on the backs of yaks.

In many ways, Rob Hall's Adventure Consultants site served as a sort of town hall for Base Camp, largely because nobody on the mountain was more respected than Hall, who was on Everest for his eighth time. Whenever there was a problem—a labor dispute with the Sherpas, a medical emergency, a critical decision about climbing strategy—people came to him for advice. And Hall, always generous, dispensed his accumulated wisdom freely to the very rivals who were competing with him for clients, most notably Fischer.

Fischer's Mountain Madness camp, distinguished by a huge Starbucks Coffee banner that hung from a chunk of granite, was a mere five minutes' walk down the glacier. Fischer and Hall were competitors, but they were also friends, and there was a good deal of socializing between the two teams. His mess tent wasn't as well appointed as ours, but Fischer was always quick to offer a cup of fresh-brewed coffee to any climber or trekker who poked a head inside the door.

The forty-year-old Fischer was a strapping, gregarious man with a blond ponytail and manic energy. He'd grown up in New Jersey and had fallen in love with climbing after taking a National Outdoor Leadership School course as a fourteen-year-old. In his formative years, during which he became known for a damn-the-torpedoes style, he'd survived a number of climbing accidents, including twice cratering into the ground from a height of more than seventy feet. Fischer's infectious, seat-of-the-pants approach to his own life was reflected in his improvisational approach to guiding Everest. In striking contrast to Hall—who insisted that his clients climb as a group at all times, under the close watch of his guides—Fischer encouraged his clients to be independent, to move at their own pace, to go wherever they wanted, whenever they wanted.

Both men were under considerable pressure this season. The previous year, Hall had for the first time failed to get anybody to the top. Another dry spell would be very bad for business. Meanwhile Fischer, who had climbed the peak without oxygen but had never guided the mountain, was still trying to get established in the Everest business. He needed to get clients to the summit, especially a high-profile one like Sandy Hill Pittman, the Manhattan boulevardier-cum-writer who was filing daily diaries on an NBC World Wide Web site.

Despite the many trappings of civilization at Base Camp, there was no forgetting that we were more than three miles above sea level. Walking to the mess tent at mealtime left me wheezing to catch my breath. If I sat up too quickly, my head reeled and vertigo set in. I developed a dry, hacking cough that would steadily worsen over the next six weeks. Cuts and scrapes refused to heal. I was rarely hungry, a sign that my oxygen-deprived stomach had shut down and my body had begun to consume itself for sustenance. My arms and legs gradually began to wither to toothpicks, and by expedition's end I would weigh twenty-five pounds less than when I left Seattle.

Some of my teammates fared even worse than I in the meager air. At least half of them suffered from various intestinal ailments that kept them racing to the latrine. Hansen, forty-six, who'd paid for the expedition by working at a Seattle-area post office by night and on construction jobs by day, was plagued by an unceasing headache for most of his first week at Base Camp. It felt, as he put it, "like somebody's driven a nail between my eyes." This was Hansen's second time on Everest with Hall. The year before, he'd been forced to turn around 330 vertical feet below the summit because of deep snow and the late hour. "The summit looked *sooooo* close," Hansen recalled with a painful laugh. "Believe me, there hasn't been a day since that I haven't thought about it." Hansen had been talked into returning this year by Hall, who felt sorry that Hansen had been denied the summit and who had significantly discounted Hansen's fee to entice him to give it another try.

A rail-thin man with a leathery, prematurely furrowed face, Hansen was a single father who spent a lot of time in Base Camp writing faxes to his two kids, ages nineteen and twenty-seven, and to an elementary school in Kent, Washington, that had sold T-shirts to help fund his climb. Hansen bunked in the tent next to mine, and every time a fax would arrive from his daughter, Angie, he'd read it to me, beaming. "Jeez," he'd announce, "how do you suppose a screwup like me could have raised such a great kid?"

As a newcomer to altitude—I'd never been above 17,000 feet—I brooded about how I'd perform higher on the mountain, especially in the so-called Death Zone above 25,000 feet. I'd done some fairly extreme climbs over the years in Alaska, Patagonia, Canada, and the Alps. I'd logged considerably more time on technical rock and ice than most of the other clients and many of the guides. But technical expertise counted for very little on Everest, and I'd spent less time at high elevation—none, to be precise—than virtually every other climber here. By any rational assessment, I was singularly unqualified to attempt the highest mountain in the world.

This didn't seem to worry Hall. After seven Everest expeditions he'd fine-tuned a remarkably effective method of acclimatization. In the next six weeks, we would make three trips above Base Camp, climbing about 2,000 feet higher each time. After that, he insisted, our bodies would be sufficiently adapted to the altitude to permit safe passage to the 29,028-foot summit. "It's worked thirty-nine times so far, pal," Hall assured me with a wry grin.

Three days after our arrival in Base Camp, we headed out on our first acclimatization sortie, a one-day round-trip to Camp One, perched at the upper lip of the Icefall, 2,000 vertical feet above. No part of the South Col route is more feared than the Icefall, a slowly moving jumble of huge, unstable ice blocks: We were all well aware that it had already killed nineteen climbers. As I strapped on my crampons in the frigid predawn gloom, I winced with each creak and rumble from the glacier's shifting depths.

Long before we'd even gotten to Base Camp, our trail had been blazed by

Sherpas, who had fixed more than a mile of rope and installed about sixty aluminum ladders over the crevasses that crisscross the shattered glacier. As we shuffled forth, three-quarters of the way to Camp One, Hall remarked glibly that the Icefall was in better shape than he'd ever seen it: "The route's like a bloody freeway this season."

But only slightly higher, at about 19,000 feet, the fixed ropes led us beneath and then over a twelve-story chunk of ice that leaned precariously off kilter. I hurried to get out from beneath its wobbly tonnage and reach its crest, but my fastest pace was no better than a crawl. Every four or five steps I'd stop, lean against the rope, and suck desperately at the thin, bitter air, searing my lungs.

We reached the end of the Icefall about four hours after setting out, but the relative safety of Camp One didn't supply much peace of mind: I couldn't stop thinking about the ominously tilted slab and the fact that I would have to pass beneath its frozen bulk at least seven more times if I was going to make it to the top of Everest.

Most of the recent debate about Everest has focused on the safety of commercial expeditions. But the least experienced, least qualified climbers on the mountain this past season were not guided clients; rather, they were members of traditionally structured, noncommercial expeditions.

While descending the lower Icefall on April 13, I overtook a pair of slower climbers outfitted with unorthodox clothing and gear. Almost immediately it became apparent that they weren't very familiar with the standard tools and techniques of glacier travel. The climber in back repeatedly snagged his crampons and stumbled. Waiting for them to cross a gaping crevasse bridged by two rickety ladders lashed end to end, I was shocked to see them go across together, almost in lockstep, a needlessly dangerous act. An awkward attempt at conversation revealed that they were members of a Taiwanese expedition.

The reputation of the Taiwanese had preceded them to Everest. In the spring of 1995, the team had traveled to Alaska to climb Mount McKinley as a shakedown for their attempt on Everest in 1996. Nine climbers reached the summit of McKinley, but seven of them were caught by a storm on the descent, became disoriented, and spent a night in the open at 19,400 feet, initiating a costly, hazardous rescue by the National Park Service.

Five of the climbers—two of them with severe frostbite and one dead—were plucked from high on the peak by helicopter. "If we hadn't arrived right when we did, two others would have died, too," says American Conrad Anker, who with his partner, Alex Lowe, climbed to 19,400 feet to help rescue the Taiwanese. "Earlier, we'd noticed the Taiwanese group because they looked so incompetent. It really wasn't any big surprise when they got into trouble."

The leader of the expedition, Ming Ho Gau—a jovial photographer who answers to "Makalu"—had to be assisted down the upper mountain. "As they were bringing him down," Anker recalls, "Makalu was yelling, 'Victory! Victory! We made summit!' to everyone he passed, as if the disaster hadn't even happened." When the survivors of the McKinley debacle showed up on Everest in 1996, Makalu Gau was again their leader.

In truth, their presence was a matter of grave concern to just about everyone on the mountain. The fear was that the Taiwanese would suffer a calamity that would compel other expeditions to come to their aid, risking further lives and possibly costing climbers a shot at the summit. Of course, the Taiwanese were by no means the only group that seemed egregiously unqualified. Camped beside us at Base Camp was a twenty-five-year-old Norwegian climber named Petter Neby, who announced his intention to make a solo ascent of the Southwest Face, an outrageously difficult route, despite the fact that his Himalayan experience consisted of two easy ascents of neighboring Island Peak, a 20,270-foot bump.

And then there were the South Africans. Lavishly funded, sponsored by a major newspaper, the source of effusive national pride, their team had received a personal blessing from Nelson Mandela prior to their departure. The first South African expedition ever to be granted a permit to climb Everest, they were a mixed-race group that hoped to put the first black person on the summit. They were led by a smooth-talking former military officer named Ian Woodall. When the team arrived in Nepal it included three very strong members, most notably a brilliant climber named Andy de Klerk, who happened to be a good friend of mine.

But almost immediately, four members, including de Klerk, defected. "Woodall turned out to be a total control freak," said de Klerk. "And you couldn't trust him. We never knew when he was talking bullshit or telling the truth. We didn't want to put our lives in the hands of a guy like that. So we left."

Later de Klerk would learn that Woodall had lied about his climbing record. He'd never climbed anywhere near 8,000 meters, as he claimed. In fact, he hadn't climbed much of anything. Woodall had also allegedly lied about expedition finances and even lied about who was named on the official climbing permit.

After Woodall's deceit was made public, it became an international scandal, reported on the front pages of newspapers throughout the commonwealth. When the editor of the Johannesburg *Sunday Times*, the expedition's primary sponsor, confronted Woodall in Nepal, Woodall allegedly tried to physically intimidate him and, according to de Klerk, threatened, "I'm going to rip your fucking head off!"

In the end, Woodall refused to relinquish leadership and insisted that the climb would proceed as planned. By this point none of the four climbers left on the team had more than minimal alpine experience. At least two of them, says de Klerk, "didn't even know how to put their crampons on."

The solo Norwegian, the Taiwanese, and especially the South Africans were frequent topics of discussion around the dinner table in our mess tent. "With so many incompetent people on the mountain," Hall frowned one evening in late April, "I think it's pretty unlikely that we'll get through this without something bad happening."

For our third and final acclimatization excursion, we spent four nights at 21,300-foot Camp Two and a night at 24,000-foot Camp Three. Then on May 1 our whole team descended to Base Camp to recoup our strength for the summit push. Much to my surprise, Hall's acclimatization plan seemed to be working: After three weeks, I felt like I was finally adapting to the altitude. The air at Base Camp now seemed deliciously thick.

From the beginning, Hall had planned that May 10 would be our summit day. "Of the four times I've summited," he explained, "twice it was on the tenth of May. As the Sherps would put it, the tenth is an 'auspicious' date for me." But there was also a more down-to-earth reason for selecting this date: The annual ebb and flow of the monsoon made it likely that the most favorable weather of the year would fall on or near May 10.

For all of April, the jet stream had been trained on Everest like a fire hose, blasting the summit pyramid with nonstop hurricane-force winds. Even on days when Base Camp was perfectly calm and flooded with sunshine, an immense plume of wind-driven snow was visible over the summit. But if all went well, in early May the monsoon approaching from the Bay of Bengal would force the jet stream north into Tibet. If this year was like past years, between the departure of the wind and the arrival of the monsoon storms we would be presented with a brief window of clear, calm weather during which a summit assault would be possible.

Unfortunately, the annual weather patterns were no secret, and every expedition had its sights set on the same window. Hoping to avoid dangerous gridlock on the summit ridge, Hall held a powwow in the mess tent with leaders of the expeditions in Base Camp. The council, as it were, determined that Göran Kropp, a young Swede who had ridden a bicycle all the way to Nepal from Stockholm, would make the first attempt, alone, on May 3. Next would be a team from Montenegro. Then, on May 8 or 9, it would be the turn of the IMAX expedition, headed by David Breashears, which hoped to wrap up a large-format film about Everest with footage from the top.

Our team, it was decided, would share a summit date of May 10 with Fischer's group. An American commercial team and two British-led commercial groups promised to steer clear of the top of the mountain on the tenth, as did the Taiwanese. Woodall, however, declared that the South Africans would go to the top whenever they pleased, probably on the tenth, and anyone who didn't like it could "bugger off."

Hall, ordinarily extremely slow to rile, flew into a rage over Woodall's refusal to cooperate. "I don't want to be anywhere near the upper mountain when those punters are up there," he seethed.

"It feels good to be on our way to the summit, yeah?" Harris inquired as we pulled into Camp Two. The midday sun was reflecting off the walls of Nuptse, Lhotse, and Everest, and the entire ice-coated valley seemed to have been transformed into a huge solar oven. We were finally ascending for real, headed straight toward the top, Harris and me and everybody else.

Harris—Harold to his friends—was the junior guide on the expedition and the only one who'd never been to Everest (indeed, he'd never been above 23,000 feet). Built like an NFL quarterback and preternaturally good-natured, he was usually assigned to the slower clients at the back of the pack. For much of the expedition, he had been laid low with intestinal ailments, but he was finally getting his strength back, and he was eager to prove himself to his seasoned colleagues. "I think we're actually gonna knock this big bastard off," he confided to me with a huge smile, staring up at the summit.

Harris worked as a much-in-demand heli-skiing guide in the antipodal winter. Summers he guided climbers in New Zealand's Southern Alps and had just launched a promising heli-hiking business. Sipping tea in the mess tent back at Base Camp, he'd shown me a photograph of Fiona McPherson, the pretty, athletic doctor with whom he lived, and described the house they were building together in the hills outside Queenstown. "Yeah," he'd marveled, "it's kind of amazing, really. My life seems to be working out pretty well."

Later that day, Kropp, the Swedish soloist, passed Camp Two on his way down the mountain, looking utterly worked. Three days earlier, under clear skies, he'd made it to just below the South Summit and was no more than an hour from the top when he decided to turn around. He had been climbing without supplemental oxygen, the hour had been late—2:00 P.M., to be exact—and he'd believed that if he'd kept going, he'd have been too tired to descend safely.

"To turn around that close to the summit," Hall mused, shaking his head. "That showed incredibly good judgment on young Göran's part. I'm impressed." Sticking to your predetermined turn-around time—that was the most important rule on the mountain. Over the previous month, Rob had lectured us repeatedly on this point. Our turn-around time, he said, would probably be 1:00 P.M., and no matter how close we were to the top, we were to abide by it. "With enough determination, any bloody idiot can get up this hill," Hall said. "The trick is to get back down alive."

Cheerful and unflappable, Hall's easygoing facade masked an intense desire to succeed—which to him was defined in the fairly simple terms of getting as many clients as possible to the summit. But he also paid careful attention to the details: the health of the Sherpas, the efficiency of the solar-powered electrical system, the sharpness of his clients' crampons. He loved being a guide, and it pained him that some celebrated climbers didn't give his profession the respect he felt it deserved.

On May 8 our team and Fischer's team left Camp Two and started climbing the Lhotse Face, a vast sweep of steel-hard ice rising from the head of the Western Cwm. Hall's Camp Three, two-thirds of the way up this wall, was set on a narrow ledge that had been chopped into the face by our Sherpas. It was a spectacularly perilous perch. A hundred feet below, no less exposed, were the tents of most of the other teams, including Fischer's, the South Africans, and the Taiwanese.

It was here that we had our first encounter with death on the mountain. At 7:30 A.M. on May 9, as we were pulling on our boots to ascend to Camp Four, a thirty-six-year-old steelworker from Taipei named Chen Yu-Nan crawled out of his tent to relieve himself, with only the smooth-soled liners of his mountaineering boots on his feet—a rather serious lapse of judgment. As he squatted, he lost his footing on the slick ice and went hurtling down the Lhotse Face, coming to rest, head-first, in a crevasse. Sherpas who had seen the incident lowered a rope, pulled him out of the slot, and carried him back to his tent. He was bruised and badly rattled, but otherwise he seemed unharmed. Chen's teammates left him in a tent to recover and departed for Camp Four. That afternoon, as Chen tried to descend to Camp Two with the help of Sherpas, he keeled over and died.

Over the preceding six weeks there had been several serious accidents: Tenzing Sherpa, from our team, fell 150 feet into a crevasse and injured a leg seriously enough to require helicopter evacuation from Base Camp. One of Fischer's Sherpas nearly died of a mysterious illness at Camp Two. A young, apparently fit British climber had a serious heart attack near the top of the Icefall. A Dane was struck by a falling serac and broke several ribs. Until now, however, none of the mishaps had been fatal.

Chen's death cast a momentary pall over the mountain. But thirty-three climbers at the South Col would be departing for the summit in a few short hours, and the gloom was quickly shoved aside by nervous anticipation of the challenge to come. Most of us were simply wrapped too tightly in the grip of summit fever to engage in thoughtful reflection about the death of someone in our midst. There would be plenty of time for reflection later, we assumed, after we all had summited—and got back down.

• • •

Climbing with oxygen for the first time, I had reached the South Col, our launching pad for the summit assault, at one o'clock that afternoon. A barren plateau of bulletproof ice and windswept boulders, the Col sits at 26,000 feet above sea level, tucked between the upper ramparts of Lhotse, the world's fourth-highest mountain, and Everest. Roughly rectangular, about four football fields long by two across, the Col is bounded on the east by the Kangshung Face, a 7,000-foot drop-off, and on the west by the 4,000-foot Lhotse Face. It is one of the coldest, most inhospitable places I have ever been.

I was the first Western climber to arrive. When I got there, four Sherpas were struggling to erect our tents in a 50-mph wind. I helped them put up my shelter, anchoring it to some discarded oxygen canisters wedged beneath the largest rocks I could lift. Then I dove inside to wait for my teammates.

It was nearly 5:00 P.M. when the last of the group made camp. The final stragglers in Fischer's group came in even later, which didn't augur well for the summit bid, scheduled to begin in six hours. Everyone retreated to their nylon domes the moment they reached the Col and did their best to nap, but the machine-gun rattle of the flapping tents and the anxiety over what was to come made sleep out of the question for most of us.

Surrounding me on the plateau were some three dozen people, huddled in tents pitched side by side. Yet an odd sense of isolation hung over the camp. Up here, in this godforsaken place, I felt distressingly disconnected from everyone around me—emotionally, spiritually, physically. We were a team in name only, I'd sadly come to realize. Although we would leave camp in a few hours as a group, we would ascend as individuals, linked to one another by neither rope nor any deep sense of loyalty. Each client was in it for himself or herself, pretty much. And I was no different: I really hoped Doug Hansen would get to the top, for instance, yet if he were to turn around, I knew I would do everything in my power to keep pushing on. In another context this insight would have been depressing, but I was too preoccupied with the weather to dwell on it. If the wind didn't abate, the summit would be out of the question for all of us.

At 7:00 P.M. the gale abruptly ceased. The temperature was fifteen below zero, but there was almost no wind. Conditions were excellent; Hall, it appeared, had timed our summit bid perfectly. The tension was palpable as we sipped tea, delivered to us in our tents by Sherpas, and readied our gear. Nobody said much. All of us had suffered greatly to get to this moment. I had eaten little and slept not at all since leaving Camp Two two days earlier. Damage to my thoracic cartilage made each cough feel like a stiff kick between the ribs and brought tears to my eyes. But if I wanted a crack at the summit, I had no choice but to ignore my infirmities as much as possible and climb.

Finally, at 11:35, we were away from the tents. I strapped on my oxygen mask and ascended into the darkness. There were fifteen of us in Hall's team: guides Hall, Harris, and Mike Groom, an Australian with impressive Himalayan experience; Sherpas Ang Dorje, Lhakpa Chhiri, Nawang Norbu, and Kami; and clients Hansen, Namba, Weathers, Stuart Hutchison (a Canadian doctor), John Taske (an Australian doctor), Lou Kasischke (a lawyer from Michigan), Frank Fischbeck (a publisher from Hong Kong), and me.

Fischer's group—guides Fischer, Boukreev, and Neal Beidleman; five Sherpas; and clients Charlotte Fox, Tim Madsen, Klev Schoening, Sandy Pittman, Lene Gammelgaard, and Martin Adams—left the South Col at midnight. Shortly after that, Makalu Gau started up with three Sherpas, ignoring his promise that no Taiwanese would make a summit attempt on May 10. Thankfully, the South Africans had failed to make it to Camp Four and were nowhere in sight.

The night had a cold, phantasmal beauty that intensified as we ascended. More stars than I had ever seen smeared the frozen sky. Far to the southeast, enormous thunderheads drifted over Nepal, illuminating the heavens with surreal bursts of orange and blue lightning. A gibbous moon rose over the shoulder of 27,824-foot Makalu, washing the slope beneath my boots in ghostly light, obviating the need for a headlamp. I broke trail throughout the night with Ang Dorje—our *sirdar*, or head Sherpa—and at 5:30, just as the sun was edging over the horizon, I reached the crest of the Southeast Ridge. Three of the world's five highest peaks stood out in jagged relief against the pastel dawn. My altimeter read 27,500 feet.

Hall had instructed us to climb no higher until the whole group gathered at this level roost known as the Balcony, so I sat down on my pack to wait. When Hall and Weathers finally arrived at the back of the herd, I'd been sitting for more than ninety minutes. By now Fischer's group and the Taiwanese team had caught and passed us. I was peeved over wasting so much time and at falling behind everybody else. But I understood Hall's rationale, so I kept quiet and played the part of the obedient client. To my mind, the rewards of climbing come from its emphasis on self-reliance, on making critical decisions and dealing with the consequences, on personal responsibility. When you become a client, I discovered, you give up all that. For safety's sake, the guide always calls the shots.

Passivity on the part of the clients had thus been encouraged throughout our expedition. Sherpas put in the route, set up the camps, did the cooking, hauled the loads; we clients seldom carried more than daypacks stuffed with our personal gear. This system conserved our energy and vastly increased our chances of getting to the top, but I found it hugely unsatisfying. I felt at times as if I weren't really climbing the mountain—that surrogates were doing it for me. Although I had willingly accepted this role in order to climb Everest, I never got used to it. And I was happy as hell when, at 7:10 A.M., Hall gave me the OK to continue climbing.

One of the first people I passed when I started moving again was Fischer's sirdar, Lobsang Jangbu, kneeling in the snow over a pile of vomit. Both Lobsang and Boukreev had asked and been granted permission by Fischer to climb without supplemental oxygen, a highly questionable decision that significantly affected the performance of both men, but especially Lobsang. His feeble state, moreover, had been compounded by his insistence on "short-roping" Pittman on summit day.

Lobsang, twenty-five, was a gifted high-altitude climber who'd summited Everest twice before without oxygen. Sporting a long black ponytail and a gold tooth, he was flashy, self-assured, and very appealing to the clients, not to mention crucial to their summit hopes. As Fischer's head Sherpa, he was expected to be at the front of the group this morning, putting in the route. But just before daybreak, I'd looked down to see Lobsang hitched to Pittman by her three-foot safety tether; the Sherpa, huffing and puffing loudly, was hauling the assertive New Yorker up the steep slope like a horse pulling a plow. Pittman was on a widely publicized quest to ascend Everest and thereby complete the Seven Summits. She'd failed to make it to the top on two previous expeditions; this time she was determined to succeed.

Fischer knew that Lobsang was short-roping Pittman, yet did nothing to stop it; some people have thus concluded that Fischer ordered Lobsang to do it, because Pittman had been moving slowly when she started out on summit day, and Fischer worried that if Pittman failed to reach the summit, he would be denied a marketing bonanza. But two other clients on Fischer's team speculate that Lobsang was short-roping her because she'd promised him a hefty cash bonus if she reached the top. Pittman has denied this and insists that she was hauled up against her wishes. Which begs a question: Why didn't she unfasten the tether, which would have required nothing more than reaching up and unclipping a single carabiner?

"I have no idea why Lobsang was short-roping Sandy," confesses Beidleman. "He lost sight of what he was supposed to be doing up there, what the priorities were." It didn't seem like a particularly serious mistake at the time. A little thing. But it was one of many little things—accruing slowly, compounding imperceptibly, building steadily toward critical mass.

A human plucked from sea level and dropped on the summit of Everest would lose consciousness within minutes and quickly die. A well-acclimatized climber can function at that altitude with supplemental oxygen—but not well, and not for long. The body becomes far more vulnerable to pulmonary and cerebral edema, hypothermia, frostbite. Each member of our team was carrying two orange, seven-pound oxygen bottles. A third bottle would be waiting for each of us at the South Summit on our descent, stashed there by Sherpas. At a conservative flow rate of two liters per minute, each bottle would last between five and six hours. By 4:00 or 5:00 P.M., about eighteen hours after starting to climb, everyone's gas would be gone.

Hall understood this well. The fact that nobody had summited this season prior to our attempt concerned him, because it meant that no fixed ropes had been installed on the upper Southeast Ridge, the most exposed part of the climb. To solve this problem, Hall and Fischer had agreed before leaving Base Camp that on summit day the two sirdars—Ang Dorje from Hall's team and Lobsang from Fischer's—would leave Camp Four ninety minutes ahead of everybody else and put in the fixed lines before any clients reached the upper mountain. "Rob made it very clear how important it was to do this," recalls Beidleman. "He wanted to avoid a bottleneck at all costs."

For some reason, however, the Sherpas hadn't set out ahead of us on the night of May 9. When Ang Dorje and I reached the Balcony, we were an hour in front of the rest of the group, and we could have easily moved on and installed the ropes. But Hall had explicitly forbidden me to go ahead, and Lobsang was still far below, short-roping Pittman. There was nobody to accompany Ang Dorje.

A quiet, moody young man who regarded Lobsang as a showboat and a goldbrick, Ang Dorje had been working extremely hard, well beyond the call of duty, for six long weeks. Now he was tired of doing more than his share. If Lobsang wasn't going to fix ropes, neither was he. Looking sullen, Ang Dorje sat down with me to wait.

Sure enough, not long after everybody caught up with us and we continued climbing up, a bottleneck occurred when our group encountered a series of giant rock steps at 28,000 feet. Clients huddled at the base of this obstacle for nearly an hour while Beidleman, standing in for the absent Lobsang, laboriously ran the rope out.

Here, the impatience and technical inexperience of Namba nearly caused a disaster. A businesswoman who liked to joke that her husband did all the cooking and cleaning, Namba had become famous back in Japan for her Seven Summits globetrotting, and her quest for Everest had turned into a minor cause célèbre. She was usually a slow, tentative climber, but today, with the summit squarely in her sights, she seemed energized as never before. She'd been pushing hard all morning, jostling her way toward the front of the line. Now, as Beidleman clung precariously to the rock a hundred feet above, the overeager Namba clamped her ascender onto the dangling rope before the guide had anchored his end of it. Just as she was about to put her full body weight on the rope—which would have pulled Beidleman off—guide Mike Groom intervened and gently scolded her.

The line continued to grow longer, and so did the delay. By 11:30 A.M., three of Hall's clients—Hutchison, Taske, and Kasischke—had become worried about the lagging pace. Stuck behind the sluggish Taiwanese team, Hutchison now says, "It seemed increasingly unlikely that we would have any chance of summiting before the 1:00 P.M. turn-around time dictated by Rob."

After a brief discussion, they turned their back on the summit and headed down with Kami and Lhakpa Chhiri. Earlier, Fischbeck, one of Hall's strongest clients, had also turned around. The decision must have been supremely diffi-cult for at least some of these men, especially Fischbeck, for whom this was a fourth attempt on Everest. They'd each spent as much as $70,000 to be up here and had endured weeks of misery. All were driven, unaccustomed to los-ing and even less to quitting. And yet, faced with a tough decision, they were among the few who made the right one that day.

There was a second, even worse, bottleneck at the South Summit, which I reached at about 11:00 A.M. The Hillary Step was just a stone's throw away, and slightly beyond that was the summit itself. Rendered dumb with awe and exhaustion, I took some photos and sat down with Harris, Beidleman, and Boukreev to wait for the Sherpas to fix ropes along the spectacularly corniced summit ridge.

A stiff breeze raked the ridge crest, blowing a plume of spindrift into Tibet, but overhead the sky was an achingly brilliant blue. Lounging in the sun at 28,700 feet inside my thick down suit, gazing across the Himalayas in a hy-poxic stupor, I completely lost track of time. Nobody paid much attention to the fact that Ang Dorje and Nawang Norbu were sharing a thermos of tea be-side us and seemed to be in no hurry to go higher. Around noon, Beidleman fi-nally asked, "Hey, Ang Dorje, are you going to fix the ropes, or what?"

Ang Dorje's reply was a quick, unequivocal "No"—perhaps because neither Lobsang nor any of Fischer's other Sherpas was there to share the work. Shocked into doing the job ourselves, Beidleman, Boukreev, Harris, and I col-lected all the remaining rope, and Beidleman and Boukreev started stringing it along the most dangerous sections of the summit ridge. But by then more than an hour had trickled away.

Bottled oxygen does not make the top of Everest feel like sea level. Ascending above the South Summit with my regulator delivering two liters of oxygen per minute, I had to stop and draw three or four heaving lungfuls of air after each ponderous step. The systems we were using delivered a lean mix of compressed oxygen and ambient air that made 29,000 feet feel like 26,000 feet. But they did confer other benefits that weren't so easily quantified, not the least of which was keeping hypothermia and frostbite at bay.

Climbing along the blade of the summit ridge, sucking gas into my ragged lungs, I enjoyed a strange, unwarranted sense of calm. The world beyond the rubber mask was stupendously vivid but seemed not quite real, as if a movie were being projected in slow motion across the front of my goggles. I felt drugged, disengaged, thoroughly insulated from external stimuli. I had to remind myself over and over that there was 7,000 feet of sky on either side, that everything was at stake here, that I would pay for a single bungled step with my life.

Plodding slowly up the last few steps to the summit, I had the sensation of being under water, of moving at quarter-speed. And then I found myself atop a slender wedge of ice adorned with a discarded oxygen cylinder and a battered aluminum survey pole, with nowhere higher to climb. A string of Buddhist prayer flags snapped furiously in the wind. To the north, down a side of the mountain I had never seen, the desiccated Tibetan plateau stretched to the horizon.

Reaching the top of Everest is supposed to trigger a surge of intense elation; against long odds, after all, I had just attained a goal I'd coveted since childhood. But the summit was really only the halfway point. Any impulse I might have felt toward self-congratulation was immediately extinguished by apprehension about the long, dangerous descent that lay ahead. As I turned to go down, I experienced a moment of alarm when a glance at my regulator showed that my oxygen was almost gone. I started down the ridge as fast as I could move but soon hit the traffic jam at the Hillary Step, which was when my gas ran out. When Hall came by, I masked my rising panic and thanked him for getting me to the top of Everest. "Yeah, it's turned out to be a pretty good expedition," he replied. "I only wish we could have gotten more clients to the top." Hall was clearly disappointed that five of his eight clients had turned back earlier in the day, while all six of Fischer's clients were still plugging toward the summit.

Soon after Hall passed, the Hillary Step finally cleared. Dizzy, fearing that I would black out, I made my way tenuously down the fixed lines. Then, fifty feet above the South Summit, the rope ended, and I balked at going farther without gas.

Over at the South Summit I could see Harris sorting through a pile of oxygen bottles. "Yo, Andy!" I yelled. "Could you bring me a fresh bottle?"

"There's no oxygen here!" the guide shouted back. "These bottles are all empty!" I nearly lost it. I had no idea what to do. Just then, Groom came past on his way down from the summit. He had climbed Everest in 1993 without supplemental oxygen and wasn't overly concerned about going without. He gave me his bottle, and we quickly scrambled over to the South Summit.

When we got there, an examination of the oxygen cache revealed right away that there were six full bottles. Harris, however, refused to believe it. He kept insisting that they were all empty, and nothing Groom or I said could convince him otherwise. Right then it should have been obvious that Harris was acting irrationally and had slipped well beyond routine hypoxia, but I was so impeded myself that it simply didn't register. Harris was the invincible guide, there to look after me and the other clients; the thought never entered my own crippled mind that he might in fact be in dire straits—that a guide might urgently need help from me.

As Harris continued to assert that there were no full bottles, Groom looked at me quizzically. I looked back and shrugged. Turning to Harris, I said, "No big deal, Andy. Much ado about nothing." Then I grabbed a new oxygen canister, screwed it onto my regulator, and headed down the mountain. Given what unfolded over the next three hours, my failure to see that Harris was in serious trouble was a lapse that's likely to haunt me for the rest of my life.

At 3:00 P.M., within minutes of leaving the South Summit, I descended into clouds ahead of the others. Snow started to fall. In the flat, diminishing light, it became hard to tell where the mountain ended and where the sky began. It would have been very easy to blunder off the edge of the ridge and never be heard from again. The lower I went, the worse the weather became.

When I reached the Balcony again, about 4:00 P.M., I encountered Beck Weathers standing alone, shivering violently. Years earlier, Weathers had undergone radial keratotomy to correct his vision. A side effect, which he discovered on Everest and consequently hid from Hall, was that in the low barometric pressure at high altitude, his eyesight failed. Nearly blind when he'd left Camp Four in the middle of the night but hopeful that his vision would improve at daybreak, he stuck close to the person in front of him and kept climbing.

Upon reaching the Southeast Ridge shortly after sunrise, Weathers had confessed to Hall that he was having trouble seeing, at which point Hall declared, "Sorry, pal, you're going down. I'll send one of the Sherpas with you." Weathers countered that his vision was likely to improve as soon as the sun crept higher in the sky; Hall said he'd give Weathers thirty minutes to find out—after that, he'd have to wait there at 27,500 feet for Hall and the rest of the group to come back down. Hall didn't want Weathers descending alone. "I'm dead serious about this," Hall admonished his client. "Promise me that you'll sit right here until I return."

"I crossed my heart and hoped to die," Weathers recalls now, "and promised I wouldn't go anywhere." Shortly after noon, Hutchison, Taske, and Kasischke passed by with their Sherpa escorts, but Weathers elected not to accompany them. "The weather was still good," he explains, "and I saw no reason to break my promise to Rob."

By the time I encountered Weathers, however, conditions were turning ugly. "Come down with me," I implored. "I'll get you down, no problem." He was nearly convinced, until I made the mistake of mentioning that Groom was on his way down, too. In a day of many mistakes, this would turn out to be a crucial one. "Thanks anyway," Weathers said. "I'll just wait for Mike. He's got a rope; he'll be able to short-rope me." Secretly relieved, I hurried toward the South Col, 1,500 feet below.

These lower slopes proved to be the most difficult part of the descent. Six inches of powder snow blanketed outcroppings of loose shale. Climbing down them demanded unceasing concentration, an all but impossible feat in my current state. By 5:30, however, I was finally within 200 vertical feet of Camp Four, and only one obstacle stood between me and safety: a steep bulge of rock-hard ice that I'd have to descend without a rope. But the weather had deteriorated into a full-scale blizzard. Snow pellets born on 70-mph winds stung my face; any exposed skin was instantly frozen. The tents, no more than 200 horizontal yards away, were only intermittently visible through the whiteout. There was zero margin for error. Worried about making a critical blunder, I sat down to marshal my energy.

Suddenly, Harris appeared out of the gloom and sat beside me. At this point there was no mistaking that he was in appalling shape. His cheeks were coated with an armor of frost, one eye was frozen shut, and his speech was slurred. He was frantic to reach the tents. After briefly discussing the best way to negotiate the ice, Harris started scooting down on his butt, facing forward. "Andy," I yelled after him, "it's crazy to try it like that!" He yelled something back, but the words were carried off by the screaming wind. A second later he lost his purchase and was rocketing down on his back.

Two hundred feet below, I could make out Harris's motionless form. I was sure he'd broken at least a leg, maybe his neck. But then he stood up, waved that he was OK, and started stumbling toward camp, which was for the moment in plain sight, 150 yards beyond.

I could see three or four people shining lights outside the tents. I watched Harris walk across the flats to the edge of camp, a distance he covered in less than ten minutes. When the clouds closed in a moment later, cutting off my view, he was within thirty yards of the tents. I didn't see him again after that, but I was certain that he'd reached the security of camp, where Sherpas would be waiting with hot tea. Sitting out in the storm, with the ice bulge still standing between me and the tents, I felt a pang of envy. I was angry that my guide hadn't waited for me.

Twenty minutes later I was in camp. I fell into my tent with my crampons still on, zipped the door tight, and sprawled across the frost-covered floor. I was drained, more exhausted than I'd ever been in my life. But I was safe. Andy was safe. The others would be coming into camp soon. We'd done it. We'd climbed Mount Everest.

It would be many hours before I learned that everyone had in fact not made it back to camp—that one teammate was already dead and that twenty-three other men and women were caught in a desperate struggle for their lives.

• • •

Neal Beidleman waited on the summit from 1:25 until 3:10 as Fischer's clients appeared over the last rise, one by one. The lateness of the hour worried him. After Gammelgaard, the last of them, arrived with Lobsang, "I decided it was time to get the hell out of there," Beidleman says, "even though Scott hadn't shown yet." Twenty minutes down the ridge, Beidleman—with Gammelgaard, Pittman, Madsen, and Fox in tow—passed Fischer, still on his way up. "I didn't really say anything to him," Beidleman recalls. "He just sort of raised his hand. He looked like he was having a hard time, but he was Scott, so I wasn't partic-ularly worried. I figured he'd tag the summit and catch up to us pretty quick to help bring the clients down. But he never showed up."

When Beidleman's group got down to the South Summit, Pittman collapsed. Fox, the most experienced client on the peak, gave her an injection of a power-ful steroid, dexamethasone, which temporarily negates the symptoms of alti-tude sickness. Beidleman grabbed Pittman by her harness and started dragging her down behind him.

"Once I got her sliding," he explains, "I'd let go and glissade down in front of her. Every fifty meters I'd stop, wrap my hands around the fixed rope, and brace myself to arrest her slide with a body block. The first time Sandy came barrel-ing into me, the points of her crampons sliced into my down suit. Feathers went flying everywhere." Fortunately, after about twenty minutes the injection revived Pittman, and she was able to resume the descent under her own power.

As darkness fell and the storm intensified, Beidleman and five of Fischer's clients overtook Groom, who was bringing down Weathers, on a short rope, and Namba. "Beck was so hopelessly blind," Groom reports, "that every ten meters he'd take a step into thin air and I'd have to catch him with the rope. It was bloody nerve-racking."

Five hundred feet above the South Col, where the steep shale gave way to a gentler slope of snow, Namba's oxygen ran out and the diminutive Japanese woman sat down, refusing to move. "When I tried to take her oxygen mask off so she could breathe more easily," says Groom, "she'd insist on putting it right back on. No amount of persuasion could convince her that she was out of oxy-gen, that the mask was actually suffocating her."

Beidleman, realizing that Groom had his hands full with Weathers, started dragging Namba down toward Camp Four. They reached the broad, rolling ex-panse of the South Col around 8:00 P.M., but by then it was pitch black, and the storm had grown into a hurricane. The windchill was in excess of seventy be-low. Only three or four headlamps were working, and everyone's oxygen was long gone. Visibility was down to a few meters. No one had a clue how to find the tents. Two Sherpas materialized out of the darkness, but they were lost as well.

For the next two hours, Beidleman, Groom, the two Sherpas, and seven clients staggered blindly around in the storm, growing ever more exhausted and hypothermic, hoping to blunder across the camp. "It was total chaos," says Beidleman. "People are wandering all over the place; I'm yelling at everyone, trying to get them to follow a single leader. Finally, probably around ten o'clock, I walked over this little rise, and it felt like I was standing on the edge of the earth. I could sense a huge void just beyond."

The group had unwittingly strayed to the easternmost edge of the Col, the opposite side from Camp Four, right at the lip of the 7,000-foot Kangshung Face. "I knew that if we kept wandering in the storm, pretty soon we were going to lose somebody," says Beidleman. "I was exhausted from dragging Yasuko. Charlotte and Sandy were barely able to stand. So I screamed at everyone to huddle up right there and wait for a break in the storm."

The climbers hunkered in a pathetic cluster on a windswept patch of ice. "By then the cold had about finished me off," says Fox. "My eyes were frozen. The cold was so painful, I just curled up in a ball and hoped death would come quickly."

Three hundred and fifty yards to the west, while this was going on, I was shivering uncontrollably in my tent, even though I was zipped into my sleeping bag and wearing my down suit and every other stitch of clothing I had. The gale was threatening to blow the tent apart. Oblivious to the tragedy unfolding outside and completely out of bottled oxygen, I drifted in and out of fitful sleep, delirious from exhaustion, dehydration, and the cumulative effects of oxygen depletion.

At some point, Hutchison shook me and asked if I would go outside with him to bang on pots and shine lights, in the hope of guiding any lost climbers in, but I was too weak and incoherent to respond. Hutchison, who had got back to camp at 2:00 P.M. and was less debilitated than those of us who'd gone to the summit, then tried to rouse clients and Sherpas in the other tents. Everybody was too cold, too exhausted. So Hutchison went out into the storm alone.

He left six times that night to look for the missing climbers, but the blizzard was so fierce that he never dared to venture more than a few yards from the tents. "The winds were ballistically strong," says Hutchison. "The blowing spindrift felt like a sandblaster or something."

Just before midnight, out among the climbers hunkered on the Col, Beidleman noticed a few stars overhead. The wind was still whipping up a furious ground blizzard, but far above, the sky began to clear, revealing the hulking silhouettes of Everest and Lhotse. From these reference points, Klev Schoening, a client of Fischer's, thought he'd figured out where the group was in relation to the tents. After a shouting match with Beidleman, Schoening convinced the guide that he knew the way.

Beidleman tried to coax everyone to their feet and get them moving in the direction indicated by Schoening, but Fox, Namba, Pittman, and Weathers were too feeble to walk. So Beidleman assembled those who were ambulatory, and together with Groom they stumbled off into the storm to get help, leaving behind the four incapacitated clients and Tim Madsen. Madsen, unwilling to abandon Fox, his girlfriend, volunteered to look after everybody until a rescue party arrived.

The tents lay about 350 yards to the west. When Beidleman, Groom, and the clients got there, they were met by Boukreev. Beidleman told the Russian where to find the five clients who'd been left out in the elements, and then all four climbers collapsed in their tents.

Boukreev had returned to Camp Four at 4:30 P.M., before the brunt of the storm, having rushed down from the summit without waiting for clients—extremely questionable behavior for a guide. A number of Everest veterans have speculated that if Boukreev had been present to help Beidleman and Groom bring their clients down, the group might not have gotten lost on the Col in the first place. One of the clients from that group has nothing but contempt for Boukreev, insisting that when it mattered most, the guide "cut and ran."

Boukreev argues that he hurried down ahead of everybody else because "it is much better for me to be at South Col, ready to carry up oxygen if clients run out." This is a difficult rationale to understand. In fact, Boukreev's impatience on the descent more plausibly resulted from the fact that he wasn't using bottled oxygen and was relatively lightly dressed and therefore *had* to get down quickly: Without gas, he was much more susceptible to the dreadful cold. If this was indeed the case, Fischer was as much to blame as Boukreev, because he gave the Russian permission to climb without gas in the first place.

Whatever Boukreev's culpability, however, he redeemed himself that night after Beidleman staggered in. Plunging repeatedly into the maw of the hurricane, he single-handedly brought back Fox, Pittman, and Madsen. But Namba and Weathers, he reported, were dead. When Beidleman was informed that Namba hadn't made it, he broke down in his tent and wept for forty-five minutes.

Stuart Hutchison shook me awake at 6:00 A.M. on May 11. "Andy's not in his tent," he told me somberly, "and he doesn't seem to be in any of the other tents, either. I don't think he ever made it in."

"Andy's missing?" I asked. "No way. I saw him walk to the edge of camp with my own eyes." Shocked, horrified, I pulled on my boots and rushed out to look for Harris. The wind was still fierce, knocking me down several times, but it was a bright, clear dawn, and visibility was perfect. I searched the entire western half of the Col for more than an hour, peering behind boulders and poking under shredded, long-abandoned tents, but found no trace of Harris. A surge of adrenaline seared my brain. Tears welled in my eyes, instantly freezing my eyelids shut. How could Andy be gone? It couldn't be so.

I went to the place where Harris had slid down the ice bulge and methodically retraced the route he'd taken toward camp, which followed a broad, almost flat ice gully. At the point where I last saw him when the clouds came down, a sharp left turn would have taken Harris forty or fifty feet up a rocky rise to the tents.

I saw, however, that if he hadn't turned left but instead had continued straight down the gully—which would have been easy to do in a whiteout, even if one wasn't exhausted and stupid with altitude sickness—he would have quickly come to the westernmost edge of the Col and a 4,000-foot drop to the floor of the Western Cwm. Standing there, afraid to move any closer to the edge, I noticed a single set of faint crampon tracks leading past me toward the abyss. Those tracks, I feared, were Harris's.

After getting into camp the previous evening, I'd told Hutchison that I'd seen Harris arrive safely in camp. Hutchison had radioed this news to Base Camp, and from there it was passed along via satellite phone to the woman with whom Harris shared his life in New Zealand, Fiona McPherson. Now Hall's wife back in New Zealand, Jan Arnold, had to do the unthinkable: call McPherson back to inform her that there had been a horrible mistake, that Andy was in fact missing and presumed dead. Imagining this conversation and my role in the events leading up to it, I fell to my knees with dry heaves, retching as the icy wind blasted my back.

I returned to my tent just in time to overhear a radio call between Base Camp and Hall—who, I learned to my horror, was up on the summit ridge and calling for help. Beidleman then told me that Weathers and Namba were dead and that Fischer was missing somewhere on the peak above. An aura of unreality had descended over the mountain, casting the morning in a nightmarish hue.

Then our radio batteries died, cutting us off from the rest of the mountain. Alarmed that they had lost contact with us, climbers at Camp Two called the South African team, which had arrived on the South Col the previous day. When Ian Woodall was asked if he would loan his radio to us, he refused.

After reaching the summit around 3:30 P.M. on May 10, Scott Fischer had headed down with Lobsang, who had waited for Fischer on the summit while Beidleman and their clients descended. They got no farther than the South Summit before Fischer began to have difficulty standing and showed symptoms of severe hypothermia and cerebral edema. According to Lobsang, Fischer began "acting like crazy man. Scott is saying to me, 'I want to jump down to Camp Two.' He is saying many times." Pleading with him not to jump, Lobsang started short-roping Fischer, who outweighed him by some seventy pounds, down the Southeast Ridge. A few hours after dark, they got into some difficult mixed terrain 1,200 feet above the South Col, and Lobsang was unable to drag Fischer any farther.

Lobsang anchored Fischer to a snow-covered ledge and was preparing to leave him there when three tired Sherpas showed up. They were struggling to bring down Makalu Gau, who was as debilitated as Fischer. The Sherpas sat the Taiwanese leader beside the American leader, tied the two semiconscious men together, and around 10:00 P.M. descended into the night to get help.

Meanwhile, Hall and Hansen were still on the frightfully exposed summit ridge, engaged in a grim struggle of their own. The forty-six-year-old Hansen, whom Hall had turned back just below this spot exactly a year ago, had been determined to bag the summit this time around. "I want to get this thing done and out of my life," he'd told me a couple of days earlier. "I don't want to have to come back here."

Indeed, Hansen had reached the top this time, though not until after 3:00 P.M., well after Hall's predetermined turn-around time. Given Hall's conservative, systematic nature, many people wonder why he didn't turn Hansen around when it became obvious that he was running late. It's not farfetched to speculate that because Hall had talked Hansen into coming back to Everest this year, it would have been especially hard for him to deny Hansen the summit a second time—especially when all of Fischer's clients were still marching blithely toward the top.

"It's very difficult to turn someone around high on the mountain," cautions Guy Cotter, a New Zealand guide who summited Everest with Hall in 1992 and was guiding the peak for him in 1995 when Hansen made his first attempt. "If a client sees that the summit is close and they're dead-set on getting there, they're going to laugh in your face and keep going up."

In any case, for whatever reason, Hall did not turn Hansen around. Instead, after reaching the summit at 2:10 P.M., Hall waited for more than an hour for Hansen to arrive and then headed down with him. Soon after they began their descent, just below the top, Hansen apparently ran out of oxygen and collapsed. "Pretty much the same thing happened to Doug in '95," says Ed Viesturs, an American who guided the peak for Hall that year. "He was fine during the ascent, but as soon as he started down he lost it mentally and physically. He turned into a real zombie, like he'd used everything up."

At 4:31 P.M., Hall radioed Base Camp to say that he and Hansen were above the Hillary Step and urgently needed oxygen. Two full bottles were waiting for them at the South Summit; if Hall had known this he could have retrieved the gas fairly quickly and then climbed back up to give Hansen a fresh tank. But Harris, in the throes of his oxygen-starved dementia, overheard the 4:31 radio call while descending the Southeast Ridge and broke in to tell Hall—incorrectly, just as he'd told Groom and me—that all the bottles at the South Summit were empty. So Hall stayed with Hansen and tried to bring the helpless client down without oxygen, but could get him no farther than the top of the Hillary Step.

Cotter, a very close friend of both Hall and Harris, happened to be a few miles from Everest Base Camp at the time, guiding an expedition on Pumori. Overhearing the radio conversations between Hall and Base Camp, he called Hall at 5:36 and again at 5:57, urging his mate to leave Hansen and come down alone. "I know I sound like the bastard for telling Rob to abandon his client," confesses Cotter, "but by then it was obvious that leaving Doug was his only choice." Hall, however, wouldn't consider going down without Hansen.

There was no further word from Hall until the middle of the night. At 2:46 A.M. on May 11, Cotter woke up to hear a long, broken transmission, probably unintended: Hall was wearing a remote microphone clipped to the shoulder strap of his backpack, which was occasionally keyed on by mistake. In this instance, says Cotter, "I suspect Rob didn't even know he was transmitting. I could hear someone yelling—it might have been Rob, but I couldn't be sure because the wind was so loud in the background. He was saying something like 'Keep moving! Keep going!' presumably to Doug, urging him on."

If that was indeed the case, it meant that in the wee hours of the morning Hall and Hansen were still struggling from the Hillary Step toward the South Summit, taking more than twelve hours to traverse a stretch of ridge typically covered by descending climbers in half an hour.

Hall's next call to Base Camp was at 4:43 A.M. He'd finally reached the South Summit but was unable to descend farther, and in a series of transmissions over the next two hours he sounded confused and irrational. "Harold was with me last night," Hall insisted, when in fact Harris had reached the South Col at sunset. "But he doesn't seem to be with me now. He was very weak."

Mackenzie asked him how Hansen was doing. "Doug," Hall replied, "is gone." That was all he said, and it was the last mention he ever made of Hansen.

On May 23, when Breashears and Viesturs, of the IMAX team, reached the summit, they found no sign of Hansen's body but they did find an ice ax planted about fifty feet below the Hillary Step, along a highly exposed section of ridge where the fixed ropes came to an end. It is quite possible that Hall managed to get Hansen down the ropes to this point, only to have him lose his footing and fall 7,000 feet down the sheer Southwest Face, leaving his ice ax jammed into the ridge crest where he slipped.

During the radio calls to Base Camp early on May 11, Hall revealed that something was wrong with his legs, that he was no longer able to walk and was shaking uncontrollably. This was very disturbing news to the people down below, but it was amazing that Hall was even alive after spending a night without shelter or oxygen at 28,700 feet in hurricane-force wind and minus-100-degree windchill.

At 5:00 A.M., Base Camp patched through a call on the satellite telephone to Jan Arnold, Hall's wife, seven months pregnant with their first child in Christchurch, New Zealand. Arnold, a respected physician, had summited Everest with Hall in 1993 and entertained no illusions about the gravity of her husband's predicament. "My heart really sank when I heard his voice," she recalls. "He was slurring his words markedly. He sounded like Major Tom or something, like he was just floating away. I'd been up there; I knew what it could be like in bad weather. Rob and I had talked about the impossibility of being rescued from the summit ridge. As he himself had put it, 'You might as well be on the moon.' "

By that time, Hall had located two full oxygen bottles, and after struggling for four hours trying to deice his mask, around 8:30 A.M. he finally started breathing the life-sustaining gas. Several times he announced that he was preparing to descend, only to change his mind and remain at the South Summit. The day had started out sunny and clear, but the wind remained fierce, and by late morning the upper mountain was wrapped with thick clouds. Climbers at Camp Two reported that the wind over the summit sounded like a squadron of 747s, even from 8,000 feet below.

About 9:30 A.M., Ang Dorje and Lhakpa Chhiri ascended from Camp Four in a brave attempt to bring Hall down. At the same time, four other Sherpas went to rescue Fischer and Gau. When they reached Fischer, the Sherpas tried to give him oxygen and hot tea, but he was unresponsive. Though he was breathing—barely—his eyes were fixed and his teeth were clenched. Believing he was as good as dead, they left him tied to the ledge and started descending with Gau, who after receiving tea and oxygen, and with considerable assistance, was able to move to the South Col.

Higher on the peak, Ang Dorje and Lhakpa Chhiri climbed to 28,000 feet, but the murderous wind forced them to turn around there, still 700 feet below Hall.

Throughout that day, Hall's friends begged him to make an effort to descend from the South Summit under his own power. At 3:20 P.M., after one such transmission from Cotter, Hall began to sound annoyed. "Look," he said, "if I thought I could manage the knots on the fixed ropes with me frostbitten hands, I would have gone down six hours ago, pal. Just send a couple of the boys up with a big thermos of something hot—then I'll be fine."

At 6:20 P.M., Hall was patched through a second time to Arnold in Christchurch. "Hi, my sweetheart," he said in a slow, painfully distorted voice. "I hope you're tucked up in a nice warm bed. How are you doing?"

"I can't tell you how much I'm thinking about you!" Arnold replied. "You sound so much better than I expected. . . . Are you warm, my darling?"

"In the context of the altitude, the setting, I'm reasonably comfortable," Hall answered, doing his best not to alarm her.

"How are your feet?"

"I haven't taken me boots off to check, but I think I may have a bit of frostbite."

"I'm looking forward to making you completely better when you come home," said Arnold. "I just know you're going to be rescued. Don't feel that you're alone. I'm sending all my positive energy your way!" Before signing off, Hall told his wife, "I love you. Sleep well, my sweetheart. Please don't worry too much."

These would be the last words anyone would hear him utter. Attempts to make radio contact with Hall later that night and the next day went unanswered. Twelve days later, when Breashears and Viesturs climbed over the South Summit on their way to the top, they found Hall lying on his right side in a shallow ice-hollow, his upper body buried beneath a drift of snow.

Early on the morning of May 11, when I returned to Camp Four after searching in vain for Harris, Hutchison, standing in for Groom, who was unconscious in his tent, organized a team of four Sherpas to locate the bodies of our teammates Weathers and Namba. The Sherpa search party, headed by Lhakpa Chhiri, departed ahead of Hutchison, who was so exhausted and befuddled that he forgot to put his boots on and left camp in his light, smooth-soled liners. Only when Lhakpa Chhiri pointed out the blunder did Hutchison return for his boots. Following Boukreev's directions, the Sherpas had no trouble locating the two bodies at the edge of the Kangshung Face.

The first body turned out to be Namba, but Hutchison couldn't tell who it was until he knelt in the howling wind and chipped a three-inch-thick carapace of ice from her face. To his shock, he discovered that she was still breathing. Both her gloves were gone, and her bare hands appeared to be frozen solid. Her eyes were dilated. The skin on her face was the color of porcelain. "It was terrible," Hutchison recalls. "I was overwhelmed. She was very near death. I didn't know what to do."

He turned his attention to Weathers, who lay twenty feet away. His face was also caked with a thick armor of frost. Balls of ice the size of grapes were matted to his hair and eyelids. After clearing the frozen detritus from his face, Hutchison discovered that he, too, was still alive: "Beck was mumbling something, I think, but I couldn't tell what he was trying to say. His right glove was missing and he had terrible frostbite. He was as close to death as a person can be and still be breathing."

Badly shaken, Hutchison went over to the Sherpas and asked Lhakpa Chhiri's advice. Lhakpa Chhiri, an Everest veteran respected by Sherpas and sahibs alike for his mountain savvy, urged Hutchison to leave Weathers and Namba where they lay. Even if they survived long enough to be dragged back to Camp Four, they would certainly die before they could be carried down to Base Camp, and attempting a rescue would needlessly jeopardize the lives of the other climbers on the Col, most of whom were going to have enough trouble getting themselves down safely.

Hutchison decided that Chhiri was right. There was only one choice, however difficult: Let nature take its inevitable course with Weathers and Namba, and save the group's resources for those who could actually be helped. It was a classic act of triage. When Hutchison returned to camp at 8:30 A.M. and told the rest of us of his decision, nobody doubted that it was the correct thing to do.

Later that day a rescue team headed by two of Everest's most experienced guides, Pete Athans and Todd Burleson, who were on the mountain with their own clients, arrived at Camp Four. Burleson was standing outside the tents about 4:30 P.M. when he noticed someone lurching slowly toward camp. The person's bare right hand, naked to the wind and horribly frostbitten, was outstretched in a weird, frozen salute. Whoever it was reminded Athans of a mummy in a low-budget horror film. The mummy turned out to be none other than Beck Weathers, somehow risen from the dead.

A couple of hours earlier, a light must have gone on in the reptilian core of Weathers's comatose brain, and he regained consciousness. "Initially I thought I was in a dream," he recalls. "Then I saw how badly frozen my right hand was, and that helped bring me around to reality. Finally I woke up enough to recognize that I was in deep shit and the cavalry wasn't coming so I better do something about it myself."

Although Weathers was blind in his right eye and able to focus his left eye within a radius of only three or four feet, he started walking into the teeth of the wind, deducing correctly that camp lay in that direction. If he'd been wrong he would have stumbled immediately down the Kangshung Face, the edge of which was a few yards in the opposite direction. Ninety minutes later he encountered "some unnaturally smooth, bluish looking rocks," which turned out to be the tents of Camp Four.

The next morning, May 12, Athans, Burleson, and climbers from the IMAX team short-roped Weathers down to Camp Two. On the morning of May 13, in a hazardous helicopter rescue, Weathers and Gau were evacuated from the top of the Icefall by Lt. Col. Madan Khatri Chhetri of the Nepalese army. A month later, a team of Dallas surgeons would amputate Weathers's dead right hand just below the wrist and use skin grafts to reconstruct his left hand.

After helping to load Weathers and Gau into the rescue chopper, I sat in the snow for a long while, staring at my boots, trying to get some grip, however tenuous, on what had happened over the preceding seventy-two hours. Then, nervous as a cat, I headed down into the Icefall for one last trip through the maze of decaying seracs.

I'd always known, in the abstract, that climbing mountains was a dangerous pursuit. But until I climbed in the Himalayas this spring, I'd never actually seen death at close range. And there was so much of it: Including three members of an Indo-Tibetan team who died on the north side just below the summit in the same May 10 storm, and an Austrian killed some days later, eleven men and women lost their lives on Everest in May 1996, a tie with 1982 for the worst single-season death toll in the peak's history.

Of the six people on my team who reached the summit, four are now dead—people with whom I'd laughed and vomited and held long, intimate conversations. My actions—or failure to act—played a direct role in the death of Andy Harris. And while Yasuko Namba lay dying on the South Col, I was a mere 350 yards away, lying inside a tent, doing absolutely nothing. The stain this has left on my psyche is not the sort of thing that washes off after a month or two of grief and guilt-ridden self-reproach.

Five days after Namba died, three Japanese men approached me in the village of Syangboche and introduced themselves. One was an interpreter, the other was Namba's husband, the third was her brother. They had many questions, few of which I could answer adequately. I flew back to the States with Doug Hansen's belongings and was met at the Seattle airport by his two children, Angie and Jaime. I felt stupid and utterly impotent when confronted by their tears.

Stewing over my culpability, I put off calling Andy Harris's partner, Fiona McPherson, and Rob Hall's wife, Jan Arnold, so long that they finally phoned me from New Zealand. When Fiona called, I was able to say nothing to diminish her anger or bewilderment. During my conversation with Jan, she spent more time comforting me than vice versa.

With so many marginally qualified climbers flocking to Everest these days, a lot of people believe that a tragedy of this magnitude was overdue. But nobody imagined that an expedition led by Hall would be at the center of it. Hall ran the tightest, safest operation on the mountain, bar none. So what happened? How can it be explained, not only to the loved ones left behind, but to a censorious public?

Hubris surely had something to do with it. Hall had become so adept at running climbers of varying abilities up and down Everest that he may have become a little cocky. He'd bragged on more than one occasion that he could get almost any reasonably fit person to the summit, and his record seemed to support this. He'd also demonstrated a remarkable ability to manage adversity.

In 1995, for instance, Hall and his guides not only had to cope with Hansen's problems high on the peak, but they also had to deal with the complete collapse of another client, the celebrated French alpinist Chantal Mauduit, who was making her seventh stab at Everest without oxygen. Mauduit passed out stone cold at 28,700 feet and had to be dragged and carried all the way from the South Summit to the South Col "like a sack of spuds," as Guy Cotter put it. After everybody came out of that summit attempt alive, Hall may well have thought there was little he couldn't handle.

Before this year, however, Hall had had uncommonly good luck with the weather, and one wonders whether it might have skewed his judgment. "Season after season," says David Breashears, who has climbed Everest three times, "Rob had brilliant weather on summit day. He'd never been caught by a storm high on the mountain." In fact, the gale of May 10, though violent, was nothing extraordinary; it was a fairly typical Everest squall. If it had hit two hours later, it's likely that nobody would have died. Conversely, if it had arrived even one hour earlier, the storm could easily have killed eighteen or twenty climbers—me among them.

Indeed, the clock had as much to do with the tragedy as the weather, and ignoring the clock can't be passed off as an act of God. Delays at the fixed lines could easily have been avoided. Predetermined turn-around times were egregiously and willfully ignored. The latter may have been influenced to some degree by the rivalry between Fischer and Hall. Fischer had a charismatic personality, and that charisma had been brilliantly marketed. Fischer was trying very hard to eat Hall's lunch, and Hall knew it. In a certain sense, they may have been playing chicken up there, each guide plowing ahead with one eye on the clock, waiting to see who was going to blink first and turn around.

Shocked by the death toll, people have been quick to suggest policies and procedures intended to ensure that the catastrophes of this season won't be repeated. But guiding Everest is a very loosely regulated business, administered by a byzantine Third World bureaucracy that is spectacularly ill-equipped to assess qualifications of guides or clients, in a nation that has a vested interest in issuing as many climbing permits as the market will support.

Truth be told, a little education is probably the most that can be hoped for. Everest would without question be safer if prospective clients truly understood the gravity of the risks they face—the thinness of the margin by which human life is sustained above 25,000 feet. Walter Mittys with Everest dreams need to keep in mind that when things go wrong up in the Death Zone—and sooner or later they always do—the strongest guides in the world may be powerless to save their clients' lives. Indeed, as the events of 1996 demonstrated, the strongest guides in the world are sometimes powerless to save even their own lives.

Climbing mountains will never be a safe, predictable, rule-bound enterprise. It is an activity that idealizes risk-taking; its most celebrated figures have always been those who stuck their necks out the farthest and managed to get away with it. Climbers, as a species, are simply not distinguished by an excess of common sense. And that holds especially true for Everest climbers: When presented with a chance to reach the planet's highest summit, people are surprisingly quick to abandon prudence all together. "Eventually," warns Tom Hornbein, thirty-three years after his ascent of the West Ridge, "what happened on Everest this season is certain to happen again."

For evidence that few lessons were learned from the mistakes of May 10, one need look no farther than what happened on Everest two weeks later. On the night of May 24, by which date every other expedition had left Base Camp or was on its way down the mountain, the South Africans finally launched their summit bid. At 9:30 the following morning, Ian Woodall radioed that he was on the summit, that teammate Cathy O'Dowd would be on top in fifteen minutes, and that his close friend Bruce Herrod was some unknown distance below. Herrod, whom I'd met several times on the mountain, was an amiable thirty-seven-year-old with little climbing experience. A freelance photographer, he hoped that making the summit of Everest would give his career a badly needed boost.

As it turned out, Herrod was more than seven hours behind the others and didn't reach the summit until 5:00 P.M., by which time the upper mountain had clouded over. It had taken him twenty-one hours to climb from the South Col to the top. With darkness fast approaching, he was out of oxygen, physically drained, and completely alone on the roof of the world. "That he was up there that late, with nobody else around, was crazy," says his former teammate, Andy de Klerk. "It's absolutely boggling."

Herrod had been on the South Col from the evening of May 10 through May 12. He'd felt the ferocity of that storm, heard the desperate radio calls for help, seen Beck Weathers crippled with horrible frostbite. Early on his ascent of May 24–25, Herrod had climbed right past the frozen body of Scott Fischer. Yet none of that apparently made much of an impression on him. There was another radio transmission from Herrod at 7:00 P.M., but nothing was heard from him after that, and he never appeared at Camp Four. He is presumed to be dead—the eleventh casualty of the season.

As I write this, fifty-four days have passed since I stood on top of Everest, and there hasn't been more than an hour or two on any given day in which the loss of my companions hasn't monopolized my thoughts. Not even in sleep is there respite: Imagery from the climb and its sad aftermath permeates my dreams.

There is some comfort, I suppose, in knowing that I'm not the only survivor of Everest to be so affected. A teammate of mine from Hall's expedition tells me that since he returned, his marriage has gone bad, he can't concentrate at work, his life has been in turmoil. In another case, Neal Beidleman helped save the lives of five clients by guiding them down the mountain, yet he is haunted by a death he was unable to prevent, of a client who wasn't on his team and thus wasn't really his responsibility.

When I spoke to Beidleman recently, he recalled what it felt like to be out on the South Col, huddling with his group in the awful wind, trying desperately to keep everyone alive. He'd told and retold the story a hundred times, but it was still as vivid as the initial telling. "As soon as the sky cleared enough to give us an idea of where camp was," he recounted, "I remember shouting, 'Hey, this break in the storm may not last long, so let's *go*!' I was screaming at everyone to get moving, but it became clear that some of them didn't have enough strength to walk or even stand.

"People were crying. I heard someone yell, 'Don't let me die here!' It was obvious that it was now or never. I tried to get Yasuko on her feet. She grabbed my arm, but she was too weak to get up past her knees. I started walking and dragged her for a step or two. Then her grip loosened and she fell away. I had to keep going. Somebody had to make it to the tents and get help, or everybody was going to die."

Beidleman paused. "But I can't help thinking about Yasuko," he said when he resumed, his voice hushed. "She was so little. I can still feel her fingers sliding across my biceps and then letting go. I never even turned to look back."

SEPTEMBER 1996

• • •

Author's Note: In this article, "Into Thin Air," I speculated that Andy Harris, one of Rob Hall's guides, walked off the edge of the South Col and fell to his death in the rogue storm of May 10. Only minutes earlier, I had encountered him in the blizzard, spoken with him briefly, and then watched him walk to within thirty yards of Camp Four, where he became enveloped in clouds.

Two weeks after the magazine went to press, I discovered compelling evidence that Harris did not walk off the Col—and that in fact the person I encountered was not Harris. In a telephone conversation, Martin Adams, a client of Scott Fischer, revealed that he had encountered a climber just above the Col at about the same time I had encountered Harris. In the stormy darkness, Adams couldn't tell who the other climber was, but their conversation, he says, was very similar to the one I reported having with Harris. Adams and I are now certain that, in my hypoxic condition, I confused him with Harris.

On July 25, in a four-hour, face-to-face discussion, Lobsang Jangbu,

Fischer's head Sherpa (who two months later would die in an avalanche just below the South Col on the Lhotse face), revealed something that hadn't come up in our previous discussions: He had spoken with Harris on the South Summit at 5:30 P.M. on May 10—about the same time I thought I saw Harris near the South Col. By this late hour Hall had been radioing for help, saying that Doug Hansen had collapsed on the Hillary Step and that both men desperately needed oxygen. As Lobsang began descending he saw Harris himself ailing, plodding up the summit ridge to assist Hall and Hansen. It was an extremely heroic act for which Harris deserves to be remembered.

As I reported, when radio contact between Hall and Base Camp was reestablished the next morning, a distraught, debilitated Hall said that Harris "was with me last night. But he doesn't seem to be with me now. He was very weak." From this snippet, which I interpreted as the incoherent babble of a severely hypoxic man, it is impossible to say what became of Harris. But the awful truth remains that he is gone.

For two months after returning from Everest, I was haunted by the thought that Harris, who'd become a close friend, had been so near the safety of camp and yet never made it. Unable to let the matter rest, I obsessively mulled over the circumstances of his death even after my article went to press—which is how I discovered my error.

That I confused Harris for Adams is perhaps not surprising, given the poor visibility, my profound exhaustion, and the confused, oxygen-starved state I was in. But my mistake greatly compounded the pain of Andy Harris's partner, Fiona McPherson; his parents, Ron and Mary Harris; and his many friends. For that I am inexpressibly sorry.

OCTOBER 1996

THE CALL OF THE HUNT

by JANE SMILEY

Back when I was on the very lowest reaches of the educational slopes, before any of my present opinions were formed, I used to ponder Oscar Wilde's characterization of foxhunting as "the unspeakable in pursuit of the uneatable." Like almost every other expression that had to do with foxhunting, Wilde's mot seemed to me like a magic charm, or what I would later know as a mantra—an almost unintelligible set of words that others seemed to understand and use with ease but that I found mysterious and fascinating. Just because I was an Anglophile (I had read all of Mary Poppins, Sherlock Holmes, and Prince Valiant by that time) didn't mean I knew what "view halloo" or "gone to earth" or "whipper in" meant. "Hounds" were not dogs. They had "sterns," not tails, and they were counted in "couples," not one by one. Red woolen hunting coats, worn only by men, were actually "pink." Before the hunt everyone partook of the "stirrup cup," which came in a chased silver vessel with a pointed bottom that couldn't be set down but had to be brought around and taken away by servants. Foxes had no tails, faces, or feet, but "brushes," "masks," and "pads," and these were ritually cut from the corpse after the "death" and awarded to especially avid members of the "field" who had been "in at the death."

I came to foxhunting through horseback riding, which was my overwhelming obsession. The hunt in my town, St. Louis, was called the Bridlespur Hunt, and most of the horsey types there, from the Busches on down, were members, whether they actually "rode to hounds" or not. If you were a member of the hunt and had "earned your colors," you could wear robin's-egg blue on the collar of your melton jacket. The western environs of St. Louis and St. Charles counties, just north of the Missouri River as it approaches the Mississippi, were and may still be good hunt country, with broad, rolling fields and open woodland, plenty of foxes, and good scenting conditions for the hounds, which I understood then to be light winds and sufficient humidity. Nonetheless, Bridlespur country was not England, and the master, the huntsman, and the members of the field spoke regular American when they weren't hunting, and sometimes when they were. They were probably less afraid of breaking the linguistic rules than I was.

Anything about hunting that other sorts of hunters might cite to justify their sport is not citable about foxhunting. The fox is truly uneatable, even for the hounds, who mill about excitably after the death until the whippers-in whip them back into a pack and the huntsmen and the master decide whether and where to find another. Besides, probably no one in the field has ever gone without a meal anyway. Foxhunters do not commune with nature. The huntsman controls the hounds, the whippers-in look for the fox, and the members of the field spend their nongalloping time gossiping among themselves or attending to their horses. The history of foxhunting (or stag hunting) over the centuries is, in every particular, the history of a privileged class riding roughshod (the horses' iron shoes caulked to provide more secure footing in the mud) over everything in its path. When I saw the movie *Tom Jones,* right in the midst of my foxhunting career, I could at least understand the moment when the farmer emerges from his hovel after the passing of the field and lifts up his prize goose, trampled and broken by the galloping horses. These days, much better read, I understand the "unspeakable" part of Wilde's remark, and I surely wouldn't go foxhunting again, but all the same, like most of the educated, I do harbor a fondness for the sins of my ignorant past.

As a parent, I cannot imagine the abdication of good sense that allowed my parents to allow me to "ride to hounds," but they did. Probably I wore them down drop by drop, as I did about every equestrian venture, overcoming their perfectly reasonable objections on the grounds of safety and expense with the sheer tenacity of my desire. I had gotten them to pay for the riding lessons, then to allow me to jump, then to let me go in the Pony Club rally, which entailed a lot of jumping. I had shown devotion to the horse. After breaking my arm high-jumping (I never suffered a single equestrian injury, but track and field was my undoing), I'd gone to the horse every chance I could anyway and cleaned her stall one-handed. That persuaded them to buy me the horse. She was a dark bay Thoroughbred mare with a kindly nature and a beautiful head. Under saddle, she was a little hot for me, but I had her in control most of the time. It didn't really matter, though, how good or bad she was objectively—she was my destined mate, and I was ready to take the good with the bad.

I rode her and jumped her all summer and into the fall. After the fields were harvested, everyone else in the barn loaded their horses into trailers on Sundays and sometimes on Wednesdays (remember, this was the leisure class) and went out to the various areas where the master had secured permission to hunt, and they galloped and jumped for hours on end. The other girls went. Surely that must have been an element of my argument, and there was probably some phoning among parents. Thanksgiving loomed, and I set my sights upon that Thursday hunt. What better way to celebrate the coming of the English to Virginia—the true origin of our country, forget those nonfoxhunting Puritans—than rising at 5:00 A.M., riding all day, and coming home too exhausted toward the late afternoon to partake of the family feast?

It seems to be the case that experienced horses do like foxhunting. Horses will respond to the sound of the horn and hounds and the sight of the field galloping away by whinnying and fighting to join the hunt. Some horses, if they lose their riders, will keep galloping and jumping with the group until caught and led away.

Writers and artists of foxhunting also maintain that the fox enjoys the hunt. There are many paintings of a fox standing alertly on a stone wall in the foreground, watching the hounds and the horses gallop into the empty distance. Certainly the fox has plenty of warning that it is being hunted—foxhunting makes a virtue of noise—the liquid call of the horn, the seismic boom of forty horses galloping over the earth, and the cry of the hounds, which is neither barking nor howling, but a high, desperate, glad yodeling called "giving voice." When the hounds are fast on the trail of the fox, they are said to be "in full cry," which means that the noise and speed and adrenaline are peaking in horse and hound and human, and possibly, too, in the fox.

There are other, more efficient mechanisms for disposing of a chicken-killing fox than foxhunting, though characterizing the fox as a verminous nuisance has always been the foxhunter's single limp rationalization for the whole colorful enterprise.

And the hounds undoubtedly like it, because, like all hunting dogs, this is what they are bred to do, and because for the rest of their time they live in the kennel, and because, unlike Labs and pointers and German shorthairs, they work in a group.

And so I set the clock for 5:00 A.M., and I rose and dressed carefully in my high black boots, my thick wool "canary" (yellow) breeches (in those days before stretch fabrics, wide-pegged at the thigh for ease in mounting), my black melton jacket, my white cotton "stock" (a four-inch wide tie wrapped two or three times around the neck, intended for use as a bandage or tourniquet in case of emergency), my hair net, and my velvet hard hat, in which my mother vested a great deal of faith concerning head injuries. I was chauffered by my mother in her robe to the stable, where I accompanied my horse and the other members of the elect to the wildlife area in St. Charles County where the hunt was to commence. We were mounted by eight.

Maybe the best thing about a foxhunt is the sight of all the horses and riders gathered together early in the morning, waiting to set off. The horses are impeccably clean and fitted out—in any equestrian endeavor there is a high premium placed on making a pristine appearance that I see now is a sort of conspicuous consumption rooted in the days of grooms and servants—and they are fresh and eager, too, striding about in an informal ballet, long-necked and long-limbed and long-tailed, giving off their horsey scent to the accompaniment of the happy chatter of many riders who know one another and are secure in sharing social rituals of long standing.

When the huntsman and the whips bring in the hounds, the hounds introduce an entirely different energy, noisy and single-minded, that focuses the field upon the task at hand and reminds them that this isn't just a ride in the park. They are giving themselves up to the fox, which, once found, will lead them across all sorts of country, and they and their horses will have to be ready for anything—any sort of ground, any sort of fence, any sort of incline, any sort of woodlot. This is the "chase," not the "stalk." Not much care will be taken once the apotheosis is achieved: the hounds in full cry.

I was nervous about the jumping. I had heard, though I hadn't told my mother, that the fences could be as high as four feet, and I wasn't used to jumping much higher than three feet. I fixed my hard hat more firmly on my head. Four feet and solid. Unlike jumps in a ring, these were not made of poles on standards that would fall if hit. They were telephone poles and chicken coops and railroad ties. I kept my fears to myself, but I did hear someone else say, "Usually there's a lower part to one side that you can go for." I decided to stay close to that woman and discreetly fell in not far from her.

I was proud of my mare. She looked sleek and fit, rangy and eager, which is often the special charm of a Thoroughbred. She was somewhat calmer than usual, probably taking pleasure and reassurance from the presence of the other horses. She had never hunted before, but she had raced. Perhaps the situation she found herself in suggested to her that there would be the opportunity to GO. Most Thoroughbreds, even failed racehorses, like very much to GO.

The huntsman set off with the hounds and the whips. When they were just out of sight, the hounds began to give voice. That was the master's signal to follow, and we followed him—more experienced members of the field in front, less experienced or less eager ones behind. It was a dank late autumn day. The sky promised to be a clear, platinum blue, but mist rose from the muddy brown fields and leafless dark woodland, softening the chilly air. The riders and the horses gave off a mist, too, of breath and evaporating perspiration. Like duck and deer hunting, foxhunting is a sport that gives late autumn and early winter a point, that lures the hunter out of the warm house into the strange, coldly lit charms of the dying year. Soon we were cantering after the hounds, which we could hear but not see. I wasn't looking for anything except the tails of the horses in front of me. I thought I would manage my horse for now, and learn about the niceties of actually chasing and killing a fox at some later date.

I should mention here that in England foxhunting is often carried out without the fox, revealing that galloping and jumping and listening to the hounds is the real point of the sport. "Draghunts" are common in England—hours before the hunt, someone drags a sack impregnated with fox scent over the countryside, more or less diabolically mimicking foxy strategies, taking care to challenge the field. Draghunting isn't the only death-free alternative. In her memoirs, Jessica Mitford, another left-winger who once adored foxhunting, recalls that her father, Lord Redesdale, was especially fond of hunting his children, a memory corroborated by Nancy Mitford in her novels.

Here is where education interferes with narrative. I know what we would have done next, but the nugget of memory has accreted too many images from later riding experiences, later experiences of horse manuals, English literature, social class, England itself, and even conversations with others. Images that arose as a response of the imagination offer themselves as memories. All I know about what happened next is that we followed the hounds for an hour or more, and that I grew more self-confident and relaxed.

The next thing I remember is the sight of a large fence, and myself pausing to wait for other riders to clear it. We gathered at the edge of the field, under the overhang of the woodland, trying to avoid the mud. My turn came up. I followed four or five strides behind the woman in front of me, knowing her horse's willingness would influence my horse. But I didn't have anything to worry about. My mare was happy to jump. The fence loomed, brown and upright, in front of us, got larger, and was gone. I felt her forelegs land and saw that we were in a wide, muddy lane that veered to the right toward a dirt road. I saw the other horses galloping away.

Of course, accompanying these visual memories are sensory ones, particularly the feeling of the presence of the horse as I gripped her sides with my legs, moved my own body with the rhythm of her gait, leaned close to her neck, felt the tug of her mouth through the reins in my hands. Two strides after the fence, our momentum was still carrying us forward. I twitched the right rein to remind her to follow the others, and I felt her right hind leg slip in the mud and go out from underneath us.

The fall was a slow one—not a toppling or a pitching forward off the horse, but a sideways fall with the horse. The mud was soft, and I was on my feet almost before I hit the ground, reassuring those who followed that I was all right. Perhaps I remember the sensation of pulling my leg from under my mare, but perhaps I don't. She was on her feet nearly as fast as I was. I do remember the strangeness of the feeling that now we were no longer going, now we were stopped, and I was standing on my feet rather than mounted on my horse. One step forward revealed that my mare was limping badly, so it was clear that going was over for the day.

The next thing I remember is the diagnosis, a break at the stifle joint of the left hind leg. The stifle joint is the joint at the top of the leg, close to the body, comparable to a human knee. I knew from all the horse stories I had read by then that a broken leg was fatal to a horse. I knew that all discussion of healing her and maybe breeding her was done for my benefit, to put off the final blow. But a broken stifle joint was too much of a challenge to veterinary medicine of the period. After pretending to consider other alternatives, my stepfather and the vet told me that the mare would be trailered out to the kennel where the Bridlespur hounds were kept, and put down. An electrical device of some sort would be put to her head, the current would run to her iron shoes, and she would die, be butchered, and be fed to the hounds, a common and entirely appropriate use for old hunters.

Early in the fall, when it was still almost summer, I had been riding my mare alone one Sunday afternoon when I saw my summer riding friend, Dorothy, being driven past in her mother's car. Dorothy's family raised Connemara ponies, and Dorothy rode a gray mare named Larkspur. She had been riding for years and had shown me all the trails and fields around the club where I kept my mare. Dorothy, teary and disheveled, didn't respond when I called out to her, but her mother stopped the car and leaned across her daughter toward the open passenger window. She said, "Dorothy's pony's just been killed hunting. She fell at a fence and broke her neck." They drove off. I'm sure I looked stricken and sympathetic, although I don't know whether, at fourteen, I knew the right thing to say. Later I heard that Dorothy had given up riding entirely, even though her family had ten or fifteen other possible mounts for her. I certainly considered forsaking all equestrian activity, a reasonable reaction to the death of one's destined equine mate, rather like taking the veil upon the death of one's spouse.

But I found myself cool and remote from my own mare. She stood still in her stall, her eyes half shut, her head down, her coat staring. She had lost her very horseness, a larger-than-human vitality that makes equine alertness and beauty compelling to people like me. I sat with her and groomed her and gave her carrots, but I wasn't drawn to her. A day and a half after her accident, she was gone from her stall, and I was back to square one, horsewise. I did not think it likely that my parents would replace her.

None of this meant that I had learned anything about the dangers and difficulties of my chosen sport. My obsession flourished as green as ever; unlike Dorothy, I was uneducable. Experience did nothing to me.

Now for the peripeteia. The damp, muddy fall progressed into a crisp, frosty winter. The once distant gray-blue sky became a brilliant glare that surrounded us with light. I was again in the field, this time on a rented horse, also a bay mare. We all, riders and horses, seemed to shine in the sunlight, from our glossy black velvet caps down to the caulked shoes of our mounts, which glinted and winked with each stride and rang on the frozen gravel roads. This was the New Year's hunt, its venue a part of the wildlife area that had no fences. For some reason, I resolved to stay near the master and watch the actual chase after the fox. I don't remember what the chase looked like. I know there was a fox out there, but I don't remember what it looked like. I know the sterns of the bunched, coursing, vocalizing hounds pointed up like miniature pikes as the pack ran and scrabbled over the countryside in glorious full cry. I do remember the sight of the master's horse in front of me, as well as the sunlight on the white stock and gold stock pin of the rider beside me. I remember the long, tireless gallop and the relief I felt at there being no jumping. Then I remember the way we came upon the hounds and the huntsman and the whips just where a clearing gave way to light oak woodlands. The liver-and-white hounds were yodeling and whining, and the huntsman vaulted off his mount and waded into the pack while the whippers-in unfurled the long lashes of their whips and began driving the hounds away from the focus of their attention. The huntsman was leaning down, and then he held the quarry aloft, a dead gray fox.

Yes, I felt exhilarated at the sight, pumped up by the vigor of the galloping and the sensation of having ridden in front of the field, of having been in at the death. I wasn't at all repelled or moved by the sight of the dead fox, and my reaction was entirely visceral, not at all intellectual. We had wanted to kill him and now he was dead, a stillness at the center of human, canine, and equine tumult. Good for us, good for me, good for my rented mount, who had been both willing and controllable. The huntsman drew his knife.

Maybe this is the ugliest face of foxhunting, the group blood-lust. How is the field different from any other mob, except that its members are mounted? A significant portion of my subsequent education would invite and even force me to conclude that the pink coats and the high boots, the elaborate costume and ritual and language of foxhunting, the very expense of it, is really the merest film of respectability designed to camouflage the mob and allow it to reassure itself that it is far more civilized than other mobs, when it is actually far worse—caught up in irresponsible and destructive blood-lust, the object of which is not social justice or even retribution for felt wrongs, but the trivial pursuit of unworthy prey. I could talk myself into class hatred here.

On the other hand, foxhunting is a form of aggression, and it seems clear by now that human aggression is so inherent that it must and will take a form. Inclination, cultural history, and education, too, predispose me to prefer elaborate forms that break down inherent drives into parts, ritualizing them and presenting them for both appreciation and interpretation. Beauty, always morally neutral, resides in rituals of aggression as much as it does in rituals of religious faith or love or art. Foxhunting need not be unmediated or mindless aggression, partly because the hunt must receive permission to ride over land owned by others. The responsibility of the master, the huntsman, the whips, and the field is to understand the potential for destruction that foxhunting presents and to mitigate the destruction—riding fit and experienced horses, taking responsibility for younger members of the field, never galloping across agricultural ground but always keeping to its margins, hunting in winter when much of the agricultural and natural world is dormant, never blocking the fox's escape strategies, promoting courtesy among the members of the field through severe social strictures. In traditional foxhunting, as in the Catholic Church, there is a name for every occasion of sin as well as every occasion of transcendence. The aggressive impulse is developed and restrained by form that may look like obscure and arbitrary formality.

My teenaged self wasn't engaging in any of these arguments. She was panting and excited, warmed in the chilly sunlight by the exertion of the chase. When the huntsman came around to "blood" me, that is, to dab my cheek with the fox's blood to signify that I had witnessed my first death, the warmth and thickness of it on my cheek and neck was an unalloyed thrill. Of course, now I read many meanings into that gory signifier—the end of virginity, blood on my conscience, feeling death as well as seeing it, making the fox's self part of my own.

I also clearly remember seeing the master look around and smile as the huntsman was taking the trophies from the fox—he smiled at me and told the huntsman to give me one of the pads, rewarding my eagerness and interest in the progress of the chase. Perhaps in addition to keeping close to the master, I had peppered him with respectful questions. I was known for asking a tiresome number of questions in those days. If I did, I don't remember it now.

I took the pad in my hand. It was the small, dark foreleg of the fox, maybe three inches long, with toes and nails like those of a little dog. It hadn't stiffened yet. It seemed marvelous to me, as exciting as any silver cup or blue ribbon. But the hunt was moving on, looking for another fox, and so I put it in my pocket. Later, I wrapped it in plastic and put it in the family freezer. Over the next two and a half years, while it stayed, untaxidermied, in the freezer, my mother would unwrap it from time to time, wondering what sort of meat was in the small package. I would unwrap it from time to time, too, and stare at its wonderfulness. I considered it very important that the freezer was close to the back door, because, should the house catch fire, the last thing I would do after saving our dogs would be to snatch my fox pad from the inferno.

Education interfered with later foxhunting in the most literal way—when I got to college, I found I had neither the time nor the money to keep riding, and I hated the dangers of hitchhiking to the stable. My mother had pressed me to go to Vassar instead of one of those horse colleges in Virginia that had been my original inclination. She beat the lure of the horses and set my walking feet on the path of learning and art. Pretty soon I was too well educated for either blood sports or Anglophilia, and so I remain. The equestrian activity that interests me now is dressage, which is to foxhunting rather what ice dancing is to hockey. Horses rarely if ever break their necks or their legs at dressage, and dressage, like all the arts (trout fishing, ballet, novel writing) is full of theorists and intellectuals, as well as practitioners, both human and equine, who are advanced in years.

My present horse is also a Thoroughbred, though, and I sometimes sense beneath his self-restraint that inbred urge to GO, to join the galloping herd, to be caught up in headlong forward motion. And I sometimes sense that inborn urge in myself, too.

NOVEMBER 1994

DAVE SCOTT, MERE MORTAL

by JOHN BRANT

It's nap time in Boulder, a little before two o'clock on a June afternoon of shifting winds and slowly massing thunderheads. With Ryan and Drew finally sleeping, the phone momentarily silent, and his plans fixed for tomorrow's coaching session, Dave Scott decides that for the first time since coming to Colorado from California ten days earlier, he can afford a bike ride.

Scott prepares slowly, somewhat fumblingly, taking time to trade jokes with his wife, Anna, and his sister, Jane. Just a few weeks ago, after months of waffling and agonizing, he announced his retirement from a twelve-year career as the world's preeminent triathlete. Now, with no apparent race to point toward, no Ironman looming at summer's end, Scott exercises out of desire rather than necessity, a shift in his life of profound, enduring, and often unforeseen consequence.

"Look at these hairy legs," he scoffs while slipping on cycling shoes. "I'll be the laughingstock of every triathlete in Boulder."

"So go ahead and shave them," Jane says. "Who's going to challenge you on it?"

"I couldn't do that," Scott protests, only half facetiously. "If I shaved my legs everyone could see that I don't have any muscles down there."

Anna, sitting at the kitchen table, shakes her head and rolls her eyes. "My husband," she says softly, so as not to disturb her sleeping children, "has more problems with body image than a fifteen-year-old."

Bearing his hairy legs (professional triathletes shave body hair to cut water and wind resistance), divided heart, and low-grade neuroses, Scott pushes away from his sister's modest north Boulder house and sets off for the mountains. In part this ride is professionally motivated; Scott's new enterprise is coaching pro triathletes, and he is scouting sites for time trials. Mostly, however, he rides to satisfy an inner hunger.

The forty-mile route he plans vectors north from town in the shadows of the Flatirons and foothills, traces a rough square on the far western rim of the Great Plains, then makes a dagger thrust up Left Hand Canyon into the eastern slope of the Rockies, eventually cresting at 10,000 feet. A year ago this ride would have represented a bare-minimum workout for Scott. More typically he would have ridden at least twice as far, and cycling, moreover, would have been just a portion of his labors. In his competitive prime Scott always ran, swam, and cycled every day; if he couldn't do all three sports, he rarely bothered doing any. His workouts blended passion, precision, volume, and quality in a combination often emulated but never matched. For a number of important reasons, Dave Scott was recognized as the first genuine triathlete, a man who stamped his imprimatur on the sport, who not only defined triathlon but redefined the way people think of human endurance and potential.

Watching him work, even knowing of his struggles during the past few years, it becomes clear why Scott still finds it difficult to think of his career in the past tense. He appears at least a decade younger than his thirty-eight years. Injury, illness, family demands, the inexorable advance of age—the factors that combined to drop the curtain on his racing days—all seem in abeyance. Yet no more, barring an unforeseen comeback, will Scott hammer the Queen Kaahumanu Highway along the Kona coast of Hawaii's Big Island, fusing his fate with that of triathlon's signature, showcase event. Scott won six Hawaii Ironmans and finished second in two others. Mention the triathlon to the average Venezuelan or Australian, Dane or Japanese, Israeli or American, and the image conjured will be that of Dave Scott pounding relentlessly through the heat, wind, and lava fields of Kona, mastering the seemingly insane distances of the Ironman in a thoroughly sane yet thoroughly compelling manner.

No more, apparently, will Scott commend himself to the harsh dictates of the Ironman. Yet in a less dramatic but still crucial sense, he will labor to lead the way. What happens to triathletes when they grow old? Or as others might put it, what happens to triathletes when they grow up? Dave Scott will live out the answers to these questions.

During the first stages of today's ride, whirring along north Broadway past Boulder's mushrooming subdivisions, auto traffic, and armies of hardworking citizen runners and cyclists, Scott appears at once tentative and steady, befitting both his long layoff and his vast reservoir of base fitness. He follows Broadway until it empties onto Highway 36, the route connecting Denver and Rocky Mountain National Park, which in its booming two-lane traffic and stark, wide-open beauty resembles certain stretches of the Queen K. Highway in Kona.

Here, not coincidentally, Scott starts to find his stroke, and his singular style begins to emerge. It is not the flashing style of a Mark Allen, who dethroned Scott in the 1989 Ironman and has since gone without a serious challenger at races of that distance, nor is it quite the rippling, muscular style of a Mike Pigg, the most prominent male triathlete of the sport's second generation. It is steadier, more deliberate, more implacable. Partly this is a function of technique: Scott always geared his bike higher than most other triathletes, so he turned his pedals more slowly. In similar fashion, he tailored his running stride and swimming stroke to take advantage of his daunting strength and compensate for his comparative lack of natural speed. The result was a pulsing yet controlled motion that, for all its studied power, seemed achievable by the common woman or man. Not the least aspect of Scott's genius for the triathlon was his ability to make it coherent to the average athlete, the average fan.

As Scott finishes the flat portion of his ride, the sky turns from patchy blue to denser pewter, and faint volleys of thunder report down Left Hand Canyon. Two miles into the ascent, at around 8,500 feet, big, cold, plashing drops of rain begin to descend. A mile farther and a few hundred feet higher up the mountain, the storm clamps down for fair. Thunder peals and booms, the leaves of creekside aspens turn and whiten and shudder, the high tips of lodgepole pines creak and toss in the driving wind.

Scott counters by slipping on a rain shell and hunkering lower over the bar. For another minute he keeps beating into the teeth of the storm, and then, after a sudden tight pivot, he is slaloming back down the road at 50 mph, now trying to outrace the weather he challenged a moment ago.

Today the weather wins. Scott stops and signals to the driver of a trailing car that he is calling off the hunt. He breaks down his bike, straps it into the trunk, and, high-colored, exultant, dripping sweat and rain, climbs into the passenger seat.

"That was fun," he says quietly, with the easy, pleasing inflections of a native Californian. Shorn of the fighter-pilot mustache of his racing years, Scott's face seems slightly fuller and decidedly more open.

"If I were still an athlete, I'd still want to be out there," he says, looking out at the rain. "But now that I'm a . . . a what? A coach?"

Scott issues a bright fusillade of laughter. He is a gifted and infectious laugher. He punctuates his conversation with laughter like another man might with nail biting or lip pulling.

"Now that I'm a *coach*, I'll take the ride."

For a few moments, with bright, avid eyes, Scott admires the storm working on the mountain. Then, in a more subdued voice, he says, "Funny thing is, now that I've finally decided to stop racing, my knee feels better than it has in three years."

Another ruminative minute passes. The car exits the valley; the rain advances along the plains toward Denver. "You start working out," Scott says, "you start getting ideas."

Only in recent years has the relationship between ideas and exercise become a source of conflict and ambiguity for Dave Scott, rather than delight and release. For more than a decade, as he labored over the roads around his lifelong home of Davis, California, Scott's ideas flowed clearly and strongly, products of his steadily accruing strength and the confidence that he was following a peculiar but correct vocation.

This stretch of California's Central Valley is a place of bitter and abiding winds, Scott explains, gesturing beyond the windshield of his Toyota to where the Sacramento River sloughs stretch northwest from Interstate 80. The prevailing westerlies cross San Francisco Bay, forty miles distant, are suctioned and condensed as they pass through the Carquinez Strait, then howl across this flat, mostly hot corner of the San Joaquin Valley. In the winter, Scott continues, other winds ride down from the Sierra, mix and swirl with the prevailing westerlies, and create bone-cold maelstroms that can knock automobiles, not to mention runners or cyclists, from one lane of highway to the next.

"My other calling was to be a weatherman," Scott says with a wry smile. It is early May, a few weeks before Scott will establish summer quarters in Boulder. He is driving from Davis to Sacramento, where he will address a team of high school swimmers. "The wind and the weather can get crazy out here, and I'm known as something of an expert on both. People would always call up and ask what the weather was going to be."

Scott's weather eye was honed during the prodigious hours he spent training over the sere, cheerless ground around Davis. It was by soldiering down the valley's windblasted roads, sweating past agribusiness fields, and humping over baked, treeless hills that he built his strength. The factors that other triathletes found repellent about Davis—its heat and cold, its winds, its relative remoteness and monotony—were the very things that Scott embraced. Antaeus-like, he drew power and sustenance from his native ground.

"Dave had a concentration level that was just amazing," says Mike Pigg, one of the few top triathletes who trained with Scott in Davis. "Day in, day out, he did it by solo training. There's only one highway you can take out of Davis, and Dave could tell you every bump and crack on it, because he'd been over it a thousand times."

Scott recalls countless nights of returning to town after an eighty-mile time trial on the bike or a hard two-hour run, and being greeted only by a changing traffic light. "Before I was married, when I was still working, I usually wouldn't finish exercising until eleven or eleven-thirty at night," he says. "Then I would go to the salad bar at Straw Hat Pizza, eat while I wrote out my next day's training, then crash into bed." Scott's monastic routine was moderated after his marriage to Anna in 1985. Still, the great bulk of his professional life was conducted in solitude.

In San Diego or Boulder, of course, Scott could have commiserated with the scores of other triathletes who gather at those favored and fashionable places. Indeed, after he won his first few Ironmans, he might have lived anywhere he pleased. He chose to remain in Davis. Through the years, people in the sport have endlessly speculated on that decision. Some have attributed it to a reclusive strain in Scott's character, and others to a Machiavellian one. Those of the latter opinion hold that Scott was deliberately trying to intimidate his opponents with his solitary habits, that he sought to create an air of mystery. Scott, however, says he remained in Davis partly because its climate and terrain closely resembled those of Kona, but mostly because it was home, because he had come to accept and regard the place on its own terms.

While the valley yawning around Davis might be unremitting and, to the eyes of most, unappealing, the city itself is a pleasing medium-size community, a quietly shining diamond in what is often considered Northern California's rough. Founded as a trading nexus for surrounding farms, Davis blossomed after World War II as the site of a campus of the University of California. Situated midway between San Francisco and the Sierra, it is a city with a strong and informed outdoor ethic. Bike lanes are ubiquitous and well traveled. Graceful oak and walnut trees give shade and deflect the heat.

Scott's parents migrated here in 1948. His father, Verne, served for forty years on the university's civil engineering faculty. Dave, born in 1954, enjoyed a high-California childhood of wholesome family activity, much of it centered on sports, particularly swimming. In high school he swam the 200 and 400 meters ("They could never get any event long enough for me," he recalls) and excelled in water polo. At UC-Davis he majored in physical education and exercise physiology and continued with swimming and water polo, earning All-American status in both sports. After graduation in 1976, he went to work full-time as coach of the city's masters swimming program.

"I was always amused to read articles describing me as a recluse because I stayed in Davis," Scott says. "In the masters program I was working with four hundred people a day, and for a lot of them I was more of a counselor than a coach. The articles said I was a hermit, but I felt more like Johnny Carson."

Those were the first flush days of the fitness movement, and after work, not content with the miles he had swum and the weights he had lifted during the day, Scott would head out on 11-mile runs. He began entering and winning long-distance swimming events, including consecutive victories in the 2.4-mile open-water swim at Waikiki, the race that inspired the swimming portion of the Ironman. It was at the Waikiki awards ceremony in 1978, in fact, that Scott was first invited to enter the fledgling Ironman, the first edition of which had just been completed.

"I looked at this flier advertising a 2.4-mile swim, 112-mile bike ride, and 26.2-mile run," Scott recalls with a laugh, "and thought that sounded like a really neat three-day workout."

When informed that the stages ran continuously on one day, Scott was more challenged than awed, and in 1979 he set out to take the Ironman's measure. He felt confident about his swimming ability, but cycling and running were still largely terra incognita. For cycling help, he turned to his friend Pat Feeney, whom he coached in the masters swimming program. "Dave hadn't done anything hard up to that point on the bike," Feeney remembers. "We went out for seventy miles over some good-size mountains. Dave was riding this rusted old forty-pound hulk of a bike, but from that first ride I could see that he had grit and he had resources. I could see that he was just very strong, mentally and physically."

As a runner, on the other hand, Scott was self-taught. After impressing himself by running a ten-mile time trial in 60 minutes, Scott ran a 2:45 marathon that September, just a few months before the February 1980 Ironman. He was continuing with his swimming, meanwhile, trying to parlay all his training so that the triathlon would be a culminating rather than a cataclysmic effort. At the same time, he was experimenting with a high-complex-carbohydrate, low-fat diet, which at that time was still considered radical.

"When I first started, there wasn't anything to read about the triathlon, no books or manuals, and no coaches," Scott explains. "It was just a question of how far I could go: four-hundred-mile cycling weeks, sixty-five miles a week running, twenty thousand yards swimming. Eight or ten hours a day. More was better, I always used to think."

All that remained was to simulate the Ironman in a single day's training. This Scott accomplished by bookending a local century bike ride with a 5,200-yard swim in the pool and a 21-mile run on the roads around Davis. That evening, coming back into town near the end of his run, he still felt fresh and strong. When he saw some friends on a street corner, he greeted them euphorically. "At that moment," Scott says, "I knew the Ironman was not going to be just a matter of survival."

That seemingly obscure moment on the dark streets of a quiet California town was in fact pivotal, perhaps *the* pivotal moment in both Scott's career and the development of the sport: From that point on, the Ironman was a *race*. An unaccomplished, unassuming young swim coach had taken the white whale of the Ironman and systematically studied how to harpoon it. He had dared to approach training as an essentially continuous enterprise. Before any physiologist or other human-performance specialist, Scott intuitively understood the Ironman distance and how his mind and body could be adapted to its demands. To this day, with the possible exception of Mark Allen, nobody has understood it better.

The seeds of that understanding sprang from favorable genes and an intellect remarkably attuned to applied exercise physiology, but they flourished because of emotion. Scott and others ultimately equate his success with his passion.

"Nobody could train with the same passion I had," Scott, by nature the most modest and self-effacing of men, states flatly. "I didn't need to have a coach prodding me and an entourage around to pat me on the back. Nothing makes me feel better than exercising for a series of days and knowing I'm getting stronger."

"Dave always raced with a little bit of rage," reflects Bob Babbitt, editor and publisher of *Competitor* magazine and a leading authority on triathlon. "He comes across as this brick, but he isn't. He had to fuel his rage somewhere. At the Ironman, his attitude seemed to be that his competitors were trying to take the bread and butter out of his family's mouth. Almost a 'this guy's out to kill me, so I'll kill him first' mentality. You never saw Dave Scott tapping anybody on the butt when he went past. I remember a comment Scott Molina made about Dave back in '85: 'That guy's racing with sincerity.'"

He also seemed to be racing with fate. Scott's first Ironman, in 1980, was also the first to be televised. A nationwide audience watched him recast the race in his own image, slashing the course record from 11:15:56 down to 9:24:33 and transforming what had been generally regarded as a bit of masochistic exotica into a legitimate and riveting sporting event. After Scott had broken the Ironman's code, distances that once engendered awe were approached with confidence. Scott's performance made the Ironman and other endurance events analogous to spacewalking: They had no sooner been dared than they seemed to become commonplace.

Five more Ironman titles followed, in '82, '83, '84, '86, and '87. Those victories—all of them televised—signed Scott's name indelibly upon the triathlon, which during those same years was growing exponentially. The men's elite competition was ruled by the "Big Four" of Scott, Mark Allen, Scott Tinley, and Scott Molina. While the latter three were far more successful than Scott over shorter courses, he, by dint of the Ironman, remained far better known.

"My career was always like this," Scott says, making an oscillating line in the air with his hand. "I wasn't nearly as consistent as Allen and Pigg. I had a lot of distractions during my career, but starting every August 1, I was always able to shut everything else out and focus on the Ironman."

That focus was manifested in the pool in Davis and on the straight, blazing roads of the Central Valley. The heat and winds toughened him, and the intimately familiar landscape provided abundant, reliable cues for measuring his progress. In Davis, Scott could work with rapt and solitary concentration, cultivating a deeply felt but unpretentious relationship with his native place. A reporter once asked Scott what he thought about during all his lonely hours working in the valley. "My rhythms," he replied, "and my lunch."

Now, driving the same valley toward the Sacramento high school, Scott looks back longingly at the fierce simplicity of those days and thoughts. Today, crowding forty, with two growing children, an uncertain agenda, and a body no longer leaping at his bidding, Scott travels with a teeming brain often at war with itself. His chief source of frustration is not the recalcitrant pain rising from his left knee, nor is it the time, energy, and sleep devoured by childrearing, nor is it his absence from the limelight, nor is it even the fact that the corporate sponsorships that sustained him so robustly in his racing prime have dwindled; it is that without hard training, without the organizing principle of the Ironman, his life seems to lack structure and coherence.

"I'm an angry, frustrated man," he says, threading his car through the thickening afternoon traffic. Scott tries to cushion his words with a dissembling boom of laughter, but the strain in his voice is evident. "My whole life has revolved around being fit—being *superfit*. Since my one Ironman-length race last year [a fifth-place finish in the Nice Triathlon], my ratio of nontraining to training days has probably been three or four to one. And I'm not talking about hard training—I'm talking about any exercise *at all*. That's been very debilitating to my self-esteem, my sense of self-worth. Whenever I used to go someplace, I was always known as Dave Scott the triathlete. Now it's Dave Scott . . . who am I now?"

While retirement has forced Scott to confront such issues directly, he has never seemed to possess an unshakable sense of self. This insecurity, perhaps, has served as the engine of his competitive drive. Scott talks often of the commingled exhilaration and anxiety with which, at age twenty-six, he set out on a completely uncharted professional course. He always enjoyed his family's support and blessing, and he made good on his gamble, but throughout his career he couldn't help comparing his mercurial progress with that of his father, who for forty years followed an established profession of unquestioned worth. Triathlon, on the other hand, has always struggled to be taken seriously, even in comparison with other sports. The best runners, swimmers, and cyclists go to the Olympics and world championships; the best triathletes go to Hawaii, where they wear flowered shorts and funny sunglasses, call their reason into question by pursuing stupendous distances, and, for their trouble, suffer indignities ranging from broken derailleurs to incontinence.

"It wasn't until the last few years," Scott says in a rather startling admission, "that I could tell people I met in airplanes what I did for a living. I would always say I was a fitness consultant. People could seem to relate to that. But a triathlete? What's that? Is that really an occupation? You can make a living doing *that?*"

Scott flicks on his turn signal, gliding across three lanes of freeway toward his exit ramp. "I never had a mentor, someone to follow," he says matter-of-factly. "All through my career I was the first. The first to make the sport a profession, the first to have an agent, the first to do a book and video. I was always paving the way, and that was always my choice. But now . . ." His voice trails off as the school comes into sight. "Now, sometimes, I just wish I had somebody telling me what to do."

Jesuit High School, the site of today's talk, occupies a giant parklike campus in an affluent suburb of Sacramento. Its athletic facilities, particularly its swimming pool, are worthy of many Division I universities. At five in the morning last winter, Anna Scott drove here to swim. At age twenty-nine, she was trying to make the U.S. Olympic team in the 50-meter freestyle. Technically she failed, finishing nineteenth in the trials (she had finished fifth in the 1988 trials), but that, as her husband suggests, pales in light of the attempt itself.

Scott's talk, a staple of the fitness-consulting business that is now his primary source of income, forms a family thank-you for Anna's use of the pool. Wearing a brightly colored floral-print sportshirt, fashionably baggy black slacks, and tasseled loafers, Scott takes the lectern in a sun-splashed classroom. His audience, twenty gracefully sprawling, chlorine-bleached teenagers, are raptly attentive. They see before them a trim, handsome, accomplished man, a world-famous athlete, an exemplar of health and fitness. Scott, accordingly, puts his diffidence and anxieties behind him and begins to exhibit the qualities that once prompted triathlon writer Mike Plant to observe, "Dave Scott has the interpersonal skills of a parish priest."

Scott *listens* to these kids, encouraging them to share their struggles as athletes, and offering the stories of his own struggles in return. He describes his tong wars with Mark Allen at the '86, '87, and '89 Ironman races. In those first two races Scott prevailed; the third was Allen's first in his current three-year skein of Ironman championships. That 1989 race was also, by general acclaim, the greatest single competition in the sport's history.

"Mark and I were together all through the bike and all through the marathon," Scott tells the kids. "Whenever I surged, Mark would answer. We both felt great. I had a plan: At twenty-four and a half miles of the marathon, I was going to throw in a surge and break him.

"At mile twenty-three I backed off just a little bit, gathering energy to make my move. But then it took me a whole mile of hard work to get back to his shoulder. Then, at mile twenty-four, he exploded. Before I knew it he'd opened ten feet on me. My first reaction was, 'Mark, come back here, I'm going to beat you!' I tried to answer his surge, but I couldn't. His lead kept widening, and there wasn't anything I could do about it. At the top of the hill going back into Kailua, Mark had a thirty-second lead, and I knew that he had won—not that I had lost. I did an 8:10, which broke the course record, but Mark did an 8:09. I had a great race; he had a phenomenal one."

What Scott doesn't tell the kids are the events of the months leading up to the 1989 Ironman, which in many ways were more phenomenal than the race itself. That summer, at age thirty-five, Scott flogged himself into an unprecedented pitch of fitness. In so doing he aggravated a long-standing knee problem, the same condition that had kept him out of the 1988 Ironman. Earlier, Scott had agreed to do the Japan Ironman at Lake Biwa in August, intending to train through that race in preparation for the Hawaii Ironman in October. Not until three days before the Japan race did Scott decide he would follow through on the commitment. The day before the race, he went out for a forty-mile leg-stretcher on the bike, got lost, and ended up pedaling one hundred hard miles. Later the same day, again by mistake, a half-mile dip in the lake became a two-mile thrash. On race day, finally, Scott embarked on his supposed train-through and came back with a clocking of 8:01:32. That mark still stands as the fastest Ironman-distance triathlon ever.

Six weeks later, on a knee that Scott says was considerably less than healthy, he engaged in his epochal duel in Kona with Mark Allen. That was his last Ironman, his last superlative triathlon of any distance. Since October 1989 his knee condition (which Scott describes as a result of biomechanical imbalance, a tracking abnormality in his patella), once aggravating, has been debilitating. Over the past year he has also suffered from chronic fatigue and a painful inner-ear infection that is exacerbated by exercise. Whether or not these woes resulted from the extreme, almost surreal stresses of that remarkable 1989 racing season, those months epitomize the Faustian undercurrent that has always run through Ironman-distance triathlons. Because Ironwomen and

Ironmen have become so relatively common, because their ranks now include grandpas and letter carriers, service reps, and algebra teachers, it is easy to lose sight of the discipline's radical nature. Such mental, physical, and emotional heights as Scott sustained do not come without some sort of bargaining.

But Scott spares the high school kids these speculations, just as he spares them the dark litany of doctor's appointments, missed races, and diminishing expectations. Nor does Scott describe the hard economic realities of triathlon. As long as he was racing, as long as his Ironman performances provided his twelve sponsors access to the mother lode of network TV exposure, Scott enjoyed a handsome income. The sponsors, in turn, had a willing and attractive spokesman for their product. For two years in the 1980s, for instance, the Dave Scott model Centurion bicycle was the top-selling racing bike in America. When the exposure ceased, however, so did the sponsors' interest. Only Brooks Shoes, InSport (which carries a Dave Scott line of athletic clothing), and Serotta Bicycles still agree with Scott that, whether racing or not, he remains the most important name in the sport.

Scott spares the kids all these considerations, but he does share a story from early in his career. It seems that just after he crossed the finish line for his first Ironman victory, a reporter asked him, "Are you going to retire now?"

"Retire?" an incredulous Scott replied. "I've only just begun!"

The reporter's question was no doubt asked out of combined ignorance and awe, yet it also seems to contain a prescient, if unconscious, wisdom that strikes close to the heart of Scott's dilemma: "Your beginning was your climax," is another way to put it. "What direction is there now but down?"

"Coaching is a science, but it's an art, too," Scott explains, sitting at the kitchen table in his sister's house in Boulder. It's the day after his ride up Left Hand Canyon. The sky has cleared, domestic rhythms have been established, and Scott seems more relaxed and confident than he has in weeks. "I think I have something to offer in both dimensions. As far as the Big Four went, Allen was always known as the mystic, Tinley and Molina were the jocks, and I was the scientist. I know about muscle and blood physiology, and I know about what kind of decisions you have to make in the heat of competition. My real strength is in developing confidence in athletes, helping them develop tenacity."

Scott explains that while he's open to working with citizen triathletes, he has most to offer to professionals. That estimation seems accurate, but it is also fraught with irony. Scott, the self-coached recluse, the legend who trained alone in a cloud of valley dust and mystery, is now offering services of the most communal variety.

There is a geographical irony working as well: that Scott, anchored so securely in Davis, would seek to ply his trade in Boulder, with which he has always maintained a layered, ambivalent relationship. His sister, Jane Scott, is a masters swimming coach for the city of Boulder. In the summer, when triathletes fly in from around the world to train here, Jane directs the swimming workouts for her brother's erstwhile competitors. This is characteristic of the genial, intense, somewhat incestuous world of big-league triathlon. Mark Allen's summer digs, to cite another example, are just 200 yards down the street from Jane's house. Dave stays with Jane whenever he's in Boulder, but the two men rarely see each other.

"I don't know if anybody really knows him well," Scott says about Allen, who uses the same phrase in describing Scott.

During his racing days Scott typically came to Boulder for a few weeks each summer. In Colorado, however, he often remained as solitary and hidebound in his habits as he was at home. While other triathletes ran on the splendid mountain trails, Scott, to his sister's embarrassment, liked to run on the flat fast-food strip of Diagonal Boulevard. While Allen, Molina, and Tinley went on weeklong, 500-mile bike tours through the Rockies, Scott always declined their invitations to join them.

"It was part of Dave's mystique to train alone," comments Bob Babbitt. "He would race poorly all season, and going into the Ironman you'd think there was no way this guy was in shape. Then in Hawaii he'd blow everybody's drawers off. Nobody ever knew what Scott was doing, and that wasn't accidental on Dave's part."

Scott acknowledges the inherent tension between his top competitors and himself. "I always got the media attention that goes with winning the Ironman, and that probably bothered the other guys," he says. "When we worked out together, it tended to get too competitive. Or else I would notice something in their training I didn't agree with and would feel awkward about saying anything."

Now, during the summerlong clinic he is conducting in Boulder, Scott's business will be to point out such flaws. Some veteran triathletes will no doubt be skeptical of his methods and motives. Others, such as Scott Molina, welcome him as a full-fledged member of their community.

"For me, there's only one coach out there I would consider working with, and that's Dave Scott," Molina says. "We all do clinics and talks, try to give advice to other people, but none of us has a background in exercise physiology like Dave's. He understands training, he's bright, and he's been putting his knowledge to use for a lot of years."

Complicating matters will be the questions and speculations that will inevitably swirl around town: Is Scott really retired? Is he really as out of shape as he says? Wasn't he out hammering Left Hand Canyon yesterday? And wasn't that Scott this morning, sharing a lane in the 50-meter pool with Molina, Tinley, Greg Welch, and Ray Browning?

It was, and just now, before heading out with client Colleen Cannon on a bike ride, Scott is drying off and powering down a bowl of whole-grain cereal. Ryan, not quite two, and Drew, age three, are barreling around the living room, Anna is on the phone with InSport discussing Dave's clothing line, while Scott himself sits contentedly in the middle of it all. For a moment—with one hard workout under his belt, another one waiting, and other triathletes whispering about his progress—it seems like the old times have returned.

The early-morning swim had consisted of grinding sets of laps totaling 3,400 meters. A year or two ago Scott would have been out setting the pace, and the workout would have escalated—or degenerated—into a race. Today, however, he puts less pressure on himself, allowing the others, mostly Molina and Welch, to pull the train.

Afterward, in the parking lot, the talk was of upcoming races in France and Japan. Clothes were hurriedly changed, one group of athletes heading off for intervals at a running track, another to take their bikes to the mountains. Scott looked on wistfully, perhaps more than a bit enviously. He, too, was heading for another workout, but one whose goal was the waxing of another athlete's strength.

His present client, Colleen Cannon, is a blond, compact, cheerful woman of thirty-two who for the last few years has been one of the world's top-ranked female triathletes. Although she's been working closely with Scott for months, she remains the slightest bit star-struck. Cannon, like Erin Baker, Mike Pigg, and many other second-generation pros, was first drawn to triathlon by watching Dave Scott and the Ironman on ABC's *Wide World of Sports.*

Their work today retraces the route Scott took yesterday up Left Hand Canyon. The heart of the session will be a six-mile time trial up the steepest part of the canyon, encompassing a rise in elevation of 2,300 feet. On the flat miles leading to the climb, Scott talks constantly, reaching over occasionally to adjust Cannon's posture or suggesting a different foot position.

As they enter the canyon, Scott's encouragement grows less frequent but more urgent. After just one day back in the saddle, his legs are already more attuned to the ascent. His instinct is to push ahead—to give vent to his competitive rage—but his coach's mission is to stay at Cannon's side. For a searing moment his inner conflict becomes palpable. Yet as quickly as it arises, it is resolved by the demands of the moment. Instead of attempting to squelch his rage, he finds a way to translate it.

Leaning close to Cannon through the heart of the climb, Scott shifts his instruction from technique to sensibility. It is confidence he is imparting, the impulse toward full extension, the art of setting and meeting a challenge by employing all of (but not only) one's physical strength. If the question were put to him, Dave Scott might say it was passion he was communicating, a passion in which past achievement and future anxiety are exultantly, if fleetingly, put to rest.

Their ride back down the mountain is swooping, playful, and breathtakingly swift. Back at Jane's house, while Cannon tends to her bike, she is asked whether, given more workouts like today's, she thinks Scott might reconsider his fitful retirement. She responds with an exhausted, hopeful smile.

Scott, meanwhile, waves and gives a hearty farewell laugh. He turns to go inside to his wife and sons and the business end of a sport that it is his continued fate to pioneer, a hybrid, arduous, and still-fledgling sport in which, to Dave Scott's credit and grief, no one waits to tell him what to do next.

OCTOBER 1992

COWGIRLS ALL THE WAY

by E. JEAN CARROLL

1.

There is a horse auction establishment on South MacArthur in Oklahoma City. It is a big white building with a dirt arena inside. Actually, there are two arenas, a large one where the horses are exercised and a smaller one that has a stage with seats around it. I mention this place because it was there that the fifty Miss Rodeo America contestants made their first public appearance. They ate the barbecue in the large arena, and then were introduced by state in the small arena with the seats. In the large arena there was an open bar, but the contestants were not allowed to drink.

"They should let us," said Miss Rodeo Pennsylvania, "to see who gets crocked and who doesn't." Then Miss Rodeo Utah introduced herself.

She had on a baby-blue western suit with white leather piping down both pant legs. Her jacket had four white arrows on the back, pointing at her bottom. She had on baby-blue boots, a white ruffled blouse, and a baby-blue cowboy hat. She wore Merle Norman's Boston Blue eyeshadow, and two hearts held her rodeo sash. She clasped her Miss Rodeo Utah purse in her baby-blue gloves.

"You look like you've won a lot of beauty contests," I said. "Have you ever entered one?"

"No," she said, "I'm a cowgirl all the way!"

In 1975 Miss Rodeo Colorado was bucked off in the grand entry of the Miss Rodeo America contest and was rushed from the arena to the hospital with fractured vertebrae. In 1976 a horse fell on Miss Rodeo Arizona and broke her back. In 1978 Miss Rodeo Kansas, who later became Miss Rodeo America, pivoted her horse to avoid hitting a contestant who had just run over a spectator in the arena. She caught her foot in the gate, was jerked off backward, and broke her arm. It's a rugged kind of competition—no cakewalk.

Before leaving the horse auction building, a man came up to me and said he was from Springdale, Arkansas, "the chicken-pluckin' capital of the world." Said he was "with the chamber of commerce there" and was on the Miss Rodeo board. Then he said, "I'm not a cowboy, but I believe in this crap."

I want to pass along these notes so you'll know what he meant by that. A lot of people are dubious about these contests. The banner on the bosom, the high-heeled hobble, the ramble down the runway. But in a very particular way, this pageant can tell you something special about these women and the way they grew up, about what someone taught them once, about a certain way of life. I mean there are things here that can cloud the issue, and it can all make for a clash in styles. But you should remember that these rodeo queens have roared into the arenas of Ranger, Texas; Ringling, Oklahoma; Roundup, Montana; and Rifle, Colorado, on the foulest, greenest, dumbest, and rankest of horses, shot their salutes to the crowd, and raced out to standing ovations. I want you to remember that Miss Rodeo America 1980 laid a leg over 200 head of weirdo horses and ran the rail in 300 rodeo performances. "Ah, the arena is a little wet, ma'am," they told her in Oregon. "The rain has made it a little *slick*. And that horse there don't like to see his reflection in no mud puddle. Makes him *hoppy*."

"Hand me the reins," said Miss Rodeo America, and half a minute later she exploded out of the gate in a gallop, her crown sparkling in the spotlights, her hips flaring over the saddle, her horse snorting and sliding, her salutes popping like cherry bombs.

I want you to remember that Miss Arkansas is a bull-riding champion and that Miss Wyoming was raised on a 5,000-acre ranch and rounds up cattle; she ropes, wrestles, brands, implants, and inoculates the calves, and runs the buck rigs, hay rigs, tractors, and stackers. I want you to remember that the queens in this contest have won barrel-racing championships, pole-bending championships, team-roping championships, and all-round cowgirl championships. I want you to recall that these queens raise, ride, race, rack, rope, rein, run, rub, reed, and sleep horses. I want you to remember that when Miss Utah was still in a baby-blue bib she took her afternoon nap in the barn on the back of a palomino. "Wasn't your mother terrified you'd fall off and get trampled to death?" I asked her.

"Well, of course, she'd put a *saddle* on him *first*," said Miss Utah, mortified that anyone would speak ill of her mother.

I want you to remember all these things because I am about to introduce you to Dorothy Alexander, the pageant coordinator.

2.

Dorothy Alexander came out of her room in a leopard-skin polyester negligee and said, "You girls have so much pep, I want you to do this all week, OK?"

The queens applauded. Dorothy had confessed to me earlier that she was once a Miss University of Montana "a thousand years ago."

The queens had changed from the three-piece suits they had worn all day to their nightgowns. They were seated on the floor in the hall in front of the elevators on the third floor of the Lincoln Plaza Hotel.

"You're the best horsewomen in America," Dorothy said, "and you've got a lot of pep!" More applause.

Dorothy had told me that the queens rode like "real ladies" but that she thought the personality competition was the most important. "We can't have a dunce for Miss Rodeo America," said Dorothy. "This is *not* a bawdy pageant!"

The elevator doors opened a few minutes later, and a television crew got off to take pictures of the "best horsewomen in America" wearing their nighties.

3.

A cowboy was once fined $200 by the Professional Rodeo Cowboy's Association for making a pass at a queen.

"Now listen," said Tom Poteet, general chairman of the pageant, "tonight you girls are going to be with the cowboys a little while. I know I can count on you to be ladies. I know I don't have to worry about any *problems*, OK?" The queens were then led into an empty room, where a buffet had been prepared for the cowboys, contestants in the National Finals Rodeo. The queens were asked to fill their plates and then were directed to four tables in the furthermost corner of the room. When the last queen was seated and had her lap covered with a paper napkin, the doors were thrown open and a hundred rodeo cowboys swaggered in.

There was a pause. A hush fell. The lone figure of Hawkeye Henson, former world champion bronc rider, emerged from the clutch of men. He started across the room, his black silk shirt pulled tight across his chest, his neckerchief arranged with the point hanging down the front, his black hat cocked, his famous eagle feather at an upward angle, his spurs softly jingling on the tiles. As he neared the queens, Miss Kentucky looked him up and down and said, "I wonder if this is the beginning of the end?"

4.

Working Cowhorse Pattern

Ride the pattern as follows:
Begin work to the right,
First figure eight,
Second figure eight; proceed to rail,
Begin run,
Sliding stop,
Turn away from rail; begin second run,
Sliding stop,
Turn away from rail; make short run,
Sliding stop,
Back up,
Quarter turn to right or left,
Half turn to opposite direction,
Half turn opposite.

That is one of the horsemanship patterns printed in the *Miss Rodeo America Official Rule Book*. The book is a white paperback with twenty-four photocopied pages, and it begins with the question: "What are we looking for in a Miss Rodeo America? Answer: An attractive, intelligent girl . . . a girl who has never been, is not now, or who will not become pregnant during her reign . . . a well-dressed girl who can ride a horse with showmanship and skill, and promote the great sport of rodeo." In other words, a beautiful, big-breasted, barrel-racing, flag-waving, fashionable *virgo intacta* with an IQ somewhere above the persons who composed the *Official Rule Book*.

The book provides a section on "dress wear for horsemanship," supplies a list of equestrian skills the queens are scored on, and concludes with two pages of diagrams illustrating the Miss Rodeo America Horsemanship Patterns Numbers 1 and 2. There is one omission, however, one fact the *Rule Book* committee neglected to photocopy: The horses in the contest are green. The Miss Rodeo America Pageant is produced in the Cowgirl Capital of the World during National Finals Rodeo Week, when the finest stock in America is stabled in the city limits, and the queens get green horses. (They are supplied by local saddle and bridle clubs, riding schools, stock contractors, and "interested individuals.") That is to say, the *Official Rule Book* tells a queen that she must wear a "form-fitting western blouse or shirt with long sleeves, any color with yoke, and shirttail tucked in" while she performs her figure eights, proceeds to the rail, begins her run, slides to a stop, turns from the rail, begins her second run, slides to a stop, turns from the rail, makes her short run, slides to a stop, and backs up; but it does not tell her that her horse might blow up.

The *Official Rule Book* was composed by persons who yearn to merge Miss America with Dale Evans, who burn to combine "The Star-Spangled Banner" and the barnyard; the breast and the breast collar. What do these people care about green horses when what they are looking for is Phyllis George Evans, her hair flashing in the floodlights and her ass fastened on anything that nickers? Next to nothing.

5.

7:30 A.M. to 9:30 A.M. breakfast. Speeches by one-third of the contestants on their respective states.

Miss Rodeo Hawaii walked to the front of the room, smiled—she had a mouthful of spectacularly large, dazzlingly white, splendidly shaped teeth with beautiful crimson gums—delivered the first paragraph of her speech, and stopped dead. "I'm sorry," she said, smiling. A half-minute passed. "I'm sorry," she said, her smile disintegrating completely, and sat down.

"Our next contestant will be Miss Nebraska!" sang Dorothy Alexander.

10:00 P.M. Pajama party. One-third of the contestants give gifts. Illinois passed out popcorn balls; Colorado, Coors T-shirts; Iowa, crocheted booties; and Tennessee, fifty bottles of Jack Daniel's.

"But you *cannot drink them*!" yelled Dorothy. She was now wearing a Mediterranean blue peignoir set. "Listen to Mother," said the television producer, who was there with his crew again.

"I'm going to come in *every* room tonight and check," giggled Dorothy.

"Hey, Texas," yelled the television producer, "hold up that bottle. Hey! Hold up that bottle."

"No pictures!" cried Dorothy.

A member of the press and a pageant official were at the gate when Miss Idaho entered the arena in the first go-round of the horsemanship competition. "This horse turns nice," said the official. The horse ducked off the wrong way four times toward the alley in the figure eight. "He's nice on the turns, though," said the official. The horse lunged at the rail, made two bounds, and blew up into a ticking gallop on the run. On the slide, he reared, nearly fell over backward. "Miss Idaho should sit more on her crotch," said the official. In the second run, Miss Idaho worked the reins, kept the horse's head low, corrected the cross-firing of his back end. On the slide, he reared again. "It's *all* in Miss Idaho's crotch," said the official. The third run was smooth—the slide was second-rate, but no rearing. "Boy, wait till you see this guy turn," said the official. Miss Idaho backed the horse, reined him to the right for the pivot. The horse stood like a post. Miss Idaho calmly worked the reins. The horse sucked in his breath, became a statue. "Where did you *find* this piece of crap?" asked the member of the press. The nine judges looked on in silence. Miss Idaho removed her foot from the stirrup and heeled the horse in the right shoulder with her boot. The horse swung to the right. The crowd applauded. "He's fantastic!" shouted the official. The horse spun left. The crowd cheered. Miss Idaho rolled him right, shot her salute, and cantered out of the arena to an enthusiastic ovation. The official shouted even more excitedly, "Oh, he's just fantastic! Fantastic, fantastic!"

6.

"You girls are out on horses all day. In the gunk. In the muck. In the manure. That's what causes blackheads."

The queens were listening to this in the hotel conference room. The room had rows of seats ascending in tiers, and on the ceiling there were the sort of circles of tiny fluorescent lights that make people who sit under them look funny. The lights in the room could be turned high or low, but either way the queens looked weird. They looked especially weird in the light because they were wearing little pink ruffs around their necks and had little pink plastic makeup trays with mirrors in front of them, and masks on their faces. It was the afternoon of the coronation, and the Mary Kay consultants were meeting with them in the conference room for a "cosmetic session."

"Have any of you dried?" asked the head consultant, at a lectern in the front of the room. The assistant consultants walked up and down the rows checking to see if any queens were dry. If they were, they were handed hot washcloths.

"Since the masks are taking some time," said the head consultant, "why don't I just give you a little history about how Mary Kay got started. Well, there was this old tanner of hides. . . ." At this point Miss South Dakota ripped off her ruff, put her head down on her tray, and went to sleep.

"I see you are dressed for the coronation," I said.

"Yes, but I don't look as good as some of the girls."

"Do you mind if I write down what you have on?"

"No. Go ahead."

"All right. You have on gold-and-silver collar tips with your initials."

"Right."

"You have on a blue silk scarf with your initials set in diamonds pinned across the knot."

"Right."

"Your buckle is gold and silver with rubies and diamonds."

"Right."

"You have blue—what are those?"

"Eel."

"Blue eel boots. Black hat. Black pants. Blue jacket."

"You forgot the buttons."

"The, ah, buttons are silver circles with raised gold flowers with rubies in the middle."

"Right."

The person I was speaking to was Joe "Sandy" Boone, president of Miss Rodeo America.

7.

There is a sound that barrel-racing horses make when they are in the alley and ready to run. It's a rapid, thumping sound of hoofs hitting dirt. The air is thick with dust, and the noise of the hoofs sounds richer in the dust, and when the dirt clods hit the iron chutes as the horses rear back and dig out, there is also a ringing sound. These were the sounds in the State Fair Grounds arena alley the night of the coronation. The horses were rank, and they didn't have fifty; and each queen had to race into the arena, fire her salute, and then gallop out the gate and dismount so that the next could ride in. But it was, as a matter of fact, the finest time of the pageant.

The ten finalists had been named. The four runners-up had been named. The reigning Miss Rodeo America had taken her last royal roar around the arena. Six rodeo clowns had competed in a bullfighting championship. And the winner of *that* had been named.

"Well, folks," said Hadley Barrett, the rodeo announcer, to a crowd that could have been larger, "is there anything else we have to do tonight?"

"I can't *stand* it any longer," said Diana Putman, the reigning queen.

"May we have the envelope, please?" said Hadley. There was a drum roll. "Who will wear the crown next? If you're too nervous to open that envelope I'll—Oh! You got it. Ladies and gentlemen, we are going to ask Diana to name her successor. Diana, we want *you* to name the 1981 Miss Rodeo America."

Diana looked down at the card in her hand, then shouted, "Miss Rodeo Colorado!"

Screams from the contestants.

Kathy Martin, five foot six, 120 pounds, dark eyes, flashing hair, a public relations major whose hobbies were "equine evaluation, training quarter horses, dancing, jogging, sewing, and trail riding," made her way toward her precursor. The band struck up "The Most Beautiful Girl in the World." Diana removed the crown from her hat and placed it on Miss Colorado's hat. The queens were screaming.

"There she is, ladies and gentlemen!" said Hadley. "The 1981 Miss Rodeo America!"

Miss Colorado walked down the steps: no train, no tears, no toppling tiaras, no scepters, no roses, no ermine. All that awaited her was the top reining horse in the country, dancing at the end of a rein held by a cowboy in white.

APRIL/MAY 1981

LIFE AMONG THE SWELLS

by WILLIAM FINNEGAN

I found a peak, a no-name wave just west of Off-the-Wall. A lifeguard told me an unusual sandbar had formed there after a recent storm and would probably be gone after the next storm. When a set caught it right, the bar produced a steep takeoff with long, tapering lefts and short, quick rights. Over the course of a week I surfed the place three times, each time alone or nearly alone. The waves weren't very big, but they were mostly clean and deeply pleasing. What I couldn't decide was whether the light edge of ecstasy I felt while riding this evanescent spot was radiating from the experience itself or from my awareness that it was happening on the holy North Shore.

If the surfing world has a shared mythology, then the North Shore of Oahu is its Olympus. For those who surf, it doesn't matter where one lives—I live in New York City—the place takes up an alarming amount of one's fantasy life. High-resolution images of waves at the Banzai Pipeline, Sunset Beach, Waimea Bay, Backdoor, and Off-the-Wall fill the collective surfing unconscious with mesmerizing caverns, pitching silver lips, and impossibly deep, dreamlike rides.

What happens there is straightforward: Winter storms in the North Pacific generate large swells that strike the coast of Hawaii, their force undiminished by a continental shelf. A fortuitous concentration of reefs and channels on the North Shore turns those swells into ridable waves, and great surfers come from all over the world to ride them. A critical mass of photographers and cameramen gathers to immortalize—and commodify—it all for the entertainment of the rest of us. The imagery produced has, at least for surfers, a power, a fascination, a *glamour* of complex transcendence.

From November to February the North Shore teems with visiting surfers. They come from Brazil and Europe and Florida and Japan and, most numerously, Southern California. This seasonal migration began in the 1950s, when a handful of California surfers first ventured over from Makaha, a West Shore spot then considered the last word in big waves. Nowadays the seasonal influx numbers in the thousands.

For the most part, it's a hard-core crowd—young, male, low-budget, dead serious about surfing. An elaborate dominance hierarchy, both in and out of the water, is constantly under construction. Hot locals and famous pros occupy the heights, but bold, talented newcomers are forever on the rise. Different surfers excel in different conditions, and each spot has its own pecking order, adjusted daily. Given the intensity of the competition, the absence of formal rules, the great cultural diversity of the players, and the sheer quantities of adrenaline being pumped, it all goes off pretty peaceably.

A few young women, some of whom surf, make the pilgrimage these days. Local nightlife, however, is nonexistent. Even in December, the peak month for visitors, the scene is decidedly tame. Short-timers stay in cramped rental cottages, eight and ten to a house. Parties tend to be muted, pot-themed affairs, ending early. A night out is pizza at D'Amicos, a no-frills joint near Sunset Point.

Surfers come for the waves. They also come to get their ticket punched: North Shore experience is indispensable on any ambitious surfer's résumé. And if they're planning to make a career in surfing (an option reserved for only the hottest of the hot), they come to perform in this, the main arena—and to be photographed doing so as often as possible.

The highest concentration of cameras usually occurs in December, at the Pipeline Masters (or the Chiemsee Gerry Lopez Pipeline Masters, as it's currently known). Held since 1971, the Pipe Masters is probably the world's best-known surf contest and is the final event of the year on the nine-country professional World Championship Tour. Insofar as most surfers take an interest in any contest, they take an interest in the Pipe Masters. When the waves are good, it can be a spectacular show.

But that's a big "insofar." I was at the 1996 Pipe Masters as part of the media mob. Though the contest was on hold for more than a week while its promoters prayed for Pipeline to break, the North Shore surf community didn't seem to be holding its collective breath. Out at Sunset one balmy, brilliant morning, I asked a local surfer about the Pipe Masters and its various affiliated events. "Next year they're going to put up a Ferris wheel," he said, jerking a thumb back toward the beach.

His tart dismissal of the pro scene captured nicely, I thought, the attitude of most surfers toward the organized, commercialized version of the sport: rumpled apathy, contempt, a whiff of envy. Contests are a scam, a distraction from more important things: the ocean, the weather, and of course that weightiest of matters, one's own surfing.

I largely shared this attitude. Indeed, just being in Hawaii heightened my ingrained suspicion of everything that seeks to package and sell surfing. I lived in Honolulu as a kid—I went to junior high school there—and it now makes me physically ill to revisit certain South Shore spots, obscure breaks where a few friends and I used to surf, and find a hundred boards in the water. The sport's salesmen have done their job too well. And the World Championship Tour is, naturally, their favorite marketing tool.

This was my first trip to the North Shore since 1978, and it too was dramatically more crowded than I remembered it. There were traffic jams and parking hassles. Surfers on bicycles, boards under arms, patrolled the coast constantly, keeping a close watch on the dozens of spots. Whenever a break got halfway ridable, people were on it, battling for waves. If the surf was actually good, it was crowded from dawn till dark.

Still, I was wildly happy to be there. Out at Sunset that morning, long, sparkling sets moved in from the north, their broad faces buffed by a light south wind. I could see army C-130s flying lazy, low-altitude circles offshore and a big green sea turtle swimming near my takeoff spot. I lucked into a solid wave alone and rode it from a big-shouldered, sapphire blue outside wall through a jacking inside bowl. On the paddle back out I was grinning like an idiot.

As I sniffed around the North Shore, I kept catching small glimpses of myself as a young dog haunting these same neighborhoods, in scenes long forgotten: riding a beloved board at a fast, shallow break known as Gas Chambers; staying in a creepy, celibate Baha'i household up at Waialee; surfing Pipeline for the first time on my nineteenth birthday; getting drubbed within an inch of my life by a ten-wave set at Sunset.

While the surf on the North Shore may be Olympian, the place itself is another matter. Beyond the cropped edges of the exquisite photos, it's a damp, semirural, rather ordinary-looking stretch of tropical coast, twelve miles long, between the old sugar towns of Haleiwa and Kahuku. Military installations and pineapple fields occupy the rolling terraces behind the coastal bluffs, and horse farms take up the verdant flats where the bluffs swing inland. There's a small harbor at Haleiwa. Otherwise, the only significant notch in the coast is the U-shaped, cliff-lined, river-mouth bay at Waimea. Beach houses, both modest and posh, fill the narrow, intermittent strip between the ocean and the only through road.

The year-round residents are native-born islanders, ex-Californians, and a scantling of transplants from farther away. Some surf, though most don't. Ethnically, it's Hawaiians, Chinese, Japanese, Filipinos, *haoles* (whites), Koreans, and every conceivable combination thereof. Some people commute to Honolulu, thirty miles away on the South Shore, or to one of the island's military bases, but local jobs are scarce, particularly since the sugar mill at Haleiwa closed last year. There's only one hotel, a Hilton near Kahuku, which seems to be struggling.

Tourism reaches the North Shore mainly in the form of charter buses, which stop in Haleiwa, where curio shops and "art galleries" lie in wait for them, or on the roadside at Sunset Beach, where they exhale packs of camera swingers in front of the famous wave every few minutes, inhale them back, and proceed.

Surfers on the North Shore, like surfers most everywhere, are often broke, or nearly so. And the winter pilgrims have tended to bring with them a motley flock of hangers-on, not all of whom leave when the winter swells end. A transient layer of nouveau poverty thus lies uneasily alongside the community's older rural Hawaiian poverty, the two worlds sharing, among other things, an underground economy specializing in crack, heroin, speed, stolen property, and above all, marijuana.

This is the non-glam North Shore, and you can scarcely be here a day without noticing it. Its denizens trip along the roadside, trade food stamps at tiny cinder-block groceries, settle domestic disputes in grubby laundromats at night. Just east of Sunset Point, near a surf spot known as Velzyland, the road passes a long row of low beige houses that could be in backwater Alabama: rotting carports, muddy trucks on blocks, chained pit bulls, large men drinking beer on a weekday morning, barefoot children in dirty shorts.

So while a Ferris wheel on the beach at Sunset obviously won't happen— that was just a metaphor—there is this other perspective on the pro surfing circus that passes through Hawaii each winter: that of the kids who live here, many of them poor.

I think it's safe to say that they're unlikely to share my bourgeois purist's distaste for crass commercialism. In fact, the local boys who've made it as pro surfers are heroes to such kids, who would no doubt be happy to join the circus and see the world themselves. And this poor-boy's perspective was really more interesting, I later decided, than my own.

But I only saw that after spending a week, waiting for the Pipe Masters to start, with one of the homeboy heroes, a young pro named Conan Hayes.

• • •

He's not one of the professional surfing tour's poster boys yet. He had a great year, though, rising from number thirty-five on the forty-four-man tour to number ten going into this, the year's final event. In an August meet in La-canau, France, he defeated, in successive heats, Kelly Slater, Sunny Garcia, and Shane Beschen, who were then ranked number one, two, and three in the world, respectively. Perhaps, I think, that's why everywhere we go on the North Shore—to the beach, out surfing, into Haleiwa for breakfast—people greet him with peace signs, double-clutch handshakes, cryptic jokes. They're drawn to him, sensing he may be the Next Big Thing. "Nah," says Conan. "It's be-cause I cut my hair."

Just yesterday he had a burgundy-tinted Afro. Now, suddenly, he has a bur-gundy tennis ball. He's obviously into abrupt revamps—in surfing magazine photos past, he had blond braids and then blond cornrows. "Experiments," he says, when I ask him about other self-adornments—a pierced nose, a pierced tongue. (His half-dozen tattoos must fall under another category.)

Conan is strangely self-possessed for a kid of twenty-two, with a quiet, watchful manner that crosscuts suavely with his flamboyance. Although he's a haole, he's got a streetwise, multicultural air. With his long arms and power-ful torso, he looks like a boxer, some junior welterweight brawler from the Bronx. At five foot seven and 145 pounds, he's one of the smaller men on the pro tour.

Conan really doesn't seem to see the North Shore through the prism of his own success—a sports-mad campus on which he is a popular jock. His humil-ity can be quite disarming. One day we're crawling down a narrow road near Pipeline in my rental car, easing past a battered sedan going the other way. Co-nan waves to the other driver, a shirtless old Filipino, who waves back. "You know him?" I ask, a little surprised.

"Nah," Conan says. "But you gotta wave to people in Hawaii. It's like super-mandatory. I was just covering for you."

Conan learned his rural Hawaiian manners on the Kona Coast of the Big Is-land, where he grew up and, when he is not out on tour, still lives. His parents were country hippies, his father a marijuana farmer. For a haole kid, Hawaiian public schools can be tough places. "Yeah, they had a Kill Haole Day at my school," Conan recalls. "But all my boys were the gnarliest Hawaiian guys, and by junior high I was known for surfing, so I was cool. I never fazed."

The Big Island doesn't have a reputation for good surf, but Conan's parents gave him a used board when he was ten, and his talent was noticed immedi-ately, even at his mediocre home break. A local surf shop and a Honolulu board company began to sponsor him when he was only eleven, flying him to Oahu for amateur contests, which he soon began to win.

John Carper, a board shaper on the Big Island at the time (he's now on the North Shore and shapes boards for Conan), remembers a whole crop of hot local kids, from which only Conan and his best friend, Shane Dorian, also now a top pro and Carper team rider, emerged. "There were so many drugs around," Carper says. "And all these other kids were turning into little jelly piles—no motivation. Shane and Conan were different. They were dead-set against drugs. They were like ghetto kids. They had that kind of determination."

When Conan was fourteen, his father got busted for growing pot. His sentence: ten years in federal prison. Conan had been largely raising himself already—"He was sleeping on people's floors, hanging with adults," according to Carper—and developing his trademark equanimity. "He was never angry or hyperactive, like a lot of kids coming out of the drug culture," Carper said. "He could always entertain himself."

After his father went to jail, Conan began raising himself for real. "My mom had no money, and she had my little sister," he says. Conan, barely five feet tall at the time, moved to the North Shore, where he scraped by on whatever his local sponsors gave him, lived off friends, became a strict vegetarian, and won every state amateur title in sight. One year he and Shane Dorian lived together in a walk-in closet. Somehow Conan managed to graduate from high school.

The adult he most credits with helping him through this hand-to-mouth adolescence is Ben Aipa, a legendary Hawaiian surfer and board maker who became his coach. "Conan was really very independent," Aipa recalls. "But I took him everywhere with me, trying to keep him busy. I was coaching Brad Gerlach"—a world-tour pro—"and I used to take Conan along. Conan already saw where he wanted to go."

Against his sponsor's advice, Conan turned professional and soon found himself with an unorthodox new sponsor: Chris Lassen, a painter from Maui who had parlayed his work—garish, tropical-fantasy fare—into a multinational schlock-art business with revenues last year of more than $20 million. Lassen, who surfs, wanted a surf team with his name on it. Conan ended up sharing a palatial North Shore beach house, just down the road from his old walk-in closet, with other Lassen beneficiaries. Lassen bankrolled his travels to contests on the World Qualifying Series, where top finishers graduate to the World Championship Tour.

Conan was in awe of Lassen's custom-car collection—Cobras, Lamborghinis—and remembers, with a rich chuckle, cruising Waikiki with Lassen's team manager in the boss's Porsche 911. This idyll ended when Lassen's corporation reorganized and disbanded the team.

By the end of 1994, Conan had qualified for the World Championship Tour. He had a board sponsor, a wetsuit sponsor, a sandals sponsor, a sunglasses sponsor—and the fees they paid him to promote their products far outpaced the prize money he won in 1995, which came to less than $30,000. Tour life was not luxurious for surfers at his level, who doubled up on hotel rooms and rental cars. Still, his income allowed him to make down payments on a house in Kona for his mother and, just down the mountain and across from the beach, a modest condo for himself.

His 1996 results were sharply better, making Conan an increasingly hot commodity. But rather than cash in on his promotional value with a clothing sponsor—the main source of most pros' income—Conan started, with several partners, his own clothing line, called Seventeen Apparel. "It's so much better than having a sponsor breathing down your neck," he says.

Conan's commitment to the company is intense. He has SEVENTEEN tattooed in large letters across his back, and "17" inside a star on one calf. He recently turned down an endorsement offer from another clothing outfit that would have paid him $450,000 over three years. "I believe in my company," he says. "And I won't always be on tour."

This odd combination of forward-looking prudence—rare, to say the least, on the pro tour—and go-for-broke recklessness (making one's body a lifelong billboard for a fledgling enterprise in a high-risk business like the rag trade) struck me as essential Conan. While his job at Seventeen is, as one of his partners put it, "to surf"—to appear in ads, to win contests with the firm's logo on his board—he is passionate about its designs as well.

"Our clothes are, like, *all basketball*," he told me, indicating the sweatpants, jersey, and sneakers he was wearing, which were, I guess, pretty basketball. He pointed to a Seventeen ad in a surf magazine, which featured a photo of him doing a spectacular snapback. "We're going for a super-clean look," he said, studying the ad. The avant-garde athlete as entrepreneur, I thought—part performer, part promoter. They had named their company Seventeen, one of his partners told me, because "that's the age when a surfer comes into his own, when the little grommet grows up, when he stops following and starts wanting his own image. Kids that age *love* Conan."

Although Conan rejected the idea, when I mentioned it, that selling surf-related products ultimately exacerbates, by glamorizing the sport, the problem of crowds in the water, he is not insensitive to the ambiguities of what people in his world, like people in the film business, call simply "the industry." He is very protective of the anonymity of surf spots on the Big Island, for instance, actively opposing any coverage of them in the magazines. When the publicity machine meets his ordinary surfer's preference for solitude, commercialism loses.

Indeed, he surprised me by saying that he had been training for the Pipe Masters not at Pipeline, the obvious place, but back on the Big Island: lifting weights, mountain biking, surfing. Why? "I hate the North Shore," Conan said. "Too many people, too much hype."

Conan and I paddled out at Pipeline one morning during the Pipe Masters waiting period. The surf was about two feet and exceedingly gentle. The swell was too small and too north for Pipeline—a spectacular, ultra-hollow left—to be breaking. And yet there were twenty guys in the water at the famous patch of reef that morning. When Pipeline is breaking, the crowd there is the most dangerous on the North Shore. Today it was just the most annoying.

My eye kept drifting down the beach to my no-name peak, on the other side of Off-the-Wall. It looked empty, as usual, and it seemed to be working. But Conan pointed out a photographer on the beach and said, "Taylor's guy's here, so I should stay here." He meant Taylor Steele, a well-known surf-video producer.

"But these waves are too small," I whined. "The pictures won't be any good."

"You'd be surprised," Conan said, with a little grimace. I guessed what he meant: The surf mags are full of shots of guys doing aerials against a blue sky with nothing in sight but a spray of salt water to indicate that there was even a wave outside the frame. And the other guys in the water with us were, I noticed, indeed launching some incredible maneuvers—"slutting out," as the pros say, meaning that the cameras present were turning them into "photo sluts."

While Conan went to work for the cameras (later, when I asked Taylor Steele about his professional relationship with Conan, he said, "I need Conan, Conan needs me"), I paddled outside and went for a swim in the clear water among the fissures and rocks of the Pipeline reef. The jagged bottom, with its holes and caves and overhanging ledges, was terrifying when one pictured ten-foot waves exploding into the thin cushion of water above it. There were so many places for a falling body to slam against or get stuffed under.

A little later, Conan, having grown bored with milking knee-high waves, joined me. He also studied the bottom. "All this sand in the gullies and inside," he said. "That all has to wash away before Pipeline will go off. We need a big west swell."

I found an area of reef that looked like it might form the head of the peak—the first place where a wave starts to break—on a good-size day. I asked if it was the takeoff zone. Conan turned and studied the shore. "Yeah, it is," he said. "But I like a boil over there better. It's a little deeper." He pointed some yards west, and I realized I had seen him take off over there, from a spot frighteningly far behind the peak, in a surf video. In that piece of footage, Conan had been rewarded for his daring with a huge backdoor barrel. It was rides like that one that had earned him his reputation for surfing Pipeline with abandon.

For the Masters, Conan was hoping that Pipeline would assume its full form.

Even among the top forty-four, having to surf big Pipe would sharply narrow the field of serious contenders. And Conan, who loves big waves, would be in that winnowed group. (The women's WCT, which normally holds contests alongside the men's tour, doesn't have an event at Pipeline. The wave, when it's happening, is considered just too hairy.)

I noticed that Conan had started shivering. I couldn't see why. The air and water were wonderfully warm. "I don't have any body fat," he explained.

We were joined by a couple of young Brazilian women on bodyboards. Like half the surfers on the North Shore, they seemed to know Conan well. Both were darkly tanned and wore almost nothing. Drifting and chatting with them, Conan seemed to forget about being cold. They hung on his words and laughed at his jokes. In the ocean, even without waves to ride, Conan, his shoulders rippling, lolled like an alpha-male dolphin.

With waves to ride, he was something else again. A few days later, the swell was bigger—though still not big enough for the contest's purposes—and he and I were surfing Off-the-Wall. It was fairly crowded, but the waves were worth competing for, so a pecking order was in place. Conan shot to the top of it without seeming to consider any other possibility. He paddled for position faster than anybody else, seemed to read the swells sooner, caught every wave that interested him, and then tore it apart. There were several other excellent surfers out, but Conan's turns, snapbacks, lip bashes, gouges, floaters, and reentries were all a solid notch sharper and more startling.

While his intensity was presumably only a fraction of what it would be in serious waves or in a contest, it was formidable. The look on his face when he dug for a wave bore a distinct resemblance to fury.

And his virtuosity, his superiority to an ordinary surfer like me, was not, I realized, simply a matter of degree. There were also basic category shifts. When I consider a wave, I ask first if I can catch it and second if I can make it (that is, stay ahead of its breaking section). Conan, it seemed, wasn't asking the same questions. Catchability, for instance, is less of an issue when you can paddle as fast as he and other pros can. You can catch almost any wave you want. Conan had been trying to explain certain tactics in three-man heats to me, and they hadn't really made much sense, but now I saw that they did make sense if the normal limits of wave-catchability were simply repealed. Clever dodges of all sorts suddenly became possible.

I noticed Conan giving me blank looks more than once when I asked him, of an approaching swell, something like, "Do you think this right looks makable?" To me this was a normal question—he knew the break well, after all, and I didn't; a lot of waves were closing out hard on the inside bar. Eventually, from some mumbled replies about "open face," I gathered that he didn't really care if a wave was makable. He wasn't looking to ride waves the longest possible distance and pull out of them cleanly before they broke—the traditional definition of a successful ride—as I was. He was just looking for some open face to shred, maybe a lip to bash, maybe a barrel to pull into. A wave that closed out was not, in his book, necessarily to be avoided.

His gravity-defying floaters and monster reentries were in fact designed for making the most of close-outs. Indeed, such maneuvers were essential to success in contests, when you often couldn't wait around for "makable" waves.

I rode in feeling old.

One reason most surfers don't care about contests is that they're usually held in mediocre surf, which even the best surfers cannot make interesting. Another is that surfing is simply not, at bottom, a competitive activity—there is no objective standard available to rate performance. Contests, furthermore, "promote the sport" at a time when the biggest problem in surfing is crowds in the water and the last thing most of us want is for more people to get turned on to our chosen obsession.

Then there are the locals at the spots where contests are held, who are often unhappy about having their home breaks rented out and closed off. Protests by what pro tour officials are pleased to call "recreational surfers" have been growing all along the WCT trail—in Australia, South Africa, Réunion, California—over contest permits and public access.

On the North Shore, enforcement of a contest's exclusion zone has traditionally fallen to a crew of local heavies who used to be known as the Black Shorts and are now called Hui O He'e Nalu ("Group of Wave Sliders") or simply the Hui. Ostensibly a Hawaiian cultural self-help group, the Hui is widely feared among both visiting and resident surfers. The Hui's franchise on contest security has been eroded by local lifeguards, only some of them Hui members, who've formed something called Water Patrol Inc., complete with Jet Skis. But this lucrative little business only underscores the tension between the contest scene and the rest of the surfing world.

Rob Machado gives this dynamic an extra twist. A brilliant surfer, Machado finished 1995 ranked second in the world after losing to Kelly Slater in what many people think was the greatest Pipe Masters heat ever. (Mediocre waves were not a problem that year.) Afterward, Machado said that the most exciting thing about the contest wasn't the prize money or the glory, but simply the opportunity to ride immaculate Pipeline for twenty-five minutes with only one other surfer. It was a peculiar form of purism, but it resonated, I think, with the masses.

Slater for his part could probably afford to rent any break he liked. Easily the biggest name in surfing, he is said to get a million dollars a year from his sponsor, Quiksilver, and to have been offered $2 million to sign with Nike. Coming into this contest, he had won the Pipe Masters three of the previous four years and had already sewn up his fourth world title in five years. While anything could happen in any given heat, Slater stood firmly as the primary obstacle between hopefuls like Conan and the Pipe Masters crown.

Conan was crashing in an empty room at the Sunset Point house of another young pro named Jun Jo. "We're all professional time-consumers," Conan said. He meant pro surfers, who spend half their lives waiting around for contests to start. Conan amused himself during the Pipe Masters waiting period by playing basketball, golf, and Hang Time, the video game of choice at Jun's place. Weight lifting and other serious training were on hold—Conan didn't want to be sore if the contest suddenly started. He listened, as always, to a lot of rap—especially Tupac Shakur—and played a lot of guitar.

One day we sat on the deck of a beach house that Rob Machado had rented for the contest. The surf had come up, finally, but so had an onshore wind. Pipeline was a foaming mess—still no lefts in sight. A fitful traffic of young pros, coaches, shapers, and photographers drifted across Machado's deck. High-performance surfboards filled the small yard. (A couple of these would later get broken in moments of pique by their owners after unsuccessful Pipe Masters heats.) In the space of an hour, the entire cast of some of Taylor Steele's surf videos wandered past—including the soft-spoken, Afro-haired Machado, a rangy Hawaiian phenom named Kalani Robb, and Conan's friend Shane Dorian, whose clean-cut charm has also landed him a leading role in a forthcoming Hollywood feature film, *In God's Hands*. Steele's videos, with their punk soundtracks, have become cult objects.

"It's weird," Conan says. "These kids in Japan and Europe and wherever know every wave, every note of every song, on Taylor's videos."

Conan and his friends are, in other words, the coolest of the cool in a large patch of youthworld. Certainly, I thought, watching them come and go, the pros—with their deep tans, their amazing physiques—carried themselves like young gods.

The way they speak about surfing is a peculiar combination of sports talk and art talk. On the one hand, there are wave conditions and training regimens and heat tactics, and on the other there are hopeless efforts to describe the indescribable: what moves them in surfing, what they love. Many young pros, I found, including Conan and Dorian, grew up idolizing an unorthodox Australian goofyfoot named Mark Occhilupo, who flourished in the mid-1980s, disappeared from the surfing scene for seven years, and recently resurfaced on the pro tour, again surfing wondrously. Occy, as he is known, was ahead of his time, his acolytes say, but when pressed to elaborate they flail, sounding a bit like art majors.

"He had no weird influences," Dorian finally told me.

Conan agreed.

But what did that mean, I asked—no weird influences?

"He came from nowhere," Dorian said. "He didn't look like he had studied anybody else's style. The way he looks at a wave is just genius."

Conan agreed. Genius.

Conan and his buddies also talk a lot of regular surf talk—with some differences. I once asked Conan about peak experiences, and he mentioned surfing in East Java last year at a remote break called Grajagan. A WCT contest was being held there, but what he seemed to treasure was simply the great waves they found. He got what was probably the longest tube ride of his life, he said, and he saw the most amazing tube ride ever. I knew the ride he meant, because I had seen it on video: Kelly Slater, insanely deep for insanely long.

"I was on the shoulder, paddling out," Conan said. "And I could see Kelly back in there, just so far back in this big, sucking-out, overhead barrel. He was actually skidding around on the foam ball. I really thought he'd never come out. And then I looked back, and—" Conan thrust his arms upward in imitation of Slater's brief, ecstatic gesture as he escaped the great tube. Conan, shaking his head, gave a vivid groan, eloquent in the preverbal language spoken by all surfers about surfing. It was notable to me that he, busy making his living from the sport, still obviously shared the basic stoke of it.

The Pipe Masters finally got under way on the ninth day of the twelve-day waiting period. You sometimes hear the Pipe Masters described by nonsurfers as the Super Bowl of surfing. The opening-day crowd for this Super Bowl numbered about 150. A few surfers—mainly friends of the contestants. A few Japanese girls, hoping to get Kelly Slater's autograph. Some confused-looking tourists. And a few clumps of idle North Shore scenesters—shaved heads and wraparound shades, ponytails and big pirate earrings, nobody stinting on tattoos.

Otherwise, it was all cameras. They lined the water's edge, practically outnumbering the spectators. The Pipe Masters is, as pro tour officials say, a "media-driven event." It lives by its TV coverage, its syndication sales. The Jet Skis of Water Patrol Inc. cruised the lineup, keeping the throngs of "recreational surfers" out of the contest site.

Unfortunately, for the start of the 1996 Pipe Masters, there was no Pipeline. There were good-size, clean waves at the place called Pipeline, but they were walled-up rights, not ultra-hollow lefts. The swell still wasn't west enough, people said. There was still too much sand on the reef. The trialists, who competed in the morning, surfed well, but many Pipe specialists got nowhere. Even Mark Occhilupo didn't make it through.

In the afternoon, as the main event commenced, though, a superb left began to fire just down the beach, at Off-the-Wall. Shawn Briley, a rotund local tube-riding wizard who had failed to survive the trials that morning, paddled out at Off-the-Wall, where he snagged barrel after barrel. I watched his performance from the judges' platform overlooking Pipeline. Nothing much was happening in the heats out front, so all eyes (and binoculars) were on Briley, with the usual chorus of screams and groans rising each time he made one of his miraculous, casual escapes. "Ten! Ten!" a judge would shout. The judges were all old surfers, clearly still not oblivious to ordinary stoke.

Only one surfer was being eliminated in the three-man, first-round heats. Still, Pipe aces were dying like flies in the chunky rights. Rob Machado and Kalani Robb, two of the contest favorites, were unceremoniously bounced. Conan's first heat wasn't scheduled until the next day.

As there was still plenty of light left when the day's competition ended, I hurried down to Sunset. The waves were bigger and much better there than they had been at Pipeline, and I ended up surfing until dark. There was a daunting array of pros in the water—I counted three former world champions—which made it difficult to get waves to oneself. So I tried to see the session as a chance to study, at close range, the moves of the masters. I even succeeded, in part.

And that's when I realized that the North Shore, the pro scene, had seduced me. My aggressive skepticism about the upper reaches of surfing—that hazy area where hot surfers turned into commercial icons and magnificent waves became some huckster's profit margin—had been undone by ten days at the circus. I was actually interested in something other than the ocean and my own surfing.

I was fascinated especially by Mark Occhilupo. He seemed unaffected by his loss at Pipeline earlier in the day. He was surfing exuberantly, anyway, with great concentration. I can't say I understood everything he was doing—his moves were so quick, so fearless, that I found them strange and hard to follow. Maybe, I thought, "no weird influences" was the best description.

Conan's opening-round heat was held in head-high, inconsistent rights. His opponents were a fellow Hawaiian named John Shimooka and a Brazilian goofyfoot, Flavio Padaratz. Both were tour veterans whom Conan had passed in the rankings over the course of the year.

All three started with a couple of low-scoring rides. Then Conan caught a bigger, longer wave and reeled off a series of wild lip bashes that scored an 8.25 and put him in the lead. He caught a second, fairly good wave, a 6.4. He needed one more decent score to be sure of advancing (heats are decided on each surfer's three best waves). Shimooka got a nice barrel for a 9, putting him in the lead and Conan in second.

Then things got interesting.

Conan and Shimooka started shadowing Padaratz. To avoid elimination, Padaratz needed a good wave. But Conan and Shimooka, working together, could prevent him, I realized, from catching one. They could do this, under the rules of the three-man heat, simply by taking off on either side of him. The way it worked was diabolical: Once Padaratz caught a wave and committed himself to riding it in one direction or the other, the Hawaiian in front of him would pull back, as if to give him the wave, but the Hawaiian in back of him would drop in. Since, in surfing, the rider in front is always wrong, Padaratz would be cited for interference—a penalty that would kill his chances of advancing.

I thought this seemed like dirty pool, and some of the Brazilians on the beach seemed to agree. But, I was informed by a contest official, it was a not-uncommon tactic. In fact, only the opening round of the Pipe Masters used three-man heats. After that, it would be man-on-man, and that, I was told, was when the serious hassling would start.

Padaratz paddled furiously up and down the beach, looking for a wave. Conan and Shimooka paddled gaily along with him. Very few waves came through. Nobody took off.

But then, with perhaps five minutes left in the heat, Conan and Shimooka seemed to relax—seemed, actually, to be absorbed in conversation—and Padaratz slipped away, getting just far enough to catch, alone, a small wave that suddenly stood up nicely. He rode it fiercely across the Backdoor sandbar and scored a 7.15, enough to move him into second place.

Now Conan needed a wave, any wave, immediately. And Padaratz was shadowing him. They charged back and forth. Padaratz's plan was brutally simple. Any wave Conan caught, he would catch, too, and surf right at him, earning Conan an interference.

There were several hundred people on the beach that day, and they were starting to yell—in Conan's favor, I thought. Conan was a faster paddler, but not so much faster that he could completely elude Padaratz in the confined space of the contest site. Whether he could outrace him by a margin large enough to catch a wave by himself began to seem, in any case, like a moot question, because no waves at all were coming through now. Shimooka seemed to be watching the whole drama passively.

It was the worst, most graphic hassling the contest had seen so far. And I found it really unsettling to watch—mainly because, if any "recreational surfer" were to do for fifteen seconds to another surfer what Padaratz was doing to Conan for minutes on end, a fight would break out. As crowd behavior, it was beyond outrageous. As contest behavior, however, it was apparently normal. So much, I thought, for contests as a respite from crowds.

And that was how the heat ended. No waves came, and Conan was out of the contest in the first round.

Pipeline never did break that week, but the Pipe Masters limped on. The beach crowd grew toward the end of the contest, though surfers on the whole seemed to stay away—other spots, after all, were getting better waves. Padaratz made it through his second heat but then lost to Shimooka man-on-man in the third round. Shimooka ended up tied for fifth. Shane Dorian, who was surfing brilliantly, made it to the third round, where he ran into Kelly Slater, who was quite unstoppable. Slater went on to win the contest for the fourth time. Of the fourteen WCT contests held in 1996, he won seven.

Watching Slater, I kept thinking about things that Conan and Shane had said about him earlier in the week. "Other guys surf incredible," Conan said. "But all that stuff *came* from Kelly."

He didn't mean specific maneuvers necessarily, he said, but a sensibility that put them together in startling, beautiful new ways, an original understanding of where certain things might be done on a wave, and the rare, even unprecedented athletic ability to realize his ideas. He made the perhaps inevitable comparison to Michael Jordan.

Shane said, "I don't know how Kelly does it. He can't look to anybody else for inspiration. He can't look to us. We have to look to him." This, coming from one of the best surfers on earth, was heavy praise.

But it seemed to me clearly warranted, as Slater burned through the Pipe Masters, surfing on a distinctly higher plane than anyone else. His turns were bigger, cleaner, more gasp-inducing, his floaters more prolonged and dazzling, his tube rides longer and more agile, his down-the-line speed measurably greater.

And within this overwhelming repertoire was a presence of mind, too, a wit that saw subtle opportunities for unexpected moves, moves that drew screams of surprise and even laughter from the crowd. I had seen Slater in many photographs and a few videos, and while he was obviously a great surfer, I had usually found his style rather odd and even ugly. Now I saw how his surfing adapted to conditions, how breathtakingly spontaneous it was. What had seemed odd to me was simply original. What had seemed ugly was simply new. And a contest situation brightly showcased his raw superiority.

One incident in the final serves as an example of that superiority. It was Slater against Sunny Garcia, a powerful Hawaiian who has the second-best record in pro surfing over the past five years. Garcia surfed well, but Slater surfed supernaturally, scoring a 10, a 9.5, and an 8.25 in waves that weren't particularly good.

As the heat wound down and Garcia lost all hope of catching Slater, a beautiful wave came through, with Slater in position. Garcia stunned the crowd by taking off in front of Slater, thus incurring an interference penalty and effectively conceding the heat. It was a kamikaze move, a measure of Garcia's frustration, but both surfers, recognizing that the contest was over, chose to surf the wave hard, for the hell of it.

They charged down the line, Slater on Garcia's tail. The wave threw out, both ducked, both disappeared. The crowd was screaming itself hoarse. Two surfers getting barreled together is extremely rare. Both of them making it out is far rarer. As the wave roared along, faint traces of the surfers inside could be seen through the curtain. Then somebody fell, and a board went over the falls. And then Slater emerged from the tube, standing tall. Garcia, surfing in front, hadn't made it. But Slater, riding behind, had.

It made no sense. But there it was.

After his first-round loss in the Pipe Masters, Conan went back to Jun Jo's house, took a nap, and shaved his head. When I saw him later and asked him why, he shrugged. Because he felt like it. His scalp was white as bone. He stuck it out the window as we drove down the road. It needed sun, he said. People we passed who recognized him howled.

Conan wanted to go home to the Big Island, but he was obliged to stick around for the pro tour's year-end banquet in Honolulu. Slater would be crowned world champ again. Conan would receive the Most Improved award. If he missed the banquet, he could be fined.

So he passed his days surfing, golfing, Christmas shopping, going to the movies—*Jerry Maguire* twice, a midnight premiere of *Beavis and Butt-Head Do America*—watching a few Pipe Masters heats, and visiting with his dad in Honolulu.

His father had just been released from federal prison, after seven and a half years. The terms of his release confined him for now to Honolulu. I spoke to him on the phone, and he told me that one of the nicer moments of his incarceration occurred in 1995 while watching television. A Hawaiian surf contest unexpectedly came on. It was the men's finals of the Town and Country Pro. And there was Conan, ripping it apart and winning the contest.

"That was a really pleasant surprise," he said. But his prison years had been made bearable, he said, mainly by the fact that he is a dedicated Buddhist. And in his calm and careful way of speaking I thought I heard the wellsprings of Conan's signature sangfroid.

Toward the end of the week, Conan finally talked to me about his lousy Pipe

Masters showing. "The bad part is that because Kalani [Robb] and Rob [Machado] were already out, all I had to do was get through a couple of heats, and I'd have finished the year at number seven." As it was, he would fall to number thirteen.

We were sitting on the beach at Pipeline, squeezed into a small patch of palm-tree shade in deference to Conan's pale melon. "What can I do?" Conan asked mildly. "I can't make the waves come." He bent forward, shut his eyes, put his fingers on his shaved head, and tried to beam telepathic orders at the ocean. We both laughed. Then he added, "All you can control is yourself."

A middle-aged photographer came padding across the beach toward us. He nodded to Conan, who nodded back. The photographer gestured toward Off-the-Wall. "The light's getting better," he said. "If you could just go out and get a couple . . ."

Conan sighed. "Sure," he said. And he grabbed a board and went surfing.

APRIL 1997

WHY DO WE FISH?

by RANDY WAYNE WHITE

I did not come directly to saltwater fly-fishing. Few do. It is a last step, not the first. About the third time a right-handed wind buries a 4/0 short shank into one's hinterlands, the sport begins to invite reinspection. It is less a matter of paying dues than of waiting until the time is right.

For me, fishing had more to do with the cleaning table than with ceremony. It was an interlude to work, then it became work. I hung corpses out to dry; I stacked them in coolers. Economic expediency influences behavior as surely as one's antecedents—fishing was a means, not an end. What I liked about it was being on the water, but you don't have to have a rod in your hand to be on the water.

For a time, I preferred a mask and snorkel. Catch the tide right, and I could drift among that which, from a boat, was only imagined. Most divers dislike turbid water, but I never fancied myself a diver. I loved sliding down a mangrove bank, my own hands ghostly in the murk, stilling myself as a big caudal fin materialized a foot from my mask, then breathless as that frail nucleus assumed mass and shape until finally it was punctuated by a solitary black eye. Spook a fish that close and the contracting of fast-twitch muscle fiber booms like a snare drum.

For many, the fascination of water lies in its potential: the opportunity to converge with elements as basic as a tidal system, the potential to intersect, in some precise way, with dynamics that may be intuited but never fully understood.

Think about that, and thrashing around with a mask on one's face will come to seem arbitrary at best. Not so with fly-fishing.

In the past two months, I've had several calls from people wanting to learn about the sport. That they would contact a journeyman saltwater caster like me marks their desperation as surely as their number illustrates the pastime's sudden vogue. The callers are mostly upwardly mobile professionals who are focused and articulate. They already know some of the questions to ask: Fin-Nor or Scientific Angler reel? Sage rod or Loomis?

I answer the questions cheerfully, happy to spur their enthusiasm a little by telling them what's going on in my own angling life. Through the window, from my desk, I can see several fly lines I have stretched from fence to house, so that they will be straight and clean when I need them. By the phone are twenty leaders I have tied and coiled. On the desk behind me, in leather cases, are my reels: a beautiful gold Sea Master, a Fenwick Big Game, and a couple of Scientific Anglers.

"I'm going to southern Mexico, Sian Ka'an," I tell each of the callers, "to fish for the Big Three." Meaning a bonefish, a tarpon, and a permit—three fish of dissimilar appearance that share similar habitat.

I don't insult my callers by explaining this. If they have any regard for saltwater fly-fishing, they know that to hit this spooky trifecta in a single day is to attain the sport's pinnacle. If they haven't, there is no way to explain why a rational person would spend good money and endure microbes and customs clerks so that he might use the most willowy of tackle to try to catch oversize fish that, if he's lucky enough to land, he'll release anyway.

Silly? Yes, so why risk the discussion.

Nor do I inform them about the sketch pad by the phone. On it I have been designing a hook that I want to make. It will not be curved into a question mark like most hooks, nor will it be forged of steel or bronze. It will be sharp as a hypodermic needle bent into two abrupt V's, and made of wire so that, instead of having to wait to release the fish, the fisherman can effect the release by tightening down on the line at any time during the fight and simply allowing the hook to bend free.

Release the fish before you land it? Ridiculous!

You bet. No matter how much they've read, my novitiate callers aren't ready for this. You have to ply the trade for years before you can come to terms with one of the sport's most alluring truths: Fishing excuses any absurdity.

· · ·

The cover of one of my fishing notebooks reads simply CENTRAL AMERICA, which is appropriate in that there are a great many entries about travel in Guatemala, Costa Rica, Nicaragua, Belize, Panama, and Mexico, but only two or three mentions of actually catching a fish.

Here's an example: "I've finally figured out that the Mayan phrase *yec-te-tan* means 'I do not understand.' It is what the Guatemalan mountain people reply when I press inquiries about a boat that will take me fly-fishing. They smile a little as I pantomime the strange casting motion—am I drunk, or just dancing? They inspect the light rod, presumably vexed by comparisons between it and the more practical hand lines used by their own fishermen. What's the purpose of these feathers tied to a hook when I could use a fresh chunk of fish as bait? Why intentionally make fishing difficult? *Yec-te-tan!*"

Indeed, what is the purpose? I might ask myself that now, standing on the dock at Casa Blanca Lodge, Quintana Roo, the Yucatán Peninsula—ask it not in a mood of self-flagellation or soul searching, but in the spirit of amused self-deprecation, aware that anyone who would go to such lengths to achieve so little is, if not already a doofus, certainly headed that way.

Yec-te-tan. And who does?

Well, maybe I understand just a little. In all directions from this dock, the Caribbean vectors away into turquoise vacuity. To be centered in it is one of the purest pleasures I know. The world is heat saturated, luminous—seabirds, mangroves, sky, wind. Salt water here is motion without essence; find a straight track of sunlight, and your eyes travel it to the bottom without any sense of penetration. But the water will float a fly line, and even small fish cast shadows.

Not that I am champing at the bit to break out the rods. We have just arrived in the little Cessna that brought us 120 miles from Cancún, and I'd like to get the feel of the place first. Normally, I avoid the Americanized fishing lodges that can be found in every Central American country but El Salvador and Nicaragua. Some people travel to fish, but I fish to travel, so time spent in an enclave of sports who are still a little hung over from the bar at the Miami airport and who talk endlessly of spinner baits and bass bustin' . . . well, it seems time misspent. I prefer the open road, where I can use my rods as devices of introduction.

Once, traveling through Guatemala, friends and I were stopped by a band of militiamen who rousted us from our pickup truck and frisked us at gunpoint. I stood with my nose to the truck until I noticed several of the men puzzling over my fishing gear. That's one of the great things about a fly rod—almost everyone suspects what it is, but almost no one knows for sure. In short order, I was demonstrating the double haul while the soldiers argued about which river I should try first. Because any discussion of fishing requires hand gestures, their rifles were leaned against the truck, where only moments before I had stood sweating, scared shitless. Even these men knew that a fisherman is not a worthy object of suspicion. He may be a fool—hell, he's almost certainly a fool— but at least he is benign, and offering assistance to benign fools is more than a good deed; it is an obligation. No matter where you go in the world, natives are proud of the local fishing. Even if they aren't, they'll still drop everything to lie about it.

This trip, though, I have intentionally sought out a place that caters to the growing ranks of saltwater fly fishermen. Built on a low promontory of sand and coconut palms, Casa Blanca Lodge is a neat collection of thatch-roofed cottages that flank a stucco dining hall. The resort has an outpost feel to it, which I like. There is no hint of pretension in its tile floors and lawn of sea wrack, no stacks of hunt-and-fish magazines to preoccupy the gut-hook-and-gaff crowd while they wait for their catches to be iced, measuring success by the blood pounds in their coolers.

"The Caribbean's Finest Light Tackle Fishing," reads the Casa Blanca brochure. Which may be true, though I won't mind if it isn't. I chose Casa Blanca because it is situated in a part of the Yucatán that I have always wanted to see. The lodge is located at the mouth of Bahía de la Ascensión, in the 1.3-million-acre Sian Ka'an Biosphere Reserve, a stronghold of indigenous people and endangered fauna, among them jaguars, tapirs, crocodiles, and more than 300 species of birds. Unlike most parks, a biosphere reserve allows human habitation, as well as the monitored use of natural resources. Which is why Casa Blanca operates with the blessing of the Mexican government and why more than 800 Maya still live and farm and fish near the fallen temples of their forebears.

Standing beside me, my twelve-year-old son, Lee, says, "I'm going to get my mask and snorkel, maybe swim out to the reef." He has already carried his bags to the room, though mine are still on the dock. He hesitates. "Unless you two want some company."

Meaning me and my friend Jeffrey. Jeffrey was one of the top flats guides in the Florida Keys before skin cancer packed him on to shadier venues, and he has come along to take photographs and offer advice, plus do a little fishing himself. He already has his gear together, standing in water up to his knees, his right arm lifting, then drifting as the fly rod arcs in sync, each false cast jettisoning deliberate increments of working line.

To Lee I say, "Good caster, huh?"

"Jeff? Yeah." He watches as Jeffrey's line oscillates, surging through the looping switchbacks, then growing taut in a haze of spray. Against a mangrove backdrop, the line is a lemon-bright filament that animates elements of flight. Lee says, "Nice." Then: "If I see a permit or a tarpon, I'll let you know."

His shirt is off, and he's already holding his mask. He waits a moment before adding, "While I'm swimming?"

"Um . . . you see one, just give a holler. I'll get my mask and come right in."

His expression reminds me of something. "I meant so you could get your rod and try to catch it." A picture of the Guatemalan mountain people pops into my mind—that bemused smile.

"Ah, my rod, right. That's just what I'll do. But maybe I'll watch Jeff cast for a while first."

Lee is walking toward the beach. On any journey to the Caribbean, the water's surface is the final leg of the trip. He looks at Jeffrey casting once more. "Real pretty," he says.

Our fishing guide, Mario Torres-Bolio, is coffee-skinned, wide bodied, and possesses a certainty of focus that I happily lack. Even so, I empathize with him. I empathize with him because for thirteen years I was a full-time floating businessman who, by taking the objectives of my trade seriously, made a decent living as a professional fishing guide—a curious occupational turn for a guy who for years hadn't much liked to fish.

Here's how it happened: In 1976 I got my Coast Guard captain's license and began to canvass marinas near my southwest Florida home, asking if there was work for my boat and me. On Sanibel Island, at Tarpon Bay Marina, the owner, whose name was Mack, said, "We could use another fishing guide; our two slot just opened. The guy blew three power heads in the past six months and decided to go into the lawn-care business."

A generous offer, but I wasn't a fishing guide. "I thought maybe I could hire out to people who want to see the backcountry, like bird-watchers. Or do history tours."

As I would learn, Mack's way of dealing with the idiotic was to act as if he took it very seriously. "Ah, history tours. That should pull in some business."

The next morning, 6:00, the phone rang. It was Mack. "Get your butt out here. You've got four people to fish for snook."

And that's the way it went for more than a decade. The worst year was the first because, though I had grown up fishing, I was a disastrously bad guide. The test is this: If in the space of four to six hours you can teach complete strangers how to cast, set, and play a fish, and then find feeding fish on a bad tide in the wind, and if finally you can position the boat so these novice casters can reach them with the proper bait, then you are a competent guide.

I wasn't, and I knew it.

To my credit, I believe, I didn't justify my own shortcomings the way most bad guides do. I didn't hang around the dock, grousing about the incompetents I had just suffered, didn't gripe about all the jerks I had to deal with—the people I took out were almost always nice, a truth that didn't vary much over the years. No, the problem was me, and more than once I dropped clients at the dock, only to sneak around the backside of the marina office to refund their money. It was humiliating. I endured it for about six months, then decided I'd better either buckle down and learn the trade, or get the hell out.

After that, I had no free days. When I wasn't chartering, I was on the water, trying to learn what I should have known in the first place. Did fish always pile on eddy lines, or were they disseminated by tide or instinct or moon stage or God knows what else to the turtle-grass flats on the flood? During cold snaps, did fish seek deeper water, or would they move to the shallows to warm themselves with sunlight? Over the next twelve months, I had slightly more than a hundred charters, but I spent 300 days on the boat. I learned knots; I studied charts. If a fisherman, expert or not, had advice to give, I listened—a habit I still practice. You can't learn anything with your mouth open.

This was bait-fishing, not fly-fishing, but some things apply to both disciplines: (1) A fisherman's ego shrinks in proportion to the actual amount of time he or she has spent in the wind, ducking hooks, being made to appear foolish by the unfathomable behavior of fish—something that in time he will no longer pretend to understand. (2) The habits of fish may be mysterious, but fishing is not; effective fishing is little more than attention to detail, one bit of knowledge linked to another. (3) Serious fishing is seriously hard work.

By my third year I judged myself a competent guide, and by my fourth I probably actually was. I was doing 300 trips a year, and while I still didn't much like to fish, I took a sort of feverish pleasure in doing it well. Depending on the species sought, and varying with the month, I broke my routine into a series of robotic moves employed to produce a maximum amount of fish in a minimum amount of time. Then it was back to the dock to rebait and re-ice for the next trip.

I had my lines down, too. When someone felt bad about the backlash they'd caused or the fish they'd missed: "If that's the worst thing you do in your life, you're in good shape." On how many pounds of fillets they could expect to ship home: "Go to a fish market. You'll save money."

These were remarks used to comfort, deflect, and amuse the steady flow of midwesterners, northeasterners, and other outlanders who were my clients, a generally pleasant bunch who ranged from beer-pounding conventioneers to Ma and Pa on a dream vacation to the famous or powerfully rich, most of whom, once isolated on a small boat in strange waters, proved to be just people, nothing less, people trying to get by in life and maybe have a little fun along the way.

It was in my fourth season that I began to think in terms of building a reputation. Fishing guides think like that, as if specialization were a way to make one's mark, even in a field where all accomplishment is as ephemeral as a scaled creature's heartbeat. I decided I wanted to be known as a light-tackle tarpon specialist. On my coast, there are no bonefish, and permit are esoteric occasionals better associated with the Florida Keys and flats pioneers such as Jimmie Albright, Stu Apte, and Chico Fernandez.

Where I worked, tarpon were the glamour species. Plus, I liked the way these giant herringlike creatures looked and moved. Each spring, tarpon would appear in the littoral: wild pods of broaching fish six feet long, chromium-bright and mindless as beams of light. They were fish that, in their behavior and prehistoric physiology, implied some recondite design. You could hook them, touch them, gaff them, stuff them, hang them, visit upon them any outrage, even dissect them, but that part of their life, the design and movement of it, was still private, beyond reach or understanding. I don't know why I found that so compelling, but I did. I do.

And so I decided to learn what there was to know about tarpon. At about that same time, a man showed up at the docks and asked in the shyest and most apologetic way whether he could hire me to take him fly-fishing. I found it touching. At that time, people didn't fly-fish Florida's southwest coast. It was too deep, too shallow, too murky, always too something. After all, saltwater fly-fishing was still in its fledgling days, gathering slow, slow momentum down on the Keys.

"We'll take some bait, just in case," I told him.

"There's no need for that. I won't use it."

"You probably won't catch anything," I said, making sure he knew in advance just exactly who was off the hook.

"I don't care."

Well, I had heard that before, but I took him anyway.

It was pretty, watching him cast. That's one detail I remember about the trip. The motion was lean and metronomic, but in a way that gave the impression of improvisation. Equally memorable was that the guy caught fish—dazzling, considering that he was making all the concessions, giving each of those small sea trout and redfish fair opportunity to go about their own lives. Unlike using bait fish in its death throes, or plastic lures punched from a mold and stamped with eyes, there seemed something bedrock honest about a small streamer fly made of game hair.

Most memorable of all was this: As the guy blind-casted the grass flats, a tarpon ate his fly, savaged the adjacent water for a microsecond, vaulted the boat, vaulted it again, popped the leader, then greyhounded off, leaving us both shivering like wet dogs, goofy with shock.

"Jesus Lord."

"Did you see that?"

"Holy shit!"

"Came out of nowhere and took."

"Did you see that!"

"That's what I'm saying!"

So much for the accepted fishing wisdom of a region.

I'd like to say that I was an instant convert to fly-fishing, that on that day I began the journey to, in this instance, Casa Blanca Lodge, in Quintana Roo, the proving ground—if such a place can exist—of my own fieldcraft.

But it's not so. I found fly-fishing intimidating. There was all that discourse about the sport being an "art," the unfamiliar terminology, the elitist feel to it that was as foreign to me as Orvis jodhpurs.

Over the next year, I pieced together the reality. Fly-fishing, at best, is a craft, not an art; memorizing a dozen words demystifies most of the nomenclature; and what's wrong with Orvis jodhpurs? Also, I learned how to cast—a skill I acquired on my own, practicing only when and where no one could see.

In the meantime, though, I stuck with matters at hand. Each spring morning, I was in my boat, bait swarming beneath the aerator spray, leaders tied, hooks sharpened, beginning to fume if my clients were even a little bit late, my patience draining with the tide. It didn't matter what excuses or disclaimers they brought aboard with them. They could wax on and on about the beauty of the day, hint that they wouldn't mind substituting a picnic for the fishing, promise that they didn't give a damn if we wet a line or not, and it was all just more catalyst in an ever-hardening resolve.

I knew what they wanted, even if they didn't.

Which is why I empathize with Mario, our guide. He met us at the Cessna yesterday afternoon, and as we walked from the packed-sand landing strip he said that he was excited about helping me go after the Big Three on fly, but that it had rained hard for the past five days.

"The fishing—maybe not so good now."

That was fine with me. "I don't care if we catch anything or not."

I recognized the dubious look he gave me.

"No, I mean it. It's of no importance."

His expression didn't change.

"Honest!"

We talked along, I speaking in poor Spanish, he answering in slightly better

English—a thing that is humorous in itself and is, in my experience, a common mode of conversation between English and Spanish speakers in Mexico and Central America.

"*En la mañana? Cuando . . . pescado . . .* I mean, *pescamos?*"

"What time to fish you mean?"

"*Sí. Hora. A qué hora?*"

"Today, we fish now. *Palometa* on fly, very difficult. Every day, all the time, we must fish."

"*Palometa?*"

"You call 'permit.' "

"Oh, *permit.*"

Yes, a permit would undoubtedly be the hardest of the three fish to take on fly. There are competent anglers who have fished permit for years, cast crab flies at thousands, and never had a single taker. But I was still feeling claustrophobic from the plane ride. I wanted to get a beer and roam around a little. Which is what I did—looking down at the dock occasionally to see Lee swimming, Jeffrey casting, and Mario futzing with his boat, probably fuming a little, too.

This morning, though, Mario is in charge, the three of us positioned just as he wants us in his fifteen-foot trihull with its thirty-horsepower Yamaha Enduro engine. Our fly rods are belted port and starboard, the water jug is full, Jeffrey has his cameras and a battery of flies, Lee has his mask and snorkel ("In case we don't have to fish all the time"), and I am equipped with the accoutrements of a modern sport: a pair of Capo Striker polarized sunglasses, shirt by Tarponwear, shorts by Patagonia, shoes by Omega—the overall effect being that of some meat hanger who probably roughed up the aisle clerks before robbing Abercrombie & Fitch. Truth is, I feel a little overwhelmed by all the equipage. Tomorrow, I've already decided, I go back to the way I normally fish: T-shirt, bare feet, and a pretty scarf I bought in Cuba to keep the sun off my head.

Mario steers us through a series of saltwater creeks, and I position myself sufficiently outboard to watch the bottom blur by: marl plateaus eroding toward copper-streaked sand basins, startlingly bright beyond the shade of mangroves. Then shoals of turtle grass, the bowed blades defining the direction of the tide in the same way wheat fields reveal wind. A pink coral head jumps past, and fish flush: small snappers, barracuda, then a few bonefish.

I glance at Mario. He has turned inward, running the boat by rote, so I know we are nowhere close to the bottom we will fish. I think of it in those terms—what bottom and where?—for if one plies the trade long enough, one ceases to think of water as water, but more specifically as an ichorous element that, because it is affected by wind and because it flows with lunar patterns, is one more factor to be considered. On the Great Lakes, the walleye-heads might fish at forty feet or sixty feet, hunting the thermoclines. In the Atlantic, billfishermen might troll the fifty-fathom line. But on the flats, you fish banks and rips and mesas, contours of land sculpted by current and closer in appearance to the sand rifts of a desert. On the flats, three feet of water is considered extreme.

We exit out into Laguna Pájaros. The water is light-saturated, a radiant gel that diffuses the boundaries of sea and space, creating pale demarcations of color. At one moment we seem to be riding through a green concavity; the next, careening down the skin of a massive blue sphere. Then Mario points to a charcoal stroke on the horizon: an island. "We fish there."

Me: *"Qué pescados . . . pescamos alli?"*

Mario: "What kind fish? *Macabí.* Bonefish." He smiles, awakening to the hunt.

I smile back, because I like Mario. On the boat he's all business, but ashore he softens a bit and doesn't mind conversation. He grew up speaking Mayan to his mother, and I think he appreciates it when I try the few Mayan words I know. When our boat first panicked a cormorant into flight, I nudged him and said, *"Cheech."*

Surprised, Mario chuckled. "Bird, yes. A bird." Then he corrected me: *"Ch-EECH."*

Lee is *impal,* my son. I am *tata,* his father. *Xtabay* is a kind of spirit, a forest ghost with silky hair like a woman but the feet of a turkey. And that's all the Mayan I know, except for *yec-te-tan,* about which Mario has already told me an ironic story. When the conquistadores arrived, he said, they asked the Maya, in Spanish, the name of their land. Naturally, the Maya did not understand, and said so.

On the conquistadores' maps, *yec-te-tan* became Yucatán.

As the boat carries us across the bay, shadows of cumulus clouds drift before us, gathering speed. The bellies of the clouds are tinted jade, holding light or water—I don't know which. Mario no longer steers by rote; his head pivots back and forth, measuring the water plain.

Though they were not a species available to me as a guide, and though I have caught only a few on fly, I still have a particular fondness for bonefish. The first bonefish I ever took was off Caye Caulker, Belize, thanks to a local who steered me by the shoulder to a muddy little water pocket and then pointed, saying, "De boneyfish, dey live dere, mon."

He meant they lived on the flats?

"No, mon—de boneyfish, dey live dere." He pointed to the mud pocket again; it covered an area no bigger than a refrigerator.

Yes, bonefish hunted close to shore. I already knew that.

"I tell you, mon, daht where dey be living! Right dere!" Finger at the mud pocket again.

My brother, who had already waded out, looked at me and shrugged. I shrugged back, and made a cast into the mud pocket, just to please the local. An instant later, a fish was on the fly, taking line—and it ran right between the legs of my brother, who in garbled surprise began to wail, "Ooh-ooh-ooh—WHOA!" as he tried, without dignity, to dismount my line.

Whenever I see a bonefish now, I grin. I hook one, I begin to chuckle.

I chuckle a lot this afternoon. At Cayo Cedros, where nesting cormorants and frigates burp and growl like lions, I take my first bone, aware that Mario is judging my casting ability, gauging his chances of connecting me with the big three. His reaction to a decent cast is, "Good! Now streep! Streep!" His reaction to a cast that spooks fish is a whispered, "Sheesh."

I hear both.

A bonefish is a strange-looking creature, with a head like that of an Amazon bird and a tail that seems too big for its body, until it meteorites across the shallows, in which case the tail, at least, makes perfect sense. When I get the first bonefish to the boat, I feel the weight of it—there is a wonderful density to even a small bonefish. "One down and two to go," Jeffrey says.

Four hours later, though, it is still one down and two to go. At Punta Hualaxtoc, north of the landing strip, Mario puts me on permit, the size of which actually makes my knees shake. Crouched beside me, his cameras ready, Jeffrey calls, "See the spike? See the spike?" meaning the cobalt point of tail or the periscoping spine of the fish's second dorsal fin. Each permit I see travels with deliberation, absolutely purposeful in its movement, displacing great volumes of water as it forages.

"Jesus, they're all so damn big."

"There's the spike again—cast!"

I cast to dozens of them, thinking, perversely, that if one hits, my light rod and I are in for serious trouble. Occasionally I can see a whole fish through the water, its body a series of crescents held together by a pearlescent skin. Seeing the fish makes my throat go dry. They are intimidating, with their scimitar dorsals and scythelike tails, and it's shameful how relieved I am when they show no interest in my fly. None do. I cast in a way so as to lead them, as a quarterback might lead a receiver. I walk the fly in, ever closer, like artillery. Balls to the wall, I throw right at them, hoping to shock them into a strike—but instead shock only Mario, who has poled his butt off to get me close enough just to have me spook them.

Sheesh!

But a permit that will eat a fly is an anomaly. Better casters than I have spent obsessive, bewildered years proving just that. And if I didn't believe it before, I certainly believe it after a few tight-sphincter hours fishing Punta Hualaxtoc.

"Ah, screw it! These fish would eat a tomato before they'd eat a fly."

Jeffrey: "We could try another flat."

"No, let's can it. Give Mario a break and just have fun. Hey, Mario—*por favor, vamos pescar sábalo? No tienen hambre.*"

"You are not hungry?"

"No, the permit, *las palometas,* they aren't *hambre.*"

"Tarpon, you fish? Go now?"

"Sure. You bet. *Es no importante.*"

Another day, we travel to a deep backcountry area called Laguna Santa Rosa, pulling the skiff through mangrove tunnels hand over hand, then exiting into lakes the color of smoky crystal. Once, after miles of nothingness, we round a bend to find the stone ruins of a Mayan temple, wild orchids and dildo cacti growing from the blocks of coquina rock, and iguanas baking themselves in the heat and silence. But no tarpon—Mario says all the rain has flushed them.

Which leaves bonefish, hundreds of bonefish, thousands of bonefish. Miss your fore cast, and they'll take on the back cast. Standing in knee-deep water, intent on the tidal guttering and sand whorls that concentrate my attention as surely as they funnel fish, I say to Lee, "You want to catch another?"

"No. It's kind of fun watching."

"You'd rather have spent more time exploring that temple, huh?"

"Yeah. I'd go back there anytime."

"Your little brother, he'd rather fish."

"For hours. I don't know how he does it."

"Miss him?"

"Um, I don't know."

"I miss him, too."

Later, in our room, as Lee begins to doze, I touch my hand to his leg, a whorled shape beneath the bed covers, and whisper, "I'll tell you a secret."

He stirs. "You'd rather have spent more time exploring the temple, too?"

I was going to tell him that, when I was his age, I didn't like to fish, either. Instead, I say, "You got it."

Two A.M., and I am wondering, Why is that true—I didn't like to fish?

My earliest memories are of fishing; it was something I learned as naturally as Colorado children probably learn skiing. For my mother, who had been obsessed and overwhelmed with work since childhood in a Carolina mill town, fishing was her only hobby. The same with my many uncles.

I remember her out digging night crawlers and cutting bamboo poles to size. My uncles collected Catawba caterpillars or used bass lures on spinning rods. Even now, if I see a worm, I picture it in the shape of a hook.

Around the dinner table, my southern family included—and still does—the funniest people I have ever known. Swirling their iced tea in mason jars, they'd get me laughing until I cried, talking about bream and sunfish (robin, we called them) and where we might fish next.

What I remember best was the porcupine quills my mother favored as bobbers. At the most delicate touch of the tiniest fish, a porcupine quill will vanish beneath water, an implosion as precise as the path of a well-thrown fly line. In a tackle shop, my eyes still linger on them, taking pleasure.

For a period, when I was old enough to fish on my own, I did a lot of it. I would make dough balls of cotton and bread and catch catfish in the town's small pond. There was a boy who got in the habit of joining me, a classmate named Perry Grey—his real name. Perry was one of those unfortunate children who, because he was tiny and not very clean, became the butt of school jokes, a pariah who could only be touched at a price.

Cooties! He's got cooties!

Once, Perry insisted that I come home with him to see the flying squirrel he had caught. His house was no smaller than my own, but I remember that it was very dark inside and that it stank of something—soured whiskey and urine? I would for years associate that odor with flying squirrels.

Each time I carried a pole to the pond, Perry would materialize. Which was OK; he loved to fish, and he was a nice kid, though I hated it when he began to trail me on the playground. Then one afternoon, when some classmates chanced upon us at the pond, I rallied the cruelty to do what I had been unable to do before. I told Perry I didn't want him tagging after me any more. "Get out of here. I didn't invite you—I mean it."

Some days later, not more than a week, my mother was reading the paper, and I heard her say, "That poor, poor child." Then she went to show the story to my father, and I heard her say, "He got the rope up, but he couldn't reach it, even from a chair, so he had to stand in his mother's high heels."

As I said, Perry Grey was a tiny boy.

It was at about this time that fishing began to create wide spaces of silence that I felt could have been better used. I fancied that it began to interfere with baseball.

My mother, though, kept right on working and fishing, fishing and working, until something had to give and finally did. My cousin Kerney (whom we call Chucky, for reasons I still don't understand) is now minister at the Church of God in Hamlet, North Carolina, and he spoke at her funeral. He looked down at me from the pulpit, grinned, winked, and said, "I bet Georgia taught most everybody in this church how to fish. Why, her boy Randy's become famous for it. Can't you just see her now, up there in heaven, with a chaw of tobacco, sayin' 'Bite fish! Dang you, bite!' Yes, sir, I bet that's what Georgia's doin' right now."

The effect of which was about the same as being with them all at the dinner table.

Jeffrey took me aside one evening and asked, "You ever think much about what it is we actually do?"

"Huh?"

"As guides. Our relationship to fish? I'm finding it harder and harder to justify hooking them, causing them to swim around at top speed, under stress, just for my own pleasure or profit."

This is what Jeffrey said, or something like it—I was drinking beer, not taking notes.

I told him, "As a matter of fact, I have." Then, with a piece of shark wire, I made the hook I had designed, the hook that would bend free at any chosen moment, the angler's personal gauge of just how long he felt good about being connected to a fish. A big tarpon, which after an hour comes up belching like a blown horse, could instead be freed after fifteen minutes. A bonefish could be sent on its way after five.

At least, that's what the hook was supposed to do.

Jeffrey considered the tiny thing with a professional eye, touched the point. "It needs to be a lot sharper."

"Of course. But you see how it works?"

"You know—it might. It might work at that. Let's make a couple, and I'll put them in the vise. Little shrimp ties for bones."

"I've already got a name for it," I said. I didn't, but I was suddenly feeling overly sensitive. I mean, we were discussing the momentary discomfort of creatures that were, after all, just fish. And it wasn't as if we hurt them, then humiliated them back at the docks by hanging them on display. "If it works," I said, "I'll call it the Premature Emancipation Hook." Which I felt gave the whole business a nice masculine flavor while also paying tribute to the absurdity of such a thing.

"We can try it tomorrow," Jeffrey said. "Can you imagine the look on Mario's face? We'll have one mad Maya on our hands."

I imagined the poor guy thinking, *Yec-te-tan.*

Actually, we tried the Premature Emancipation Hook on our last day at Casa Blanca. More accurately, Jeffrey tried it, not me. Fishing affords many kinds of intersections. It provides continuity, one filament linking decisions to lives. My decision was to spend the day with Lee, swimming and walking the beach.

Jeffrey said the hook worked OK, and our guide wasn't mad a bit.

Like me, Mario was probably still feeling a little giddy from the morning before, when, *boom-boom-boom-boom*, just like that, I landed a mutton snapper, a bonefish, a tiny tarpon, and a permit—the saltwater trinity, plus one, all on fly.

MAY 1993

THE KING OF THE FERRET LEGGERS

by DONALD R. KATZ

Mr. Reg Mellor, the "king of ferret-legging," paced across his tiny Yorkshire miner's cottage as he explained the rules of the English sport that he has come to dominate rather late in life. "Ay lad," said the seventy-two-year-old champion, "no jockstraps allowed. No underpants—nothin' whatever. And it's no good with tight trousers, mind ye. Little bah-stards have to be able to move around inside there from ankle to ankle."

Some eleven years ago I first heard of the strange pastime called ferret-legging, and for a decade since then I have sought a publication possessed of sufficient intelligence and vision to allow me to travel to northern England in search of the fabled players of the game.

Basically the contest involves the tying of a competitor's trousers at the ankles and the subsequent insertion into those trousers of a couple of peculiarly vicious fur-coated, foot-long carnivores called ferrets. The brave contestant's belt is then pulled tight, and he proceeds to stand there in front of the judges as long as he can, while animals with claws like hypodermic needles and teeth like number 16 carpet tacks try their damnedest to get out.

From a dark and obscure past, the sport has made an astonishing comeback in the past fifteen years. When I first heard about ferret-legging, the world record stood at forty painful seconds of "keepin' 'em down," as they say in ferret-legging circles. A few years later the dreaded one-minute mark was finally surpassed. The current record—implausible as it may seem—now stands at an awesome five hours and twenty-six minutes, a mark reached last year by the gaudily tattooed seventy-two-year-old little Yorkshireman with the waxed military mustache who now stood two feet away from me in the middle of the room, apparently undoing his trousers.

"The ferrets must have a full mouth o' teeth," Reg Mellor said as he fiddled with his belt. "No filing of the teeth; no clipping. No dope for you or the ferrets. You must be sober, and the ferrets must be hungry—though any ferret'll eat yer eyes out even if he isn't hungry."

Reg Mellor lives several hours north of London atop the thick central seam of British coal that once fueled the most powerful surge into modernity in the world's history. He lives in the city of Barnsley, home to a quarter-million downtrodden souls, and the brunt of many derisive jokes in Great Britain. Barnsley was the subject of much national mirth recently when "the most grievously mocked town in Yorkshire"—a place people drive miles out of their way to circumvent—opened a tourist information center. Everyone thought that was a good one.

When I stopped at the tourist office and asked the astonished woman for a map, she said, "Ooooh, a mup eees it, luv? No mups 'ere. Noooo." She did, however, know the way to Reg Mellor's house. Reg is, after all, Barnsley's only reigning king.

Finally, then, after eleven long years, I sat in front of a real ferret-legger, a man among men. He stood now next to a glowing fire of Yorkshire coal as I tried to interpret the primitive record of his long life, which is etched in tattoos up and down his thick arms. Reg finally finished explaining the technicalities of this burgeoning sport.

"So then, lad. Any more questions for I poot a few down for ye?"

"Yes, Reg."

"Ay, whoot then?"

"Well, Reg," I said. "I think people in America will want to know. Well . . . since you don't wear any protection . . . and, well, I've heard a ferret can bite your thumb off. Do they ever—you know?"

Reg's stiff mustache arched toward the ceiling under a sly grin. "You really want to know what they get up to down there, eh?" Reg said, looking for all the world like some working man's Long John Silver. "Well, take a good look."

Then Reg Mellor let his trousers fall around his ankles.

A short digression: A word is in order concerning ferrets, a weasel-like animal well known to Europeans but, because of the near extinction of the black-footed variety in the American West, not widely known in the United States.

Alternatively referred to by professional ferret handlers as "shark-of-the-land," a "piranha with feet," "fur-coated evil," and "the only four-legged creature in existence that kills just for kicks," the common domesticated ferret—*Mustela putorius*—has the spinal flexibility of a snake and the jaw musculature of a pit bull. Rabbits, rats, and even frogs run screaming from hiding places when confronted with a ferret. Ferreters—those who hunt with ferrets, as opposed to putting them in their pants—sit around and tell tales of rabbits running toward hunters to surrender after gazing into the torch-red eyes of an oncoming ferret.

Before they were outlawed in New York State in the early part of the century, ferrets were used to exterminate rats. A ferret with a string on its leg, it was said, could knock off more than a hundred street-wise New York City rats twice its size in an evening.

In England the amazing rise of ferret-legging pales before the new popularity of keeping ferrets as pets, a trend replete with numerous tragic consequences. A baby was killed and eaten in 1978, and several children have been mauled by ferrets every year since then.

Loyal to nothing that lives, the ferret has only one characteristic that might be deemed positive—a tenacious, single-minded belief in finishing whatever it starts. That usually entails biting *off* whatever it bites. The rules of ferret-legging do allow the leggers to try to knock the ferret off a spot it's biting (from outside the trousers only), but that is no small matter, as ferrets never let go. No less a source than the *Encyclopædia Britannica* suggests that you can get a ferret to let go by pressing a certain spot over its eye, but Reg Mellor and the other ferret specialists I talked to all say that is absurd. Reg favors a large screwdriver to get a ferret off his finger. Another ferret-legger told me that a ferret that had almost dislodged his left thumb let go only after the ferret and the man's thumb were held under scalding tap water—for ten minutes.

Mr. Graham Wellstead, the head of the British Ferret and Ferreting Society, says that little is known of the diseases carried by the ferret because veterinarians are afraid to touch them.

Reg Mellor, a man who has been more intimate with ferrets than many men have been with their wives, calls ferrets "cannibals, things that live only to kill, that'll eat your eyes out to get at your brain" at their worst, and "untrustworthy" at their very best.

Reg says he observed with wonder the growing popularity of ferret-legging throughout the seventies. He had been hunting with ferrets in the verdant moors and dales outside of Barnsley for much of a century. Since a cold and wet ferret exterminates with a little less enthusiasm than a dry one, Reg used to keep his ferrets in his pants for hours when he hunted in the rain—and it always rained where he hunted.

"The *world record* was sixty seconds. Sixty seconds! I can stick a ferret up me ass longer than that."

So at sixty-nine, Reg Mellor found his game. As he stood in front of me now, naked from the waist down, Reg looked every bit a champion.

"So look close," he said again.

I did look, at an incredible tattoo of a zaftig woman on Reg's thigh. His legs appeared crosshatched with scars. But I refused to "look close," saying something about not being paid enough for that.

"Come on, Reg," I said. "Do they bite your—you know?"

"Do they!" he thundered with irritation as he pulled up his pants. "Why, I had 'em hangin' off me—"

Reg stopped short because a woman who was with me, a London television reporter, had entered the cottage. I suddenly feared that I would never know from what the raging ferrets dangle. Reg offered my friend a chair with the considerable gallantry of a man who had served in the Queen's army for more than twenty years. Then he said to her, "Are ye cheeky, luv?"

My friend looked confused.

"Say yes," I hissed.

"Yes."

"Why," Reg roared again, "I had 'em hangin' from me tool for hours an' hours an' hours! Two at a time—one on each side. I been swelled up big as that!" Reg pointed to a five-pound can of instant coffee.

I then made the mistake of asking Reg Mellor if his age allowed him the impunity to be the most daring ferret legger in the world.

"And what do ye mean by that?" he said.

"Well, I just thought since you probably aren't going to have any more children. . . ."

"Are you sayin' I ain't pokin' 'em no more?" Reg growled with menace. "Is that your meaning? 'Cause I am pokin' 'em for sure."

A small red hut sits in an overgrown yard outside Reg Mellor's door. "Come outa there, ye bah-stards," Reg yelled as he flailed around the inside of the hut looking for some ferrets that had just arrived a few hours earlier. He emerged with two dirty white animals, which he held quite firmly by their necks. They both had fearsome unblinking eyes as hard and red as rubies.

Reg thrust one of them at me, and I suddenly thought that he intended the ferret to avenge my faux pas concerning his virility; so I began to run for a

fence behind which my television friend was already standing because she refused to watch. Reg finally got me to take one of the ferrets by its steel cable of
a neck while he tied his pants at the ankle and prepared to "put 'em down."

A young man named Malcolm, with a punk haircut, came into the yard on
a motorbike. "You puttin' 'em down again, Reg?" Malcolm asked.

Reg took the ferret from my bloodless hand and stuck the beast's head deep
into his mouth.

"Oh yuk, Reg," said Malcolm.

Reg pulled the now quite embittered-looking ferret out of his mouth and
stuffed it and another ferret into his pants. He cinched his belt tight, clenched
his fists at his sides, and gazed up into the gray Yorkshire firmament in what I
guessed could only be a gesture of prayer. Claws and teeth now protruded all
over Reg's hyperactive trousers. The two bulges circled round and round one
leg, getting higher and higher, and finally . . . they went up and over to the
other leg.

"Thank God," I said.

"Yuk, Reg," said Malcolm.

"The claws," I managed, "Aren't they sharp, Reg?"

"Ay," said Reg laconically. "Ay."

Reg Mellor gives all the money he makes from ferret-legging to the local children's home. As with all great champions, he has also tried to bring more visibility to the sport that has made him famous. One Mellor innovation is the
introduction of white trousers at major competitions ("shows the blood better").

Mellor is a proud man. Last year he retired from professional ferret-legging
in disgust after attempting to break a magic six-hour mark—the four-minute
mile of ferret-legging. After five hours of having them down, Mellor found that
almost all of the 2,500 spectators had gone home. Then workmen came and
began to dismantle the stage, despite his protestations that he was on his way
to a new record. "I'm not packing it in because I am too old or because I can't
take the bites anymore," Reg told reporters after the event, "I am just too disil-
lusioned."

One of the ferrets in Reg's pants finally poked its nose into daylight before any
major damage was done, and Reg pulled the other ferret out. We all went
across the road to the local pub, where everyone but Reg had a drink to calm
the nerves. Reg doesn't drink. Bad for his health, he says.

Reg said he had been coaxed out of retirement recently and intends to break
six—"maybe even eight"—hours within the year.

Some very big Yorkshiremen stood around us in the pub. Some of them claimed they had bitten the heads off sparrows, shrews, and even rats, but none of them would compete with Reg Mellor. One can only wonder what suffering might have been avoided if the Argentine junta had been informed that sportsmen in England put down their pants animals that are known only for their astonishingly powerful bites and their penchant for insinuating themselves into small dark holes. Perhaps the generals would have reconsidered their actions on the Falklands.

But Reg Mellor refuses to acknowledge that his talent is made of the stuff of heroes, of a mixture of indomitable pride, courage, concentration, and artless grace. "Naw noon o' that," said the king. "You just got be able ta have your tool bitten and not care."

FEBRUARY/MARCH 1983

PRIVATE LANDSCAPES

THE HIGH COST
OF BEING DAVID BROWER

by DANIEL COYLE

September dusk in the hills of Berkeley, California, and David Brower is work-ing in his office. He is writing a letter, and it's getting late.

He pauses often, pen tapping as he summons the rhythms and imagery to transform a string of mere words into something more powerful: a message. When he makes the slightest move to the side, his old swivel chair yowls in protest. Anne, his wife, has asked him several times to oil the bearings, but she doesn't mention it anymore. The screech of metal has become for her a kind of code: Short screeches mean her husband is working; a long screech means he is turning away from his desk and perhaps coming to bed. When she hears nothing, she comes to check, cane thumping down the dim hallway, to make sure her husband is where he should be, head bent over his papers, white hair ablaze in a cone of lamplight.

Brower works through sunset. After the letter, there's a book to look at, a luncheon to arrange, a grant proposal to examine, a radio interview to do, and then, perhaps after a martini, the real work begins.

Each afternoon, Brower's desk receives a stack of environmental journals, magazines, books, newsletters, updates, pamphlets, and broadsheets from all regions of the globe, reams of paper deepening at the steady rate of four inches a day. About twice a week, Brower dives in, tearing out pages, pressing down sticky notes, performing hasty origami on countless leaves of newsprint, cutting and pressing the anonymous flow with an imperial hand until only the vital information remains. Governments proclaim, scientists reveal, ambassadors declare, activists denounce, politicians waffle, and rebellions are crushed; human civilization gushes along on a torrent of print, and Brower inhales all of it in great thirsty gulps. Once he has done that, his instinct calls for utterance, expressive action. To tell them, all of them: *Can't they see what's happening?* Within the walls of his modest home there are eleven telephones, a fax machine, a typewriter, a laser printer, and a PowerBook. His latest goal is to write a newspaper column, preferably syndicated worldwide. He is learning his way around the Internet. He is eighty-three years old.

If there's enough time, Brower will fax some of his findings to one of the hundreds of environmental organizations with which he is affiliated, perhaps with a note: *You have to see this.* Maybe they'll turn up in the Sermon, the stump speech that Brower delivers in various forms a hundred or so times a year, a witty assemblage of eco-parables and scary statistics that says, in essence (1) the Earth's living body is under dire attack and (2) with energy and boldness it can be healed.

But there's never enough time. That is the point. So Brower simply reads the stack of mail and keeps going, making speeches and writing letters until there's more mail to wade through, more speeches to give, more letters to write. It never ends; if it did, so would Brower. He has made a preacher's bargain with life. He constructs messages—on biopreserves and hypercars, wilderness restoration and population control—and messages, in turn, construct him. They form the framework of his days, magnetically coupling him to thousands of anonymous faces with brief, intense sparks, each spark affirming his identity as the most charismatic, controversial environmental leader of the century.

Brower is wholly or partly responsible for what the movement considers many of its greatest rescues—the Grand Canyon, Kings Canyon, the North Cascades, Point Reyes, Redwood National Park, and Dinosaur National Monument—and equally responsible for some of its most tragic losses, including Utah's Glen Canyon. He founded Friends of the Earth and Earth Island Institute and helped start the League of Conservation Voters. More important, Brower is a visionary in the most fundamental sense of the word. In the late fifties and sixties, using film, books, and the persuasive resonance of his voice, he taught the American public how to see and relate to wilderness—a skill being appreciated anew by activists dissatisfied with today's bloodless, technocratic approach. He is a cultivator of talent—"soft path" physicist Amory Lovins and population guru Paul Ehrlich were first recognized and encouraged by Brower—and of an endless fount of ideas awaiting fruition, including the National Biosphere Reserve System and the World Ecological Bank, which would provide funding for preservation projects. Not all of his ideas take root, and Brower doesn't seem to expect them to. He is, as he puts it, a catalyst, a coaxer, a pied piper whose main function is "to turn on the lights."

He is also, as numerous people will testify, holy hell to work with. Beneath his genial veneer lies an obsessive, uncompromising drive that led to a series of bitter disputes and his unhappy departures from both the Sierra Club and Friends of the Earth. Prickly and single-minded, Brower seems always to move too fast, want too much, push too hard. No one can keep up. His sense of mission comes before allegiances, before friendship and family, before everyday comfort and affection. He's given a million dollars of his own money to support small environmental projects. Year by year, he has purified his life until all that remains is the David Brower ecological gospel in excelsis, the totality of which is contained in the most primal of assertions: *I know.*

But there is one reality that cannot be disguised. Slowly, inevitably, Brower's body is beginning to fail. He fights these changes as he fights everything he despises: stiff-arms them with clever wordplay, obliterates them with sheer will, steadfastly refuses to alter his course. His death, when it comes, will undoubtedly set off a rush to embrace his ideals and his memory—both of which are safe, easy to love. But for now there is just the old man in the lamplight, existing on the periphery of the movement he helped create, etching out messages for an unseen audience. Before our eyes, Brower is being transfigured into the embodiment of his own sermon, a living metaphor for a planet being consumed by itself. The difference, of course, is that his body cannot be healed. And Brower, the visionary, seems the last to see.

"How late will he work?" I ask. Anne shrugs. "I never know. Sometimes till two or three in the morning. Sometimes later."

We walk to the back patio, and Anne pours strawberry-banana nectar into tiny glasses. She talks of their upcoming trip to the eastern Sierra Nevada, a reunion with old Sierra Club friends. She is looking forward to it warily. Brower's 1969 split with the Sierra Club was an earthshaking event, a source of such anger and sadness that tempers still flare despite courteous exteriors. "It could be wonderful," she says. "Then again, it could be horrid. One never knows."

Anne Brower is a small woman with shrewd, knowing eyes. She has been married to David for fifty-two years. Her friends call her a saint, because they can conceive of no one else who would have stayed with him. She won't agree, of course. To be a saint, one must *do* something.

"I'm very uninteresting compared to David," she says firmly. "Everything has always been connected to his work. I've lost my identity.

"There was one time when I thought we'd finally get away for a vacation together," she says. "It was back in 1969, after David was fired. I saw an ad for a beautiful house on Big Sur. We rented it for the year, and I even bought towels, thinking, 'Well, now he won't have to work so much anymore.' We stayed there one night. He went right on doing what he had been doing."

After a while, the conversation turns to a more somber subject. From deep within the house, there's a faint squeak, and Anne nods as if to confirm it: He's still there.

"David doesn't think about death at all," she says. "I think at my age there's nothing more exciting that's going to happen to me except dying. But he believes that if he were to think about death, it would keep him from accomplishing things. He wants to work up to the bitter end."

"But why? Can't he rest awhile?"

Anne's eyes move quickly to mine. She looks mildly surprised.

"Why, he has to save the world."

David Brower is not a hard man to meet. He is hard to catch. He spends half the year voyaging on a dizzying wave of conferences, retreats, book readings, film festivals, lectures, and benefits. It's been said that he never met an invitation he didn't like. His quotidian duties include the chairmanship of Earth Island Institute, which he founded in 1982, and membership on the board of the Sierra Club, to which he was reelected this year. When in town, he can be spotted buzzing around the Bay Area in his slightly beat-up 1983 Corolla, the one with the FREE AL GORE bumper sticker. He drives the Berkeley hills like a dervish, accelerating into blind corners, downshifting on the fly. Following Brower is frightening, though the feeling is slightly attenuated by the realization that he was born four years after the introduction of the Model T.

Brower loves restaurants, particularly fifties-era seafood-and-steak joints with studded-leather booths and bartenders who know his preferences—Tanqueray martinis straight up, no distractions. He doesn't like to dine with just one other person, so he typically invites a crowd. More sociable, he says. Sinbad's, on the Embarcadero, at one.

The voice is what one notices first. Not that the rest slips past. He's a big man, with the rawboned physicality of a former football star. The unclimbable crag of a face, totemic cheek-creases, wild blooms of eyebrows, glistening blue eyes, and a halo of pearly hair combine to create such an aura of spiritual heft that it's a good ten minutes before one notices that Brower is something less than an image of sartorial splendor, outfitted in his customary garb of a T-shirt and well-frayed blazer, mismatched polyester pants, and inexpensive running shoes with Velcro closures. Bowed legs and a sore knee—the latter partly a result of a 1936 ski injury—lend a hint of a John Wayne saunter. When he walks across a room, eyes track him, and Brower looks resolutely at the floor. It's hard to tell whether he's shy or just looking where he's going.

But the voice, so vigorous and yet so intimate, is what stands out. Brower begins each sentence in the tenor register and slides into a velvet baritone, looping melodies around themselves, hitting words with unexpected emphases so that the listener has the sense of hearing them for the first time. He doesn't speak words so much as play his voice, a cornetlike music that spirals above the atonal chug of normal conversation. There is no gap between Brower's public and private dialects, as sometimes occurs with public figures. Furious, depressed, or asking would you please pass the salt, Brower sings. "When he's speaking to a crowd, it's like he's whispering to you," says Patrick Goldsworthy, an old friend from the Sierra Club. "He says things with feeling."

Brower found the voice in the early 1940s when, as a shy mountaineer, he was asked to talk in front of two hundred people on a Sierra Club High Trip. He doesn't remember much about what he said—something about the landscape, the mountains. But standing there, in front of the campfire, something inside him awoke. "He used to be so quiet," Anne says. "Now you just drop in a nickel and the cassette plays."

"Now, take a bird's feather, for instance," Brower says, spearing a shrimp. "I just marvel at that structure—the hairs, the spacing, the pattern. It's a very nice bit of design, enabling it to fly, to handle temperature changes. Or look at beetles. Did you realize that there's a beetle that can produce steam to fire at enemies? There's a clam that can manufacture cement at the temperature of seawater. What's the trick? We have no idea. If we found out, we might pave everything in sight." He chuckles, with a quick glance to make sure I'm chuckling, too.

"There are certain advantages to being an octogenarian. For instance, I can be outrageous. I was only mildly outrageous before eighty, but now there's nothing they can do to hurt you. They might, of course." He smiles into his Tanqueray. "But probably not."

He recites poetry. He counts pelicans, noting that his all-time Sinbad's lunch record stands at 176, happy hour included. He seems content, an emotion that militant environmentalists—militant anybodies, for that matter—aren't supposed to possess after a half-century of throwing themselves into the establishment's toothy maw. Even his pacemaker, recently implanted to correct a mild fibrillation, is charmingly evoked. "My doctors told me to get this pacemaker so I could keep up with myself," he says.

But between the riffs, there's silence. Long, awkward, fork-scraping silences. Anne shoots guests a sympathetic look. Words possess tremendous power with Brower, but he cannot or will not employ them for small talk. He won't ask about you, and he would prefer if you didn't ask too deeply about him. His words fly up and out; they soar like so many pelicans. Then you wait until more appear.

Even with his closest friends, Brower can sit for an hour and not speak. He's ephemeral at social gatherings, preferring to avoid them or linger in a corner. At conferences he hovers near the door, unless he's at the podium. He's more at ease with a thousand people he doesn't know, his friends say, than with one person he does.

His behavior forces his friends to explain, and so they do. *He's shy. He's preoccupied. He's aloof. He's humble. He's arrogant. He's honest. He's scared to death of people.*

Some boil over in frustration. "He could have become a nationally known leader," says former Sierra Club colleague Jim Moorman. To Brower, however, speculation is moot. He can't change—and even if he did, what would be the cost? What places wouldn't get saved? What ideas wouldn't be born? Besides, as he likes to say, "I don't like people telling me what to do."

Of course, personal costs have piled up, but Brower, ever optimistic, ever in control, has always managed to deal with them. Friends no longer speak to him? Forgive them, then find new ones. Environmental groups fire him, call him selfish and irresponsible? Start another group. Start two—they'll come around. Children grow distant in your absence? Take them on unforgettable adventures; they'll come around, too. But keep moving forward. "A ship in harbor is safe," he likes to say. "But that's not what ships are built for."

While Brower remains for the most part in good health, his body has suffered breakdowns: bladder cancer ten years ago, recurrent sciatica, a fainting spell before the pacemaker was implanted. In public he deals with mortality in typical Browerian style, kidding about applying for a twenty-year extension and stating his fervent hope that the recipient of his dust will have as much fun with it as he himself is currently having. But mostly he deals with it by not dealing with it, traveling incessantly.

"Some people need money, some people need power," says Edwin Matthews Jr., a former Brower protégé at Friends of the Earth who split with him over management style. "What Dave needs is to be appreciated. Or maybe to be loved. He's in his element telling a story he's told five hundred times to a group of people fifty years younger sitting around him in a circle, listening."

Part of his work is to oversee the creation of his own legacy. The two volumes of his 904-page autobiography, *For Earth's Sake* (1990) and *Work in Progress* (1991), are less the story of Brower's life than a meticulous exhibition of his old writings, reflections, and wish lists, a kind of museum of the interpreted self. He wrote his most recent book, an extended sermon titled *Let the Mountains Talk, Let the Rivers Run,* in a focused stretch of four months, giving coauthor Steve Chapple the distinct impression that this was "his last shot at getting it right."

"He has faith in his destiny," says Martin Litton, an old friend and ally who served on the Sierra Club board from 1964 to 1972. "He feels he was placed on Earth to do these things that no one else can do."

Those close to him say that even as Brower continues at an unrelenting pace, he has also begun to repair broken relationships. He is paying more attention to his family. A few years ago Anne began accompanying him on some of his travels. He says "love you" when he tells his children good-bye, and he looks them in the eye when he says it. He attempts what for Brower borders on the inconceivable: He sits around and talks about nothing at all. The old ship is trying, with supreme difficulty, to get accustomed to harbor.

"I like him a lot better now," says his daughter, Barbara, a professor of geography at Oregon's Portland State University. "He's a more attentive father, and he's turned into a good grandfather. His humanity has increased."

To Brower's surprise and pleasure, his forty-nine-year-old son, Bob, has offered to accompany him and Anne to this weekend's High Trip reunion in Lone Pine, California. The second of their four children has been beset by what are gently called "Bob's troubles"—a head injury from a motorcycle accident, bad luck with jobs and women, and other, more personal demons.

"This trip will be good for Bob," Brower pronounces, draining his coffee. "Getting out into the wildness will help Bob be Bob again."

Another long silence. Chairs shift. Then Brower stands abruptly, announces that it's time to go, and walks toward the restaurant door.

Strawberry Creek was a fine place to grow up. Its upper reaches were a rolling paradise of trails, and that's where David Brower spent his days. The Browers were like other families who lived in the crude Victorian houses on Haste Street, a stubborn and religious mix of third- and fourth-generation immigrants. His father, Ross Brower, taught mechanical drawing at the University of California, Berkeley, on whose undeveloped campus Strawberry Creek flowed. David, one of four professor's kids, had the run of the hills, bicycling, hiking, and catching butterflies, which he pinned on cardboard. He was a solitary boy, and this was his kingdom.

Things got tough when David was in the third grade. The university fired his father, who had to manage apartments to get by. Around the same time, his mother fell ill. Her vision slipped away—an inoperable brain tumor, they were told. One day David stood wordless at the foot of her bed as she peered at him, trying to guess who he might be.

Their walks began as a way for David to escape chores around the apartments. But his mother loved the hills and found the strength to walk for hours. They went again and again, the tall woman and her bowlegged boy, as far as they could walk, past the farthest reaches of Strawberry Creek to the top of Grizzly Peak, where you could see the whole world. She gripped his left arm and he led the way, telling her where the rough places were. And other things, too.

Now we're in the pines. The fog is clearing. There are some wildflowers in the clear-

ing, and a red-tailed hawk flying above them, looking for field mice. There's a breeze coming off the ocean. It'll be beautiful at the summit. This way.

It was good preparation, walking those hills. His boyhood friends used to joke, "He who follows a Brower never follows a trail," and their words would remain true throughout his life. Whenever Brower reached a personal or professional crossroads, he could sense where he was—and, more important, where he wanted to be. To others he would sometimes look foolish, lost. But Brower didn't mind: He was in motion, rising above the rest, and if his friends didn't come along, well, he would wave to them when he got to the mountaintop.

After dropping out of college during the Depression—the established road to higher education never suited Brower—he paired with various friends and disappeared into the Sierra for weeks. Toting *Survey of Sierra Routes and Records* and a bag of small notebooks to leave as registers, they set out to leave their names on as many peaks as possible. They cached food in candy cans and huddled through storms without tents. Brower was nearly six foot two, 170 pounds, and rawhide-strong. He was the happiest he had ever been.

Inevitably, he met people who liked to do the same thing. Sierra Club members traveled in big groups, wore jaunty alpine hats, sang campfire songs, and talked about the sainted founder, John Muir, who had implored them to "explore, enjoy, and preserve" these mountains. It became their trinity. Gradually Brower grew to like their gracious camaraderie, their clannish verve. These were talented, first-rate people—lawyers, doctors, writers from pedigreed California families. And they liked him. Put him anywhere in the Sierra at night, they said admiringly, and he would know where he was by sunrise.

The club became family, and soon Brower was wearing an alpine hat and leading High Trips, the 200-person, two- and four-week outings. Scissoring along on his bowed legs, he walked faster than anyone, and more optimistically. "Brower miles" became a running gag. *Dave's got a place that ain't on the map—he says it's just a mile away.* Then they'd bushwhack a half-dozen miles and find themselves someplace unforgettable, Brower yodeling in triumph. Roping up with fellow Sierrans, he tackled difficult first ascents, like that of Shiprock in New Mexico, for which his team employed a new device called an expansion bolt. With his long reach and flowing style, Brower usually climbed lead, and he scored more than seventy first ascents. Camel Cigarettes wondered about the possibility of his becoming a spokesperson, and with good reason. Club women swooned over the tousle-haired Adonis; they would lie down in the trail for him, it was said. But he stepped over. There were always more places to go.

For Brower, the only thing that compared with climbing was writing. He spent winter nights bent over his desk at home, transforming the sensory clutter of his expeditions into words, images, and stories. On the expanse of the page, the expeditions were different, more clever, tidy, as if he had tapped into a sort of parallel reality that stripped away all the nonsense and cut immediately to the important things: beauty, truth, heroism, wilderness. He liked it immensely, this word magic, and he could tell that he was good. He landed a job as an editor with the University of California Press in 1941 and, at about the same time, won a seat on the Sierra Club's board of directors. On High Trips, people began asking him to speak. They sat around him in a circle, and Brower could see their eyes shining in the firelight.

At his new job, he shared an office with a woman named Anne Hus. She was an editor, too, worldly and whip-smart, and they sipped sherry at her parents' house. Brower, now twenty-nine, needed near-violent prodding from his Sierra Club friends to keep up the pursuit—after all, he was heading off to fight the Germans, and she was engaged to another. But her engagement broke apart. From a train on the way to officer candidate school, he wrote a letter proposing marriage. She wrote back. Two weeks after their wedding, they went to a movie. It was their first real date.

When Brower returned from the war, he threw himself into Sierra Club works. But he was interested in fulfilling the last part of Muir's trinity. Mountains could be ruined—he had seen it in Europe—not by bombs, but by far more dangerous weapons: roads and bridges, ski chalets and power lines. Now here was a cause to believe in.

His timing was perfect. Fueled by postwar expansion, the Bureau of Reclamation was looking to dam the Colorado River in Utah's Dinosaur National Monument. The club's leadership decided to organize, to motivate, and Brower took the lead. They made him executive director in 1952. Nobody knew what an executive director did, since the club had never had one before. But whatever Brower did, that was it. Give riveting testimony before Congress. Make headlines. Build public support. He filmed and narrated wilderness-awareness movies on Yosemite and the North Cascades. He invented a new genre of book, monstrously big, wildly expensive exhibits of heartbreakingly beautiful wilderness photos by his friend Ansel Adams and others. The books were Brower's special pride. He determined the tint of each photo, the placement of each comma. Move the readers to tears, he said, and their action will follow. He was resoundingly right. Club membership increased from 7,000 to 77,000 during his tenure (today it hovers at around a half-million). Pundits say he invented environmentalism for the media age, but what he really did was something simpler: He took the American public by the hand and showed it what he saw.

Meanwhile his own family was growing up. Most of the childrearing fell to Anne, of course. David was too busy, too involved. Anne uses the word "encapsulated." She could drop a dinner plate behind him and he'd keep working. Sometimes birthdays and other special occasions slipped past. "You don't know me from the girl next door!" his daughter, Barbara, screamed at him. "Of course I do," Brower replied without missing a beat. "She's a little taller and has blond hair."

There was so much to do. When the bureau tried to dam the Colorado River near the Grand Canyon, he ran full-page ads in *The New York Times*, one of which read, "If They Turn Grand Canyon into a Cash Register Is Any National Park Safe?" Perfect! Public sympathy swelled, the dam was scuttled, and though the club was stripped of its valuable tax-deductible status (IRS regulations prohibit direct political action), the loss was more than offset by small, nondeductible contributions. Brower called for more books, more words, more pictures. More action! He was featured in *Life* magazine. When the board of directors—some of whom were old climbing pals—objected over the tax issue or worried that too much of the club's budget was tied up in books, he ignored them, or threatened to resign, or used that voice of his. *Is it more important to keep the bottom line black or the earth green?*

Battles were being won: Dinosaur, the Wilderness Act of 1964, Point Reyes National Seashore. Lost battles, like that over Glen Canyon in the late fifties, held even more power—Brower never visited the canyon but agreed to its being dammed in exchange for the cancellation of two other dam projects in northeastern Utah's Echo Park and Split Mountain. When the dam that would soon create Lake Powell was being built, Brower made repeated pilgrimages to the place, compiled films, commissioned books, and transformed his shortsightedness into a cross that he still bears. "Glen Canyon died in 1963 and I was partly responsible for its needless death. So were you," he wrote in *The Place No One Knew* (1963). He vowed never to commit the same sin again.

Relations with the club's board, however, worsened. Friends wrote him letters, pleaded with him to change his ways. ("Please take a good, long, objective look at the present aspect of the club, its finances, and its programs—and, very important, at yourself! As ever, Ansel.") But Brower wouldn't change. He ignored lines of authority and spent money without board approval. Seemingly oblivious to rising financial problems—the club lost $100,000 a year in 1967 and 1968—Brower demanded a costly international series of books. How could he change? The bastards weren't resting, and relentless action was the best way to get more money. Couldn't they see?

In 1969 they fired him. Technically it was a resignation, but everyone knew the truth. First a coldly worded telegram relieving him of fiscal responsibilities, then a series of votes. "The Happening," Sierrans called it in hushed tones. Almost all of Brower's friends voted against him, including Adams. The Sierrans salved their doubts by talking of "cleansing" the club, by comparing Brower to a noble but foolish climber who got too far above his protection, who hurt the club by taking selfish risks. How could they understand that there was no self left to risk? He was on a mission they couldn't imagine. This was bigger than rivers, bigger than any lines on the map. They would see, once he got to the mountaintop.

As we get ready to leave for the Sierra Club High Trip reunion in Lone Pine the next morning, Brower putters around his house, looking for something. He moves carefully in the labyrinthine spaces of his living room, bending into corners as if he were sniffing orchids in a garden.

"I know where it is," he says. "It should be right here."

Elbow-deep in a stack of papers, he extracts his quarry, a magazine story on Yosemite. He places it carefully on another stack and moves on, tracking down something else.

"Could you give me a tour of the house?" I ask. Brower does not turn. After a moment I ask again, and he looks at me incredulously. Where would he begin? With the hundred or so file boxes stacked in every possible cranny—ten under the baby grand piano, six behind the couch—which serve as the repositories of his daily clipping and filing? Or with the warrenlike basement, where Bob Brower resides, its windows covered by more boxes? Or perhaps with the rocks, the hundreds of granite, limestone, quartzite, agate, and sandstone keepsakes, many from Glen Canyon, which lend the distinct impression that a glacier has just receded through his living room? Or out on the patio, with the four garbage cans brimming with golf balls, the fruit of Brower's morning strolls near the links, colors in one can, whites in the others? Or perhaps the bedroom, the door of which is papered with dozens of tattered name tags, each reaffirming the identity of the person within: HELLO MY NAME IS DAVID BROWER. Brower cannot give a tour because the meaning of his home, like the meaning of himself, is not found in any individual object. Everything here is equivalent, possessing significance only within the arc of relentless action that created it.

"Here are some pictures," he says finally. He points them out, one by one: black-and-white portraits of him and Anne the year they married, smiling grandkids captured in a snapshot, the surreal poise of an Ansel Adams landscape, images of family closeness, of wilderness, of a life rich in people.

But these images aren't complete, not as a record of relationships. Where are Dick and Doris Leonard, his best friends during the early Sierra Club years? Where is Dan Luten, his old next-door neighbor, fellow mountaineer, and longtime colleague? Where is Edwin Matthews? Where are Wallace Stegner, Phil Berry, Mike McCloskey, Dr. Luna Leopold, all the others?

Unlike his wife ("I hated them all," says Anne of the Sierrans who voted against her husband), Brower says he holds no grudges. In the months after the Happening, he was determined not to become a pariah. He kept his membership and did his best to maintain the social ties despite lingering tensions. In 1983, when the petition was circulated to renominate him to the board, he made a special point of obtaining the signatures of old friends such as Adams. When Brower encounters former colleagues—as he will this weekend at Lone Pine—he exudes cordiality, and it is usually returned in kind. After all, there's important work to be done, work that transcends personal disputes. But no cordiality can resurrect the promise of these relationships. They are shadows, ghosts of a time long past.

"Brower overlooked certain aspects of human relations that are important," says Hal Gilliam, former environmental columnist for the *San Francisco Chronicle*. "He never made amends, never apologized for his mistakes. I know so many people who worshiped him and then were turned off."

Some ghosts are more corporeal than others. Dick Leonard was Brower's strong-minded mentor and climbing buddy; people said they seemed like brothers. In 1952 Leonard pushed for Brower to become the club's executive director, and in 1969, saying he had to preserve the organization, he orchestrated Brower's removal. Brower carried no rancor, making a point of celebrating each New Year's Eve with the Leonards, as always. But a few years ago Dick fell ill. It was a long and painful ordeal; friends wept at seeing the once-powerful climber trapped at home in a wheelchair, blind. But Brower never wept with them. Though he lived less than a mile away, he never visited. Doris Leonard, puzzled and saddened, could only conclude that it wasn't her husband Brower was avoiding; it was the other presence in that house.

Brower has a recurring nightmare. In it, he is trying to get something done—packing for a trip, cleaning the house—and he can't finish in time. He is sweating and trying hard, but the work keeps piling up and the clock keeps ticking. The harder he tries, the worse things get. And then it's time.

Within days of leaving the Sierra Club in 1969, Brower was on the move. With a few loyal staffers and thousands of disaffected members, he set out to realize his vision of what the Sierra Club could have become: a global, media-savvy, politically muscular activist group. He called the new organization Friends of the Earth, and it would be the first truly international environmental group. Newly christened the archdruid of environmentalism by John McPhee's *New Yorker* profile, Brower attacked on all fronts: Nuclear weapons. Solar energy. Population control. The California condor. The Alaska Pipeline. Toxics. Whales. Brower's role was to act as visionary and catalyst, traveling widely, casting his net. He preached the Sermon to thrilled campus crowds, always ending with the Goethe couplet that had become his credo: "Whatever you can do, or dream you can, begin it. Boldness has genius, power, and magic in it."

Then he'd look at the rapt faces and say, "There's magic in you. Let it out." You could hear a pin drop. It was marvelous.

Meanwhile his children had grown up. The three boys, like their father, weren't overly enamored with college. Ken worked on his writing (which like his father's was concerned with the environment), Barbara studied geography, and Bob and John pursued less structured endeavors, dabbling in electronics and recycling, respectively. They were too old to go on summer trips now. There were the usual modern family pains—hospital visits, broken relationships, fumbling for careers—and David simply didn't have time to come home and play catch-up. He would later calculate that in the first forty years of his marriage, he spent an aggregate of twenty-five years away.

Almost from FOE's beginning, board members were worried. Money came rapidly—the group had a $1.5 million budget within a few years—and departed just as quickly. Led by Brower's enthusiasm, FOE started dozens of new projects each year. Every few weeks or so, some young person would walk into the Pacific Avenue headquarters: *Hi. Dave, uh, hired me to work on overgrazing.* The staff swelled to fifty, triple that of comparably budgeted environmental groups. But every time FOE tried to get its financial house in order, there was Brower, eyes glistening, singing in that incantatory voice. *We can work faster, better, harder. We'll get more members, sell more books, take on more projects.* He was unstoppable.

But by the mid-eighties the FOE board had heard the voice too often. The coffers were nearly empty, and the staff had divided into virulent pro- and anti-Brower factions. Three successive presidents had resigned, chorusing protests that their work was being undercut by Brower. New kids kept strolling in. "Founder's syndrome," pronounced a management consultant, diagnosing a disease with only one known cure. So in 1986 it happened again. Another board vote, another ousting, another round of damaged friendships and bitter recriminations.

Within months, Brower emerged with another group. This time, he swore, he was through with bureaucracies and boards. Earth Island Institute would be built according to the Brower model: an umbrella organization for small projects, each responsible for its own staffing and its own wallet. The scheme has worked out pretty well. EII has made a name for itself through the dolphin-safe tuna campaign and other successes. Brower gets to be Brower, shaking up worldviews with big ideas. Infuriated as ever by inaction, he still makes noise at board meetings, threatening to resign three times in recent years. "He gets frustrated that Earth Island doesn't have the infrastructure like he had at his other groups," says Chris Franklin, Brower's personal assistant. "He stands up at meetings and does an I'm-going-to-take-my-ball-and-go-home sort of thing."

These flare-ups are part of the primal drive that has defined the course of Brower's life from mountain climber to environmental agitator to ethereal visionary, the same drive that in its intransigence created a place like Earth Island Institute. This is where he belongs, among people, yet profoundly apart. He does not wish to cause distress; he simply has no choice. He must take people by the arm and lead. *This way.*

The tiny town of Lone Pine, California, lies on the border of two universes. To the east stretches some of the harshest desert in America, trailing down to Death Valley, 104 miles away. To the west swells the 14,000-foot rampart of the southern Sierra, including Mount Whitney, the highest peak in the Lower 48. Lone Pine sits in a narrow shelf between the two worlds, cushioned by chaparral and cottonwoods, fully belonging to neither.

It's a good setting for a High Trip reunion. Club members have come from as far away as Maine. They gather outside town on Friday evening, next to a small lake in the shadow of Mount Whitney, about fifty people in all. They arrive wearing trail regalia, neckerchiefs and too-snug jeans, toting coolers of beer and dilapidated photo albums. Teeth flash in shouts of greeting; bear hugs knock hats to the dirt.

The Brower family arrives late, just before sunset. Quietly, with David leading, they pick their way to the edge of the group. David seats his wife in a comfortable chair before finding an adjacent log for himself and Bob. He deftly fixes drinks from his nylon daypack, an old-fashioned for her, a martini for himself, straight up, no distractions. Then he leans forward, elbows on his knees, and looks around. A warm wind blows from the desert; the air tastes of sage. The noise of the far-off highway is hard to distinguish from the papery rev of dragonflies. Brower's eyes move around the campsite, taking it all in.

He looks at the people. There are no ghosts here, no old rivals of battles past. These are only faces, some recollected, some new. Brower waits for them to come over. By and by, they do.

"Do you remember me? I was twelve when you led us on a Yosemite trip."

"You always walked so fast, Dave—and it don't look like you've slowed down much."

Brower smiles and nods, and the visitors wait expectantly for small talk. A colorful story, perhaps, or a fond recital of names and reminiscences. Anne smiles at them. "Aren't these gnats amazing?" Brower says.

He's looking at the small cloud of insects hovering off his shoulder, a mad tornado of feathery motes. He lifts his big hand and slowly moves it through the gnats; they repool instantly. He does it again and then stares at the creatures. "What's their method of communication?" he asks. "What sort of compass do they use to figure out where they need to go? How do they talk to one another? These are some of the things I'd like to know."

Hands rise and touch gnats. Brower smiles and raises his martini in a toast. "Amazing. If we humans could only communicate half as well, everybody might get along a little better."

People chuckle. Brower chuckles. Alone at the other end of the log, Bob sips his beer and watches his father. Brower leans forward, and the words begin to pour forth. He talks about the Internet, the importance of learning multiple languages, the foolishness of Bob Dole, and the role of religion in society. He talks, and people gather, dragging lawn chairs, magnetized by the passion of his voice. Then Brower notices something.

"Look!" The group follows his outstretched hand. "Look!"

Brower is pointing at the hills a few miles to the east, over which a glowing rim has appeared. The harvest moon. Round and opalescent as the iris of some monstrous eye, it slides into view, decorating the windblown lake with a thousand glittering replications. The air resounds in childlike coos and adolescent howls. But Brower's voice chimes above them all, calling out numbers: the distance between Earth and the moon, the distance between each and the sun. He is letting this little gathering know, within a few miles, precisely where they stand in relation to the rest of the galaxy. He stands, his hair lustrous in the moonlight. *I know.*

Later, in the flicker of the campfire, someone pulls out a guitar. With rusty voices, the group launches into the old hiking songs. They sing "The Twelve Days of Hiking" to the Christmas tune, jubilantly hollering, "Five *Brow-er* miles!"

Then Brower sings. It's an old song from the beginning of the century, a ballad whose words nobody else could remember, a tragic song about a family broken apart by love and fate. The guitarist tries the first verse, but then loses the melody. Brower keeps going. Lit by firelight, holding a little dog that has found its way to his lap, Brower sings sweetly and alone.

The next morning Brower has bristlecone pines on his mind. The organizers have scheduled a slot of free time, and he's planning to drive the hour north to Bishop to check up on the planet's oldest living inhabitants. It's been fifty years since he's seen them. "I want to see how they're doing," he says.

Brower is sitting in a small deck chair next to the outdoor pool at the Dow Villa Hotel, where the group has gathered for sweet rolls and coffee. Bedecked in shorts and a shortsleeved sportshirt, Brower blends faultlessly with the camera-necked specimens of *Turista americana.* He's also as antsy. "Where's your son?" he asks Anne. She shrugs. Bristlecone pines can wait.

Bob finally arrives and settles in for coffee. Brower shifts his chair so he can see Whitney's summit and talks about the speech he is going to give at tonight's dinner. He wants to ignite the revival of full-scale High Trips, which were discontinued in the early seventies because of the Forest Service's concerns about impact, among other things. It's an old issue, and in all likelihood a dead one, as mule-supported group tours have gone hopelessly out of fashion, supplanted by mountain bikes, ultralight packs, and other so-called advances. But nothing is hopeless.

"We allowed ourselves to be stopped, and we shouldn't have," he says. "High Trips were exactly what John Muir intended—they were the first ecotours. And we let somebody tell us we couldn't do them?"

Then something makes him stop. He takes a few deep breaths and attempts to speak.

He can't. The words won't work. They come out garbled, insane, sputtering off his lips.

He sits up straighter and inhales deeply, filling his chest with oxygen. His right hand feels for his left wrist. He tries to count the beats of his pulse, but the numbers won't fall in line.

Bob notices. "Dave, you OK?"

His father manages a nod. But his vision blurs and shimmers; he can't see Bob, Anne, anything. He needs something immovable, something real. He turns and looks up, past the cool white metal of the swimming pool fence, to the Sierra. But Mount Whitney buzzes and wavers. He stares for more than a minute, squinting and glaring ferociously, attempting by force of will to make the mountains stop. They will not.

"Dad, you OK? You need some oxygen?"

Brower doesn't hear. He steeples his hands around his mouth, his lips moving. He is not praying.

When the paramedics arrive, his pulse is fifty-eight and weak, his respirations shallow. They strap an oxygen mask over his face and wrap him in a rough blanket. Since he is conscious, they ask questions: *Who are you? What day is it?* He answers only one. "I'm David Brower," he says.

In the waiting room at Southern Inyo Hospital in Lone Pine, there's ranch oak furniture, a soda machine, and a softly humming clock. The nurse asks what religion she should write on the admission form. "None," says Anne, and then corrects herself. "Put 'Lapsed Presbyterian.' "

Anne and Bob sit quietly, having shifted into the unnatural placidity that emergency rooms require. Bob flips through an electronics magazine; Anne taps her cane handle. Encouraged by the reviving effect that the oxygen seemed to have, they haven't permitted themselves to consider the possibility that this could be anything more than a faint.

"I think all he needs to do is go back to the hotel and sleep a little," says Anne. "Then he'll feel better." Then to me: "I'm sorry you didn't get to see the bristlecone pines."

The doctor comes in, a lean young man with sympathetic eyes. Gently, he asks a few questions and then sums up the situation. Anne and Bob listen intently, comprehending only scraps of meaning. *Possible blood clot. Brain. Aphasic—he's having trouble using words.* These things often pass, he tells them, but it's best to let him sleep here and then go to Bishop for a CAT scan in the morning.

"Your husband is one of my heroes," he says.

"Oh, you're another one of those," replies Anne.

An hour later in the waiting room, the situation begins to sink in. Deprived of oxygen, part of her husband's brain has stopped functioning. It may function again. It may not. Anne's eyes focus on the clock. For the first time, she looks weary.

"He suppresses the idea of his dying because he has so much he wants to do," says Anne. "I think it may not be good to suppress those thoughts. I don't. I think about it every now and then. He never does, and it comes out in bad ways, like it did today. In his feeling really . . . lonely."

"I knew it was serious when the paramedics were talking to him and he says, 'Bob, what should I do?'" says Bob. He shakes his head. "He's never asked me that before. Not ever."

"I plan to have, at his memorial service, great big baskets of rocks," says Anne. "I'll say, 'I know David loved those rocks, he got them all, so please take thirty or forty with you when you leave.' I hope to get them all out of the house then."

Brower's condition steadily improves. When Anne comes to his bedside, he recognizes her and speaks clearly. His strength seems to be coming back, though his vision hasn't. When he looks into someone's face, he can see only one eye.

Through the night, every hour or so, a nurse wakes him. *Where are you? What day is it? What's your name?* They carry pen and paper to write down his responses should he make any mistakes. Earlier Anne asked him if she could bring any books or newspapers from the hotel. He said no, not tonight.

The next morning Brower is sitting up in his hospital bed. His legs are casually crossed, the remains of his breakfast scattered on the tray in front of him. Wires trail from beneath his polka-dot gown, sending information to unseen machines. Anne is relieved to see that he looks himself.

"They seem to water the lawn here a great deal," he says, pointing out the window. "I hope it's just in the morning and evening and not in the heat of the day. That would be a waste."

Without prompting, he takes us through the incident in vivid detail, as if he were talking about one of his climbs: the initial dizziness, the inability to speak, his attempt to make Whitney sit still. The sentences stream forth in a smooth narrative flow, each word carefully chosen. With image and rhythm, he is creating a story to obliterate the ravages of his body.

But there comes a point in his telling when everything stops, when he arrives at a nothingness where words don't exist. He doesn't know what happened, because he wasn't there. This is where his story ends. This is where Brower cannot be Brower anymore. He can only be human.

"It was scary," he says. "I didn't like it at all." Then, more plaintively, "I want to go home."

"Poor dear," says Anne, laying her hand upon his.

And after a while, he will go home. He will go home where the doctors will tell him he has suffered a stroke and give him pills to thin his blood. His daughter will fly in from Portland and straighten the office up, and he won't particularly mind. Though spelling will confound him for a while, his speech will come back with full vigor. Soon he will joke with audiences about his "conking out," using his story to create sparks of energy and affection. This incident will be folded into his identity and will provide him with new words to loft out into the night from his old swivel chair, new messages to tell us where we are and where we need to go.

But for now he needs a CAT scan in Bishop, and the ambulance thrums outside. Brower looks at the gurney disdainfully but realizes that he has no choice. Straight-backed, with great dignity, he sits down and swings his legs up. The paramedics touch a hidden lever, and the gurney springs skyward, raising him four feet off the floor. He leans back, knits his fingers behind his head, and looks toward the door.

"Here we go," he says.

DECEMBER 1995

KEEPING AMERICA'S TREES SAFE FROM SMALL-CURD BUBBLE WRAP

by IAN FRAZIER

In New York City, where I live, plastic bags get stuck in trees. Especially in the winter, the wind lifts them and fixes them by their handles in high upper branches, where they become, compared to ordinary litter, immortal. Nobody touches them. They rustle and luff in the breeze; they age to gray, fright-wig shreds. Something about them has always bugged me. I've thought about them, written short pieces about them, mentioned them to my friend Tim. We speculated about how to get them down. Tim is a jeweler. In his studio he made a snagging device of several short wire grapplers set at right angles to a rod ending in a sharpened, curved hook. We put the snagger on the end of a long, stout aluminum tube and fit that into another piece of tube. We now had a tool with which we could reach nearly twenty-five feet off the ground. We tried it first on old familiar landmark bags in my neighborhood. It worked great—the grapplers would inveigle the bag with a twist of the pole, and then the blade would cut it free. In just a morning we debagged almost the whole neighborhood.

Tim's brother Bill joined us, and we began to go bag-snagging all over greater New York. The three of us have known one another since we were kids; we've always liked to fool around outdoors. Bill is a musician, with good dexterity for removing the finer plastic shreds. Tim is tall and sometimes would stand on teetering chunks of concrete atop upended trash cans to set new height records for bag-snagging. Then we wanted to go higher and higher. We added more poles to the snagger until we could reach to almost fifty feet. On midsummer evenings we would go snagging until late, when the light faded, in the emptying streets of downtown Manhattan and along the Bronx-Queens Expressway and in parks in New Jersey. From a tree by a construction sight we snagged a heavy-gauge burlap bag that we used to carry the other bags. We also brought down plastic drop cloths, crime-scene-marker tape, sneakers, extension cords, promotional flags, bicycle chains, a part from a baby's crib, and a pair of extra-large forest green stretch pants. Most people who saw what we were doing seemed to take it as a matter of course. We never came across or heard about anyone else doing it. After a while we had to conclude that at taking plastic bags and other trash out of trees, we were very likely the best in the world.

We began to think about expanding our range. What about the rest of the country? Maybe there was a mother lode of bags and other stuff in trees out there someplace. I happened to mention this to a guy from Chattanooga, Tennessee, and he said that in river valleys, floods often leave debris in the trees. I made some calls to towns along the Mississippi River between St. Louis and Memphis, where the flooding was bad in the summer of 1993. A woman who answered the phone at the city hall in Ste. Genevieve, Missouri, said there was still a lot of stuff in the trees around there—plastic, paper, clothes. Bill and Tim and I all had some free time in August. We decided to take a road trip to the Mississippi, snagging any bags we saw along the way.

We loaded the snagger and poles into Bill's Taurus wagon and hit the highways in full bag-snagging fever. Bill drove; I scanned the roadside trees. (Tim, who had some last-minute work, would fly out to join us later.) Periodically we pulled over at rest areas and truck stops to check the trees there. We saw no bags, no bags, and more no bags. Bill was braking in high-speed traffic for bag sightings that turned out to be patches of yellow leaves or tent-caterpillar webs. In 1,059 miles between the Holland Tunnel and the Mississippi River, we snagged exactly three plastic bags. One was a classic white bag with handles, such as Korean markets use—perhaps the most common of tree bags, we call it the undershirt bag—in an elm beside the westbound lane of the Pennsylvania Turnpike in the middle of the state. One was a Superior Ice Company bag in a honey locust on Highway 231 in rural Indiana; on the bottom of the bag it said, enigmatically, IS ONE ENOUGH? The third was a standard black plastic leaf bag in an ash beside Highway 50 in Illinois. As we crossed the Mississippi at Chester, Illinois, we were wondering whether bags in trees might turn out to be just a New York phenomenon. Then, in the cottonwoods along the Missouri shore, we saw it: plastic sheeting, reams of it, scrolls of it, exploded strands of it; filmy strips of plastic strewn and draped among the trees, dangling and drooping and corkscrewing around the trunks as if left by a welcoming committee just for us. A side benefit of being able to take stuff out of trees is that objects that would be eyesores to most people represent challenge and delight for us. We shouted for joy.

We spent about a week along the middle Mississippi, mostly in the broad floodplain on the Missouri side. The year before, parts of the plain had been under fifty feet of water. Here, as in New York, our main quarry was bags, but here they were sandbags. Sandbags are made of coarse-woven nylon sewn with heavy thread. During the flood, more than a million were used in the defense of Ste. Genevieve alone. Broken open, emptied, in colors of olive drab and soot black and khaki and beige and linen white and banana yellow, fraying sandbags flew from the branches of trees like stateless flags. We snagged them by the score. We found more trot lines, floats, and cane fishing poles than you're likely to see in trees in New York; also more tugboat hawsers. The Mississippi is stronger than the average New York gust of wind, and the objects it deposits in trees are bigger—milk crates, pallets, coolers, a sawhorse, a shopping cart, sixty-five feet of garden hose, a small room. Just downstream from the Ste. Genevieve ferry landing I found a tractor-tire inner tube well up in a cottonwood. After a lot of cutting and wrangling, I yanked the monster free, and I carried it out slung over my shoulder on a section of the pole. A man who had been fishing along the river was driving out on the field. He saw me in his rearview mirror, hit the brakes, and backed up. He was red-faced, with a rooster-comb of white hair and a potbelly. He leaned over to the open window: "What kind of a catch do you call that?"

"You call that a river rubber," I said.

"A river rubber," he repeated slowly, considering it. "What do you do with it?"

"Well, you can eat 'em, but you have to soak 'em a really long time."

"I imagine you do," he said. "I imagine they'd be kind of stretchy and tough."

The river is as muddy as advertised, and all business. The breeze carries the smell of diesel exhaust and fresh paint. Tugboats push coal barges rafted together five across and five deep, a piece of horizon that approaches, fills the landscape, and throbbingly recedes. Local people do not swim in the river or water-ski in it. When we asked a waitress at the Anvil Restaurant in Ste. Genevieve why, she said, "Are you for real? It's gross!" They do fish in it. Forked sticks used to hold still-fishing poles line the riverbanks. While we were there, large mayflies were hatching, and fish were popping the surface inshore and well out in the current. I saw an expanse of back rise silently out of the water, followed by a dorsal fin, followed by more back—the largest fish I've ever seen in fresh water. I asked Bill and Tim whether they'd seen it, and they said they'd only seen the expression on my face. Over the years, the river has writhed so much in its bed around here that people generally don't live right next to it. This means that for long stretches between the fortresslike docks of coal yards and limestone quarries the riverbank still looks much as it did to Mark Twain—except for the occasional banner of drift plastic waving from the trees.

We followed the riverbank on foot for some miles, through groves of hard-used cottonwoods and willows, across flats where the mud was dry on top and squishy and wet underneath, through forests of weeds twice our height laced through with morning glory vines. Most of the bags were on low branches; some were in bushes we could reach by hand. Generally we took everything. Sometimes we stopped to look back at the improvement; trees from which bags have been removed are prettier than trees that never had any to begin with. In a bag-free landscape, imagination can pick its century. The marshy shallows simmered between the river and the levee: Birds sang, herons roared, turtles splashed, insects whirred, wildflowers puckered. The air was like something a dry cleaner would do to a stain when all milder measures had failed. After a while we went back to the car for some maximum air-conditioning and John Anderson singing "Seminole Wind" on the tape deck and a quick run to the convenience mart for two twenty-ounce Frescas that I drank within seconds of buying.

Many houses on the floodplain are abandoned. The flood left mud up to the second stories; a dead, gray, dried wash of mud also marks barns and trees. Grain silos are crushed and sagging, a school building is a tangle of wreckage under a roof. In what used to be the town of Kaskaskia, Illinois, only a few houses, all of them damaged, remain. Kaskaskia is one of the oldest towns on the river. It was a fur-trading settlement in the seventeenth century, and later a Jesuit mission, an English fort, and the first capital of the state. (A jump of the river in 1881 made Kaskaskia an island that sits closer to the Missouri side, but it is still legally part of Illinois.) The river flooded it in 1844, 1881, and 1973. A new fifty-foot levee broke during the high water of July 22, 1993, and water up to twenty feet deep filled the town.

Bill and Tim and I walked on the open lawns by the brick Church of the Immaculate Conception (damaged, but still standing) and the boarded-up two-story colonial brick structure where the state legislature once met. We snagged some high sandbags, a length of red nylon cord, a doll's straw hat, beige plastic sheeting, and a catastrophe of a disintegrated black plastic tarpaulin—the last from an immense Missouri elm. Nearby, a shirtless man rolled a ride-around mower from a pickup bed and started the engine. We walked over to talk to him. He was mowing the strip that would have been his side lawn, if he still had a house there. He told us that his name was Robert Doza and that the flood had taken the house, which had been in the family since 1957, and a two-car garage with a Pontiac inside. He had a broad, tan, soft face with rueful lines around the eyes. The house had been all paid for, he said. When the water was deep, he'd come over to the house in a barge and stood on his roof and piled it with sandbags in an attempt to keep the house from floating away. He'd sawed off the side porch with a chainsaw and tied the porch, the garage, and the house to tall trees. He showed us the ropes still hanging from cottonwoods nearby. But storms had come, and waves had beaten the roof to pieces, and the water had twisted and wrung the house so badly that when he'd found it afterward in the neighbor's yard there wasn't even any lumber he could salvage. He said that unfortunately he had let his flood insurance lapse just before the flood—missed his renewal deadline by just ten hours, and State Farm wouldn't bend an inch. He said he knew it was his fault. He tried to return to the house after the levee had broken and the water had started to rise, he said. He took his four-wheel-drive ATV and put a life jacket on it and on himself and drove toward Kaskaskia, along the levee and on back roads, keeping to the high ground. In a few places the current was so strong over the road that he almost got washed away. He reached his driveway finally and tried to hook a little trailer to the ATV, but had to give up because the water was too deep. He said, "I thought if I could get the trailer hooked up, maybe I could at least save some clothes. . . ." He looked away; his eyes teared; he turned both his lips into his mouth and pressed them together.

We drove as far north as St. Louis and as far south as Cape Girardeau, Missouri, looking for stuff in trees—or, often, just looking for the river itself. Roads don't go very near the river, usually. You can hunt for the river a long time in a car without catching a glimpse of it, and then suddenly you turn down a side road, come around a corner, and the wide brown bulk of it lunges at you like something out of a closet. Sometimes a side road leads you to a place on the river that used to be a steamboat landing. At a spot once known as Brickey's Landing, about ten river miles north of Ste. Genevieve, we found an abandoned inn from the last century and some foundations and structures of rusted iron. The channel swung conveniently near a sound limestone bank; from the falling-down porch along the inn's front you could see a long way across the river and upstream. The place was a nineteenth-century version of a rest stop on the highway. Mud in the inn's upstairs showed that it had been underwater for some time. There was a lot of plastic in the trees, and we spent a while with the snagger taking it out.

A badger-shaped man with a drooping mustache and a muscle shirt that said PETER FRAMPTON ON TOUR was digging in a midden just below the inn. In one hand he had a long, narrow trowel and in the other the butt section of a two-piece fishing rod, which he used to poke through the dirt. He said that after the flood, the eddy there had left so much stuff that he would have needed a U-Haul to carry it all away. He told us that he had once found the trigger mechanism from an old flintlock rifle at this spot, that he was a butcher, that he liked to read Hermann Hesse, that someone had swiped an arrowhead collection he'd spent twelve years building up, that he came out here to get away from his troubles, and that he was fucked up in the head over women. He said that after the flood he had found a 250-pound drift log here and had carried it out and dumped it in the front yard of a woman who had recently broken up with him—"a lot of work, actually, but it was good for me."

Often the only way to follow the river was by driving on the levees. Some levees are paved with a single lane of crushed limestone; rolling along it, a car is at the same height as an elevated train. You can look down into the rows of corn filing past, and through second-story windows of farmhouses on the inland side. Mourning doves and pigeons sometimes flush from the levee's sides as you approach, and rise from beneath the car. The land that was flooded is fertile. On one side of the levee are acres of gold-green milo, and dusty green soybeans, and corn tassels reddened by the declining sun. On the other side are cottonwoods, willows, marsh, and river. We scanned both sides with binoculars. Sometimes a scrap of black plastic trash bag on a branch turned into a crow and flew away. In many places, we found nothing at all in the trees—which, when I think about it, is actually good.

On County Road H leading to Belgique, Missouri, we came across the most spectacular stuff-in-trees location ever. It was an elm grove draped in what turned out to be sheets of bubble wrap. We found the remains of a roll of bubble wrap on the ground. Evidently, the full roll had floated into the grove during the flood and then had come undone and trailed itself through the branches as the water went down. It was the kind of wrap with smaller bubbles—"small-curd bubble wrap," Bill called it—and not a bubble was unpopped. We snagged bubble wrap from the elms for much of an afternoon. Teasing a long strand of it from benighted upper branches was a satisfying thing. Sometimes the wrap put up a fight. Tim broke the cutting blade of the snagger in a tussle with it. Finally we subdued the garbage all into about eight large leaf bags.

In former years our enthusiasms have sometimes been of a less constructive sort. For example, we used to get up early on weekend mornings and hit golf balls into the water from the shoreline of lower Manhattan, sometimes ricocheting them off piers, bridge supports, and once a passing ship. We have also golfed in the more regular way, played baseball, fished, and shot guns. Now all we want to do is go bag-snagging. As a companionable outdoor pastime, bag-snagging is ideal. It carries a bit of the willful excitement of vandalism, yet is its opposite. It lets you go places where people would otherwise stop you, lets you participate in the landscape without need for a tee time or a game license. It establishes small pieces of the country—the particular places where you have snagged bags—firmly in your mind. You feel differently about a place once you have snagged there. And when you take a big piece of plastic from a tree, you affect the look of the landscape in a dramatic way. The grove on the road to Belgique is now permanently affixed to my own map. After we had un-bubble-wrapped the elms, we stood around admiring them. The next day we came back to admire them some more. I could have sat among them all day.

APRIL 1995

MOMENTS OF DOUBT

by DAVID ROBERTS

A day in early July, perfect for climbing. From the mesas above Boulder, a heat-cutting breeze drove the smell of the pines up onto the great tilting slabs of the Flatirons.

It was 1961; I was eighteen, had been climbing about a year, Gabe even less. We were about 600 feet up, three-quarters of the way to the summit of the First Flatiron. There wasn't a guidebook in those days; so we didn't know how difficult our route was supposed to be or who had previously done it. But it had gone all right, despite the scarcity of places to bang in our Austrian soft-iron pitons; sometimes we'd just wedge our bodies in a crack and yell "On belay!"

It was a joy to be climbing. Climbing was one of the best things—maybe the best thing—in life, given that one would never play shortstop for the Dodgers. There was a risk, as my parents and friends kept pointing out, but I knew the risk was worth it.

In fact, just that summer I had become ambitious. With a friend my age whom I'll call Jock, I'd climbed the east face of Longs Peak, illegally early in the season—no great deed for experts, but pretty good for eighteen-year-old kids. It was Jock's idea to train all summer and go up to the Tetons and do *the* route: the north face of the Grand. I'd never even seen the Tetons, but the idea of the route, hung with names like Petzoldt and Pownall and Unsoeld, sent chills through me.

It was Gabe's lead now, maybe the last before the going got easier a few hundred feet below the top. He angled up and left, couldn't get any protection in, went out of sight around a corner. I waited. The rope didn't move. "What's going on?" I finally yelled. "Hang on," Gabe answered irritably, "I'm looking for a belay."

We'd been friends since grade school. When he was young he had been very shy; he'd been raised by his father only—why, I never thought to ask. Ever since I had met him, on the playground, running up the old wooden stairs to the fourth-grade classroom, he'd moved in a jerky, impulsive way. On our high school tennis team, he slashed at the ball with lurching stabs, and skidded across the asphalt like a kid trying to catch his own shadow. He climbed the same way, especially in recent months, impulsively going for a hard move well above his protection, worrying me, but getting away with it. In our first half-year of climbing, I'd usually been a little better than Gabe, just as he was always stuck a notch below me on the tennis team. But in the last couple of months—no denying it—he'd become better on rock than I was; he took the leads that I didn't like the looks of. He might have made a better partner for Jock on the Grand, except that Gabe's only mountain experience had been an altitude-sick crawl up the east side of Mount of the Holy Cross with me just a week before. He'd thrown up on the summit but said he loved the climb.

At eighteen it wasn't easy for me to see why Gabe had suddenly become good at climbing, or why it drove him as nothing else had. Just that April, three months earlier, his father had been killed in an auto accident during a blizzard in Texas. When Gabe returned to school, I mumbled my prepared condolence. He brushed it off and asked at once when we could go climbing. I was surprised. But I wanted to climb, too: The summer was approaching, Jock wasn't always available, and Gabe would go at the drop of a phone call.

Now, finally, came the "on belay" signal from out of sight to the left, and I started up. For the full 120 feet Gabe had been unable to get in any pitons; so as I climbed, the rope drooped in a long arc to my left. It began to tug me sideways, and when I yanked back at it, I noticed that it seemed snagged about fifty feet away, caught under one of the downward-pointing flakes so characteristic of the Flatirons. I flipped the rope angrily and tugged harder on it, then yelled to Gabe to pull from his end. Our efforts only jammed it in tighter. The first trickle of fear leaked into my well-being.

"What kind of belay do you have?" I asked the invisible Gabe.

"Not too good. I couldn't get anything in."

There were fifty feet of slab between me and the irksome flake, and those fifty feet were frighteningly smooth. I ought, I supposed, to climb over to the flake, even if it meant building up coils and coils of slack. But if I slipped, and Gabe with no anchor . . .

I yelled to Gabe what I was going to do. He assented.

I untied from the rope, gathered as many coils as I could, and threw the end violently down and across the slab, hoping to snap the jammed segment loose, or at least reduce Gabe's job to hauling the thing in with all his might. Then, with my palms starting to sweat, I climbed carefully up to a little ledge and sat down.

Gabe was now below me, out of sight, but close. "It's still jammed," he said, and my fear surged a little notch.

"Maybe we can set up a rappel," I suggested.

"No, I think I can climb back and get it."

"Are you sure?" Relief lowered the fear a notch. Gabe would do the dirty work, just as he was willing to lead the hard pitches.

"It doesn't look too bad."

I waited, sitting on my ledge, staring out over Boulder and the dead-straw plains that seemed to stretch all the way to Kansas. I wasn't sure we were doing the right thing. A few months earlier I'd soloed a rock called the Fist, high on Green Mountain, in the midst of a snowstorm, and sixty feet off the ground, as I was turning a slight overhang, my foot had come off, and one hand . . . but not the other. And adrenaline had carried me the rest of the way up. There was a risk, but you rose to it.

For Gabe, it was taking a long time. It was all the worse not being able to see him. I looked to my right and saw a flurry of birds playing with a column of air over near the Second Flatiron. Then Gabe's voice, triumphant: "I got it!"

"Way to go!" I yelled back. The fear diminished. If he'd been able to climb down to the snag, he could climb back up. I was glad I hadn't had to do it. Remembering his impatience, I instructed, "Coil it up." A week before, on Holy Cross, I'd been the leader.

"No, I'll just drape it around me. I can climb straight up to where you are."

The decision puzzled me. *Be careful,* I said in my head. But that was Gabe, impulsive, playing his hunches. Again the seconds crept. I had too little information, nothing to do but look for the birds and smell the pine sap. You could see Denver, smogless as yet, a squat aggregation of downtown buildings like some modern covered-wagon circle, defended against the emptiness of the Plains. There had been climbers over on the Third Flatiron earlier, but now I couldn't spot them. The red, gritty sandstone was warm to my palms.

"How's it going?" I yelled.

A pause. Then Gabe's voice, quick-syllabled as always, more tense than normal. "I just got past a hard place, but it's easier now."

He sounded so close, only fifteen feet below me, yet I hadn't seen him since his lead had taken him around the corner out of sight. I felt I could almost reach down and touch him.

Next, there was a soft but unmistakable sound, and my brain knew it without ever having heard it before. It was the sound of cloth rubbing against rock. Then Gabe's cry, a single blurt of knowledge: "Dave!"

I rose with a start to my feet, but hung on to a knob with one hand, gripping it desperately. "Gabe!" I yelled back; then, for the first time in half an hour, I saw him. He was much farther from me now, sliding and rolling, the rope wrapped in tangles about him like a badly made nest. "Grab something," I yelled. I could hear Gabe shouting, even as he receded from me, "No! Oh, no!"

I thought, there's always a chance. But Gabe began to bounce, just like rocks I had seen bouncing down mountain slopes, a longer bounce each time. The last was conclusive, for I saw him flung far from the rock's even surface to pirouette almost lazily in the air, then meet the unyielding slab once more, headfirst, before the sandstone threw him into the treetops.

What I did next is easy to remember, but it is hard to judge just how long it took. It seemed, in the miasma of adrenaline, to last either three minutes or more than an hour. I stood and I yelled for help. After several repetitions, voices from the Mesa Trail caught the breeze back to me. "We're coming!" someone shouted. "In the trees!" I yelled back. "Hurry!" I sat down and said to myself, now don't go screw it up yourself, you don't have a rope, sit here and wait for someone to come rescue you. They can come up the back and lower a rope from the top. As soon as I had given myself this good advice, I got up and started scrambling toward the summit. It wasn't too hard. Slow down, don't make a mistake, I lectured myself, but it felt as if I were running. From the summit I down-climbed the eighty feet on the backside; I'd been there before and had rappelled it. Forty feet up there was a hard move. *Don't blow it.* Then I was on the ground.

I ran down the scree-and-brush gully between the First and Second Flatirons, and got to the bottom a few minutes before the hikers. "Where is he?" a wild-eyed volunteer asked me. "In the trees!" I yelled back. "Somewhere right near here!"

Searching for something is usually an orderly process; it has its methodical pleasures, its calm reconstruction of the possible steps that led to the object getting lost. We searched instead like scavenging predators, crashing through deadfall and talus; and we couldn't find Gabe. Members of the Rocky Mountain Rescue Group began to arrive; they were calmer than the hiker I had first encountered. We searched and searched, and finally a voice called out, "Here he is."

Someone led me there. There were only solemn looks to confirm the obvious. I saw Gabe sprawled face down on the talus, his limbs in the wrong positions, the rope, coated with blood, still in a cocoon about him. The seat of his jeans had been ripped away, and one bare buttock was scraped raw, the way kids' knees used to look after a bad slide on a sidewalk. I wanted to go up and touch his body, but I couldn't. I sat down and cried.

Much later—but it was still afternoon, the sun and breeze still collaborating on a perfect July day—a policeman led me up the walk to my house. My mother came to the screen door and, grasping the situation at once, burst into tears. Gabe was late for a birthday party. Someone had called my house, mildly annoyed, to try to account for the delay. My father took on the task of calling them back. (More than a decade later he told me that it was the hardest thing he had ever done.)

In the newspapers the next day a hiker was quoted as saying that he knew something bad was going to happen, because he'd overheard Gabe and me "bickering," and good climbers didn't do that. Another man had watched the fall through binoculars. At my father's behest, I wrote down a detailed account of the accident.

About a week later Jock came by. He spent the appropriate minutes in sympathetic silence, then said, "The thing you've got to do is get right back on the rock." I didn't want to, but I went out with him. We top-roped a moderate climb only thirty feet high. My feet and hands shook uncontrollably, my heart seemed to be screaming, and Jock had to haul me up the last ten feet. "It's OK, it'll come back," he reassured.

I had one friend I could talk to, a touch-football buddy who thought climbing was crazy in the first place. With his support, in the presence of my parents' anguish, I managed at last to call up Jock and ask him to come by. We sat on my front porch. "Jock," I said, "I just can't go to the Grand. I'm too shook up. I'd be no good if I did go." He stared at me long and hard. Finally he stood up and walked away.

That fall I went to Harvard. I tried out for the tennis team, but when I found that the Mountaineering Club included veterans who had just climbed Waddington in the Coast Range and Mount Logan in the Yukon, it didn't take me long to single out my college heroes.

But I wasn't at all sure about climbing. On splendid fall afternoons at the Shawangunks, when the veterans dragged us neophytes up easy climbs, I sat on the belay ledges mired in ambivalence. I'd never been at a cliff where there were so many climbers, and whenever one of them on an adjoining route happened to yell—even if the message were nothing more alarming than "I think it goes up to the left there!"—I jerked with fright.

For reasons I am still not sure of, Gabe became a secret. Attached to the memory of our day on the First Flatiron was not only fear, but guilt and embarrassment. Guilt toward Gabe, of course, because I had not been the one who went to get the jammed rope. But the humiliation, born perhaps in that moment when the cop had led me up to my front door and my mother had burst into tears, lingered with me in the shape of a crime or moral error, like getting a girl pregnant.

Nevertheless, at Harvard I got deeply involved with the Mountaineering Club. By twenty I'd climbed McKinley with six Harvard friends via a new route, and that August I taught at Colorado Outward Bound School. With all of "Boone Patrol," including the senior instructor, a laconic British hard man named Clough, I was camped one night above timberline. We'd crawled under the willow bushes and strung out ponchos for shelter. In the middle of the night I dreamed that Gabe was falling away from me through endless reaches of black space. He was in a metal cage, spinning headlong, and I repeatedly screamed his name. I woke with a jolt, sat shivering for ten minutes, then crawled, dragging my bag, far from the others, and lay awake the rest of the night. As we blew the morning campfire back to life from the evening's ashes, Clough remarked, "Did you hear the screams? One of the poor lads must have had a nightmare."

By my senior year, though, I'd become hard myself. McKinley had seemed a lark compared to my second expedition—a forty-day failure with only one companion, Don Jensen, on the east ridge of Alaska's Mount Deborah. All through the following winter, with Don holed up in the Sierra Nevada, me trudging through a math major at Harvard, we plotted mountaineering revenge. By January we had focused on a route: the unclimbed west face of Mount Huntington, even harder, we thought, than Deborah. By March we'd agreed that Matt Hale, a junior and my regular climbing partner, would be our third, even though Matt had been on no previous expeditions. Matt was daunted by the ambition of the project, but slowly got caught up in it. Needing a fourth, we discussed an even more inexperienced club member, Ed Bernd, a sophomore who'd been climbing little more than a year and who'd not even been in big mountains.

Never in my life, before or since, have I found myself so committed to any project. I daydreamed about recipes for Logan bread and the number of ounces a certain piton weighed; at night I fell asleep with the seductive promises of belay ledges and crack systems whispering in my ear. School was a platonic facade. The true Idea of my life lay in the Alaska Range.

At one point that spring I floated free from my obsession long enough to hear a voice in my head tell me, "You know, Dave, this is the kind of climb you could get killed on." I stopped and assessed my life, and consciously answered, "It's worth it. Worth the risk." I wasn't sure what I meant by that, but I knew its truth. I wanted Matt to feel the same way. I knew Don did.

On a March weekend Matt and I were leading an ice-climbing trip in Huntington Ravine on Mount Washington. The Harvard cabin was unusually full, which meant a scramble in the morning to get out first and claim the ice gully you wanted to lead. On Saturday I skipped breakfast to beat everybody else to Pinnacle Gully, then the prize of the ravine. It was a bitter, windy day, and though the gully didn't tax my skills unduly, twice sudden gusts almost blew me out of my steps. The second man on the rope, though a good rock climber, found the whole day unnerving and was glad to get back to the cabin.

That night we chatted with the other climbers. The two most experienced were Craig Merrihue, a grad student in astrophysics, said to be brilliant, with first ascents in the Andes and Karakoram behind him, and Dan Doody, a quiet, thoughtful filmmaker who'd gone to college in Wyoming and had recently been on the big American Everest expedition. Both men were interested in our Huntington plans, and it flattered Matt and me that they thought we were up to something serious. The younger climbers looked on us experts in awe; it was delicious to bask in their hero worship as we nonchalanted it with Craig and Dan. Craig's lovely wife, Sandy, was part of our company. All three of them were planning to link up in a relaxing trip to the Hindu Kush the coming summer.

The next day the wind was still gusting fitfully. Matt and I were leading separate ropes of beginners up Odells Gully, putting in our teaching time after having had Saturday to do something hard. I felt lazy, a trifle vexed to be "wasting" a good day. Around noon we heard somebody calling from the ravine floor. We ignored the cries at first, but as a gust of wind came our way, I was pricked with alarm. "Somebody's yelling for help," I shouted to Matt. "Think they mean it?" A tiny figure far below seemed to be running up and down on the snow. My laziness burned away.

I tied off my second to wait on a big bucket of an ice step, then zipped down a rappel off a single poorly placed ice screw. Still in crampons, I ran down into the basin that formed the runout for all five gullies. The man I met, a weekend climber in his thirties who had been strolling up the ravine for a walk, was moaning. He had seen something that looked like "a bunch of rags" slide by out of the corner of his eye. He knew all at once that it was human bodies he had seen, and he could trace the line of fall up to Pinnacle Gully. He knew that Doody and Merrihue were climbing in Pinnacle. And Craig was a close friend of his. During the five minutes or so since the accident he had been unable to approach them, unable to do anything but yell for help and run aimlessly. I was the first to reach the bodies.

Gabe's I had not had to touch. But I was a trip leader now, an experienced mountaineer, the closest approximation in the circumstances to a rescue squad. I'd had first-aid training. Without a second's hesitation I knelt beside the bodies. Dan's was the worse injured, with a big chunk of his head torn open. His blood was still warm, but I was sure he was dead. I thought I could find a faint pulse in Craig's wrist, however, so I tried to stop the bleeding and started mouth-to-mouth resuscitation. Matt arrived and worked on Dan, and then others appeared and tried to help.

For an hour, I think, I put my lips against Craig's, held his nose shut, forced air into his lungs. His lips were going cold and blue, and there was a stagnant taste in the cavity his mouth had become, but I persisted, as did Matt and the others. Not since my father had last kissed me—was I ten?—had I put my lips to another man's. I remembered Dad's scratchy face, when he hadn't shaved, like Craig's now. We kept hoping, but I knew after five minutes that both men had been irretrievably damaged. There was too much blood. It had been a bad year for snow in the bottom of the ravine; big rocks stuck out everywhere. Three years earlier Don Jensen had been avalanched out of Damnation Gully; he fell 800 feet and only broke a shoulder blade. But that had been a good year for snow.

Yet we kept up our efforts. The need arose as much from an inability to imagine what else we might do—stand around in shock?—as from good first-aid sense. At last we gave up, exhausted. I could read in Matt's clipped and efficient suggestions the dawning sense that a horrible thing had happened. But I also felt numb. The sense of tragedy flooded home only in one moment. I heard somebody say something like "She's coming," and somebody else say, "Keep her away." I looked up and saw Sandy, Craig's wife, arriving from the cabin, aware of something wrong, but in the instant before knowing that it was indeed Craig she was intercepted bodily by the climber who knew her best, and that was how she learned. I can picture her face in the instant of knowing, and I remember vividly my own revelation—that there was a depth of personal loss that I had never really known existed, of which I was now receiving my first glimpse.

But my memory has blocked out Sandy's reaction. Did she immediately burst into tears, like my mother? Did she try to force her way to Craig? Did we let her? I know I saw it happen, whatever it was, but my memory cannot retrieve it.

There followed long hours into the dark hauling the bodies with ropes back toward the cabin. There was the pacifying exhaustion and the stolid drive back to Cambridge. There was somebody telling me, "You did a fantastic job, all that anybody could have done," and that seeming maudlin—who wouldn't have done the same? There were, in subsequent weeks, the memorial service, long tape-recorded discussions of the puzzling circumstances of the accident (we had found Dan and Craig roped together, a bent ice screw loose on the rope between them), heated indictments of the cheap Swiss design of the screw. And even a couple of visits with Sandy and their five-year-old son.

But my strongest concern was not to let the accident interfere with my commitment to climb Huntington, now only three months away. The deaths had deeply shaken Matt; but we never directly discussed the matter. I never wrote my parents about what had taken place. We went ahead and invited Ed, the sophomore, to join our expedition. Though he had not been in the ravine with us, he too had been shaken. But I got the three of us talking logistics and gear, and thinking about a mountain in Alaska. In some smug private recess I told myself that I was in better training than Craig and Dan had been, and that was why I wouldn't get killed. If the wind had blown one of them out of his steps, well, I'd led Pinnacle the day before in the same wind and it hadn't blown me off. Almost, but it hadn't. Somehow I controlled my deepest feelings and kept the disturbance buried. I had no bad dreams about Doody and Merrihue, no sleepless nights, no sudden qualms about whether Huntington was worth the risk. By June I was as ready as I could be for the hardest climb of my life.

It took a month, but we climbed our route on Huntington. Pushing through the night of July 29 and 30, we traversed the knife-edged summit ridge and stood on top in the still hours of dawn. Only twelve hours before, Matt and I had come as close to being killed as it is possible to get away with in the mountains.

Matt, tugging on a loose crampon strap, had pulled himself off his steps; he landed on me, broke down the snow ledge I had kicked; under the strain our one bad anchor piton popped out. We fell, roped together and helpless, some seventy feet down a steep slope of ice above a 4,500-foot drop. Then a miracle intervened; the rope snagged on a nubbin of rock, the size of one's knuckle, and held us both.

Such was our commitment to the climb that, even though we were bruised and Matt had lost a crampon, we pushed upward and managed to join Ed and Don for the summit dash.

At midnight, nineteen hours later, Ed and I stood on a ledge some 1,500 feet below. Our tents were too small for four people; so he and I had volunteered to push on to a lower camp, leaving Matt and Don to come down on the next good day. In the dim light we set up a rappel. There was a tangle of pitons, fixed ropes, and the knots tying them off, in the midst of which Ed was attaching a carabiner. I suggested an adjustment. Ed moved the carabiner, clipped our rope in, and started to get on rappel. "Just this pitch," I said, "and then it's practically walking to camp."

Ed leaned back on rappel. There was a scrape and sparks—his crampons scratching the rock, I later guessed. Suddenly he was flying backward through the air, down the vertical pitch. He hit hard ice sixty feet below. Just as I had on the Flatiron, I yelled. "Grab something, Ed!" But it was evident that his fall was not going to end—not soon, anyway. He slid rapidly down the ice chute, then out of sight over a cliff. I heard him bouncing once or twice, then nothing. He had not uttered a word.

I shouted, first for Ed, then for Don and Matt above. Nothing but silence answered me. There was nothing I could do. I was as certain as I could be that Ed had fallen 4,000 feet, to the lower arm of the Tokositna Glacier, inaccessible even from our base camp. He was surely dead.

I managed to get myself, without a rope, down the seven pitches to our empty tent. The next two days I spent alone—desperate for Matt's and Don's return, imagining them dead also, drugging myself with sleeping pills, trying to fathom what had gone wrong, seized one night in my sleep with a vision of Ed, broken and bloody, clawing his way up the wall to me, crying out, "Why didn't you come look for me?" At last Don and Matt arrived, and I had to tell them. Our final descent, in the midst of a raging blizzard, was the nastiest and scariest piece of climbing I have done, before or since.

From Talkeetna, a week later, I called Ed's parents. His father's stunned first words, crackly with long-distance static, were, "Is this some kind of a joke?" After the call I went behind the bush pilot's hangar and cried my heart out— the first time in years that I had given way to tears.

A week later, with my parents' backing, I flew to Philadelphia to spend three days with Ed's parents. But not until the last few hours of my stay did we talk about Ed or climbing. Philadelphia was wretchedly hot and sticky. In the Bernds' small house my presence—sleeping on the living room sofa, an extra guest at meals—was a genuine intrusion. Unlike my parents, or Matt's, or Don's, Ed's had absolutely no comprehension of mountain climbing. It was some esoteric thing he had gotten into at Harvard; and of course Ed had completely downplayed, for their sake, the seriousness of our Alaska project.

At that age, given my feelings about climbing, I could hardly have been better shielded from any sense of guilt. But mixed in with my irritation and discomfort in the muggy apartment was an awareness—of a different sort from the glimpse of Sandy Merrihue—that I was in the presence of a grief so deep its features were opaque to me. It was the hope-destroying grief of parents, the grief of those who knew things could not keep going right, a grief that would, I sensed, diminish little over the years. It awed and frightened me, and disclosed to me an awareness of my own guilt. I began remembering other moments. In our first rest after the summit, as we had giddily replayed every detail of our triumph, Ed had said that yes, it had been great, but that he wasn't sure it had been worth it. I hadn't pressed him; his qualifying judgment had seemed the only sour note in a perfect party. It was so obvious to me that all the risks throughout the climb—even Matt's and my near-disaster—had been worth it to make the summit.

Now Ed's remark haunted me. He was, in most climbers' judgment, far too inexperienced for Huntington. We'd caught his occasional technical mistakes on the climb, a piton hammered in with the eye the wrong way, an ice ax left below a rock overhang. But he learned so well, was so naturally strong, and complemented our intensity with a hearty capacity for fun and friendship. Still, at Harvard, there had been, I began to see, no way for him to turn down our invitation. Matt and I and the other veterans were his heroes, just as the Waddington seniors had been mine three years before. Now the inner circle was asking him to join. It seemed to us at the time an open invitation, free of any moral implications. Now I wondered.

I still didn't know what had gone wrong with the rappel, even though Ed had been standing a foot away from me. Had it been some technical error of his in clipping in? Or had the carabiner itself failed? There was no way of settling the question, especially without having been able to look for, much less find, his body.

At last Ed's family faced me. I gave a long, detailed account of the climb. I told them it was "the hardest thing yet done in Alaska," a great mountaineering accomplishment. It would attract the attention of climbers the world over. They looked at me with blank faces; my way of viewing Ed's death was incomprehensible. They were bent on finding a Christian meaning to the event. It occurred to them that maybe God had meant to save Ed from a worse death fighting in Vietnam. They were deeply stricken by our inability to retrieve his body. "My poor baby," Mrs. Bernd wailed at one point, "he must be so cold."

Their grief brought me close to tears again, but when I left it was with a sigh of relief. I went back to Denver, where I was starting graduate school. For the second time in my life I thought seriously about quitting climbing. At twenty-two I had been the firsthand witness of three fatal accidents, costing four lives. Mr. Bernd's laborious letters, edged with the leaden despair I had seen in his face, continued to remind me that the question "Is it worth the risk?" was not one any person could answer by consulting only himself.

Torn by my own ambivalence, studying Restoration comedy in a city where I had few friends, no longer part of a gang heading off each weekend to the Shawangunks, I laid off climbing most of the winter of 1965–66. By February I had made a private resolve to quit the business, at least for a few years. One day a fellow showed up at my basement apartment, all the way down from Alaska. I'd never met him, but the name Art Davidson was familiar. He looked straight off skid row, with his tattered clothes and unmatched socks and tennis shoes with holes in them; and his wild red beard and white eyebrows lent a kind of rundown Irish aristocracy to his face. He lived, apparently, like a vagrant, subsisting on cottage cheese in the back of his old pickup truck (named

Bucephalus after Alexander's horse), which he hid in parking lots each night on the outskirts of Anchorage. Art was crazy about Alaskan climbing. In the next year and a half he would go on five major expeditions—still the most intense spate of big-range mountaineering I know of. In my apartment he kept talking in his soft, enthusiastic voice about the Cathedral Spires, a place he knew Don and I had had our eyes on. I humored him. I let him talk on, and then we went out for a few beers, and Art started reminding me about the pink granite and the trackless glaciers, and by the evening's end the charismatic bastard had me signed up.

We went to the Cathedral Spires in 1966, with three others. Art was at the zenith of his climbing career. Self-taught, technically erratic, he made up in compulsive zeal what he lacked in finesse. His drive alone got himself and Rick Millikan up the highest peak in the range, which we named Kichatna Spire. As for me, I wasn't the climber I'd been the year before, which had much to do with why I wasn't along with Art on the summit push. That year I'd fallen in love with the woman who would become my wife, and suddenly the old question about risk seemed vastly more complicated. In the blizzard-swept dusk, with two of the other guys up on the climb, I found myself worrying about *their* safety instead of mere logistics. I was as glad nothing had gone wrong by the end of the trip as I was that we'd collaborated on a fine first ascent.

Summer after summer I went back to Alaska, climbing hard, but not with the all-out commitment of 1965. Over the years quite a few of my climbing acquaintances were killed in the mountains, including five close friends. Each death was deeply unsettling, tempting me to doubt all over again the worth of the enterprise. For nine years I taught climbing to college students, and worrying about their safety became an occupational hazard. Ironically, the closest I came during those years to getting killed was not on some Alaskan wall, but on a beginner's climb at the Shawangunks, when I nearly fell headfirst backward out of a rappel—the result of a carabiner jamming in a crack, my own impatience, and the blasé glaze with which teaching a dangerous skill at a trivial level coats the risk. Had that botched rappel been my demise, no friends would have seen my end as meaningful: instead, a "stupid," "pointless," "who-would-have-thought?" kind of death.

Yet in the long run, trying to answer my own question "Is it worth it?," torn between thinking the question itself ridiculous and grasping for a formulaic answer, I come back to gut-level affirmation, however sentimental, however selfish. When I image my early twenties, it is not in terms of the hours spent in a quiet library studying Melville, or my first nervous pontifications before a freshman English class. I want to see Art Davidson again, shambling into my apartment in his threadbare trousers, spooning great dollops of cottage cheese past his flaming beard, filling the air with his baroque hypotheses, convincing me that the Cathedral Spires needed our visit. I want to remember what brand of beer I was drinking when that crazy vagabond in one stroke turned the cautious resolves of a lonely winter into one more summer's plot against the Alaskan wilderness.

Some of the worst moments of my life have taken place in the mountains. Not only the days alone in the tent on Huntington after Ed had vanished—quieter moments as well, embedded in uneventful expeditions. Trying to sleep the last few hours before a predawn start on a big climb, my mind stiff with dread, as I hugged my all-too-obviously fragile self with my own arms—until the scared kid inside my sleeping bag began to pray for bad weather and another day's reprieve. But nowhere else on Earth, not even in the harbors of reciprocal love, have I felt pure happiness take hold of me and shake me like a puppy, compelling me, and the conspirators I had arrived there with, to stand on some perch of rock or snow, the uncertain struggle below us, and bawl our pagan vaunts to the very sky. It was worth it then.

DECEMBER 1980

VOYAGE OF THE SMITHEREENS

by CRAIG VETTER

**A bitter night in Chicago . . . Grenadine dreams . . . a chance
to learn port from starboard.**

You have to try to imagine the trip the way I did that cruel winter evening in
Chicago when Jack and I dreamed it up. We had a nice big *National Geographic*
map open on the table in front of us, and there they were—the West Indies,
the Windwards, the Grenadines—arching down the blue page from fifteen degrees south to twelve degrees south. Just the island names warmed the room:
Martinique, St. Lucia, St. Vincent, Bequia, Mustique, Canouan, Union, Carri-
acou, Grenada. I pictured the big equatorial sun in the big Caribbean sky, felt
the big, steady push of the trades riding into the sails of our forty-seven-
foot sloop till the beak of the thing was down into the swell like a plow in a
furrow, bucking warm spray into my nut-brown face where I stood at the
wheel like every Spanish explorer, every French pirate, every English mer-
chantman who ever slid a ship on these perfect turquoise waters, past these
green volcano islands, into glassy little bays where huge crowds of coco palms
come right down to the beach to meet you, where the natives are so friendly,
so gentle, that even when they talk about money it sounds like they're
singing.

And on top of all that, my old friend Jack, who'd spent ten years of his life as a boat hobo on these particular seas, had promised he'd teach me the what's-that and the how-to of this big old bareboat, from the pointy front porch to the stubby rear end and every last yo-ho-ho in between.

As a fantasy, the whole thing was—how you say in the languages of the Caribbean?—perfecto. Magnifique. Smashing. Nobody should have so much fun. Well . . . as it turned out . . . nobody did.

It's a squalid little story, I swear.

Roosters . . . dogs . . . thieving frogs . . . and drawers like they have at the morgue.

There was a waning moon in the warm starry sky when Mrs. Babbs and I arrived at the dock in Rodney Bay, St. Lucia. The *Indies Adventure* was lashed to a pier along with half a dozen other fiberglass rent-a-yachts, and she looked pretty good to me. Forty-seven feet is a lot of boat if most of your sailing experience has been on little day sailers. Of course you don't have to make a *life* among five other people on those little boats, either.

But if I didn't yet know the potential for peevishness among otherwise decent people who go cruising together, Jack had said he did. In his many years before the mast he'd seen more than a few pleasure voyages sail straight into the jaws of hell when those aboard discovered they just didn't like one another enough to put up with the relentless intimacy of life on a boat. Jack and I would be fine together, we knew that. We'd been pals for twenty years, we'd traveled together, we'd even shared my small apartment for several weeks. But the rest of the crew was going to have to be chosen carefully, and that night in Chicago, Jack said he thought he'd come up with a mix that was just right. Along with himself, me, and Mrs. Babbs, he'd invited an illustrator friend of his from London named Fran, a boat builder named Buzz, and Buzz's friend Sonny, who would do the cooking. All of them had been cruising before, he said, and Buzz was one of those mellow salts who'd actually made a voyage around the world. A good group, Jack thought. Then he made a quick sketch of the boat, including kitchen, bathrooms, and beds. He and Fran would take the aft cabin, which was the largest on board and had a double mattress and a single. Mrs. Babbs and I could have the fore cabin with its double bed, and Buzz and Sonny would take the single bunks just aft of the salon on the port side.

It all looked fine to me, but that's only because nowhere in any of the hundred sea stories I'd grown up on had anyone bothered to mention that, to an experienced sailor, where you end up sleeping on a boat is more important than a working compass, and that there has probably been more grisly death at sea over the allotment of beds than from storms or scurvy or the division of plunder.

Unfortunately for Mrs. Babbs and me, all the experienced sailors were on board when we arrived. Everybody said hi, then Jack took our bags and led us below. "Here's your cabin," he said, nodding his head into a room that was just slightly larger than one of Houdini's trunks. There was a little built-in wardrobe adjacent to over/under bunks, which had approximately the same quality of light, the same headroom, as those drawers they have in the morgue. Mrs. Babbs, a Chicago woman who grew up in a family of eight in a two-bedroom apartment under the el tracks, looked at me as if she might weep, or maybe kill someone.

"Jack, you don't expect us to live in there for twelve days," she said.

"You'll get used to it," he told her.

"Maybe we could rotate cabins or something," she said.

"Oh, I don't know," he said. "You might get Buzz and Sonny to trade with you now and then . . . we'll see. Meanwhile, don't live out of your suitcases . . . unpack . . . settle in . . . get comfortable." Then he disappeared topside, leaving me with the vague feeling that I'd just been swindled in some sort of nautical bait-and-switch.

Ah, but that first night, as we sat on deck meeting each other, the soft Carib air made everything seem possible. The Big Dipper was low enough and close enough that you could have swung on the handle, and the warm breeze carried that wonderful jungle smell of something green somewhere smoldering. Now and then, one of the roosters in the hills around the bay would screech something about his territory, then another, then a hundred others would take up the argument till every skinny little fish-eating dog on the island felt compelled to come howling into the riot. Then it would die and leave only the chucking of the water against the hull, and the wind-chime tink of the lines on the tall aluminum masts.

The six of us talked about our possible route among the islands . . . maybe north to Martinique, then south toward the bright water and deserted islands of Tobago Cays. Everything depended on the wind, of course, which was usually straight out of the northeast this time of year . . . but you never know. Jack said we were going to have to lock our dinghy to the boat every night because word on the island trotline had it that the filthy French yachties were stealing them, and he and Buzz remembered back to a time in the southern Caribbean when you didn't have to lock anything. Then, at a certain point, Jack put in that all of us were going to have to make some sacrifices, that things were a bit Spartan on a boat this size. We were going to have to be stingy, for instance, about the way we used water: no long showers. Then he added, "This is not the Love Boat . . . this is not a honeymoon cruise." He didn't look at Mrs. Babbs or me when he said it, but he didn't have to, because as it turns out, on a crowded boat, pointy little remarks like that just sort of fly up into the rigging and hang there like signal pennants that finally spell out "bad blood aboard."

Mrs. Babbs and I made our separate beds that night on either side of the wheel, on the long benches in the cockpit, listening to the barking and the crowing and the occasional resonant bray of a single donkey who could out-shout the whole hillside when he got going.

"I didn't come down here," hissed Mrs. Babbs, "to sleep in an airless little closet for two weeks."

"Don't worry," I told her. "We'll work it out." And I thought we would. But that was only because nowhere in any of those goddamn sea stories did Melville or Conrad or C. S. Forester bother to mention that the sea hates an op-timist.

The next morning broke like that fantasy I'd had standing over the map in Chicago: 80 perfect blue-sky degrees with a few puffy clouds on the horizon for effect. We drove into the crowded little port town of Castries to shop for ba-nanas, mangoes, papayas, cinnamon, and paprika, and to change our money into the eastern Caribbean currency, which is worth about thirty-seven cents to the American dollar. A huge white cruise ship towered over the foot of the main drag looking like something Bugsy Siegel might have built if he hadn't settled on Las Vegas to play out his vision. The disgorged passengers moved in packs along the sidewalks, through the hawk and bustle of the St. Lucians.

We sailed out of Rodney Bay about two that afternoon. Actually we motored out. There's a lot more motoring on a large sailboat than you'd think, because you have to run the big diesel engine two hours a day to keep the batteries charged. Even after we got the sails up and came south onto the light wind along the lee coast of the island, it was hard to tell how much of our four knots was sail and how much was screw, and in the still air belowdecks while we were under power, it smelled a little like we were sailing an oil rig.

Martinique lay off our stern, its beautiful volcanic hump shrinking against the northern horizon. Jack had made a command decision to skip the French island and take us three hours south, down the coast of St. Lucia, for an overnight at a small deepwater bay that was towered over by two huge rock cones called the Pitons. We spotted them an hour away: beautiful, overgrown pinnacles that could have been brought from Yosemite. About three miles from the anchorage, a long, narrow open boat with an outboard came cutting toward us at high speed. She was flying French, German, and American flags from her gunwales, and the two St. Lucians aboard hailed us with big smiles as they came alongside. They wanted to know if they could help us park in the cove, which was going to take a deep anchor and a bowline to one of the palms on shore. Jack said no, that we ought to be doing this sort of thing for ourselves. The men persisted. How much? Ten dollars, E.C. Oh, all right, Jack told them, and they sped off waving happily, yelling they'd meet us there.

As soon as we got the anchor down, other merchants came alongside offering us marijuana, then fresh tuna, which we bought for dinner. Over the rest of the afternoon, we barbecued the fish on the afterdeck, we swam, and we visited an elephant that was rocking neurotically back and forth under the palm forest above the beach. Buzz and Jack said that the absentee owner of the cove had brought the poor young pachyderm from Africa years before and stranded it for reasons nobody understood.

Just before sunset, Buzz and I rowed the dinghy around the limits of the cove to stretch our arms and backs. We watched as the boat boys escorted ship after ship into the cove and moored them with an efficiency that reminded me of the parking lot at Le Dôme or Ciros. By the time the sun hit the sharp blue horizon, they had thirty yachts anchored cheek by jowl between the rock pinnacles that flanked the cove. A rainbow formed itself to the west. A northbound cruise liner turned to silhouette against the intense red splash of the last of the sun. As we pulled back toward the ship, Buzz noted that Jack seemed very uptight to him, and that the two of them were already into a running antagonism over the finer points of how to sail. He said he thought the best thing for him to do was just to fade into the background and let the captain have his way. I told him the captain's way was getting on my nerves.

We ate dinner at the cockpit table in a wind that was beginning to smell like rain, to the beat of Bob Marley and the Wailers coming out of a huge sound system on shore. The local boatmen were camped around a big yellow fire at the base of the North Piton, which was bouncing the reggae across the cove as if it were coming from the rock itself.

"No woman, no cry," sang Marley as Mrs. Babbs and I made our bed on deck, this time on the space just forward of the mast. Sonny and Buzz had rhapsodized to us about how wonderful it was to sleep topside in the open air, and then had added that tonight they might just try it themselves. But after dinner, when Mrs. Babbs had asked the cook if she and her boyfriend were indeed going to take a turn on deck, Sonny hemmed and hawed, saying they hadn't decided and that she didn't know when they'd decide.

Our berth on the bow turned out to be comfortable enough, though, and for half an hour we lay listening to the languid music as it mixed with the happy jabber of French and German coming from the neighboring boats. Now and then the smell of elephant dung swept by on the stiffening breeze. Then it started to rain. Lightly at first, then a little heavier, and by the time our thin blanket was soaked, I knew it was hopeless. We gathered the mattresses and bedding and took them below. I pitched mine on the floor under the dinner table. Mrs. Babbs slept on a couch.

The horrible truth about sailing . . . roosters in the barnyard . . . the wisdom of old Sam Johnson.

I caught Jack in the cockpit first thing in the morning.

"Listen," I said. "You're going to have to work out some sort of cabin rotation."

He went into his little speech about how sacrifices had to be made on a boat, and I told him fine, as long as sacrifice got shared there was no problem. "Fair is fair," I said.

"It doesn't necessarily work that way on a boat," he told me.

"Well it damn well better work that way on this boat," I said, as Mrs. Babbs clambered up the gangway and jumped into the fray. If he'd told her she was going to be stuck in a closet on an airless little bunk bed, she said, she never would have come. Jack looked at the two of us as if he really didn't understand the squall of outrage that had just broken on him; as if we had missed some crucial truth about boats and the sea, a truth so obvious and fundamental that it hadn't occurred to him that he would ever have to speak it.

"Look," he said. "Sailing isn't supposed to be *fun*." He hit the word *fun* as if it were for wimps.

Thinking back, of course, that was the moment at which we should have just spit in each other's eye, said thanks, and scuttled the whole voyage. And actually, we did try to end it. Jack let my stunned silence hang in the beautiful morning air for a few seconds, then said, "I mean if it's going to be like this, I'd just as soon turn around and sail back to Rodney Bay."

"If we can't work it out," I said, "that's just what you're going to have to do."

There was a heavy pause while the implications of our words worked on us.

"Of course we can work it out," Jack said in a tone that called up the original fantasy, and all the planning we'd done, all the warm anticipation that had carried us through the long, cold winter. It couldn't end like this, could it? Barely twelve nautical miles into the cruise? Two old friends standing there in everything that is perfect about the tropics crowing at each other like a couple of roosters at war over some invisible line in the barnyard dirt?

Nothing had been resolved by the time we pulled anchor and struck south on an eight-hour course for Bequia, but at least, I thought, bearings had been taken, positions were known. I spent some of the morning on the fantail watching the wake, thinking that Sam Johnson had been right when he said, "Being in a ship is being in jail, with the chance of being drowned." I think I would have welcomed the threat of drowning that morning; at least it would have broken the sloshing boredom of the day. Truth is, there isn't much to do on a sailboat while you're under way in a light wind. Jack gave each of us a turn at the wheel, but on a straight reach like ours, even that is an uneventful meditation on compass and landmark.

Around noon, Jack got out the sextant and showed me how to shoot the sun with it. It was an academic exercise, since we were never out of sight of one island or another, but I'd always wanted some sense of what it was to steer by the stars, and celestial navigation was one of the things Jack had offered to teach me on the trip. After we'd taken a few sightings, though, he suggested we leave the calculations for later, then slipped back into his funk, whatever it was. When I asked him what was wrong, he said he was fine, just fine, in the tone people get when they don't want to have the conversation you're trying to open. He told me Mrs. Babbs and I could have the aft cabin that night, then went below for a nap.

A wide gray squall brushed us in the last few miles across the channel where the Atlantic and the Caribbean meet between St. Lucia and St. Vincent. The wind came up to about thirty knots, the ship heeled over, got its bow down into the four-foot seas, and for about an hour there was some rodeo to it. Everybody's spirits rose to the action: We trimmed the sails, braced the mast, and then hung on while Jack manhandled the wheel.

"Put another quarter in," I said as the muscle went out of the wind in the lee of St. Vincent, but the high ride was over. We gentled along for another three hours or so, then caught sight of a cruise ship at anchor just outside the mouth of Admiralty Bay, Bequia.

The girl they took to Vegas . . . ugly people ashore . . . Captain Bligh kicks the ladle out of Fletcher Christian's hand.

As we came around the headlands, another ship came into view, this one a huge schooner belching smoke out of one of its four great masts.

"Oh no," said Buzz. "Not that abomination . . . that pig . . . that sorry excuse for a ship . . . *Windstar.* We ought to come back after dark and sink her."

As we motored through her shadow, Jack joined in the litany of nautical disgust. It wasn't really a sailing ship, he explained, it was a cruise liner disguised to look like a sailing ship: 440 feet long, four 200-foot masts that double as smokestacks for the huge engines, seventy-four cabins, the whole thing completely computerized right down to the joystick where the wheel ought to be.

As Jack and Buzz went on about the horridness of the big ship, Mrs. Babbs's sense of kitsch kicked in. "I think it's beautiful," she said. "I bet the beds are *huge*."

A half-hour later we had our anchor down near the head of the bay, and were surrounded on three sides by the palmy hillsides that enfold the thatch and stucco of the little village called Port Elizabeth. Bequia has always been the yachties' favorite among the Grenadines, probably because it is accessible only by boat and has a long maritime tradition back to the days when it was a whaling port. Twenty or thirty ships rode at anchor around us, bobbing on the wakes of the small-boat traffic in the harbor: water taxis, dories selling fruit and knickknacks, shore launches from the cruise ships, even a boat to take you waterskiing.

It was all a bit much for Jack and Buzz. It had been several years since either of them had been to Bequia, and they didn't like the squeeze that had come on the place. "Yeah, it's still pretty," Jack told me when I marveled at the lazy green perfection. "But to me it's like a girl you knew when she was young and beautiful and innocent. Now," he said as we watched a dozen pier boys scrambling and fighting for the bowline of a shore launch, "it's like somebody's taken her to Vegas."

The same theme was echoed that night in a small waterfront restaurant called Mac's. Buzz and Jack had found three old friends in the harbor: an American couple named Bob and Sandy who had lived in Bequia for years, and a photographer from Grenada named Joe. "Speed boats in the bay and ugly people ashore," was the way Bob put the changes. Sandy added that you could actually see a personality change come over the local kids at high season. They worked the bay and the piers like bellboys. "You say hi to some kid you've known for years, a sweet kid," she told us, "and he'll look at you as if to say, 'Not now. I'm working.' Then, come May, the sweetness returns."

Sunset that night was obliterated by *Windstar* as she sat at the mouth of the harbor, her shrouds lit like a Mexican plaza by long strings of bright bare bulbs.

"Gorgeous," said Mrs. Babbs. "I love it."

Jack's mood was not good when he woke from his night on deck. He repossessed his cabin, then took off with the dinghy to visit friends in the harbor, which pretty much stranded the rest of us and left me with the feeling that I was living in a one-car family in Los Angeles.

Mrs. Babbs and I hailed a water taxi and spent the morning on a wild, empty windward beach with Buzz and Sonny. We body-surfed for a while on the small waves, then Buzz and I sat out of the sun in an abandoned stone building, where he talked about his adventures in the Caribbean among the colorful and generally misanthropic characters who are attracted to sailing.

Somewhere in the conversation he asked me why I thought things had grown so brittle on our ship, and I told him I was damned if I knew, but that it didn't seem to be getting any better. He agreed, and when the subject of the water supply aboard the *Indies Adventure* came up, he said he thought Jack's attitude had become a bit strange. I told him I thought "strange" was a kind way to describe it and that the whole thing was starting to remind me of *Mutiny on the Bounty.*

Which it was. Jack had been starchy about our 200 gallons of water before we left the dock, but it had gotten to the point where every time he heard a tap go on for even a moment, he'd yell, "Mind the water, now." Mrs. Babbs and I hadn't even taken a shower since we'd sailed, and as far as I could tell everyone else was using the supply just as carefully. Nevertheless, shortly after we'd sailed out of the Pitons, Jack had gone nuts on Mrs. Babbs as she stood at the sink in the galley. No one had told her that when the engine is running, *all* the water on this boat was hot, and she had opened the tap and given it about ten seconds to run cool. When Jack saw what she was doing, he'd yelled, "What's the matter with you? Don't do that . . . my God . . ." And on and on, too long and too loud and too crazy. I stood silent a few feet away, trying to match the outburst with the incident, and feeling very much as if I had just watched Captain Bligh kick a ladle out of Fletcher Christian's hand.

On the beach that morning, Buzz said that Jack had told him that he wasn't going to top off the tanks in Bequia because it cost something like sixteen cents a gallon, and, besides that, he just didn't think it was good sailing form to fill up every time you had a chance.

The whining conch . . . the death of yo-ho-ho . . . rats on a rope in Union Island.

Mrs. Babbs and I spent the afternoon walking the island, but no matter what stunning panorama, or perfect beach, or great green jungle gully we came onto, the conversation always pulled back to the pissy little details of life aboard our humorless barge.

In a way, I knew the situation was classic: groups, friends, couples go out camping, river running, sailing, under the cruel delusion that they know each other and can pull together happily, only to come back wishing death and pestilence on one anothers' heads. I've even heard of expeditions hiring psychologists onto their trips to cool hot blood and bandage torn egos. Still, it had never occurred to me that such contentiousness would overtake this trip, in this place. I felt as if I'd traveled to paradise, found a perfect conch, put the shell to my ear, and heard the sound of children arguing over a nickel.

It wasn't all Jack's fault, I knew that. I'd become pretty pugnacious myself when efforts at conciliation had failed, and had even begun looking for trouble. But something about taking on the captaincy of our voyage had turned Jack, my old buddy, a guy who had spent years telling me how he'd chased a disorderly kind of fun across the Caribbean, into somebody I didn't know: a stiff, moody, abrupt character who seemed to have turned back on the original spirit of the enterprise before we even set sail. I tried to talk to him about it, but it didn't work. Instead, he kept telling me that life on a ship wasn't a democracy and didn't include the normal civilities, the manners, you could expect on land; and I kept telling him that in close quarters, the small courtesies seemed to me all the more important. When it became clear that neither of us was listening to the other, a poisonous silence took up between us.

Mrs. Babbs and I decided to take a hotel room that night to avoid another snarling spat over bunks. We had dinner on board, then, just after dark, as we prepared to go ashore, a local dinghy pulled alongside and the boys in it launched into a sorry version of "Yellow Bird." They finished and asked for money.

"We didn't ask you to sing," Buzz tried to tell them.

"You should have stopped us," they said.

The exchange turned bellicose after that, and when Buzz finally shined a flashlight in their eyes and told them to shove off, one of them raised a large stumpy stick and shouted, "You see this club? I will remember your face. I will remember your dinghy. I take care of you when you come ashore."

I came on deck just as they rowed off, just in time to hear one of them yelling, "We come back later tonight and blow your boat to *smithereens.*"

As their nasty laughter receded across the dark bay, I thought to myself, save yourself the trip, boys, because as far as I can tell this boat is going to blow *itself* to smithereens, and the blast is going to shred every sail and sink every dinghy in this harbor.

In the morning all of us agreed that another day on the island was a good idea, and we pretty much went separate ways. Jack changed his mind and filled the water tanks, then disappeared with the dinghy again. Mrs. Babbs and I walked, spent some time on the beach, and that afternoon found Fran in one of the waterfront bars. She had managed to stay almost entirely apart from the bad feelings aboard, spending long hours alone with her book. When the inevitable subject came up, she said that nothing was much different than it had been the other times she'd sailed with Jack. "It's just the way he is on a boat," she said. "You just have to sort of ignore it. Everyone who's ever sailed with him calls him Captain Bligh. It's his nickname."

We ended the conversation holding out the hope that things might get better, but I didn't believe it, and in a way it was a relief that night when I started yelling at Jack, who started yelling at Mrs. Babbs, who started yelling at Sonny over the music of steel drums at a hotel jump-up in Friendship Bay. Fran and Buzz had stayed on the ship, perhaps because they sensed that the huge billious bubble of acrimony was about to explode, and they were right. It got nasty early. It got cheap and it got low. In fact, it occurred to me several times in the angry free-for-all that fists and feet would have done much less damage than the verbal slash-and-slur that got loose that night. It was amazing: The band played "Down the way where the lights are gay" while the four of us sat there and beat the crap out of each other's spirits.

Exhaustion finally ended the mayhem. Nothing had been resolved. Jack suggested we wait till the next day to make any decisions and I agreed, although it felt like the death of yo-ho-ho to me.

Ah, but these things are never over when they're over, and somehow the next morning everybody was urging everybody to make another try. Jack drew up a rotation schedule for the big beds, and I decided what the hell . . . one more island . . . one more bead on this fool's rosary . . . why not? Who knows, I thought, it might even give me a chance to smooth my neck feathers back down into a more gentlemanly nap, maybe give me time to accept that common points of decency get left on the dock when you cast off, that sailing is supposed to be punishment, not fun.

Yeah, right.

It was four hours to Union Island, and five minutes out Jack made a remark that convinced me that we were going to find about as much union at Union as we had found friendship in Friendship Bay. He spotted a ship he had once sailed on, a lovely sleek clipper, and he said, "I'll bet they're headed for Antigua. I wish I were going with them."

"Well then, get out the goddamn flare gun," I almost said. "Rig the boatswain's chair, hail them on the radio, whatever it takes."

Instead I got out the map, and when I saw there was a small airport on Union, I knew it was just a matter of waiting for the right moment to run like a rat across the next line that connected us to land.

It came around noon, a day later. Mrs. Babbs and I were on the beach, waiting for Jack to pick us up in the dinghy. After a while, Mrs. Babbs decided she'd swim out and get him while I waited with our packs on shore. When she was about halfway to the ship, I saw Jack set out in the little boat, saw Mrs. Babbs wave to him from the water, and watched as he ignored her and made for the shoreline where I stood waving and pointing.

"Was that Mrs. Babbs?" he said as he drifted into the beach. "I saw somebody waving, but I thought, I don't know anybody out here, so I just kept going."

It was an awkward moment, and it grew worse when he suggested that Mrs. Babbs was the problem, that she didn't seem to be a boat person, and that perhaps I ought to consider putting her on a plane and flying her out. I said that sounded like a great idea . . . and that I'd be getting on it with her. Other things were said; hard things, some of them. But finally there wasn't a lot of anger left in either of us. Mostly, I think, we were just deeply relieved to be out from under the grinding failure of what had seemed like such a sunny plan as we stood over that map sailing our index fingers from island dot to island dot, unable to imagine the trouble that lay for us in every blue half-inch.

DECEMBER 1988

THE SKIING LIFE

by JAMES SALTER

We left Munich in the morning and had lunch near Garmisch at a restaurant on the edge of a frozen pond. From there we drove on to Innsbruck and toward the Arlberg and St. Anton. By then it was late in the day.

How pure it all was, how carefree. The road had begun to be icy. It started to snow. Three or four miles from St. Anton a train went past us in the dusk, the lighted windows, the swift, slender cars. In town the streets were snow covered and there were barns mixed in with the houses and hotels.

We were skiing for the first time, or almost the first—I had previously gone for a day or two—moved by images of elegant-looking people and the glamorous names of certain towns. The instructors—farmers and carpenters—spoke English, since the British had been coming there for years. We went up with unfamiliar equipment in a cable car, a long, unsettling ride. It was just ten years after the war, and life in Europe was still hard. There were people who had walked up, not able to afford a ticket, starting before daylight and sitting in the sun at the top eating bread and cheese from their knapsacks before starting down. There were others with only one leg.

The snow was deep that first day. I was in the wrong class; I fell at every turn. The head instructor motioned me over after lunch. "I thought you could do stem turns," he said, since that was what I had told him. "I thought so, too," I said.

In the beginning it seems so difficult, the sequence of things escapes you, the snow grabs your edges or slips from beneath, the falls are exhausting. What enables you to learn? It's simple: desire. Twenty years later I sat in a small hotel in Wengen listening to Ingemar Stenmark, a Swedish idol if there ever was one—it is not an unknown breed—talk about his career. He was unmistakable in a race. He came down as if he owned the course, in powerful gulps and with incredible authority, slamming the poles aside with his shoulders as if he were batting balls. He had fallen in the slalom that day, which was rare—he was twenty-five years old and nearing the end of his career but still skiing as if everything in the world depended on it. He was asked, among other things, what he felt had given him his greatness. "Desire," he said, and added, "I don't think I have talent to an extraordinary degree." It was desire and work, he said, as one of the rewards, a tall blonde, came in and put his running jacket on the couch beside him in preparation for supper.

You continue to try. This snow is windswept, the instructor explains. This is called marble. This is powder. Follow me closely, he says, as if you can, turn where I turn. Somehow you follow, trying to do what he does, forgetting some things, remembering others. The trail is narrowing, you are going faster than you should and farther, beyond your endurance. Suddenly he swings against the slope, comes to a stop, and looks back as astonishingly you do the same. *"Jawohl!"* The sweetness of that word.

One morning you wake unaware that, mysteriously, something has changed. This day it comes to you, the ability to slip where he slips, to turn where he turns, to begin to imitate the set of his shoulders, the resilience of his knees. All day, run after run, filled with an immense, unequaled happiness, and at the end into town together, down the last, rolling slopes, and so weary that you fall asleep after supper in your ski clothes, the lights burning throughout the night.

In April we skied again and afterward went down to Venice. The Gritti was inexpensive then. The floors were marble and the hallways lit by lanterns held by gilt Moorish hands. Anyway you can say you've been there. In fact it was dull. We drove back through Udine and Cortina. I was thinking about the following year and asked the prices. Room, bath, and demipension in season was 3,600 lire, at the time about six dollars.

We never made it back to Cortina. We skied in many other places in Europe over the years, including Kitzbühel and Wengen, where the big races are held, the Hahnenkamm and Lauberhorn, the classics, always in the middle of January.

Racing in Europe is a heroic sport, more popular than it is in America and far more rewarding. Huge crowds gather along the course, ringing cowbells and shouting "Hopp! Hopp! Hopp!" as the racers come down, and hundreds of reporters are there.

I skied the Hahnenkamm once with Toni Sailer. He was a member of Kitzbühel's famous *Wunderteam:* Hinterseer, Pravda, Sailer, Leitner, Huber, and Molterer, all of them young and hard. Molterer won a silver and a bronze in the 1956 Olympics in Cortina. Hinterseer won a gold medal in 1960 at Squaw Valley. Sailer did what no other man but Killy has ever done. He swept the three events at the Olympics, winning the downhill, slalom, and giant slalom at Cortina, and two years later at the World Championships won two more golds. It was not only the victories but the margin of them that is legendary—he won the Olympic downhill by three full seconds, the slalom by four, and the giant slalom by six. As I recall, Killy won the Olympic downhill at Grenoble by a slim two or three hundredths of a second.

By the time I met Sailer he was in his early forties, handsome, laconic, and very fit—following his successes he had for a while been a movie actor. We went up early in the morning, in silence, before sunrise.

The Hahnenkamm is the undisputed king of the downhills. It is especially difficult at the top and also near the finish. The women don't race it; they don't have the physical strength for it, the compressions where the terrain suddenly flattens after a steep pitch, or the fall-away turns. When a racer first comes to Europe all he hears about is the Hahnenkamm and the horror stories, "I was going eighty miles an hour in the fog," the terrible crashes, bodies covered with blood borne away on stretchers. Twenty-five or thirty thousand people come to see it, and millions more watch on television.

There was no one there that morning. The starting hut was empty. As we walked toward it I heard Sailer sniff and mutter, "Cold."

"You have a cold?"

"No, the weather."

I asked him as a matter of, to me, historical interest how many times he had skied the course. He took this to mean races, but I wanted a broader figure, like the number of consecutive games Lou Gehrig had played; I said not just races, practice, too.

"That doesn't count," he said.

We cruised down the course, naturally. Rather, he was cruising, and we stopped two or three times en route. The top was as menacing as its reputation. Somewhere along in the middle was the Alteschneise, the Old Cut, where he had fallen one year in a race, and it was there that he let slip a pronouncement of, up to that point, record length. "You're skiing very well," he said. I may have been—I didn't feel it. I felt like the boxer who has a cold bucket of water thrown on him and hears someone say, "Wake up, you won the fight." I also felt lucky he hadn't seen me go down on a hand and one knee at the first turn on top.

We stopped at the final pitch, the Ganslern, out of the bottom of which, in a race, they hit ninety miles an hour. "Where the shadow of the trees is," Sailer said, pointing out the spot. The snow was perfect here, none of the ice there had been at the start. Down we went.

He became amiable afterward. I asked him some questions about racing. Though he had been more or less superhuman, he confessed that it was hard to bring yourself to believe you were the best. What was the most important quality of all? I asked. He cited virtually the same thing Stenmark did: will. Then becoming almost chatty, he said, "There are things you can learn in ski racing and things you can't learn. They could all be good downhill racers if they had the guts and the will."

A Frenchman I sat next to once on a plane joined me, out of sheer boredom probably, in a discussion about life. To throw him off I took the position that life in Europe, in his own country in particular, was in many ways better than life in the United States, a perhaps exuberant view but I was just seeing how things would go. "The bread is better," I said.

"The bread? Yes, perhaps."

"The food is better," I continued. He shrugged and almost at the same time nodded a little. Between us there was the enthusiasm of men comparing wives. "The attention to the details of life," I went on.

"Yes, yes," he said, "but the United States has given something more important to the world. The modern world would not exist without it."

"What's that?"

"They invented credit."

Plastic. It applies to more than credit cards in the modern world. There was a time before the advent of crowds, when Europe was not awash in money—in fact when there was something of a drought—when ski boots were made of leather, often to order and delivered within two or three days. They put your foot down on a piece of brown wrapping paper, traced it, took a few measurements, and when you came back, there were your boots. That was the ancient regime. Karl Molitor, who lives in Wengen, had a factory and used to manufacture leather boots. He was also a racer and had an idea of what a boot should be. He raced in the Lauberhorn, of course, which is above Wengen, and as with Sailer I once went down the course with him on a *Besichtigung*, as he said, a reconnaissance. Accompanying us was a beautiful Swiss woman in a close-fitting ski suit. I never quite understood what relationship she had to the course or to Molitor, but I accepted it as part of national enthusiasm for the race, which is of such dimension that if a Swiss wins there is no closing time for the bars.

You reach the start of the course by taking the train from Wengen up to Kleine Scheidegg, and then a ski lift. The Lauberhorn is a very long race, about 2.7 miles, some 30 percent longer than most races, and it has, as one racer described, everything: changes in terrain, difficult turns, steepness in places, and the hardest part at the end. "You have to pace yourself more," he said. "Decide how much you can give." This makes it a bit more strategic than a simple all-out assault.

The morning we skied was the day of the race, and we were allowed on because Molitor was the chief of the course. At the time he was in his early sixties, though he appeared at least ten years younger. It had snowed; there was a cold, fresh layer on the ground, the first snow in several weeks. Molitor took a turn or two in it. "The snow's too good for racing," he commented as we started down.

The beginning is gradual. The first big pitch is the Dog's Head—the racers would be in the air here, Molitor called out. The turns before the bridge, he said a little later, were critical. "You can lose more time on the slow part than you can gain on the fast."

The most famous feature is a place on the course called the Austrian Hole, where one year the entire Austrian team crashed. Finally there is a last, steep schuss, not particularly long, but thought-provoking. "No turns here," Molitor warned; this was to avoid any marring of the surface. I watched him go down, then the Swiss woman. Then I went. It felt fast.

Molitor had won the race six times, he admitted. "When was that?" I asked. "A hundred years ago," he said carelessly.

Later that day I watched the race. There was a mist—actually thin, low-hanging clouds on the upper part of the course, out of which the racers shot in their skin-tight suits, past crowds and black trees, flying in the air at top speed, curving around crucial turns. As it happened, the bars didn't stay open late; an Austrian won that year.

For several weeks before the 1968 Winter Olympics in Grenoble, Robert Redford—who was to be the star of *Downhill Racer*, the movie we were working on—and I traveled with the U.S. ski team, taking in the daily routine and avidly listening to conversations, in defiance of Matisse's famous dictum that exactitude is not truth. The most visible and important figure on the team was Billy Kidd; there were hopes he would win the downhill or slalom. He was from New England, a region of damp, bitter winters and often icy runs. I saw him and the associated bleakness as being the right thing for the movie's hero. I never had an opportunity to talk much to Kidd, who was either arrogant or shy, possibly both, but I had worked it all out in my mind and one night at dinner explained it at length to Redford.

He shook his head, No, not Kidd, he had someone else in mind.

"Who?"

"At the end of the table there."

He was referring to a blond, virtually unacknowledged member of the team whose principal distinction, as far as I could tell, was the number of times he boasted he had broken his leg. His name was Spider Sabich. Like Redford he was from California, and I realized that Redford had picked him out because he saw in him a type he knew very well: himself.

Over the next few years I got to know Sabich and it became obvious that Redford's judgment was good: He was an admirable fellow. He raced professionally; in fact he was largely responsible for the popularity of professional ski racing and became its world champion, a somewhat dubious title, but like Redford he achieved stardom. (Redford did not become a star because of *Downhill Racer*. Against all advice from his agent he grew a mustache to play the Sundance Kid opposite Paul Newman, and it was this that did the trick.) Sabich was not as lucky with his own costar, Claudine Longet, who during an argument and out of jealousy shot and killed him one day in Aspen, Colorado. Sabich had made a business of winning, often by the smallest margin, and it was by a very small margin that he died—Longet had shot him with a .22 pistol, which ordinarily would not have done much damage, but the bullet just nicked the aorta and he bled to death before anything could be done.

I went to Aspen to ski the first time in 1959 and immediately broke my arm, though that did not color my impressions. There were two doctors in town at that time, neither of them millionaires, and you did not have to have an appointment. One of them put the arm in a cast, and I went back to skiing a day or two later at reduced proficiency. There was also a fellow in those days who parked his car at the foot of the mountain and for the annual premium of a dollar would drive you to the hospital if anything happened to you on the slopes. In short, it was cozy.

When we moved there about ten years later, they had paved the streets but dogs still walked across as if they owned them and sometimes sat down to meditate in an intersection.

The early glory of Aspen had been intense but brief. The town was born in 1878 and from the beginning flourished, but with the collapse of silver in 1893 there was a long, slow decline like that of a car abandoned in a field—the seats disappear, the steering wheel, the tires and doors; finally there is only a rusted skeleton, even the engine gone. In the same manner the wooden houses of Aspen, the streetcar lines and hotels, melted away.

The old crowd, members of the generation that was born in town after the silver boom, was still around at the end of the 1960s, though thinned by adversity and the years. A bartender I knew took me around to the office of one of the heirs to a great Aspen mining fortune. He was one of two brothers who had owned a renowned mine, the Smuggler, as well as others. When we arrived he was wearing a pearl gray, wrinkled suit, a white shirt with the collar points askew, and a wide silk tie. His pants, I noticed, were fastened with a large paper clip. He wore a hat on the side of his head and there was an aroma in the air of tobacco and whiskey. "Rick," he said to the bartender, "you'll help me move some things out of here, won't you?"

The things turned out to be a huge horsehair couch at least sixty years old and a set of large matching chairs. We managed to get them down three flights and onto the street, where a truck was waiting. It was evidently some sort of corporate relocation. "They're heavy," we remarked as we struggled outside with the last chair. "You're lucky he's not sitting in it," said the truck driver, who seemed to have some knowledge of things.

Coming back upstairs, damp with sweat, Rick said offhandedly, "Is that all? How about the safe?"

"No, no," the old magnate said, "but you're going to help me unload everything, aren't you?"

There was no one at the apartment we drove to, so we left the furniture outside. Afterward he wanted to pay us. "How much do you boys want?" he said.

"How much have you got?" Rick asked.

"Will two dollars be enough?"

"Two dollars! That's an insult."

"Come on over to the Onion," the tycoon offered genially, "and I'll buy you some drinks."

The Red Onion was a bar from the mining days and one of the best restaurants in town. I don't remember now who paid for the drinks. The old veteran had very little money, it turned out. He'd been married to a girl from Leadville, and when they were about to divorce he signed his half of everything over to his brother so she wouldn't get it. The brother never gave it back.

We lived in the west end of Aspen, which was the old residential section. The town was still relatively indifferent to fashion. Skiing began on Thanksgiving Day when you came down from the mountain, face seared by the cold, unseasoned legs weary, and sat down to the most memorable of meals. Around Easter, skiing ended—in early April, when occasionally some of the biggest storms came.

When we lived in the East you drove for hours to ski and often waited in long lines. Skiing was a kind of pilgrimage. In Aspen it was different, it surrounded you, winter and skiing. There were the still hot days of early October cutting wood in the forest and the first white dusting of distant peaks, the nights growing colder, autumn ending, the blizzards and epic days, the evening fire soaring around logs you had split yourself, breakfast in town with exhaust drifting up in the cold from cars with glazed windows. The world was far away; in fact this was the world. To the south and west the clouds would turn dark blue, and a certain smell, like the smell of rain, lay in the air. Tremendous storms coming, the roofs piled high with snow.

There are days, months, even years when you feel invincible, dropping down the back of Bell, Corkscrew, Moment of Truth as if slipping down the stairs, edges biting, bumps disappearing in your knees. The memory of it all will stay forever. You hate to have it end. You are slicing the mountain as if with a knife. Of course even on great days there is always that lone skier, oddly dressed, off to the side past the edge of the run, going down where it is steepest and the snow untouched, in absolute grace, marking each dazzling turn with a brief jab of the pole—there is always him, the skier you cannot be. Afterward the hotness of the bath, darkness falling, the snow deep outside, couples in the street downtown, the restaurants filled, faces you know.

There are dull days on the mountain and days of indescribable joy, the runs empty, the air speckled with cold. People come to town who've been given your name, people come to dinner—the winter brings you together, somehow makes you friends. You become a kind of guide. Ex–hot shots on their college ski teams, confident despite years in the city and wiggling their hips in anticipation, say, "Let's go" and "You lead the way." In a minute or two they're passing by in an approximation of their old form, still ready to compete. Skiing is a little like dancing, grace seeks to be admired. "Where to?" they cry. "What next?"

"Oh, let's go straight ahead, there's a run just over the crest." It's a narrow, bumpy chute, invisible until you are practically on it, and will instill a sense of moderation—for a long time it also had a tree in a very inconvenient spot. At the bottom when they arrive, you merely remark, "That was great, wasn't it?"

"What's that called again?"

"Blondie's."

At dinner once there was a movie producer, a charming man naturally, with a good-looking girl he had found in Vail. She'd been working in a lodge there. "There are two things I like about Vail," I acknowledged, but the talk rushed on, they wouldn't let me finish. Later she leaned over to me. "Tell me something," she said.

"What?"

"I want to know what the two things are."

"Two names," I said, "the names of two runs, Adios and Forever."

And so it seems—the years cannot touch you, the disasters roll past. Jack Nicholson reigns in the Jerome Bar wearing a baseball cap and an uncynical smile. He is king of the place and even the town, a new king, everyone eager to be touched by his existence, young men in cowboy hats, doe-eyed girls. A page has been turned; new people are coming, the terrifying young splendid in their clothes, men in their twenties with their hair gathered tight in back, girls like addicts, *Vogue* on the outside, vague on the inside, as they say. I think back to the casual days. On a bulletin board outside a place called the Mineshaft I once saw a piece of paper pinned among the For Sales that said, WANTED, RIDE TO THE EAST, TWO GIRLS, WILL TRADE ASS FOR GAS.

There was a woman I knew who used to ski every day, all season long, whatever the weather, whatever the conditions. She was born to it, you might say— her father had been a racer on the Austrian team. Tall and sleek, she was married and had two small children; I often saw them on the slopes. Of course, she skied wonderfully, a natural. If you were too busy to ski, disinclined, or away, you knew she was there nevertheless. It was a kind of pact. One didn't know the terms, but they could be guessed at—her father had been killed while skiing, caught in an avalanche. She was being faithful to that, somehow. Other aspects of her life were in turmoil.

One afternoon I was in Denver and the phone rang. A friend was calling to say there had been an accident, an avalanche, and Meta had been caught in it. They were all up searching for her, probing the snow with long poles. I looked out the hotel window as we talked—it was already dark.

She had gone off by herself, skiing down out of bounds. Lots of people did it. Her husband had been worried when she hadn't come home at the usual hour. It was her husband who found her. They dug her out in the dark and carried her body down. There are people killed every year in snowslides in Colorado and throughout the West, but not always emblematic people, not always goddesses. Later someone told me that she died on the very same day her father had, years before. I never bothered to confirm it, but I think it must be true; I think it was part of the pact.

Times change and things change. It was a beautiful town once, comfortable and decayed. The winters were long and dazzling, no one locked anything, we were countrymen. Slowly it altered. They brought the cities with them and the cities' ways. Meta Burden is gone, Ralph Jackson, Fred Iselin, Bugsy. Not everyone has died, but they seem to have vanished, gone away. Sometimes the old town appears again, for a few moments, like a ship seen at sea in the mist. The snow is falling, you are on the mountain, and there, half-blurred and thrilling, it lies at your feet.

I gave, over the years, a lot to skiing, by which I merely mean time and certain broken bones. The bones have healed—I can't even say which shoulder or leg it was—and the time was not wasted. I say that because so much of it is remembered and what is truly wasted is time you have nothing to show for and cannot recall. I never went on the Haute Route or to the Bugaboos, but the rest of it is part of me.

I was going up on the lift one time with a young boy—this was in Vermont long ago—who was about eight or nine years old. He had blond, English hair and a nice face. He turned to me as one would to a friend, and, snowy world all about us, confided, "It's quite fun, isn't it?"

He was quite right.

DECEMBER 1992

PERUVIAN GOTHIC

by KATE WHEELER

Geographers writing in Spanish often refer to Peru's eastern Andes as *muy accidentado*, "very accidented." The same could be said of the lives shaped in these devastating mountains. If you live between Cajamarca and Chachapoyas, between the Marañón and Huallaga Rivers, you could have as a neighbor a man whose name is Hitler, or Himmler, or Lenin, or Nixon, but who's never heard of the famous man he's named after. Or a nun who fell in love with a terrorist, left the convent, and became the leader of a hit squad. Or an ex-soldier who wanted to make his fortune but instead was sold as a slave to a gold mine and barely escaped with his life.

Those people live relatively close to roads, police, schools—civilization. But as you travel east from the sere peaks of the Andes and fall into the green-black, steaming jungle, the lives become even more excessive, filled with more danger. This tropical montane forest contains some of the thickest under-growth in the world. Within six months, any machete-cut trail utterly disappears. Unless you count survival, revenge, and desire as laws, no law has penetrated this region since Inca totalitarianism fell apart more than four centuries ago. For a time in the 1700s, Spanish Franciscans tried to convert it into a paradise of cinnamon, coca, and cotton plantations farmed by Indians, but forest and natives alike proved inhospitable to life on any terms but their own. The priests fled in the early 1800s. Soon the natives were all gone, too; some migrated, and the rest died of smallpox and other European-borne diseases.

This wilderness had been literally empty of human life for the better part of 200 years when Benigno Añazco, a determined mestizo from a small highland village, began chopping his way into the no-man's-land of the forest, reopening the Inca roads of stone.

Nearly everyone who lives in this part of northeastern Peru has heard the story of Añazco, or at least some version of it, and he is known, with some affection, as Don Beni. Sometime around 1960, they say, the devout Seventh-Day Adventist gathered his wife and children and vanished into the woods. He built one house, then another. Around house number three his wife tired of their hacking progress and took most of the kids back to town. Añazco kept one daughter for himself and pushed on for twenty years more. Now he lives in a remote corner of Peru's San Martín Department with his Bible, his transistor radio, his daughter-wife, and their four (of eight) surviving children.

People say that Añazco killed his son-in-law, shot him point-blank in the chest with a shotgun. The young man wanted to put in a cocaine airstrip, and Añazco would not abide drugs in his kingdom.

He's got 800 head of cattle, they say. Owns more than a dozen houses, each piled high with dried meat and fortified with guns. They say he can tell a man to stand at the edge of a stream, close his eyes, and count to 500, and by the end of that time Añazco can show him ten fresh trout laid out on the riverbank. They say he has the pelt of a humanlike being that he shot in the wilderness; the beast was hiding behind a tree, whistling.

For years at a time, he would pause to farm, always near ruins: Ancient terraces, he discovered, mark fertile soil. Once he deviated from the Inca roads and spent years on a detour that took him into a maze of swamps that proved impassable. There was no food; several of his children died. He backtracked to his original course and continued on, sacrificing everything, including his family's well-being, for a vision: He would open the jungle all the way to the city of Saposoa, sixty miles east, founding villages along the way. Pineapples would be exchanged for potatoes. The poor of the highlands would farm on land where seeds wouldn't go to waste. Soon the government would build a modern highway. Hunger would disappear. The glories of the Inca empire would live again.

Peru is unmapped south of the Ecuadoran border, between the Marañón and the Huallaga, north of Cajamarca. Political maps are mostly blank, except for rivers that tend to be misnamed and shown running north-south, 90 degrees off course. Due to the difficult surveying conditions, topographic maps simply don't exist. And because archaeologists have generally avoided the region, the ruins dotting the valleys and drainages east of the Andes are encrusted with the opinions of weird amateurs, self-serving mystics, corrupt officials, and superstitious peasants.

Yet there is at least one independent scholar, a German-born ethnohistorian named Peter Lerche, who has made it his life's work to study the region. He married locally, renounced his German passport, and now lives along the edge of the rainforest on an isolated farm, where he returns from explorations to write up his findings in various self-published pamphlets and books.

I met Lerche in 1994 on an archaeological tour of the Peruvian city of Chachapoyas. He was a muscular, eerily concentrated man with blue tattoo lines fanning down his cheekbones in imitation of the Machiguenga people of Ecuador and Peru. Lerche claimed he was the only outsider who had seen Añazco in decades. It had been back in 1989. He was scouting from a tree in an area of jungle he thought was uninhabited when he spotted Añazco's cattle herd. Añazco spent weeks showing Lerche the local ruins, including one Inca sacred site whose exquisite polygonal stonework, in pink sandstone, rivals that of Cuzco. Lerche calls it Puca Huaca (Red Temple) and thinks its presence shows that Inca power extended deeper into the eastern forests than most scholars had assumed.

Yes, he said, Añazco had murdered his son-in-law. Yes, he'd had children with his daughter. "But the world would be a poorer place without such people," he contended. "Añazco is in his late sixties now. People don't last long out there. You want to meet him?"

It was more than a year before we could arrange an expedition. Besides Lerche, photographer Steve Alvarez, and me, our six-person party included my old friend Oscar Arce, a local guide and outdoorsman who first told me Añazco's tale; Segundo Huamán Huamán, a soft-spoken twenty-year-old peasant and a friend of Arce's; and Julio César Soto Valle, an ambitious radio repairman from Chachapoyas who'd once worked in a cocaine factory to assist his family's fortunes. For our safety, we brought along two shotguns and a 9-mm Beretta pistol.

It took eighteen hours in an open truck to reach our takeoff point, the highland town of Bolívar, not far from Añazco's birthplace. From here, Lerche said it would take eleven hard days to reach Añazco's log cabin, on a tableland known as La Meseta—that is, if he was still there and hadn't moved even deeper into the wilderness. A major Inca highway begins in Bolívar, leading eastward over a 13,000-foot pass and down into the jungle. The road is part of the vast, 15,000-mile network of amazingly well built highways that held the ancient empire together. Cubic paving stones are visible at the edge of town, though there's been no maintenance since the Spanish Conquest diverted Inca energies from public works.

We followed this route down the backside of the mountain, spending the first night in a ruined Inca *tambo*, or guest house, at 10,000 feet. Then we dropped into the forested Yonán River valley and followed this to the confluence of the Yonán and Huabayacu, where another Inca road was visible running southeast toward La Morada, a village founded by Añazco's former wife. She still lived there, or so we were told, along with several sons and daughters. We hoped they'd be willing to tell us Añazco's present whereabouts.

Up close, the forest had little romance. Rain, mud, slopes, vines, cliffs, sinkholes, swamps, thorns, ants, mosquitoes, and biting flies. We crossed whitewater canyons on bridges made of rotten logs, pulled ourselves up cliffs on pencil-thin roots, and fought our way through thickets of bamboo. Any Inca highway that may have existed along the river valley had long since sunk into thigh-deep bogs. No imagination was required to see how Añazco could have spent a lifetime hacking through this terrain. Alvarez and I soon learned to stuff one cheek with an enormous wad of coca leaves, activated with powdered lime. Drooling green, looking like old-style toothache cartoons, the expedition chugged along, our optimism mildly enhanced.

One horrid day we found ourselves shuddering in a cave, trapped for hours, watching the endless sheets of rain. Lerche chose this place to tell us the story of what had happened to the last U.S. citizens who tried to cross through this area. In 1913, two engineers from Chicago, William Cromer and William Page, formed a partnership with the brothers Mirko and Stevo Seljan, two Croatian engineers who had successfully explored the Sudan, Central Africa, Patagonia, and Brazil's Xingu River. With sponsorship from Chicago investors and the Vienna and Lima Geographic societies, the expedition hoped to sell land to eager colonists from the United States. "Virginal, luxurious, rich, and inviting" was how their expedition's prospectus described this swath of jungle.

The Croatians and Americans split up, planning to meet halfway between the Huallaga and the Andes. The two parties were never heard from again, and no bodies were found. A 1920 report in the bulletin of the Lima Geographic Society says, somewhat cryptically, that "the Americans were more or less assassinated near [Bolívar]." In 1922, the bulletin noted that a British World War I pilot had gone in search of the 1913 expedition, finding nothing but a hand-drawn map and rumors of foul play that seemed to point to a porters' mutiny. The bulletin then went on to note, "The very nature of the ground, quite sinuous and accidented, seems to take pleasure in crushing adventurers who cross it for the first time, heaping upon them all of its penalties and plagues."

• • •

Within a few days we had slipped into Añazco's kingdom. One afternoon we met a family of settlers living in a small cabin set in a slash-and-burn clearing. They were not relatives of Añazco, but they knew about him, knew that he had come before them, opening up the jungle. Lerche had brought along snapshots of Añazco, his daughter-wife, and their pale, expressionless children. The family pored over the photographs, mesmerized. "So that is him, and that is Margarita. And look, there are the children, poor little things." They sang us a ballad about Don Beni and gave us directions to La Morada.

All places were marked by Añazco's imagination. Osiris, House of Gold, the Enchanted City, the Vineyard, the Garden, Angola. Añazco's place names were culled from his dreams, fantasies, convictions, or the war reports he listened to on his transistor as he began to work new land. In this country without maps, directions were poetic: A couple hours' walk downriver, we'd see Orpheus across the valley. After nine bridges we'd reach Israel.

Orpheus, an abandoned cabin used as a travelers' rest stop, sat on a lawn as green and misty as any in England, overlooking the Huabayacu. The Añazcos got there in 1960, their first year of exploration. A day's journey downriver, Israel was substantial, a house of rammed earth. The Añazco family lived there longest, from 1966 to 1972.

The Huabayacu Valley must have been densely populated during Inca and pre-Inca times. Our trail passed by innumerable ruined dwellings, crumbled walls, and terraces. Along the cliffs were many tombs, often decorated with ocher paintings of jaguars and scorpions. High along the far shore, we traced the indentation of an Inca highway that Añazco had cleared and followed. Yet these signs of domestication and culture, while everywhere, were barely discernible behind the scrim of foliage. It was oddly comforting to be so thickly surrounded by evidence that ecosystems recover, if left alone. I imagined rediscovering my own Massachusetts neighborhood centuries after invasion and plague, its driveways filled up with weed maples, its aluminum-sided houses swallowed in green.

Civilization! La Morada (the Purple One) is a town of more than 200 people, pioneering families that Añazco's ex-wife somehow managed to recruit from villages to the west. It's named for the purple flowers that cover a nearby limestone cliff in the spring. The town contains the ruins of a Spanish church as well as a denser share of ancient stones. No accident: In this part of the world, a flat spot the size of a soccer field is cause for major settling-in.

To us, La Morada looked like heaven. Children raced around the school grounds. Arce and Huamán went to buy cane liquor and a chicken. Hymns resounded from Seventh-Day Adventist gatherings. Pigs are commonplace in most Peruvian villages, but here we saw only one hog wandering the lanes: Adventism maintains that pork fills the body with demons.

La Moradans presented a united façade. Theirs was a town of goodness. They insisted we ignore any rumors we might have heard that La Morada was a stronghold for drugs or terrorism—never would they allow such things. Here lived Añazco's former wife, Noelita Bardales; his oldest daughter, Cayade Añazco; sons Zacarias, Silver, Alejo, David, and Mercedes; and thirty grandchildren. La Morada was the site of the major Añazco family tragedies: bitter quarrels, divorce, murder. A miasma of propriety filled the air whenever these events were in danger of being mentioned. Town identity seemed to depend on suppressing all memory of Añazco's actions.

Cayade Añazco, thirty-seven, told me that her childhood had often been frightening. "Very difficult it is to walk," she said in her hill woman's mild voice, "when there is no one to guide us. We placed our faith in God, and in that way we lived, all alone, for many years." When I asked what she had learned from her father, she began to list herbal cures. "Mud on the stomach lowers the worst of fevers. Eucalyptus for cough, cedar for pimples of the skin."

"I'd like to ask you about something that might have been sad in your life," I finally forced myself to say. We were sitting on a log, yards from where her father shot her first husband, José Aliaga.

"I have to serve dinner," she said, and walked off.

The matriarch, Bardales, sent word she would receive me. I was led to her compound, which was large if not especially tidy, with several spacious houses built around it. Bardales sat on a bed, a sixty-three-year-old woman surrounded by daughters-in-law and infants, in a windowless, unpainted room. She had a pleasant, open face and an easy smile that revealed a number of missing incisors. Heavy-breasted, big-boned, she was an imposing presence, her body still showing vestiges of what must once have been formidable toughness.

In her courtyard, one son circled, gripping a corncob; another sat in a doorway smiling gently. They both were in their twenties, and both were retarded— the result, most likely, of malnutrition during infancy. "My little dummies," Bardales tenderly called them. "They'll never leave their mother."

Refusing to discuss the killing of her son-in-law, she waxed lively on the subject of her husband, presenting an unheroic portrait. In 1960, she said, she and Añazco and their three children were living in the town of Chuquibamba, some twenty-six crow-miles west of here. One morning after she had stayed out all night at a dance with her brothers, Añazco furiously announced that he was heading off into the jungle and that he was taking the children with him. Bardales begged not to be left behind. Añazco agreed to let her come, on condition that she accept thirty lashes with a mule's rein. She agreed. "He only gave me about twenty," she said, "not too hard."

As they cut their way into the woods, Bardales worked and suffered at least as much as her husband. She bore and raised nine children in the uninhabited forest; she also broke trail, cleared land, helped with construction. Her husband would walk ahead with the machete while she followed with a hoe, flattening a path for a nasty mule named Camión, or Truck, loaded with babies and corrugated roofing.

Whenever Añazco went for supplies, Bardales and the children stayed alone in the forest, eating seeds and leaves for a month at a time. Wild pigs attacked them. Jaguars ate the calves. (Bardales once chased after one with her machete.) Bird cries spooked them, and they imagined ghosts, dwarves, and walking spirits.

Just across the valley from La Morada, the family lived together for the last time. Bardales decided to give up the journey and leave her husband in 1975. Bushwhacking had become too hard for her, she said; the change of life had come upon her, and she could no longer wield a machete. Besides, she said, the children needed school. Bardales moved here with most of the children and a small herd of cattle. She and her sons officially incorporated the town, and eventually the government sent a teacher. Forty families now live there.

Añazco, meanwhile, continued traveling eastward with their youngest daughter, Margarita, then thirteen, and one retarded son. They established themselves up on the tableland of La Meseta. The last time he visited La Morada was in 1986, and it was on that visit, Bardales said, that he shot Cayade's husband.

Bardales was proud of La Morada. Her ex-husband, she pointed out, hadn't succeeded in recruiting any new settlers to live with him. It seemed he and she were competing to see who could create the more lasting civilization. "When my town started to grow," Bardales says, "he got jealous. Last time he came he said, 'You have filled this place with your grandchildren.' Well, he had his chance."

I offered her the photo of Añazco with Margarita and the children. Her gaze grew profound, and she surprised me, suddenly, with a burst of candor. "I cried for years over that. That man stole my daughter. He treated me badly. Well, in God's house you can't push the women around. On Judgment Day, when God comes back with the Great Carpenter, we're *all* going to have to be on our knees, praying that we'll be in heaven together."

No one in La Morada was certain where Añazco might be. Some said that he might be a week's walk away, maybe farther. We decided to climb up to La Meseta and look for Añazco's son Fabián in the hope that he might lead us to his father. Crossing the Huabayacu, two of us were nearly swept into the next box canyon, the edge of the unexplored country where the Croatian explorers vanished in 1913. On the far shore, we climbed 1,200 feet to the top of the tableland. Later in the day we came to a cabin that Lerche quickly recognized as the place where he had visited Añazco back in 1989. But it was abundantly clear that Añazco had moved on. The shrubbery was overgrown, and there were no signs of cattle. All the old landmarks were gone.

By a lucky choice of trails, we reached Fabián's compound in three days, including one day of vain machete work in search of Lerche's favorite temple, Puca Huaca. Fabián lived with his extended family in log cabins strung out along a stream that Añazco named the River of Repose. He wore an emerald green poncho, soccer shorts, and rubber tire sandals. He had a mop of hair like the leprechauns in fairy-tale books, and a feral gleam in his eye. At first Fabián was suspicious of our motives, and he carefully shielded his two teenage daughters from our porters. He defied us to imagine a life like his. "Words are easy," he said, "but one who creates reality is called crazy." Whenever he ventured to towns outside Añazco's realm, he heard strangers talking behind his back: "There goes an Añazco. You know they're savages. They can't even talk."

Inside the main cabin, Fabián's wife was lying in quiet agony on an enormous bed. A cow had stepped on her foot, and she was feverish, her leg badly swollen. We gave her antibiotics and aspirin. Perhaps it was because of this that Fabián decided to trust our intentions and agreed to lead us first to the Red Temple and then to his father. "No one of low character would come this far," he reasoned, grinning a snaggy, elfin grin. "And if you think it takes willpower to get here, think about what it takes to live here."

Fabián hacked at the underbrush for nearly an hour before he found Puca Huaca. It was covered with green moss, which Lerche scraped off, almost worshipfully, with handfuls of fern. The salmon pink stones had softly rounded contours, as if warm dough had been patted into shape and then hardened into rocks. We pressed our hands against them, amazed to consider how few people's touch intervened between us and the ancient dead. The quarry for this sandstone was twelve miles away, and many of the blocks weighed several hundred pounds.

"It's incredible how it's been covered up," Lerche said. This entire part of the forest had been gnawed down by Añazco's cows, so that the temple and its surrounding cell-like structures were plainly visible. Had it not been for Añazco's cows, I could see how another few centuries could go by without Puca Huaca ever being found.

The following morning, Fabián led us down the River of Repose, and after four hours of walking, we spotted a large cedar log that appeared to be the outer barrier of a domestic compound. Arce spun around and said, "It's him! It's him!" Alvarez and I looked at each other, grinning as we walked across the log bridge that led into Benigno Añazco's courtyard.

Perhaps it's always a shock when a myth turns out to fit into a human body. Añazco was golden-skinned, whip-strong, far handsomer than his picture. But he'd aged. His beard was white and stringy. He no longer gave the impression of truculent power we'd projected into the shadowed, bluish images that Lerche had snapped, in forest light, at the entrance to Puca Huaca. He looked more like a Taoist sage than a murderous mountain man. Behind him, tending the fire in a tan skirt and rubber boots, was Margarita. And all about the courtyard were the children: Idmas, sixteen, a silent boy in a maroon poncho; Adan, nine, and Zoila, four, gyrating in excitement; and Luisa, a six-month-old with enormous cheeks.

Añazco seemed overjoyed to see us. He invited us into his house, a one-room cabin of well-fit logs, with a bed and a table inside. He apologized for the corn husks on the floor. He sent Idmas to cut sugarcane and promised to kill a heifer the next day. Soto and Huamán dropped their packs and began playing with the children.

He spoke eagerly, as if we'd been waiting years to resume an urgent conversation that had been interrupted. I showed him a government satellite map from Lima, and he traced his thumbnail across the indistinct image, determining our precise location: on this river, below that mountain. He told Lerche that his dream of opening the jungle all the way to Saposoa had failed. A new breed of settlers was flowing into the next few valleys, he said. Drug workers, unrepentant terrorists. Outsiders had taken over his rice farm to the east and set up a primitive cocaine factory. After they threatened to kill him, Añazco abandoned it. "The ambition for easy money is the worst disease on earth," Añazco fumed. "The smugglers lack a full sensibility. They think happiness lies in money."

We washed up in the river and sat down in front of Añazco's cabin to resume the conversation. His benches were enormous logs of tropical cedar, hand-split and smoothed, protected from rain by a corrugated overhang. We didn't chat for long: Añazco's favorite child, Zoila, gave her father no peace. Climbing onto his lap, she seized his wrist, jumped down again, yanked him with her whole weight. Añazco ignored her cries as long as possible and then explained that this child could not sit still: She was like him.

Following Zoila's exuberant lead, we ducked through canopies of wild plants into field after field where beans, sugarcane, and potatoes grew in neat rows. It was summer, and the farm looked its best. In a month it would be time for the harvest; from October to May, torrential rains would flood the trails waist deep. The Añazcos would hole up with stores of salt and radio batteries, plowing during breaks in the weather.

Añazco was clearly the hardest-working man in the region, and the wealthiest. His farm rose above the muck and exigencies of pure survival. Fat cattle—85 head, not the rumored 800—grazed on the bank of the River of Repose, quietly gnawing back the jungle. "Cows," he said, "are the great discoverers." Wooden bridges eased hard spots on the trail. Perhaps it was the bridges, an effort any other peasant would consider unnecessary, that made Añazco's sense of destiny most clear. He worked not only for himself, but for an abstract ideal of civilization; not just for the present, but for the future. "People who have no vision," he said, "have doubts."

Schooled for just two years in his hometown of Chuquibamba, Añazco's active mind had patched a vision out of local legends, Bible reading, personal ruminations, and the advice of the grandparents who raised him. (His mother lost her health after bearing Añazco at age forty; his father was a womanizer who left his children "nothing more than a name.") His grandmother had been an extraordinary woman. A mule breaker, livestock castrator, and midwife, Mama Josefa carried a bayonet in her waistband, and a whip she was not afraid to use on evildoers. Some people said she was a saint. When Añazco was six, Mama Josefa prophesied that he "possessed her sign" and was destined to explore the eastern mountains. She counseled little Benigno to get used to walking, to ignore hardships, to become a soldier defending goodness everywhere.

In 1942, when he was fifteen years old, Añazco entered the forest with three friends. Turned back once by cliffs, again by swamps, the friends gave up. Añazco went on alone, discovering a pasture, which he called the Garden, and then several tombs at Osiris. He sighted the flat, fertile La Meseta through binoculars in 1955. He and Bardales had three children, but his attentions were increasingly focused on the mountains. His trips grew longer, and his solitude became excessive. After hallucinating his children's laughter on an extended outing in 1960, he returned to town and took them out of school, and the family set forth as a unit.

He explained the thinking behind some of the names he'd given his farms. "I named Orpheus because of a dream," he said. "A man came giving me advice. I forgot the advice, but I remembered the name. When we came down to Israel, it was the time of the Six-Day War. It made me want to cry that they would destroy this tiny nation. I said, 'If they erase it there, I will do everything possible to create Israel here.' "

Altogether, Añazco had chopped fourteen farms out of the jungle. "I fall in love with land as if it were a woman," Añazco said. "When I find a nice piece of land, I don't want to go on without working it a little. I build a house, and then, because I must keep going, I move on with pain in my soul." It was for the sake of others, he said, that he moved on: "God gives some of us an inclination. When we see that we cannot take it in our bellies when we die, it becomes our pleasure to leave something behind for others."

He was bitter, though, that others hadn't responded to his dream of founding towns. He once sold eight cows to buy 2,000 acres of La Meseta from the government and set aside much of that land for the poor, anyone who'd claim it. One group traveled from the Marañón valley after Añazco circulated a cassette tape extolling the virtues of the virgin jungle. He helped them build houses, but in a year they all went back. "They were worried about bears and diseases, where to get batteries and store-bought clothes," Añazco said with contempt.

We assured him that all the people we'd met had come down the river valleys following his example, that one lifetime was not enough to see the effects of work like his. Privately, though, we wondered whether he had driven neighbors away with his pet theories. He could go on for hours about how air becomes water deep inside the mountains, why there is a heaven but no hell, why the Virgin Mary was no saint.

The next morning, we killed the brown-and-white heifer. Añazco donned an apron and rolled up his sleeves. Entwining the cow's legs and body with rope, Arce pulled her down easily. She lay snorting in the grass. Lerche held her horns flat against the ground, exposing her throat. Añazco sliced through her skin. Then, with a long knife, he dug expertly for the spinal cord. Death came a minute and a half after the first cut. Once the belly was open, exposing pink and white organs, Añazco called softly for Margarita. "Marga," he said, "you've got the delicate hand." She selected cuts with quiet efficiency. For lunch, we ate the traditional first stew, flesh from the neck. For dinner, Idmas charred the head in the fire to get rid of its hair and Margarita served it with beans. That night we snored heavily next to the carcass, cut up and preserved in the rising smoke of the cooking fire.

All the next day it rained. We sat on the benches, eating beef with fresh yucca and sweet potatoes, listening to Añazco's life story, and watching Idmas collect rainwater from an ingenious wooden sluice. Pentatonic Andean music issued thinly from the black transistor radio. Across the brown, swollen river, toucanets cried, and scarves of mist threaded slowly among the opulent trees.

Timidly, I asked Añazco whether he could accept a difficult question.

"For me, miss, I think there are no hard questions," he replied. Long ago, he'd asked pardon for his evil acts—murder, incest, cruelty. "God is something superior," he said, "like electrical waves. If electricity can light a bulb, how can God not be in contact with our hearts? And so, if I have sinned, God must forgive."

"How was it that you got together with your daughter?" I asked.

Añazco didn't flinch. He began by explaining his relationship with Bardales. He was her last choice after she had pursued four other men. "So when I took her on, I made her swear she'd never make me jealous. She remembered for a while, but after some time, that woman, she made my life a hell with her character. And so we separated. After that, I tried to find another woman. I went to town and I tried my best. I thought, 'Only death can stop me in these works of the mountain. But I cannot live alone. I need the help of a woman. I will take my daughter.' You don't expect children to fall in love. You expect them to obey, to resign themselves. 'People will repudiate me,' I thought, 'but how can I die alone?' I thought about it very well, and I decided. She had judgment. She said that she would attend me, but that if I could find another woman, then we'd separate."

Añazco told us that Lot, the righteous man who was saved from the burning of Sodom, had a child with each of two daughters after his wife was turned to salt. "One of those sons went on to become the father of the Moabites," Añazco challenged. "If it's in the Bible, what is your opinion?"

Quiet, shy, and a little stocky, Margarita trundled through her daily tasks, usually with Idmas at her side in silent communion. She harvested beans and potatoes, tended the fire, crocheted baby clothes, and discreetly listened to Añazco as he told their story. She was thirty-three. She'd been with her father for twenty years. Though her legs were splattered with mud, she was not immune from concepts of glamor. When she smiled, she always remembered to tighten her lip to hide her bare upper gum.

That afternoon, as gently as I could, I asked her about her life. We were cutting up more of the heifer, flicking botfly eggs into the waiting jaws of Pinochet and Seguidora, Añazco's two dogs. Her voice was barely a breath, but she came straight to the point, bluntly summing up her painful history. "My mother left," she said, "because everyone thought my father was a madman. People look at me with contempt because I went with him. My mother said, 'You are no longer my daughter.' I suffered for many years over that. But I came out of duty to my father, not out of hatred for my mother.

"When I was small, we always thought we would come to a town one day. But not now. Now I am of the mountains. I hear on the radio how people live in towns. They steal, kill, take each other's land. They have no peace." She had learned to cope with her pain, she said, through resignation. She had no one to confide in, and so, when something bothered her inside, she had to rely only on herself. "I get used to it," she said.

We invited Añazco to come out to one of his pastures, alone, for a portrait, and while Alvarez was setting up his equipment, I took advantage of our solitude to ask Añazco about the murder of Cayade's husband.

He said that his son-in-law, José Aliaga, was one of those ambitious village youths who went to the coast to discover that where jobs are scarce, crime could be the most direct way of obtaining a living. "He came back saying that he had specialized in all the ways of evil, robbery, rape, and drugs," Añazco said. "He said it was my duty to help people rise. He wanted me to protect this mafia thing. Either I would run it or he would run it. I said no. He said no one was going to stop him. He had a plot to get me alone—I heard he'd been bragging how he would kill me. So then I realized it was him or me."

One day, Añazco said, Margarita had just given birth, and he traveled to La Morada for supplies. He went to Cayade's house, and she and José came out. "Bang! I got him. I got him in the heart. Bang! To the ground. I made a death." Añazco's voice quivered with remembered passion. Though he didn't mention it specifically, other relatives had insisted that in addition to his criminal leanings, Aliaga had been sleeping with Bardales.

How did he feel about killing another human being?

"I felt, 'I have gotten rid of my problem.' As soon as I killed him, my whole body relaxed. I'd been watching my back for years. To this day, I feel nothing but relief about it." Añazco's only regret was that his fugitive status now impeded him from gathering settlers for his towns. He planned to stay here for the rest of his life, on the land named after his mother, Pascuala. "Pascuala," he said, "will feed me until I die."

I would later learn that the murder case against Añazco, filed in 1989, remains mired in a Kafkaesque limbo. Since the police won't go and get him, the suspect must present himself, and since he does not present himself, nothing can be done. But after meeting with the subprefect of Chachapoyas, Manuel Paredes Rodriguez, I doubted that Añazco would ever be prosecuted. "There, where justice does not arrive, to kill a wicked man is justice," Paredes said. "We should give that man a parchment, not a prosecution. He has served as an agent of development, an example of work and perseverance for all Peruvians."

Down the hall, attorney Conrado Mori leafed through the law on incest, discovering that the statute of limitations had elapsed. Margarita had been an adult for too long. "Well, the Incas used to practice incest deliberately," Mori mused. "Brothers would marry sisters. They'd get one superintelligent one and six idiots, throw away the idiots and make the good one emperor."

I thought of Añazco standing alone in his field, waiting for vindication before he dies. Waiting, amid the cries of the emerald toucanets, the lowing of his broken-legged mule, the laughter of his beloved children—amid all of his kingdom's lovely, awful splendors, Añazco had his own summation. "On the seventh day," he said, "God surveyed all of the creation that he had made, the good and the bad, and he sanctified all of it equally."

That's not exactly what it says in Genesis. But surely, in the end, only God is qualified to judge Benigno Añazco.

NOVEMBER 1996

AT SEA

by **JONATHAN RABAN**

In maritime law, a ship is a detached fragment of the society under whose flag it sails, a wandering chunk of Britain—or Liberia, or Panama. However far it travels overseas, it's an ark containing the laws and customs of its home port. Here is the happy paradox of seagoing: Nowhere on Earth can you be as exposed to and alone with wild nature as at sea, yet aboard a boat you never leave the culture of the land.

Cruise ship passengers know this. A mile offshore, the ship skirts the coast of an alarming and exotic country, famed for its unpronounceable language, its foul drinking water, its bloody coups and casual thievery. High on C Deck, a steward bears gin-and-tonics on a silver tray; the tourists, snug in their four-star world of comforts and deference, see the dangerous coast slide past like a movie. They're home and abroad in the same breath.

On an autumn Atlantic crossing in 1988, in a British cargo ship, we ran into a declining hurricane in mid-ocean. For twenty-four hours, the ship was hove-to, going nowhere, while the sea boiled around us like milk and the wave trains thundered. In the officers' mess, the floor rolled through 75 degrees of arc, and tropical fish spilled onto the carpet from their tank beside the bar.

"Bit of a windy day we've got today," the captain said from behind his preluncheon glass of dry sherry, and the two junior deck officers, stumbling crazily up the sudden hill toward the framed portrait of the Queen and Prince Philip, tried as best they could to nod vigorously and smile, as junior officers must when spoken to by their captain. The radio officer landed, from a considerable height, in my lap. "Oh, pardon! Whoops! Do please excuse me!" he said.

Had the *Atlantic Conveyor* been registered in excitable Panama, the scene might have been different, but we were flying the Red Ensign, and the more the ocean tossed us about like bugs in a bucket, the harder we all worked to maintain the old-fashioned prim civilities of our little floating England. Every student of the British class system, its minuscule distinctions of rank and precedence, its strangulated politenesses, its style of poker-faced reticence, should get a berth aboard a Liverpool-registered merchant ship in a severe storm.

The last case of cannibalism to be tried in Britain came to hinge on this conflict between the culture of the ship and the untamed nature of the sea. In 1884, the yacht *Mignonette*, on passage from Tollesbury, in Essex, to Sydney, Australia, met heavy weather in the South Atlantic. Caught by an enormous breaking wave, the yacht foundered, and her professional crew (which was delivering the boat to its new Australian owner) took to the thirteen-foot dinghy, where they drifted for three weeks on the empty ocean under a hot and cloudless sky. On the twenty-fourth day of their ordeal, the four emaciated mariners cast lots. The cabin boy, Richard Parker, seventeen years old, drew the short straw, and the captain slit his throat with a penknife. The survivors dined gratefully on the boy's remains.

A German ship eventually picked them up and took them back to England. Their trial was a sensation of the day. The first line of the defense was that there was no case to answer: The *Mignonette*, a registered British ship, had sunk, and the killing of the cabin boy had taken place in an unflagged open boat on the high seas. The law of the land, argued the defense, had no jurisdiction over the men's conduct in a dinghy in international waters. On the ocean, a thousand miles from the nearest coast, the law of the wild prevailed.

Unfortunately for the men (and for those of us who would like to get up to mischief in dinghies beyond the twelve-mile limit), this reading of the law ran counter to a section of the British Merchant Shipping Act of 1854, which held that a British seaman was subject to English law whether he was on or off his ship—and the dinghy, flag or no flag, was, legally speaking, an integral part of its parent yacht. The captain and mate of the *Mignonette* were found guilty of murder, sentenced to death, and then granted a royal pardon. The sympathy of the court (and British public opinion) was with them, but a guilty verdict was required to prove that the long arm of the law can extend far out to sea.

The ocean itself *is* a wilderness, beyond the reach of the morality and customs of the land. But a boat is like an embassy in a foreign country. So long as you are aboard a boat, you remain a social creature, a citizen, answerable to the conventions of society. You might as well sally forth alone across the trackless ocean in a clapboard cottage with a white picket fence and a mailbox.

I am now readying my own boat for a sea trip (I can't quite call it a voyage) from Seattle to Juneau, Alaska, and I'm living day to day on the slippery interface between the nature and culture of the thing. My boat, a thirty-five-foot ketch, is Swedish built and American registered; like its owner, it is a native of one country, resident in another, and not quite a citizen of either. I never fly a flag, except under official duress, preferring to think of the boat as an independent republic, liberal-democratic in temper, easygoing in its manners, bookish in its daily conversation. My slovenly Utopia.

On a wall of the saloon, between the fire extinguisher and the VHF radiotelephone, is mounted a 1773 cartoon of George III—Farmer George, the obese, rubber-lipped, mad king of England—our gentlest, most generous monarch, who lost the American colonies and was in the habit of putting grave constitutional questions to the wise shrubs in his garden. Every British ship has its royal portrait. George III seems the right king for me. His erratic captaincy of the ship of state is an apt emblem for my own, often fumbling, command of my vessel.

The real heart of my boat is its library. There are few sea books in it—the inevitable coastal pilots, tidal atlases, and one or two grim volumes with titles like *The 12-Volt Bible.* But when I'm galebound on the dank and gloomy Northwest Coast, I'm in no mood to read Conrad or Melville. At anchor in a lightless British Columbian inlet, where matte black cedars crowd 'round the ruins of a bankrupt salmon cannery and the rain falls like ink, I shall pine for brilliance and laughter, for rooms full of voices. So, on the long shelf in the saloon, overhung by the gimballed oil lamp, are *Lolita* and *Madame Bovary,* the novels of Evelyn Waugh (all of them), Dickens's *Great Expectations,* Trollope's *The Way We Live Now,* Thackeray's *Vanity Fair,* Byron's *Don Juan.* There are books by friends and acquaintances, like Paul Theroux, Richard Ford, Cees Nooteboom, Ian McEwan, David Shields, Martin Amis. I rejoice in the thought that my eye might lift from a page of Waugh (let it be Julia Stitch, in bed, at the beginning of *Scoop*) to the sight of a black bear snuffling in the driftwood at the water's edge: nature outside the boat, society within, and just an inch of planking between the world of the one and the world of the other. The essence of being afloat is feeling the eggshell containment of an orderly domestic life suspended over the deep. The continuous slight motion of the boat, swinging to its anchor on the changing tide, is a reminder of how fragile is our tenure here—aloft with a novel, coffee cup close at hand, while the sea yawns underfoot and the bear prowls through its dripping wilderness on shore.

I love the subtlety and richness of all the variations on the theme of society and solitude that can be experienced when traveling by sea. It is like living inside a metaphor for the strange voyage of a human soul on its journey through life.

Out on the open sea, with a breaking swell and the wind a notch too high for comfort, you are the loneliest fool in the world. You are trying to follow the vain hypothesis of a compass course. It's marked on the chart, 347 degrees magnetic, a neat pencil line bisecting the white space of the ocean. The absurd particularity of that number now seems to sneer at you from the chart as the boat blunders and wallows through the water, its hull resounding like a bass drum to the impact of each new ribbed and lumpish wave. The bow charges downhill on a bearing of 015 degrees. Ten seconds later, it's doing 330 degrees, up a potholed slope. Abandoning the helm to the autopilot, which at least will steer no worse, if little better, than you do, you go below.

Slub . . . thunk. Dickens, Thackeray, Trollope, and the rest lurch drunkenly in line along the bookshelves. Two oranges and an apple chase each other up and down the floor. Your morning coffee is a jagged stain on the oatmeal settee. The decanter has smashed in the sink. The closet door is flying open and shut, as if a malevolent jack-in-the-box were larking among your shirts. A dollop of green sea obscures the view from your living-room window. Your precious, contrived, miniature civilization appears to be falling to pieces around your ears, and you can't remember what madness drove you to be out here in the first place.

Then you hear voices. For a moment, you fear that you're losing your wits; then you realize that the voices are coming from the VHF set: a captain calling for a harbor pilot or a fisherman chatting to his wife in the suburbs. It is, after all, just a dull morning at sea, with the invisible community of the sea going about its daily business. You turn up the volume on the radio, climb the four steps to the doghouse, and regain control of the wheel. Three or four miles off, a gray, slab-sided bulk carrier shows for a few seconds before being blotted out by a cresting wave, and you find yourself watching the ship with a mixture of pleasure at finding a companion and rising anxiety at encountering a dangerous intruder.

Letting out the sails to steer clear of the big stranger on your patch, you quickly recover your taste for solitude—and the waves themselves seem to lose their snarling and vindictive expressions. In the society of the sea, it is the duty of every member to keep his distance from all the others. To be alone is to be safe. It's no coincidence that those two most English of attitudes, being "stand-offish" and "keeping aloof," are nautical terms that have long since passed into the general currency of the language. Standing off is what a ship does to avoid the dangers of the coast; aloof is a-luff, or luffing your sails, head to wind, to stay clear of another vessel. The jargon of the sea is full of nouns and verbs to describe the multitude of ways in which a ship can keep itself to itself. The ocean is, in general, a sociable and considerate place, where people (professional mariners, at least) treat each other with remarkable courtesy. But this civility is based on distance and formal good manners. Always signal your intentions clearly. Always know when to give way and when to hold your course. If people on land behaved like ships at sea, they'd look like characters in an Italian opera, or members of the Japanese imperial court.

I've never crossed an ocean under my own steam—never, really, more than nibbled at the ocean's edge. The longest open-sea crossing that I've made was from Fishguard, in Wales, to Falmouth, in Cornwall: 200 miles, thirty-five hours; a day, a night, and most of the next day, with a dream-harrowed sleep (full of collisions, groundings, swampings, and founderings) at the end of the trip. Cowardice is one reason for my failure to tackle an ocean; my passion for arrivals is another. When the light begins to fail and the sea turns black, I yearn to make landfall—to pick out the winking entrance buoys and find my way into a strange port. The intricate, heart-stopping business of coastal pilotage is for me the great reward for a day spent jouncing about in the waves offshore.

Dusk is a good time (though just before dawn is best), when lights stand out but the shape of the land is still clearly visible. You bring one shadowy headland into line with another, then find the lazy flash of the fairway buoy, timing it against your watch to check its ID. Cautiously standing off, you wait until the pinpricks of light ahead resolve themselves into a narrow, winding lane, into which you thread the boat, moving under engine, at half speed.

The most satisfying harbors are those that are fringed with a maze of shifting sandbars, like the entrance to the Somme estuary in northern France or the approach to Wexford in Ireland, where buoyed channels take one on bafflingly serpentine routes into town. Each channel represents a pooling of knowledge by the local pilots and fishermen and is a path whose broad outline has been trodden for hundreds of years. But sandbars alter their positions after every gale, and the buoys are never exactly in the right places. As so often at sea, you are at once in good and experienced company and entirely on your own.

Inching warily from buoy to buoy, you watch the shivering needle on the depth sounder. It is your blindman's stick, with which you have to tap-tap your way, feeling for deep water as you go. Twelve feet. Ten feet. Eight feet—and you've lost the channel. Nine feet. Ten feet—and you breathe again. Now you're inside the line of breakers, in a broad, lakelike sea, with the lights of the town silvering the water in the distance. In a moment of inattention, the bow of the boat suddenly climbs as the keel scrapes sand, but it settles back, the buoy slides past, and the floating town drifts slowing toward you, taking you in.

Anyone who has struggled into a harbor out of a bad sea will understand why the words "heaven" and "haven" are closely cognate. A dismal slate-roofed town (visit the Methodist chapel and the fish-and-chip shop) is paradise itself when you find shelter there after a day of being cold and frightened aboard a lurching boat. You'd willingly kneel to kiss the stones of the dock, you are so full of gratitude for the fact of Dulltown's existence. Its people are so friendly! So attractive! Its Methodist chapel is, as Methodist chapels go, a very cathedral! Its fish and chips are, without doubt, the best fish and chips in the world!

Few travelers have ever felt this way about Dulltown. You are privileged. Your means of arrival has revealed to you a place hidden from the mass of humanity: Dulltown Haven . . . Dulltown as heaven. For a writer, such an epiphany is pure gift—and it will save you from the addled cynicism that is the usual curse of traveling.

Yet we were, a few moments ago, on the Somme estuary and the mouth of the River Slaney, and neither St. Valery nor Wexford is in the least like Dulltown. They are beautiful and complicated places even if you reach them dully, by car. The miracle of coming into them by sea is that as soon as your boat is attached to the dock by a trapeze of ropes, it becomes part of the architecture and skyline of the town. You belong to the working fabric of the community as no ordinary visitor can aspire to do. Your neighbors (at least in places unspoiled by yachting marinas) are fishermen, longshoremen, local boat owners; and the more difficult the harbor approach, the more nearly will you be accepted as a resident. In the more remote communities, your patience and skill as a navigator (you wouldn't be there if you were a total buffoon) is an automatic ticket of entry to society.

For a day, or two, or three, or as long as the weather outside remains discouraging, you settle into dockside life. You go visiting in the afternoons. You work on your boat. You learn a dozen names. In the evenings, you go with your new neighbors to the bar across the street, where (if you are a writer) you try to listen harder than you drink. You hear things that no one would dream of telling you had you come here by car.

Then, at five o'clock one morning, in the final hour of the flood tide, you untie the damp ropes in the dark and steal away from the place without saying good-bye. You leave behind a small gap, like a missing tooth, in the shape of the town as you will come to remember it.

At the fairway buoy, the sea is oily, with curlicues of rising mist. The remains of a big swell make the water surface bulge and contract, like a fat man breathing. Visibility is down to a mile or less. A moderate westerly is forecast.

Ahead lie the open sea and a day like a blank slate. But some things are certain. There will be—as now—moments of wonder and elation such as rarely visit you on land. There will be the building magnetic power of the unknown port across the water. There'll be at least one serious cause for alarm, and at least one unpleasant surprise.

You kill the engine and let the boat drift on the tide, waiting for enough wind to hoist the sails. The town you left is now hidden in haze. Alone in a circle of diffuse light, you float in silence. In time, the sea and the day will begin to impose their own narrative order on your life; but for now, you are a character as yet unformed, awaiting the sequence of events that will define you.

Bon voyage!

SEPTEMBER 1996

ETERNAL BLISS OR BUST

by CHIP BROWN

Zho ba! We are walking at last in the land of the lotus, looking for the jewel, or something, anything really, after the ordeal of getting here: the warp journey to Shanghai, then west again to Chengdu, capital of Sichuan Province, and then the twelve-hour trundle on a train painted the green of a placid dragon, south through miles of tunnel to Xichang, where we spent the night by a lake and sucked intestine-friendly yogurt through straws and started west in the morning in a convoy led by a six-wheel equipment truck laden with gear and supplies like rice, extra gasoline, and two magnums of Chinese champagne, which were wildly overpriced at seventy-five cents a bottle. One of the trio of four-wheel-drives was a Chinese Bai Lou that ran dutifully as long as Mr. Deng kept the fuel pump cool with mud packs. West and west and west on roads lined with masonry tombs and rice paddies that looked like golf greens. Plains yielded to bleak hills, hills heaved into mountains. Hour after hour, for two days, we skidded and jounced and swayed around switchbacks, six mountain ranges, a measureless world of gorges and forests and epic rivers flowing off the Plateau of Tibet. Dust sifted into everything; it got behind your eyes, it came out on the floss when you cleaned your teeth. This was April, the dry season. The roadway straggled onto a hacked-up cobble creekbed that looked like the mouth of an ogre with the tongue chopped out; by late summer, runoff would be thundering in the stony gullet. We skirted the wreck of a bus in which four people had died. Blue and pistachio green log trucks came rushing around blind one-lane bends. There was no margin for error; our white-gloved drivers worried their horns, and at rest stops they spit on the wheels to gauge how hot the brakes were. When the Chinese feel anxious, they say, "There is a tiger in my heart." None of us who leaned toward Buddhist teachings were such masters of nonattachment that we could keep the tigers out of our hearts on the drive in. It was 1,100 crooked, ragged kilometers from Chengdu to Beiyangping, the lumber camp on China's frontier where the road ended and we began—hallelujah!—to travel under our own power. Perhaps this is the jewel in the lotus: a new pair of boots and solid earth under foot. *Zho ba!* Let's go!

Our leader, fittingly, was bringing up the rear; his assistant had forged ahead to leave little blaze orange strips of supposedly biodegradable tape wherever the trail forked. Five thousand feet below, the foamy blue-green water of the Shou Chu glittered in a V-shaped river valley.

"Dabney, this is Peter. Do you copy? Over," said Peter Klika, fiddling with his prized two-meter-band walkie-talkie.

"Peter, this is Dabney. Over."

"Where are you?"

Those of us who had followed Dabney Eastham out of Beiyangping had to blunder through the thorns in the wrong direction for a couple of minutes, unwilling to trust the amused villagers who were gesturing vigorously in the other direction. Dabney, a former patent lawyer who'd taken up gold mining, was down by a stream and didn't have much to report after a scant fifteen minutes on the trail.

"OK, Dabney," said Peter. "I'll talk to you at six. Over and out."

The trail dived into the woods, picked up a logging road, and then plunged back into the pines again. The juncture was marked by fluttering Tibetan prayer flags and mani stones. The Tibetan writing on the flags and stones repeats a central mantra of Buddhism, *om mani padme hum,* "the jewel is in the lotus."

Peter is a free-spirited, forty-six-year-old, Chinese-speaking former State Department diplomat and onetime robber of Inca graves. When not tending his Los Angeles real estate law practice, or expanding his collection of sexually explicit pre-Inca pottery, or adding to a store of adventures on seven continents, from hitchhiking across Afghanistan to a solo traverse of Baffin Island on foot in celebration of his fortieth birthday, he runs China Trek. He founded the company in 1982, and after twenty-five trips he's become fairly adept at sidling through the Middle Kingdom bureaucracy. "We're not backpackers," Peter said. "We're cultural voyagers."

It was a distinction his recruits could appreciate during the luggage weigh-in before the flight to Chengdu. Big, bulging duffels tipping the scale at . . . *two kilos!* What the Commerce Department might wish to believe was ultralight American backpacking technology in action had actually been Peter with his foot discreetly wedged under the scale.

The trail dropped through a dappled forest of spruces and pines and blossom-splashed rhododendrons. The land looked like Colorado. Anywhere else, one gray, 14,000-foot limestone mountain would have been the main attraction, webbed with trails and climbing routes. Here, it was a nameless extra making way for the stars, the sacred peaks of the Konka Risumgongba range, still offstage. We'd had but one glimpse of them on the way in: Shenrezig, Jambeyang, and Chanadordje, the holder of the thunderbolts, their sharp, unclimbed 20,000-foot snow summits glittering in the distance like the sails of giant schooners.

As dusk drew down, a crumbling masonry tower loomed in the inky light. It had been mortared together about 1,000 years ago by the Naxi people, one of China's many ethnic minorities. From a series of watchtowers joined by strategic lines of sight, the Naxi could keep an eye peeled for enemies and summon help with signal fires. We meant to camp in a nearby field but were waiting for our gear. China Trek trips have a history of getting to camp after it's too dark to clear the yak dung away from your tent site. Soon enough, however, the ridge we'd come over began to ring with a cacophony of tinkling bells and wild, half-sung, half-yodeled cries—and down through the willows and the prickers snaked a train of Tibetan horsemen and nineteen duffel-laden mules and donkeys. The pasture was suddenly as hectic as a train station at rush hour. The animals were unloaded and set loose to graze; tents sprang up. Mr. Zhang and Mr. Wang, our assigned Chinese "liaison officers," uncrated the kitchen. The cook, an unhappy urbanite exiled to mountain duty, started chopping turnips. Kerosene lamps were lighted, and Dr. Nie Ming, a Chinese urologist, listened to knee complaints. With some passes near 16,000 feet, we were more likely to come down with elevation-related disorders than kidney stones or urinary tract infections. But Dr. Nie was so aghast that a dozen Americans were heading into one of the most remote mountain ranges in the world with no medical support that he volunteered to take his vacation from surgery duties at Chengdu Hospital No. 4 and serve as our unpaid expedition doctor.

We were a curious bunch, those of us from the States preparing beds in a Chinese pasture. It was a West Coast group with pronounced New Age tendencies and plenty of mystical experience. Jasmine Lutes, who runs a personal-growth training company with her husband, Tom, once had a vision of him as a golden energy field. And one time in Hawaii, Joan and Jim Channon—she's a filmmaker, he's an artist—ate some mushrooms and started speaking Japanese, which neither one of them knew a word of, ordinarily. Sybil Malinowski, well versed and seemingly grounded in real estate law, confided to me that she aspired to elevate her vibrational level and ascend to heaven without dying, à la the Virgin Mary. As the only easterner—worse, the only New Yorker—I was quickly stereotyped as the cynic in the lotus.

The other couple was David and Susan Stone, an accountant and teacher, respectively, from Seattle. David, a tall, shambling fellow, knocked over the rice at dinner and then got on his knees, prepared to pick up every last grain. Zhang waved him away. There was plenty of rice.

"I don't want to get a reputation for spilling things," David said.

"Too late," said Peter.

Peter can talk New Age in a pinch, dropping quotes from Milarepa about the "stony fastness of the mountains where there is a secret marketplace where one can barter the vortex of life for eternal bliss," but in general he prefers to do his celestial navigation with a sextant. He made an exception once, when he went to a monastery in Taiwan to see a monk said to be adept at reading past lives. "Can you tell me what I was in my previous incarnation?" Peter asked, expecting to hear something grand about his karma. The old man wrinkled his nose and said, "You were the elbows of a worm."

The three couples had new North Face domes, the nylon equivalents of honeymoon suites. Dabney shared a Kelty tent with his young climbing partner, Steve Thompson. Sybil was tenting with her Walkman. And in what the Chinese might call Documentary Tent No. 1, I was billeted with Rob MacKinlay, a San Francisco photographer. The jewel in Rob's lotus was a magazine cover shot that would earn him the bonus he needed to feed his wife, Mimi, and their poor hungry kitten, Ansel. Ansel mewed needfully in Rob's thoughts with every lens change.

The Chinese team had its own camp of nylon tents; the bronze-faced Tibetan packers bedded down under horse blankets and a gray canvas tarp. And Peter retired to his "Minstrel Hut." Cursed with a deafening snore, he considerately segregated himself from the rest of us. Not far enough away, however. Our lullaby that first night in the wilds of western China was a three-part fugue of trilling sinuses, ringing donkey bells, and the mercifully soothing murmur of the river below.

Faint though they were, we were traveling in the footsteps of Joseph Rock, the Austrian botanist who, under the aegis of the National Geographic Society, was the first Westerner to explore the Konka Risumgongba and to visit many of the remote villages just to the southeast in the kingdom of Muli. Muli, about the size of Massachusetts, was set up under the reign of Genghis Khan in the thirteenth century. It was one of several autonomous states in the region and served as a politically expedient buffer between China and Tibet when Rock made three expeditions there between 1924 and 1928. He took extensive notes on geography, plants, and Tibetan and Naxi cultures. He endured the considerable hardships of crossing mountain passes and traveling during monsoon season. In places, his mules had to be pushed through snow and hauled on lines across rivers. There was the ever-present danger posed by bands of murderous outlaws. All the more reason to travel in style: Rock loaded his huge pack trains with such ultralight items as iron bedsteads, bathtubs, and camp tables. He had himself tendered into some villages on a sedan chair. He introduced his muleteers to the phonograph and the voice of Caruso. His cooks prepared multicourse Austrian meals, which the moody explorer ate with real silverware and capped with a nice liqueur (no Chinese champagne for him).

Until Rock's exploration, the Konka Risumgongba was a mystery to the outside world, glimpsed from a distance and mentioned but in passing by missionaries and travelers. Many of Rock's maps and photographs were published in his epic July 1931 *National Geographic* article, which for many years was the only detailed description of the area and is still the most informative write-up.

Lacking a road to Beiyangping, Rock started his journeys into the Shou Chu drainage 130 kilometers south at the Muli monastery. In those days the monastery, at the foot of 15,000-foot Mount Mitzuga, was a thriving walled community of 700 monks; it served as the capital of the theocratic state and as a way station for pilgrims intent on circumambulating the sacred mountains. Muli has been off limits to Westerners since Rock's day—hidden behind political sensitivities after the 1949 revolution and the Chinese invasion of Tibet ten years later, and the fact that authorities didn't want foreigners poking around the gold mines in the area. The kingdom and the Konka Risumgongba disappeared into one of those blank spots on the map; despite numerous trips in four of China's mountain provinces, Peter Klika had never heard of the place.

And then one Saturday in 1983, in a used-book store in Pasadena, California, Peter stumbled onto a copy of Rock's article. He couldn't reconcile Rock's descriptions and coordinates with his own maps. The more he looked for information about Muli and the Konka Risumgongba, the less he found. So he began worming around for information about the area and elbowing the Chinese for permission to visit the range. Five years later he received a letter from the Chinese Mountaineering Association saying it would grant a permit and sponsor a trip to Muli if Peter could obtain permission from two other branches of the bureaucracy. With the help of his Chinese law partner and a Chinese word-processing program, Peter wrote to each pertinent bureau, saying the other two had granted him permission to visit Muli—would they do the same? He got his permit.

He made his first trip with a party of climbers in 1989. Everywhere he went, Peter inquired about the fate of the Muli king, whose reign had ended in 1949, and every time he got a different answer: The king had been killed by the Chinese; the king had died a natural death; the king had voluntarily abdicated and was living in Muli with his family. "What king?" one man said. Even the whereabouts of the monastery were in doubt. What was marked "Muli" on the map was not the monastery Rock had described, but a raw administrative capital filled with Han Chinese loggers and foresters. The monastery was another three hours up a ragged road.

A year later the second expedition met with abysmal fall weather. The four-wheel-drive trucks sank up to their axles in mud; it rained relentlessly; and one of the expedition members, a California state senator, whined so much that it became difficult for the others to barter the vortex of life for eternal bliss.

Ours was Peter's third expedition to Muli. He had put forth the possibility that we would circumambulate the range, but when it became clear that most of his trekkers didn't have the time, the stamina, or the desire to undertake such a venture—and that the Tibetan horsemen were loath to risk their ponies in the snowy, avalanche-prone passes—he improvised a less ambitious plan: We would proceed along a route new to Peter himself into the village of Garu, which Westerners had last entered, officially at least, when Joseph Rock passed through sixty-four years earlier.

Tibetan Buddhism distinguishes eighteen varieties of void, but the maps of Muli and the Konka Risumgongba surely constitute yet another. We were relying heavily on Rock's article and the maps compiled from his field notes. Maps from the U.S. Defense Mapping Agency were worse than bad, misplacing rivers and omitting towns and leaving whole sections blank or shaded with a bizarre "reliability index" that offered travelers the cold comfort of being able to quantify the number of Buddhist voids they were experiencing simultaneously. Peter had obtained a Chinese military contour map that gave survey heights for some mountains, but it couldn't have been more obscure if it had been designed to disinform NATO tank crews. Between the pictograph place names and the blurry lines, it was like trying to read a palm through a shower door. So, cartographically at least, it was hard to get a fix on Muli; the place seemed to shift and dissolve like the juniper smoke sent up each morning at the monastery to underscore the illusoriness of life.

There at the monastery, before the leg to Beiyangping and the start of the trek proper, we spent the night with the lamas at the heart of the once and former kingdom. The convoy climbed the foothills of Mount Mitzuga at dusk, a winding drive past green rice fields and groves of walnut trees and tidy homes with Shiva's tridents poking up from tile roofs. Dozens of young monks in crimson robes stopped in their tracks as we pulled in. One of the younger ones ran for the main temple. Peter, twice a visitor here, advised us to stay by the vehicles until it was clear that we were welcome. A moment later a senior lama emerged in his bloodred robe, arms extended in that cradling wave with which Tibetans greet one another and that makes them look like they are trying to gauge the weight of an imaginary watermelon. The lama greeted Peter in Chinese, clasping his hands and bowing slightly, a breakaway smile lighting his face. And then he greeted each of us in like manner. "His eyes were so full of love I thought I was going to burst into tears," Tom said later. Indeed, the lama had the most astonishing brown eyes, radiant and serene. It seemed he could see into you for a thousand miles—could see what there was in you that was also in himself.

All but destroyed during the Chinese invasion of Tibet, and again during the cultural revolution, the monastery was being resurrected next to the ruins of the old buildings whose shattered walls and roofless rooms stood as haunting testimony to the campaign of repression. Peter had counted just thirty lamas and novices during his first visit, and only a handful of elders left to lead and teach the arcana of the religion. Now the community had grown to fifty, and the main temple, a handsome tile-roofed structure with white plaster walls and red and yellow eaves, had been finished. Spanking new banners billowed in the cool evening air.

We were shown to one of the rooms off the courtyard, three spare beds under a dangling lightbulb. A young novice toted in a pitcher of jasmine tea. We were welcome to stay the night, we learned. "We're like pilgrims," Peter said. "They are moved that we have come so far to see them." Zhang advised us to be careful not to give the monks pictures of the Dalai Lama. However much they might have appreciated photographs of the Tibetan leader, the monks might be arrested should the photographs be discovered by Chinese authorities.

Around 7:15 P.M. two dozen novices seated themselves under the temple portico and began to chant. A few shouted at first in counterpoint. More voices joined in. Melodies emerged, and the chanting modulated on unknown cues, swelling and resonating through the courtyard. One of the lamas walked among the novices, observing and instructing them as they swayed and rocked. When darkness fell, he turned his flashlight on them. They chanted on. A dog in the village below barked in answer. After an hour and a half the chanting abruptly ceased, and those of us who had been listening in—and mumbling along—could feel the force of the silence: a spirit-laden hush flowing from religious discipline. A headlamp came bobbing across the courtyard. It was our driver Mr. Deng. *"Chr ba!"* he shouted: Let's eat! The horrified Americans shushed him furiously. Peter jumped up, put his arm around the driver, and smoothed him out of the courtyard.

We were woken the next morning by conch-shell blasts and the shivery din of gongs, and shortly thereafter were ushered inside the monastery. Rows of monks sat cross-legged in front of golden effigies of Buddha, his attendants, and incarnations of various lamas. We were given sticks of incense and took seats behind the last row of young monks, who had a hard time keeping themselves from peeking at the hairy giants in their midst. The lama who had greeted us the evening before punctuated the chants with deep bass overtones. Prayers were chanted for each of us. The abbot, dressed in a flowing crimson robe and a yellow crescent-shaped hat, draped muslin shawls and thin red scarves around our necks.

Peter wanted to make a donation to the collection box. A sum of 600 yuan—about $110—was presented, but it was a contretemps: The monks could only accept odd sums. Peter kicked in another yuan to make it 601. As the little monks filed out, one of their older brethren stood by the door and gave each of the buzz-cut little shavers a bit of pocket money.

Two days after we struck the tents under the Naxi watchtower, we established a base camp in a pasture at 10,260 feet, overlooking the green barley terraces and the mud-masonry houses of the village of Garu. We had come about twelve miles through three other villages and regained most of the altitude we lost dropping into the valley. We crossed the Shou Chu on a rickety swinging bridge of cables and planks strung between two stone piers. Tattered prayer flags fluttered over the torrent. By midday we'd made the first village, Lama. Some of us who dawdled were invited inside a house. The ladder up from the wood-chip barnyard was hewn from a log. It was as cool and shady inside the main room as it was hot and bright outside. Our host directed us to sit by the smoky hearth; he filled china cups with a yellow barley wine called *chang* and demonstrated how to take a pinch of toasted barley from a pot and sprinkle it in our drinks. The chang was sweet; we sipped it carefully, worried about bacteria.

"I think it's just alcoholic enough to be safe," Peter said.

The man said something in Chinese that Peter could make out despite the dialect.

"He says his heart is bitter because he does not have more to offer us."

When Peter brought the Polaroid camera out, our host and his wife went off to change. Heaven help the trekkers who venture into the Shou Chu valley without Polaroid cameras. Take only pictures and leave only footprints are not the watchwords of modern cultural voyaging—leave footprints and pictures is more like it. Peter's two previous expeditions Polaroided most of the valley, and now when a camera clicks people there expect a print to materialize immediately. To meet a demand he created, Peter was carrying dozens of packs of film.

Our hostess returned in a magnificent, long, black skirt with red and yellow stripes and a top fashioned of gold brocade. Her wrists and neck were ringed with silver and nickel-brass jewelry. Tufts of green and yellow yarn swung from delicate silver chains attached to her ears. Her husband looked equally resplendent in a chartreuse tunic, his ornately sheathed foot-long knife gleaming across his waist.

We trooped up to the roof on another notched-log ladder so our hosts could pose. Rice straw was drying in the sun. Every house in the valley had a small furnace built into the wall, from which the family sent sacrificial smoke into the sky void. A boneless pig was hanging from the rafters of a rooftop shed. It had been gutted, cleaned, salted, sewn back up and hung out to dry, perfectly intact—tail, snout, ears, everything but the squeal.

We went on through Woati toward Turu, six miles up the trail. Whenever we would stop to fill water bottles and shake in the little iodine tablets, people would gather, wave, and smile. Occasionally Jim would sketch their faces. All was right with the world: Men were fascinated by gadgets, women by fabrics. Kids got Joan to repeat Tibetan phrases and nearly fell down in the dirt from laughing. "I'm probably saying something like 'I am the daughter of a pig,' " she said.

We stayed that second night at the house of a Turu villager, sleeping on his roof. Peter found a little store, run by a Mongol, where *pijou* in big green bottles could be bought for five yuan—less than a dollar; he later learned that the price for locals was two yuan. The beer was strong, and after a bottle, Stoney the rice-spiller lost his glasses. (He saw them for sale in the Mongol's store on the way out and bought them back for forty yuan.)

On toward sunset our spiritual aspirations gave way to a gross eruption of materialism, as the cultural voyagers did land-office business, trading cash for horse blankets, knives, money belts, bracelets, chunks of turquoise, and stirrups. What jewels Turu villagers couldn't pluck from the lotus they stripped from their fingers and offered for sale. A better mantra for Shou Chu mani stones would have been, Do you want to buy? What one of us might spend on dinner for four in Manhattan is a good year's salary there. The shopping frenzy finally cooled when Peter and Zhang discovered that they had drained most of the expedition bank. A big sum had gone to have Jasmine's hair braided in the Tibetan fashion. It took many hours that night and the next morning to complete the job; expensive as it was, the effect was priceless when Tibetan women who had never seen Westerners came face to face with a gorgeous black American wearing her hair like theirs.

From then on, however, money would be tight. The Chinese were counting on supplementing the trip larder with local produce, maybe a chicken or two, and if we didn't rein in the acquisitions we might be testing the claim of some Tibetan lamas that it is possible to get all the protein you need simply by breathing airborne bacteria.

We set out for Garu early the next morning, a long uphill haul. We turned out of the valley of the Shou Chu and into the valley of the Konkaling River, a rollicking green flow in a bed of ginger boulders, then left the river quickly, angling up a ridge on long switchbacks. Rain squalls damped the dust in the afternoon and put a chill in the air. The group strung out, each of us moving at his own pace. Jasmine, beginning to feel dizzy and nauseated, fell to the rear. When I reached the village, a crowd of fifty people had gathered around Rob. I took off my hat. The eyes of the villagers went wide, some gasped, some laughed uproariously. They had never seen blond hair before. Or maybe they'd never seen thinning blond hair before.

It was getting close to sundown when the rest of the group arrived. Jasmine was experiencing mild hypothermia and was faint, possibly from altitude sickness. Peter and Zhang arranged with a local homeowner to let her lie in a sleeping bag by a hearth. Mr. Su, our Yi guide who had been all over this country hunting, had taken the horses up to the pasture above town, another half-hour of walking. Jasmine was weak, but after a few hours of rest she felt able to ride up on a mule and made a quick recovery over the next twenty-four hours. Tom said later that she'd been overwhelmed by the blessing at the monastery, the exertion of the travel, the intensity of the reception she'd received. "She feels like she has a responsibility to be an ambassador of her race," he explained.

"Aw, come on," said Steve. "Nobody feels a responsibility to be the ambassador of their race." At twenty-three, Steve was half the age of most of us. He was a chain smoker, aghast that the New Agers were supplementing their meals with blue-green algae. He'd been grousing loudly about the donkey bells, and several times Dabney had to chide him to keep his thoughts to himself.

The village of Garu, home to about 350 people, sits on a shelf above a deep defile with mountain walls to all points of the compass. It's too high to grow rice; the billowing green fields, cleverly irrigated by culverts that bring water down from the mountains, are mostly planted with wheat and barley.

The pasture that was base camp for us also seemed to have become the village green, as people flocked up to eyeball the circus. We were getting an idea of what it's like to be Michael Jackson. Crowds gathered around our camp table to watch us drink coffee and hot Tang. When they heard the sound of a tent fly unzipping, they would dash over to see the new arrival. They knelt over duffels, mating and unmating strips of Velcro. They rubbed Gore-Tex like tailors taking the hand of gabardine. An old woman found an empty Evian bottle in my duffel, unscrewed the top, and pocketed it. Her face was as leathery and worn as an old catcher's mitt, but there was something in her eyes that made me think of the light in the middle of the ocean. Everyone had large, liquid eyes, and most flashed smiles when you met their gaze. As Rock had remarked, the people of Garu bear a startling resemblance to the Apache. A few were dressed in Mao jackets and caps and the rubberized sneakers that are ubiquitous in rural China, but many wore traditional clothes—the men in skin vests, their calves wrapped in woolen leggings tasseled with colored yarn, the women in brilliant flowing skirts, their hair woven into thin braids and tied with pieces of turquoise and yellow bulbs of amber and strands of wool—108 braids in all, one for each chapter of the Kanjur, the most sacred book in Tibetan Buddhism. In the mornings old women marched their flocks up to the threadbare pasture where our tents were pitched—pigs, sheep, goats, and black cows all tangled up together. At night, the people of Garu built fires and invited us to dance, men with men, women with women. Step, step, kick, circle right, arms interlocked. The evenings of song and merriment and cross-cultural rapport were so similar to Wildman weekends and women's Esalen workshops that the New Agers floated out of their sandals. The lotus was spitting up jewels.

Treasures of cultural voyaging aside, Dabney, Steve, Rob, and I wanted to get up into the realm of the snow and ice, if only for a look. Dabney and Steve had an extra week and were planning to explore the Duron Valley on the other side of the range. The four of us left Garu in midafternoon, accompanied by Su, who spoke Chinese, some Tibetan, and even a little English, and Wang, the assistant liaison officer, plus three Tibetan horsemen. We trudged uphill for three hours, through sweet-smelling pine forests. The trail was a daily commute for sawyers from Garu who humped the ridge to cut beams for construction in the village. We pitched tents that night at 13,250 feet, just below a pass slung between two wind-sheared hills. Here at last was our gate into the high country where the thunderbolts were stored. I could feel the air getting rare in my lungs, and the strange pull of the pass, still in the light when the camp was dark.

You can seek out mountains all your life and strive for summits and all the time not know what you want or why you do it, beyond the bald explanations of the challenge or the need for some dimly understood sense of renewal. So few things ever said about mountains seem equal to the intensity of being in them. I'm no clearer about my motives now than I was twenty years ago; in fact what I wonder about now is this compulsion to know why, this restless impulse to dig out the logic of a life, when what anyone ought to do is wage it unself-consciously, without equivocation, as a cat leaps or a flower blooms, or lightning strikes. *Why, why, why* is the West's great mantra. Even after a little while in China you begin to see how unimportant *why* is. Chinese consciousness is organized not around causes, but around balance and order and, above all, harmony. One strives to wear fate easily and not moan and whine like a state senator for its rationale. It's one thing to meet the principle of the Tao in a book; it's another to draw it out of the air and drink it down when you sip from the streams that run from the mountains in the land it came from.

I spent three days on the far side of the gate, released from the need to make a coherent story of my being, adrift in the paradoxes of Lao Tzu: "He who strides forward does not go." I wanted to climb, but my lungs burned and my head throbbed. "Galling limitations," the *I Ching* had prophesied. I rejoiced in my aspirin. Much of the time I was alone—Dabney and Steve had cruised on into the Duron Valley, and Rob was off taking pictures—and it was a kind of bliss to barter company for solitude, to get clear of human voices. There is no premium on privacy in China; in the mountains I had all I wanted. Snow fell each night and melted in the afternoon. My companions were crows, rocks, silence, and a jar of aspirin.

On the first of May Rob got up at one in the morning. He wanted to hike to the Duron Valley divide and climb one of the peaks for a view of the sacred mountains in the light of dawn. Our camp was at 14,350 feet, and the pass into the Duron Valley lay four miles and some 1,500 feet above. It was pitch dark, about 20 degrees, and the fresh blanket of snow was ankle deep.

A line from the *I Ching* came to me. "Rob," I said, "in all his transactions, the superior man carefully considers the beginning."

But Ansel was mewing. Rob marched into the darkness, his headlamp lighting the way. I went back to sleep and rose just before sunrise. I had not planned to again attempt to climb the nameless 17,000-foot castle of gray slate that sat astride the divide. The day before, I had turned back at the pass, exhausted, sunburned, and nauseated. But for a westerner there must be some higher harmony in fulfilling goals, because I found myself plodding uphill again.

Rob's boot-trail stretched across the snow. The valley was a staircase of four giant steps. Wending my way up the third, I walked in the tracks of a lone brown wolf and, in a brilliant basin of snow, met Rob coming down. Clouds swirled downvalley. I turned back to the labor of ascending, cutting up onto the shoulder of the peak and scrabbling up a steep chute of gray stones. I leaned over to rest on my ice ax. It made me ill to look too far up the talus slope. Just before the summit there was a band of rock. I ate an aspirin and worked up through a chimney, breaking off icicles with my shoulder, feeling every heartbeat in my temples. Ten feet and rest. Ten feet and rest.

And here was the top. It was noon.

Mists rose from the abyss on the north face, obscuring the distant massif of Minya Konka, but south and west and east the weather was clear. Endless ridges ran to the ends of the earth, and the white giants glittered as if rinsed in liquid steel: Shenrezig, Chanadordje with its chisel-shaped summit, and Jambeyang, half again more beautiful, an immense fang of ice and snow and rock bared against an azure sky.

I ate another aspirin and started down on my own version of the Long March. The snow had melted. Leaping from tussock to tussock was like hopscotching on the heads of blond owls. I passed the witchy pinnacles and the couloirs and the empty stone yak-herder huts at our camp, and curved around the dramatic ravines and saddles, and dropped through the high-country gate we had breached three days before, the seam between realms. Down to 13,250 feet, where there was supposed to be a tent and some supper but wasn't because some crucial piece of information had been lost in the translation from English to Chinese to Tibetan, and so there was nothing to do but ignore the cries of Mayday! Mayday! that were coming from my knees and plow on, through the rhododendrons and the piney air to the camp at Garu, twelve miles and 7,000 feet below the aerie where I had stood at noon.

And so in reverse. We descended from Garu, each of us a bit wistful to be coming down. We pitched camp outside Kana Radja, a little monastery mentioned but never visited by Rock, where we had stopped on the way in. There were just four monks, three of whom were really novices, ages thirteen, nine, and eight. I had slipped them some Chinese cookies. Had they ever tasted cookies? From their expressions you would have thought they were awakening to the glory of Mahler or reading Joyce, especially the littlest fellow.

A Tibetan man who lived below Kana Radja invited us to his house that night. Galoom the Cosmic Cowboy, a trader whom we had met on the way in and who had sold practically everything but his horse to Tom, tagged along. We went down before dark, crossing the crib of animals inside the gate as our host gripped the collar of his mastiff even though the dog was already held back by a thick chain. As I passed, the animal lunged and furiously exercised his jaws. I had the very New Yorkish thought that it was not going to be easy to escape the party with that dog around. We all found seats to the right of the hearth, sitting on pads or cross-legged on the plank floor. Evening light filtered through the few glassless windows and slanted down the smoke hole in the roof. The smoke in the room was not unpleasant. Our host, a tireless, agile man, could not do enough for his guests. He circulated continuously with a kettle of chang. When the light was gone from the windows, he pulled a piece of pitchy wood from the fire and set it on a hanging metal stirrup; it cast a lovely light. Zhang and the cook arrived with a butane lantern. Our host doused the hanging fire. Oh, no, no, we said. Zhang snuffed the bleaching light. Our host left the room and returned with a lantern of his own—cultural wire-crossings had become a trip motif. The room was a babble of languages—who knew what was being said. It didn't matter, really. The party was made not of dialogue, but of presences.

Tom had Peter lie face down on the floor and began to massage his scoliotic back. Jim took a place in support at Peter's head. And though no one explained it to him, Galoom the Cosmic Cowboy held on to Peter's feet.

"Breathe into the tension," said Tom, performing slow and subtle maneuvers to get Peter to release the physical and mental stress locked in the curvature of his back. The process was as much concerned with emotions as with the body and very much rooted in the Eastern principle that physical disorder reflects frictions on the higher planes of the mind and spirit. However, it was too slow and subtle for our cook, who jumped up, shouldered Tom and the New Age out of the way, and had at Peter's back like it was a cutting board of fresh vegetables. Galoom frowned, and Jim retreated. The cook pounded, kneaded, and chopped with the sides of his hands. He gulped a mouthful of chang, and then, with a loud rasp such as can be produced only by a race of people who are ankle-deep in hocked phlegm, he spit it all over Peter's back. Oh, what a stunning move! The fan of aerosol chang gleamed briefly in the hanging fire. The cook gulped another mouthful and spit again. Peter sighed pleasantly. Later he decided that Chang Expectoration Massage was the essence of cultural voyaging, and he resolved to mention it in China Trek's promotional literature.

We ended that night with the Cosmic Cowboy leading a session of chanting. Long *om* sounds swelled and subsided. I decided to start looking for a wholesale deal on blue-green algae. It was hard to know what our host and his family made of the performance, especially as the volume grew and the *om*ing was overtaken by freelance forays into stranger sounds and harmonies, chang-fired birdcalls, percussive mouth noises. Maybe to them this was the anarchic cacophony of free-market capitalism, the cult of the individual. Maybe it was just the music of a zam blowout.

And so in reverse: Turu, Woati, Lama. The rice crop was being harvested now. Women trudged uphill under bulging sacks of grain. I hiked with Sybil, who insisted that it was only our belief in the firmness of the earth underfoot that kept us from plunging through the molecular interstices of the trail.

We camped along the Shou Chu short of the swinging bridge. And then we made the 5,000-foot grind uphill to Beiyangping. How different the place seemed now, shocking in its contrast to the neat harmonious villages, an oozingly raw, rip-and-run boomtown of tar-paper shacks and palpable boredom.

I was in a sour mood anyway. Some spiritual heir of Joseph Rock's

Konkaling bandits had stolen my brand-new boots out of my duffel; my property was going up like sacrificial furnace smoke. (My sleeping pad and shaving kit had already been filched.) The boot theft seemed to reflect the foot of karma kicking me for disdaining to join the shopping spree on the way in.

But Beiyangping didn't need any help appearing hateful. A black-haired boy was jerking a lesser panda around on the end of a rope, to the amusement of a desultory crowd. The animal looked like a cross between a ferret and a racoon. It kept trying to get away, and the boy couldn't have been having more fun jerking it back. He picked it up by the tail and flung it at some dogs. When the exhausted animal quit fighting for freedom and lay in a shivering heap, near death, the boy dragged it around on its back. Men laughed. The town was mostly men—men with ill-fitting dentures and grinning, masklike faces. We found a store where we could draw up chairs outside, shell peanuts, and celebrate the end of the trek with tall green bottles of Chinese beer, but the boy dragged his prize over to our circle.

"Maybe we could buy it from him," said Peter.

"That's a great idea," said Joan.

"How much?" asked Peter in Chinese. A murmur ran through the sea of bystanders: This was a twist! The boy named a price, Peter named another. And then it was agreed: forty yuan for the animal's freedom. The villagers were tickled silly, as no doubt any of us would have been had twelve Chinese backpackers materialized in New York and offered $8 to ransom a cockroach. The boy removed the rope, nervous about being bitten. The animal scuttled into a ditch beside a shack, and ran around the corner; the townspeople ran after it. It stopped to drink some water under a stoop, then huddled in a hole. Joan got up to check on it. Another kid ran up with a stick and threw it at the creature. Five grown men watched.

"If you throw that stick again, I'm going to throw a stick at you," Joan said in a level voice, even though she could not hope to be understood. Five minutes later she checked on the creature again. The crowd had doubled; there was a wicker cage over the hole, and a drunken man in a black sweater was jabbing at the animal with a stick. Joan picked up her own stick, went to the man, and yanked the prod from his hands.

"Get out of here!" she said in a steely voice, brandishing her stick. "You people deserve what's happening to you! You people deserve to live under communism! You deserve Tiananmen Square! You deserve to be killing each other!"

Incomprehensible words again, but there was no mistaking her meaning. The drunk in the black sweater backed off, and the crowd dispersed. One man came forward and by a mix of translation and gesture made it known that if the animal was to go free, it had to be prodded out of the hole first. He helped

Joan coax it out. She led it nervously to the forest's edge and watched the creature flee. When she returned she found the same man approaching with a thermos of hot water for tea. He was a tractor driver. He'd been living in Beiyangping for twenty years. His wife was in Chengdu. He was allowed to see her once a year. He ventured to hope that his countrymen's attitude toward animals had not offended Joan irreparably. He gave her a small silver dagger—a present, he said, on behalf of friendship between their two countries.

"Easier to climb to heaven than to take the Sichuan road," wrote Li Bai 1,200 years ago. The Tang Dynasty poet knew of our present-day travail. The Tao can count dust and ruts among its verities. And bandits. Our drivers were nervous, for they had heard reports of highwaymen rolling rocks into the road and robbing people when they got out of their cars. The ace at the wheel of the Nissan was in such a hurry that he crashed into a log and crumpled the bumper. Not long after, we skidded around a hairpin—and lo! Rocks in the road! Before our driver could say anything, the Cultural Voyagers, who knew nothing of bandit reports, had jumped out and were shouldering boulders aside. I'm convinced the outlaws had abandoned the ambush when they got word that my boots had already been stolen. Rocks cleared, we resumed the trip, composing limericks to kill the pain:

> Dr. Nie said I'm no normal GP.
> I lug bags, boil water, make tea.
> Vacations are clover
> But if this one's not over
> I'll soon need a doctor for me.

And so we made our way back to Chengdu along the Sichuan road. And what I remember now is this: not the dust, not the headaches, not even the feeling of being in the mountains, but the afternoon on the way down, when we were approaching the monastery at Kana Radja. I had been thinking of the littlest monk and the power of cookies. All of a sudden here he was, scurrying up the trail as fast as his legs could carry him. He was wearing his oxblood robe; no shoes; hair growing back from a boot-camp cut. "Lama!" he shouted. I took it as an invitation—Come to my place!—not an appraisal of my spiritual station. "Lama!" He was beside himself with happiness. The circus was returning to pitch its tents nearby and slip him sweets and take his Polaroid as he wobbled under the weight of the sacred books. "Lama!" he said again, and then he took my hand and skipped and ran me to the homely little temple that was his home.

There is rapture in mountains, but none like what I could see on the face of that little monk beaming up at me with his big Tibetan eyes and clinging to my hand as if it were all that he could ever want of fortune—this happiness that I had come back. I gave him a Frisbee later and showed him how to throw it to his pals. They sailed it into Void No. 19, and I was sure it was gone for good, but they went in after it, and when they came out they had it in their hands and held it up for me to see, as if it were the jewel itself.

SEPTEMBER 1992

EVERYBODY COMES TO BELIZE

by EDWARD HOAGLAND

In Belize you will meet determined birders working on their life lists, trying to sight a jabiru stork. You'll meet a roofer from Milwaukee taking the winter off, a junk-bond salesman who has lost his job for "liquoring the Indians" (selling to execs from bankrupt savings and loans), a cashiered chef from Santa Monica, an advertising person jettisoned in an agency shakeup. I, too, had lost my job, as a college professor, for political incorrectness, and was looking for a rainforest respite, coral sand beaches, Mayan ruins, preferring a mainland landfall to an island destination because of the resonance of continents—jaguars and mountain lions, whole Indian nations, and the knowledge that I could walk from these mangrove swamps and limestone plains clear to Alaska or Argentina, should I so choose.

What I did was get myself to Miami and on board a SAHSA jet for Belize City. SAHSA is Honduras's airline, and after crossing the aquamarine Caribbean to Quintana Roo and paralleling the heel of the Yucatán—the flight attendants serve Rock Cornish hen at any hour—it dropped me off in Belize, an English-speaking democracy formerly known as British Honduras. The country achieved independence from Great Britain in 1981, but, being coveted by Guatemala, it still keeps 2,000 of Her Majesty's troops on its soil to thwart these designs. About the same size as El Salvador, which has 6 million people, and Vermont, which has 600,000, Belize is only a third as populous as Vermont. It boasts 700 species of trees, as many as in the entire continental United States, and 90 kinds of bats, 54 of snakes, 6 of opossums, and 5 types of wildcats. Though regarded as a political anomaly by Honduras and Mexico too, it won admission to the Organization of American States in 1991, partly by denying U.S. forces landing rights during the invasion of Panama. (The British are said to have coached the Belizeans on this.)

As an oasis of tranquillity, far less populous now than when a million Mayans lived here a thousand years ago, Belize has lately received some spurts of anxious refugees from civil wars in El Salvador, Honduras, Guatemala, and Mexico. From the seventeenth century it was a hideout for the so-called Baymen, Scottish and English privateers who hid in the river mouths that indent the mangrove swamps and robbed Spanish merchant ships. The world's second-longest barrier reef further sheltered the Baymen from retaliation, and one buccaneer in particular, Peter Wallace, who is said to have arrived with eighty companions at the mouth of the area's most navigable river in 1638, may have given that river and the country his name (Wallace; Wilis; Belis). On the other hand, a Mayan word for "muddy" is *beliz*.

Jamaica's governor, the nearest British authority, intermittently put the kibosh on such freebooting, whereupon the Baymen would buy slaves to cut logwood, a small, locally abundant tree whose heartwood provided red and purple dyes for Europe's woolen industry. When new technology eclipsed this livelihood, they shipped mahogany, Spanish cedar, pine, oaklike Santa Maria trees, and sacred Mayan ceiba or "silk-cotton" trees (for their fluff), at the lofty top of which godlings once dwelled. Slavery among off-duty pirates in the woods became more of a meritocracy, a looser, more rascally, rum-punch, miscegenetic operation than regimented plantation slavery, and white supremacy was hard to maintain. Kidnapped Mayans and escaped slaves from elsewhere were added to the Creole brew, and Carib Indians began arriving about 1802, after surviving tribal annihilation on some of the Lesser Antilles islands, which they in turn had conquered from the Arawaks. (*Carib* meant "cannibal" in Arawak, and thus the Caribbean vacationlands have an ambiguous semantic ring.) Later additions included Sepoy mutineers deported from India, Chinese coolie wanderers, Miskito Indians from Nicaragua, Mexican mestizos fleeing the Caste War in the Yucatán, and Confederates deserting the ruined South.

In 1798 the Baymen had secured their hold on the territory by beating off a fourteen-vessel Spanish fleet at St. George's Caye, near Belize City, and by 1871 the uncharacteristically reluctant Crown was persuaded to formalize its relationship with the colony. Bananas, citrus fruits, cacao beans, sugar, molasses, coconuts, and tortoiseshell in dribs and drabs were not exports to make a merchant banker's mouth water, and the market for mahogany petered out. Chicle tapped from sapodilla trees as a base for chewing gum then replaced mahogany, but after a boom of thirty years or so, synthetics were invented, which by World War II had rendered chicle superfluous too. Sugar and citrus are the main crops now, and—in the forests—ecotourism and marijuana. Ecotourism, indeed, may have supplanted marijuana. You meet rapscallions aiming to run ecotours who seem not altogether unlike eighteenth-century logwood buccaneers.

Hard-drug courier planes, however, drop off enough white powder when refueling that Belize City has a cocaine problem. It has become Footpad City, which is a shame because it has a flavor otherwise like that of Dar es Salaam a couple of decades ago, with a peaceable and planetary hum that can transport you out of the Americas for the price of a cheap plane seat. Stay awhile, but seek security.

From the airport go to the 4 Fort Street Guesthouse, if you are midscale. (Head to the Fort George Hotel if you are upscale; or to Mom's, on Handyside Street, if you are traveling light.) In a wicker chair on the Fort Street veranda, with a margarita and a glass of iced rainwater and a lovely bouillabaisse in front of me, I found my cover pierced immediately. A British naval officer seconded to Belize's navy paused in flirting with my traveling companion to say, "You look like a college professor who's just been sacked. That special seediness."

There on the veranda I also met a local beer brewer, and an elderly butterfly hunter who was rumored to have been cashiered from his job only four months short of when his pension should have kicked in, and then Sharon Matola, who is the soul of conservation in Belize. She is a thirtyish woman who ran away from Baltimore with a Romanian lion trainer, toured with a circus in Mexico, then came to Belize as a jaguar trainer for a movie company. She cajoles party ministers to set aside swathes of rainforest in reserves, and British soldiers to help her build the Belize Zoo. And there was a Yorkshireman who flies Puma helicopters for the Royal Air Force. He told me of the fun of lowering a snake scientist into the jungle to capture boas, imitating the man's herculean rassle with a thirteen-footer until the shy herpetologist himself showed up for supper.

Belize City has 60,000 people. Hurricanes flattened much of it in 1931 and again in 1961, so the seat of government has been moved fifty miles inland to a village called Belmopan, though no one who had a choice moved. At the Swing Bridge over Haulover Creek you are in the center of town. Putt-putts and pitpans (river craft), lobster boats, sailing sloops, and dive boats tie up here. Banks, the post office, the police station, Lebanese shops, Hong Kong restaurants, the green Catholic church, the president's green frame house, and the

People's United Party's blue headquarters are close at hand. You can buy papayas and Bombay cloth, see Ibo and Ashanti faces speaking Jamaican patois, overhear lots of Spanish, and visit the Mennonite furniture mart nearby. Pale, burly, blond, in straw hats and bib overalls, Belize's 6,000 Mennonites came from Manitoba by way of Chihuahua in search of clean living. They raise Belize's chickens, breakfast eggs, and green vegetables, converse in a sixteenth-century Dutch-German dialect, and look at you aware that you are going to hell. Some are such fine mechanics that they are called Mechanites. Others use a horse and buggy and are departing for Bolivia or Paraguay to start pioneering primeval jungle all over again.

Colorado surfers, Gurkha artillerymen, Boston remittance men, pass slowly by, as the muggers with shoeshine kits circle them. I'd heard of Belize on the Yukon River, where some of the young placer miners spoke of winters in Placentia like a luscious secret, ducking south when the creeks froze up and paying in gold nuggets. It was twice as expensive as the rest of Central America yet half as expensive as North America, they said, and no need to feel sorry for anyone: Just sun, swim out to wrecks, eat fish, smoke dope. Red parrots, blue grottoes, Indian pyramids. Buy in dollars, not quetzals, cordobas, lempiras, balboas.

Haulover Creek is lined with slapped-together shacks of misfitted boards in cheap landsmen's pastels or deeper mariners' colors, some built of salvagers' booty off the teeth of the reef, some out of junkyard crating and hurricane damage. Nothing to make you weep unduly if it blew down again, but handy and homey, set up on stilts; people run for the concrete schools in a flattening storm. The gardens are hedged with conch shells, turtle skeletons, shark and crocodile skulls. South of the Swing Bridge, on Albert and Regent streets you've got more substantial white clapboard two-story houses, in the modestly porticoed, gingerbread-and-iron-railing style of superseded British colonial ports worldwide.

After a day or two you may want to head for the bus station, or go to a gray house on stilts at the corner of Euphrates and Orange and talk to George Young, an ambulance driver who also runs a couple of ramshackle station wagons and may be pleased to drop everything and take you on a chartered tour of the country. My traveling companion, Trudy, a college psychologist, and I spent four good days with him. George is fiftyish, a black Creole, the son of a sailor who would sometimes come home from the Seven Seas and ship out the same night and who had an "outside family" to keep up with, too. But George has paid school fees for six kids, maintains close relations with them, and got to know his father fondly and his half-brothers also, before the old man's death. His mother and three brothers live in the United States, but George chose what he calls "the slow lane," staying here as a family man and taxiing the occasional tourist around.

George drove us north to Crooked Tree, Guinea Grass, Orange Walk, Sarteneja, and the ruins at Altun Ha, two excavated ceremonial plazas with pyramids, temples, ball courts, and palaces covered with irrepressible greenery and imbued with a marvelous seabed smell. In the ball-game plaza would-be kings competed in life-and-death matches. Crooked Tree, a placid village bordering a waterfowl sanctuary on a lagoon, grows cashews and mangoes. Guinea Grass is Wild Westville, by contrast, druggy and close-mouthed; and you can see a fortified, floodlit villa gleaming white behind razor wire. You can also rent a skiff for the twelve-mile trip up the New River, through mazy lambent sloughs to the ridge and ruins at Lamanai, or Submerged Crocodile, some of which are 2,500 years old. As recently as 1867 Mayans fought the British here (5 million people in Mesoamerica still speak Mayan dialects), but with the huge, orchid-stippled trees, the vivid river, the lakelike lagoon, and the sun on the marshlands beyond, a quietude prevails. The two-square-mile center of Lamanai seems scarcely excavated, though more than 700 building sites have been identified and there are three temple pyramids that you can climb, decorated with jaguar and crocodile and sun-god masks. It was here in the sixties that archaeologists found the largest piece of carved jade in Central America: a nine-pound head of the sun god, Kinich Ahau. Palms, ferns, and philodendrons swarm nearly everywhere, fountaining vegetation at each cleared spot, and spider monkeys gab and amble in the canopy overhead. In the limey lichen-covered rubble you can find sea fossils inches from the honey smell of brilliant flowers. The scents of soil and sea are blended, and nature here is veined with history. We tasted custard apples (like warm ice cream) and soursop fruit, admiring the clouds reflected on the water, and the sailing trees.

Sarteneja, east of the mouth of the New River, is an isolated fishing village a couple hours' drive from Guinea Grass through large sugarcane plantations, the marl road strewn with cane leaves where the big trucks have passed. Wages are $10 or $20 (U.S.) a day, though illegals from El Salvador may work for only $3, which is about the price of a pack of Independence cigarettes and a bottle of Belikin beer. George talked about how many cane-cutters get bitten by "tommygoffs," or fer-de-lances. "Wowlas" are boas. The king vulture is called "King John Crow"; the screech owl, the "monkey bird"; the osprey, the "billy hawk"; the toucan, the "bill bird"; the blue heron, the "full pot" (because it's so big its meat fills a pot). The otter is the "water dog." The kinkajou is the "nightwalker." The tapir is the "mountain cow." Howler monkeys are "baboons." Pumas are "red tigers." We saw cornfields and beehives, and little *milpas* growing yams and plantains. "Lots of sweets in this soil," George said.

Being black in Belize is never as dicey as it is in Guatemala or Mexico, but the two major parliamentary parties do tend to divide along racial lines. This northern part of the country is largely Hispanic, the heartland of the United

Democratic Party, whose colors are red and white, and party officials' houses are sometimes painted that way. George's Creole Party, the People's United Party, uses blue and white. "But your feet be lifted off the ground here if you make much noise about that," George said. "You might wind up in a well. They's a lot of wells around. You can't ax them about politics. Very distressful if you did."

Sarteneja is a beach town of 1,600 souls on Chetumal Bay. It's got blue water, a row of coconut palms and almond trees, and some fishing sloops from which people go out in dories to dive for conch or lobster (called crawfish) or angle for red snapper, bluefish, shark, and mullet. There are two dirt streets of tin-roofed, cement-block houses; some hungry dogs; a nondescript one-story hotel; and several vacation huts going up. The gringos who've discovered this place— schoolteachers, diner owners—seem mostly from upstate New York, though I met a stone-broke Quebecois whose single asset seemed to be a sailboat he had built; he was awaiting a buyer. In countries like Belize no particular relationship exists between a gringo's income and how imaginatively he travels.

I'd come to meet Jan and Tineke Meerman, a stringbean fortyish couple from the Netherlands who manage the 22,000-acre Sarteneja Reserve on nearby Shipstern Lagoon. Sarteneja Reserve is owned by a group of Swiss butterfly fanciers, and Jan and Tineke raise and mail out the pupae of perhaps 30 of the reserve's 200 species to commercial butterfly farms in Europe, where visitors enjoy the relaxing ambience of greenhouses full of tropical plants, waterfalls, exotic birds, and so on. The pair can also, of course, cater to the bottomless market for dead butterflies, which are collected like stamps worldwide. But what has happened to Jan and Tineke—very tall, he wears a U-shaped beard; very precise, she clips her hair short—corresponds to Sharon Matola's transformation from jaguar trainer to conservationist. Jan, a carpenter's son, arrived in Belize as an amateur lepidopterist, but in the process of going into the forest and marsh after butterflies (catching 30 quick species in any morning) he too became a committed ecologist. He speaks of reintroducing howler monkeys to the 8,000 acres of gallery forest within the reserve, and of the necessary education program that would involve the surrounding villages. His recreation used to be collecting lucrative butterflies for the carriage trade— with a graceful tweaking motion he catches them by the wings between his fore- and middle fingers. Now it's sleeping on jaguar and puma trails in the rainy season, when the tracks show up well, and studying the habits of several individuals he knows.

Married nine years, Jan and Tineke are a good team and have a "night" dog and a "day" dog to perform different duties outdoors (bite and wag). They have a pet wowla, a small croc, some turtles, and a collared peccary. We ate a shrimp-and-grouper dinner and talked about Belize's three coral snakes and

four tommygoffs, and why hot countries have a slow pace, and how Mennonite apostates, as George put it, "try to get bad," going to bars, flirting clumsily.

We slept in the bunkhouse and in the morning walked the nature trail that
Jan maintains, labeled with dozens of trees. Trumpet tree, bullet tree, mimosa,
waterwood, poisonwood, strangler fig, sapodilla, ceiba, gumbo-limbo, mother-
of-cocoa, royal palm, finger palm. Then we wound down the old Northern
Highway, through a pleasant backwater of cane fields, little cattle ranches,
shallow wetlands, and second-growth woods, back to Belize City, where a cab-
driver excitedly hailed George to tell him that another driver, using George's
other station wagon, had been arrested for running drugs. "He wants you to
bail him," he said. It seems that George's own good reputation had prevented
the car from being impounded, however, and George was disinclined to extract
the man from jail immediately. The trouble was, George suggested, that jail was
too soft. Imprisoned British soldiers still are forced to dig graves for a coffin full
of stones and dig it up again, or build a mountain of sand and run up and
down with their packs on. *That* is jail, he said.

At the airport, Mennonites in severe frocks and blocky shoes were meeting
new pilgrims from Canada who looked as raptly distracted by God as they,
while Trudy and I rendezvoused with our new guide, Neil Rogers. Neil, a
rolling stone and Englishman with years of tourist-herding in India under his
narrow belt, seemed as symmetrical a type to my own as were the residents to
the visiting Mennonites.

Just as I like to eavesdrop to get an inkling of what's in store, Neil was eaves-
dropping on us from behind a door as we approached. Life here, he said after
introducing himself, was lived "on the knife edge," either going beautifully or
awfully, which was how he preferred it. He, too, had arrived "at loose ends" in
this spot where reef-divers "bubble around" and the sky seems so big and the
world só small.

Travelers aim for salient sights and memorable days that slice through a
cross-section of a new country. In the Pyrenees they want to spend a sunny
hour with a goatherd who has been hiking those same meadows for half a century, or will barge in on a glassblower on the island of Murano who's been doing that since before they were born. Spanish lace-workers who have gone
blind making tablecloths in the service of m'lady; fisherfolk in the Bay of
Fundy whose ancestors were riding the tides when King George squabbled
with George Washington. Old wines, tapestries, porcelains, and cathedrals:
Continuity and devotion are what tourists are after, because they're gone at
home. Ah, the peasants in the fields, *they* still believe!

Of course, the rainforest is so old it's where snakes chose to lose their legs.
They were lizards who found that wriggling on their bellies through the tum-

bled vegetation was faster to begin with. Animism, pythonic religion, a faith older than Christ or Moses, is what we look for in the jungle. Otherwise we want to chop it down.

Neil, in his Land Rover, sped us west from Belize City toward the Guatemalan border, an eighty-mile trip that till the 1930s could take two weeks of poling up the Belize River, with landings at Double Head Cabbage and More Tomorrow, at Burrel Boom, Dancing School Eddy, and Never Delay, at Black Man Eddy and Bullet Tree Falls. In the Valley of Peace, Salvadoran refugees grow peanuts. Neil spoke of the virginal spelunking in the mountains to the south and maybe ten days' wilderness walking either north or south. His boss, Mick Fleming, at Chaa Creek Cottages, where we were headed, had recently been on an expedition along the Raspaculo branch of the Macal River, an area where some said no human beings had set foot for probably a millennium.

Fleming had left Uganda because of Idi Amin, and Chaa Creek is an African-style lodge with round, whitewashed, thatch-roofed cottages. There is a raised patio for having drinks on, and breadnut trees spread overhead with parrots and keel-billed toucans feeding in them. The river flowing by in front needs only a couple of hippos.

Next door to Chaa Creek, an herbalist from Chicago named Rosita Arvigo will give you a massage and an infusion of tonics learned from a genuine Mayan shaman named Eligio Panti. She runs a research facility called Ix Chel Farm, which has been collecting medicinal plants for the National Cancer Institute in the United States. Rosita has also cleared out a nature trail in the bush, where you can examine rubber and allspice trees, mahogany and bay cedar, fiddlewood and custard apple, and the give-and-take tree, a handsome palm whose spines can deliver painful wounds that its own bark will cure. She's a tously, somewhat offish woman who lived for years with a tribe of Indians in Guerrero, Mexico, before moving here.

Next day, a retired British tank sergeant named Dick Strand, from Bath, took a group of us bumping by Land Rover to admire the 1,000-foot Hidden Valley Falls on the Río On and then a sumptuous cave through which the Río Frío slips, sandy-bottomed and radiant with leafy-green backlighting at both ends. He took us up on the Mountain Pine Ridge to watch British cannonfire and to see where survival teams live off iguanas, armadillos, and coatimundis. Strand has done this, and has five tours of duty in Northern Ireland to reflect on, plus better stints in Germany and Cyprus. But he came back, married a Belizean, fathered two daughters, and bought a comfortable house on which his property tax is $27 a year.

Then Neil piled Trudy and me into a car and took us upriver till the track petered out on a fertile plain by the Macal, probably the site of the Mayan capital of Tipú. The Classic period sites of Tikal and Caracol, as well as Xunantunich, are not far off.

A young man, William Morales, met our Jeep with his mule at a modest melon-and-squash farm, strapped our bags on the beast, and led us up a limestone gorge. The river sashayed, ran like puppies, leapt down rock ledges through tawny pools with tarpon and snook in them, past rock facings and great sacred cotton "world trees," bullhoof trees, palms, figs, and Santa Maria trees, my favorites because the trunks are like oaks. Palmettos and ferns were underfoot, and vines draped everywhere, over tapir and tayra tracks.

Most days, William rides seven miles at dawn to chainsaw a piece of the jungle for a hydroelectric project, hearing the howler monkeys holler as he goes and comes. We climbed a bluff to his parents' pretty farm at the lip of a waterfall. Antonio and Leah Morales had tried to raise cattle, but the jaguars kept killing their stock; now they were trying coffee. By candlelight we dined on homegrown corn, beans, peppers, chicken, pineapple, and coffee, and Antonio told how, when he and his brothers built watch fires to protect their cows, the biggest jaguar just sat down by one of them and warmed his back—then splashed vigorously through the stream, his colors gorgeous in the firelight, and loped away. Even hunting opossums and white-lipped peccaries ("warree") for the pot is an adventure, because the men go barefoot at night on paths where tommygoffs—the proverbial "two-hour snakes"—are also hunting. Tommygoffs can give birth to as many as seventy young, and Antonio had seen one strike an agouti just as he himself had drawn a bead.

In the morning, with a hundred birds sounding like tin whistles and all the world a stage for them, Antonio led us through the woods to a cave he'd found while gathering roof thatch and tie-tie vines. Head-high once we'd crawled inside, it wound down for maybe 200 yards, with stone shelving providing niches for occasional polychrome pots painted with monkeylike or humanoid figures. There were a couple of low-ceilinged side chambers that you could scramble up into, marked by ceremonial fire rings (these caves were underworld religious sites, never places Mayans slept), and behind an impressive stalactite an offshoot passage sloped into an ultimate cul-de-sac, which had an altar in it.

I'm crepuscular by nature and feel at peace in caves, and Antonio likes the night. He told about how as a child he'd led mule trains through the dark forest to the *chicleros'* camps, with just a bell mare to help him, the big cats never attacking. Starlight can belong to people, too.

Back at Chaa Creek, the supple Neil Rogers put Trudy and me into the hands of a driver named Elmo Richards, who had grown up in a hamlet called Las Vegas, near Bullet Tree Falls. His father had been a hunter, selling crocodile hides at $3.50 per foot, fer-de-lances for $12, boas for $5, puma skins for $50, and one-hole jaguars for $75. (Now a good woodsman is more likely to grow "Belize Breeze" in an off-road patch.)

Elmo had worked with his father in a slaughterhouse in San Ignacio (100 lambs a week for the British military). Soon restless, he went to Los Angeles to visit a cousin. But like so many Belizeans I met, he found the United States scary. When he went out-of-doors, young toughs would home in on him, reaching for his beer money, his pizza money, asking with death in their voices whether he was a Crip or a Blood. Life was so cheap and there seemed so little space for him to squeeze into that he was relieved when his cousin simply gave him a secondhand truck to take back to San Ignacio. At the slaughterhouse there he would load it with meat and drive southeast to the coastal town of Dangriga, selling wholesale at every crossroads shop. In Dangriga he'd pick up a load of fish and start back, a twelve-hour round-trip. Because his sister had married a Dangriga politician, he was well rooted at either end.

From the nondescript capital of Belmopan, a barracks village, we turned onto the so-called Hummingbird Highway, which is so rich in hummingbirds, orioles, laughing falcons, blue-crowned motmots, and swallow-tailed kites that the name seems not a hype. The gravel road swings past a dozen quick and amber creeks, pocket valleys, minijungles, past grapefruit and lime groves and sweet-potato milpas. Good Living Camp. The Sibun River. Over-the-Top Camp. Alta Vista. We saw a drug czar's *finca*, a Hershey chocolate farm, a Nestlé orange juice factory. The Maya Mountains to the west lent the scenery a panache, and finally we turned toward them and drove into the 102,600-acre Cockscomb Basin Wildlife Sanctuary, named for Victoria Peak, the country's highest mountain (3,675 feet), whose profile is like a rooster's comb. Elmo, pleased with us, invited us to his family's next boil-up—his father dumped in pigs' tails, peppers, palm oil, opossums, chocolate, bananas, everything.

There were three cabins at the reserve, one for the wardens, one for us, and one for the three soldiers guarding us from bandits. Walking out, we swam idyllically in South Stann Creek under a spreading bri-bri tree and smelled the droves of warrees that had been eating palm nuts underneath the cohune trees. The soldiers (Belize remains a democracy partly because it has only a 600-man army) included a Creole corporal, tall, black, and street-smart, from Belize City; a slim, straight-shooting mestizo from Orange Walk, or "Rambo Town," as George Young had called it; and a Mayan from the Punta Gorda district. The four wardens were small-framed, muscular, round-faced Mopan Mayans with the bark of woodsmanship on them and an air of watchful stillness. These canebrakes and "tumble" forests (so called because the hurricanes bowl them down) were their home, and like good wardens they had hunted jaguars before the preserve was established, using a large gourd with buckskin drawn across its mouth that grunted like a rutting *tigre* when you scratched your nails across the top.

After a balmy night of insect songs and bat activity under the panoply of stars, and some more walking in the morning, Elmo drove us to Dangriga (a Garifuna word meaning "standing water"), whose population is climbing toward 9,000. Sun-soaked in February, the reddish streets were a promenade for ladies carrying black umbrellas to block the heat. (The men we saw were mostly drunk.) We ate lunch in the Starlight Cafe, a Chinese restaurant next to the Local Motion disco. At night, Elmo said, some drugs or sex may be peddled, but in a more good-humored spirit than Belize City's melee. We heard that a local obeah man rises from the image of a coiled snake if you go to consult him in his cabin, that the boas grew venomous fangs at nightfall, and that a Welsh woman had been living alone in the mangrove swamps for two decades.

The Chinese fled here from the Japanese in World War II, and now a second wave is leaving Hong Kong in fear of the Communist takeover. Lebanese own many of the citrus farms; they arrived as storekeepers but have lately sold their businesses to "Hindoos" (East Indians) to become landowners. You see them less often, Elmo said, but everybody eats Chinese.

The Garifuna, or Black Caribs, as the English called them, arrived on this coast in the early nineteenth century. They were seafarers, dugout-paddlers, island raiders, cannibal warriors. At the time of the European conquest, the Caribs, paddling from South America, had swept the Arawaks from the Lesser Antilles and were perhaps prepared to move on Haiti and Cuba. Instead they were decimated and temporarily given St. Vincent's Island as Indian territory, though scalawag French and English and blacks from a slave ship that wrecked just off the island in 1675 joined the brew. The Yellow Caribs, those with white blood, were permitted to stay after the British reassumed control, but the Black Caribs were deported in 1797 to Roatán, an island off Honduras, and some wandered here to the mouth of Stann Creek, a former trading post set up by English Puritans from Nassau. The Mayans still seem metaphorically stunned at their self-inflicted decline as a civilization, which began 500 years before Columbus, but the Garifuna, whose conquest of the Caribbean was arrested at full tilt by the English, French, and Spanish, have energy to spare. They go to sea, or colonize Brooklyn (which has more Garifuna than Belize) or become schoolteachers, merchants, government clerks.

In Belize we are thrust into nearly the climate in which we were born—body temperature, like the womb, like Olduvai Gorge. And the pyramids have such basic forces inscribed on them as the sun, the tiger, the croc. Friends whom I met in Belize City like to swim nude every morning near the mouth of the brawny Belize River, five fathoms deep where it enters the sea, and dolphins and sharks and whatnot show up, fast mountain currents joining the punch of the tide.

Stann Creek and Dangriga are gentler. We hired a boat from Ringo Usher, the son of the local dentist, and headed twelve miles out to Tobacco Caye, a seven-acre island where those seventeenth-century Puritans grew tobacco and where Garifuna turtlers later settled. Now Ringo and his father are building tourist cottages in Dangriga. All up and down this coast, old sea-snake and saltwater-crocodile islets are being converted to money, though we did see one that has been preserved for the boobies and frigatebirds to nest on. Hundreds wheeled over it, landed to roost; at one end was a special tree where, Ringo said, the birds went to sit when they were sick and preparing to die.

The frigatebirds steal fish from the boobies by "beating on them till they spit it up," as Ringo said, and we saw other avian and piscine dramas. Ospreys diving. Herons. Water birds, from limpkins to soras, loons to grebes to whistling swans, have celebrative cries, saluting the dawn or the rising moon as if God were alive in the world. But we—lizards that we are—tend to hoard the sun, gaze out with a basilisk's impassive stare from our beach towel, bathing in a kind of fugue of memories while feeding heat to our cold bones. And the breaking surf eases our hearts. *Thump. Thump.* Its failure to accomplish anything except in a cosmic time frame is comforting, yet the energy soothes and reassures us.

Tobacco Caye sits right atop the barrier reef, so swimming from the beach you can dive a few fathoms down the splendidly awesome wall or paddle about in the shallows on top. Or you can do what I did, which was to step from Ringo's skiff straight into the hammock that Winnie and Nolan Jackson, his grandparents, have rigged on their dock, and stay there awhile. The surf thundered hard, the wind blew boisterously, the sun skidded off the tossing waves. With a bit of thatch shading me, I was in heaven, though Nolan grumped that if the wind always blew like this, "We would go crazy."

It was suppertime, and going off to collect two lobsters from one of his traps for Trudy and me to eat, Nolan remarked over his shoulder, "It's a shame these poor lobsters have to die for you." Because he didn't know us from Adam, his grouchiness seemed refreshing. People come to his hammock and little hotel for their honeymoons or divorces or a cancer recuperation or to celebrate a cash bonus, dressing in beachcombers' sweats as if they were pleasantly indigent. Winnie said she'd moved out here for her asthma, but demurred when we complimented the view. "It's just pretty; it's not beautiful," she said.

She baked johnnycake, fried plantains, and boiled rice and beans to go with the lobsters, while the wind blew pelagically, the thatch over us rattled, and the Atlantic crashed against the rim of the reef. Nolan told us he had grown up on an island on Glover's Reef, eighteen miles farther out, an island his brother has now "thrown away to an American for $75,000." Nolan himself shipped out in 1945 with Panamanian papers to see the world. Making friends, he soon acquired a dead American's papers too, and worked on American ships as Josnik Kowalski, pretending his accent and darkish skin were Polish in origin, at twice the money. For seven years he traveled to Europe and the Far East, a deckhand in the summer, a fireman in the warm engine room when the weather turned cold, and stayed at the Seamen's Church Institute in New York, taking astronomy courses and studying for a mate's license between jobs. It was a fine spell, but so many regular navy men were demobilized that ships became hard to find. He remembers the brutal glitter of New York with a certain startled pleasure—the "rum shops" selling beer for "a shilling" (twenty-five cents), the museums, the social possibilities, the excitement of the uptown streets, the breakneck competition—but marginal folk like him felt crowded out.

He came back to Glover's Reef and fished for red snapper, grouper, and tuna till he lost his boat off the beach one night in 1978 when a north wind blew. Tobacco Caye, where he and Winnie started over, had been Winnie's grand-parents' home, though "if you lived here you were nothing," she says. "If you lived in town you were something." Back when tortoiseshell was worth $10 a pound, the village would send two big schooners down the Mosquito Coast to Nicaragua after hawksbill turtles. Though small and built up with holiday houses, Tobacco Caye has a nesting pair of ospreys, sixty feet up in a coconut palm, and catbirds, tanagers, grackles, turnstones, pelicans, herons. The houses have solar panels for electricity, and tubing to carry rainwater from the roofs to cisterns.

I roamed the island, admiring the palm trees' idiosyncratic windblown slant, and imagined drifting ashore here as a castaway, trying to crack a co-conut open for water to survive, then hoping that another would fall before I collapsed. I swam, lazed in the hammock, and met Elwood and Sandra Fair-weather, Belizeans who, like Nolan Jackson, made me a bit homesick. Elwood, in a foundered leather easy chair next to his beach shack, said in a gravelly, im-penitent voice: "Twenty-eight years in New York." He and Sandra, a pretty woman with a red ribbon in her hair, had been married fifteen years, and had just had a baby daughter. Sandra laughed at how long they'd delayed, and showed me some charcoal drawings she'd made, and a jaguar cub skin. Elwood had three grown kids from his first marriage, to an Italian woman in Brooklyn; he'd worked in a bookstore for eight years and then as a typographer, until computers made him redundant.

I sat in a broken wooden chair next to him and met his chums who wan-dered by: a dugout lobster fisherman, a diving guide, a buffaloed Texan who had sailed down here from Galveston and had just lost the motor off his boat. (He had a charter arriving, a woman from Minneapolis—what would she think? Would she advance him money?) Elwood dispensed a fatalistic calm. In New York he'd haunted Greenwich Village, he said, "and generally was a beat-nik." Bleecker Street, the New School, St. Mark's Place, Washington Square—we found we'd shared some city sites and obsessions of the sixties; and like Nolan, he didn't seem to have returned to Dangriga by fervent choice.

Elwood's ancestors fought the Spanish at St. George's Caye in 1798. Later another, as treasurer, signed British Honduras's paper money. His father is a distinguished Anglican minister, who worked in New York for many years and whom I visited at the cathedral in Belize City. But with that lineage also goes the proud tradition of "going for a stick"—a cotton tree—for a dugout canoe, and the obeah stories. Even in New York, Elwood informed me, an obeah woman could retain her powers, could walk down the street with a gold chain on and no snatcher would grab it lest it turn into a poisonous serpent in his hands. One obeah man, however, got his comeuppance, despite his supernatural powers. He liked to sleep with married women, after first slipping out of his skin so they didn't know who he really was. But he ran afoul of a clever husband who discovered where the obeah man had hidden his skin and who had sprinkled salt on it so that it shrunk. The poor lover snuck back from his dalliance and couldn't put it on. It didn't fit! *Skinnee, Skinnee, Skinnee, don't you know me?* he cried—a song still sung by schoolkids.

Sandra, who is a dancer and a Belize City Creole, not a Garifuna, draws some wicked-looking nudes, and there are Garifuna stories of young girls propitiately fed to crocodiles. These perhaps balance the apparent likelihood that Garifuna men who captured Arawak women for wives in pre-Columbian times first ate the Arawak husbands, thus adding a certain vividness to life and making the victory memorable. Though not much more than do the gastronomical rituals of success and failure in New York.

We tourists wear bifocals. Pious about the survival of the sixty species of coral in the Caribbean, we nonetheless want a strobe-light vacation, both light and dark. Ecotourism, and yet with malice aforethought for when we get back and start scrambling for money and status again. Eat well, dress well, and strip the earth to pay for it—and not just for lucre, but the endless OJ and burgers grown in the tropics on bulldozed rainforest, the gas guzzling, shrimp guzzling, resort rambling. Tourists come from consuming countries, and once they pass Passport Control and get home again, they are Central America's problem, not yet its solution.

FEBRUARY 1992

THE BLACKFOOT YEARS

by ANNICK SMITH

I am not a fisherwoman. I have tried many times to catch fish on a line—sometimes to please others, sometimes to satisfy myself—but I do not like to snap the necks of wiggling cutthroat trout, or rainbows, or Dolly Vardens.

"You eat them, you can kill them," my husband, Dave, would scold me.

Where I live, you learn that tracking and killing wild game is more honest than buying domestic meat—better for the world, perhaps, better for the soul. But killing is never a matter of logic. My squeamishness goes back to a bookish childhood in Chicago, where I grew up in an apartment on the North Side. The closest I came to fish was when my fat little Grandma Deutch would take me to the Jewish fishmonger's shop on Broadway for smoked whitefish in wax paper: smelly, greasy, delicious. Still, I attach myself to men who love to fish. And it has been my good fortune to live along trout streams.

When my young family came to Montana in the fall of 1964, we spent our first day fishing Rock Creek, a blue-ribbon stream in the Clark Fork drainage. Dick Hugo, the Northwest poet, took us. He had convinced Dave to leave Seattle and join the English department at the University of Montana. We could have looked for houses to rent, or checked out the campus where Dave would teach on Monday.

"Let's go fishing," said Dave.

Dave and Dick and our eldest son, Eric, fished the narrow canyon while I untangled six-year-old Steve's line. We stayed until dark. The valley was streaked with the red of vine maple. The burnt-grass hillsides were fringed with ponderosa pine, western larch, and Douglas fir. God or nature, certainly not accident, had endowed the land with the same colors and markings as the trout.

We spent every off-day fishing Rock Creek, and within a year we had rented a streamside bungalow at the Valley of the Moon Ranch. I was still in my twenties, only a few years removed from innocence. That was before our twins were born, before my black hair turned gray, before Dave realized he had a fatal heart disease.

But those were the Rock Creek years, and they are not part of this story. This story begins six years later and is about my family and neighbors, a way of life, a book, and a river we sometimes call the Big Blackfoot to distinguish it from the Little Blackfoot.

In western Montana, all highways run along pine-forested river routes carved through mountains by ice and running water. The Big Blackfoot empties into the Clark Fork of the Columbia a few miles from Missoula. You can turn off I-90 at Milltown and drive along the river on Highway 200 through a narrow, winding canyon. Where the land opens into prairie, turn right on Bear Creek Road if you are coming to visit me.

Dave and the boys and I built our recycled hewn-log house in the midst of our meadow. The main door faces the morning sun. We never use that door, though, because the best entry is from the path that links the driveway to the kitchen, which looks north toward the river. I sit on our deck on summer evenings and watch night crawl up Bear Creek from the blue-black Blackfoot Valley.

Sometimes the night sky pulses green in rhythmic waves of patterned light, passing over fixed points of starlight, reminding me of rivers, of blood and sap, of the flowing patterns of life. The river hides rocks, snags, and drowned creatures. This secrecy draws me to waters. I believe we are much more like rivers than we are like meadows.

My best friend has studied interpersonal psychology. "Do you know what your name means to Buddhists?" she asked me once. "*Onnica* means flux," she said. "And flux means chaos." I'm not much given to believing such things, but the river has become my metaphor for change and connection. It seems I have been standing in the same place for twenty years watching the chaos of my life flow by.

There's an idyllic morning I carry around with me like a lucky rubbing-stone. It was 1971, our first summer at the ranch, and we'd gone fishing on the Blackfoot. The salmon fly hatch was about over, but a few of the heavy, orange-bodied insects hung on to willow branches in the cool, dewy air. When their wings dried, they would beat them suicidally over riffles where the rainbows were waiting.

We drove our Land Rover to the edge of a high bank upstream from where Belmont Creek flows into the big river. Dave and the older boys scrambled down to the rocky shore, shadowed by great-branched ponderosa pines and pink-and-yellow cliffs embroidered with lichen.

"Use live ones for bait," shouted Dave.

The boys and I hopped through willows and serviceberry and chokecherry bushes, grabbing for sluggish salmon flies. Dave immediately hooked and netted two twenty-inch rainbows. Eric and Steve, with their squiggling flies, caught smaller trout. Even I got a good bite. Then it was over.

I brought out tuna sandwiches and peaches and chocolate-chip cookies. A thermos of hot coffee. A jar of lemonade. After lunch, with the sun high and the water cool, I was happy to lie on the damp sand, the older guys gone downriver in search of big ones, the four-year-old twins making dams out of colored river stones—aquamarine, rose, jade green.

Norman Maclean memorialized those Late Precambrian rocks "almost from the basement of the world and time" in the title story from *A River Runs Through It*, in the passage about *logos*, the Word. He described the Blackfoot's deep patterns: the "unity" of a three-part fishing hole, its billion-year geologic history. He connected the act of fishing to his father's Presbyterian notion of grace. Readers who never hefted a rod or cast a line identified fly-fishing with craft and art and beauty—and Maclean's story of brotherly love and death.

But on that long-ago summer morning, I knew nothing of Maclean. I did not know that his wife had recently died or that he had retired from teaching at my old alma mater, the University of Chicago. I would never have guessed that some sixty miles upcountry, in a log cabin at Seeley Lake, at the age of seventy-three, the crusty old Montana teacher was beginning to write his great book about family and fishing and love. Or that the book's culminating scene would take place exactly where I lay daydreaming in the Blackfoot breeze.

Dave grew up along the Mississippi in Hastings, Minnesota, and loved to skate. He read the boys *Hans Brinker or the Silver Skates* so they would get the idea of his life on the river. "We kids'd skate the backwaters," he said. "We would build big fires and tease the girls." It was a vision from Currier & Ives, or Brueghel.

Dave bought secondhand skates at the Salvation Army. Black hockey skates for himself and the boys, white figure skates for me. I cannot remember Dave ever putting his on. Snow stood four feet deep in our field that year, and Dave was too ill. His arteries were clogged with the cholesterol that we could see in patches under his deep-circled, pale blue eyes. He didn't have the energy to clear an ice rink on the river, and I didn't care enough to do it.

"Live fast, die young, and leave a good-looking corpse" was Dave's self-mock-ing motto. He had given me *The Amboy Dukes* when we were high school lovers, and I had hidden the bad-boy book under a rubber girdle in my bureau. But now he had fallen victim to familial hypercholesterolemia, a genetic metabolic disease that would endanger our children. Buying our 163 acres with a down payment borrowed from my parents and building our log house were bets against mortality. "It makes me feel better," Dave told a friend, "to imagine Annick and the boys on that place. To know they'll be there . . ."

There were other reasons. Dave had grown up poor and illegitimate and wanted land with his name on the deed. I have come to realize that he also wanted to cheat fear and fate by returning to a time when death was a fairy tale. He was intent on living out the most vivid fantasies of his rural midwestern childhood.

"What do you want to be when you grow up?" It was a joke. Eric posed the question to his father because Dave changed professions—lawyer, professor, filmmaker—the way other restless men change wives. Dave's answer became a family catchword. "I want to be a cowboy."

The Blackfoot Valley offered a haven where the Cowboy could fish, hunt, ride his horses, own land wild enough to harbor elk, whitetail and mule deer, black bear. My dreams of escape joined easily with his, and I became the Ranch Wife. Land is safer than blood or love. It is not like a river.

Dave would spend two Christmases on the ranch. The first was in 1971, when a German shepherd, a black Lab pup, two Siamese cats, four boys, and Dave and I shared an old one-room bunkhouse to which we had added a sleeping loft and deck. We melted snow for water and tramped a path through the drifts to our open-air outhouse while we built the big house on the meadow.

The second Christmas was in 1972, when we finally moved in. We slept on mattresses on a floor salvaged from the gym at Hellgate High School. The worn maple was marked with random green and yellow stripes, red numbers. It was cold, but we were breathing the perfume of red cedar from our new shake roof, and we rejoiced in flush toilets and electric heat. We could not know that this would be our last winter on the ranch together, or that the following winter Dave and Steve and the twins and I would be living in Hollywood.

The City of Angels was about as far as you could move from our Blackfoot homestead. We rented a furnished one-bedroom apartment in a transients' building on Orchid Street, leaving Eric to finish high school and caretake the ranch. Dave had quit his tenured job at the university, and we embarked on a last desperate try to make daydreams come true; we were going to break into the movies. If life is a river, you have to learn how to float.

"It's Disneyland," said Dave. "We can always go back to Montana." He wrote scripts and I looked for film work and Steve endured Hollywood High. We bought the twins a foam-rubber football and tossed it around in a park lined with palm trees. The lawn was full of dog turds and held a plaque dedicated to Rudolph Valentino.

By April Fools' Day we were back in Montana, broke and stripped of illusions and wondering what our next move should be. Dave never got a chance to decide. Just after his forty-first birthday, on the eighth of May, his heart stopped. He fell down on the maple kitchen floor. While the six-year-old twins watched, I pumped at his chest and breathed into his mouth. I neglected to hold his bleeding nose and have always felt guilty, but Dave was a drowned man, and I could not save him.

We held a wake at the ranch. Neighbors I knew only slightly brought food: macaroni casserole, banana bread, a sliced ham. The cardiologist came. His wife wore white gloves. He had convinced me to approve an autopsy. "Not for me or you," he said. "For the boys." Now he pulled me aside. "The arteries were so diminished. I don't know how he could live at all." Luckily, Dave had not known that, because of a birth defect, his coronary arteries were shrunk to half-size, like a withered arm. It must have been stubbornness that kept him moving, dreams. I was glad he had spent his last days fishing and working our Blackfoot ranch. When David Smith died, he was wearing black rubber boots caked with Blackfoot mud. He had just come in from irrigating our meadow.

My vaulted, pine-paneled bedroom was garlanded with loops and streams of work print. After two years in Spokane producing a series of documentaries, I was home and editing a film about Dick Hugo. The twins had memorized Hugo's poems backward from hearing them over and over on the Showcron editing table. I still slept with Dave's pajamas (the scent of him) under my pillow. I had met Dave when I was sixteen, borne two of our four children by the time I was twenty-two. Now I was a liberated woman of forty with a new life and career, and I was having a hard time separating the core of me from him.

All four boys and I were together for the first time in months: Eric and Steve home from their colleges for Christmas. We gathered around our new fireplace. It was made of salvaged red bricks; I had designed it, with Steve the hod carrier. It was the first addition to our home to be built without Dave's supervision.

The moment becomes a Polaroid picture: distorted and transient. We sat around a fire, played word games, listened to a scratched recording of Dylan Thomas reading *A Child's Christmas in Wales*. We did our best to drive off melancholy.

There was a book I intended to give to one of the boys as a present, but once I started reading it, I could not let it go. In a few years I would come to know Norman Maclean as a friend and business partner in our efforts to make a movie based on his book. But first and most important, he was the voice of *A River Runs Through It*. I read aloud: "In our family, there was no clear line between religion and fly-fishing."

"Your father would have loved this book," I said.

Fourteen years later, snow is falling outside my bedroom window so thick I see nothing but ghosts. April blizzards are common in the Blackfoot Valley. I have seen snow on Memorial Day, snow on the Fourth of July. I open the pages of my first copy of Maclean's book, inscribed years after I bought it, by the author: "To Annick Smith, who lives where it is more beautiful but so tough the Finns and the Serbs lined their fields with rock-piles and then gave up."

The day Norman Maclean signed my book, I had gone to visit him again at Seeley Lake. The lake is fed by the Clearwater River, which is a tributary of the Big Blackfoot and part of the same fierce snow country. Five-hundred-year-old larch climb from the lakeshore, and each fall the larch shed golden needles on the shingled roof of Norman's log cabin, which he helped his father build in 1922. When I arrived I was shocked to see the eighty-five-year-old author descending a ladder from the roof, broom in hand.

"You should take care!" I admonished.

"I *am* taking care," the old man snapped back.

We walked to his dock, gazed across Seeley Lake to a peak in the Swan mountains where a fire was burning unchecked. As a young man, Norman worked for the Forest Service in the Bitterroots, and he has come to detest its cut-down-the-trees-and-make-money politics. He has been writing a book about the Mann Gulch fire of 1949, where thirteen young smoke jumpers died senselessly. Norman is ill now and confined to his Chicago home. I hope he lives to see the book in print. It is another great cautionary tale.

I think about living along the Big Blackfoot. If the river is important, so is the wild country around it, and so are the people who live off the country. Is it possible to preserve all three?

In western Montana the economic rule is real estate for capital, trees for decent work. There is logging and mill work, driving log trucks and building roads. Then there's splitting shakes and peeling posts and poles and—if you're a kid or really hard up—selling firewood for $65 a cord, cut and split. The best deal is packaging log houses and selling them to Japan.

Blackfoot country has been logged for a hundred years. The virgin timber was hauled by horse teams and floated downriver to the mill at Bonner. Much of the forest is private, first owned by Anaconda Mining, now by Champion International and Plum Creek. Only a few stretches of old growth remain. I am fighting to preserve a few acres of yellow pine, Douglas fir, and larch in the

Bear Creek drainage that borders my homestead. I cannot stand the whine of chain saws, the shudder and rumble of earth as the great trees fall, the sharp odor of sap running like blood.

"We're managing for regeneration," a company forester told me recently. "It's an *industrial* forest. Trees will grow back."

"Not in my lifetime," I say. "Not in my children's lifetime."

Even if the forester is correct, the primeval forest is gone. Trees that grow back will be a uniform crop, planted to harvest in fifty years. The industrial managers hire gyppo outfits and pay by the piece, no benefits, no security, and no motive to care for the land. Remote ranges are laid open with raw roads; the skinned earth is pink. Old-time loggers like my neighbors are disgusted, for they love the wild woods. But who wants to go to a big city? Wrassle burgers at McDonald's?

Sometimes I think the West has gone pure loco. Neither the environmentalists' angry clichés nor the businessmen's pipe-dream colonialist economics work. We must sit down together to preserve what we have in common. Every year brings less cover for elk and bear. More erosion. Mud and silt choke creeks and settle in the river. With the climate warming, perhaps, from accumulated need and greed and the cutting of forests worldwide, our snow runs off in a week, leaving little moisture in the soil.

What will happen next, I wonder? Are we making a desert where only knapweed can survive? Will old photos and memories and Norman's book be the only ways to salvage the beauty? Can we exist on nostalgia and art?

If you are to avoid complicity in destroying the sacred, you must adhere to the rules of right conduct. Take the day William Hurt came to Montana to fish the Blackfoot with Norman Maclean.

This was in 1983. Hurt, along with about a dozen Hollywood stars and studios, wanted to make a film based on *A River Runs Through It*. He is a fine fly fisherman and had been anxiously preparing to show Norman that he could play Norman's legendary fisherman brother, Paul. It took some doing, but finally, just above Sperry Grade, Norman and Hurt and Norman's old fishing-crony George Croonenberghs set off in George's raft.

Minutes later, they were paddling back to shore. Hurt bounded out and came racing up the steep bank.

"Forgot to buy a license," he huffed.

"No fishing without a license," Norman had ruled. No matter who you are.

Hurt raced some fifty miles and returned with his license. The two old fishermen had pulled onto a gravel beach and were calmly pitching stones into the Big Blackfoot. Hurt scrambled down the bank and the expedition was off again.

Several hours and six downstream miles later, I stood on the Clearwater Bridge, squinting into late afternoon sunlight reflected from the rapids and spray and riffles of the bright river running under us. Our fishermen came bobbing down the stream and pulled into the shore.

"He can fish," pronounced Norman as Hurt held up a modest twelve-incher. George nodded agreement, and Hurt grinned.

The deal was on. Hurt went off to Brazil to make *Kiss of the Spider Woman*, certain that he would come back to produce, direct, and star in *A River Runs Through It*. The trip to Brazil won him an Oscar but cost him Norman. Hurt had lost touch with Norman, who had lost faith in Hurt, and within a year the deal was off.

We need pilgrims in our valley more than we ever needed settlers. The run of river that Hurt traversed with the two old men is protected by the Nature Conservancy. Other stretches are being conserved through easements or purchase by state and federal agencies and private environmental groups. There are fishing- and boating-access sites and restrictions on development. And two of Montana's largest wilderness areas, the Scapegoat and the Bob Marshall, border the upper reaches of the Big Blackfoot in a region so cold, snowy, and rugged that real estate developers have left it alone. The coldest temperature in the Lower 48—70 degrees below zero—was recorded on the Continental Divide on Highway 200 at Rogers Pass.

A few years ago, my friend Bill Kittredge and I took a producer and a director on a scouting expedition with Norman Maclean. We came to where the Clearwater River flows into the Blackfoot, and the director was snapping photos of a great rock, water swirling, picturing Norman's brother Paul shadowcasting in the spray.

A young couple in perfect Orvis fishing outfits came striding up the bank, wicker creels over their shoulders, rods in hand. We stopped to chat with them. In the pocket of the woman's fishing vest was a familiar paperback.

"What's that book?" asked the producer.

The young couple were high school teachers from Colorado, religiously tracking the fishing spots in *A River Runs Through It*.

"Would you like to meet the author?" asked the producer.

They were awestruck. Norman cracked jokes and signed their dog-eared book.

Other pilgrims are not so literate. Norman might call them desecrators. In his youth an occasional canoeist might have driven a Model T up the narrow, twisting Blackfoot Canyon to shoot Thibodeau Rapids on a summer Sunday afternoon. It would be a dusty, all-day excursion. This July, when the water is high, hundreds of sweaty Missoulans will take half an hour to drive the same route. They will parade down the Blackfoot in orange, yellow, or black rubber rafts. They will drink beer and pop from floating coolers and trail strings of children in inner tubes. Some will troll with bait, others will cast flies. Most will come up empty, because the fishing has become erratic; the river is overused.

I've felt outraged, too, at what Norman calls "Moorish invaders from California." But I am not sure of my moral ground. I have rafted the river with my own cooler and kids in inner tubes. We shoot the rapids for the fun of it.

One July evening not long ago I decided to try my hand at casting with the new fly rod my fisherman son, Eric, gave me for my fiftieth birthday. Now that my boys are grown and gone, I have decided to give fly-fishing one last try. I am no longer a squeamish city girl. It's been twenty-five years since I threw my first line into Rock Creek, and I am far more experienced in life and death.

Bill Kittredge and I crossed the Blackfoot a mile or so down from the fishing hole at Belmont Creek, where Norman Maclean described his sacred last expedition with his brother Paul. We did not want to intrude on a spot that held so many memories: where my little boys hopped through willows to catch salmon flies while Dave hooked big rainbows; where Bill had fished with his own brother, Pat, during his first years in Montana.

We walked through the dusky woods toward a sandbar. Long-stemmed daisies and yellow buttercups glowed in the leafy light. A few mosquitoes circled, whining. At the head of the hole, a well-muscled young man stood with his left arm around a woman. Her blond hair was wet. Both were tanned. Both buck naked. With his right hand, the man was casting a fly rod. "Let's get the hell out of here," Bill said. I turned. Bill was already twenty yards back the way we had come.

I wanted to stand in the shadows and watch. I wanted to see if a red Hills Bros. can, full of worms, lay at the man's feet. Could this be a scene straight from Norman's book?

We walked softly on decaying cottonwood leaves. I inhaled the sweet, acrid odor, which triggers memories of Dave Smith and Dick Hugo, who are dead, and Alex and Andrew and Eric and Stephen, who are grown up. I thought of dogs who walked with us.

Bill stooped to pick up an object in the weeds. It was a soggy wallet. Inside was a driver's license, dated three years before; a man's picture was barely visible through mildewed plastic covering it. Was this a relic of a drowned man? We had visions of death on the river, and of love, at the same moment.

Out my bedroom window, April snow is falling again, and I rejoice because the moisture will help ease three years of drought. Things change, and do not change. I live alone most of the time in our log house up Bear Creek, although my son Steve is here now, and my friend Bill comes to spend some nights. The twins have graduated from college, and we celebrated Eric's wedding on Memorial Day with softball, champagne, and dancing to the Big Sky Mudflaps.

Robert Redford has bought the rights to *A River Runs Through It* and we will film it on the Blackfoot one of these summers. Norman Maclean likely will never make it back home to Montana for one last fishing trip.

When I go for my daily walk, I often head down Bear Creek to the river. I take my dog. I pick wildflowers or berries or mushrooms. Once I talked to a great horned owl. I rarely fish.

Each of us has memories we sing over and over like a song in our inner ear. The place where my life connects with its stories is the Big Blackfoot River in western Montana. It is real. I want my grandchildren to fish in its green waters and to float its rapids in inner tubes. I hope strangers will dive into pools smelling of fish and build play dams with stones that go back to the beginning of time. Boys and girls should skate on the river, make love on its banks. I don't mind if they are naked.

APRIL 1990

THE WORLD OUT THERE

IT'S A FUN, FUN, FUN, FUN COUNTRY

by ANNIE PROULX

We're sitting there, Collins and I, in Rip Griffin's truck stop in Moriarty, New Mexico, the so-called Pinto Bean Capital of the World, taking a break from looking for people having fun. It's the height of American vacation time, mid-August. I came down from Newfoundland to Albuquerque, cutting the long angle across the continent, through the White and Green mountains, along lakeshores and into the oak forests of the Ozarks, up the Pecos River on the route of the Spanish conquistadors, into the Sangre de Cristo Range, and in all these places the parks and campgrounds were strangely empty. Where the hell is everybody, I ask Collins.

We tried for directions to the rattlesnake man's house, but it seems he's long gone. The woman at the Moriarty Museum said, "Once everybody kept rat-tlesnakes as a tourist attraction—you'd have a pit with snakes in it and the tourists would lean over and look. Now the SPCA would get on you. Those days are over." We admired the collection of 1,440 ballpoint pens and a fifty-three-year-old coconut and said, well, what about the Love House built out of motor-oil cans?

"There it is." She pointed at an old stucco bungalow across the street. "Be-longed to a man named Love. You never could see any cans."

There weren't any pinto beans, either. The town quit growing them a generation ago, and one irritable farmer, perhaps harassed by journalists' jokes about flatulence, shouted at us, "I don't 'preciate you askin' 'bout pinto beans. I grow corn! Why should a farmer be any different than a doctor?"

Now, elbows on the table among a clutter of cameras, notebooks, and newspapers, we're drinking coffee and looking out the window at the road where it hooks out of the western mountains in a long, sweeping bend. It's hot, southwestern August hot, and the big stainless semis peeling into the parking lot catch on fire from the sunset. There are forty-odd trucks parked on the oily dirt, and another pulls in every few minutes, air brakes hissing. The drivers stiff-arm the back door, walk past the TRUCKERS CHRISTIAN CHAPEL HELD IN TV LOUNGE sign, past the packets of bee pollen, the rack of *Truckers News*, swing into booths, and pick up phones—fifty, sixty truckers and every one of them pouring it into the gab line. A guy in cutoff jeans with a bleached mustache and a Texas accent saws at a problem.

"Gotta get my goddamn daughter out of jail. Stole John's car . . . tried but she got busted up and drug down the road. Slammed her head on the side of the . . . yeah." He seems to be talking to a lawyer he knows well. "She don't have no respect for herself. Nah, I talk to her but she won't listen. . . . Could buy a bicycle on layaway down at Wal-Mart but she'd rather steal a car. . . . Whaddaya think we oughta do?"

Here comes another, hard-bitten face, wet hair furrowed by comb marks, clumping in on cowboy boots, lips already moving. There are tattoos on his arms, his shirt is open to the navel, and he's wearing a silver-and-turquoise belt buckle the size of an omelet. Sits next to us, ring flashing, calls for coffee and food, looks our way.

"Let me tell you something." He shakes his finger at Collins. "I hate a big truck stop. Reason why is I was in Mississippi one time, ordered catfish, smelled funny. I took a bite down near the tail, I smelled that smell again, poked it with the knife, the guts all came out. Let me tell you something. They never took the guts out. I eat the vegetables, calls the waitress over and show her the guts. She sees I eat the vegetables, she says, 'I notice it didn't slow you down any.' They didn't charge me for the goddamn catfish, but I got to thinking about it as I walked out to the truck and then BRAGGH! Right in the parking lot. Let me tell you something, the parking lot's the only reason you stop at a truck stop. Think about it. Where the hell you gonna park the truck if you want to eat at a good place?"

He is Bill Holland from the Texas Panhandle, an independent trucker, one, he says, of only a hundred heavy haulers in the country. He tells us stories about run-ins with mean-spirited cops, the sufferings of truckers, his design modifications to his rig, a 1984 four-axle (eight axles with trailer) limited-edition Autocar with 879,000 miles on the motor and a decal that says YES, AS A MATTER OF FACT, I DO OWN THE WHOLE DAMN ROAD.

He complains to the waitress: "Let me tell you something. This iced tea is sour." She shrugs and we ask him what he does for fun.

"I don't have any fun at all." His voice is virtuous. "I drive twelve hours a day, seven days a week, 365 days a year so other people can have fun." He says he is paying alimony to five ex-wives and the IRS has a piece of the action. "Champagne tastes," he says, implicating both the tax men and his exes. "Let me tell you something. I took a vacation in 1969. Went to the beach and almost died after three days, I was so bored." His only pleasure now, he says, is an occasional alligator hunt and the feast that follows it. "I love gator tail." He aims an imaginary .22. "If I had my druthers I would be down in East Texas in the swamp right now. That's my fun." Then he's on the phone, says he has to get out of town before it's too late. He's in the truck and away into the night, grinding up through the gears, fifteen, twenty-two, thirty miles an hour.

Collins and I have a plan now, which is not to have a plan. We drift east, still in New Mexico and still on a piece of old Route 66 chopped up by bigger highways like a dismembered rattlesnake. The towns are white-hot and empty; heat waves shudder up from the blistering tarmac. The landscape is the color and texture of dried orange peel. No one is outside. A few cars lurch down the potholed main street of Santa Rosa. It is the kind of place where shade is worth money.

"Not much fun in Santa Rosa today," I say. Collins, half asleep with his wreck of a straw hat tipped over his eyes, sits up and points his finger at me. "Let me tell you something," he says. "I don't 'preciate you saying they don't know how to have fun in Santa Rosa." He rolls down the window and calls to a man coming out of the laundromat.

"¿Qué se hace aqui en Santa Rosa para divertirse, señor?"

"El charco azul, señor." He points.

"The Blue Hole," says Collins. "That way."

The Blue Hole is a cold artesian well, 200 feet across, bubbling up from limestone caverns. Willows bend over the water. The eye is drawn into the relentless blue, an ethereal and exquisite cerulean. Maybe thirty feet down, a tiny passageway leads to a deeper underwater room. There is a grate over the entrance. The Blue Hole attracts divers from all over the West, and before the grate was put in, some ran out of air in the lower cavern and drowned. Today there are no scuba divers, but a dozen Santa Rosa kids with clacking teeth mumble from blue lips that they come here every day and swim. The girls melt away. One of the boys, Chris Foust, tells us he has a famous ancestor who sold his soul to the devil for magical powers; another says the skeletons of the drowned divers are still down there.

Jesse Akina and Cherise Kukua from Hawaii show up, and Cherise, who has lightning bolt designs painted on her fingernails, dazzles everyone with her perfect dives. Her Aunt Charlene and Uncle Mark Shear hold their fat, good-natured baby up to see the swimmers. Charlene dips the baby's toes in the water, and he shrieks at the horrible coldness. It is 62 degrees, tepid to a Maine coast swimmer.

"Life goes on!" one of the kids cries, and leaps into the chill blue.

We're in the Texas Panhandle now, as flat as it gets, as far as it gets. The *llano estacado* rolls on and on—pale buffalo grass, distant windmills, a few cattle, the nodding heads of oil pumps against a white sky. Out of Amarillo we turn south and the landscape roughens, yawns into startling chasms and brushy canyons. This is Palo Duro Canyon, once a Comanche stronghold, later part of legendary cowman Charles Goodnight's ranch, the first in the Panhandle. There is good shade, shelter, and water in the canyon's wrinkled hide. The strange red landscape is like a crumbly layer cake cut by a blindfolded cook. The black New Deal workers who built the road into Palo Duro Canyon Park called the bizarre minarets and stacks that are the cake's crooked slices "hoodoos," a word that has entered the language of rocks and climbing.

We are in the park by dawn's early light, looking for evidence of people at play in the Great Outdoors. The place is deserted. We see a roadrunner, two deer, sage grouse, rabbits, but no human life until we head for a cloud of dust and find the riding stables. Two cowboys with brooms are sweeping the corral to keep the dust and flies down. Foreman Mike Wesley says this is work, not fun, and when he wants the latter he goes "to the show or the bars, but not like I used to—the previous owner broke me of that. I come in with a hangover and he put me out breaking a colt. I said, 'Nevermore.' " The second broom, Bo "Stud Man" Peters, says his idea of fun is "to git drunk and git laid," and that both of these activities can be practiced outside.

Customers who come to ride the horses hope for fun, although "ninety percent don't know the front end from the back end," says Wesley. He's saddling horses now, getting ready for "about forty air force brats" who've arrived for a ride. An early-bird party, including a tense, rein-clutching kid about nine years old in a red shirt, starts down the trail. A man and a woman are walking away from the corral toward a yellow van.

"Quit your damn worrying, Sherry."

"The horses are so big."

"He's just gonna trail, that's all. Looks like a little cowboy up there!" The van backs, turns, and drives away. Five minutes later here's Red Shirt again, lying

low on his horse's neck and holding on. His steed spooked and broke into a gallop, and he held tight, terrified, until somebody whoaed the horse and sent him
back home. There's nothing the kid can do now but sit on the porch, waving at
flies and waiting for his parents. "I had a life experience," he tells us.

The air force kids are anxious, waiting for their horses. All of them pat their
horses. They say the name of the horse again and again. Knowing the name,
saying the name, is important.

Kid: My stomach's starting to hurt.

Kid: You ever rid a horse?

Kid: What if you got to go? What do you do then?

Kid: Just get off.

Kid: Not me. I'm gonna pee on the horse. I don't care.

Cowboy: You look mean enough to take this one.

Kid: I hate this horse. He's gonna bite me. I want Sundance.

Kid: Can you wind up this horse?

Kid: I don't like it.

Kid (sobbing): Excuse me, mister, I don't want to ride this horse.

But they are all loaded on, and the horses start down the dusty trail in the
torrid heat. Before they are out of sight, there is a rumpus and a kid yells. Mike
Wesley goes running. He's back a few minutes later with a horse and a kid lagging on foot.

"Shirley started to roll" is all he says.

An hour later the parents of Red Shirt, who's still sitting on the porch swatting at flies, come back. The kid stalks over to his mother.

"Terrific, Mom, terrific!" he says in a sarcastic voice.

"I'm so proud of you."

"Mom, I didn't ride the horse."

The father stops smiling. "You didn't ride the horse?" The kid explains that
the horse started galloping, that he couldn't hold it, that he was scared.

"Look," confesses the father. "I cried the first time I got on one. I apologize,
it was not a good idea." They all get in the yellow van and drive away. Nobody
is smiling. The kid looks back at the horses.

It's a funny thing. The Panhandle Plains Historical Museum in Canyon has an
exhibit of photographs and objects showing how Panhandle Texans had fun
earlier in the century. There are sepia pictures of church and family picnics at
the Devil's Kitchen, cowboy reunions, rock climbers, croquet fiends, women
seesawing on double planks set on a fence rail, iceboaters sailing on frozen
playas, grown-ups spinning tops at the LX Ranch, swimmers splashing in Tub
Springs. Here are people fishing, squirting themselves with garden hoses, riding in sleighs and buggies and on horses and burros, playing baseball, smiling

at each other at garden parties, swinging in cottonwood shade, hiking, racing homemade scooters, riding in rowboats pulled through shallow water by horses, ice skating, riding bicycles, going off on a hunt, and stoking the fire for a barbecue.

Pretty soon we're running north through the Oklahoma Panhandle, and it makes Texas look steep. The state is crisscrossed by the old cattle trails—the Chisholm, the Santa Fe, the Western. Now it's wheat, natural gas, and oil; the livestock stays on the ranch. From the dead, flat fields, flocks of small birds fly up like pepper specks.

Texas County proclaims itself the Saddle Bronc World Center, but in two hours of driving over the prairie we see no beast, equine or human. It is incredibly, incendiarily hot. Every little cafe and restaurant brings you a clinking pitcher of ice water. Chilled water is deep pleasure in Oklahoma. We seem to be heading for Boise City, for no good reason except that on the far side of the old Santa Fe Trail the map shows a green state park splotch labeled "Black Mesa, 4,973 feet," the high end of the state getting into the mood of the Rockies.

Then we're in Cimarron County, a place where more Indian arrowheads have turned up than in any other Oklahoma county and where there are still no traffic lights. We register at a motel that resembles a storage depot for used electric chairs. There is a feeling of time rushing forward, of imminent catastrophe. We've got to stay out of these rooms until it's time to sleep. Collins squints, says there is still enough light to take pictures. We might as well drive out to Black Mesa now. Maybe we'll catch ranchers in rowboats being pulled through the shallows by saddle broncs.

The road to Black Mesa bisects a circle of flat earth surrounded by indigo thunderheads. The landscape darkens; we are alone on the dipping and rising road except for stray cattle. We pass a set of signs:

I RAISE COWS
THEY EAT HAY
DON'T THROW
TRASH ON
THE RIGHT-OF-WAY

The bruise-colored clouds, riven by incessant lightning, close the horizon with no exit. The wind claws the fields. At Black Mesa we see no one but a man walking a dog. He turns away when we slow down, probably doesn't want to be asked what people here do for fun. We loop the park, go out to the primitive camping sites: empty, nobody, nothing but signs of prohibition—no fires, no fishing. Then the clouds open, and as the Boise City paper succinctly put it, "Hard rain fell quickly."

Next morning we are in the local eatery: a few booths, Formica tables with ashtrays, chairs with chrome legs. The waitress brings us ice water and weak coffee. Collins is having one of his spells; he has blended the personalities of Red Shirt's mother, who worried too much, and Shirley, the horse that rolled. He points and says, "Let me tell you something." The restaurant fills up with Oklahoma farmers. They all look the right age to have inhaled pounds of prairie soil in the Dust Bowl days. They all smoke and cough. The air is blue. A farmer, tanned as black as charred toast except for the dead white forehead of the tractor-cap wearer, walks in; he is wearing a shortsleeved pink shirt, purple shorts, and purple suspenders. Three tractor drivers in kidney belts follow him and order pie, and then comes a knot of older farmers, one in bright green pants and a striped shirt, another in age-yellowed white patent-leather loafers. They limp in on canes and with walkers, greet everyone in hoarse voices, light cigarettes, and begin to cough, deep, terrible coughs that rack them and set off a round of sympathetic coughing through the whole restaurant. Hack, hack, hack, hack. Collins, a nonsmoking vegetarian (though I have seen him declare a lobster to be a vegetable), wants simultaneously to get out of the place and to stay and take photographs of Decayed Rural Civilization. Instead he drinks his water and calls for more. Later he says, "Farmers are the unhealthiest people in the country."

Don't know why, but the Cimarron National Grasslands up beyond Elkhart, Kansas, looks good to us. The Cimarron River flows through, and they say it's a good place to camp or have a picnic.

The river runs under willow shade, and the picnic ground is a cool, grassy refuge in the blasting heat. We drive past empty picnic tables and the new SSTs (Sweet Smelling Toilets), which resemble giant trout-smokers with big stacks, and come to a bend in the river that flattens into a small pool. There are no willows here. The water is sluggish. On the muddy bank upstream, a man is baiting a hook.

He is V-8 Stevens, born near Abilene, Texas, but now of Hugoton, Kansas, spending his day fishing for channel cat. He has a thermos of coffee and a sandwich, two poles, two tackle boxes. "In 1923 I was working for the pipeline, welding, but I hurt my eyes," he says, "and I became a painter. Painted big engines." The horseflies loop around like electrons, attracted by the pieces of raw liver that V-8 has arranged on top of one tackle box. So far V-8's luck is out, but any hour now a big channel cat might seize the underwater liver. He offers us coffee and the loan of one of his poles, but we have to move on.

Later, Collins says, "If you'd taken V-8 up on his offer of a pole, I bet you would have had a life experience." No doubt about it.

We are beginning to shape a theory: People in the United States do not have fun except on weekends; they have fun only in authorized big recreation places that have high "fun" profiles or are heavily advertised or have natural-disaster news value: Yellowstone National Park, the Grand Canyon, Mount St. Helens, Mount Rushmore. And it is necessary, in America, to leave home to have fun, to drive a long way to a different part of the country before the sense of pleasure kicks in. The familiar is never fun. Why go to the picnic grove on the Cimarron when you can drive to Oregon and have a picnic on the Clackamas?

We stop in Rolla beside the railroad tracks. It's one of those places where you do stop. There are a few disintegrating grain elevators that look as though they've been through a tornado, say around 1957. I stand in the hot weeds, looking at the elevators, while Collins wanders the streets. The town is half boarded up. Collins drifts back in half an hour, shirt soaked with sweat, says he met a kid and had this conversation:

"Passin' through?"

"Yep. You?"

"No, but wish I was."

We drive on. We are getting into big fields here, corn, sunflowers, wheat. Collins is developing an obsessive interest in fields of sunflowers, and we search for hillocks with photographic vantage points. There are none. Someone is burning stubbled fields, and we drive toward them, looking for flames but finding dense smoke. We cough like Oklahoma farmers.

Hugoton, Kansas, bills itself as the Gas Capital, but the gas museum is closed. No telling when it is open. The sight of tents and plastic flags marking the Stevens County Fair has the same effect on Collins as a rattling feed bucket has on a pig. He presses his face against the window and struggles to get at it and, once out of the car, rushes at its heart. I study rocket models, the insects on pins, a board with gauges of wire glued on, and move on to the prize-winning vegetables. All the wheat seed entries, bagged in plastic, look identical. Earl and Darrell Teeter grew Eagle for first place, but the Scout, Lamar, Ike, and Karl 92 cultivars also got blue ribbons. It looks like you can't lose growing wheat in Stevens County, Kansas. The big raffle prize is a potato basket. Outside, people walk slowly, eating funnel cakes, a German pastry resembling albino snakes sprinkled with powdered sugar.

Collins is where the action is, in the pig tent. Here are kids and pigs—spotted, pink, brown pigs of all ages, temperaments, and sizes. The pig owners steer their animals into the ring with slender sticks, and in the audience proud mothers with video cameras catch the moment. A dog trots past wearing a hat that proclaims, I DON'T NEED NO STINKIN' LEASH. We've seen it all in an hour.

We're ripping up the Wyoming interstate and talking about Basque shepherds—there are 870,000 sheep in Wyoming, most of them raised by Basques—when Collins spies one with a flock of sheep and two dogs at the edge of the four-lane. Fifteen miles later I begin to understand why writers and photographers rarely work together. We turn back. For a long while Collins wanders among sheep. Through the binoculars I watch him wandering. The sheep scatter in a panic. The shepherd approaches Collins. Collins approaches the shepherd. I wait for the dogs to tear Collins's throat out, but instead an amiable friendship springs up between the photographer and the shepherd, and the latter casts his dogs out after the sheep. While the dogs herd the wool-lies, the shepherd poses, lights a cigarette, walks about, peers at the horizon. This all happens several times for Collins's benefit. As a finale the shepherd throws the small dog into a water hole. This happens several times as well. At last Collins pulls away and returns.

"I was afraid he was going to drown the little dog," he says. "But the big dog rescues the little one." The shepherd, it seems, was extraordinarily cooperative, for only last year a photographer from *People* magazine, hurtling down this same highway, also saw him and turned back.

"He may be the only professional Basque shepherd model in the world," says Collins.

An hour later we're almost out of gas on a long, empty, lonesome road. We offer fluttering prayers from dry lips.

"If we hadn't gone back for that shepherd . . ."

"Let me tell you something," says Collins. "We'll make it."

We make Kaycee, favorite hangout of Butch Cassidy and You-Know-Who, catch the gas station about three minutes before it closes, get some supper at the cafe. There are posters of coming entertainment plastered all over the front entry, and we're going to miss a good one. It is too damn bad.

6TH ANNUAL
HOLE-IN-THE-WALL
PIG WRESTLING
& TESTICLE FESTIVAL

This lurid festival (it is not clear whether the testicles being celebrated are those of the contestants or the pigs) will be followed the very next weekend by the Big Horn Mountain Polka Day, an accordion extravaganza I've longed to attend for years. It's been like this all the way—either something has just hap-pened or it's going to happen after we're gone—the Oklahoma Cow Chip Throw, the horseback hypnotist show, a gathering of crush freaks who watch women step on grapes. But up the road in Buffalo, it turns out, tomorrow is Basque Day.

It is hotter than hot, a crushing, blaring, sunstroke heat that comes with flies, sun blindness, and depression. Buffalo has a fine shady park, but the Basque Day festivities are set up on a shadeless, vacant midtown lot. The dancers, in red costumes and long stockings, look sweated out, and a Great Pyrenees dog pants against a wall. Basques smile and greet us as though the world were not about to explode in flames.

Michael Camino, a sheep rancher, stops to say hello. He gives us a thumbnail sketch of the economic vice that is squeezing western sheepmen. "Running sheep is a hard, hard job these days," he says. When pressed to describe the Basque character, he laughs. "Hardheaded, stubborn, short, stocky, big-nosed, with large families—and good Catholics. We like handball, jai alai, singing, cards, wood chopping, weight lifting, rowing—on the coast—and fishing. Our play, what we do for fun, comes out of work. You can see that."

The music begins, and the dancers leap and twirl under the fierce sun. A man turning lamb burgers at the grill lets out a shrill, ululating cry—the *ir-rintzi*, or Basque yell, a quavering, prolonged yodel with a shriek at the end that grew from the shepherd's long-distance calls to his dog. We learn that there is more to sheep than wool and leg of lamb; add crayons, bone china, marshmallows, chewing gum, antifreeze, photographic film.

I meet Joseba Etxarri, a Basque journalist, visiting from Spain, who specializes in Basque history and culture. I ask him about Basque music, especially the accordion, and about the irrintzi. Suddenly he throws back his head and lets out a sustained, warbling cry. When he catches his breath, he says, "If you want to hear Basque music, you must hear Kepa Junkera, a young man, maybe twenty-eight, who is the best accordion player in the world. He is unbelievable. It is worth it to buy an airplane ticket and fly to Europe to hear him, for he does not come to North America."

That night we hit the 14th Annual Sheridan County Rodeo for a few hours. The crowd is not as jovial and good-natured as the Basques, and there's an atmosphere of intense competition. The T-shirts have tough slogans: ROADKILL BAR & GRILL; ALL MUSTANG; IF YOU CAN'T RUN WITH THE BIG DOGS STAY ON THE PORCH; NO FEAR, DANGEROUS SPORTS GEAR; STURGIS BLACK HILLS MOTORCYCLE RALLY. Three or four security guards walk up and down and back and forth, talking to one another on their holster phones, and a crew of professional video people get the action and rodeo royalty. Queen Cedar Moore is quoted as saying, "It's an experience of a lifetime."

The announcer, a key figure at any rodeo, has a blaring voice, and his jokes and patter are professional cornpone, his routine with the clown a combination of ancient insults, bathroom and animal jokes. But he keeps things rolling, gets the contestants in and out of the box. "He broke the pattern, what a shame, he'll have to take a no score, and NOW . . ."

The kids care passionately, and winning or placing well means everything. They ride broncs bareback and saddled, ride bulls and rope calves and steers solo and in teams. They tie goats' tails, barrel race, bend poles, race mules, and milk wild cows with everything they've got, and when they are thrown or fall dazed with bone-jarring thuds they do not cry, but get up and limp out with their heads high. Unaccountably, I think of those guys you see out west hitch-hiking along the highways with saddles on their shoulders, thin, lamed-up, dead-eyed. They probably had their bull-riding days when all that mattered was doing it the best. Deep play.

The idea of deep play comes from economist-philosopher Jeremy Bentham and has to do with betting absurd amounts at odds that translate into either a negligible win or a devastating loss—an irrational pursuit in the utilitarian view, and philosophically immoral. Cultural anthropologist Clifford Geertz applied the concept to Balinese cockfighting. In deep games, he found, "Where the amounts of money are great, much more is at stake than material gain: namely, esteem, honor, dignity, respect—in a word . . . status." Geertz saw that the combination of risk, danger, humor, skill, and double entendres translated into the "fun" of deep play. Folklore scholar Beverly Stoeltje held this outline up against the Texas rodeo and saw, in the risks and rewards, the elements of deep play. Threads of deep play seem knotted through many kinds of outdoor "fun"—risky, dangerous, crowd-attracting performance enmeshed with rough joking—and the big payoff is admiration and status.

Cloud peak wilderness in Wyoming is the high central ridge of the Bighorns. At 8,000 feet, it's chilly, and the weather is a defiant mix of storm and sunshine. Even though it's a weekend, we don't see many vehicles on the road. Campsites are deserted, and there are no hikers at the trailheads. We're alone in the mountains until we find the Marathon Pipeline Company of Findlay, Ohio, gnawing on roast pig bones. They've come all this way for the Marathon company picnic. The atmosphere is one of comfortable pleasure, a kind of volleyball-and-horseshoes lite fun, nothing deep. It is deliciously cool under the pines. A man wearing a cap emblazoned OLD FART. NOTHING FINER THAN A PIPELINER comes over to see what I'm writing in my notebook.

"We just took two hogs off the rotisserie," he remarks. "They are all et up now. You missed it." Over by the volleyball court I see Collins. He has a yearning look on his face, as if he wants to put his camera down, rush up to the net, and spike the ball.

Hard rain falls quickly somewhere, and by the time we get to Clear Creek we're driving through deep puddles. Cruising downgrade, we glance up a muddy track where mountain bikes and riders sprawl in a tangle under the lodgepole pines. Another rider bumps down the wet trail, spattered with mud. They are Jehovah's Witnesses, says Larry Connolly, making their annual bike ride "from Powder River Pass over forty miles of hellish, grueling logging roads, rained on and hailed on, to Trigger Lake Road.

"We do a lot of riding," says Connolly, "and some of us did this one last year. This afternoon we picked up a water bottle we dropped last year. It's rough across streams, then there's a corduroy road at the top of the pass. The deceiving thing about the pass is there seems to be more uphill coming down than going up." They are tired, grubby, scratched, hungry, and say they're having fun.

The Lakota name for this massive tower, the porphyry throat of an extinct volcano, was Bear Lodge. It was renamed Devils Tower in 1875 by the infamous gold-scouting expedition escorted by Col. Richard Dodge in flagrant violation of Lakota treaty rights. The group declared the formidable rock columns to be "inaccessible to anything without wings." But in 1893 two local ranchers made the ascent with a homemade ladder on the Fourth of July.

Five thousand climbers a year tackle Devils Tower, and climbing parties stand in line every morning for a chance at the muscular rock. There are more than a hundred routes up, and their names tend to be twee: La Vaca Solitaria, Digital Extraction, Adrenaline Surfer, Lack of Enthusiasm, Pee Pee's Plunge, B.O. Plenty.

There is a mob of people here, the biggest recreational crowd we've seen on this journey. The parking lot is jammed, and tourists speaking many languages and dressed in everything from spike heels to turbans jostle and climb and pant in the baking heat. There is a sign at the bottom: PLEASE DO NOT DISTURB PRAYER BUNDLES AND PRAYER CLOTHS. A neurosurgeon from Punjab and his party pose for photographs on a tumbled stone column. Hundreds of tourists trudge around the base, cricking their necks as they stare up at the climbers. Six- to eight-year-old boys walking with their parents hate this place. Nowhere else do they feel so little and kidlike. They behave badly and run through the extensive poison ivy that grows under the lodgepole pines.

The sun bores out of the cloudless sky like a drill. Rock is too hot to touch. We look up. There are climbers on every side of the Tower, some on the sizzling stone in full sun. It must be like climbing an upended fajita pan. Above, turkey vultures circle and soar; below, people jabber and click cameras. Collins is clicking, too, at the base of the Durrance Approach, access point for a dozen routes. A woman comes down, streaked with sweat and chalk and grime, her flame-colored legs abraded and scraped. She looks cooked. She is Sparky Colby, from Jackson Hole, and says it is about as hot as it can get up on the rock. She's climbed in the Tetons and the Black Hills, and climbed ice in Conway, New Hampshire. She clerks and works in restaurants to support her climbing habit. Her friend Brian Moore slides down the hot dirt, shaking blood from his knuckles.

"Hey, you ever bite warts?" he asks. "I bit the top off a wart and it's bleeding." He washes dishes, works as a carpenter, and climbs every chance he gets.

"I eat beans and rice and try to work as little as possible. Climbing—it's a kind of . . . it's different than anything else."

One after another, sweat-drenched, dirt-streaked, abraded humans come off Bear Lodge, their muscled legs like anatomy illustrations. We ask Daniel Doolittle, president of Wave Rave Snowboard of Colorado, what it's like on top. "It's high desert," he says, "prickly pear, sagebrush. It looks like a mesa. And the screeching raptors. The best and the worst of the climb is that the whole time you've got the river watching you."

Down in the parking lot, where it's about 200 degrees in the shade, a man and a woman and their grown-up son are having a little car trouble. The car is a 1980 Mercury Zephyr, and it won't start. The front of the Zephyr is jacked up, and the father is underneath. His voice comes out.

"Have to tighten the starter. Do it all the time."

The son is anxious and says, "If it slips, it'll crush your laigs." The jack handle projects into the thronged walkway that leads to the Tower. The son turns to his mother. "Don't you let no kids bump that handle. Kick 'em in the face if you have to, but don't let 'em bump it."

There is a cry of pain from under the car. "Take my glasses! A rag!" A heavy torso wriggles out and father gets up, red suspenders swinging free.

"It doesn't look like much fun," I remark.

"Well, it *is* fun. I rebuilt my own car when I was fifteen. Yes, fooling with cars is fun, but I got to give it up. I got an incurable disease—something wrong with my laigs and they can't find out what. I got two Seventh-Day Adventist doctors taking care of me, and they're all that's keeping me alive. I was a contractor. I can't work now. But as long as the Lord's on my side, I'm happy. It could come any day, my time, could be thirty or forty years."

The son lowers the jack. The father gets in, turns the key, and the car starts.

We're standing on Crow Flies High Butte in New Town, North Dakota, just north of the Fort Berthold Reservation, looking down far below at a houseboat on the Missouri River. We can see a dog on the houseboat, an American flag, and four people. A man's arm lifts as he casts a fishing pole, and his watch face flashes.

On the other side of Four Bears Bridge is the new Four Bears Casino, owned by three affiliated tribes, the Mandan, Hidatsa, and Arickara. The casino is part gambling hall, part hotel, part restaurant, part museum, part gift shop, and, down by the river, part campground. On the other side of the highway is a flat field that resembles a fairground the day after it's all over. There's paper and plastic in every direction, bits of rope and empty cans. A few tents still stand. We wander through the trash toward Grace "Charging" Henry, who is taking down her canvas tent. She tells us the Little Shell Pow Wow ended last night. There were drum groups, grass dancers, eagle-feather dancers, fancy-feather dancers, shawl and jingle-dress dancers. There was singing and fried bread. It was a lot of fun, but we missed it. There'll be another one next weekend, the Crow Pow Wow, a really big one, and in September the United Tribes Pow Wow in Bismarck. We'll miss them, too. The light is fading, and the bent paper plates in the grass look like birds from a distance.

We drive down along the river in the dusk, through the empty campground on the high banks of the Missouri, and come to a point where a few cars are parked, some people sitting or standing near the water. The sky over the river holds a silvery light tinged with raspberry juice. Vietnam veteran Bobby Finley and his son-in-law Frank Lockwood and Frank's children are fishing. Bobby's cigarette end glows red. He points at the water. "This used to be our powwow ground," he says. "It's under water now. And there were gardens all along there. In 1944 they flooded part of the area, and in 1990 it was all under water. So now we have the powwows across from the casino. But this is where they should be. Food, feather powwow, traditional dancing—that's what we call freedom, what we call fun." As a veteran, he can dance the warrior's eagle-feather dance, always moving forward, never back.

Frank is a fast talker and has plenty to say about having fun, which was in greater supply in earlier generations. "Our ancestors used to wrestle bears for the fun of it—down in the bars. My great-grandfather, James Conklin, 'Big Wolf,' used to wrestle the boxing bear." The bear was trained to swing.

But Bobby looks moodily over the water and says, "Our old powwow ground. And we got sections in here where we used to farm. If I could walk on water, I'd walk right over to it and stand there." The kids run back and forth on the damp sand, climb on Bobby. In the half-dark it looks like they are wrestling with a bear.

Life on the road is disappearing into the rearview mirror as we roll through sunflower country and into prairie wetlands, potholes full of ducks and herons. It's getting on toward Wednesday, the hump of the week when everybody works and nobody thinks of the outdoors and fun. We pass a sign advertising a Polish shake and try to guess what it is. A kielbasa milk shake? Wild polka action on the dance floor? How about a handclasp that makes your knuckles pop?

Everything has changed. It is freezing cold, and we're shivering at the marina on Barker's Island in Superior, Wisconsin, on the shore of the great, fierce lake. The wind is terrific, and spume blows off the ragged tops of the whitecaps. The lines and rigging of hundreds of moored yachts clatter and rattle and clink against the aluminum masts with an extraordinary sound not unlike the chirping, twittering music of the slot machines in the Four Bears Casino. We wander through the S. S. *Meteor,* last of the whalebacks to ply the Great Lakes, now a floating museum exhibiting bits and pieces of the wrecks of other ships, a catchall of marine disaster mementos. Later, eating Chinese noodles in the Choo-Choo Diner and listening to the radio, we notice that all the songs sound like Gordon Lightfoot singing "The Wreck of the Edmund Fitzgerald." The people here are good glarers, or maybe they've set their faces against the bitter wind.

For nearly two weeks we've been looking at empty campgrounds, driving down lonely roads, walking up silent trails. Every motel has a vacancy sign glowing in the night. But we don't need to wonder where everybody is anymore. They are in Bayfield, Wisconsin, one of the country's hot vacation spots, fishing and windsurfing, kayaking and canoeing, hiking and taking the excursion steamer, planning day trips to the Apostle Islands, sailing, eating whitefish and whitefish livers at Grunky's. There is not a damn place to stay within a hundred miles. We have to move on, but not before we go down to the edge of the lake, working itself up again into large, thrashing waves.

It is cold and violently windy, yet two kayaks turn and maneuver in the rough waves. Frank Koshere, a water-quality biologist for the state, says this is the maiden voyage of his kayak, the first he has built. His partner is Jan Pearlman. They stand in the water, blue with cold but laughing and pleased.

A few hundred feet offshore, a big solo kayak is pivoting and slipping through the graybeards. Whoever is paddling it, wet suit gleaming in the watery light, is in the fast lane of kayaking. He is Doug Liphart, who has moved up here from south of Minneapolis, works in a local paddle shop, and teaches problem kids winter survival, dogsledding, outdoor skills. He is a passionate kayaker who looks for difficult water. He paddled the coast of Wales last summer and finds the stormy waters of Lake Superior excellent fun. "You've got to respect the water, but I really get a kick out of this," he says.

Hours of driving before we find a place to sleep. Is there time to come back the next day? We want to go to the Apostle Islands, to watch the divers sinking into the chill depths of Superior. But I've got to be in Quebec in a few days, and then on to Maine. We've been thwarted by bad timing and long distances. Never found the whitewater bodysurfer somewhere in Colorado, didn't reach the BASE jumper planning a parachute leap from a transmission tower; the wheelchair mountain racers were in an impossible future. Instead we got powwow dreamers and little kids on stick horses.

We'll split up. Collins will go back to Bayfield in the morning to find the divers, and I will go on to *la belle province* and the *carrefour mondial de l'accordéon*. The last I see of Collins, he is being followed by a car with a license plate that reads THE FLY.

The accordion festival in Montmagny features virtuoso players from a dozen countries. The first night, at the opening dinner, over *la grande valse des fromages*, an accordionist walks onto the stage and begins to play notes and runs and rhythms it is not possible to play. The audience shrieks and stamps its feet. I look at my program: "Kepa Junkera, Pays Basques Español." Whaddaya know.

Labor Day weekend, the end of the summer, and I am in Greenville, Maine, for the 21st Floatplane Fly-In. A sawed-off guy named John "Snaps" Knapp, in a pair of black rubber boots, is sloshing around in the water. His little Avid, drawn up near the shore, collects a crowd. "Why do I fly?" he says. "Same reason Harley people have bugs on their teeth—for fun. This plane is ten years old, and I've had a thousand and ten hours of fun in it."

Snaps built the plane himself from a kit, and for the sake of more power installed a snowmobile engine. He gives us a demonstration by standing on the pontoon, reaching in, and yanking the starter cord. The plane sounds exactly like a snowmobile. His signature landing is to hit the water on one pontoon. It's fitting, he says, because he's only got one foot.

"I used to be a motorcycle racer. Then I had an accident—not at a race, no, somebody got me out on the highway. My foot was hanging by a thread. I pulled it off myself. They fixed me up with a prosthesis. This happened in September. I told the doc, 'I'll be skiing by Christmas.' He said it couldn't be done. But I did it.

"Had to figure out what to do for fun," he continues. "First I looked at boats. Boats are not fun. Boats are one-dimensional. Then I got interested in flying. I took up floatplanes for the food. Ever go to an airport restaurant? They're terrible. Yeah, I got into seaplanes because marinas have great restaurants."

He takes somebody up for a ride, telling him it's not *if* the engine conks out, it's *when*. "Sheer terror, that first time! It was! And I love it." Long after they're out of sight, you can hear the snowmobile engine in the sky.

Yeah, I think, all the deep players love it. Too bad Collins isn't here. Then I get a flash recollection of a license plate I saw somewhere on the road: U NEVER NO.

JUNE 1995

THERE MUST BE A GOD IN HAITI

by BOB SHACOCHIS

I knew this road, Route Nationale One—this beautiful, perilous road, my nightmare road, a dark journey toward the light threading humanity's most fundamental aspirations, the road the American soldiers had nicknamed Highway to Hell; I knew it better than I knew the streets of my hometown. It originated in the fetid harborside slums of Port-au-Prince, where the poorest of the hemisphere's poor bathed in sewers and homeless children fought one another for the feral right to lick the residue out of the brown plastic pouches of MREs—spaghetti and meatballs, chicken à la king—they'd scavenged from the military's garbage. Here the road boasted the world's biggest pothole, dredged out by runoff from the eroding mountainsides and a death trap during storms. Hours-long traffic jams billowed diesel soot, and along the quayside it was not unusual to see, throughout the infinite years of the tyrants, bodies bobbing in the otherwise tranquil harbor. Yet everywhere here the roadside was thick with human vitality, thousands of *marchands*, energetic with desperation and gifted with tenacious, earthy humor, hawking what a world they had never seen had thrown away—a national yard sale of grease-caked junk and hand-me-downs.

From city center the road headed north, past the walls of Fort Dimanche, where for twenty-nine years the Duvaliers in their madness had murdered friend and foe alike; past the sugar refinery and warehouses and foreign-owned assembly plants; past the airport with its fleet of derelict planes; past the newly paved October the 15th Boulevard, commemorating the date of President Aristide's return from exile; past the Barbancourt rum factory and the once stately neo-Colonial Ministry of Agriculture, big as a football field, half of it roofless and charred from a fire, the other half still occupied by bureaucratic zombies. Finally, through the crazy dodge of traffic, the road arrived at the leafy outskirts of town, a small village called Titanyen, which is also the name of the vast coastal plain nearby, mostly methane-whiffy mangrove swamp, where the Haitian military would dump its flood of victims, the corpses eventually shrouded by land crabs and consumed by free-ranging pigs.

The capital and its singular urban miseries left behind, Route Nationale One arrowed ahead, squeezed between a barren ridge of mountains and the coast until, an hour north, it passed the Côte des Arcadins, site of Haiti's all-but-abandoned beach resorts. The road skirted crystal blue shallows, reefs you could swim to from shore; occasionally you glimpsed high walls that enclosed *ti paradis*—little paradises, the seaside hideaways of Port-au-Prince's oligarchy, its shoulder-board putschists, its drug kingpins. Farther along was the once lovely port of St. Marc, where you began to notice the frequency of *hounfours*, voodoo temples, identified by their gay flags and symbolic wall paintings. From there the road curled inland and then flattened out through the malarial Artibonite Valley, Haiti's breadbasket, so overtly primitive that the Special Forces who patrolled the valley called it, unsympathetically, Dinosaurland; its industrious inhabitants, toiling in rice paddies from dawn to dusk, were "mud people."

Beyond the Artibonite was the Savane Désolée, its rainless, infertile soil clumped with cactus and thorn acacia. From there began the radical ascent into the mountains of the north, the road a continuous challenge of switchbacks and plunges, blind curves and breathtaking views of the impossibly rugged interior. Travelers invariably battled both nausea and fascination as, for the next two hours, the road slalomed past packs of uniformed schoolchildren on their daily vertical treks to and from literacy, the pavement diving toward transparent rivers and rising up again to a bowled horizon of overcultivated slopes and lush, shadowy ravines. A few miles past the town of Limbé, Route Nationale One crested a final ridge and foreshadowed its terminus on the shores of the Windward Passage: to the northwest, the pendant-shaped bay where Columbus dropped anchor to praise this once most Rousseauean of isles; straight below, the idyllic vista of the coastal savanna, the fertile Plaine du Nord that once made Haiti—Ayiti—imperial France's most lucrative colony. Finally, the road quit at Cap-Haïtien, touted in centuries past as the

Pearl of the Antilles, the Paris of the New World, but now certainly the most exhausted, depleted city in the Americas.

My first trip on Route Nationale One, in the spring of 1986, was not uneventful. I had come with Yves Colon, a Haitian-American friend and fellow journalist, to report on the people's revolution, the *dechoukaj*, the "uprooting," of Baskethead, aka Baby Doc: Jean-Claude Duvalier. Leaving the wreckage of Port-au-Prince, we stopped for lunch in the town of Gonaïves, where a Duvalierist death squad threatened us for giving food to a hungry child who came crying to our table. Farther on in the mountains, we were confronted by several roadblocks manned by machete-waving peasants. No, we were not the hated bourgeoisie, Yves would respectfully explain; we'd then make a small "donation" to the local youth committee and drive on, passing truckloads of Haitian soldiers, temporarily at peace with their countrymen. At last we entered Cap-Haïtien, intent on climbing to the Citadelle, the largest mountaintop fortress in the New World, built by Henri Christophe, the first elected president of the world's first free black republic.

I would not travel Route Nationale One again until September 1994, the first week of the American intervention. This time it would be the most unforgettable ride of my life: running police roadblocks with the correspondents from *Time* and the *Miami Herald*, inching our way through villages where thousands of euphoric people jammed the road to cheer us. After so many years of neglect, the road between St. Marc and Gonaïves had become impassable without a four-wheel-drive vehicle. A CBS film crew had rolled its Land Cruiser a few hours earlier, trying to navigate the archipelago of holes and trenches, yet we raced ahead recklessly, bruised and jolted, trying to reach Cap-Haïtien before the pitch black wildness of nightfall.

During the sixteen months of the American occupation, I traveled Route Nationale One dozens of times, sometimes in the back of Humvees, sometimes in a Pathfinder with Gary, my interpreter. By the time the troops pulled out last January, I had internalized this road; it had become a path through my own moral and physical frontiers. I knew its flashpoints, its *zenglendoes* (bandits), its heroes, and its martyrs. I knew where it measured my courage and where it mocked my wavering fortitude. I knew its hostility as well as its hospitality, its bloodstains and its celebrations. I had so accepted this road that I would find myself driving through the countryside after dark, not recommended, alone and mindless, knowing only not to stop, for any reason, no matter what—you could kill but not save, you could pity but not help. I realized then that I had succumbed to the fatalism that was Haiti, which was not necessarily a mistake. The mistake was, I had begun to believe I could finesse it.

Which is perhaps why my last trip on Route Nationale One, this past spring, felt like a small redemption. The country was mango-ripe with small but ephemeral redemptions, recuperating from the three years it had been buried alive under the de factos, trying hard to believe it had been reborn into grace. This time I was taking my wife along. She had flown down from Florida for a long weekend, an anniversary present of sorts, her first trip to the island. It was a place she'd always dreamed of visiting and somehow expected to love. And despite my misgivings, I was determined that she be given that chance: to embrace the Haiti that might have existed in a tourist brochure, had the centuries not left it so cursed. "There are no people in the world who are as nonviolent as these people," I remember Bernie Diederich, the godfather of all foreign correspondents in Haiti and one of Graham Greene's drinking buddies, telling me during the first days of the invasion. "They've never been able to get rid of the stigma of 1791." The year of payback—slave uprising, the massacre of whites.

When I thought of the many thousands slaughtered in Rwanda, Bosnia, Chechnya, Afghanistan—so much of the world—I knew Bernie had a point, but it didn't change the fact that on too many of my trips to Haiti I had seen someone violently killed before my eyes. Now the troops had gone home, and the newly formed Haitian National Police—rookies with handguns—had assumed tenuous control. Was the road safe? I wondered as we packed the car that Saturday for the trip north. No one could say, and normally I wouldn't care. My wife was game but made me promise to play the adventure straight down the middle, no steering toward the edges, no looking for trouble in a country where trouble customarily looked for you. I agreed without a hint of protest because, if only for a weekend, I needed a Haiti that needed my wife, someone seeing the island with fresh eyes, someone whose experience might counteract the myths, connect with Haiti's magical brilliance, and leave behind a blessing.

I was sitting on the veranda of the Hotel Oloffson, our first night there, comforting my wife as we waited to be served rum sours. Incredibly, while walking across the hotel grounds to our room, she had been bopped on the head by a brace of coconuts dislodged from a tree by gusty winds. Fortunately, they were *coco yay*—hollow husks—and had struck a glancing blow, more alarming than anything else. Yet still I had to wonder, what sort of welcome was this from the *loas*, the Haitian spirits: roughhouse flirtation or warning? A woman approached, exuding camaraderie, certain we were of her tribe, and I invited her to sit down.

"Coco yay," she said, making the anecdote of my wife's small misfortune self-referential, "that's what people have been calling me all day long!" Her droopy eyes and flat mouth became animated, made happy with unlikely pride. Dry coconut—Creole slang for a tightwad, someone stingy, juiceless. Apparently it was in her nature to nickel-and-dime the dispossessed. She was an editor on the foreign desk of one of the globe's most influential newspapers, in Haiti for the first time, "on vacation" and why not, clearly pleased to have escaped her office for the field, the front lines, here at the Caribbean's most famous hotel.

The very design of colonialism—the gingerish Victorian charm, the gabled Edwardian panache—achieved its ultimate seduction in those venues once renowned, with brazen overconfidence, as oases of civilization. The Kiplingesque Windamere Hotel in Darjeeling. Somerset Maugham's steamy haunt, the Raffles Hotel in Singapore. Outposts of faded authority and funky grandness banding the girth of the planet, their architecture and ceiling-fan ambience created an indelible vision of exotic intrigue.

The Hotel Oloffson—a whitewashed, three-tiered tropo-Gothic fantasy nestled in its own jungle in a high-walled enclave in downtown Port-au-Prince—was just such a place, or rather the illusory variation of just such a place, since it was built atop a history that didn't quite fit the groove of what was once called the white man's burden. The hotel was a native hybrid, an imitation that became authentic through the grind and twist of desperate events, "a folly," as a travel writer once observed, "of spires, crotchets, finials, and conical towers."

This folly was the extravagant vision of the Sam family, which constructed the mansion at the turn of the century and subsequently abandoned it in 1915, when the family's dubious contribution to the nation, President Guillaume Sam, was dragged into the street, his body rent to pieces by a mob, and then paraded around on sharpened poles. The U.S. Marines seized the occasion as an excuse to invade, and into the capital they marched, leasing the future hotel as a hospital. The rear wing became a maternity ward; Room 20, now the Graham Greene room, was an operating theater. In his novel *The Comedians*, Greene described the Oloffson, alias the Hotel Trianon: "You expected a witch to open the door to you or a maniac butler, with a bat dangling from the chandelier behind him."

Personally, I had never thought of the Oloffson as spooky, but surely it must have been in the summer of 1994, when the attachés—the Cédras regime's paramilitary assassins—would come by to dance to the house band and get liquored up before hitting the streets to do the death-squad thing. The band canceled its regular Thursday-night performances when Uzi-toting Macoutes began turning over tables and abducting guests.

The Oloffson was where I preferred to stay in town; the other predictable choice was the Oloffson's antithesis, the Hotel Montana, up the mountainside in Pétionville, the provenance of the ruling class, otherwise known as MREs—Morally Repugnant Elites, so named by State Department wags over at the embassy. The atmosphere at the Montana was triumphantly corporate. Television networks rented entire floors; phone service was fairly reliable; security was tight.

Besides serving as a sort of crash house for the shaggier species of reporter and foreign-aid entrepreneur, the Oloffson doubled as an art gallery and celebrity watering hole. Fetishes, artifacts, and relics abounded, perhaps none more curious or enduring than the highly literate chameleon Aubelin Jolicouer, aging spy, former Duvalierist apparatchik, and gossip columnist for one of Haiti's two daily newspapers, transformed only slightly by Greene into the fictional Petit Pierre. Any day you could sit on the airy veranda and observe Jolicouer mounting the Oloffson's steps, bald head and gold-knobbed cane gleaming, his spidery body impeccably suited, to hold soirees in the hotel's wicker-and-rattan drawing room or play backgammon with cronies from the CIA. Quite the cocksman, in years past Jolicouer would gravitate toward the *femmes blancs* flitting through the hotel, though now he shunned white babes—a form of protest against American intervention, his patriotic, private sacrifice for Haitian sovereignty.

Jolicouer had been a fixture at the Oloffson for decades, just as the foreign correspondents had returned year after year, dining on the veranda at twilight, their conversations interrupted by sudden bursts of automatic-weapons fire from the National Palace, where still another coup was unfolding, each journalist pausing with fork in midair, wondering, "Didn't I order a double?"

The Oloffson liked to boast of its glamorous guests: Malcolm Lowry, Mick Jagger, Irving Howe, Noël Coward, Ali MacGraw, John Gielgud, the list goes on. Back in the early seventies, when Baskethead first came to power, Haiti enjoyed a relatively brief but successful tenure as a jet-set destination. The casinos, the privacy, the security, the servile population, the hypnotic appeal of the culture, all proved irresistible to the rich and famous. In the mid-eighties, at a New Year's Eve dinner in the Turks and Caicos, the former manager of one of Haiti's most exclusive resorts proclaimed to me that he loved Port-au-Prince because it was the only city in the world beside Geneva where he felt safe enough to walk around after dark with $10,000 in cash in his pocket.

But the *blancs*, the foreigners, didn't come to Haiti anymore, not as tourists anyway, except a handful of hard-wired voyeurs—like myself, perhaps—who seemed to thrive on cruising the world's most fucked-up places. For a generation, for many generations, there had been the killings, the state-sponsored violence, the crushing poverty, the inaccessibility of the Creole language. In the mid-eighties the Centers for Disease Control in Atlanta made matters worse with an AIDS scare. Hollywood and the missionaries bogeyfied voodoo, Haiti's syncretic and wildly creative version of animism, an ancient view of the universe that Western societies seem compelled to shit upon. "Haiti," a Baptist mission's stationery warned, "6.5 million souls in Catholicism and witchcraft." And of course there's the racial dynamics—an insurmountable barrier to many whites—and now the military occupation of the island, its political instability, and once again its uncertain future.

Haiti was different, way different, but it wasn't the last refuge of barbarism, as so many otherwise decent folks seemed to think. The Haitian people led recognizable lives, although in stratified, polarized worlds. Still, tourism was a questionable commodity, if not an altogether frivolous pursuit. The country was by no means a bargain, and it's doubtful you'd have what is commonly regarded as "a good time." Like a disturbing dream, Haiti brimmed with contradictions. It was archaic, alarming, fabulous, and strange, home to a state of permanent upheaval and permanent transcendence, a nation with an accomplished artist and incipient dictator in every family. From the veranda of the Oloffson, it was inevitable that you would entertain the self-congratulatory thought that you'd landed at Hip Central, come to feel the jungle beat, hear the bullets sing, party with saints and vampires, good and evil, either one, here at the Edge-Dancers' Ball, Neo-Bohemian Pavilion Number One, Hemisphere Number One, Zone D—as in Democracy, as in Delusion.

If you wrote about Haiti as a "writer"—that is, not as a journalist, a reporter—it seemed impossible you could convince a reader that such a place truly existed.

My wife, however, was enchanted, eating griot, glancing down at the tiny swimming pool that glowed serenely in the darkness like a lozenge of blue mountain sky, the same pool, once drained, where the protagonist of Greene's *The Comedians* discovers the corpse of a government minister who fell out of favor with Papa Doc. Through the Port-au-Prince grapevine, I had asked my sidekick Gary to join us, and he finally came, big-hearted and soft-spoken, sweeping food into his mouth, making my wife laugh by telling stories on me. At some point, after we had stopped counting rum sours, we fell silent as Manno Charlemagne, Haiti's Bob Marley, waltzed across the veranda with his Uzi-slung entourage and disappeared into the hotel. Ever since Manno had been elected mayor of Port-au-Prince, he had confronted the remnants of the old regime head-on, bulldozing a strip of Macoute-owned honky-tonks in Champ Mars, whipping the whores and pharisees off the streets, trying to turn the vast plaza in front of the National Palace into a Haitian Central Park. His enemies had quadrupled, and now he lived at the Oloffson, suddenly fond of its high walls.

"Gary," I asked, as I asked each time I returned to Haiti, "how is it out there?"

"You know. You know how it is," he said as I watched his face harden for the first time since he sat down. "Bob, the people are suffering with hope."

• • •

There were no reports of trouble in the north, so off we went early Saturday morning, myself at the wheel, Gary riding shotgun, my wife and the editor in the backseat, clucking their tongues at my one caveat: "It's a long, hot, arduous trip, and anything could happen. Please, no whining," I said, though I needn't have bothered. Gary laughed knowingly. The two of us had endured plenty of hours on Route Nationale One, shrugging off the complaints of various passengers, always worldly macho males, while the women we occasionally traveled with seemed far more adaptable, rising stoically or even playfully to Haiti's challenge.

I hated going anywhere in Haiti without Gary, not because I was dependent on his trilingual skills, but because I craved his companionship, his abiding decency, his gentle humor and unwillingness to despair, even though, like most Haitians, he had nothing, and no visible prospects for the future. The first thing I always did in Haiti was to go find Gary, asking around for him on the streets of the slums behind the National Palace, where he lived with his senile grandmother. In 1963, when Gary was three years old, his father was murdered at Fort Dimanche by François Duvalier; his mother abandoned him and fled to Miami. His hapless grandmother sent him to an orphanage run by Pentecostal missionaries when he was eight, an experience so traumatic it was the only subject he refused to talk about. One day last summer, I unthinkingly took Gary with me to Fort Dimanche, where a team of forensic anthropologists was preparing to exhume one of Papa Doc's mass graves. As we stood on the edge of the site, watching the laborers scrape the muck with their hoes, Gary, always stalwart in the face of Haiti's cruelties, seemed to stiffen with pain. "Oh shit, shit!" I said, realizing what I had done, tugging Gary back toward the car, away from the marshy, putrescent ditch where his father had likely been buried.

In some all-important ways, Gary and I knew one another better than anyone else on earth. Together we had been stoned and shot at. Together we had stumbled through riots and scenes of devastation. We had shared the same bed when lodgings were scarce, got silly drunk and talked about love, music, politics, white men and black men, about the distances that separated us. And I had wondered, time and again, How the hell do we spring you out of here, my friend? because Gary longed to travel, to touch and taste the planet like any intelligent, curiosity-driven human being. But no country in the world granted visas to rank-and-file Haitians. Which is to say, finally, that for Gary and me, any trip on Route Nationale One was a trip down memory lane.

But today we were hauling newborns. As the Haitian countryside unscrolled itself so clemently before my wife's absorbing eyes, she murmured her appraisals. The landscape so much more clean and tended than she had expected; such spectacular beauty, dramatic panoramas; such handsome people who carried themselves with vibrant dignity; such a sense of community—everybody pulling together in the fields. When I heard her say, "I don't think I've ever been in a place where I've felt such a strong creative spirit," I was reminded of a trip Gary and I had taken with Macduff Everton, a photographer I had worked with in South America and the Himalayas. Back in the States, people would look at Macduff's slides and ask themselves with incredulity, This is Haiti? because the pictures were unequivocally sublime.

Yes, this too was Haiti, the one that existed behind the stereotypes, behind the bloody ethos of hate and avarice and race. Macduff's images served to humanize a nation that since its inception had been treated by the Western world, with calculation, like a nigger. Excuse me, but like a savage, filthy nigger. Haiti: the nigger of nations, or so the white man's regard for the world's first free black republic would lead you to conclude. "Imagine," said William Jennings Bryan in 1920, "niggers speaking French." "I don't care if you dress them up and put them in the palace," opined the commander of the 1915 Marine occupation, "they're still nigs."

Against this odious background, Macduff's images were more than mere counterpoint. They were, I think, therapeutic, restorative, perhaps even a shade triumphant, penetrating the layers of white mythology. The irony was, Macduff couldn't get off the island fast enough. "I don't think I've ever been to a place where I felt such evil," he told me afterward. "Do you know what I mean?" I couldn't really answer yes, any more than I could tell him no. Certainly his photographs, their aesthetic radiance, told a different story. Since what he saw through his lens seemed in opposition to his feelings, I had to conclude that for whatever reason, the interior process by which Macduff experienced things was somehow reversed in me and that Haiti was in fact a construction of whatever eye took it in. Which doesn't explain why Haiti had trudged through history draped in blood-stained rags; no confluence of words or images could transform the country or undo the moral default it represented. "If democracy comes," a pretty young mulatto woman told me last year, "the blacks will kill us all." The oppressed become the oppressors, et cetera. This was a nation that once ass-whipped Napoleon, a nation whose revolution caused the Americans and the French to stumble on their pretty words: Of, by, and for the people. *Liberté, égalité, fraternité.* Slaves had made themselves free, and their freedom was unforgivable. Thus a 200-year-long impasse, a land defined by collective *maroonage,* shipwrecked in the exclusive harbor of Western civilization.

My wife's glance out the window was guileless and embracing and gay, even when, stopping atop the pass into the northern mountains to buy oranges, we were swarmed by market ladies, pleading and persistent. *"Mwen pa vle, cherie,"* I was forced to say as they thrust half the produce of Haiti into the car. "I don't want." Gary knew what was going on, but still he sighed with embarrassment. The marchands couldn't hear me through my whiteness; I stopped seeing them through the blurring bottomlessness of their need.

Throughout the ride north, the editor had taken pleasure in recognizing what she knew, or thought she knew, in the passing landscape, and as we entered Cap-Haïtien she became excited. For her this was a type of homecoming, because she had visited the city many times, vicariously, in the course of her work. As we fell in with the traffic weaving through the battered streets, she told an anecdote that left me deep in cynicism. Her paper's Pentagon correspondent, a seasoned journalist whose reportage I knew well and admired, had come ashore with the Marines at the start of the intervention and filed a story stating in its lead that the city had descended into chaos. The editor had considered this a dubious assertion and, despite the reporter's objections, had rewritten the lead.

"Wait a minute," I bristled. "I was here then. Gary was here. It was chaos. Gary, what did you see?"

"I saw chaos, man."

"*Chaos,*" said the editor, "has a specific meaning, and the reporter couldn't provide enough evidence to justify its use." Sitting in her office, she had refused to accept her own correspondent's eyewitness account, had thought nothing of reshaping the on-the-ground reality. How many times in Haiti had I overheard reporters arguing on the phone with their foreign desks, trying to contain the spin?

OK, so forget it. With Haiti and the foreign press, power flowed unmeasured and unchecked through many hands. Besides, we had come to Cap-Haïtien as tourists, to enjoy ourselves, if such a thing could be done in so broken a place. The city was a mini Port-au-Prince: garbage-piled streets, boarded storefronts, crowds of unemployed. It was now midafternoon, too late for an assault on the Citadelle but early enough, after we secured rooms at the Hôtellerie du Roi Christophe, for a jaunt to the beach. Cormier Plage, a small resort owned by an old associate of Jacques Cousteau, was a half-hour west on a rocky, unpaved road that snaked along the sheer mountainous headlands of the coast. During the heyday of the intervention, Cormier was packed with UN observers, international police monitors, NGOs, PVOs, pick a group; now we found it returned to its customary idleness, deserted but for three American soldiers who had been scuba diving and a minibus of German tourists on a side trip from the Dominican Republic. At twilight, as we headed back toward Cap-Haïtien, we saw the Germans at a nearby fishing village, being treated to a "voodoo ceremony," drums and dancing on demand, and we would see them the next day at the Citadelle, mounted on paso fino horses. A few days later, back in Port-au-Prince, we would awake to news of their charter jet taking off from Puerto Plata and crashing into the sea.

• • •

Early the next morning we set out for the Citadelle, certainly one of the wonders of the world, a monument to the genius of paranoia. You could see it from
the plains below, a man-made nipple atop the cone of Pic Laferrière. The road
brought us first to the village of Milot, at the base of the peak, where the imposing excess of the fortress in the sky is prefaced by an onion-domed chapel
and the ruins of Sans-Souci—Christophe's palace, built when the former president declared himself king of northern Haiti in 1811. From Milot, a steep serpentine track had been cobbled into the slope, ending four-fifths the way up the
mountain at a dusty parking lot. From here you advanced on foot along a trail
worn marble-smooth, like cathedral steps, by the legions of barefoot men who
hauled the fortress piece by piece up the crag. Or, if you had no shame or were
otherwise feeble, you rented a short, scabby horse to haul you upward, your
feet scraping the ground. Before I even turned off the ignition, our car was engulfed by a ragtag entourage of chatty kids and "helpers," several of whom attached themselves to the unathletic editor. They were as yet unaware that she
was coco yay and had no intention of rewarding them for their good-natured
but superfluous attentions.

We'd been given a peaceful and fragrant morning, sunny but not too hot,
and up we marched as if we were on a school field trip, only the chaperones
were feisty, sharp-witted children. As the path steepened, Haiti unfolded below
us like an emperor's map in relief, mesmerizing, growing more beautiful with
the perspective of elevation.

What does Haiti mean to you? I'm often quizzed by friends back in the States,
puzzled by my attraction to the island. If I knew what Haiti meant to me, I'd
probably stop going. Or maybe not. Haiti, much like the Balkans, is a place
where history has a parasitic lock on the present, where everyday life crashes
back and forth across slippery moral thresholds, shattering and reshaping values, identities, hearts. One moment, children were sheltering you from gun-
men; the next moment, those children were dead. One week, you were cheered
by elated crowds manning the roadblocks on Route Nationale One; the next
week, the same people were angrily pounding your car, screaming unintelligible grievances into your face. "Haiti," wrote the novelist Herbert Gold, "is the
best nightmare on earth." Rather, it was an honorable dream, cruelly deferred,
populated for the most part by honorable people, cruelly denied.

As I labored toward the Citadelle, I asked myself the same question: What
does Haiti mean to me? Nothing. Everything. I imagined, when I came back
home after the first month of the invasion, having witnessed so many horrific
acts and so many heroic efforts, that I'd find a difference in myself, I'd be a better person somehow. But this metamorphosis never happened. I remembered
reading one of Annie Dillard's "found" poems, extracted from the letters of
Vincent van Gogh: "It may be true that there is no God here, but there must be

one not far off." And, farther on: "This is not a thing I have sought, but it has come across my path and I have seized it." Dillard's title was "I Am Trying to Get at Something Utterly Heart-Broken." For me, the poem was a convergence, a moment when I thought, Haiti. The associations were infinite; hope and heartbreak have always been part of every story, whatever the story was when God and man colluded in negligence.

Sweaty and light-headed, we finally stood beneath the magnificent shiplike prow and towering bastions of the Citadelle. Naturally, my wife and the editor wanted a room-by-room tour, but lacking such patience, I left them with Gary and slipped off through the vaulted passageways. I climbed up to the roof and, overcoming vertigo, crept out to the edge of the highest battlement.

From my position atop the fortress, the view had a deceptive magnitude. The surrounding mountains stacked one on top of the other, higher and higher until they disappeared, like runaway slaves, into the scouring clouds. The flanks of the hillsides were mosaics of failed agriculture: red scabs of depleted land, fields of bedrock where the soil had washed away. Muddy rivers twisted across the plains on their way to the Atlantic.

So much of the country looked ruined—blowtorched, gouged, raked, and blasted. But there was another Haiti, a lost Haiti, in those dense, misty mountains on the horizon. Gary and I had gone there, to the proverbial end of the road and beyond, in search of the infamous Marc Lamour, alleged to be Haiti's one and only guerrilla fighter. During the Cédras regime, the Haitian army had launched a´ massive assault on Lamour and his small band of followers, marching up roadless valleys into his mountain sanctuary, burning entire villages to the ground in a futile attempt to hunt him down.

Gary and I had made our way to Lamour's hideout shortly after the American intervention. These were maximum hinterlands, haven for the maroons, the escaped slaves whose furious lust for freedom evolved into mass insurrection against the French. To get to Lamour we had to make a four-hour drive from Limbé to the world-forsaken town of Bois de Caïman, where we started walking. We quickly attracted the inevitable entourage—a pack of young boys, a man herding a pig, a man carrying a stool on his head, a little girl in a powder blue dress and black baseball cap who held my hand firmly the entire way. Within minutes we had passed through the envelope, out of the commonplace Haiti, and entered the most paradisiacal valley I'd seen anywhere in the tropics. For an hour and a half we hiked among the round, skull-white stones of the river's alluvial plain and splashed thigh-deep into its refreshing blue pools. Here was the virgin splendor of pre-Columbian Ayiti, a vestigial Eden tucked away and shielded from the devastation of 500 years of genocide and greed.

Slowly we ascended the densely timbered slopes and finally came to a burned-out clearing in the jungle. One by one, peasants in tattered clothes, internal exiles, began to emerge from behind the curtain of flora, marveling at our otherness. Lamour, secure in his court, eventually appeared to grant us an audience, and it really doesn't matter what he said, because in the end the journey to find him would always mean as much if not more to me than the words that he spoke. The man and the land shared an identical point of view.

Survival. Maroonage. The lost memory of Haiti's soul.

Atop the Citadelle, my reverie was a sentimental indulgence, I know, but one that seemed to offer at least the illusion of healing.

Back at the Roi Christophe, I couldn't impress upon the editor how hazardous it was to travel after dark. She dallied at lunch, took forever to check out of her room, and so we left Cap-Haïtien to return to Port-au-Prince much later than I had planned. Still, the loas, despite pitching coconuts at my wife, had been benevolent, and it was I who suggested we stop along the Côte des Arcadins for a drink. From the grand veranda of a resort called Moulin-sur-Mer we sipped our rum sours, watched the sun set over the Golfe de la Gonâves, then went on. A few miles later, we came upon a ghastly accident. Only minutes earlier, two large trucks had collided head-on, their wreckage crisscrossing the road. Several villagers stood nearby, doing nothing, for there was nothing they could do. The nearest police station was a good half-hour away, and not one of the villagers had any EMT training. I had been on the scene of many accidents like this in rural Haiti, had even participated in triage with the Special Forces, but I had no medical expertise to speak of, and the victims in this wreck were doomed long before anyone could show up with the equipment to cut them out of their pancaked cabs.

The moment seemed to provide the editor with an epiphany. "So what do you do if you're in a bad accident?" she wondered out loud. "Isn't there someone you can call?"

"Not out here there isn't," I said. "Not anymore. Not since the troops left."

"You just sit there and die?"

"Yes. You die. You're fucking dead."

Safely back at the Oloffson, we blindly stumbled into an argument, the editor and I. On the walk down from the Citadelle, she said, she had observed me discreetly slipping money into selected pockets. She thought my behavior was misguided. That was not the way to help anybody, she asserted. It only made matters worse, this personalizing of macroproblems; the most meaningful way to change things was to pay your taxes and lobby for legislative reform.

You're absolving yourself of any face-to-face responsibility, I replied hotly. Your sense of altruism is a comfortable abstraction. You detach yourself from individuals as if they were sorry apparitions, congenitally nameless.

Throughout my early twenties, I had lived and worked in the black island-nations of the Caribbean: I had been the grain of salt in a sea of pepper. Whatever insights I might have about race and poverty won't satisfy me or anybody, but it's clear that of all the burdens fate had placed on humanity's shoulders, whites have borne a featherweight load. In Haiti, my name was and always would be *blanc*. In Creole, the words for "man" and "black" were identical: *neg*. In Haiti, black was the color of man, and white, unfortunately, was the color of both abandonment and salvation. Please, don't, I would find myself saying to a weathered old peasant showering me with gratitude for some petty and thoroughly inadequate act of charity: a match, a cigarette, a lift. Most often, however, I pushed silently through the shoals of beggars, ignoring their extended hands.

"You gave them money because it makes you feel warm and fuzzy," said the editor, and that made me hit the roof.

My wife intervened, attempting to explain whatever it is about me that requires explanation, and Gary looked on, dismayed, as two more blancs in a centuries-long procession of blancs squabbled over the methods and mechanisms they might best apply, like bandages, when they were intermittently inspired to repair the world.

NOVEMBER 1996

A REFLECTION ON WHITE GEESE

by BARRY LOPEZ

I slow the car, downshifting from fourth to third, with the melancholic notes of Bach's sixth cello suite in my ears—a recording of Casals from 1936—and turn east, away from a volcanic ridge of black basalt. On this cool California evening, the land in the marshy valley beyond is submerged in gray light, while the far hills are yet touched by a sunset glow. To the south, out the window, Venus glistens, a white diamond at the horizon's dark lapis edge. A few feet to my left is lake water—skittish mallards and coots bolt from the cover of bulrushes and pound the air furiously to put distance between us. I am chagrined, and slow down. I have been driving like this for hours—slowed by snow in the mountains behind me, listening to the cello suites—driving hard to get here before sunset.

I shut the tape off. In the waning light I can clearly see marsh hawks swooping over oat and barley fields to the south. Last hunts of the day. The eastern sky is beginning to blush, a rose afterglow. I roll the window down. The car fills with the sounds of birds—the nasalized complaints of several hundred mallards, pintails and canvasbacks, the slap-water whirr of their half-hearted takeoffs. But underneath this sound something else is expanding, distant French horns and kettledrums.

Up ahead, on the narrow dirt causeway, I spot Frans's car. He is here for the same reason I am. I pull up quietly and he emerges from his front seat, which he has made into a kind of photographic blind. We hug and exchange quiet words of greeting, and then turn to look at the white birds. Behind us the dark waters of Tule Lake, rippled by a faint wind, stretch off north, broken only by occasional islands of hardstem bulrush. Before us, working methodically through a field of two-row barley, the uninterrupted inquiry of their high-pitched voices lifting the night, are twenty-five thousand snow geese come down from the Siberian and Canadian Arctic. Grazing, but alert and wary in this last light.

Frans motions wordlessly to his left; I scan that far eastern edge of Tule Lake with field glasses. One hundred thousand lesser snow geese and Ross's geese float quietly on riffles, a white crease between the dark water and the darkening hills.

The staging of white geese at Tule Lake in Northern California in November is one of the most imposing—and dependable—wildlife spectacles in the world. At first one thinks of it only as a phenomenon of numbers—it's been possible in recent years to see as many as three hundred thousand geese here at one time. What a visitor finds as startling, however, is the great synchronicity of their movements: long skeins of white unfurl brilliantly against blue skies and dark cumulonimbus thunderheads, birds riding the towering wash of winds. They rise from the water or fall from the sky with balletic grace, with a booming noise like rattled sheets of corrugated tin, with a furious and unmitigated energy. It is the *life* of them that takes such hold of you.

I have spent enough time with large predators to know the human predilection to overlook authority and mystery in the lives of small, gregarious animals like the goose, but its qualities are finally as subtle, its way of making a living as admirable and attractive, as the grizzly bear's.

Geese are traditional, one could even say conservative, animals. They tend to stick to the same nesting grounds and wintering areas, to the same migration routes, year after year. Males and females have identical plumage. They usually mate for life, and both sexes care for the young. In all these ways, as well as in being more at ease on land, geese differ from ducks. They differ from swans in having proportionately longer legs and shorter necks. In size they fall somewhere between the two. A mature male lesser snow goose (*Chen caerulescens*), for example, might weigh six pounds, measure thirty inches from bill to tail, and have a wingspan of three feet. A mature female would be slightly smaller and lighter by perhaps half a pound.

Taxonomists divide the geese of the Northern Hemisphere into two groups, "gray" and "black," according to the color of their bills, feet, and legs. Among black geese like Canada geese and brandt they're dark. Snow geese, with rose-pink feet and legs and pink bills, are grouped with the gray geese, among whom these appendages are often brightly colored. Snow geese also commonly have rust-speckled faces, from feeding in iron-rich soils.

Before it was changed in 1971, the snow goose's scientific name, *Chen hyperborea*, reflected its high-arctic breeding heritage. The greater snow goose (*C. c. atlantica*)—a larger but far less numerous race of snow goose—breeds in northwestern Greenland and on adjacent Ellesmere, Devon, and Axel Heiburg islands. The lesser snow goose breeds slightly farther south, on Baffin and Southampton islands, the east coast of Hudson Bay, and on Banks Island to the west and Wrangell Island in Siberia. (Many people are attracted to the snow goose precisely because of its association with these little-known regions.)

There are two color phases, finally, of the lesser snow goose, blue and white. The combined population of about 1.5 million, the largest of any goose in the world, is divided into an eastern, mostly blue-phase population that winters in Texas and Louisiana and a western, white-phase population that winters in California. (It is the latter birds that pass through Tule Lake.)

The great numbers of these highly gregarious birds can be misleading. First, we were not certain until quite recently where snow geese were nesting, or how large their breeding colonies were. The scope of the problem is suggested by the experience of a Canadian biologist, Angus Gavin. In 1941 he stumbled on what he thought was a small breeding colony of lesser snow geese, on the delta of the McConnell River on the east coast of Hudson Bay—14,000 birds. In 1961 there were still only about 35,000 birds there. But a 1968 survey showed 100,000 birds, and in 1973 there were 520,000. Second, populations of arctic-breeding species like the snow goose are subject to extreme annual fluctuations, a boom-and-bust cycle tied to the unpredictable weather patterns typical of arctic ecosystems. After a series of prolonged winters, for example, when persistent spring snow cover kept birds from nesting, the Wrangell Island population of snow geese fell from 400,000 birds in 1965 to fewer than 50,000 in 1975. (By the summer of 1981 it was back up to 170,000.)

The numbers in which we see them on their wintering grounds are large enough to be comforting—it is hard at first to imagine what would threaten such flocks. Snow geese, however, face a variety of problems. The most serious is a striking loss of winter habitat. In 1900 western snow geese had more than 6,200 square miles of winter habitat available to them on California's Sacramento and San Joaquin rivers. Today, 90 percent of this has been absorbed by agricultural, industrial, and urban expansion. This means 90 percent of the land in central California that snow geese once depended on for food and shelter is gone. Hunters in California kill about 20 percent of the population each year and leave another 4 to 5 percent crippled to die of starvation and injuries.

(An additional 2 to 3 percent dies each year of lead poisoning, from ingesting spent shot.) An unknown number are also killed by high-tension wires. In the future, geese will likely face a significant threat on their arctic breeding grounds from oil and gas exploration.

The birds also suffer from the same kinds of diseases, traumatic accidents, and natural disasters that threaten all organisms. Females, for example, fiercely devoted to the potential in their egg clutches, may choose to die of exposure on their nests rather than to abandon them in an unseasonable storm.

In the light of all this, it is ironic that the one place on earth a person might see these geese in numbers large enough to cover half the sky is, itself, a potential threat to their existence.

The land now called Tule Lake National Wildlife Refuge lies in a volcanic basin, part of which was once an extensive, 2,700-square-mile marshland. In 1905 the federal government began draining the area to create irrigated croplands. Marshland habitat and bird populations shrank. By 1981 only fifty-six square miles of wetland, 2 percent of the original area, was left for waterfowl. In spite of this reduction, the area, incredibly, remains an ideal spot for migratory waterfowl. On nearly any given day in the fall a visitor to the Klamath Basin might see more than a *million* birds—mallards, gadwalls, pintails, lesser scaups, goldeneyes, cinnamon teals, northern shovelers, redheads, canvasbacks, ruddy ducks; plus western and cackling Canada geese, white-fronted geese, Ross's geese, lesser snow geese, and whistling swans. (More than 250 species of birds have been seen on or near the refuge and more than 170 nest here.)

The safety of these populations is in the hands of a resident federal manager and his staff, who must effectively balance the birds' livelihood with the demands of local farmers, who use Tule Lake's water to irrigate adjacent fields of malt barley and winter potatoes, and waterfowl hunters, some of whom come from hundreds of miles away. And there is another problem. Although the Klamath Basin is the greatest concentration point for migratory waterfowl in North America, caring well for birds here is no guarantee they will fare well elsewhere along the flyway. And a geographic concentration like this merely increases the chance of catastrophe if epidemic disease should strike.

The first time I visited Tule Lake I arrived early on a fall afternoon. When I asked where the snow geese were congregated I was directed to an area called the English Channel, several miles out on the refuge road. I sat there for three hours, studying the birds' landings and takeoffs, how they behaved toward each other on the water, how they shot the skies overhead. I tried to unravel and to parse the dazzling synchronicity of their movements. I am always struck anew in these moments, in observing such detail, by the way in which an animal slowly reveals itself.

Before the sun went down, I drove off to see more of the snow goose's landscape, what other animals there might be on the refuge, how the land changed at a distance from the water. I found the serpentine great blue heron, vivacious and melodious flocks of red-winged blackbirds, and that small, fierce hunter, the kestrel. Muskrats bolted across the road. At the southern end of the refuge, where cattails and bulrushes give way to rabbit brush and sage on a volcanic plain, I came upon mule deer, three does and four fawns standing still and tense in a meandering fog.

I found a room that evening in the small town of Tulelake. There'd not been, that I could recall, a moment of silence all day from these most loquacious of geese. I wondered if they were mum in the middle of the night, how quiet they were at dawn. I set the alarm for 3:00 A.M.

The streets of Tulelake are desolate at that hour. In that odd stillness—the stillness of moonlit horses standing asleep in fields—I drove out into the countryside, toward the refuge. It was a ride long enough to hear the first two movements of Beethoven's Fifth Symphony. I drove in a light rain, past white farmhouses framed by ornamental birches and weeping willows. In the 1860s this land was taken by force from the Modoc Indians; in the 1940s the government built a Japanese internment camp here. At this hour, however, nearly every landscape has a pervasive innocence. I passed the refuge headquarters— low shiplapped buildings, white against a dark ridge of basalt, facing a road lined with Russian olives. I drove past stout, slowly dying willows of undetermined age, trees that mark the old shoreline of Tule Lake, where it was before the reclamation project began.

The music is low, barely audible, but the enthusiasm in some of the strong passages reminds me of geese. I turn the tape off and drive a narrow, cratered road out into the refuge, feeling the car slipping sideways in the mud. Past rafts of sleeping ducks. The first geese I see surge past just overhead like white butterflies, brushing the penumbral dimness above the car's headlights. I open the window and feel the sudden assault of their voices, the dunning power of their wings hammering the air, a rush of cold wind and rain through the window. In a moment I am outside, standing in the roar. I find a comfortable, protected place in the bulrushes and wait in my parka until dawn, listening.

Their collective voice, like the cries of athletic young men at a distance, is unabated. In the darkness it is nearly all there is of them, but for an occasional and eerie passage overhead. I try to listen closely: a barking of high-voiced dogs, like terriers, the squealing of shoats. By an accident of harmonics the din rises and falls like the cheering of a crowd in a vast stadium. Whoops and shouts; startled voices of outrage, of shock.

These are not the only voices. Cackling geese pass over in the dark, their cries more tentative. Coyotes yip. Nearby some creature screeches, perhaps a mouse in the talons of a great horned owl, whose skipping hoots I have heard earlier.

A gibbous moon shines occasionally through a winddriven overcast. Toward dawn the geese's voices fall off suddenly for a few moments. The silence seems primordial. The black sky in the east now shows bloodred through scalloped shelves of cloud. It broadens into an orange flare that fades to rose and finally to the grays of dawn. The voices begin again.

I drive back into Tulelake and eat breakfast amid a throng of hunters crowding the tables of a small cafe, steaming the windows with their raucous conversation.

Bob Fields, the refuge manager, has agreed to take me on a tour in the afternoon. I decide to spend the morning at the refuge headquarters, reading scientific reports and speaking with biologist Ed O'Neill about the early history of Tule Lake.

O'Neill talks first about the sine qua non, a suitable expanse of water. In the American West the ownership of surface water confers the kind of political and economic power that comes elsewhere with oil wells and banks. Water is a commodity; it is expensive to maintain and its owners seek to invest the limited supply profitably. A hunting club that keeps private marshland for geese and ducks, for example, will do so only as long as they feel their hunting success warrants it. If the season is shortened or the bag limit reduced by the state—the most common ways to conserve dwindling waterfowl populations—they might find hunting no longer satisfying and sell the marsh to farmers, who will turn it into cropland. Real estate speculators and other landowners with substantial surface-water rights rarely give the birds that depend on their lands a second thought when they're preparing to sell. As O'Neill puts it, "You can't outweigh a stack of silver dollars with a duck."

The plight of western waterfowl is made clearer by an anomaly. In the eastern United States, a natural abundance of water and the closure of many tracts of private land to hunting provide birds with a strong measure of protection. In the West, bird populations are much larger, but water is scarcer, and refuge lands, because they are largely public, remain open to hunting.

By carefully adjusting the length of the hunting season and the bag limits each year, and by planting food for the birds, refuge managers try to maintain large bird populations, in part to keep private hunting clubs along the flyway enthusiastic about continuing to provide additional habitat for the birds. Without the help of private individuals, including conservation groups that own wetlands, the federal and state refuge systems simply cannot provide for the birds. (This is especially true now. The Reagan administration has proved more hostile to the preservation of federal refuges and their denizens than any American administration since the turn of the century.)

Some birds, the snow goose among them, have adapted to shortages of food and land. Deprived of the rootstocks of bulrushes and marsh grasses, snow geese in the West have switched to gleaning agricultural wastes and cropping winter wheat, a practice that has spread to the Midwest, where snow geese now feed increasingly on rice and corn. A second adjustment snow geese have made is to linger on their fall migrations and to winter over farther north. That way fewer birds end up for a shorter period of time on traditional wintering grounds, where food is scarcer each year.

As we spoke, O'Neill kept glancing out the window. He told me about having seen as many as three hundred thousand white geese there in years past. With the loss of habitat and birds spreading out now to winter along the flyway, such aggregations, he says, may never be seen again. He points out, too, looking dismayed and vaguely bitter, that these huge flocks have not been conserved for the viewer who does not hunt, for the tourist who comes to Tule Lake to see something he has only dreamed of.

We preserve them, principally, to hunt them.

In broad daylight I was able to confirm something I'd read about the constant, loud din of their voices: Relatively few birds are actually vocalizing at any one time, perhaps only one in thirty. Biologists speculate that snow geese recognize each other's voices and that family units of three or four maintain contact in these vast aggregations by calling out to one another. What sounds like mindless chaos to the human ear, then, may actually be a complex pattern of solicitous cries, discretely distinguished by snow geese.

Another sound that is easier to decipher in daylight is the rising squall that signals they are leaving the water. It's like the sustained hammering of a waterfall or a wind booming in the full crowns of large trees.

One wonders, watching the geese fly off in flocks of a hundred or a thousand, if they would be quite so arresting without their stunning whiteness. When they fly with the sun behind them, the opaque white of their bodies, the white of water-polished seashells, is set off against grayer whites in their tail feathers and in their translucent, black-tipped wings. Up close these are the dense, impeccable whites of an arctic fox. Against the grays and blues of a storm-laden sky, the whiteness has a surreal glow, a brilliance without shadow.

I remember watching a large flock rise one morning from a plowed field about a mile distant. I had been watching clouds, the soft, buoyant, windblown edges of immaculate cumulus. The birds rose against much darker clouds to the east. There was something vaguely ominous in this apparition, as if the earth had opened and poured them forth, like a wind, a blizzard, which unfurled across the horizon above the dark soil, becoming wider and higher in the sky than my field of vision could encompass, great swirling currents of birds in a rattling of wings, one fluid recurved sweep of ten thousand passing through the open spaces in another, counterflying flock, while beyond them lattice after lattice passed like sliding walls, until in the whole sky you lost your depth of field and felt as though you were looking up from the floor of the ocean through shoals of fish.

At rest on the water the geese drank and slept and bathed and preened. They reminded me in their ablutions of the field notes of a Hudson's Bay trader, George Barnston. He wrote of watching flocks of snow geese gathering on James Bay in 1862, in preparation for their annual two-thousand-mile, non-stop thirty-two-hour flight to the Louisiana coast. They finally left off feeding, he wrote, to smooth and dress their feathers with oil, like athletes, biding their time for a north wind. When it came they were gone, hundreds of thousands of them, leaving a coast once "widely resonant with their petulant and incessant calls" suddenly as "silent as the grave—a deserted, barren, and frozen shore."

Barnston was struck by the way snow geese did things together. No other waterfowl are as gregarious; certainly no other large bird flies as skillfully in such right aggregations. This quality—the individual act beautifully integrated within the larger movement of the flock—is provocative. One afternoon I studied individual birds for hours as they landed and took off. I never once saw a bird on the water move over to accommodate a bird that was landing; nor a bird ever disturbed by another taking off, no matter how tightly they were bunched. In no flight overhead did I see two birds so much as brush wing tips. Certainly they must; but for the most part they are flawlessly adroit. A flock settles gently on the water like wiffling leaves; birds explode vertically with compact and furious wingbeats and then stretch out full length, airborne, rank on rank, as if the whole flock had been cleanly wedged from the surface of the water. Several thousand bank smoothly against a head wind, as precisely as though they were feathers in the wing of a single bird.

It was while I sat immersed in these details that Bob Fields walked up. After a long skyward stare he said, "I've been here for seven years. I never get tired of watching them."

We left in his small truck to drive the narrow causeways of Tule Lake and the five adjacent federal refuges. Fields joined the U.S. Fish and Wildlife Service in 1958, at the age of twenty-two. His background is in range biology and plant ecology as well as waterfowl management. Before he came to Tule Lake in 1974, to manage the Klamath Basin refuges, he worked on the National Bison Range in Montana and on the Charles Sheldon Antelope Range in Nevada.

In 1975 a group of visitors who would profoundly affect Fields arrived at Tule Lake. They were Eskimos, from the Yukon-Kuskokwim delta of Alaska. They had come to see how the geese populations, which they depend on for food, were being managed. In the few days they were together, Fields came to understand that the Eskimos were appalled by the waste they saw at Tule Lake, by the number of birds hunters left crippled and unretrieved, and were surprised that hunters took only the breast meat and threw the rest of the bird away. On the other hand, the aggregations of geese they saw were so extensive they believed someone was fooling them—surely, they thought, so many birds could never be found in one place.

The experience with the Eskimos—Fields traveled north to see the Yukon-Kuskokwim country and the Eskimos returned to Tule Lake in 1977—focused his career as had no other event. In discussions with the Eskimos he found himself talking with a kind of hunter he rarely encountered anymore—humble men with a respect for the birds and a sense of responsibility toward them. That the Eskimos were dumbstruck at the number of birds led him to a more sobering thought: If he failed here as a refuge manager, his failure would run the length of the continent.

In the years following, Fields gained a reputation as a man who cared passionately for the health and welfare of waterfowl populations. He tailored, with the help of assistant refuge manager Homer McCollum, a model hunting program at Tule Lake, but he is candid in expressing his distaste for a type of hunter he still meets too frequently—belligerent, careless people for whom hunting is simply violent recreation; people who trench and rut the refuge's roads in oversize four-wheel-drive vehicles, who are ignorant of hunting laws or who delight in breaking them as part of a "game" they play with refuge personnel.

At one point in our afternoon drive, Fields and I were watching a flock of geese feeding in a field of oats and barley on the eastern edge of the refuge. We watched in silence for a long time. I said something about the way birds can calm you, how the graceful way they define the sky can draw irritation right out of you. He looked over at me and smiled and nodded. A while later, still watching the birds, he said, "I have known all along there was more to it than managing the birds so they could be killed by some macho hunter." It was the Eskimos who gave him a sense of how a hunter should behave, and their awe that rekindled his own desire to see the birds preserved.

As we drove back across the refuge, Fields spoke about the changes that had occurred in the Klamath Basin since the federal reclamation project began in 1905. Most of the native grasses—blue bench wheat grass, Great Basin wild rye—are gone. A visitor notices foreign plants in their place, like cheatgrass. And introduced species like the ring-necked pheasant and the muskrat, which bores holes in the refuge dikes and disrupts the pattern of drainage. And the intrusion of high-tension power lines, which endanger the birds and which Fields has no budget to bury. And the presence of huge pumps that circulate water from Tule Lake to farmers in the valley, back and forth, back and forth, before pumping it west to Lower Klamath Refuge.

It is over these evolving, occasionally uneasy relationships between recent immigrants and the original inhabitants that Fields keeps watch. I say good-bye to him at his office, to the world of bird poachers, lead poisoning, and politically powerful hunting and agricultural lobbies he deals with every day. When I shake his hand I find myself wanting to thank him for the depth with which he cares for the birds, and for the intelligence that allows him to disparage not hunting itself but the lethal acts of irresponsible and thoughtless people.

I still have a few hours before I meet Frans for dinner. I decide to drive out to the east of the refuge, to a low escarpment that bears the carvings of Indians who lived in this valley before white men arrived. I pass by open fields where horses and beef cattle graze and cowbirds flock after seeds. Red-tailed hawks are perched on telephone poles, watching for field rodents. A light rain has turned to snow.

The brooding face of the escarpment has a prehistoric quality. It is secured behind a chain-link fence topped with barbed wire, but the evidence of vandals who have broken past it to knock off souvenir petroglyphs is everywhere. The castings of barn owls, nesting in stone pockets above, are spread over the ground. I open some of them to see what the owls have been eating. Meadow voles. Deer mice.

The valley before me has darkened. I know somewhere out there, too far away to see now, long scarves of snow geese are riding and banking against these rising winds, and that they are aware of the snow. In a few weeks Tule Lake will be frozen and they will be gone. I turn back to the wall of petroglyphs. The carvings relate, apparently, to the movement of animals through this land hundreds of years ago. The people who made them made their clothing and shelters, even their cooking containers, from the lake's tule reeds. When the first white man arrived—Peter Ogden, in 1826—he found them wearing blankets of duck and goose feathers. In the years since, the complex interrelationships of the Modoc with this land, largely unrecorded to begin with, have disappeared. The land itself has been turned to agriculture, with a portion set aside for certain species of birds that have passed through this valley for no one knows how many centuries. The hunters have become farmers, the farmers, landowners. Their sons have gone to the cities and become businessmen, and the sons of these men have returned with guns, to take advantage of an old urge, to hunt. But more than a few come back with a poor knowledge of the birds, the land, the reason for killing. It is by now a familiar story, for which birds pay with their lives.

The old argument, that geese must be killed for their own good, to manage the size of their populations, founders on two points. Snow goose populations rise and fall precipitously because of their arctic breeding pattern. No group of hunters can "fine-tune" such a basic element of their ecology. Second, the artificial control of their numbers only augments efforts to continue draining wetlands.

We must search in our way of life, I think, for substantially more here than economic expansion and continued good hunting. We need to look for a set of relationships similar to the ones Fields admired among the Eskimos. We grasp what is beautiful in a flight of snow geese rising against an overcast sky as easily as we grasp the beauty in a cello suite; and intuit, I believe, that if we allow these things to be destroyed or degraded for economic or frivolous reasons we will become deeply and strangely impoverished.

I had seen little of my friend Frans in three days. At dinner he said he wanted to tell me of the Oostvaardersplassen in Holland. It has become a major stopover for waterfowl in northern Europe, a marsh that didn't even exist ten years ago. Birds hardly anyone has seen in Holland since the time of Napoleon are there now. Peregrine falcons, snowy egrets, and European sea eagles have returned.

I drive away from the escarpment holding tenaciously to this image of reparation.

OCTOBER 1982

TODAY MANY PROBLEMS

by LAURENCE SHAMES

I know I am in trouble from the way Clive looks at Allison.

It is a look beyond lust, beyond longing. It is a gagged, moony, brain-dead sort of stare: the look of a man who's been in the African wilds too long and is suddenly—slam!—confronted by a lissome twenty-six-year-old Connecticut blond as eager for adventure as any naughty milk-bathed debutante out of Fitzgerald. Allison has long legs and a Minolta. I have a spiral notebook and a sinking feeling. Clive may be a hale fellow and a charming raconteur, but I know from this moment that he won't be worth squat as a safari guide.

This is in Kigoma, a miserable outpost of stomped red dirt and frying fish on the eastern shore of Lake Tanganyika. Some years ago, the Red Chinese decided to make friends in Tanzania by building a railroad that connected nothing to nowhere. Mercifully, this madness had to have an ending, and Kigoma is it. Thousands of miles of track culminate at one dinky pier with splintered pilings and a single rusty crane. At the Railway Hotel, Kigoma's finest, a handscrawled sign advises that clothes must be worn in the disco.

Clive (OK, not his real name) pushes his sunglasses up above his eyebrows and sips his beer. He is improbably handsome—square-jawed, with curly black hair and violet eyes—and has led an improbably interesting life. He is telling

Allison (not hers, either) about an evening at Nairobi's fabled Muthaiga Club, an evening when he and several other scions of Britain's prodigal aristocracy emerged, in black tie, at 3:00 A.M., to tap-dance on the bonnets of Land Rovers under a flame red setting moon. Allison is rapt. This is bad. We haven't even left for camp yet and he's practically in her tent.

To be fair, I must say that Clive is not getting paid to lead this expedition. He's doing it to promote his luxury accommodations—four canvas boxes on a leopard-infested beach—at the foot of the Mahale Mountains, some fourteen hours away by water. I have flown in from Dar es Salaam to trek said mountains and to hang out among the world's greatest remaining population of wild chimpanzees. As for Allison, she has wafted down from Burundi on a tour around the lake. She is, she says, on assignment for the in-flight magazine of an airline that does not serve Africa. OK, it's a strange business. It's a strange world.

The sun sets behind the blue hills of Zaire on the other side of the lake. Almost instantly the breeze drops, and the churning water of the world's longest freshwater lake—420 miles north to south—calms to a baylike surge. In surface area, Lake Tanganyika is much smaller than nearby Lake Victoria; in volume, it is eight times bigger. Formed more than 10 million years ago by the geothermal upheavals and cavings-in that created the Rift Valley, Lake Tanganyika has been sounded to 4,710 feet; its bottom, pockmarked with geysers, is sunk 2,148 feet below sea level. Laced by swirling winds, stung by lightning that moves in from the mountains to the west, it is an altogether imposing body of water—and we will be traveling it in a glorified canoe with a fifteen-horsepower outboard that looks like a relic from colonial days.

But no problem. Clive has made this trip many times—well, OK, twice. So we splash aboard over the stern platform and settle in among the provisions, which consist almost entirely of cabbages, milky green, their outer leaves already showing spots of ooze. Clive's Tanzanian staff, smiling broadly and smoking blithely around the gasoline cans, gesture kindly toward the boat's more comfortable gunwale—a lapse in judgment, since that will be the windward, splashward side as we journey south.

But no problem. I produce a liter of Glenlivet from my duffel. I like scotch. It travels well. When I go to the duty-free shop at Heathrow and buy my cardboard tube, that's when it really dawns on me that I'm on safari. Anyway, I take a pull, then hand the bottle to Allison, who gulps like a knight in a mead hall. She passes it on to Clive, who takes it with the hand that's not steering the boat. With what seems to me exaggerated attention to the rim where Allison's lips have lately been, he hauls his ration and passes it back. I moistly recline, to stargaze at the upside-down constellations of the Southern Hemisphere. Allison takes the bottle and sidles to the stern, to put less distance between her mouth and Clive's. I fall asleep to the gentle dance of the canoe as it proceeds by S-curves through the mile-deep waters of the lake.

Dawn. An African with rheumy red eyes is piloting the boat, and the Mahale Mountains are jutting in a lavender promontory that protrudes from the coastline like the prow of a ship.

The Mahales are a great geobiological crossroads. They retain examples of West African flora—remnants of that distant time before the Rift cleaved the continent into two largely separate systems. The hills, which rise as high as 8,075 feet above sea level, represent the southernmost range of certain animal and plant species and the northernmost of others. Since the chain is the only real mountain mass within hundreds of miles of Tanganyika's eastern shore, it attracts much of the available rainfall and furnishes that vivid and peculiarly African image of wildly fertile land slipping foot by foot into aridity. To the tall haven of moisture flock colobus monkeys, yellow baboons, spotted hyenas, buffalo, elephants, lions—55 species of mammals in all. Add to this 120 kinds of birds, among them palm nut vultures, Goliath herons, and the crowned hawk eagle, which is bold and strong enough to pluck monkeys from the tops of trees. Deeply moved by the nearness of so much life, I pee over the side of the canoe.

It then occurs to me that we have lost Clive and Allison.

I look around the boat for them, but all I see are cabbages. Cabbages stacked in the bow. Cabbages wedged under the seats. Finally, poking coyly from under a swath of burlap, two heads appear that are not cabbage-green. My guide and my colleague. At their side is my nearly empty bottle of Glenlivet.

We reach camp around eight. By way of greeting, the cook runs over and tells us a leopard chased him into the lake last night. Then we go to our tents—those truly wonderful safari dwellings with folding cots and shaving mirrors hung on pegs, with zippered windows over mosquito netting, with canvas basins slung on tripods. Camp is on a thin, beautiful crescent of sandy beach between the forest and the emerald green and shockingly clear water. Waterbucks sometimes come down to drink here in the evenings; lions occasionally follow to eat them.

Clive, having changed into a *kikoi*, comes by to announce that we'll stay in camp today. "You must be tired," he tells me. No, I think, *you* must be tired. *I* feel great. But I let it go. I simply say that I'll have a swim. "Oh, good idea," says Clive. "The water is sublime here. And we have a species of water cobra found nowhere else. Six feet long. Very deadly."

Early next morning, before the sun has topped the hills, Clive tells me that he will not, after all, be hanging around to trek after the chimps with me. Rather, he'll be taking the boat, the rifle, the fishing gear, most of the food, and Allison to do some exploring down the lake. But no problem. He'll be leaving me in the care of Mkumbwe, a local fellow who is in fact a respected employee of the Mahale Mountains National Park and as fine and knowledgeable a tracker as the country possesses.

Mkumbwe bows his head under the weight of these compliments and extends a hand in one of those gentle, almost boneless African handshakes. He has a winning smile, a well-fed girth, and a large panga, or bush knife, hanging from his belt. Yet my immediate response to Mkumbwe is lack of confidence. Why, I wonder? Good liberal that I am, I do not let this troubling reaction go unexamined. Why this unease about going into snake-ridden, lion-hiding, unmapped jungle in the sole care of a black man? Am I being racist? Or is it just that Mkumbwe has only one eye? I mean, he has two eyes, but one of them, opalescent, just wanders off to the port side.

I take Clive aside. "Don't kid me, now. Can he see?"

"Has a little trouble with depth perception," my guide allows.

"Like on the edges of ravines?" I ask.

"Very surefooted," Clive says. "Not to worry."

I watch as he and Allison board the motor canoe to head south. With a touch that has already become proprietary, he helps her hoist her butt over the stern. Frankly, I don't expect to miss them. But as I watch them vanish around the first curve in the shoreline, I feel a certain desolation, as if my best friends in the whole wide world have abandoned me. I have a certain fleeting image of myself, as if seen from a great distance, standing alone between the vast lake and the mountains, and boy, do I look tiny.

"So, Mkumbwe," I bravely say, "we find the chimps today?"

That, after all, is the object of the exercise. But finding the chimps at Mahale is by no means a sure thing. Mahale is big: 622 square miles, as opposed to the suburban 20 at Jane Goodall's famous Gombe Stream preserve. Mahale is tall, with almost 5,000 vertical feet through which the animals can wander. The chimps move great distances in accordance with the availability of food and water and the presence of predators. While they have grown accustomed to people, they are not dependent. They travel fast, making far greater headway across the canopy than humans can manage through the undergrowth.

Still, Mkumbwe is confident. "We find them easy. Hour. Hour and half. You stay long as you like. Then I take you to meet Nishida."

"I don't want to meet Nishida," I say.

"But Nishida is great man."

"That's why I don't want to meet him."

What, after all, did I have to say to the eminent Dr. Toshisada Nishida of Tokyo University, the man who established the Kasoge Research Camp in

1965, who has lived in the jungle ever since, and who would certainly be an international celebrity were it not for Japanese reticence about making scientists into stars? I'm no primatologist, God knows; in fact, I learned only recently not to call apes monkeys. So I could picture the awkward moment: I execute a clumsy little bow, while Nishida-san shyly extends a hand; then he bows while I extend a hand. Then I ask a couple of stupid questions. Then the interview is over. What for?

"OK," says Mkumbwe agreeably. "No Nishida. Just chimps. We leave after breakfast."

"Maybe we should leave now," I say. "Before it gets too hot."

"Not too hot," says Mkumbwe, presumably unaware that not all of us grew up on the equator. "Besides, short walk."

"OK," I say. "What's for breakfast?"

"Cabbage."

At the base of the Mahale Mountains there is a swath of hummocky grasses that, in this dry season, have been sunbleached to the color of lions, and from this grass comes a somewhat distant, but not very distant, sound of growling.

"Mkumbwe," I ask my one-eyed tracker, "what's that?"

"Lion," he says affably. "Do not worry. Mr. Lion, he very afraid of Mkumbwe. Mr. Lion see Mkumbwe, he run away."

"Promise?"

"Oh, yes. And it is good thing that Mr. Lion is down here."

"Why is that, Mkumbwe?"

"Because chimpanzees no like lion. If lion is high up, chimps go higher up. If lion is by lake, chimps go not so high. We find them soon."

At this stage, you understand, I still believe Mkumbwe. He has given me lots of good advice. He's spared me the trouble of carrying water, for instance, by telling me we'll find plenty of clean, fast-moving streams along the way. He's saved me from a turned ankle by counseling the wearing of boots that weigh a ton and are already squishing with sweat. So why shouldn't I believe that 400-pound lions turn tail and flee at the sight of him?

Two hours later, we are climbing through gallery forests a quarter-mile or so above the lake. Humidity does strange things here. In the shade, it is slimily steamy; in the smallest clearing, the sun is as sharp and the air as cloyingly dry as in the desert. We have found no water save for one fetid, greenish pool, from which I would not moisten my bandana, let alone drink.

"Today many problems," says Mkumbwe, and he casually swings his panga so that its hooked end catches in the sappy bark of a miombo tree. "Those chimps, they silly. We listen awhile, till they call Mkumbwe."

So we sit. Far off, a colobus chatters, a moorhen clucks. But there are no screams of chimpanzees. My patience thin, I stand up and pace. Mkumbwe's panga works loose from the tree and falls, burying itself haft-deep exactly where I've been sitting. My tracker fixes me with his one good eye while seeming to regard the nine inches of sunken steel with the blind one. "You lucky man, bwana. That panga silly."

We climb, using vines to clamber up the steep sides of knife-edge valleys. My shirt is soaked, and I am tempted to suck on it. Then, as we top a small rise, I hear a rustling off to the left. I am sure it is the chimps, and I take imbecilic pride in being the first to hear them. "Mkumbwe," I whisper, putting a finger to my lips. We freeze. The rustling gets louder, closer. In my mind's eye, I can already see the loping, loose-armed creatures with their leather faces, their sad eyes. I picture them sliding into sunshine, pink legs flashing through thin fur, shoulders bunched. I can picture the leader bursting into startled alertness, springing up, twirling in the air, screeching out a warning.

Instead, Professor Nishida comes walking jauntily down an intersecting trail. He is wearing a khaki hat primly tied beneath his chin, and he is smoking through a cigarette holder that he clutches from below, in the manner of Hirohito. He has small, round, wire-rimmed glasses and the quietly berserk affect of those soldiers who occasionally emerge from a Philippine jungle, unaware that the war has been over for some time. He is flanked by two porters, and he is chatting with them in musical and unmistakable Swahili.

So I will meet the great man after all. I promise myself not to ask any stupid questions. Steer clear of primatology, I counsel myself. Nishida approaches, his step light and indefatigable. We do the I-bow-he-shakes routine. He asks where I am from. I compliment him on his fluent Swahili. He looks at me as if I am demented or have given mortal offense. "I not speak Swahili. They speak Japanese." He touches the brim of his bush hat and bounds off. He offers no advice as to where the chimps are, and he doesn't invite us to walk with him.

"Nishida," says Mkumbwe in a reverent whisper. "He very great man."

"I'm sure that's so. But where are the chimps?"

He shakes his head sadly. "They silly. They go way high. You want to turn back?"

"No. I want to find them."

"You thirsty?"

"Yes."

"Today many problems. Streams dry. They silly."

The sun is at its zenith now, but at the higher elevations a cooling mist reaches down in fingers from the treetops. We climb another hour. Here and there, breaks in the forest afford views down to the lake. It looks thirst-quenching and compact. Through holes in the mist, it looks like you could skip a stone to Zaire, twenty-six miles away.

We find the chimps.

Forgive me, after all this time, for stating the fact so undramatically. But the truth is that, while finding a lion may be dramatic, stumbling across an elephant may be dramatic, coming upon a troop of chimps feels—no offense, Mom—like going home. More than anything, it's relaxing. It all seems so familiar.

There are some twenty apes in the group, and they are arrayed around a small clearing as if in Aunt Margaret's living room after a holiday meal. A few lounge in trees. A few nap on the ground. Little ones chase each other. Their hands are exactly like our hands. They have little wrinkles on their knuckles, just like we do.

The chimps seem neither bothered by nor especially curious about Mkumbwe's and my arrival. They glance up with their dark, wet eyes, and go back to their grooming. I sit down on the ground, staying very low, in token submission. The chimps let me sidle over very close, almost touching-close—I can hear their fingertips rustling softly through one another's hair as they clean away bugs and bits of leaf. A baby rides its mother's back. Two adolescents, for no apparent reason, hug each other.

Suddenly I am embarrassed for my species. Chimps are a lot nicer to each other than we are. True, they pilfer food, they fight sometimes, they masturbate in public. I hear they even go to war on occasion. But they're considerate, patient; they look out for each other. Would two chimps with the hots for each other go off with the rifle, the fishing gear, and the food, leaving the odd chimp out to stay behind and die? Would a chimp think the worst of another chimp just because the poor thing was half blind? For that matter, if chimps could write, would they be so snide?

I lie back in the grass to learn kindness. The apes circle softly. They groom, they kiss, they baby-sit. They chatter, and they scratch their elbows and their armpits, which are just like ours.

Mkumbwe approaches and tells me softly that the light is going and we'd better head back down the mountain. I feel loss at having to leave.

"Can we come tomorrow?"

"If you want. Tomorrow we find them easy."

He's lying, of course. He doesn't have the faintest idea if we'll find them easily, or at all. But what the hell. He's only trying to be a gracious host, trying to make the visitor happy. He means well. Almost everybody does.

SEPTEMBER 1990

TORCHED

by MICHAEL PATERNITI

Out of Louisiana frog swamp and Kentucky canebrake, Kansas cheatgrass and Dakota badland, they appear on the bright cusp of summer, marked like exotic birds in their Forest Service pickle suits or pressed fire shirts. Men and women, flying west, flushed out by lightning. In the airport lounges of Salt Lake City, Denver, and Missoula, they gather in circles, chewing gum, their clean hands looping with the punch line of some random joke. Their faces are weathered and open, reflections, to a large degree, of the landscapes that have shaped them. Their last meal may have been salmon; it may have been a good piece of sirloin. They may have slept eight hours; if they did, many of them won't again until the first snow falls.

Between now and that snow, however, these men and women—the ones known as helitacs and hotshots and the elite firefighting crews called smoke jumpers—will hump thousands of backcountry miles, dig fire lines until their backs are wrecked, and push through so many days of fatigue that the snake-hiss and flicker of flame will seem like a fever-dream. Some of them will be injured; some will die—their bodies identifiable only by dental records. And yet they will go on chasing the erratic mind of wildfire: to the top of the next spur ridge, to the bottom of the next gully.

As it has been for years, this chase often plays itself out most dramatically through the gasoline forests of the West, where a decade of all-time drought conditions and insect infestations has left some forests up to 90 percent dead. It begins with the lightning storms that crash the Southwest during the spring dry season, igniting the chaparral and mesquite of New Mexico, Arizona, and Texas until the summer monsoons douse everything with driving rains. The fires move through the mixed conifers of the Rockies—Colorado, Wyoming, Idaho, and Montana. Washington and Oregon flare simultaneously, and the Northwest may burn until Halloween. With the October Santa Ana winds in Southern California fanning new blazes, the season's end is punctuated by some of the wildest and most dangerous fire, often in heavily populated areas. And every year, the gypsy caravan mobilizes: the fire-command officers, the PR staffers, the caterers and contractors, the helicopter pilots and water-tender operators.

As the months pass, the men and women begin to reappear in the airport lounges. This time they stand in tighter circles, raccoon-eyed, inside themselves. They smell of ash, their fingernails are black crescents, their hands are marked by nettles and scabs and bee stings. They have hacking coughs from weeks of breathing smoke; because of it many of them will come down with low-grade fevers and unshakable colds. When they finally arrive back home, they may sleep for eight hours or eight days, floating in a Rip van Winkle haze, until one night they dream of a burning twig and then flaming leaves and then finally a full-blown fire that eats trees, flowers, rabbits, bones. When they wake up months later, on the bright cusp of summer, the mad circus—the barbecue to end all barbecues—has begun again.

Several weeks after the tragedy at Colorado's Storm King Mountain that left fourteen firefighters dead in July 1994, I drive west out of Missoula, crossing Idaho's panhandle beneath high kingdoms of cloud and smoke. It's a hot day near the end of August, and the wind hurries loamy whiffs of burning cedar through the car window. I drop to the tumble-rock bottom of Hells Canyon, en-shrouded by smoke, and pass into the deep spruce forests near Burgdorf, which are burning a few miles back from the road. Another twenty miles south and I'm in McCall, a town of 2,200 set beside a mountain lake, which has become command central in the effort to control more than a quarter-million burning acres in nearby Payette National Forest.

I arrive during the high point of one of the worst fire years of the century, one that will claim thirty-four lives, burn more than 4 million acres, and cost about $925 million to fight. McCall's main street is choked with army trucks, while helicopters buzz over the lake and planes full of slurry, a bubble-gum-pink fire retardant, dematerialize on the horizon. Buses ferry personnel between town and ten fire camps set in the woods, each one a mosaic of Navajos and Mexicans, homeboys and white boys, part of the America that exists inside the burning America.

Out at the airport, the jumper base looks like little more than a big Amish barn with two planes parked nearby, a Douglas DC-3 and a DeHavilland Twin Otter. Yet this is the home of one of the country's elite firefighting tribes, the McCall Smokejumpers—the shock troops, scramble squads, and aerial ambulance crews that respond to the first sign of dysfunction in our forests.

This morning, however, the jumpers are killing time in a few rare moments of calm before the next onslaught of lightning, predicted to hit sometime overnight. Bodies are strewn on the lawn, starfished and basking in the sun to the cranked-up groans of Tom Petty's "Freefalling." On the tarmac, Zach Morrow, the towheaded young son of two married jumpers, is spinning under the wing of the Doug, arms outstretched. A handful of jumpers take turns wobbling down the runway on a unicycle while others hoot encouragement.

Through a garage door, I pass into what's called the ready room, a cavernous, cement-floored hangar with parachutes stacked like mailbags against one wall. On hooks around the room hang Kevlar jumpsuits, padded, puffy numbers with big Elvis collars. The jumpers' lockers—those belonging to Koy, Outlaw, Hog, Catfish, Hurricane, Real McCoy, Ghost, Sparky, the Human Rototiller, and about sixty others—are small wooden cubbies, stacked in threes. Some are messy with fire gear; some are full of reminders of who the jumpers are when they aren't jumping: There are pictures of children swimming and men fishing, a photo of a dog in an inflatable pool, and a blue psychedelic tie. A Post-it Note is scribbled with the phone number of a woman, Marla. There's an onion, an orange, postcards from Fiji and Tonga, more pictures of children splashing in a lake, a girlfriend on a sailboat. So many images of water, it seems, to balance the constant specter of fire.

Two of the lockers are conspicuously empty but for a few items; they belonged to Roger Roth and James Thrash, who died at Storm King Mountain. While Roth was younger and quiet and lived in Florida during the off-season, Thrash was in many ways the heart and soul of the McCall jumpers. A forty-four-year-old father of two and a hunting guide in nearby New Meadows during the off-season, he was legendary for his cool head in chaotic situations. Thrash's bones were found inside his fire shelter, near what was left of another body, that of a woman hotshot he apparently tried to save from a fire that tore uphill at thirty miles per hour. Thrash's locker still bears his name, and inside it are a pair of folded jeans, a pair of sneakers, a toothbrush, and a Frank Thomas baseball card. A few weeks ago, he might have been the first person I met walking in.

Instead, it's Captain Jack, who lives in an Airstream trailer across from the base. "Where've you been?" he hollers when he spots me loitering in the maze of lockers. "Got worried. Thought we'd send a search party." At fifty-two, Jack Seagraves is still jumping, something of an anomaly among his McCall colleagues, whose average age is thirty-six. He has gray wisps of hair sticking out of a Casey Jones hat and is fit and slap-happy, with a perpetually ironic grin.

"I've always been a rebel," says Captain Jack, leaning both elbows on the operations desk, behind which hangs the jump list, a batter's lineup, more or less, for who will go to the next fire. "I've been a dentist and a minister. But I gave it all up to come back to jumping. I'm a traveling man."

Standing nearby, Rob Morrow, the stubble-faced father of Zach, diagnoses the smoke jumper's chronic wanderlust as a Christmas syndrome. "When you're a little kid, you're hoping that Santa's going to bring you that bike," he says. "You're pretty sure you're going to get that bike. And then Christmas morning—bingo! Smoke jumping is like that all summer. You keep hoping for that phone to ring the night before work, that voice telling you that you're going somewhere—Anchorage, Missoula, Redding, maybe Yellowstone or Silver City, New Mexico."

Preparing for the boondoggle of those little Christmases, however, is a major part of a smoke jumper's life. Captain Jack leads me into the rigging room, where the fine art of parachute-packing takes place on four long tables. As the cultic piece of equipment that separates jumpers from other firefighters, the parachute is handled here with reverence; each one has a log entry that details the fires it's been used on and the repairs it's undergone. The walls of the rigging room are festooned with photographs of various jumper teams, hung like fraternity composites, dating back to 1943, the year the base opened in McCall. Each new generation bears a striking resemblance to those that preceded it, with the one exception that in the past seven years three women have joined the group.

We pass through a door into the sewing room, crowded with ironing boards and heavy-duty sewing machines. Five jumpers are hard at work, repairing pack-out bags, chutes, and jumpsuits. Another sews tie-dyed curtains for his Microbus.

"About a third of the jumper bros are good seamsters," says Louis Hartjes, stroking his blond General Custer goatee. "Another third can hold their own in here, and the rest frankly just haven't mastered it."

There is something at first funny and touching about these muscly men hunched over their machines, trading their most intimate sewing secrets—everything from bobbin tensions to complex stitches. But sewing duty is a symbol of real status, and McCall's four year-round jumpers spend the winter right here, repairing chutes, jumpsuits, packs, boots, and whatever else needs fixing to get the show ready for next season. At one point Bob Charley, perched on a stool and reverently watching Hartjes execute a difficult bar-tacking stitch, sighs wistfully and says to no one in particular, "It'd be damn nice to have your own sewing machine at home."

Back at the operations desk, Scott Anderson, a thirty-six-year-old jumper who lives in Boise, is checking the day's fire update, as well as infrared aerial photographs that mark new spot fires. Every few minutes he glances at the clock and then taps his pencil on the desk. "As we say, smoke jumping is prolonged hours of boredom punctuated by stark moments of terror," he says. "There may be a lot of bureaucracy and bullshit here, but it would take dynamite to blow me out of this job."

Captain Jack hustles me into his yellow 1974 Chevrolet conversion van for a trip to a basin meadow five miles away where the smoke jumpers are planning a practice jump. Inside, the van has wood paneling and gold shag carpet covered by a throw rug depicting an Indian chief wearing a headdress. In a cup holder by the driver's seat there's an insulated coffee mug that reads I'M A MAVERICK. A jar of kalamata olives rolls back and forth under the seat.

By the time we get to the jump spot, Tom Koyama—Koy—is already there, pacing alone in the beargrass dotted by rocks and stumps. Koy is acting as fire-drill instructor today, dressed casually in a T-shirt, shorts, and sandals. He's been jumping for twenty-two years and, having survived more than 350 jumps, is regarded as one of the high lamas around the base.

We hear the Doug before we can see it, and when it comes into full view, the engines cut down and the plane begins to wheel in a wide circle over the meadow. Koy props himself up on an enormous fallen spruce and speaks by walkie-talkie to the spotter, who's poised at the plane's backdoor, ready to send the jumpers out two at a time.

Before the jump, the spotter lobs two sets of weighted streamers out of the plane—unfurling yellow and pink snakes that drift toward the ground. If it takes them seventy-five seconds to land, then the spotter knows the jumpers will have enough time to react should a chute fail to open. If the streamers land directly in the clearing, then it's assumed a human body will, too—which is not always the case if the jump spot is postage-stamp size or on an incline or if the wind is shifting in such a way that it seems a near-impossible feat of acrobatics to land anywhere but in a forgiving tree. The spotter will often look for a flat landing site a safe distance from the fire, though on occasion jumpers will be forced to descend through smoke, landing close enough to the inferno to feel hot cinders rising up against their skin. Today, however, the streamers float lazily to the ground, the plane loops around once more, and Koy grumbles into the walkie-talkie: "Winds out of the northwest at five miles per hour. Let's go 142-Zulu."

Above us, at about 1,500 feet, the first jumper, who's now perched in the backdoor, checks the topography below and evaluates wind conditions: Is it rushing fast? Is it burbling? Is it up-air or down-air? Then he passes the word back. The spotter sends him out the door with a slap on the back of his leg.

"When you first start jumping as a rookie, the spotter says, 'There's your jump spot,' and you find the meadow and you jump into it," says Rob Morrow. "But over time, you begin to see the bigger rocks and bigger logs and bigger trees and the better part of the meadow, and then maybe a couple more years and you're seeing everything, including the trail that gets you out of there. You size up the fire, the fuels next to the fire. The whole jump becomes highly analytical. It turns into a video game."

In that perilous moment when the jumpers step free of the plane, when they take what amounts to their own private leaps of faith, they seem shot from a cannon; the parachute, nothing but a rippling ribbon strung out behind the jumper's body, which may reach immediate bullet-speeds of up to 100 miles per hour. Within seconds, however, there's a loud *fuup* as the chute blossoms and the jumper is suddenly pulled up, bobbing in the air.

"The heavy guys hit like sacks of shit," says Koy, watching his comrades pendulum down in a rain of hoots and hollers. "That's where you get all kinds of sprained knees and ankles." Others land funny—on rocks or stumps or hornets' nests. Should a jumper come down in a tree, which is commonly the last resort for someone barreling earthward in tricky winds toward a tricky spot, the chute may fail to catch in the branches and the jumper may "burn through," falling straight to the ground. Compressed lumbar spines, broken ankles and tibias, and major back traumas are often the result, which is why jumpers look for lodgepole pines and Douglas firs, both softer trees with sturdy canopies, and hope to avoid ponderosa pines and western larches.

"Smoke jumping is a lighter, smaller man's business," says Koy. By and large, jumpers are wood-strong, lithe, and fit. Few are taller than five foot nine in stocking feet, though there's a compaction of muscle to their torsos and legs that creates an illusion of bigness. They can motor up a 35-degree slope at 8,000 feet without puffing. Watching them work, you get the feeling that Seneca might have been on to something when he claimed that all living beings are made of fire. The jumpers make a strong case for it—restless, darty, explosive.

Now in full swing, the practice jump seems to be going smoothly. Ten jumpers have landed on the ground and are in various stages of peeling off their jumpsuits and rolling up their chutes. Some pull out tins of chewing tobacco. Some are bare-chested, tanning in the blazing sun. But when one jumper comes blitzing down, running with the wind, everyone freezes.

"Schaeffer, whataya trying to do, end your career?" growls Koy loudly, adding under his breath: "Son of a bitch." Schaeffer lands hard, rolls, and comes up smiling, an embarrassed grin that's part cocky sneer. And even as he begins to remove his jumpsuit, bodies keep falling from the sky, peony after peony, bright white against the deep blue ether.

"You know what they say about us, don't you?" asks a jumper, winking as he trudges past me on his way to the lime green Forest Service rigs that will drive everyone back to the base. "They can't send us to hell, because we'd put it out."

It's been two months of orange moons and red suns and trees flaring like torched cathedral spires within sight of McCall's main drag. At night, smoke creeps down from the molten forests into town. Drift smoke, mountain smoke, and lake smoke commingle in slow fingers through the streets and wisp over neatly trimmed lawns, brushing up against house foundations. If you sleep with a window open, you inevitably wake up coughing in the night, adrift in blue clouds.

It's six o'clock on a Sunday morning, the sky a bruised purple, and the first of the jumpers begin straggling into the base for a crew briefing. Overnight, lightning has bombarded the high desert of eastern Oregon and the rolling hills near Council, Idaho, twenty-five minutes west of here by plane, and plans for a jump have changed several times. While the big blazes in the McCall area have been raging out of control for nearly four weeks, the smoke jumpers are often more valuable rushing out to meet the new, incoming fires, swatting them down before they turn big and break away.

The meeting is brief and all business, run by Scott Anderson. He has a brown mustache, a smudge of ash on his nose, and pale blue eyes that are deep-set by hard, high cheekbones. He runs the meeting efficiently but accommodates all questions as the jumpers scramble to find out where they're going and how long they'll be stuck in the woods. Thirty of them crowd the operations desk, and when Anderson announces that both planes will fly within the half-hour the whole place takes on new voltage.

After the meeting, the jumpers mill around excitedly, throw high-fives, share orange wedges, sip coffee, glance at the morning's sports page. "It's back to freeze-dried," laments one jumper as he stuffs a box of cookies into his pack. "The Fig Newtons are key." Another pauses near Thrash's locker, picks up the Frank Thomas baseball card, and then puts it back between the old sneakers.

When the hangar door goes up and the chill morning air invades the ready room, the jangle and click of buckles and zippers is counterpointed by the heavy thud of boots on the cement floor. Outside, the plane props begin to sputter; we can smell cooking spruce and see a pink brain of smoke hovering over Chicken Peak in the distance. In their outsize jumpsuits and Bell helmets with caged face guards, the jumpers line up for an equipment check. There's something both clownish and solemn about them as they make the transition from bed and home to the possibility of weeks away in the woods, the scent and weight of their lives and lovers and kids and dogs still on them but dissipating with the wind kicked up by the whirring propellers of the planes.

"Smoke jumping can be extremely difficult on a marriage, because you never know where a jumper is going to be," says eight-year veteran Brad Sanders. He gestures with his hands when he talks, fingers wide and callused. "Some jumper spouses just get hardened and say, 'Hey, why aren't you out on a fire? We need a new couch.' Others spend the season wanting their husbands or wives back." Sanders claims that in a "boomer" summer—one that might include more than twenty jumps and lots of overtime—a jumper can make as much as $25,000. This can also create a dilemma: While jumpers, like most seasonal employees, hope to work as many overtime hours as possible, many are foresters and have come to realize that, in some respects, firefighting is futile, if not damaging to the forests.

"On ninety percent of my jumps, I get to the ground, I look at the trees, and they're on the verge of dying," says Sanders. "By nature's way, it's time for that forest to burn, yet I'm trained to put out fires and that's exactly what I do. In your mind, though, there's that constant nagging doubt about whether you're right."

One by one the jumpers make their way across the tarmac now and vanish into the bellies of the Otter and the Doug. Both planes begin to taxi and then, in quick succession, rise from the ground, tippy-winged. Once they're gone, Captain Jack and I commandeer a Forest Service four-wheel-drive and head west in hopes of meeting four jumpers who are planning to land in the Hornet Reservoir area, eighty miles away by car. When we see a trail of smoke rising from the woods, we leave the truck on a ridge and pick our way through jackstrawed downfall, the sun breaking through the canopy in bright bolts.

In a small clearing we find two helitacs, firefighters who have been ferried in by helicopter, working on a piece of land the size of a large garden plot. They're armed with Pulaskis (part ax, part hoe) and use them ferociously as they turn the soil in search of smoldering leaves and twigs. A helicopter buzzes back and forth between the scorched plot and the reservoir, dumping seventy-five-gallon loads from a Bambi bucket with each run. Captain Jack works the walkie-talkie, trying to contact the jumpers, and it's not long before Brad Sanders comes crashing through the brush on foot. He and three other jumpers have just finished working on the other side of the ridge at a spot not unlike this one. He points to the top of one tree, to the place where lightning struck—the bark and meat of the tree exploded as if it's taken a bullet—and the jumpers debate whether the inside of the trunk could be on fire, only to catch later when they're gone.

"What people don't realize is that a lot of our calls are like this, mostly small, creeping fires," says Sanders. "But we need to get around the fire as quickly as possible, cutting the brush to make a control line. Out here you're away from the headaches and politics. You're your own boss, and the job becomes pure again."

After a decision has been made to leave the tree standing, Captain Jack, Sanders, and I climb up the hill and drive back down the road to where the three other jumpers are lounging in the shade, their heads propped on their packs. The fact that they've been caught slacking, having done their job quickly and efficiently, and are now waiting for a ride home seems to strike them as the worst possible unveiling. They glare and then try as best they can to ignore me. We stay long enough to clip some M&M's for the ride back and leave the jumpers as we found them, dirty-faced and spitting, looking more and more, in the rearview mirror, like a surly portrait of extras from a spaghetti western.

Beneath an arcane nimbus of numbers scrawled on a chalkboard and an oil painting of a fire by his wife, Richard Rothermel sits in his cramped office at the Intermountain Fire Sciences Lab in Missoula. He wears a plaid shirt with a single pen in his pocket and has a hearing aid in his right ear; his bottom teeth make a crooked corn row. Depending on whether fire is the topic of conversation, he comes off as the consummate physics teacher or someone's kindly grandfather. While some scientists embrace their celebrity, however cultish, with grandiose proclamations and gestures, Rothermel, sixty-six, remains ever diligent, soft-spoken, lost in the derivatives and energy balances that, for him, divine fire.

What has brought Rothermel such notoriety, and what inspires fire behaviorists from as far away as China, South Africa, and Australia to travel to the lab to meet him, is his 1972 invention of a versatile mathematical model that attempts to predict what a fire will do and is used on every continent except Antarctica as part of a computer program called BEHAVE. "In the beginning, I approached fire less as a scientist and more as an engineer," he says, looking out his window at the browned-over hills of another scorching summer day. "I figured, even if we didn't have all the answers to fire, we should at least try to help those firefighters out in the field."

To that end, Rothermel put himself on the fire line, traveling for three decades to some of the century's wildest fires, among them the Yellowstone fires, Sundance in Idaho, Mink Creek in Wyoming, and Hog in California. Season after season, he broke fire down, analyzing it like an unruly patient, parsing out its most important variables—flame length, intensity, and spread life. He then plugged those variables into complex equations that accounted for drought conditions, fuels, and even cloud cover, all in an attempt to codify the countless incarnations of fire.

On this particular afternoon, Rothermel has just returned from giving a talk to the Missoula smoke jumpers about crown fires, the kind that often travel rapidly through treetops and that killed eleven smoke jumpers at Montana's Mann Gulch in 1949. "A jumper's job is full of risks," he says. "Especially now, with the unusual dryness and the intense number of lightning strikes, they have to watch for things like plume-driven fires, ones that burn heavy fuels and create a thunderhead. The fires literally make their own weather, mostly rain and winds called downbursts. That's how they suddenly blow up."

Rothermel leads me up to a room where six fire behaviorists sit in the dark against one wall, their faces lit orange. Across from them is a plate-glass window that runs nearly the length of the room, and behind it a fire flares in a wind tunnel, catching and then burning through a bed of ponderosa pine needles laid out over a long platform. A computer races with data—colored bars bouncing frenetically on a graph—and one behaviorist barks out numbers like an auctioneer as the others nod knowingly. The radiant heat is intense enough to feel through the glass, and I can't help but think that we're witnessing the computer death of the fire gods—Hephaestus, Vulcan, and Mulciber—caught behind glass for closer observation. When I ask Rothermel if he believes that fire is a supernatural force, he laughs: "No, no. In fact, I try not to think of it at all in religious or personal terms, because the fire isn't trying to do anything. It doesn't have a memory or ambition. It just behaves in peculiar ways based on the physical conditions in which it finds itself."

Yet for thousands of years fire has been viewed mythologically. As fire historian Stephen Pyne points out in his book *World Fire*, nearly everyone—from the Aztecs to the Stoics, the Christians to the Norse—has been haunted by visions of "world-beginning or world-consuming fire." The cosmologies of fire, in turn, are endless. It has been sexualized by poets from Homer to Rilke. The Egyptians thought fire was a ravening monster that would sooner consume trees and humans than die without food. In the Middle Ages, as Gaston Bachelard mentions in his quirky 1938 book *The Psychoanalysis of Fire*, it was considered a "terrestrial exhalation" meant to nourish the stars, traveling by comet, as if by spoon, to the distant hungry mouth of the sun. And ever since Zeus thumped the Titans with lightning bolts, fire has been seen, and used, as a weapon of war.

Given these multifarious, if at times paradoxical, guises, fire has been more deeply understood as a social, political, and cultural event than a natural one. In America, where our wildlands are regarded as museum pieces—or "vignettes," in the infamous words of the Leopold Report, whose namesake, Aldo Leopold, died in a 1948 blaze—fire has worn the dark cowl of an intruder. And since fire shows no regard for muscle, bone, and sinew, it's the one thing that annually reduces our swaggering selves to a mad scramble of scarecrows. So we've looked to quash it—as if by beating the holy crap out of it, we might teach it a thing or two about etiquette.

Even the 1988 Yellowstone fires—a media-saturated event that ostensibly made a case for the necessity of fire and a let-burn policy in our nation's forests—seemed to have left only a faint mark on our psyche. "When the temperatures go up and the humidity drops, suddenly all this stuff we talked about all winter long in the Forest Service—ecosystem management and using fire to our advantage—goes out the window," says jumper Brad Sanders. "We suddenly need to suppress everything, because the public says there's too much smoke in the valley or the local landowners say their homes are threatened."

Perhaps this is partly because fire creates a convenient Manichaean universe of good and evil, glorifying anyone who stakes a claim against it. And in many ways the war against fire serves as a reminder that American might makes right. Smokey Bear, as the ranger-general in a cold war state of mind, has often mixed his antifire messages with religion and nationalism, advertising the fight against fire as nothing less than a jihad sanctioned by the long-suffering furry creatures of the burning woods.

Since 1908, when Congress established a limitless emergency fund for fire suppression, the Forest Service, among other fire agencies, has aggressively fought fire and, in the process, has profited with equipment, aircraft, and personnel. Meanwhile, tax dollars funnel into the local economies of many western fire towns—$7 million found its way to McCall in 1994. Helicopter service, mostly provided by private industry, totaled $80 million in the West. "It's a potlatch—massive, ritualistic spending in a ceremonial way," says Pyne. "Though crazy, it's not necessarily malevolent; it's just the logic of the situation." Carl Pope, executive director of the Sierra Club, argues that years of fire suppression have created "an incendiary-industrial complex" responsible for about $6 billion spent over the past decade on an effort that has left the forests of the West ragged with spruce beetle infestations and acres of dry downfall.

At its ugliest, the fire industry has also fostered profit-mongering. In the summer of 1994, federal prosecutors charged Ernest Ellison, a former mill worker, with arson on public lands in Northern California, claiming that he'd been hired by a group of private contractors to set at least three Trinity County blazes in 1992. Arson fires became so severe that summer that the Forest Service set up surveillance cameras in remote areas in the hopes of catching other culprits.

Back in the lab, Rothermel returns to his office and resumes his seat behind his desk. "We need to think about fire simply as an expression of the earth," he says. "Fire's been here ever since we've had trees and vegetation and lightning to start it. For some reason, this has been one of the most difficult things for modern people to deal with: Many of our forests have evolved because of their relationships to fire, and continually suppressing it has badly hurt them. What we're seeing now is that the West not only wants, but needs, to burn. And so it is."

He remembers sailing backward over the football field in New Meadows during a demo jump, working his toggles, thinking, Yes, something has gone terribly wrong. The wind was howling and all the schoolkids gathered in the grandstand for Career Day were screaming and suddenly power lines and street signs and cars were passing beneath his feet. Instead of landing at the fifty-yard line in a tumble of glory, he crashed down in someone's backyard and she came out in a bathrobe wielding a mean broom. "We call it the *Red Dawn* jump," says Scott Anderson. "Guys got bit by dogs, hit jungle gyms, held up traffic. It was ugly. Only three of us made the football field. But it was still better than the rodeo jump, where we landed in cow manure."

Anderson and his girlfriend, Sandie Waters, are sitting across the table from me at the McCall Brewing Company, a big, bustling room finished in wood, warmly lit, with two copper beer tanks behind the bar. Every few minutes the couple greets another friend, another jumper, an old-timer who trades a quick jumping story. There are jumpers at the next table and more perched on high stools, drinking cold wheat beer, sacrificing, as they say, to Big Ernie, the fire god. It is a group with deep family ties and rituals. From the Big Flip, an elaborate coin toss that ends up with a night of revelry in town, to the termination party—what's called the T-party—a year-end gathering turned rowdy love-in, the social network, the push and pull of razzing and respect that governs the days here, is necessary to balance the long hours and heavy work on the fire line.

And with the twin death-blows at Storm King Mountain, the McCall family has become that much closer. In fact, Jim Thrash's funeral, attended by hundreds, turned into a spectacle of small-town jumper solidarity, as much a tribute to the jumper life as to Thrash himself. The jumpers, including the pastor, wore their fire boots in honor of Thrash and used their fire shovels to bury him. His casket was draped with a parachute, and he was buried with a Dodgers baseball cap, a fire shirt, a bottle of scotch, and a eulogy read by jumper Greg Beck.

"I know some people may not have thought of it this way, but Jim Thrash and Roger Roth fulfilled every jumper's fantasy," says Anderson, sipping his beer. "Everyone wants to live forever, and in dying on that hill, they became immortal."

Later, when I ask Rob Morrow and Karen Dorris how they've been affected by the tragedy, they admit that they've just drawn up a will that will take care of their son, Zach. "It was a moment when your place on the jump list determined how you went out," says Morrow, who discovered Thrash's body. "It could have been Karen or me, and that lottery concept is something that slaps you. It's something you have to learn to live with, something we're still trying to learn to live with. Walking up on Storm King Mountain and finding those bodies, I thought, Shit, this could've been my wife.

"I've jumped with one of Thrash's reserve parachutes all summer long," Morrow continues, clearing his throat. "He rigged it, and I've kept it all summer, and it's like jumping with an angel."

With the death of the three smoke jumpers at Storm King Mountain—the third was Don Mackey, from the Missoula base—the media drew immediate if obvious comparisons to the 1949 Mann Gulch catastrophe. In many ways, the two bear little resemblance, yet thanks in part to the acclaim of Norman Maclean's 1992 book *Young Men and Fire*, Mann Gulch remains a brutal emblem of how a bad day's work can end for a smoke jumper.

"When you think about Storm King, as when you think about Mann Gulch, you wonder why it happened and why some of us were lucky to live and some weren't," says Bob Sallee, the only living survivor of Mann Gulch.

My conversation with Sallee takes place in a silver twilight outside the Spokane paper mill where he works as an executive. The mill is a big brick building, the grounds are lush, and he wears dress slacks and a white shirt open at the collar. His eyes are rheumy and his hair is shock white, as is his neatly trimmed mustache. And while Sallee, who's now sixty-four, jumped for only two years, he became famous because he miraculously survived Mann Gulch with Walter Rumsey and Wag Dodge and showed up as an eighteen-year-old kid on a "full-page spread" of *Life*, his lips pressed in an ironic grin for the camera.

When I ask if the survivor's plight is a life of nightmares, he says he never dreams about Mann Gulch. "But I've had one picture all my life," he says. "The cleft in the rocks that Rumsey and I went through. Just a narrow break in the rocks, a goat trail up through it, only wide enough for one person. The rocks, the arrangement of the rocks, is what I remember. We saw fire below us in the canyon and then flanking us. When it blew up it was like a jet airplane taking off, a huge explosion and roar, and I knew something bad was happening and I didn't look back anymore and I just went for those rocks."

Sallee is pensive for a moment; the sun sinks suddenly, erasing the shadows thrown by the huge oaks surrounding us. "The problem today is that when you teach people to fight fire, they go into it expecting to win," he says. "If a tree flares up and singes your whiskers, you don't think much about it—

you just hurry on a little faster. If a tree falls, it's an adrenaline rush, and then you go about your business. What we forget is that this is all deadly stuff."

When lightning first struck a mile north of McCall three weeks ago, the Corral blaze was nothing but a few flickers in the duff; seven days later, after it over-powered a group of smoke jumpers, the blaze jumped 32,000 acres and now has gobbled almost double that again, making it one of the biggest fires of the summer. Twenty homes have been evacuated, and 150 firefighters were rushed from their camp when the supply lines were overrun; meanwhile, as the fire runs north, it threatens the spawn on the Salmon River.

"You've seen a polite fire," says Captain Jack, gesturing toward the black moiling clouds that rise off the hills and dissipate into a bluish gray haze. "Now you'll meet the delinquent." Our party today includes photographer Raymond Meeks and his assistant, David Herwaldt. We've been issued itchy Nomex pants, fire shirts, and helmets that we wear uncomfortably now. Instead of the moonscape that we've expected to see, the fire actually burns in a mosaic pat-tern, penetrating the wilderness in separate, serpentine strands that occasion-ally come together when the wind blows hard. In every acre that the Forest Service counts as burned, there are often a surprising number of trees left in-tact.

As we hike to the edge of the furnace, Captain Jack locates Dave Reeder, a gray-bearded gnome who looks as if he's been living the last month inside a fallen tree. As the division group supervisor who calls the shots over these four miles of forest, Reeder is in constant dialogue with his walkie-talkie, ever watchful of the hodgepodge of firefighters and army troops under his com-mand. "Part of the adrenaline rush comes from worrying about everyone," he says, glancing quickly up the hill and then back over his shoulder. "It gets pretty heavy out here. More than thirty people have been injured; one guy's jugular was cut by a chain saw, but somehow he lived. There was a Chinook helicopter that disintegrated; the rotor went right through the cockpit and killed a man."

According to Reeder, the Corral fire is one of the most unpredictable he's seen in years, superheating the forest to temperatures in excess of 2,000 de-grees Fahrenheit. Above our place on the valley floor, spruce trees flash and make loud ripping sounds in the air. When we move up into the fire, the sounds thicken, more like heavy rainfall, and the flames flower wildly in the trees. Flakes of ash sift down in a constant shower, into our mouths, down our backs. Widowmakers—slender burned stubs of tree—are strewn over the hillside or totter on the dangerous edge of falling; Captain Jack and Reeder kick them down as we go. The heat, which is enough to melt a lens cap, concerns Meeks and Herwaldt, who go through the motions of fretting before diving deeper into the flames. At one point the tape recorder in my hand becomes so hot that I stuff it into my pocket.

In our attempt to get intimate with fire, we get lost. Captain Jack and Reeder are traipsing around somewhere that's not here, and here has suddenly become a forgotten closet of the woods where the fire rushes, swells, and then avalanches over one tree, hungrily catching in the next. The flames repeat themselves, tree after tree, moving swiftly along the trunk and up to the crown, shriveling branches as they go. They burn around us now like a maze of Roman candles, and we're bombarded by shooting colors—bright pumpkin orange, lurid red, cobalt blue, tea green. In the face of it, we're tempted to stand still, to let the quasars and white dwarves of fire have their way with our euphoric skinny bones.

But a quick blast of heat later we come to our senses, stumbling backward in search of the others. When we find them, we stick close, shuffling down to a clearing out of the fire just as Mark Benz, an army chaplain, approaches, carrying hoses and shovels and Pulaskis. Nothing about him indicates that he is clergy except for a cross on a chain around his neck, but even this he keeps tucked under his fire shirt. Benz, fifty-two, has an expressive Tom Waits face and tells me he served in Vietnam. "This is like going to war," he says as a helicopter skims overhead and dumps water up the hill. "Dresden, Hamburg, Hiroshima, Tet. Thank God, fire can't shoot back."

We stand watching three firefighters run a hose from a stream to a patch of burning grass. I ask Benz if fire has a soul, and he smiles, kicks his boot at the ground, rubs the side of his mouth with his finger as if he has a fat lip. "Yeah," he says. "Yeah, it does. When the forest torches up, there's a moment of ecstasy. You hear the crackling, and there's something ancient in it."

He pauses for a moment, takes in the burning landscape. "The spirituality of fire makes the world physical for me," the chaplain says. "I'm not sure that describes it. But the soul of fire is a divine one. It humbles you. Makes you human."

We linger for a moment more, and then I head down the hill with the others. When I look back up, I see the chaplain moving in on the fire, alone and flickering among the flames, swinging his Pulaski.

The T-party is held across the tarmac from the jumper base in a hangar owned by Karen Dorris's family. It's the end of September, and a sharp chill in the air has brought out the wool sweaters and fleece. With five inches of snow in the forecast, the season seems on the verge of ending. Outside, against an orangy purple sunset and a distant curtain of black clouds, Captain Jack keeps solemn counsel with himself, nervously pacing the runway, checking his notes, taking long sucks of rum from his I'M A MAVERICK cup. As the emcee for tonight's hootenanny, he's begun to feel the pressure of the spotlight.

Inside the hangar, two dopey-looking moose trophies watch over the proceedings from the wall, the jumpers' pink and yellow streamers are strewn festively in the rafters, and a row of taped-up drawings offers a tableau of the season—a midair collision that left two jumpers unharmed but rattled, one jumper's trip to Russia as part of a fire education program, a kindled romance, a portrait of Jim Thrash and Roger Roth with the words CLOSE TO GOD across the bottom. A cornucopia of fried chicken, ribs, salad, cole slaw, potatoes, soda, brownies, booze, and more booze is strewn over three long picnic tables.

I sit at a table with jumper Pat Withen and his family, as well as Holly Thrash, Jim's widow, and her two children. Holly, forty-three, is a handsome woman with a calm, strong presence that doesn't go unnoticed in the room: From time to time, people approach and offer a hug or clasp her hand. Her two children, a boy and a girl, are blond-headed and well behaved, and she talks to them with a fond directness—tousles her son's hair, hugs her daughter.

Meanwhile Captain Jack has stepped to the podium, taking everyone on a loopy, Mount Gay–inspired ride through the season. At one point he does ventriloquy in a Pepe LePew accent, using his fist as a puppet; at another he presents Mr. Thrifty, a two-foot-high plastic skeleton with labels that indicate the broken sternums and broken teeth and broken shoulders of the McCall jumpers this season. He raises a glass and toasts all "the broke jumpers," and everybody responds with a primal grunt.

At our table conversation is interspersed with Captain Jack's patter, and when I ask about the disparity between Smokey Bear's antifire message and the Forest Service's supposed desire to implement a more active let-burn policy, Holly Thrash says, "We're fighting almost every fire because we've had fifty years of Smokey Bear, one of this country's most successful and misleading ad campaigns. Urban people don't know what wildland fire is really all about, and so they want it stopped. The regeneration of the forest is something we'll never see in our lifetime. It's a shame." She says this tersely but not impolitely, and then says no more. She might be alluding to the chain of controversial decisions that endangered the firefighters on Storm King Mountain; the fire was fought within sight of the homes and highways of Glenwood Springs. Not long after Captain Jack offers a toast to her late husband, she gathers up her kids and leaves, smiling good-byes as she goes.

Shortly after the ceremony, the DJ strikes the mother lode of seventies rock, sending most of the jumpers to the far side of the room, closer to the kegs. Zach Morrow, however, dances until he's hauled off by his parents. Judging by the high-fives and handshakes and hugs all around, everyone seems pleased to have crawled through this season, and the jumpers linger late, reveling, slapping backs, singing comically to the music. And despite the music a few of them even start dancing; several others wrestle on the floor.

By the time I'm thinking about bed, sometime after midnight, the hangar is hot and loud, throbbing with music and laughter, the party still on its way to some unknown, bacchanalian climax. When I open the door, the voices from behind rush out into the cool night—"I'm hurt, motherfucker, I'm hurt!"— and drift across the empty tarmac. Above, the stars are shot through with light like so many falling parachutes. More roughhousing, a plaintive cry, and then laughter. In the distance to the south, in the blue-black shadows of Payette National Forest, there's a stark bone of lightning. Then another.

SEPTEMBER 1995

HUMBLE IS THE PREY

by DAVID QUAMMEN

The carcass of a freshly killed goat flies through the air, cartwheeling upward and outward over the heads of a phalanx of tourists. Ninety pounds of inert protein, it ascends toward its apogee bearing the weight of a ponderous question: Is there a place in our world for the great flesh-eating predators that make no distinction between goat, deer, and human?

It rises through the hot tropical air above a deep gully, and my attention, until now diverted elsewhere, shifts to fix on it. "The goat," says a voice in my brain. "I didn't realize that they'd *throw* it." Spotlighted by shafts of sunlight penetrating the tamarind trees, it floats through a backward somersault. For an instant it hangs. We tourists, all seventy-some, gape. On one level, what's being offered is just bait. On another, it's a proxy for ourselves. And then the goat falls. It lands with a meaty wallop on bare dirt.

Nine giant reptiles pile onto it like NFL linemen.

Nine giant reptiles snarf and gobble. They chomp. They gorge. They thrash, they scuffle, they tug and twist. They stir up one hellacious ruckus. The goat, or whatever's left of it after a minute of this, is invisible now, and the reptiles have composed themselves into a neat radial pattern, jaw-locked side by side, tails swinging, like a monstrous nine-pointed starfish. Their round-snouted faces, which looked amiable as old work boots until just a moment ago, have gone smeary with blood. When the goat rips in half, they split into two mobs and the tussling continues. They have each seized a mouthful, but the mouthfuls are still held together, barely, by a battered skeleton. They wrestle. They lunge for new jaw-grips and clamp down, straining greedily against the tensile limits of goat bone and sinew. It all happens fast. The lucky ones snatch away big gobbets, swallow hastily, and dive back for more. They climb over one another, foot to face, elbow to eyeball, for second helpings. Their teeth are terrible little knives, serrated along the cutting edge, perfectly suited for slicing out great whonks of meat, yet despite the wild scramble they manage somehow to avoid mutilating one another. They compete madly, but they don't fight. They ignore the five dozen Nikons and Minoltas that crackle above them like Chinese firecrackers. They polish off the goat—flesh and offal, skull and backbone, hide and hooves—as thoroughly as if it were a hamburger. Only about twelve minutes pass, maybe fifteen, until two of the more tenacious animals are scuffling over a last slimy bone. The others splay out onto their bellies, relaxing on the bare cool dirt of the gully in patches of shade. They rest and digest.

These aren't crocodilians. They're something more extraordinary: dry-land reptilian predators that lurk in savanna forest within one small region of eastern Indonesia, where they reign at the top of the food chain, eating any and every sort of red-blooded victim that's reckless enough to give them a chance. They are the largest and most fearsome of all lizards, cartoonishly notorious, almost legendary, though not well or widely comprehended in their herpetological actuality. What I mean by that: Everybody's heard of them, but nobody's heard much. Truth is, they're even more astonishing, in the flesh, in the wild, than their reputation would seem to promise.

It's Sunday on the island of Komodo, and I've come here to ask the ponderous question: Can humanity live with dragons?

Can we live without them? What will we lose from the wild places on Earth—from our sense of the word *wild* itself—when we lose all prospect of being devoured by homicidal beasts?

In the local dialect, Mangarrai, their name is *ora*. Mangarrai speakers don't call them Komodo dragons—no more than do English-speaking biologists. Science knows them as *Varanus komodoensis*, grandest of all living representatives of the varanid family of tropical lizards. Varanids in general are far-flung throughout the Asian and African tropics, but this particular giant is confined within a very small range. Isolated for millennia, adapted to certain special circumstances, it's a species almost synonymous with a single locale. Within the towns and villages of the region, a slang usage seems to have supplanted the traditional Mangarrai word, and nowadays people call them, simply, Komodos.

Komodo itself is a tiny island of sharp volcanic peaks, grassy hillsides, and forested valleys, a place that at first sight looks ordinary. Less than 200 square miles in area, it's smaller than Oahu but larger than Alcatraz. It lies in a gap of shallow tropical ocean between the islands of Sumbawa and Flores, north of another big island called Sumba, about halfway out along the great Indonesian archipelago that stretches from Sumatra to New Guinea. Unlike Sumbawa to the west, Sumba to the south, or Flores to the east, Komodo catches scant rainfall and holds few permanent sources of fresh water. Lontar palms mark the high ridges, sparsely, like candles on a cake. The hillside savannas are interrupted in some spots by igneous bluffs, big brows of rough gray rock looming out over the slopes. The valley forests are dry and deciduous, dominated by tamarinds and a few other trees. Tall piles of bare dirt and compost, shoveled up by mound-building birds of the species *Megapodius freycinet* for incubating their eggs, bulge from the forest floor like giant anthills. Sulphur-crested cockatoos, beautiful but hopelessly unmusical, skrawk in the treetops. Wild pigs and rusa deer forage through the understory and roam upward on faint trails into the savanna. On the east coast is one fishing village, made possible there by grace of a rare, precious well. Fortunately for the giant lizards, Komodo's scarcity of water has always discouraged human settlement. Farther north along the coast, in a forested valley called Loh Liang, is another small cluster of buildings. This is where tourists step ashore.

Twenty years ago, Loh Liang was the main research site during the first thorough study of the ecology and behavior of *V. komodoensis*, conducted by an American herpetologist named Walter Auffenberg. Nowadays it's the site of a visitors' camp (simple cabins, an office, an open-air cafeteria) that serves as headquarters of Komodo National Park. Since the island has no airstrip and no roads, the Loh Liang compound is reachable only by boat. A public ferry, running between Sumbawa and Flores, stops here several times each week. Old wooden cargo boats stand ready to cruise over from Flores whenever an impatient traveler (like me) cares to charter one.

Loh Liang is slightly atypical of Komodo as a whole. Half-tame deer stroll on the beach and loiter between the buildings, accustomed to handouts. For several hours each evening, the cabin rooms are lit by electricity. Bottled water is available at the cafeteria. And twice every week, Sundays and Wednesdays, at a chain-link corral overlooking a gully less than two miles' walk from the compound, park officials offer the dragons a dead goat.

To some people that sacrificed goat might seem deplorably artificial—or barbaric—but in fact it's a sensible management compromise, done at the imperative of ecotourism, which is crucial to the conservation of this otherwise inconvenient, expendable species. And it certainly makes for a good public spectacle: reliable, vivid, photogenic, safe. It allows modestly adventuresome travelers to glimpse the behavior and the anatomical tools that make *V. komo-doensis* one of the most formidable predators on the planet. No zoo visit, no na-ture film seen on PBS is adequate substitute for this artificial but very real event.

The tourists and the park rangers gather *inside* the corral, from which the dead goat is to be heaved *out*. That arrangement is nicely symbolic of who owns the forest, who doesn't, but it's also quite practical. The Komodos emerge from their secret retreats, evidently alerted by the tempting goat smell and the general human hubbub. One animal appears, then another. Then, by God, a whole gang of them. The largest are ten feet long and weigh 200 pounds, big as adolescent alligators. Unlike alligators, they walk high on their legs with a steady, surging stride. They surround the corral. Expectant but calm, they pose obligingly for everyone's camera. They nose up to the fence, almost like pup-pies. Their tongues, which are bile yellow, forked, thick as Polish sausages, flap out languidly and then withdraw, tasting the air for aromas. The goat flies, with no warning, and suddenly these lummoxy reptiles become very damn quick and scary.

That's been the scenario this morning: another Sunday, another goat. They've attacked, performing all those Komodoesque verbs you've already read. The calm has returned almost as abruptly as it left.

The Komodos rest briefly while the tourists, sated by spectacle, drift away. The corral empties. The mob scene is over, the Fujichrome has been shot, and I've got the overlook to myself. After another few minutes the Komodos too wander away, all except one placid individual who continues basking. Finally, a pair of rangers approach to pry my hands off the chain-link fence. They in-form me in polite Indonesian that the show has ended. They want to finish their morning's work by escorting me back to camp: They carry forked staffs, a nice low-tech precaution against any lingering Komodos that might come lurching out of the brush.

Most of the tourists depart on the next boat. Kamp Komodo becomes bless-edly deserted, except for the rangers, myself, the cafeteria workers, four English kids disconsolate at having missed their ferry, and my own pal Nyoman the Ba-linese Tailor, whom I've hornswoggled into making this trip as translator. No, we can't leave yet, I tell Nyoman. We've only begun to address the ponderous question.

A Komodo hatchling is just a foot long, cute as a chipmunk, and no danger to anybody. Walter Auffenberg found that the hatchlings eat insects and small lizards, for which they forage beneath the loose bark of dead trees. They also hunt grasshoppers in the savanna. The grasshoppers, Auffenberg wrote, "are captured by stealth." Smallish and medium-size Komodos feed mainly on rodents (several species of which have invaded the island along with humanity) and on native birds that feed or nest on the ground. As Komodos grow larger— so much larger—the identity and the size of their prey changes, while their hunting strategy becomes more refined. Too big for arboreal foraging, too big for a prolonged chase, they specialize in the lurking ambush. Adult Komodos are patient predators, slow-moving over medium distances, lacking the stamina for pursuit, but godawful quick on the first lunge. Also they're strong. They're deadly effective at close quarters. A full-grown Komodo, according to Auffenberg, often feeds on animals as large as or larger than itself. These prey "are obtained through both stealth and surprise," he wrote, with eloquent redundancy. A favorite Komodo trick is to hide in thick brush at the edge of a trail, waiting for some unsuspecting creature to pass.

Their ambush technique yields the larger Komodos an occasional dog, an occasional civet, an occasional goat. They eat carrion, too, and sometimes they cannibalize another Komodo. Their primary food items, as reported by Auffenberg, are wild pig and rusa deer. They have also been known to kill horses and to wait brazenly near a mare in labor, ready to scarf up the newborn foal. They have been known to kill and eat water buffalo. They have been known, yes, to kill and eat humans.

If these dietary proclivities sound ambitious, consider one other: elephants.

Five years ago, in the journal *Nature*, a scientist named Jared Diamond published a short article titled "Did Komodo Dragons Evolve to Eat Pygmy Elephants?" They did indeed, Diamond argued. Auffenberg himself had first suggested the possibility, based on paleontological evidence of two now-extinct elephant species that had inhabited the island of Flores (and probably also Komodo) during the Pleistocene. The smaller of those two elephants, *Stegodon sompoensis*, may have stood only five feet high and weighed no more than a buffalo. Diamond reasoned that Komodo dragon ancestors must have fed on the pygmy elephants during their own evolutionary progress toward gigantism, because there were no other big animals available within the reptile's native range. Buffalo, rusa deer, and wild pigs probably didn't reach Komodo and Flores until shipped in by humans, just a few thousand years ago. That was many millennia too late for the evolution of *V. komodoensis*.

Why did the ancestral Komodos evolve into giants? Those dainty and succulent elephants may have furnished a necessary condition, but not a sufficient one. Why didn't the varanids of Komodo remain small, subsisting comfortably on a diet of insects and geckos and ground birds? If they were destined to enlarge, why didn't they enlarge only so much as their cousin species, such as *Varanus indicus* and *Varanus mertensi*, which are big but not gigantic lizards that would never dream of attacking a horse?

"That size is related to predation is obvious," Auffenberg wrote. "In almost all organisms, optimal predator size is largely determined by the interaction of both the abundance of different prey size classes and the relative energy extractable from them by predators of a given size." Roughly translated: Evolution enforces efficiency, so if larger body size allows a predator to victimize large-bodied prey and to do that more efficiently than it could victimize small-bodied prey as a small-bodied predator, then evolution may well produce gigantism.

Two other variables can't be ignored, not even in this breezy summary. The first is competition. If the large-predator niches are already filled by other species, then a flesh-eating varanid lizard is not likely to find an advantage in gigantism. Better to stay small, in that situation, living efficiently at the scale where competitors are abundant but prey is more abundant still. Within the insular ecosystem of Komodo, however, to the good fortune of *V. komodoensis*, there are no big native predators offering competition. Tigers and leopards didn't make it this far out into the Indonesian archipelago because tigers and leopards, unlike varanid lizards, unlike elephants, are reluctant to swim across ocean gaps.

The other variable is hunting strategy. Does a given predator spend its time and its energy chasing one potential victim to the point of exhaustion? Or does the predator spend more time, and less energy per unit of time, waiting in ambush? Auffenberg cited a study of hunting behavior among spiders—spiders, yes, and it's not such a far-fetched comparison as it seems. Spiders are all predators, diverse and successful enough as a group to have explored a huge variety of life-history strategies. The study, by an arachnophilic ecologist named Frank Enders, featured the Salticidae family, commonly known as the jumping spiders. Salticids don't catch their prey in webs; they rely instead on stalking and sudden attack. Enders's paper included a wide-ranging discussion of other predator groups and suggested to Auffenberg that "ambush and surprise behavior tended to increase the size of the prey taken." If that's true for salticid spiders, it might also be true for varanid lizards.

Whether it is true, or just plausible, this is how I prefer to see *V. komodoensis*, based on the best (or at least the most interesting) scientific work available: as a flesh-eating lizard, grown huge on a diet of elephants, that behaves like the world's largest jumping spider.

Ho ho, we're in luck. Midafternoon Sunday now, and Nyoman has scored us an invitation to hike over the mountains with a backcountry ranger and explore a more remote valley. On that side of the pass there will be no contrived spectacles, no chain-link fences, no tourists, and plenty of Komodos. The ranger is a friendly young Floresian named David Hau, and the valley is called Loh Sabita. Within an hour, having stuffed our packs with malt biscuits and sardines and bottled water from the cafeteria, we start walking. For reasons of safety, we want to reach Loh Sabita before dusk.

Not far from the feeding corral, we leave the main trail and turn north on a much fainter track. The brush is thick on both sides of us. "Good cover for an ambush," says the voice in my brain. "If I were a Komodo, this is where I'd be, waiting for witless Americans." When we move into forest, where the under-story is sparse and the sight lines are longer, I feel slightly more comfortable. We cross a dry streambed, in the dust of which we see tracks: the sinuous mark of a dragging tail, with clawed footprints along each side. The stance is narrow, the stride short.

"Komodo?"

"Ya," David says.

"Kecil?"

"Ya, ya."

In Indonesia, *kecil* means small. In Komodo specifically, it means too small to bite off your leg. We pause to watch cockatoos. We sample the serikaya fruit, cobbled green globes filled with sweet pulp like vanilla yogurt. We pass the tall earthen hump of a mound-builder's nest. The nest is defunct, dug open by some egg-robbing predator.

"Komodo?"

"Ya," David says.

"Kecil?"

No answer. Maybe he didn't hear me.

We climb out of the forest onto a grassy slope and follow the trail upward, toward a mountain saddle between the two valleys. It's not a long climb, but the sun is blastingly hot. My shirt is soaked, and Nyoman, a city boy, looks ill. At the crest, we pause for breath and water, savoring the view back toward Loh Liang. A white wooden cross stands here, propped with a cairn. The plaque on it says:

IN MEMORY OF
BARON RUDOLF VON REDING, BIBEREGG,
BORN IN SWITZERLAND THE 8 AUGUST 1895
AND DISAPPEARED ON THIS ISLAND
THE 18 JULY 1974
"HE LOVED NATURE THROUGHOUT
HIS LIFE."

And nature, in the end, had a gustatory fondness for him. I've read about the Baron. He stopped for a breather hereabouts while the rest of his party hiked on; two hours later, when the others came back, there was nothing left but a Hasselblad with a broken strap.

We top over the saddle and descend through savanna, into the valley called Loh Sabita, where the deer are not tame, the water is not bottled, goat carcasses don't fall from the sky, and the Komodos still live by their skill as hunters.

There's a select category of animal that cuts across phylogenetic groupings to encompass the following: *Panthera tigris, Carcharodon carcharias, Ursus maritimus, Crocodylus niloticus, Ursus arctos, Galeocerdo cuvieri, Carcharias gangeticus, Crocodylus porosus, Panthera leo*. More familiarly: the tiger, the great white shark, the polar bear, the Nile crocodile, the brown bear (including those subspecies known as grizzlies), the tiger shark, the Ganges River shark, the saltwater crocodile, the lion. Reptiles, fish, bears, cats—what's the common link? They're all solitary predators that are big enough, fierce enough, hungry and indiscriminate enough, to kill and eat a human.

Elephants have committed many lethal tramplings, but elephants don't feed on the victims. Buffalo and rhino can be as dangerous as runaway trucks, but they aren't carnivorous. Buzzards eat human flesh, but they don't kill for it. Hyenas have been reported to kill and eat humans, but hyenas are pack hunters, not solitary predators. The leopard might qualify, and several additional species of shark, and possibly the anaconda or the reticulated python, but precious few other living creatures belong to this category. *V. komodoensis* does.

Beyond the sheer luridness, this list has a special potency. The capacity for treating *Homo sapiens* as prey has given at least some of these ultimate predators a mythic status, a transcendent sort of mojo, and that mythic dimension has arguably played a significant role throughout the dawning of human self-consciousness, as our species deduced—and later, defined—its position in the world.

Folk beliefs from all across Southeast Asia portray the tiger as a preternatural beast of humanlike motives and magical powers. The crocodile was once considered a water divinity by the Dayaks of Borneo, exempt from killing by Dayak hunters except in very particular circumstances of revenge. The brown bear has held great prominence in the rituals and legends of native peoples across Asia and North America, from the Bear Mother story as told by the Utes, to the bear festival celebrated by the Ainu on Hokkaido. The prospect of that mythic dimension is part of what drew me to Komodo.

I didn't aspire to any serious anthropological study of local beliefs and legends. My chief purpose was simply to see *V. komodoensis* as a real animal within its ecosystem. What did it eat, where did it hide, how did it hunt? But I was curious, too, about its transcendent mojo.

The ranger post at Loh Sabita consists of two thatch-roofed cabins on stilts, an outdoor kitchen, a rough wooden table, and a kerosene lamp. Nearby is a spring. In front of the cabins, a broad estuarine mud flat stretches off toward a fringe of mangroves along the beach. We arrive just before dusk, with the distant tree line beginning to go dark and the cockatoos, as they move toward their roosts, looking grayish pink. Loh Sabita is a lovely place. I can understand why David seems glad to be back.

His three colleagues—Ismail, Johannes, the avuncular Dominikus—greet us warmly and insist on sharing their dinner. Dried fish and rice have never tasted better. Then Dominikus serves tea, a mosquito coil is lit, and they all roll clove cigarettes and sit back to talk. I follow as best I can with my thirty-word Indonesian vocabulary. It emerges that a friend of Ismail's was attacked, just two weeks ago, by a Komodo. Yes, the man survived. He's in a hospital on Flores, Ismail says.

Such attacks are uncommon, but they happen. Auffenberg mentioned a handful, including the case of a fourteen-year-old boy who met an especially bad-tempered Komodo in the forest. Auffenberg got his account from the victim's father. The boy, trying to run away, had tangled himself in a vine. "The vine stopped the youngster for just a moment, and the ora bit him very severely in the buttocks, tearing away much flesh. Bleeding was profuse, and the young man apparently bled to death in less than one-half hour." In other cases death may be less prompt, caused by a massive infection of pathogenic bacteria, which Komodos carry like a form of toxic halitosis.

David tells of another. This one occurred seven years ago at a village called Pasarpanjang, not on Komodo itself but on Rinca, a smaller island nearby that also harbors *V. komodoensis.* It was noontime, a family had just finished lunch, a six-year-old child sprang up from the table and ran down the outside steps. A Komodo had skulked into the village and hidden itself under those steps. It stopped the child somehow, maybe with a swat of its tail, and then pounced. It had the child half swallowed by the time help arrived. The whole village turned out. They pried open the animal's jaws, got the child free, killed the Komodo. But the child, David says, was already dead.

After a halcyon night at Loh Sabita, I hear still another. Some fishing people have beached nearby to take on fresh water from the rangers' spring, and in thanks for this hospitality the women among them are fixing us lunch. One of the women has a Komodo-attack story, but she's too shy to tell it to an American journalist. Her name is Saugi. She wears an orange sarong and an acerbic, self-conscious grin. While Saugi cleans and fries fish, hiding herself back by the fire, gentle Dominikus teases the narrative out of her, to be translated in fragments by Nyoman. It all happened to Saugi's mother.

Her mother was cutting thatch. "Suddenly, the Komodo come from the hill." A puppy was playing nearby, and Saugi's mother thought that the Komodo would eat it. "But dog is too quick. Komodo is get there, and maybe angry or disappoint." So instead, switching targets abruptly, it struck the woman. Clamped its jaws onto her arm and held. She struggled. "Is like a dance," reports Nyoman. In a far corner of the kitchen, Saugi works vehemently on a fish. She mumbles. "The mouth of the Komodo is already bite, and stop, and just stay there," Nyoman says. Saugi's mother pushed a sarong over the animal's eyes (which must have seemed horribly near, gazing up into hers) and attempted to wrench free. The jaws wouldn't unlock. She tried to pull herself up into a tree. "And she is, *swooosh*, like this"—Nyoman sweeps back his arm, as though pulling a rabbit from a hat, and glares at me wide-eyed. Why must we torment this woman? asks his sensitive Balinese heart. "And the meat of mother is already in mouth of Komodo." Half the flesh of her arm had been stripped away. But Saugi's mother was luckier than some others; she survived. She spent a month in the hospital, managed to keep her arm, and even recovered the use of it, more or less.

Saugi goes silent. The cold-minded stranger with the notebook, namely me, gapes demandingly at his translator. "Now is still can see . . . ," says Nyoman, hesitating. "Still can see . . . how you say? Spots? If you cut, and can see later?" Scars, I say. Saugi finishes her task, washes her hands, wraps an end of her sarong onto her head like a turban, and stalks away.

Later that day, David and I hike out into the habitat. We follow a set of Komodo tracks along a dry streambed through the forest. We come to a wall of lava, the vertical face of a volcanic bluff rising far above us and out over the treetops. At the wall's base, David shows me several small caves where Komodos have denned. He shows me a pile of Komodo dung. The pale grayish white color indicates a high concentration of digested bone. Other dung piles nearby, more than a few, suggest that this is a well-favored piece of terrain. We circle around the wall, coming out of the forest into sunlit savanna, and then we climb up to a flat spot atop the bluff. Here we find bleached bones. They look to be fragments of femur or humerus, dry as tinder and light as balsa, half crushed by mastication. "Deer. Komodo is here one time." David lifts a piece. "He can eat all."

From this quiet moment, events surge forward rapidly.

As I inspect the bone fragments, David glasses the opposite slope of the valley with my binoculars. "Ah, Komodo!" he chirps. "Komodo!" With his guidance, yes, I can barely spot it: an elongated form, dark, almost a half-mile away, on a light patch of dirt. It doesn't budge. It's basking. Or maybe I've trained the binoculars on a Komodo-shaped log. "All right," says the voice in my head. "Better than nothing. Can't expect the same artificial immediacy as produced by a dead goat." We climb off the rock and ascend toward another large bluff. There's a commotion just ahead of us in the brush. And then a full-grown Komodo breaks into view, spooked by our noise, scrambling straight up the face of vertical lava. Lumps of rock crumble and fall. My jaw drops like the lid of a Dumpster.

This animal is as big as any I saw at the feeding, but for God's sake it's climbing a cliff. Think of an alligator galloping up the side of a four-story building, and you have roughly the image. I get my binoculars up just in time to see the Komodo summit. It pauses there, a giant reptilian silhouette against the bright sky. Then it tops over, disappearing beyond view. At that moment, I hear David scream . . . as another full-grown Komodo charges out of its hiding place, ten feet behind us, and makes a split-second decision against carving six pounds of flesh either from David's buttocks or from mine. Yaaaggh. We whirl.

Too late for defense, but we've been spared.

Through our carelessness and its own stealth, this animal got exactly the opportunity for which all hungry Komodos reportedly yearn: ambush advantage against walking meat. But it chose not to capitalize. Instead, it has peeled a sharp turn and set off downslope toward the forest. It moves as discreetly as a rhinoceros. It seems even more badly startled than we are. David and I run after it. We see it plunge down a gully. We give chase for fifty yards at precisely the right pace to ensure that we won't catch up.

When my breath is coming normally again, I'm aware of mixed feelings about this encounter. The thrill value has been high. But I really don't want to check into some Flores hospital with a massive leg wound, blood loss, and bacteremia, and I'd sworn that I was going to be faultlessly cautious. The lesson, I suppose, is an obvious one: that these animals are good at what they do and that what they do, though spectacular, can be risky to humans.

We return to search for the other Komodo, the cliff-climber. No sign of it on top of the bluff, except for some large claw marks carved into the brow of the rock. We scout the area timidly. Then we work our way down off the savanna. At the head of another dry streambed, near the forest edge, David stops.

He picks up a bone. This one is tacky with dried blood and saliva. Again he grows excited. "Too late!" he says. "Late one day. Eating in the night. Maybe yesterday." It's the site of a fresh kill, he means, and the Komodo has only just finished its meal.

Or maybe it hasn't quite finished. A strong, sweet, bad smell floats in the afternoon air.

Twenty steps on, we find the head and neck of a three-point rusa stag, attended by a million hysterical flies. The deer's upper ribs dangle raggedly from a stub of spine. Its eyes are sticky and black. Its body is gone. It looks like it was hit by a train.

He can eat all, I remember David saying. We abandon the deer head to its flies—and to its other claimants, wherever they lurk—and we get the hell out.

• • •

I collect one further account of Komodo predation against humans. For this story, though, I'm obliged to leave Loh Sabita, leave Komodo altogether, and sail back to Flores.

It's a fact generally unknown to those who have heard of this animal, but who haven't heard much, that Komodo dragons aren't native only to the island of Komodo. They also inhabit Rinca (where the six-year-old child was killed, where Saugi's mother was injured) and a tinier island named Gilimotang and some forested areas of western Flores. The total population is roughly 4,000. Indonesian officials estimate that the island of Komodo itself supports about 2,500; Rinca, about 800; Gilimotang, maybe 100; and in western Flores is a wildlife refuge, Wae Wuul, where the latest census found 129. The species is protected by law, but it's still perilously rare.

The Wae Wuul area includes several villages. The local people are obliged to share their forest trails and their meadows, sometimes their chickens and their buffalo, with the local Komodos. Three years ago, a man from one of those villages was mauled.

Wae Wuul is unreachable by road, so Nyoman and I come by boat and hike in from the coast. We walk up a small mountain, down again, then along a narrow brushy trail through a verdant valley. At the Wae Wuul ranger post we find more than I'd hoped for: the typewritten original of an incident report, composed and signed by the village chief one day after that latest mauling.

The report tells of a man named Don Lamu, who strolled out one afternoon to move his buffalo onto pasture and (as translated from careful Indonesian into imperfect but vivid English) "got an attack from a Komodo which caused a very serious pain which needed a very long cure." The date was September 1, 1989. Don Lamu and a friend were fetching the buffalo from a wallow. They heard a dog bark insistently. They went to look, assuming that the dog had cornered a wild pig. No pig. For a moment they were distracted and unwary—like Saugi's mother, like the child who dashed down the steps, like David and me at the Loh Sabita bluffs. "Suddenly," says the report, "a Komodo appeared between the two people. One of them run away, but Don Lamu couldn't do anything because the distance between Don Lamu and Komodo about six inches." Six inches sounds odd, but the essence is that this animal appeared from nowhere and struck at short range. Don Lamu tried to kick, but the Komodo "fall upon back of Don Lamu's knee until it serious injured." He kicked with the other leg. "But the animal gave respond by its teeth so that his left leg was also torn by the Komodo's teeth." With its second lunge, the Komodo had seized hold. Here the report adds a sentence that hints at the lonely intimacy between predator and prey: "Then Don Lamu sat down and held the Komodo's mouth while he was shouting asking for help."

His friend returned with a chopping knife and whacked at the animal until its jaws opened. He moved Don Lamu some yards away. But the Komodo came at them again. "Don Lamu's friend was angry and a fight happened," says the report. The unnamed friend plays a heroic role, no doubt partly because Don Lamu himself was in serious condition when the report was composed and the friend, as sole witness, supplied the narrative. With only his chopping knife, the friend stood off the Komodo. He killed it.

This story raises several questions. Among them, though not at the top in humanitarian terms: Should we mourn that dead animal?

V. komodoensis is, to my mind, one of the most magnificent species on Earth. That only 4,000 individuals exist, and that many of those 4,000 live at the outskirts of villages on Rinca and Flores—where they face immediate risk and eventual doom in the unequal battle between humans and nature—is a sorry circumstance. "Problem" dragons, like "problem" grizzly bears, will be disposed of, though the real problem is an elementary conflict between species. The Komodos of Rinca and of Flores may suffer total extirpation within a decade or two, by habitat loss if not by chopping knife. The tiny population on Gilimotang could disappear at any time. When the species is eliminated from these three other locations and confined solely to the island of Komodo, it will face additional sorts of jeopardy related to catastrophe theory and genetics. And we will have arrived, to my mind, at the threshold of another sad diminishment of the vitality and charm of our planet. But then again, my mind has the luxury of inhabiting a body that's not obliged to move water buffalos or raise children in the meadows near Wae Wuul.

Cold as it may be, my mind can't forget the measured but poignant plea in the village chief's closing statement. *Demikia hal ini Kami sampaikan dihadapan Bapak untuk bersama memikirkanya.* "That's our report. We hoped that everyone would try to find out the way how to overcome the problem."

Before visiting Komodo, I harbored the notion that large predators have played an important role, over the past 20 or 30 millennia, in shaping the way *Homo sapiens* thinks of itself as an inhabitant of the biosphere. I still harbor that notion. Have tigers and lions and bears made the forests and the savannas scary? They have indeed, and that's probably been a good thing. Have crocodiles and sharks committed ugly, horrific acts of homicide and anthropophagy? They have indeed, and by doing so they have probably helped us to keep ourselves in perspective. Humans are part of the natural world. We've arisen from it, as the giraffe and the emu have, and we live even now as part of it, though God knows we've cut it and burned it and shoveled it away from us on all sides as far as possible. We are part of the natural world, but we are not—though we tend to presume otherwise—its divinely anointed proprietor, nor its evolutionary culmination. One reminder of our real status, one corrective to our presumption, is that human beings, sometimes, within some landscapes, have served as a middling link in the food chain. We have been treated as prey by animals that are bigger and more fierce.

Those times and those landscapes are becoming rare. Large predators face higher jeopardy of extinction than most other categories of species. Large predators that are native only to small zones of circumscribed habitat face the highest jeopardy of all, and many among that group—the Bali tiger, the Japanese wolf, the Newfoundland white wolf, the warrah, the Barbary lion, the Kamchatkan bear, the thylacine of Tasmania—are already extinct. The Komodo dragon is an exception, so far.

As we continue losing the large predators, I suspect, we'll lose something else, too: the important spiritual influence that they have exerted, throughout thousands of years of human history, toward keeping us humble. When we lose what remains of that, we'll sashay toward new dimensions of hubris.

Spiritual influence, transcendent mojo: same thing in different words. What I'm referring to is the heightened appreciation bestowed on an animal as it turns up in rituals, legends, cave paintings, creature masks, tall tales, totem poles, festivals, epic poems, amulets, medicinal recipes, and scripture. The 41st chapter of the Book of Job, for instance, contains a wonderful paean to the leviathan, that fire-sneezing monster with armored skin, heart firm as stone, eyes like the eyelids of morning. The leviathan is a mythical creature, maybe part whale, maybe part reptile, that was conjured up for spiritual purposes from materials of psychological and zoological reality. It's mentioned at several points in the Bible, but Job 41 is its résumé:

> When he raiseth up himself, the mighty are afraid; by reason of breakings
> they purify themselves.
> The sword of him that layeth at him cannot hold; the spear, the dart, nor
> the habergeon.
> He esteemeth iron as straw, and brass as rotten wood.
> The arrow cannot make him flee: slingstones are turned with him into
> stubble.

The speaker is God, lecturing Job on the terrible majesty of this beast. The lecture's purpose, at least initially, is to deepen Job's humility and his reverence toward his Creator:

> None is so fierce that dare stir him up: who then is able to stand before me?

But God, to His credit, gets carried away, rambling on into a celebration of the leviathan for its own sake:

Darts are counted as stubble; he laugheth at the shaking of a spear.

Sharp stones are under him: he spreadeth sharp pointed things upon the
mire.

He maketh the deep to boil like a pot; he maketh the sea like a pot of oint-
ment.

He maketh a path to shine after him: one would think the deep to be
hoary.

Upon earth there is not his like, who is made without fear.

He beholdeth all high things: he is king over all the children of pride.

The leviathan of the Old Testament was invented to keep humans humble.
Meanwhile, real animals with big teeth and long claws and hungry bellies
were prowling the forests and savannas, making the dark waters boil like oint-
ment, and accomplishing a similar function.

What's the transcendent mojo of a giant lizard that eats deer, pigs, goats,
horses, pygmy elephants, men, women, and children? What's the mythic importance of *V. komodoensis* among those rural Indonesian folk who suffer its
terrors? To this question, I've got no answer. Walter Auffenberg couldn't find
one either, and his inquiry was more thorough than mine. "A search of all the
old literature on tribal customs and beliefs of inhabitants of Sumba, Sumbawa,
and Flores did not disclose any legends or myths reporting the ora," he wrote,
"nor did the missionaries with whom I talked on Flores know of any." Maybe
the animal has no mythic role in that culture. Or maybe the written sources
are incomplete and anthropologists haven't yet done justice to the oral tradi-
tions of the region. But if the people of Komodo, Flores, and Rinca venerate
their dragon with the same imaginative ambivalence as addressed elsewhere to
tigers and bears, I won't be surprised to hear it.

Still, there's another perspective on large predators. It's directly opposed to
what I've just offered. This other view was well expressed by a biologist named
Alistair Graham in a wondrously garish book titled *Eyelids of Morning*, about
the mingled destinies of crocodiles and humans:

> So long as one is constantly threatened by savage brutes
> one is to some extent bound in barbarism; they hold you
> down. For this reason there is in man a cultural instinct to
> separate himself from and destroy wild beasts such as
> crocodiles. It is only after a period of civilization free of
> wild animals that man again turns his attention on them,
> seeking in them qualities to cherish.

Graham is right. But his truth, I persist in believing, isn't the sole and complete truth.

It's late afternoon in Komodoland. Nyoman and I have a boat to catch. To-morrow morning we'll return to the world of airports, taxis, hotels, genteel gardens within stone courtyards, goldfish and ferns and tiny geckos—and to the privileged situation of cherishing *V. komodoensis* from afar. But first we've got to hike back down the narrow trail from Wae Wuul, through miles of prime habitat. I'll be acutely aware of blind corners, bearing Don Lamu's story in my notebook, and hoping for some piece of reconciling wisdom to come jumping out of the bushes.

OCTOBER 1992

OVERTHRUST DREAMS

by WILLIAM KITTREDGE

See them coming, headlights out of the dusk over the Wyoming desert north of Evanston. These are the roughnecks, oil-field hands, our latter-day warriors in this combat zone of American energy solutions. They are coming off shift and burning with real money and fine, innocent hubris. Later tonight in the barrooms they will grin and look you in the eye and call themselves cannon fodder. But you know, goddammit, that they don't mean it. They are boomers, and they are spinning through the urgent main adventure of their manhood, and they love these days without shame.

The broken-fingered youngsters here are the princes of our latest disorder. And this is Christmastime, our most hopeful season. They stomp the streets of Evanston in their moon boots, felt-lined Sorels like the ones you can buy from the L.L. Bean catalog, their uniform a pair of damp coveralls sheened and splattered with drilling mud. They tip their yellow hard hats to the ladies while they figure some way to feed themselves in a town without franchise foods, and they get revved up for another night of shooting pool in some joint like the Pink Pony, or for courting the Mormon girls who flock up the sixty miles from Ogden to the Whirl Inn Disco Bar. Roughnecks. They like the name.

• • •

Me and The Honorable Schoolboy, my friend and guide in this land, were picking up some fried chicken breasts from the deli in the Evanston IGA store. We were going to carry our food a couple of blocks to the Laundromat and eat there in the bright warmth amid odors of detergent and bleach, sharing space with the young oil-patch wives and their knots of beggar children. A clean, well-lighted place, a haven. *Got those all-night Laundromat blues, washed everything but my shoes.* Christmastime in Evanston.

Out on the main drag, 90 percent of the vehicles were 1980-model 4x4s, tape decks squalling some symbolic version of "Sympathy for the Devil," most of them burning diesel pumped from tanks alongside the great Caterpillar and White engines that power the drilling rigs. In a stricter, less dynamic world, that would be called theft. Here in the heartland of our heedlessness it is called small potatoes. *Forget it Jake, it's Chinatown.*

American dreams are woven, like strands in a rope, from two notions: radical freedom and pastoral communalism. These cold boomtown distances in the West have always been traveled and inhabited by those who want both in an improbably happy package containing money and something else, something more complex, something that stays secret, sensed rather than known, always there to be yearned toward.

My own great-grandfather left Michigan in 1849 to travel down the Mississippi and across to Panama, where he hiked west through the jungles on the route Balboa had blazed and caught a ship north to California and the gold camps. After a long and bootless career of chasing mineral trace in the mountain streams, first in the central Sierra and then up around the foothills of Mount Shasta, he gave it up and turned to ranching and school teaching, one place after another around the Northwest, until in 1897 he died white-trash poor in the sagebrush backlands near Silver Lake, Oregon, leaving a family determined to shake his suicidal despair.

It wasn't just gold that he never found—such instant boomer riches were to have been only the beginning. The ultimate reward for his searching was to have been the green and easy dreamland fields of some home place, the grape arbor beside the white house he would own clear and outright, where he could rest out his last serene years while the hordes of grandchildren played down across the lawns by the sod-banked pond where the tame ducks swam and fed and squawked in their happy, idiot way. The pastoral heaven on this earth— some particular secret and heart's-desire version of it—has time and again proved to be the bottom line in American dreams.

An old sweet story. Our central privilege as Americans has always been our luck—the spectacular heritage of the great good places in which we live. Since the days of the Puritans, we have been defoliating that heritage, mining it in one sense or another, as if it were inexhaustible. As if there were no tomorrow.

That which is not useful is vicious—Cotton Mather. For most of 350 years, Americans have acted as if he were right, not insane, as if the spaces amid which we reside, outside Evanston or anywhere else, were as alien as the moon.

And we still do, which accounts for the voices in Evanston. "Well, shit," you hear them say. "It's just the goddamned desert. They really aren't hurting nothing."

The local folks do know what they are losing, but they seem unwilling to recognize how very expendable the homeland of their childhoods has become, how truly it is being sacrificed. Even when home is some sagebrush Wyoming foreverland.

However big the rewards of petroleum may figure in imaginations around Evanston—airline tickets to romantic places and new hay balers for the ranchers, easy sex and pure, clean drugs and booze and the dancing beguilements of rock and roll for the roughnecks—they are not the final prizes, either. Maybe, just this once—the reasoning goes—we can drill and grade this little bit more of desert to death, and then we will quit. Then we will be home, to live out our lives in harmony with the dictates of our secret hearts, at peace with the blossoming earth.

The Young Roughneck, a crony of The Honorable Schoolboy, was talking about Christmas. About tree decorating and the strings of popcorn they used to drape on the boughs back when he was a hired-hand poorboy in the wholesome dairy country of Wisconsin. Before he got wise and went chasing over to Madison for the strobe-light concerts and rebellion in the parking lots, the small-time dope peddling and a couple or so counts of car theft before he was voting age.

But all that was behind him now. The Young Roughneck was talking household gifts, like maybe a little battery-powered coffee-bean grinder of modernistic NASA-inspired design. On the shopping-center hippie fringes of Salt Lake City he had discovered the pleasures of fresh-ground Viennese Blend. So no more Instant Folgers for this roughneck child. Not after Xmas.

"Just going to buy me that little whirring son of a bitch," he said. "Cash money." He looked across the breakfast table and grinned. A roll of folding money like the one he dug out of his pocket equals a start toward shareholding in America. No more teacher's dirty looks.

Outdoors, the morning was bright clean bluebird, four inches of glittering old snow and zero degrees. We were thirty or so miles north of Evanston, in the gut of the drilling country, where The Young Roughneck and The Honorable

Schoolboy and some others had spent the previous summer camped on BLM land while they worked the towers—squatters alongside a spring some rancher dug out and piped into troughs for his livestock in the old days, before Amoco and Chevron started deep drilling in a serious way.

Shaking the chill and some hungover nerves, we were sipping coffee laced with Crown Royal and sitting jammed into the jacked-up pickup camper where The Young Roughneck resided full-time with his wife, The Cornflower Bride, a pretty girl of nineteen with a blue cornflower tattooed onto her right breast, and their year-old son, The Oilfield Urchin, a bright-eyed winsome lad. The seating was a little cramped, but the hospitality was generous, and we were plenty warm. Could be more desperate.

Down the road a mile or so, in what they called Ragtown, where drifting roughnecks had lived all last summer in tents or less, packing water from the rancher's spring and cooking over open fires when they came off shift, there was still one stalwart living in his automobile, a late-model General Motors product. The exact make was hard to fix, since it was covered over with old blankets and tarps for insulation. The only heat in there was a two-burner Coleman stove. Light up and risk asphyxiation. Or stay tough and freeze a trifle.

The idea being to live close to the work and the time-and-a-half for overtime, which could often amount to sixty hours and a thousand dollars a week for even the mildly skilled.

"Yeap," The Young Roughneck said. "Executive wages."

Well, maybe not quite, but freedom. Last summer one of the boomers from Ragtown took his big-tired diesel Ford pickup down to Ogden and hauled back about $3,000 worth of motel furniture from a wholesale outlet, everything but a TV, and set up housekeeping in the sagebrush around a fire ring. He lived there like a crowned king of the imagination until October, when the rains commenced. He sold the stuff and headed back to winter in Texas. Radical freedom, a deer rifle you feel no need to fire, a fly rod from Orvis, and a $600 tape deck and transoceanic radio, everything on rubber, and open roads.

The Young Roughneck and family said they were staying until spring, according to latest plans, and then they were taking a vacation tour of national parks in their pickup camper. For Christmas they were going to go down to Salt Lake City and rent the best motel room in town for two or three days and buy presents and set up a tree. The Oilfield Urchin was going to have himself a traditional time, tearing up bright tissue-paper wrappings. And the first package they would open was going to be the Polaroid camera.

The bottom line out here is beyond all sensible reckoning, too long for a lifetime of finger counting, something reasonable only to the make-believe of computers: One Hundred Billion Dollars.

One hundred times a thousand million dollars. That is how much, in 1980, we in the United States spent importing foreign petroleum. That's a hellacious load of economic thrust, much of it aimed into these boomtowns like Casper and Evanston and Gillette and Wamsutter in Wyoming, and in Rangely down in Colorado.

The Ryckman Creek oil field north of Evanston has estimated reserves worth far more than $500 million, at present prices, and in the Whitney Canyon field there is an estimated reserve of natural gas worth more than $800 million. Amoco predicts that the area's total reserves will amount to the energy equivalent of about one quarter of the reserves in Prudhoe Bay, the Alaskan field now producing almost 10 percent of the nation's oil.

Though reports vary wildly, oil companies have spent at least $250 million in the Evanston area. Only the beginning. This Wyoming cow town—four or five blocks of hardware stores and notions shops, a single theater, a half-dozen bars, neat houses under Chinese elms and lilac blooming in springtime, a string of motels out by the freeway off-ramp, and a population of 4,500 only three years ago—this town has 4,000 transient newcomers already, and another 4,000 expected this year with 60 to 100 new drilling rigs. It's an old western story: the boomtown syndrome.

The litany of ills has always been much the same, whether we're talking about old-time cow towns like Caldwell, Kansas, or contemporary company towns like Colstrip, Montana; lumber towns like Mabel, Oregon, or military communities like Mohave, Arizona. In *Roughing It* Mark Twain talks about the town of Unionville in Nevada, where "we were stark mad with excitement—drunk with happiness—smothered under mountains of prospective wealth."

The beginning has always been characterized by careless haste in the expectation of landing in the chips, quick profit for the skillful and lucky, city planning generally nonexistent or close to it, and residents willing to pay almost any price for whatever it was they wanted, from dentistry in the old days to cocaine in Evanston. The central theme is easy money, followed by large numbers of people, gambling, prostitution, sewage problems, and all the macho you could hope for—all combining to make law enforcement nearly impossible, all undermining respect for what have been called the civilized virtues of home, the arts, regular bathing, and literature.

And then the money runs out, and everybody leaves for somewhere else. Look even at the towns that lasted a long time, like Butte, or even worse, Anaconda, where ARCO shut down the company plant, tossing most of the town's employees into the arms of Unemployment Compensation.

The city fathers of Evanston are aware of all this. A couple of years ago they were shocked into a possible vision of the future by the drug-crazed, cathouse horror show in Rock Springs, eighty miles east on Interstate 80 and already deep in the energy boomtown syndrome, as depicted by Mike Wallace on *60 Minutes*. Not here, they said, and they have done a reasonable job of holding the line. That's why there are no fast-food franchises in town. Outsiders have an expensive time getting building permits.

But already raw sewage is being dumped into Bear River, which runs through the outskirts of town, and older single-story houses cost nearly $100,000, with damned few on the market. Parking space for a mobile home costs $250 a month, without water and sewage connections, and the waiting list runs as long as your arm. Living in a motel room decorated with plants to make it feel like a home will cost you a thousand a month. The Ramada Inn, when I was there, had no rooms and didn't expect to have any soon. Hundreds, including company men from the oil towers, get their mail general delivery because all the post office boxes have long since been subscribed. The roads are torn up, the schools are jammed, property taxes have gone beyond all reason, bar fights and family shoot-outs and all-around thievery are becoming commonplace—the old community trying to hold on but increasingly engulfed, at the same time growing richer and richer, some say sacrificed.

"They have strung us up," a hardened downtown Evanston businessman told me, "and take or leave it, like it or maybe, they are skinning our hides. Right away they're going to start cutting steaks." At the time he was buying drinks for the house about every twenty minutes, paying for them with one $50 bill after another.

Outside The Young Roughneck's jacked-up camper, after one final pull straight from the Crown Royal bottle, we watched a seismic survey helicopter lift from a hilltop over north toward the Chase tower, the drilling rig where my friends had worked until the previous week.

During deer season last fall some hunter brought down one of the helicopters. One high-powered rifle shot to the guts, smoke and explosions and a modified crash landing. Late last summer a rancher from down on the hayland flats beside the Bear River drove up in midday and dropped a dead and reeking badger into the tank of fresh spring water all the campers here were using for drinking and cooking. The snowy Uinta Mountains down across the Utah border gleamed in the sunlight, and we were reminded that problem solving tends to run toward direct action in places where the air is so clean.

My friends were not working because they'd got themselves fired for fighting on the rig. They'd been working a morning tower from midnight until eight, and one of the hands showed up drunk with four of his friends and started beating on the motor man. That led quickly to group loyalties and bloodshed. One fellow took a ball-peen hammer to the head, and it will be some time before he remembers his name.

But not to worry. The cops ran those boys out of town, and in this boomer world jobs are never a problem. At least not for long. Just start roaming around from rig to rig after the midnight shift change, and you will find some crew where a man showed up drunk or too stoned to function, or not at all, and they will be coming out of the hole with 10,000 feet of five-inch pipe, getting ready to replace the triple-headed Howard Hughes drilling bit, and right away you will have a job. Downtime on these rigs costs about $1,000 an hour, so they like to keep them turning.

But The Honorable Schoolboy didn't want a job. Starting in June as a green hand, he'd learned to work every spot on the rig—"from the crown to the ground," as they say—and he'd saved up better than $10,000 by the winter. That was enough for a year in film school at UCLA, with some weeks in the summer for climbing in Yosemite.

The Young Roughneck, who had never finished his third year of high school, did not have those options, and things between them, on this score, were a little tricky. But what the hell, this is a world of come and go, and they both knew that the sons of stockbrokers and physicians don't look to spend the rest of their lives roughnecking on the towers. In winter there is a limit to the utility of romance.

They shook hands and looked away. Catch you later.

"He's got that girl," The Honorable Schoolboy said as we drove away. "Out here that's like a gift. Most of them just got the work, and that's a hard place to find your pride. Out here." Then he smiled at himself for having absorbed too much Hemingway. Men without women, and work, the complex attractiveness of combat zones.

When they asked me what I was doing in Evanston I would say anthropology. Journalists and sociologists have a history of getting beat up around here. It's a new roughneck sport—thumping on the pudgy creeps who come to study them as if they were a hill of ants.

When I told the woman down the bar that I was an anthropologist, she looked as if she didn't believe me.

She was one of a tribe called morning-tower widows; at least that's how I saw her at first glance. Married to men who work the morning tower, these women sleep out the days and drink away the evenings. This one was attractive in a lean and redheaded thirty-seven-year-old way, all her visible parts covered with freckles the size and color of pennies, and she was well into a red beer at 9:15 on a Saturday morning, wiping her lips with a napkin after each sip.

"God's truth," I told her. "Anthropology."

"If it gives them something," she said, "why not."

Turned out she was talking tattoos. People bouncing trailer court to trailer court can lose track of every blessed thing but themselves, and they start having multicolored pictures engraved on their skin. "Only thing they got," she said. "Keeps them company at night, while they are praying to themselves."

She was married to a helicopter pilot, and they lived sixty miles down the road in the Utah ski resort town of Park City. "No more of these rat towns," she said, twisting her mouth as if the beer had gone sour. "We drink in them class bars, and we own the condo. So things are just fine. Them hippie girls got themselves to blame. Some gotta win and some gotta lose."

She looked dead into me with her dry, gray, redhead eyes and bought me a drink as she was walking out. So much for the romance of morning drinking, morning-tower widows, and the anthropology of inky self-deception.

The Honorable Schoolboy and I headed to the Chase rig on the hill. Most of the leases around Evanston are held by Amoco and Chevron, but the actual drilling is done under contract by specialty firms such as Brinkerhoff and Chase and Parker. The Schoolboy was hoping to pick up his last paycheck, about $1,500 earned before the fighting broke out.

But right away we saw that the drilling pipe was stuck in the hole, and he got worried. They were fishing, as they call it on the rigs, sending complex tools down the hole, to about 9,500 feet in this case, latching on to the pipe and trying to break it loose from whatever formation it was locked into by a series of complex twistings and jerkings. The basic idea in this kind of operation is to get the pipe up so the drill bit can be replaced. So far they'd had about 30 hours of downtime, at the infamous $1,000 an hour, and tempers were most likely running frothy.

These deep holes, down to 15,000 feet in many wells around here, are tough propositions, hard to hold straight as the bits cut through the slanting ledges so far below. The rigs are enormous steel-girder structures towering 120 feet above the desert, and they work in a long, repetitive rhythm—at most 200 hours through the entire cycle. That's the best you'll ever get from one of those high-rental Hughes drill bits.

Most of the work takes place on what is called "the floor," a wide, enclosed platform some thirty feet off the ground, atop the substructure that houses the huge flower of blow-out protection valves designed to prevent the tremendous hydraulic pressures of the earth from blowing deadly H_2S gas into their faces. In case the valves don't work, there are gas masks. It's like war. In case of gas, the rule is: Kill for a mask, if you must. Repent later.

All the work is dangerous on these small-scale factories in the wilderness. Enormous weight hangs above the floor on cables—the Kelly gear head that turns the drilling, the huge block and tackle used to lift the tons of drilling pipe from the hole while they are changing bits—and cables can break; everything can come down. The wrap of chain used to turn the pipe into its threads can fly loose from the hands of the chain man and take off your head. Or the derrick man, ninety-five feet above your head, can drop a Coca-Cola can just after he pops the top.

Going out to such work, shift to shift, breeds hardness, and contempt for those who give it up. The Tool Pusher on the Chase rig that morning didn't have much time for The Honorable Schoolboy. Class differences, if you will, matters of vocabulary. And he was pissed to be bothered with the trivialities of a boy seeking a paycheck.

And the paycheck, the $1,500, was not there. The Tool Pusher, an old Texas professional, exasperated by all these longhaired dropout newcomers, finally recalled that he had sent it back to the drilling company. "Shit," he said, grinning cold at The Honorable Schoolboy. "I got no time to baby-sit your money."

Comes with the territory. The money, which he would no doubt recover in time, didn't bother The Honorable Schoolboy so much as this shitty way of leaving a line of work he had gone at with pride and determination. "That's Evanston," he said, and my mind heard Chinatown.

The Boeing 707 lifted from Salt Lake International into a bright morning. The flats below were covered with the undulations of a luminous ground fog that had burned at our eyes, and off west the snowy mountains of desert Utah and Nevada stood shattering white and intricate against the sheltering endlessness of clean sky, each rockfall precisely defined by shadow. Bingham Canyon—the world's largest open-pit mine—was also lovely in its unnatural way, down there under the new snowfall, a vast spiral of earth sculpture, like the Tower of Babel turned upside down.

These occasional visions of our landscape are another sort of bottom line. Those of us who live in the West, our better selves mirrored in a great and clean good place, must weigh that image against a long history of rootless boomtown extravagance that is equally our heritage.

The locals try to pretend their lives aren't changing; the boomers swagger through town with burning money in their pockets; and the professionals do their work and try to live somewhere else, maybe down in Park City, among the skiers.

And the sociologists and journalists, the people like me, come to view the rush of vitality and rich-kid chaos as if it were theater, another episode in the Wild West Extravaganza. Out along the frozen-over ranchland meadows along Bear River north of Evanston I rode a creaking hay wagon with a man who had been born in the house where he lived. "The sons a bitches," he said. "I got some of their lease money, and I like it fine . . . and you think you shouldn't stand in the way, with gas the price it is.

"But goddamn," he said. "That was country I knew, each and every rise and fall of it, and now she is roads and derricks and a lost cause. The only pretty thing about it is those towers out there at night, lighted up like Christmas trees."

JUNE/JULY 1981

THE BIG BUZZ

by ED ZUCKERMAN

Here are the intrepid killer bee researchers, relaxing over a few chilled Carta Blancas from the minibar in their room in the best hotel in Jalapa, Mexico, comparing notes on where they least enjoy being stung.

Orley R. "Chip" Taylor, Jr., a large and jovial insect ecologist from the University of Kansas who has been tracking the killer bees through Latin America for fifteen years, has just finished demonstrating the little dance he does when a bee gets into his pants and starts crawling up his thigh. Now he explains that some stings don't matter. "When you're intently working on something, sorting through a colony to find and mark the queen, and you start getting stung on your hands, maybe once a minute—ten, twelve, fifteen times—you just keep going. It doesn't bother you."

Glenn Hall, a sober bee geneticist from the University of Florida, nods in agreement. "Back of your hand, no problem. But the stings on your fingertips are painful."

"The ones I don't like are just *under* your fingernail," says Chip. "Or on the nose here"—he points just inside a nostril. "Your eyes water and you start to sneeze, and you have to stop whatever you're doing."

"Yes," says José Antonio Gutiérrez, a hyperactive graduate student at the

National University of Mexico. "And when they go in your ears, you try to get them out." He demonstrates by waggling a finger in his left ear.

"I talked to someone who did two autopsies in Tanzania," Chip says, "and there were bees in every orifice—eyes, ears, mouth, nose, anus."

"That's the one that seems to get people," says Glenn, "the anus."

"Right," says Chip, and he issues a mock threat to an invisible foe: "How would you like a bee up your anus?"

Everybody laughs. Ho ho, say I. Nothing like a little bee humor before an encounter with the killer bees. Of course, these guys have all been working with bees since junior high. (There seems to be a beekeeping gene that guides certain adolescent boys to the hobby.) These guys *like* bees. They all get stung, all the time, both by the relatively gentle European bees that have been raised in the Americas for centuries, and by the more temperamental African killer bees that have been sweeping north, as much as 300 miles a year, ever since twenty-six colonies imported for research by one Warwick E. Kerr were accidentally released in Brazil in 1957. Their northernmost column is now on the Mexican Gulf Coast, less than a year away from Texas and just a short drive from our hotel room.

Here we are, on the killer bee front line, relaxing over beer and bee jokes. Chip opens a can of roasted peanuts—which, he notes, taste very much like the sautéed bee larvae he serves when entertaining back home in Kansas. I break the mood by asking about a particularly nasty stinging incident that my pretrip research turned up. I've got a couple of clippings about a University of Miami botany student named Inn Siang Ooi, who was walking in the woods in Costa Rica one day in 1986 when he was unlucky enough to stumble upon a killer bee colony. The sting of an individual killer bee is about as toxic as that of any other honeybee, but killer bees are prone to attack in larger numbers and for a longer time than other honeybees when an intruder threatens—or when they *think* an intruder threatens—their hive.

Chip knows about the incident; several months after it happened, he visited the site, spoke to witnesses. Now, all laughter finished, he tells me and Glenn and José Antonio how Ooi had been climbing on a rock over a cave when he came upon the nest; how the bees attacked and Ooi couldn't run away because the rock face was steep; how his friends threw butterfly nets over their heads and tried to get to him but were driven back by the bees, three of them stung so seriously that they collapsed; how Ooi climbed or fell into a vent in the rock while the bees stung him still; how rescuers heard him moaning but could not find him until they saw one of his feet dangling into the cave below; how rescuers had to wait until dark (when the bees returned to their hive) to retrieve Ooi's body; how it was carried out of the forest in a procession behind a white horse; how it had been stung 8,000 times or, as one report observed, "an average of 46 stings per square inch."

• • •

There they are—the killer bees.*

On a dry yellow hillside east of Jalapa, Chip has established an apiary of forty-five bee colonies. A year ago, shortly before killer bees reached this area, he stocked it (and four others at varying altitudes) with local European bees. Now some of those bees have bred with killer bees, and we have come visiting to see how the apiary has changed.

We arrive at the edge of the apiary—Chip, Glenn, José Antonio, an enthusiastic Mexican student named Felipe Brizuela, and I—and climb out of our van. The morning was cool, but the day is hot. Yellow grasses and bare-limbed trees stretch over the surrounding hillsides. The apiary is in the sun, the hives clustered around short, leafless trees with sharp thorns. We are fifty feet away. Figuring 40,000 bees per colony, we are looking at 1.8 million bees. None of them seems to have noticed us.

Good.

The twenty-six colonies of African bees that escaped in 1957 in Brazil, 7,000 miles south of here, have made ecological history by taking over most of a hemisphere: French Guiana, Surinam, Guyana, Venezuela, Colombia, Panama, Costa Rica, Nicaragua, Honduras, El Salvador, Guatemala, Belize, and now Mexico. They found their niche in the wilds of the American tropics, where European bees never thrived. The Africans were tougher than the Europeans; they could get by on less nourishment and could fly farther—up to twelve miles or more without a rest—to seek out what nourishment there was. They reproduced more prolifically than Europeans; while Europeans stockpiled honey, the Africans used their honey to nurture more bees. Africans sometimes invaded and took over European colonies, killing the resident queens. And when domesticated European queens flew off to mate in areas where Africans lived in the wild, they mated with African drones, and so did their daughters and their daughters' daughters.

At one time, entomologists expected that this crossbreeding would result in a diminution of the killer bees' fierceness, a genetic legacy of their ancestors' lives in Africa, where men and animals routinely raid hives for honey. But after thirty-two years of crossbreeding, the killer bees are as testy as ever. Chip

---

*A note on nomenclature: Generally, the respectable press has used the term "Africanized bees" for these insects—after, of course, an initial reference to "so-called killer bees" so that readers will know what the article is talking about. Only trashy tabloids use the term "killer bees" all the way through. Now, however, a scientific debate has arisen as to whether the bees are more correctly called "Africanized" or "African." To use one term or the other would amount to taking sides. Therefore, in the interest of objectivity, I feel compelled to refer to the insects as killer bees, except where context requires that they be referred to as "the little bastards."

estimates that they have killed between 700 and 1,000 people in Latin America and stung another 70,000 to 200,000 severely enough to require medical attention. Since arriving in Mexico two years ago, the bees have killed five people, all of whom were elderly and some of whom had provoked colonies by attempting to capture them or steal their honey.

The death toll is likely to be lower in the United States, where few people steal wild honey or capture wild bees. But when the first death does occur—and some will inevitably occur after the killer bees cross the Rio Grande sometime around March 1990—it's going to be big news. (As many as eighteen killer bee swarms have already reached the States as stowaways on cargo ships, but as far as is known, American authorities have found and destroyed them all.)

American beekeepers are dreading the day. They fear an anti-bee hysteria that will put many of their number out of business. But the killer bees themselves will accomplish that; faced with feistier bees than they have ever worked with before, some beekeepers will close up shop rather than try to adapt.

Honey production is a relatively minor industry in the United States, and any honey lost could easily be replaced from the world market, but American honeybees play another, far more indispensable role: They pollinate $20 billion worth of fruits, vegetables, and other crops. Some farmers hire beekeepers to drive truckloads of bees to their farms and park them there. European bees can be trucked with impunity, but killer bees are likely to take violent exception to going on the road.

No one knows how widely the killer bees will spread in the United States. Chip thinks the climate will confine them to the Deep South; the U.S. Department of Agriculture says they may spread through the forty-eight contiguous states. The USDA is working on various schemes to slow or modify the bees. Chip has little confidence in the USDA, but he is optimistic that the bees *can* be modified in the United States, where they will encounter large numbers of wild European bees for the first time. With that in mind, he is working on selecting and positioning European drones to maximize their chances of mating with killer bee queens.

To study mating behavior, Chip has developed a plastic tube (dubbed Chip's Master Mater by his students) that slips over the sex organs of a queen bee. When drones attempt to mate with the queen, they stick to the tube, making them available for scientific scrutiny. To locate "drone congregation areas," Chip has walked the hills of Kansas towing helium-filled weather balloons from which he has suspended sexy queen bees in cages. He has modified old army radar units to track the flights of drones, and he has experimented with police radar guns. All the while, he has kept up his visits to Mexico to keep an eye on the progress of the killer bees.

Chip hasn't been in this apiary for several months, so he doesn't know what we can expect today. I suit up for the worst in full bee garb: white coveralls, leather gloves, a pith helmet, a mesh veil that attaches to my pith helmet with an elastic band and zips directly to my coveralls, and Velcro straps that seal the bottoms of my pants. The researchers don similar suits, and then we're off, ambling among the bee boxes, which are painted green and blue in cheerful Mexican style.

The researchers set immediately to work. Chip, José Antonio, and Felipe take the covers off bee boxes, shoot puffs from handheld smokers to subdue the bees, and start pulling out frames. Hanging from each frame is a bee-built wax comb, its individual cells filled with honey, pollen, or wormlike larvae (which are excellent sautéed, as Chip has pointed out). There are also a thousand or so bees on each frame, scurrying from cell to cell on bee business. Chip, José Antonio, and Felipe brush through the bees with their hands, looking for queens.

A bee colony's character is established by its queen, the mother of every bee in the hive. She lays eggs full-time after an early-in-life mating flight during which she copulates—some forty feet above the earth—with several drones and acquires a lifetime supply of semen; the lucky drones who manage to reach the mating queen literally explode their genitals into her and die.

When a colony prospers and grows full of bees, it "swarms." The queen flies off with 10,000 to 15,000 of her children to find a new home, leaving behind the rest of the colony and several larvae that workers will nourish into new queens. One of the new virgin queens will kill the others, embark on her mating flight, and then return to begin laying eggs, as the cycle begins again.

Some of the queens in this apiary have been here since Chip established it; they are European bees, and so are all of their offspring. But some of the colonies have new queens that have taken their mating flights since wild killer bee colonies moved into the neighborhood, and some of the drones they mated with were killer bees. Some of their children, therefore, are half killer bee. Those offspring are likely to have inherited their fathers' disposition.

Chip, José Antonio, and Felipe are having trouble finding some of the queens in the masses of bees running around on the frames. They pull out frame after frame, virtually disassembling some of the hives. This is just the kind of thing that pisses bees off, and a few fly up to attack the researchers—and me, the innocent bystander. But our suits protect us.

Glenn, meanwhile, is using a squirt bottle to flush larvae out of their cells. He will take them back to Florida, grind them up, and analyze their genes. His work along these lines so far seems to have provided an answer to the puzzling question: Why, after thirty-two years of crossbreeding with European bees in the Americas, haven't the killer bees been "gentle-ized" by all that European blood?

Because, Glenn has concluded, that European blood ain't there. Genetically, the killer bees at the leading edge of the invasion have shaken off any European influence picked up by their ancestors on the flight from Brazil. The bees now heading toward the Rio Grande, he says, are nearly pure African.

Chip concurs. The African bees, he and Glenn contend, have genetically swamped the relatively few European bees they have encountered. Family lines resulting from African-European crosses have died out in the wild, apparently less able to compete for resources than their pure African cousins.

These findings have been disputed by USDA researchers, who insist that the bees are not African but "Africanized" hybrids. The USDA does concede that these hybrids retain the character traits of their African daddies, so the debate seems a little academic. But it is intense. Chip and Glenn have few kind words for their colleagues at the USDA, which funded Chip's killer bee research until 1981 and then cut him off to move its program in-house; USDA researchers for their part have few kind words for Chip and Glenn. The two sides exchange cutting remarks in the *Bulletin of the Entomological Society of America* and wherever killer bee people congregate for scientific conferences.

All that seems far away from the apiary, where Glenn gathers more larvae and the others continue to search for queens. Queens that have been in this apiary since the beginning are marked with yellow dots; younger ones are marked with blue or white. The yellow-dot queens definitely preside over all-European colonies. The domains of the other queens are questionable.

Like Colony 47. When Chip opens this box, the bees do not continue about their business like mild-mannered Europeans; instead, a battalion flies up to attack him. They go for his head (rampaging bees are attracted to dark spots like hair, eyes, ears, and mouths) and run across his veil, trying to get inside it.

Mine, too.

"You know what I'd do with these bees in Kansas?" Chip calls out over the angry buzzing. "I'd kill them all." Back in Kansas, he raises gentle European bees. *These* bees are stinging his ankles (he has forgotten to bring his high white boots). Wincing, he pronounces the colony a "pecky" one.

Glenn, who has been working barehanded—he finds it awkward to manipulate his samples while wearing thick leather gloves—is suddenly stung about twenty times on each hand. He decides that gloves wouldn't be so bad after all.

Chip moves on to other boxes, calling out the colors of the dots on the queens he finds, and I, trying to make myself useful, record them in a logbook. It's difficult to do with gloves on, especially with bees running over the book and my gloves.

As the researchers open more boxes, the attack grows more intense; the bees are stirring each other up. Chip has four bees inside his veil but continues working unfazed. José Antonio is getting stung through his coveralls whenever he bends over and the cloth is pulled taut against his skin. I stand ramrod straight—no taut bee suit on me. Bees are attacking a black pen in my pocket. Angry bees are buzzing all around me, crawling on my veil, fuzzy shapes in front of my eyes and at the edges of my peripheral vision. Bees are defecating on my gloves. The pages of the logbook are smeared with crushed bees.

Felipe has picked up a dead wasp the size of a tennis ball and truly beautiful, an iridescent blue-black. Chip identifies it as a tarantula killer and says it may have been killed by the bees, which are busy stinging the dead wasp as we examine it. Glenn decides to take a picture. The camera pushes his veil against his nose, and a bee immediately stings him in the nostril.

I feel a sharp pain in the top of my head, and I jump. "Yowch!" I remark. The researchers look at me. "Stung through my pith helmet!" I comment. The helmet is mesh.

"We all know the fireman's carry if you fall over," Chip says cheerfully. He opens another box and the bees rush out at him in such an intense wave that he is rocked backward. "That's a new queen," he says. "She mated with some bad boys."

No shit. "Yowch!" The little bastards sting me again. Through the hat again.

I look over at Chip, who has hundreds of bees swarming over his hat and veil. Glenn, José Antonio, and Felipe are under siege as well. The bees are trying to kill us all, and Glenn is taking pictures so that he can remember it. Chip patiently sorts through the bees in the box that exploded at him. He is fifty-two and has been working with bees for forty years, with killer bees for fifteen. Ever since he lost his USDA funding, he has scrounged for grants (he once made a direct appeal to readers of a journal called *The Speedy Bee*) and has forked out $25,000 of his own money to continue his research.

The top of my skull is throbbing. "Tell me again why you do this," I shout to Chip, who is less than twenty feet away but can barely hear me above the buzzing.

"Don't forget," shouts Glenn, "we beg people for money so we can do this."

"It gives intense sexual pleasure," Chip shouts. "It's a secret. We don't tell anybody."

Ho ho. I have had enough. I walk out of the apiary and down a dirt track. Bees pursue me. I walk half a mile, and three or four of them are still bouncing off my veil, trying to sting me in the eye. After another few hundred yards they fall away, and I find a patch of shade under a tree.

Down a short slope, trucks are whining up the highway from Veracruz to Jalapa. This is the very route that Cortés took in his cruel conquest of Mexico. This is the route that the Americans took when they invaded in 1847, that the French took in 1862. And now, the killer bees.

I remove my gloves and hat and veil and pull two stingers out of the top of my head. With my pocketknife, I start to scrape stingers out of the narrow cloth strip that borders the mesh in my veil. Many of the stingers trail yellow bee-guts (bees literally pull themselves apart when they sting); one has an entire dead bee attached.

Sitting in the dust, pulling out stingers, I reflect.

I have a long and sorry history with the killer bees. I first encountered them—and Chip—in 1977 in French Guiana, a backwater colony on the northern coast of South America where Chip was doing some of his early research. I was sent down to write a magazine article, and I came home with a hot idea for making a fortune: Why not import and market genuine killer bee honey as a novelty/gift/gourmet item? I did it—sold several thousand bottles—and Killer Bee Honey became briefly famous (in a product review, *Outside* called it "thick, tasty, [and] overpriced"). And I lost my shirt.

What else had I accomplished in the twelve years since I'd last seen the killer bees? I'd done some good work, but I hadn't accomplished some of the things I thought I would have done by now. I hadn't found . . . but you don't want to hear about it. You know how it is. One day you're twenty-eight and tramping around a French Foreign Legion post in South America being attacked by killer bees, and your whole life is ahead of you and you have time to do anything, even sell killer bee honey; and then suddenly you're forty and everything is starting to look a little familiar, even killer bees, and you measure out your projects carefully, because there are more projects than time. You're older and different. But the killer bees are exactly the same. Glenn's genetic research has established what everybody knows: Creation is constant. Only you and I come and go.

I finish pulling the stingers out of my veil. There are 204 of them—204 of the little bastards tried to get me. They all died, and I'm still here. For the moment.

Here is the press corps, descending on the killer bees. Three days after my visit to the apiary, I am back, with colleagues.

"Sarah, dear," calls the *Outside* photographer, "will you come over here?" He is trying to get a picture of Chip being attacked by killer bees, and Sarah, a reporter for the *Philadelphia Inquirer Magazine*, is in the way. The photographer wants to get cracking; for the past two hours he has been moved out of shot after shot by a four-person video crew from a PBS science show, but for the moment the crew is occupied with Glenn a few bee boxes away. This is the photographer's chance to shoot Chip, who is hunched down looking for the queen in a fairly ornery colony. Sarah obliges and moves out of the way, but the bees are being difficult. They are attacking Chip most photogenically, but they are also attacking the photographer's camera, maddened by its blackness. "You've got so many bees on your lens . . . ," Chip says dubiously.

Howard Kerr, a nuclear engineer from Tennessee who has shown up in Mexico to promote sales of a killer bee detection device called the Buzzbuster, volunteers to help. He appears at the photographer's side with a piece of cardboard, ready to brush bees away. "Tell me when," Kerr says. The photographer aims. Chip looks up. A bee stings him in the back. Chip yelps. The photographer shoots. The video crew cues Glenn. Sarah and I take notes. The killer bees attack everybody, and everybody is very happy.

Thanks to their impending arrival in the States, killer bees are beginning to be big news. Local television crews from Texas have been trooping through Mexico demanding to be shown the carcasses of cows stung to death by killer bees. One crew, leaving nothing to chance, tossed its own live chicken against a hive and filmed the result.

Our own little media circus began yesterday, in a small apiary behind the Conafrut Research Center, where Howard Kerr—no relation to the Kerr whose bees in Brazil started all this mess—set out to demonstrate his Buzzbuster. Kerr works at the Oak Ridge National Laboratory, where he has lately been employed developing the Star Wars antimissile system. He is also a longtime beekeeper, and during his lunch breaks from plotting the destruction of incoming Soviet nuclear missiles, he used to stroll the woods around the laboratory looking for wild bee colonies. His basic technique—find a bee, see which way it flies, and move in that direction—was slow and uncertain. One day he had a better idea: Why not set out some sweet bee-bait laced with radioactive isotopes, let the bees ingest it, and then track them with radiation monitors? Thinking about it, it finally occurred to Kerr why not.

His next idea was to take sound-detection equipment used to monitor the performance of nuclear reactors and adapt it to recognize the sound of bees. He was working on this when he heard an expert speak on the killer bees. She mentioned that, because they beat their wings about fifty more times per second than European bees do, they sound different. Kerr jumped on this, and he and two colleagues developed a little electronic box that can distinguish the sound of a killer bee from that of a European bee (the sound of European bees makes a green light go on; killer bees trigger a red light). Kerr began to consult with Chip Taylor on this project—Chip suggested the name—and Kerr and his colleagues formed a company called B-Tec to market the Buzzbuster.

One day Kerr asked Chip what other kind of hardware might be useful in his research. Chip said he would love to have a device that could track the flights of individual bees. Queens fly off to mate at fourteen miles per hour, and it's hard for a fifty-two-year-old entomologist to keep up.

Kerr, eager to help, came up with an infrared transmitter in the form of a microchip that can be glued to a bee's back and tracked with ground-based receivers. He found this project especially interesting because of its similarity to the work he had been doing on Star Wars. Indeed, he's received funding from his lab. "Mathematically," he told me, "the problem of having a one-meter-long object [like a nuclear warhead] at one hundred kilometers is the same as a one-centimeter-long object [like a bee] at one kilometer. If I can direct a beam that will solve either of those problems, that beam should solve the other."

The microchip, however, is still being tested. Yesterday was the Buzzbuster's day in the sun. Kerr was hoping to sell a few hundred of the things to the USDA, and two officials flew down to see what it could do. The PBS video crew wanted to see, too. So did the reporter from the *Philadelphia Inquirer*, the photographer from *Outside*, and I. We all observed as Kerr grabbed bees and stuck them into a little plastic cylinder attached to the Buzzbuster's microphone. Kerr had a little problem—one of his prototypes apparently had a short circuit—but it was nevertheless clear that the device could tell you when you were in the presence of killer bees, in case the fact that they had just chased your grandmother from Texas to Louisiana hadn't already clued you in.

But today is the day the reporters in town had really looked forward to, when they were to visit an apiary chock-full of killer bees. Ever since the video crew arrived in Mexico, Chip, hoping to inculcate a properly cautious attitude, had been doing his best to scare its members with stories of how other film crews had gotten bees inside their veils, how they'd been stung, and how they'd panicked. This crew's cameraman, a genial and sturdy fellow, had been especially impressed by Chip's account of the cameraman from *National Geographic*, a man renowned as a fearless rock climber, who took a painful sting in the ear, worked for a while unaffected, and then keeled over, unconscious.

Arriving at the edge of the apiary, the crew had suited up with extreme thoroughness. I was envious of their brand-new equipment—nifty nylon coveralls and Velcro spats to cover gaps between their shoes and pants. Methodically, they tucked their pants into their boots, pulled their coveralls over their pants, affixed their spats over their boots and coveralls, and then wrapped tape around their spats. Then they set upon themselves and each other with a passion, taping their zippers, taping their veils, taping their hats to cover every conceivable gap. The cameraman put tape on his face where his veil might be pushed in as he looked into his camera (and promptly sweated the tape off). The sound man put tape on his ears. In an excess of caution, he wore two pairs of pants and a jacket under his coveralls. (He didn't get stung, but he did get seriously overheated.)

In the bee yard, all went well. The researchers opened hives and looked for queens. Glenn extracted larvae for genetic sampling. Howard Kerr listened to bees on his Buzzbuster. The bees attacked everybody. The cameraman got stung twice, but he didn't miss a shot.

As the sun dipped behind a ridge, Glenn stood beside a bee box, pumping smoke from his smoker. The smoke fools bees into thinking the forest is on fire;

they rush inside to suck up their honey stores and get too busy to sting. So a beekeeper usually applies smoke before starting to work on a colony. But Glenn was not planning to work on this colony. He was done for the day. He was pumping his smoker—pumping it more than any smoker is usually pumped—because the video crew had asked him to. The smoke looked nice in front of the rosy light from the ridge. It was a very pretty shot.

Here are the killer bee killers, Pablo Aranda and Manuel Rodriguez, two pleasant and intelligent young men, driving around the state of Veracruz in a white Dodge pickup. They are employees of a joint U.S.–Mexican program designed (according to whom you talk to, and when) either to stop the killer bees, to slow them down, or to do nothing at all.

In 1987, thirty years after the bees started flying toward Texas and three years before they were expected to arrive, the USDA launched an action program. In cooperation with Mexico, the USDA decided to battle the bees at the Isthmus of Tehuantepec, Mexico's narrowest point. It would set out traps to attract and kill migrating killer bees. It would offer bounties (key chains and hats adorned with the program's logo) to peasants who reported the presence of swarms that missed the traps. It would flood the area with European bee colonies and gentle European drones. It would work with local beekeepers to help them keep their apiaries pure. USDA officials announced at first that the program could stop the killer bees, or at least slow them down for ten years.

Before the program could be established in the Isthmus of Tehuantepec, the bees were already there, and it was too late. So the program set up a Bee Regulated Zone (BRZ) to the north. It was divided into two "operational units": one on the west coast around Puerto Escondido, the other on the east coast around Jalapa and Veracruz. (The Sierra Madre mountains keep the bees from moving up the middle of the country.) Nobody talks about slowing the bees down for ten years anymore—a good thing, since the first bees zipped through Veracruz in less than six months—but the program's stated purpose is still to slow the bees . . . somewhat.

Several key elements of the program have never been put into place. The BRZ was never flooded with European colonies because local beekeepers objected to the competition for a finite amount of nectar and because the program never got the funding to acquire and distribute the bees anyway. But the bee killing has proceeded. In the Veracruz unit, 22,000 cardboard boxes designed to look like good homes to bees have been hung from trees to lure migrating swarms. Each box is checked monthly by one of twenty-five teams that destroy any bees they find. Between December 1987 and March 1989, the Veracruz teams destroyed 2,500 bee colonies, 500 of them colonies of killers. (Another 2,500 colonies, including 2,000 killer bee colonies, were destroyed in the Puerto Escondido unit.) The program has its detractors, who argue that the number of swarms caught is an insignificant fraction of the number in the area and that, since some swarms die anyway in a process of natural selection, the USDA is not reducing the killer bee population but only substituting its selection for that of nature. "It's a kill-now, ask-questions-later system," says Chip Taylor. "We're blowing six million dollars in a program where we learn almost nothing—it's like stepping on ants."

Pablo and Manuel have some sympathy for these arguments—they have no idea how many swarms they're *not* catching, they say—but it's not their job to worry about that. It's their job to drive around the state of Veracruz day after day, checking 700 bee boxes and killing any bees they find inside them.

So here we are—Pablo, Manuel, and three members of the killer bee press corps—bouncing along a rough dirt road through a steep, rugged canyon with a spectacular waterfall below.

Manuel drives nonstop to the end of the road and the village of Xoltepec, a dusty hamlet of 300 souls where radios play from cinder-block houses and turkeys and chickens scratch for crumbs in the dirt. He and Pablo consult with a peasant beekeeper who has two colonies of tame European bees in rough-hewn hives he built himself; a small boy throws stones at a turkey nearby and other boys set off firecrackers to welcome us to town. Pablo arranges to return another day to give the beekeeper some modern modular bee boxes, and we prepare to depart with two new passengers. José Juan, a shy ten-year-old, wants a lift to the river at the bottom of the canyon, where his mother and sisters are washing clothes, and the village schoolmaster is heading to Jalapa with a large red poster of the Virgin Mary for *his* mother. The boy, the schoolmaster, and the Virgin join the press corps in the back of the truck, Manuel starts the engine, and off we all go, off to kill killer bees.

A quarter-mile down the canyon road, Manuel brakes to a halt, gets out of the truck, ducks under some barbed wire, and walks to a tree from which the first of twenty-nine traps on this route is suspended. He finds no bees. We take off again. He stops and looks again. No bees.

Manuel does find a trap that has fallen out of its tree. He shakes it and finds a large spider. He inserts a fresh capsule of synthetic bee pheromone, the orientation signal that scout bees release when they find a good spot for a hive, then uses a long stick with a bent wire on the end to replace the box in the tree.

In fifteen months on the job, Pablo and Manuel have found forty-five colonies, thirty of them killers, and the pace is picking up. One day a few months ago, during the wet season, they found eight bee colonies—five of them killers—along this road.

Not today.

Manuel stops and looks. No bees.

We pass an old woman on a burro.

Stop. Look. No bees.

José Juan gets out to find his mother.
Stop. Look. No bees.
The wind blows the schoolmaster's hat off.
Stop. Look. No bees.

Finally, here we all are—researchers, media, killer bee killers, and the killer bees. The bees' presence has been stage-managed. Pablo and Manuel found a colony in a box a few days ago, but they spared it on instructions from their supervisors: Save it for the television crew.

So here are all the human players, bouncing across a dry field in two vehicles, pulling to a stop between the carcasses of two dead horses. We disembark, and Pablo and Manuel lead us all on a long downhill march into the same canyon we have seen before, past rows of mango and coffee trees.

The killer bee swarm is in Box 51, hanging twenty feet up in a spindly tree on the right side of the trail. Pablo and Manuel and José Antonio pull on their bee suits for the benefit of the video crew. (They ordinarily wouldn't bother; migrating swarms and newly established colonies with little honey to protect rarely attack.) They walk toward the tree.

The video crew makes them come back and do it again.

Then the video crew makes them do it again.

A few bees are flying casually in and out of a hole in the bottom of the box, which Manuel now pokes with his long stick. The box drops to the ground. José Antonio cuts it open to take a sample. Bees fly out, but they circle harmlessly. Pablo finds the queen and holds it up for the camera. Then Manuel dumps the entire colony into a black plastic garbage bag.

The coup de grâce is delivered off-camera. Back at the trailhead, Pablo opens the buzzing bag and pours in water and detergent, a fatal blow. He dumps the dead bees onto the ground near one of the dead horses in an inelegant clump.

One killer bee colony has been terminated.

Down in the canyon, the other killer bees chortle over refreshing drafts of nectar. Tomorrow, they move north.

JULY 1989

THE STORM

By SEBASTIAN JUNGER

"They that go down to the sea in ships . . . see the deeds of the
Lord. They reel and stagger like drunken men, they are at their
wits' end."

—Psalm 107

Gloucester, Massachusetts, a town of 28,000 people, is squeezed between a
rocky coast and a huge tract of scrub pine and boulders called Dogtown Common. Local widows used to live in Dogtown, along with the forgotten and the
homeless, while the rest of the community spread out along the shore. Today
a third of all jobs in Gloucester are fishing related, and the waterfront bars—
the Crow's Nest, the Mariners Pub, the Old Timer's Tavern—are dark little
places that are unmistakably not for tourists.

One street up from the coastline is Main Street, where the bars tend to have
windows and even waitresses, and then there is a rise called Portugee Hill.
Halfway up Portugee Hill is Our Lady of Good Voyage Church, a large stucco
construction with two bell towers and a statue of the Virgin Mary, who looks
down with love and concern at the bundle in her arms. The bundle is a
Gloucester fishing schooner.

• • •

September 18, 1991, was a hot day in Gloucester, tourists shuffling down Main Street and sunbathers still crowding the wide expanses of Good Harbor Beach. Day boats bobbed offshore in the heat shimmer, and swells sneaked languorously up against Bass Rocks.

At Gloucester Marine Railways, a haul-out place at the end of the short peninsula, Adam Randall stood contemplating a boat named the *Andrea Gail*. He had come all the way from Florida to go swordfishing on the boat, and now he stood considering her uneasily. The *Andrea Gail* was a seventy-foot longliner that was leaving for Canada's Grand Banks within days. He had a place on board if he wanted it. "I just had bad vibes," he would say later. Without quite knowing why, he turned and walked away.

Long-liners are steel-hulled fishing boats that can gross as much as $1 million in a year. Up to half of that can be profit. Swordfish range up and down the coast from Puerto Rico to Newfoundland, and the long-liners trail after them all year like seagulls behind a day trawler. The fish are caught with monofilament lines forty miles long and set with a thousand hooks. For the crew, it's less a job than a four-week jag. They're up at four, work all day, and don't get to bed until midnight. The trip home takes a week, which is the part of the month when swordfishermen sleep. When they get to port the owner hands each of them several thousand dollars. A certain amount of drinking goes on, and then a week later they return to the boat, load up, and head back out.

"Swordfishing is a young man's game, a single man's game," says the mother of one who died at it. "There aren't a lot of Boy Scouts in the business," another woman says.

Sword boats come from all over the East Coast—Florida, the Carolinas, New Jersey. Gloucester, which is located near the tip of Cape Ann, a forty-five-minute drive northeast from Boston, is a particularly busy port because it juts so far out toward the summer fishing grounds. Boats load up with fuel, bait, ice, and food and head out to the Grand Banks, about ninety miles southeast from Newfoundland, where warm Gulf Stream water mixes with the cold Labrador current in an area shallow enough—or "shoal" enough, as fishermen say—to be a perfect feeding ground for fish. The North Atlantic weather is so violent, though, that, in the early days, entire fleets would go down at one time, a hundred men lost overnight. Even today, with loran navigation, seven-day forecasts, and satellite tracking, fishermen on the Grand Banks are just rolling the dice come the fall storm season. But swordfish sell for around six dollars a pound, and depending on the size of the boat a good run might take in thirty thousand to forty thousand pounds. Deckhands are paid shares based on the catch and can earn ten thousand dollars in a month. So the tendency among fishermen in early fall is to keep the dice rolling.

The *Andrea Gail* was one of maybe a dozen big commercial boats gearing up in Gloucester in mid-September 1991. She was owned by Bob Brown, a long-time fisherman who was known locally as Suicide Brown because of the risks he'd taken as a young man. He owned a second long-liner, the *Hannah Boden*, and a couple of lobster boats. The *Andrea Gail* and the *Hannah Boden* were Brown's biggest investments, collectively worth well over a million dollars.

The *Andrea Gail*, in the language, was a raked-stem, hard-chined, western-rig boat. That meant that her bow had a lot of angle to it, she had a nearly square cross-section, and her pilothouse was up front rather than in the stern. She was built of welded steel plate, rust-red below the waterline, green above, and she had a white wheelhouse with half-inch-thick safety-glass windows. Fully rigged for a long trip, she carried hundreds of miles of monofilament line, thousands of hooks, and ten thousand pounds of bait fish. There were seven life preservers on board, six survival suits, an emergency position-indicating radio beacon, and one life raft.

The *Andrea Gail* was captained by a local named Frank "Billy" Tyne, a former carpenter and drug counselor who had switched to fishing at age twenty-seven. Tyne had a reputation as a fearless captain, and in his ten years of professional fishing he had made it through several treacherous storms. He had returned from a recent trip with almost forty thousand pounds of sword-fish in his hold, close to a quarter of a million dollars' worth. Jobs aboard Tyne's boats were sought after. So it seemed odd, on September 18, when Adam Randall walked back to the dock at Gloucester Marine Railways and returned to town.

Randall's replacement was twenty-eight-year-old David Sullivan, who was mildly famous in town for having saved the lives of his entire crew one bitter January night two years before. When his boat, the *Harmony*, had unexpectedly begun taking on water, Sullivan had pulled himself across a rope to a sister ship and got help just in time to rescue his sinking crew. Along with Sullivan were a young West Indian named Alfred Pierre; thirty-year-old Bobby Shatford, whose mother, Ethel, tended bar at the Crow's Nest on Main Street; and two men from Brandenton Beach, Florida—Dale Murphy, thirty, and Michael "Bugsy" Moran, thirty-six.

On September 20, Billy Tyne and his crew passed Ten Pound Island, rounded Dogbar Breakwater, and headed northeast on a dead-calm sea.

For several generations after the first British settlers arrived in Gloucester, the main industries on Cape Ann were farming and logging. Then around 1700 the cod market took off, and Gloucester schooners began making runs up to the Grand Banks two or three times a year. French and Basque fishermen had already been working the area since 1510, perhaps earlier. They could fill their holds faster by crossing the Atlantic and fishing the rich waters of the Banks than by plying their own shores.

The Gloucester codfisherman worked from dories and returned to the schooners each night. Payment was reckoned by cutting the tongues out of the cod and adding them up at the end of the trip. When fog rolled in, the dories would drift out of earshot and were often never heard from again. Occasionally, weeks later, a two-man dory crew might be picked up by a schooner bound for, say, Pernambuco or Liverpool. The fishermen would make it back to Gloucester several months later, walking up Main Street as if returning from the dead.

The other danger, of course, was storms. Like a war, a big storm might take out all the young men of a single town. In 1862, for example, a winter gale struck seventy schooners fishing the dangerous waters of Georges Bank, east of Cape Cod. The ships tried to ride out fifty-foot seas at anchor. By morning fifteen Gloucester boats had gone down with 125 men.

At least four thousand Gloucestermen have been lost at sea, but some estimates run closer to ten thousand. A bronze sculpture on the waterfront commemorates them: THEY THAT GO DOWN TO THE SEA IN SHIPS 1623–1923. It shows a schooner captain fighting heavy weather, his faced framed by a sou'wester hat.

In the early days, a lot of superstition went into seafaring. Occasionally men stepped off ill-fated boats on a hunch. Captains refused to set sail on Fridays, since that was the day their Lord had been crucified. Boats often had lucky silver coins affixed to the base of their masts, and crew members took care never to tear up a printed page because they never knew—most of them being illiterate—whether it was from the Bible.

The *Andrea Gail* took nearly a week to reach the fishing grounds. The six crewmen watched television, cooked and ate, slept, prepared the fishing gear, talked women, talked money, talked horse racing, talked fish, stared at the sea. Swordfishermen seldom eat swordfish when they're out. Like many ocean fish, it's often full of sea worms, four feet long and thick as pencils, and though the worms are removed prior to market, many of the men who catch swordfish consider it fit only for the landlubbing public. At sea a fisherman will eat steak, spaghetti, chicken, ice cream, anything he wants. On ice in the *Andrea Gail*'s hold was three thousand dollars' worth of groceries.

The boat arrived at the Grand Banks around September 26 and started fishing immediately. On the main deck was a huge pool of six-hundred-pound-test monofilament, the mainline, which passed across a bait table and paid out off the stern. Baiters alternate at the mainline like old-time axmen on a Douglas fir. They are expected to bait a hook with squid or mackerel every fifteen seconds; at this rate it takes two men four hours to set forty miles of line. After they are done they shower and retire to their bunks. Around four in the morning, the crew gets up and starts hauling the line. A hydraulic drum on the wheelhouse deck slowly pulls it in, and the crew unclips the leaders as they come. When there's a fish at the end of a leader, deckhands catch it with steel gaffs and drag it, struggling, aboard. They saw the sword off, gut and behead the fish with a knife, and drop it into the hold.

The crew has dinner in midafternoon, baits the line again, and sets it back out. They might then have a couple of beers and go to bed.

The *Andrea Gail* had been out thirty-eight days when the National Weather Service suddenly started issuing fax bulletins about a low-pressure system that was building over southern Quebec and heading out to sea: "DEVELOPING STORM 45N 73W MOVING E 24 KTS. WINDS INCREASING TO 35 KTS AND SEAS BUILDING TO 16 FT." Meanwhile, the Weather Service was keeping a close eye on the mid-Atlantic, where Hurricane Grace, which had developed in the vicinity of Bermuda two days before, was now tracking steadily northwest toward the Carolina coast.

It was Sunday, October 27, very late to be pushing one's luck on the Grand Banks. Most of the fleet was well to the east of Tyne, out on the high seas, but a 150-foot Japanese swordboat named the *Eishan Maru* and the 77-foot *Mary T* were fishing nearby. Tyne told Albert Johnston, the *Mary T*'s captain, that he had forty thousand pounds of fish in his hold—an impressive catch—and now he was heading home.

The question was, could he make it through the Canadian storm that was rapidly coming his way? He would have to cross some very dangerous water while passing Sable Island, a remote spit 120 miles southeast of Nova Scotia, whose shoals are known to fishermen as the Graveyard of the Atlantic. That night Linda Greenlaw, the captain of Bob Brown's other long-liner, the *Hannah Boden*, radioed in and asked Tyne if he'd received the weather chart. "Oh, yeah, I got it," Tyne replied. "Looks like it's gonna be wicked." They set some channels to relay information to Bob Brown and decided to talk the following night.

Though Billy Tyne had no way of knowing it, the heavy weather that was now brewing in the North Atlantic was an anomaly of historic proportions. Three years later, professional meteorologists still talk animatedly about the storm of '91, debating how it formed and exactly what role Hurricane Grace played in it all. Generally, hurricanes this late in the season are anemic events that quickly dissipate over land. Hurricane Grace, though, never made it to shore; a massive cold front, called an anticyclone, was blocking the entire eastern seaboard. Well off the Carolinas, Grace ran up against the cold front and literally bounced off. She veered back out to sea and, though weakened, churned northeast along the warm Gulf Stream waters.

At the same time, the low-pressure system that had developed over Quebec and moved eastward off the Canadian Maritimes was beginning to behave strangely. Normally, low-pressure systems in the region follow the jet stream offshore and peter out in the North Atlantic, the usual pattern of the well-known nor'easter storms. But this system did the opposite: On Monday, October 28, it unexpectedly stalled off the coast of Nova Scotia and began to grow rapidly, producing record high seas and gale-force winds. Then it spun around and headed back west, directly at New England, a reversal known as a retrograde.

Meteorologists still disagree about what caused the storm to grow so suddenly and then to retrograde. But the best theory offered by the National Weather Service and its Canadian equivalent, Environment Canada, is that it was caught between the counterclockwise spin of the dying hurricane and the clockwise swirl of the anticyclone, creating a funnel effect that forced it toward the coast at speeds of up to ten knots. The farther west it tracked, the more it absorbed moisture and energy from the remnants of Hurricane Grace—and the more ferocious it became.

The technical name for the new storm was *midlatitude cyclone*. The people in its path, however, would later call it the No Name Hurricane, since it had all the force of a hurricane but it was never officially designated as one. And because the brunt of the storm would strike the eastern seaboard around October 31, it would also acquire another name: the Halloween Gale.

Around 6:00 P.M. on Monday, October 28, Tyne told the skipper of a Gloucester boat named the *Allison* that he was 130 miles north-northeast of Sable Island and experiencing eighty-knot winds. "She's comin' on, boys, and she's comin' on strong," he said. According to Tyne, the conditions had gone from flat calm to fifty knots almost without warning. The rest of the fleet was farther east and in relative safety, but the *Andrea Gail* was all alone in the path of the fast-developing storm. She was probably running with the waves and slightly angled toward them— "quartering down-sea," as it's called—which is a stable position for a boat; she'll neither plow her nose into the sea nor roll over broadside. A wave must be bigger than a boat to flip her end over end, and the *Andrea Gail* was seventy feet long. But by this point, data buoys off Nova Scotia were measuring waves as high as one hundred feet—among the highest readings ever recorded. Near Sable Island the troughs of such monsters would have reached the ocean floor.

Tyne would have radioed for help if trouble had come on slowly—a leak or a gradual foundering, for example. "Whatever happened, happened quick," a former crew member from the *Hannah Boden* later said. Tyne didn't even have time to grab the radio and shout.

• • •

Waves of unimaginable proportions have been recorded over the years. When Sir Ernest Shackleton skippered an open sailboat off the South Georgian Islands on May 1916, he saw a wave so big that he mistook the foaming crest for a break in the clouds. "It's clearing boys!" he yelled to his crew, and then, moments later: "For God's sake, hold on, it's got us!" By some miracle they managed to survive. In 1933 in the South Pacific an officer on the USS *Ramapo* looked to stern and saw a wave that was later calculated to be 112 feet high. In 1984 a three-masted schooner named the *Marques* was struck by a single wave that sent her down in less than a minute, taking nineteen people with her. Nine survived, including a strapping young Virginian who managed to force his way up through a rising column of water and out an open hatch.

Oceanographers call these "extreme waves" or "rogues." Old-time Maine fishermen call them "queer ones." They have roared down the stacks of navy destroyers, torn the bows off containerships, and broken cargo vessels in two.

When the rogue hit the *Andrea Gail*, sometime between midnight and dawn on October 29, Tyne would probably have been alone in the wheelhouse and already exhausted after twenty-four hours at the helm. Captains, unwilling to relinquish the wheel to inexperienced crew, have been known to drive for two or even three days straight. The crew would have been below deck, either in the kitchen or in their staterooms. Once in a while one of the men would have come up to keep Tyne company. In the privacy of the wheelhouse he might have admitted his fears: This is bad, this is the worst I've ever seen. There's no way we could inflate a life raft in these conditions. If a hatch breaks open, if anything lets go . . .

Tyne must have looked back and seen an exceptionally big wave rising up behind him. It would have been at least seventy feet high, maybe a hundred. The stern of the boat would have risen up sickeningly and hurled the men from their bunks. The *Andrea Gail* would have flipped end over end and landed hull up, exploding the wheelhouse windows. Tyne, upside down in his steel cage, would have drowned without a word. The five men below deck would have landed on the ceiling. The ones who remained conscious would have known that it was impossible to escape through an open hatch and swim out from under the boat. And even if they could, what then? How would they have found their survival suits, the life raft?

The *Andrea Gail* would have rolled drunkenly and started to fill. Water would have sprayed through bursting gaskets and risen in a column from the wheelhouse stairway. It would have reached the men in their staterooms, and it would have been cold enough to take their breath away. At least the end would have come fast.

• • •

It wasn't until Tuesday afternoon that the boats on the Grand Banks were able to check in with one another. The *Eishan Maru,* which was closest to Billy Tyne's last known location, reported that she was completely rolled by one huge wave; her wheelhouse windows were blown out, and she was left without rudder or electronics. The *Lori Dawn Eight* had taken so much water down her vents that she lost an engine and headed in. The *Mary T* had fared well but had already taken $165,000 worth of fish in nine days, so she headed in, too. The *Hannah Boden,* the *Allison,* the *Mr. Simon,* and the *Miss Millie* were way to the east and "had beautiful weather," in Albert Johnston's words. That left the *Andrea Gail.*

By Wednesday, October 30, the storm had retrograded so far to the west that conditions at sea were almost tolerable. At that point the worst of it was just hitting Gloucester. The Eastern Point neighborhood, where the town's well-to-do live, had been cut in half. Waves were rolling right through the woods and into some of the nicest living rooms in the state. On the Back Shore, thirty-foot waves were tearing the façades off houses and claiming whole sections of Ocean Drive. The wind, whipping through the power lines, was hitting pitches that no one had ever heard before. Just up the coast in Kennebunkport, some Democrats cheered to see boulders in the family room of President Bush's summer mansion.

"The only light I can shed on the severity of the storm is that until then, we had never—ever—had a lobster trap move offshore," said Bob Brown. "Some were moved thirteen miles to the west. It was the worst storm I have ever heard of, or experienced."

By now the storm had engulfed nearly the entire eastern seaboard. Even in protected Boston Harbor, a data buoy measured wave heights of thirty feet. A Delta Airlines pilot at Boston's Logan Airport was surprised to see spray topping two-hundred-foot construction cranes on Deer Island. Sitting on the runway waiting for clearance, his air-speed indicator read eighty miles per hour. Off Cape Cod, a sloop named the *Satori* lost its life raft, radios, and engine. The three people in its crew had resigned themselves to writing good-bye notes when they were finally rescued two hundred miles south of Nantucket by a Coast Guard swimmer who jumped, untethered, from a helicopter into the roiling waves. An Air National Guard helicopter ran out of fuel off Long Island, and its crew had to jump one at a time through the darkness into the sea. One man was killed; the other four were rescued after drifting throughout the night. All along the coast, waves and storm surge combined to act as "dams" that prevented rivers from flowing into the sea. The Hudson backed up one hundred miles to Albany and caused flooding; so did the Potomac.

Brown tried in vain all day Wednesday to radio Tyne. That evening he finally got through to Linda Greenlaw, who said she'd last heard Billy Tyne talking to other boats on the radio Monday night. "Those men sounded really scared, and we were scared for them," she said later. Later that night Brown finally alerted the U.S. Coast Guard.

"When were they due in?" the dispatcher asked.

"Next Saturday," Brown replied.

The dispatcher refused to initiate a search because the boat wasn't overdue yet. Brown then got the Canadian Coast Guard on the line. "I'm afraid my boat's in trouble, and I fear the worst," he told the dispatcher in Halifax. At dawn Canadian reconnaissance planes, which were already in the area, began sweeping for the *Andrea Gail.*

Two days later, a U.S. Coast Guard cutter and five aircraft were also on the case. But there was no clue about the missing boat until November 5, when the Coast Guard positively identified the *Andrea Gail's* radio beacon and propane tank, which had washed up on Sable Island. "The recovered debris is loose gear and could have washed overboard during heavy weather," said Petty Officer Elizabeth Brannan. "No debris has been located that indicates the *Andrea Gail* has been sunk."

The search had covered more than sixty-five thousand square miles at that point. In heavy seas it's hard for a pilot to be sure he is seeing everything—one Coast Guard pilot reported spotting a five-hundred-foot ship that he had completely missed on a previous flight—so no one was leaping to any conclusions. Two days and thirty-five thousand square miles later, though, it was hard not to assume the worst: Now the *Andrea Gail's* emergency position-indicating radio beacon (EPIRB) had been found. It, too, had washed up on the beaches of Sable Island.

An EPIRB is a device about the size of a bowling pin that automatically emits a radio signal if it floats free of its shipboard holster. The signal travels via satellite to onshore listening posts, where Coast Guard operators decode the name of the boat and her location to within two miles. EPIRBs have been required equipment for fishing vessels on the high seas since 1990. The only catch is that the device must be turned on, something captains do automatically when they leave port. ("It's not the sort of thing you forget," says one captain.) Though Bob Brown insists that the *Andrea Gail's* EPIRB had been turned on when it left port, it was found on Sable Island disarmed.

The Coast Guard called off the search on November 8, eleven days after the *Andrea Gail* had presumably gone down. Search planes had covered 116,000 square miles of ocean. "After taking into account the water temperature and other factors, we felt the probability of survival was minimal," Coast Guard lieutenant Brian Krenzien told reporters at the time. The water temperature was forty-six degrees. When a man falls overboard on the Grand Banks that late in the year, there usually isn't even time to turn the boat around.

• • •

"I finally gave up hope after the Coast Guard called the search off," says Ethel Shatford, Bobby Shatford's mother, at the Crow's Nest. "It was very hard, though. You always read stories about people being found floating around in boats. The memorial was on November 16. There were more than a thousand people. This bar and the bar next door were closed, and we had enough food for everyone for three days. Recently we had a service for a New Bedford boat that went down last winter. None of the crew was from here, but they were fishermen."

The Crow's Nest is a low, dark room with wood-veneer paneling and a horseshoe bar where regulars pour their own drinks. On the wall below the television is a photo of Bobby Shatford and another of the *Andrea Gail*, as well as a plaque for the six men who died. Upstairs there are cheap guest rooms where deckhands often stay.

Ethel Shatford is a strong, gray-faced Gloucester native in her late fifties. Three of her own sons have fished, and over the years she has served as den mother to scores of young fishermen on the Gloucester waterfront. Four of the six men who died on the *Andrea Gail* spent their last night onshore in the rooms of the Crow's Nest.

"My youngest graduated high school last June and went fishing right off the b-a-t," she says. "That was what he always wanted to do, fish with his brothers. Bobby's older brother, Rick, used to fish the *Andrea Gail* years ago."

She draws a draft beer for a customer and continues. "The *Andrea Gail* crew left from this bar. They were all standing over there by the pool table saying good-bye. About the only thing different that time was that Billy Tyne let them take our color TV on the boat. He said, 'Ethel, they can take the TV, but if they watch it instead of doing their work, the TV's going overboard.' I said, 'That's fine, Billy, that's fine.'"

That was the last time Shatford ever saw her son. Recently, a young guy drifted into town who looked so much like Bobby that people were stopping and staring on the street. He walked into the Crow's Nest, and another bartender felt it necessary to explain to him why everyone was looking at him. "He went over to the picture of Bobby and says, 'If I sent that picture to my mother, she'd think it was me.'"

Linda Greenlaw still comes into the bar from time to time, between trips, swearing that someday she's going to "meet the right guy and retire to a small island in Maine." Bob Brown settled out of court with several of the dead crewmembers' families after two years of legal wrangles. Adam Randall, the man who had stepped off the *Andrea Gail* at the last minute, went on to crew with Albert Johnston on the *Mary T.* When he found out that the *Andrea Gail* had sunk in the storm, all he could say was, "I was supposed to have been on that boat. That was supposed to have been me."

During the spring of 1993 the *Mary T* was hauled out for repairs, and Randall picked up work on a tuna long-liner, the *Terri Lei*, out of Georgetown, South Carolina. On the evening of April 6, 1993, the crew of the *Terri Lei* set lines. In the early morning, there were reports of gusty winds and extremely choppy seas in the area. At 8:45 A.M. the Coast Guard in Charleston, South Carolina, picked up an EPIRB signal and sent out two aircraft and a cutter to investigate. By then the weather was fair and the seas were moderate. One hundred and thirty-five miles off the coast, they found the EPIRB, some fishing gear, and a self-inflating life raft. The raft had the name *Terri Lei* stenciled on it. There was no one on board.

OCTOBER 1994

GOING PLACES

by JIM HARRISON

Everyone remembers those kindergarten or first-grade jigsaw puzzles of the forty-eight states, not including Hawaii or Alaska, which weren't states when I was a child and perhaps for that reason are permanently beyond my sphere of interest. I'm not at all sure at what age a child begins to comprehend the abstraction of maps—Arthur Rimbaud's line about the "child crazed with maps" strikes home. Contiguous states in the puzzle were of different colors, establishing the notion that states are more different from one another than they really are. The world grows larger with the child's mind, but each new step doesn't abolish the previous steps, so it's not much more than a big child who finally gets a driver's license, certainly equivalent to losing your virginity in the list of life's prime events.

It is at this point that pathology enters: Out of a hundred drivers the great majority find cars pleasant enough, and some will be obsessed with them in mechanical terms, but two or three out of the hundred will be obsessed with going places, pure and simple, for the sake of movement, anywhere and practically anytime.

"You haven't been anywhere until you've taken Route 2 through the Sand Hills of Nebraska," they're liable to say, late at night.

"Or Route 191 in Montana, 35 in Wisconsin, 90 in West Texas, 28 in the Upper Peninsula of Michigan, 120 in Wyoming, 62 in Arkansas, 83 in Kansas, 14 in Louisiana," I reply, after agreeing that 2 in Nebraska is one of my favorites. To handle Route 2 properly, you should first give a few hours to the Stuhr Museum in Grand Island to check on the human and natural history of the Great Plains. If you don't care all that much about what you're seeing, you should stay home or, if you're just trying to get someplace, take a plane.

There is, of course, a hesitation to make any rules for the road; the main reason you're out there is to escape any confinement other than that of change and motion. But certain precepts and theories should be kept in mind:

• Don't compute time and distance. Computing time and distance vitiates the benefits to be gotten from aimlessness. Leave that sort of thing to civilians with their specious categories of birthdays, average wage, height and weight, the number of steps to second floors. If you get into this acquisitive mood, make two ninety-degree turns and backtrack for a while. Or stop the car and run around in a big circle in a field. Climbing a tree or going swimming also helps. Remember that habit is a form of gravity that strangulates.

• Leave your reason, your logic, at home. A few years ago I flew all the way from northern Michigan to Palm Beach, Florida, in order to drive to Livingston, Montana, with a friend. Earlier in life I hitchhiked 4,000 miles round-trip to see the Pacific Ocean. Last year I needed to do some research in Nebraska. Good sense and the fact that it was January told me to drive south, then west by way of Chicago, spend a few days, and drive home. Instead I headed due north into a blizzard and made a three-day backroad circle to La Crosse, Wisconsin, one of my favorite hideouts. When I finished in Nebraska, I went to Wyoming, pulled a left for Colorado and New Mexico, a right for Arizona, headed east across Texas and Louisiana to Alabama, then north toward home. My spirit was lightened by the thirty-five days and 8,000 or so miles. The car was a loaner, and on deserted back roads I could drive on cruise control, standing on the seat with shoulders and head through the sunroof.

• Spend as little time as possible thinking about the equipment. Assuming you are not a mechanic, and even if you are, it's better not to think too much about the car over and above minimum service details. I've had a succession of three four-wheel-drive Subaru station wagons, each equipped with a power winch, although recently I've had doubts about this auto. I like to take the car as far as I can go up a two-track, then get out and walk until the road disappears. This is the only solution to the neurotic pang that you might be missing something. High-performance cars don't have the clearance for back roads, and orthodox four-wheel drives are too jouncy for long trips. An ideal car might be a Saab turbo four-wheel-drive station wagon, but it has not as yet been built by that dour land without sunshine and garlic. A Range Rover is a pleasant, albeit expensive, idea, but you could very well find yourself a thousand miles from a spare part.

• A little research during downtime helps. This is the place for the lost art of reading. The sort of driving I'm talking about is a religious impulse, a craving for the unknown. You can, however, add to any trip immeasurably by knowing something about the history of the area or location. For instance, if you're driving through Chadron, Nebraska, on Route 20, it doesn't hurt to know that Crazy Horse, He Dog, American Horse, Little Big Man, and Sitting Bull took the same route when it was still a buffalo path.

• Be careful about who you are with. Whiners aren't appropriate. There can be tremendous inconveniences and long stretches of boredom. It takes a specific amount of optimism to be on the road, and anything less means misery. A nominal Buddhist who knows that "the goal is the path" is at an advantage. The essential silence of the highway can allow couples to turn the road into a domestic mud bath by letting their petty grievances preoccupy them. Marriages survive by garden-variety etiquette, and when my wife and I travel together we forget the often suffocating flotsam and jetsam of marriage.

If you're driving solo, another enemy can be the radio or tape deck. This is an eccentric observation, but anyone under fifty in America has likely dissipated a goodly share of his life listening to music. Music frequently draws you out of where you belong. It is hard work to be attentive, but it's the only game in town. D. H. Lawrence said that "the only true aristocracy is consciousness," which doesn't mean you can't listen to music; just don't do it all the time. Make your own road tapes: Start with cuts of Del Shannon, Merle Haggard, Stravinsky, Aretha Franklin, Bob Seger, Mozart, Buffett, Monteverdi, Woody Guthrie, Jim Reeves, B. B. King, George Jones, Esther Lammandier, Ray Charles, Bob Wills, and Nicholas Thorne. That sort of thing.

If you're lucky, you can find a perfect companion. During a time of mutual stress I drove around Arizona with the grizzly bear expert Douglas Peacock, who knows every piece of flora, fauna, and Native American history in that state. In such company, the most unassertive mesa becomes verdant with possibility.

• Pretend you don't care about good food. This is intensely difficult if you are a professional pig, gourmand, and trencherman like I am. If you're going to drive around America you have to adopt the bliss-ninny notion that less is more. Pack a cooler full of disgusting health snacks. I am assuming you know enough to stay off the interstates with their sneeze shields and rainbow Jell-Os, the dinner specials that include the legendary "fried, fried," a substantial meal spun out of hot fat by the deep-fry cook. It could be anything from a shoe box full of oxygen to a cow plot to a dime-store wig. In honor of my own precepts I have given up routing designed to hit my favorite restaurants in Escanaba, Duluth, St. Cloud (Ivan's in the Park), Mandan, Miles City, and so on. The quasi-food revolution hasn't hit the countryside; I've had good luck calling disc jockeys for advice. You generally do much better in the South, particularly at barbecue places with hand-painted road signs. Along with food you might also consider amusements: If you stop at local bars or American Legion country dances don't offer underage girls hard drugs and that sort of thing. But unless you're a total asshole, *Easy Rider* paranoia is unwarranted. You are technically safer on the road than you are in your own bathroom or eating a dinner of unrecognizable leftovers with your mother.

• Avoid irony, cynicism, and self-judgment. If you were really smart, you probably wouldn't be doing this. You would be in an office or club acting nifty, but you're in a car and no one knows you, and no one calls you because they don't know where you are. Moving targets are hard to hit. You are doing what you want, rather than what someone else wants. This is not the time to examine your shortcomings, which will certainly surface when you get home. Your spiritual fathers range from Marco Polo to Arthur Rimbaud, from Richard Halliburton to Jack Kerouac. Kerouac was the first actual novelist I ever met, back in 1957 or 1958 at the Five Spot, a jazz club in New York City. I saw him several times, and this great soul did not dwell on self-criticism, though, of course, there is an obvious downside to this behavior.

• Do not scorn day trips. You can use them to avoid nervous collapse. They are akin to the ardent sailor and his small sailboat. You needn't travel very far unless you live in one of our major urban centers, strewn across the land like immense canker sores. Outside this sort of urban concentration, county maps are available at any courthouse. One summer in Michigan's Upper Peninsula, after a tour in Hollywood had driven me ditzy, I logged more than 5,000 miles in four counties on gravel roads and two-tracks, lifting my sodden spirits and looking for good grouse and woodcock cover (game birds literally prefer to live in their restaurants, their prime feeding areas). This also served to keep me out of bars and away from drinking, because I don't drink while driving.

• Plan a real big one—perhaps hemispheric, or at least national. Atrophy is the problem. If you're not expanding, you're growing smaller. As a poet and novelist I have to get out of the study and collect some brand-new memories, and many of our more memorable events are of the childish, the daffy and irrational. "How do you know but that every bird that cuts the airy way is an immense world of delight closed to your senses five?" asked Blake. If you're currently trapped, your best move is to imagine the next road voyage.

I'm planning a trip when I finish my current novel, for which I had to make an intense study of the years 1865 to 1900 in our history, also the history of Native Americans. I intend to check out locations where I sensed a particular magic in the past: certain culverts in western Minnesota, nondescript gullies in

Kansas, invisible graveyards in New Mexico, moonbeam targets in Nebraska, buffalo jumps in Montana, melted ice palaces in the Dakotas, deserted but well-stocked wine warehouses in California. Maybe I'll discover a new bird or animal. Maybe I'll drive up a gravel road that winnows into a two-track that stops at an immense swale, in the center of which is a dense woodlot. I'll wade through the bog into the woods, where I'll find an old, gray farmhouse. In this farmhouse I'll find all my beloved dead dogs and cats in perfect health, tended by the heroines in my novels. I'll make a map of this trip on thin buckskin that I'll gradually cut up and add to stews. Everyone must find his own places.

JUNE 1987

NO CANNIBAL JOKES, PLEASE

by TIM CAHILL

It was, I suppose, a single piece of ineptly executed and cynically fashioned art that sent me fleeing five hundred miles upriver, back into time, and deep into the malarial heart of the swamp. The people I wanted to meet—it was only later that I would come to know them as Karowai—lived a Stone Age life and knew almost nothing of the outside world. They were, some said, headhunters, cannibals, savages. If so, they still owned their own lives.

Which didn't seem to be the case with the people who lived in the administrative center located at the mouth of the great river that drained the swamp. It was only my second night in the town of Agats, and it was raining, again, here on the southern coast of Indonesian Irian Jaya, the western half of the island of New Guinea. Torrential rain hissed into the Arafura Sea, and it pounded down onto the slick brown tidal mudflats. This area, known as the Asmat, is named after the region's most famous inhabitants and is the world's largest swampland.

The electricity in the town dimmed, sputtered, and died. It was 100 degrees at eight in the evening, and the wooden boardwalk, set fifteen feet above the mudflats, was slick and treacherous as I followed a man who called himself Rudy past darkened and shuttered clapboard buildings. There were fine things Rudy thought I needed to see. Artifacts I should buy.

Rudy's aboriginal art shop was another clapboard affair, and rain thundered down on the galvanized-tin roof of the place. The electricity in the town blinked on for a second—a flash of sickly orange—then coughed piteously and died for the night.

This was not unexpected, and Rudy carried a flashlight. He was an Indonesian but not a native inhabitant of Agats; Rudy came from Java, the capital island of the Indonesian archipelago. He was a short, slender man with burnished golden skin and straight black hair. He wore a lime-green polo shirt with an alligator over the place where his heart might have been, and his shirt was open to display a small gold Playboy bunny hanging from a thin chain around his neck.

Rudy was in the business of selling native Asmat art. The Asmat are Papuans, sturdy black people related to Australian aboriginals and thought to be linked to the "Java Man" who lived over half a million years ago. The word "Papuan" derives from a Malay word, *papuwah*, meaning "frizzy-haired."

Throughout the whole of recorded time—and as recently as the 1960s—the Asmat people were the most feared cannibals in the southern swamps. Head-hunting formed the core of a complex system of survival designed to appease various malevolent spirits. Art was essential to that life, and the Asmat were master carvers. Their ancestral columns—which look a bit like totem poles as envisioned by Giacometti—were delicate, flowing poems of war and revenge. Asmat carvings, coveted by collectors, are included in the permanent collections of the Museum of Primitive Art and the Metropolitan Museum in New York.

By the 1990s, tribal warfare was very nearly a thing of the past, and the spiritual impetus that fashioned Asmat art had been degraded. Javanese sharpies like Rudy hired villagers to hack out sad, uninspired pieces that could be sold to unwary visitors, most of whom came off adventure cruise ships.

Rudy's darkened shop was filled with carvings piled one atop the other and marked with tags that read SHIP, PRICE, CABIN NUMBER. Broken pieces lay in a pile and occupied a corner of the shop. The replications of ancestral carvings, the bis poles, had been fashioned quickly, out of soft wood—not the traditional ironwood—and the spirits did not dwell in them.

Rudy sensed my growing irritation and turned the yellowing beam of his flashlight onto a squat wooden carving he imagined I might be inclined to purchase. I stared at a blocky chunk of wood, coarsely chiseled to represent a man and a woman locked in a carnal embrace. The soulless figure was as crude as something scrawled on a bathroom wall and had nothing to do with the delicacy of traditional carving that did, indeed, sometimes encompass copulatory scenes. Rudy's dying light illuminated the clunky travesty and lingered on splotches of black paint meant to represent pubic hair.

"Sexy," he whispered.

I thought for a moment of Michael Rockefeller, who had visited the Asmat in 1961 as part of a Harvard Peabody expedition, and returned soon after to purchase art for an exhibition in the United States. Rockefeller planned to visit some of the more remote villages near Agats, but his boat capsized in a fierce tide and was driven out into the Arafura Sea. His two Asmat guides swam to shore, where they summoned help. Rockefeller and a Dutch art expert, René Wassing, stayed with the overturned boat. The next morning, Rockefeller, tired of waiting, left Wassing with the boat and began to swim toward shore, which was four to seven miles away. He was never seen again.

Rockefeller was a good swimmer, and he had rigged up a flotation device out of two empty jerricans. There are sharks in those waters, as well as man-eating crocodiles. The tide was also very heavy.

Nevertheless, at least one local missionary believes Rockefeller was a victim of ritual cannibalism. Had he made it to shore, Rockefeller would have washed up near the village of Otsjanep. At the time Irian Jaya was a Dutch colony, and some years earlier Dutch police investigating a head-hunting incident at Otsjanep had killed the local chief and four others. The Asmat believe that a man killed in war will not rest until avenged by the death of an enemy. Rockefeller, naked and defenseless, would have been seen as a representative of the "white tribe."

Whatever the truth of the matter, it can be argued that Michael Rockefeller died for art.

Rudy moved in close to the sad, sorry copulation figure, trained his light on the genitals, and said again, "Sexy."

It was not a piece to die for.

"Rudy," I said. "I gotta get out of here."

I wanted to go upriver. Back in time.

The boat was a forty-foot-long dugout, no more than three feet wide, and powered by a forty-horsepower kerosene Yamaha engine. My traveling companion, photographer Chris Ranier, had wanted to get out of Agats very badly. He is best known for his documentation of endangered and disappearing cultures, and Agats was a town where you went to the Asmat museum because traditional culture was, as they say, history.

We had no radio in the big dugout, only a bit of rice, one spare propeller, and two burlap bags full of trade goods. Our guide, William Rumbarar, was a Papuan from the nearby island of Biak, and it was William who hired two local Asmat boatmen to accompany us: Conrados Kamau was a slender, clever man, good with engines, and Stef Metemeo was a short, muscular gentleman with an infectious smile, who functioned as the Minister of Morale for our trip back in time.

There were plenty of Javanese guides available in Agats, but the native Papuans seemed to distrust all Javanese out of hand, reason enough to choose a Papuan guide. And William, for his part, knew his stuff. One recent book on the Asmat, for instance, suggested that there were neolithic peoples living in tree houses only a few hundred miles upriver and that these Stone Age tribes were friendly and welcomed visitors. William had been there.

"Gone," he told us. "All modern now." By which he meant that the people had come down out of the trees and that they now lived in clapboard houses with tin roofs. The children all went to school, the adults went to church, and everyone wore missionary-clothing-drive T-shirts and shorts. It wasn't that my book was incorrect: All this had happened in the five years since it was published. "Change is very fast now," William said.

That change—the homogenization of humanity—seems to be the direction of history. There is a certain sad inevitability about it all. For the upriver people in the Asmat, it happens like this: Missionaries come, followed by the government in the form of soldiers and policemen and bureaucrats. And then the multinational developers arrive, hard on the heels of the government, and they promise a better life to anyone who wants to log the forest and farm the waste. Perhaps the development would involve mining or petrochemical exploration, but the result has always been the same. Everywhere. The living culture is entombed within museums.

Still, William explained, if we wanted to go farther upriver, deeper into the swamp, he knew of some people who still lived in the trees, people who used stone tools and were largely ignorant of the outside world. If this was, in fact, the case—the irony wasn't lost on me—I would be an agent of the changes that offended my romantic notions of human diversity. I would personally entomb some of the living culture in prose, and Chris would document it on film. Perhaps, several generations down the line, young people in the Asmat would study his photographs in an attempt to understand what had happened to them.

"How far upriver are these people?" I wanted to know.

"Past Senggo."

Senggo? Where had I read about Senggo? I paged through the best and most recent guidebook I had been able to find, *Irian Jaya*, by Kal Muller (Periplus Editions, Berkeley, California). The book, published in 1990, said, "Some unacculturated ethnic groups live in the jungles upriver from Senggo." Very good. However: "Cannibalism is frequently reported and surely practiced here."

"Who are these people you know upriver?" I asked William.

He said, "Care-oh-eye." Karowai.

Muller's book didn't have a lot of encouraging things to say about Karowai hospitality. It said, in fact, that they were cannibals. The Dutch Reformed

Church has been proselytizing among the estimated 3,000 or so Karowai for ten years and has yet to celebrate a single baptism. One missionary, the Reverend Gert van Enk, calls Karowai country "the hell of the south." Van Enk himself, according to Muller, "is not allowed into most of the tribal territory, and if caught there would be pin-cushioned with arrows." Confirming other sources, van Enk says that cannibalism is still common among the Karowai. A death is believed to be caused by witchcraft, and a culprit (or scapegoat) must be found, killed, and eaten by the relatives in revenge. This leads to a never-ending cycle of cannibalism.

"You sure this is, uh, safe?" I asked.

William said, "Oh yes, very safe, no problems, don't worry." And then his body was shaken by a sneezelike convulsion followed by a series of helpless, high-pitched wails. It was, I understood after thirty seconds or so, the way William laughed.

The rivers of the Asmat, seen from the air, are milky brown, the color of cafe au lait, and they meander drunkenly through varying shades of green in great loops and horseshoes. The water comes from the central highlands of New Guinea. It flows from glacier-clad peaks 15,000 feet high, and plunges through great canyons into the flatland swamps, where it forms dozens of interconnected waterways that empty into the Arafura Sea.

The Asuwetz River (also called the Baliem) is a mile wide near Agats, on the coast, and at low tide the banks are a sloping wall of slick brown mud twenty feet high. Mangrove trees, buttressed by high exposed roots, brace themselves against flood tide.

Women in long, thin dugout canoes that were the same gray-brown color as the river stood to paddle against the flow of the river. Thirty years ago, the handle of a paddle would be carved in the visage of an ancestor's face. That ancestor would have died in war and the paddle would have served to remind everyone of the necessity for revenge.

Nóne of the paddles I saw were carved in this way. Such artwork is now against the law, part of the Indonesian government's push to finally end head-hunting.

Upriver villages consisted of several poor huts set on stilts above the swampy ground. Some of the villages were arranged around rectangular houses 150 feet or more long, called yews. There were doors evenly spaced along the length of the yews, one for each family group, though only men are allowed inside. In past times, head-hunting raids were planned in the yews, and the Indonesian government sent soldiers in to burn most of them down years ago. The upriver longhouses, however, were too remote to attack and exist much as they must have centuries ago.

At the Asmat village of Kaima, we pulled into the beach fronting the yew. Mean, slinking, skinny little dogs battled pigs loudly for garbage under the yew. Women and children sat on the porch, weaving string bags made from orchid fibers.

One of the men issued a sort of command, a grunting hiss. Instantly the women and children were gone, clambering six feet down notched poles to the ground. Suddenly there were several dozen men standing on the porch. They wore shorts in varying degrees of repair, and some of the men sported T-shirts with such cryptic messages as JEAN-CLAUDE VAN DAMME—KARATE. A few of the men stood with their arms crossed over their chests, a defiant and aggressive stance in this culture.

We stopped because the chief here was said to possess five human skulls. We wanted to talk with him about the skulls, about the old ways, about the time before the missionaries. The men of Kaima, for their part, saw three strange Papuans, expensively dressed (shoes!), and two white men. It was unlikely that much good could come of such a visit.

There was an uncomfortable aura of suspicion and distrust. Conrados talked with the chief, a powerful-looking man of about thirty-five with fine, regular features and wary eyes. The chief was wearing yellow shorts and dried rattan strips around his considerable biceps.

I hunkered down by one of the dozen hearths in the yew. There were beautifully carved spears against one wall, some polished black ironwood bows, a variety of arrows with different bone points for different prey, and at least one polished but uncarved drum near each fire. All the woodwork was finer by far than any of the carvings I had seen in the boardwalk shops of Agats.

Conrados squatted by my side and explained that the chief might, in fact, have one skull. The chief didn't know for sure. Because of the missionaries and the government, he didn't know. For 20,000 rupiah (about $10) he could look.

"Tell him it's twenty thousand rupes only if he finds the skulls."

The chief disappeared. The rest of the men stood around silently. They didn't talk with Conrados. I glanced over at the finely carved weapons. It was all very uncomfortable. We seemed to frighten the men of Kaima just about as much as they frightened us.

Presently, the chief returned with the improbable information that he couldn't find his skulls. Misplaced the pesky buggers. There were, he told Conrados, too many people around for him to be able to find his skulls. The missionaries. The government.

We had already seen an illegal Asmat skull outside of Agats, in the village of Syuru. It was a twenty-minute walk from town over a wide, well-maintained boardwalk set variously five and fifteen feet above the boggy ground. After about ten minutes, the wooden walkway began to deteriorate precipitously.

There were missing planks, rotted planks, broken planks, and then no planks at all, only a few sticks. One of these broke under my weight, and I grabbed at something that held and then swung there for a moment, like a kid on the monkey bars.

Syuru was a small, traditional village of thatched-roofed huts on stilts. There were no boardwalks in the village itself, only a series of half-submerged bark walkways. As I wobbled my way over narrow tree trunks—small children took my hand to steady me in this process—a humming, murmurous sound I had been hearing for some time began to separate itself into individual moans and wails.

An important man had died the day before. Now the women had covered their bodies with ashes and soot. They would mourn in this fashion for seven days. The sounds were coming from several houses at once. Wailing and moaning would build to a crescendo and then subside for a moment. Suddenly a loud voice from one of the houses—sometimes it was a man's voice; sometimes, a woman's—would shout out a hoarse, anguished speech in Asmat. I had no translator, but I imagined the words were something like: "He was a good man; he worshipped his ancestors, he fed his family, and now he's gone." And the moaning and wailing and shrieking would start all over again.

In the swamplands of the Asmat, all the dead return as ghosts, but those improperly mourned can be malevolent. They can make a living relative's life hell. A cranky ancestor strews banana peels across the path of life. Literally. People in the Asmat don't fall down without a reason.

When someone dies, a proper show of grief makes a favorable impression on the recently deceased, who can then protect his descendants from all those evil spirits that populate the netherworld.

The yew at Syuru was separated from the village proper by the boardwalk. The night before, Conrados, a local Asmat, had spoken to the men of Syuru. Here the men were expecting us, and there were no women on the porch in front of the dozen doorways. It was 9:00 A.M. and most of the children were in school. It was a good time to talk heads with the guys.

The yew was two hundred feet long, at a guess, with high rafters, and there were at least fifteen fires, all set in a row, in the center of the structure and neatly spaced along the length of the floor. Only a few of the older men were present, and when a couple of schoolchildren stopped on the boardwalk to see what was going on, a thin, muscular man in threadbare gray shorts ducked through the door. He stood on the porch and said "Scram" in Asmat. The sound, the same one I heard in Kaima, is a grunting hiss. The children hurried off down the boardwalk without looking back.

The men squatting around the fires in the yew wore shorts, and they smoked clove-scented Indonesian cigarettes called kreteks. This smell mingled with the odor of woodsmoke and singed pig fat. No doubt human flesh—locally called "long pig"—had been cooked over these fires in past generations.

An older man in faded beige shorts smeared his face and chest with white ashes. He put on a feathered headdress made of bird-of-paradise feathers and produced a fire-blackened human skull from the bag. It was all very surreptitious, and there was a good deal of looking around, because we were engaged in something everyone knew was illegal. The sounds of mourning, across the way in the small huts, rose to another tormented crescendo.

I noticed that the skull lacked the lower jaw, which meant it was the trophy of a head-hunting raid. The skulls of powerful ancestors, sometimes kept as safeguards against evil spirits, are invariably intact, the lower jaw lashed to the skull with strands of rattan. Head-hunting trophies, on the other hand, are invariably missing the lower jaws, which are detached and worn on a necklace: a fearsome emblem of proficiency in war.

The man with the skull—no names: the missionaries; the government—demonstrated the value of the powerful skull. He rolled out a palm mat and lay down with his head balanced atop the blackened skull. It did not look like a comfortable way to nap.

During sleep, I had read, a man is most vulnerable to the evil influence of the spirit world. Therefore it is wise to keep a skull nearby during sleep. Men formerly slept in the yew using the powerful skulls of their ancestors, or their enemies, as pillows. Across the rotting boardwalk, a man's rich baritone voice called out a long, sing-song lament. And then, from twenty houses, the sobs and shrieks and wails began anew.

I stared at the man on the mat, whose eyes were closed and who might have actually been asleep. He seemed perfectly serene.

We were well above Kaima and had been motoring against the current for ten hours. Here, about 250 miles upriver, the villages generally consisted of a yew and four or five huts. They were separated, one from the other, by twenty or thirty or fifty miles. There had been two short afternoon rainstorms, tropical downpours accompanied by rumbling, ominous thunder. The sky was all rainbows and bruised Wagnerian clouds. The forest overhung the river and it seemed to me, in my ignorance, all of a piece: unvariegated greenery.

The river was flowing down to the now distant sea at about three or four miles an hour, but it looked sluggish, weighted down with brown silt, and its surface was a viscous brown mirror reflecting the overhanging greenery and the operatic sky. Yellow leaves, like flowers, floated among the reflected clouds. A swirling mass of neon-bright blue butterflies swept across our bow in a psychedelic haze. The world felt like the inside of a greenhouse, and the air was heavy with moisture and the fragrance of orchids.

A snowy egret kept pace with the boat, and blue-gray herons, looking vaguely prehistoric, rose from the banks of the river in a series of horrid strangled croaks. In the forest, cockatoos screeched loudly enough to be heard over the laboring of our kerosene engine. The cockatoos bickered among themselves: ridiculous, self-important dandies with their white feathers and marching-band topknots.

Chris and I bickered with a good deal more dignity, I thought. He likes to sing, and has a completely monotonous voice, which is entirely beside the point. The point is—and this can't be stressed too strongly—*Chris Ranier gets the words wrong.*

"Wooly wooly, bully bully . . ."

"Chris."

"What?"

"It's 'Wooly bully, wooly bully.' "

"That's what I was singing."

"You weren't. You were singing, 'Wooly wooly, bully bully.' "

" 'Wooly wooly, bully bully'?"

"Yeah. 'Wooly wooly, bully bully.' Not 'Wooly bully, wooly bully.' "

" 'Wooly bully, wooly bully'?"

In the midst of this perfectly asinine conversation, William erupted in a convulsive sneezing snort, followed by a series of high-pitched wails. And then Stef and Conrados buried their heads in their hands and wailed, as if in helpless grief.

"Bully bully," Chris sang, "wooly wooly."

I moved to the bow of the boat and sat sulking about this insult to Sam the Sham when what appeared to be the soggy brown remnant of some flood-felled tree suddenly disappeared from the surface of the river with a faint splash and a swirl of bubbles.

Crocodiles were once plentiful in these rivers, and local people considered them something of a bother. One famous beasty took up residence near the Asmat village of Piramat and killed fifty-five human beings before it, in turn, was killed in 1970. The animal was twenty-three feet long.

These days, crocs are seldom seen in the larger rivers. They were hunted for their hides in the late 1970s, and now, William said, they are usually found only in narrow backwaters, deep in the swamp.

Just before sunset we passed a village where a thin, attenuated man who might have been painted by El Greco paddled out to sell William some fish in exchange for a quarter-pound of tobacco. It cost another quarter-pound of the stuff to buy a large black bird with a blue mane like a stiff doily that ran from just above its eyes to the back of its neck. The bird was about the size of a large duck. It had bright red eyes with black pupils. William said that the bird was a mambruk and that it was going to be our dinner. I thought: I can't eat this. It would be like chomping down on the goddamn *Mona Lisa.*

The water took on the impressionistic pinks and yellows of a pastel sunset, so the reflected greenery on its surface was alive with color. Our wake, in the pink-yellow water, was for a moment bloodred.

There was a half moon already rising in the pastel sky. A huge bat, the size of a goose, passed overhead and was silhouetted against the moon. These mammals, sometimes called flying foxes, are nothing like the horrors in Grandma's attic. They're actually kind of cute, with velvety, foxlike faces, and they fly in straight lines or great curving swoops, beating their wings slowly, with eerie deliberation, like pelicans. I caught the acrid stench of ammonia— bat droppings—and guessed that the flying foxes probably roosted in some nearby trees. And then there were hundreds more of them, passing across the moon, in the final dying of the light.

The river was milky in the moonlight, incredibly bright against the black forest that blotted out the sky to either side. Stef knelt in the bow of the boat, watching for floating logs and fallen trees. It seemed to me that some of the logs simply swam away, though the rippling lunar ribbon that stretched out ahead of us set the mind whirling through various fandangos of fancied dread.

Senggo, the only upriver settlement marked on most maps, was a neatly arranged village of about twenty houses positioned face-to-face across a muddy raised-grass track flanked by irrigation ditches on both sides. The place was quite "modern" by William's definition: clapboard houses; tin roofs; a two-story residence; two homes with glass windows; latrines built over deeply dug trenches; large, adequately drained agricultural projects; a resident missionary; and even a policeman available to stamp and sign our *surat jalan* (literally: "travel letter") in exchange for only a very minor bribe.

No one seemed particularly concerned when I told them we were going upriver to see the Karowai, though nuances of meaning were a bit difficult to discern with my Indonesian vocabulary of about a hundred words.

"*Karowai bagus orang-orang?*"

No, they're not good.

"*Karowai tidak bagus orang-orang?*"

No, they're not bad.

"*Apa?*"

They're Karowai.

The storekeeper—he stocked bottled water, Lux soap, canned corned beef, sardines, margarine, T-shirts, towels, and shorts—welcomed us into his home, where we slept, sweating, on rattan mats as clouds of mosquitoes had their bloody way with us.

A goodly number of roosters spent the entire evening practicing for the dawn, so we were up before first light and back out onto the river at sunrise. A horde of schoolchildren stood on the dock and shouted good-byes. We had spent almost twelve hours in the company of dozens of people. The Stone Age was only a few more days upriver.

William spent several hours teaching me to finally see the swamp. The tall trees? The ones over there that grow from a single white-barked trunk and have elephant-ear-size leaves? Those are called sukun, and the Karowai eat the fruit, which is a little like coconut.

Stands of bamboo often grew on the banks of the river, in a green starburst pattern that arched out over the water. Banana trees also grew in a starburst pattern of wide, flat leaves. They reached heights of seven or eight feet, and yielded small three- and four-inch-long bananas.

Rattan, a long, tough vine used to lash homes together, to string bows, or to tie off anything that needed tying—the local equivalent of duct tape—was identifiable as a slender, leafless branch, generally towering up out of a mass of greenery like an antenna.

Sago, the staple food, was a kind of palm tree that grew twenty to thirty feet high, in a series of multiple stems that erupted out of a central base in another starburst pattern. The leaves were shaped like the arching banana leaves but were arranged in fronds.

When sago trees are cut, William explained, the trunks are split open and an ironwood stick is used to pry out the pith, which is forced through a fiber screen to separate the fibrous material from the sappy juice. The juice is a sticky blue-gray starchy fluid, about the consistency of library glue, and the Karowai eat it every day of their lives.

The pith is pounded into a starchy extract that looks like a ball of chalk. It can be baked into a kind of doughy bread. A single sago tree yields about seventy pounds of starch. Karowai villages are located near large stands of sago.

So—sukun, rattan, bamboo, banana, sago—the forest was no longer a mass of unvariegated green. Naming things allowed me to see them, to differentiate one area of the swamp from another. I found myself confirming my newfound knowledge at every bend in the river. "Banana, banana," I informed everyone. "Sukun, sago, sago, rattan, sago, bamboo . . ."

William, like any good teacher, seemed proud enough of my accomplishment for the first half hour or so, then the process began to wear on him. I was like some five-year-old on a drive in the country, pointing out every cow in the pasture to his weary parents.

A river lunch: one nice hot sun-baked tin of dog-food-like corned beef with a rather mournful-looking cow on the label, a little of last night's rice, a couple of pygmy bananas. Mash it all up in a bowl, and watch the egret above, impossibly white against the blue of the sky and the green of the sago.

When the outboard began to splutter, Conrados stopped abruptly, in midriver, and began to tinker. It was unbearably hot, well over 100 degrees, and I broached the idea of a brief swim. The possible presence of crocodiles was debated. I reminded William that there were hardly any left. He reminded me that we had seen at least one the day before. Stef, standing on the gunwale of the boat, settled the debate with a front flip into the silt-laden brown water, and then, somehow, we were all in the river, splashing each other like children, surely immortal (it couldn't happen to *me*), and secure in the knowledge that the resident crocs would take someone else, a fact that would certainly sadden those of us who survived. And besides, it was *incredibly hot.*

Sometime later that afternoon, after Conrados cured the Yamaha, we traded a length of fishing line and a dozen hooks for what William assured us was *the* local culinary treat: two pounds of fat sago beetle larvae wrapped in sago leaves and secured with a thin strip of rattan. The maggoty-looking creatures were white, with brown heads, and about the size of my little finger to the second knuckle. William mimed popping one into his mouth, nodded, made a yummy-yummy sort of face, and sneezed out his good-natured laugh.

He apparently thought I'd be horrified at the idea of eating bugs. In point of fact, I'd rather eat bugs than that damn beautiful bird we had devoured the night before.

We passed men standing on rafts of five or six large logs, stripped of the branches and peeled of their bark. The logs were roped together with thick strands of rattan. Further upriver, the rafts were larger: twenty or thirty or even eighty logs. Sometimes there was a small A-frame shelter made of sukun sticks and sago leaves on the rafts.

The logs, I learned, were floated down to Senggo from here—one man said it would take about four days—where they were purchased by "men from Java" for 5,000 rupes apiece, about $2.50.

At the next raft, one of the larger ones, William had Conrados turn back, and we picked up one of the loggers, a thin young man named Agus. He was wearing a gray, tattered T-shirt and shorts. He was, William explained, one of his Karowai friends and our local contact.

The Karowai village, situated on a bend of the river, was a miniature Senggo: just a few houses on stilts facing one another across a raised path, and a flooded-out field of yams where a few men with metal shovels were digging drainage ditches. It occurred to me that cannibals aren't generally interested in yams. A blackboard in one of the open-sided buildings probably functioned as a community center and school. The men, about a dozen of them, wore shorts, and the women wore knee-length grass skirts. There were no tree houses in evidence. It seemed, all in all, a fairly civilized sort of place here in the hell of the south.

And the people, once they learned we had tobacco to trade for a place to sleep, welcomed us as brothers. Chris and I were assigned a private room in the men's house, but I felt like wandering around a bit. I saw Agus chatting urgently with a local man who wore an earring fashioned from the silver pull-tab from a softdrink can. The pull-tab glittered in the slanting light of the late afternoon sun. The man nodded several times, then dashed off, at a dead run, into the forest. The entire encounter had looked vaguely conspiratorial.

Stef cooked a dinner of fried catfish, along with a healthy portion of sago beetle. The larvae were fried brown in the pan. They were crisp and sort of fishy-tasting on the outside, probably because they had been sautéed in fish oil. Inside, the larvae were the color and consistency of custard. They were unlike anything I'd ever eaten before, and the closest I can come to describing the taste is to say creamy snail.

The people in this village, I told William after dinner, weren't the Karowai I had read about in Muller's book.

"Change is very quick now," William reminded me. Two years earlier, just after Muller published his book, the government had instituted a program designed to stop ritual warfare among the Karowai and to get people to stop eating each other. They had summoned all of the Karowai chiefs and provided transportation down to Senggo, where everyone could see the tangible benefits of civilization, like canned corned beef and Batman T-shirts. If the chiefs would agree to end their deadly feuds, the government would help them. It would provide agricultural experts, and it would help the people build grand towns like Senggo. We were, William explained, staying in one such town.

There were, however, still people who lived in the trees. They built their houses deep in the swampy forest, well away from the river, which meant well away from the government and well away from the missionaries. Tomorrow we'd take a nice little stroll through the swamp and meet them. William said that Agus lived there, in one of the tree houses. When he wasn't logging.

"Where?" I asked. "Which way?"

William pointed off in the direction that the pull-tab man had taken. And it became clear to me that Agus wanted his relatives to know that we were coming. The message was probably something like: "Yo, we got honkies; hide the heads."

We didn't actually stroll through the swamp. The forest floor was a mass of knee-high grasses, spongy marsh, and low bushes. The understory hid an uneven surface, full of brackish potholes and unexpected tussocks. The exposed roots of the larger trees humped up out of the ground in a series of ankle-breaking traps. It was much easier, all in all, to simply walk on fallen trees that happened to point off in the right general direction, and it was not easy to walk on the fallen trees at all. The larger ones were slippery with moss and the smaller ones tended to crumble under my weight.

I thought, As soon as we get through this shit, we'll be on the trail. About an hour later, it occurred to me that this shit *was* the trail. Fallen trees were the equivalent of Agats's wooden walkways.

William cut me a good walking stick, which was helpful. I liked the stick and thought of it as a scepter, a symbol of dignity: Behold, it is Tripod, Mighty Jungle Walker.

Prolonged log walking is a bit like riding a bicycle: Speed equals stability. And I was, in fact, moving pretty fast on a large mossy log that spanned the narrowest section of a deep, foul-smelling scummy black pond when William and Stef and Conrados and Agus all began screaming, "Sago, sago, sago!"

"I see it," I called back. The sago tree was at the end of my log, on the bank of the pond, and I leaned out to grab it, because I was going just a little too fast.

"Tidak!" No!

The trunk of the sago palm, I discovered to my regret, is the vegetable equivalent of a porcupine. They are thorny sons of bitches, sago palms, extremely uncomfortable to grab for stability on mossy logs, and I had to listen to William sneeze about this prickly lesson, on and off, for over an hour.

And, of course, it rained on us. And then we could see the arc of a rainbow through the trees, and then it rained again, and suddenly we were in a large clearing surrounded by tall white-barked trees 150 feet high. In the middle of the clearing, fifty feet in the air, was a house with open sides and a thatched roof. The main support, set directly in the middle of the floor, was one of the white-barked giants that had been cut off at the fifty-foot level. The corners of the house were supported by convenient smaller trees and stout bamboo poles. The floor, I could see, was made of crossed sticks of sukun, and the thatch was sago frond.

There was a bamboo ladder up to about the twenty-five-foot level and that gave way to a thick rounded pole with notches for steps. Agus shouted some words in Karowai. Someone shouted back from above. There seemed to be a bit of negotiation going on. Mosquitoes in thick clouds attacked those of us on the ground. They were very naughty, and probably malarial.

And then I was clambering up the bamboo ladder and making my careful way up the notched pole. There were nine people sitting on the platform: two infants, two nursing mothers in knee-length grass skirts, two little boys about three and four, one boy about nine, and two naked men, each of whom had a leaf tied tightly around his penis. There was no one who might have been a grandmother or grandfather. Anthropologists who have studied tree dwellers on the nearby Brazza River figure the average life expectancy of these semi-nomadic hunters and gatherers is about thirty-five years.

One of the men, Samu, wore a ring of bamboo in his nasal septum and a double ring of rattan through the sides of his nostrils. He was, William said, the chief of this house. Three families lived here, and each of the three men had two wives.

The tree-house platform was rectangular: about twenty feet by twenty-five. The bones of several small fish hung from the ceiling, secured by rattan strings. I saw no human skulls, but there were dozens of arrows fitted into the ceiling and piled in the corners. There were two fires—a men's fire and a women's fire—and both were built on beds of small rocks over a reinforced triple-thick area of flooring. The children sat with the women, around the women's fire.

Agus and William continued to negotiate with the Karowai men. We were not the first white people these tree dwellers had ever seen. The year before, William had brought in two European groups, seven people, though no one ever stayed for more than a few hours. We wanted to hang out for a day or so, stay the night, shoot the shit. Which complicated matters.

In his two previous visits, William had learned precisely what the Karowai require in terms of trade goods. The swamp here does not yield good stone, and in the very near past, the Karowai had had to trade with outside tribes for stone axes. We had steel axes for them (I could see another steel ax set in a corner of the platform, next to an ironwood bow with a rattan pull-string and a set of arrows made from reeds and tipped with sharpened bone).

Aside from the axes, the Karowai were pleased to accept fishing line, metal hooks, salt, matches, rice, and tobacco. These were acceptable gifts, much admired and appreciated. We were welcomed to stay the night. They didn't accept credit cards here at the Karowai Hilton.

Samu, as headman, got first crack at our tobacco. He packed the rough-cut leaf into the end of a narrow bamboo tube, which fit into a wider tube that was etched in geometric red-and-white designs. He put the wide tube to his mouth, placed the narrow end against a hot rock, inhaled, then rocked back onto his heels. His face was beatific.

One of the women, Pya, reached up into a string bag hanging from the roof of the house, fished around a bit, and came up with a white ball of sago pith, which she dropped onto the embers of her fire. After a short time, I was offered a piece the size of a tennis ball. The food had the consistency of doughy bread and was very nearly tasteless. The term "half-baked" kept clattering through my mind, but I smiled and complimented Pya on her culinary skills. I used one of the few words of Karowai that I knew.

"*Manoptroban.*" Very good.

It was the first word I had uttered in the tree house, and as soon as it tumbled out of my mouth, I wanted to call it back, because it was, of course, a lie. The older of the two men, Samu, stared at me. His expression was that of a man whose intelligence had been insulted. Sago? Good? People eat this soggy crap every day. All the time. They do not sit down for regular meals, but eat only when they have to, because there is no pleasure in the taste of sago. They eat it because there is nothing else. Good? It's not good, you imbecile. It's sago.

I felt chastened and reluctant to say anything else, maybe for the rest of my life. It was better to just sit there and pull sago thorns out of my hand with my teeth.

The Karowai exchanged a few words. There was a failed attempt to remain dispassionate, and then all of them were laughing. The laughter was aimed at Chris and me. This familiar teasing and testing of strangers seems to be a universal human trait, and Chris, in his many travels, has learned to defuse it by laughing right along with everyone else. My strategy exactly. Soon enough the laughter became genuine, and we were all giggling and poking one another in the hilarity of our mutual insecurity.

There was a nice breeze fifty feet above the ground, and no mosquitoes at all. Chris asked William if the Karowai live in trees to avoid mosquitoes. William transferred the question to Agus, who was learning Indonesian, and Agus— although he knew the answer—respectfully asked Samu. Samu nodded and said a single word in Karowai.

And the answer came back—Karowai to Indonesian to English: "Yes."

There was a very long silence.

Samu finally added that it was also safer in the tree, by which he meant, I think, that in this boggy flatland the tree house had the military significance of being high ground. A single man with a bow and a sufficient supply of arrows could hold the fort against any number of similarly equipped attackers. There were even strategic holes in the floor, places where a skilled archer could pick off anyone foolish enough to try to hack down the columns that support the house.

"So there's still war?" I asked.

Samu's reaction might have been a case study for Psychology 101: Here, students, is a man about to tell a lie. The chief shifted his gaze, he stared at the ground, he coughed lightly and occupied himself for some time bringing up a great gob of phlegmy spit that he lofted off into the forest below.

"No," he said finally. No more war.

William took a hit of tobacco from Samu's pipe and attempted to defuse the situation with what he took to be an innocuous question. Where did Samu get his penis leaves? There was a string bag full of them hanging from the roof.

Samu fidgeted uncomfortably, stared at the ground, coughed again, spat again, and finally allowed that he didn't actually recall where he got the leaves.

I thought: God knows, Samu, your secret would be safe with us. The pure hard fact of the matter was that Samu would likely lose his leaves to one of the massive timbering operations now just cranking up in the Asmat. Indeed, only three years earlier Agus had lived in this very tree house. Now he had given up his penis leaf for shorts and a T-shirt that read PIECE. It was a simple, sad irony: Agus, having encountered civilization in the person of William two years ago, was now cutting down the forest that had fed him and his people for centuries.

Agus used the money he made to buy steel axes. Generally, the Karowai move every two years, after they have exhausted the local sago. It takes about a month to build a new tree house. With a steel ax, the process takes only two weeks.

The Karowai didn't like coffee or tea, but they craved tobacco. Traditionally, they had smoked dried bark.

And rice! When William fixed Agus his first bowl of rice, the Karowai had burst into tears, it was so good. It was William who had brought him all these things, awakened him to the world as it existed beyond his village: showed him steel axes and rice and matches and canned corned beef. And though Agus and William were about the same age, Agus called his benefactor Father. He was a sweet man, Agus, ambitious and bewildered at the same time. He wept every time William had to go away.

"I get the leaves," Samu said by way of accommodation to the question that had been asked some time ago, "from the trees." He nodded out toward the forest.

And then there was another long silence. Several hours' worth of it. The Karowai seemed perfectly comfortable just sitting around, smoking, enjoying their company in a haze of tobacco smoke and self-contained neolithic composure. I, on the other hand, felt constrained to fill up the fleeting hours with productive activity. To that end, I spent a good deal of time scribbling in my notebook:

I. Karowai culture
  A. Inappropriate comments
    1. Eat me.
    2. Sago is good.
  B. Inappropriate questions
    1. Been in any wars lately?
    2. Where you guys get them dick leaves?
  C. Inappropriate subject matter
    1. Cannibal jokes

    D. Appropriate behavior
      1. Sitting in a hunkering squat
      2. Smoking
      3. Spitting
      4. Being silent
      5. Keeping the fire going
      6. Tending to the fussy child or infant
      7. Smiling dreamily for no particular reason

About midafternoon, unable to sit still any longer, Chris and William and I took a walk through the swamp to visit one of Samu's neighbors. It was another hour or so to a second clearing, where there was another tree house, which was probably only thirty-five or forty feet high. Our host was named Romas, and he had a pair of what appeared to be red toothpicks sticking out of the top of his nose. The toothpicks were, in fact, bones from the wing of a flying fox, colored reddish brown in the smoke from the fire.

There were fish bones hanging from the ceiling, as in the first Karowai house, along with a turtle shell and a number of pig jaws hanging from a rattan rope. We had a long conversation about these trophies, which seemed a little anemic to me. The fish looked like ten-inchers, little guys, but the Karowai-to-English translation suggested that they were, in fact, the remnants of memorable meals. When Samu came to visit, Romas said, his neighbor always noticed a new set of bones. And the needlelike bones, going dark red in the smoke from the fires, became an occasion to engage in hunting stories. They were, these pathetic remains, conversation pieces. Interior decorating.

Against one wall was a war shield, four feet high, decorated in geometric designs, colored white and red. Next to the shield were several bows and several bunches of arrows, all of which were unnotched and unfeathered, so that when Romas allowed me to fire one off into the forest, it began to wobble after only fifty feet or so. The arrows do not fly true for very long, which is probably not much of a problem in the forest, where there are no long vistas.

Some of the arrows were tipped with cassowary bones. Cassowary are ostrichlike birds whose powerful legs end in claws that are capable of disemboweling a man. Next to the armaments were several seven-foot-long tubes of bamboo that contained drinking water.

The men in the tree house assured me that we were not disrupting them in the least and that they were doing what they ordinarily would be doing, which was precisely what everyone in Samu's house was doing. Romas reached into the embers of his fire and pulled out a bug that looked a good deal like a large iridescent grasshopper. He stripped off the wings and popped it into his mouth, like a piece of candy.

I was given a wooden bowl of the blue-gray glue that is sago sap. Sago, in fact, was all I'd had to eat over the past twenty hours. It wasn't unpleasant, just tasteless, and I fully understood why a man who had eaten nothing else in his life would burst into tears over a bowl of rice.

Romas said he hunted wild pig and cassowary. He also ate bananas, cassowary eggs, insects, and small lizards. The only sure thing to eat, however, the only dependable crop, was sago. Sago sap. Sago pulp. An endless diet of sago.

It rained three times that afternoon, and each downpour lasted about half an hour. In the forest there was usually a large-leafed banana tree with sheltering leaves where everyone could sit out the rain in bitter communion with the local mosquitoes.

Just at twilight, back in Samu's house, where everyone was sitting around eating what everyone always ate, a strong breeze began to rattle the leaves of the larger trees. The wind came whistling through the house, and it brought more rain, cooling rain, so that, for the first time that day, I stopped sweating. My fingers looked pruney, as if I had been in the bath too long.

Samu squatted on his haunches, his testicles inches off the floor. The other man, Gehi, sat with his back to the wall, his gnarled, callused feet almost in the fire. It was very pleasant, and no one had anything to say.

After the rain, as the setting sun colored the sky, I heard a gentle cooing from the forest: mambruk. The sky was still light, but the forest was already dark. Hundreds of fireflies were moving rapidly through the trees.

William rigged up a plastic tarp so the Karowai could have some privacy. Chris and I could hear him chatting with Samu and Gehi. They were talking about tobacco and salt, about steel axes and visitors.

Chris said, "I don't want them to change."

We watched the fireflies below. They were blinking in unison now, dozens of them on a single tree.

"Do you think that's paternalistic?" he asked. "Some new politically correct form of imperialism?"

"I don't know," I said.

But I thought about it. I thought about it all night long. When you suspect that your hosts have eaten human flesh in the very recent past, sleep does not come easily. It seemed to me that I was out of the loop here, not a part of the cycle of war and revenge, which was all just as well. I had expected to meet self-sufficient hunter-gatherers, and the Karowai were all of that, but they wanted more. They wanted steel axes, for instance, and did not equate drudgery with any kind of nobility.

I tried to imagine myself in an analogous situation. What would I want?

What if some alien life force materialized on earth with a superior medical technology, for instance? They have the cure for AIDS, for cancer, but they feel it is best that we go on as we have. They admire the spiritual values we derive from our suffering; they are inspired by our courage, our primitive dignity. In such a case, I think I'd do everything in my power to obtain that technology— and the hell with my primitive dignity.

I thought about Asmat art and what is left in the world that is worth dying for. I thought about Agus, who wept over his first bowl of rice and whose first contact with the outside world set him up in the business of cutting down the forest that had fed him all of his life.

I thought about the butterfly I had caught when I was a child. My grand-mother told me to never do it again. She said that butterflies have a kind of powder on their wings and that when you touch them, the powder comes off in your hand and the butterfly can't fly anymore. She said that when you touch a butterfly, you kill it.

Butterfly; Karowai.

Sometime just before dawn, I heard a stirring from the Karowai side of the house. Samu moved out from behind the plastic tarp and blew on the embers of his fire. Gehi joined him. The two naked men squatted on their haunches, silent, warming themselves against the coolest part of the forest day. Presently, the stars faded and the eastern sky brightened with the ghostly light of false dawn.

A mist rose up off the forest floor, a riotous floral scent rising with it, so I had a sense that it was the fragrance itself that tinged this mist with the faint colors of forest flowers. The mist seemed the stuff of time itself, and time smelled of orchids.

As the first hints of yellow and pink touched the sky, I saw Samu and Gehi in silhouette: two men, squatting by their fire, waiting for the dawn.

OCTOBER 1992

Contributors

EDWARD ABBEY, a contributor to *Outside* in its early years, wrote numerous books, including *The Monkey Wrench Gang, Desert Solitaire, Fire on the Mountain, Abbey's Road,* and *The Fool's Progress.* Several works have been released since Abbey's death in 1989; the most recent include *Earth Apples: The Poetry of Edward Abbey* and *The Serpents of Paradise: A Reader by Edward Abbey.*

JOHN BRANT is an *Outside* contributing editor and the magazine's former "Bodywork" columnist. His work also appears in *The New York Times Magazine, Worth,* and other publications.

CHIP BROWN, a frequent contributor to *Outside,* won the 1989 National Magazine Award for Feature Writing. He is currently working on a book about alternative medicine, to be published by Putnam Riverhead next fall.

TIM CAHILL was one of *Outside's* founding editors and for several years was its "Out There" columnist; he will resume the column in early 1998. Many of Cahill's *Outside* pieces are included in his books *A Wolverine Is Eating My Leg, Jaguars Ripped My Flesh, Pecked to Death by Ducks,* and *Pass the Butterworms: Remote Journeys Oddly Rendered.* He is currently working on a book about the Ndoki Forest in the Republic of Congo.

E. JEAN CARROLL is an *Outside* correspondent and the author of *Elle* magazine's advice column, "Ask E. Jean." Her most recent book is *A Dog in Heat Is a Hot Dog and Other Rules to Live By.*

DANIEL COYLE is an *Outside* contributing editor. His book, *Hardball: A Season in the Projects,* was named *The Sporting News's* 1994 Book of the Year.

WILLIAM FINNEGAN, a *New Yorker* staff reporter since 1987, is the author of *Dateline Soweto, Crossing the Line, A Complicated War,* and, most recently, *Cold New World.*

IAN FRAZIER is the author of *Great Plains, Family,* and two humor collections, *Coyote v. Acme* and *Nobody Better, Better Than Nobody.* He and coinventor Thomas McClelland recently received a patent for their tree-cleansing Bag Snagger, featured in Frazier's article in this anthology.

JIM HARRISON is a poet, novelist, and screenwriter. His books include *Legends of the Fall, Just Before Dark, After Ikkyu, Dalva, The Woman Lit by Fireflies, Julip,* and *The Theory and Practice of Rivers.*

EDWARD HOAGLAND, an essayist and novelist, is the author of fifteen books, including *The Courage of Turtles, African Calliope, Notes from the Century Before, Heart's Desire,* and *Balancing Acts.* He is currently working on a memoir about three years during which he was legally blind.

SEBASTIAN JUNGER is the author of the book *The Perfect Storm,* based on his story that appears in this collection.

DONALD KATZ, a longtime *Outside* contributing editor, is the author of *The Big Store: Inside the Crisis and Revolution at Sears, Just Do It: The Nike Spirit in the Corporate World,* and *Home Fires: An Intimate Portrait of One Middle-Class Family in Postwar America.* In 1994 he won, along with editor-at-large David Quammen, the National Magazine Award for Special Interests. Katz is cofounder and president of Audible Inc., a media company that provides audio programs via the World Wide Web.

WILLIAM KITTREDGE, an *Outside* correspondent, is the author of several books about the West, including *We Are Not in This Together, Owning It All,* and *Hole in the Sky,* a memoir about growing up on an Oregon ranch. His forthcoming book, *Reimagining Desire,* will be published next year by Alfred A. Knopf.

JON KRAKAUER is an *Outside* contributing editor and author of the book *Into Thin Air,* based on his eyewitness account of the 1996 Mount Everest tragedy. Krakauer won the 1997 National Magazine Award for Reporting for his *Outside* article detailing the event, which is included in this anthology. He is also the author of *Into the Wild* and *Eiger Dreams,* a collection of his magazine work.

BARRY LOPEZ is an *Outside* correspondent and a contributing editor of *Harper's.* His books include *Arctic Dreams, Of Wolves and Men, The Rediscovery of North America,* and *Field Notes,* a collection of short stories. His latest work, *Lessons from the Wolverine,* will appear in fall 1997, followed in 1998 by *Apologia,* both published by University of Georgia Press.

THOMAS MCGUANE, one of *Outside*'s earliest contributors, is the author of many novels, including *The Sporting Club, The Bushwhacked Piano, Keep the Change, Panama,* and *Ninety-two in the Shade,* which was nominated for the National Book Award. He is also the author of *To Skin a Cat,* a collection of short stories, and *An Outside Chance,* a collection of essays.

SUSAN ORLEAN, a staff writer for *The New Yorker*, is the author of *Saturday Night*. Her forthcoming book about an orchid smuggler, *The Millionaire's Hothouse*, will be published by Random House in spring 1998.

MICHAEL PATERNITI, a former executive editor of *Outside*, is a frequent contributor to the magazine. His work also appears in *Harper's*, *The New York Times Magazine*, and *Rolling Stone*.

ANNIE PROULX is the author of *Heart Songs and Other Stories*, *Postcards*, and *The Shipping News*, which won both the 1993 National Book Award and the 1994 Pulitzer Prize for fiction. Her most recent novel is *Accordion Crimes*. Proulx is currently working on a collection of short stories set in Wyoming.

DAVID QUAMMEN wrote *Outside*'s "Natural Acts" column for fifteen years and is currently an editor-at-large. He has won two National Magazine Awards, in 1987 for Essays and Criticism and in 1994, with contributing editor Donald Katz, for Special Interests. Quammen's "Natural Acts" columns have been collected in two books, *Natural Acts* and *The Flight of the Iguana*; a third collection, *Wild Thoughts from Wild Places*, will be released early next year by Scribner's. He is also the author of *The Song of the Dodo*, a book about island biogeography; three novels; and a collection of short fiction.

JONATHAN RABAN is the author of several books, including *Coasting*, *Hunting Mister Heartbreak*, and *Bad Land: An American Romance*, which won the 1997 National Book Critics Circle Award.

DAVID ROBERTS, an *Outside* contributing editor, has written several books, including *Once They Moved Like the Wind*, *In Search of the Old Ones*, and *Escape Routes*, a collection of adventure essays. He is currently working on a book about Kit Carson and John Frémont.

JAMES SALTER is the author of several novels, including *A Sport and a Pastime*, *Light Years*, and *The Hunters*. He won the 1989 PEN/Faulkner Award for *Dusk*, a collection of stories. His memoir, *Burning the Days*, has recently been published by Random House.

BOB SHACOCHIS is a contributing editor of *Outside*, *Harper's*, and *GQ*. He is the author of several books of fiction and nonfiction, including *Swimming in the Volcano*; *Easy in the Islands*, nominated for the National Book Award; and a collection of essays titled *Domesticity*. A forthcoming book, *Immaculate Invasion*, about the U.S. military intervention in Haiti, will be published in 1998 by Viking Penguin.

LAURENCE SHAMES, a longtime *Outside* contributor, is the author of *The Hunger for More: Searching for Values in an Age of Greed,* as well as many novels, including *Florida Straits, Tropical Depression,* and *Virgin Heat.* His book *Sunburn* won the 1995 British Crime Writers Association Last Laugh Dagger for best comic mystery. A forthcoming novel, *Mangrove Squeeze,* will be released by Hyperion in spring 1998.

JANE SMILEY is the author of eight works of fiction, including *A Thousand Acres,* which won the 1992 Pulitzer Prize, and *The Age of Grief,* nominated for a National Book Critics Circle Award. Her upcoming novel, *All True Travels and Adventures of Liddie Newton,* about a frontierswoman out to avenge her husband's death, will be published in 1998 by Alfred A. Knopf.

ANNICK SMITH, an *Outside* correspondent, is the author of *Homestead,* a memoir, and *Big Bluestem,* a book about the grass prairies of Oklahoma, which won the American Booksellers Association award for best environmental book by a small press. She was the executive producer of the film *Heartland* and coproducer of the film *A River Runs Through It.* She is coeditor, along with William Kittredge, of *The Last Best Place: A Montana Anthology.*

CRAIG VETTER is a longtime *Outside* contributing editor and author of the novel *Striking It Rich,* about an oil boomtown in Wyoming. He is currently working on a book about his father, who was killed in the World War II battle of Okinawa.

RANDY WAYNE WHITE, an *Outside* contributing editor, was the "Out There" columnist for eight years. He is the author of a collection of nonfiction work titled *Batfishing in the Rainforest,* as well as a series of novels. His most recent novel is *North of Havana.*

KATE WHEELER is the author of *Not Where I Started From,* a collection of short stories. Her novel, *When Mountains Walked,* will be published in 1998 by Houghton Mifflin.

ED ZUCKERMAN, a longtime *Outside* correspondent, is the author of *The Day After World War III* and *Small Fortunes: Two Guys in Pursuit of the American Dream.* He has worked as a writer-producer for the television series *Law and Order* and is the executive producer of a new NBC series, *Players.*